# BATMAN
# ARKHAM

## HUGO STRANGE

# TABLE OF CONTENTS

Brian Bolland
Collection Cover Artist

BATMAN CREATED BY BOB KANE WITH BILL FINGER

CHRIS CONROY, MARK DOYLE, DENNIS O'NEIL, JULIUS SCHWARTZ,
 VIN SULLIVAN, LEN WEIN, ROBERT GREENBERGER Editors – Original Series
E. NELSON BRIDWELL, JOSEPH ILLIDGE Associate Editors – Original Series
FRANK BERRIOS, NICOLA CUTI, DAVE WIELGOSZ Assistant Editors – Original Series
JEB WOODARD Group Editor – Collected Editions
ALEX GALER, PAUL SANTOS Editors – Collected Edition
STEVE COOK Design Director – Books
MEGEN BELLERSEN Publication Design

BOB HARRAS Senior VP – Editor-in-Chief, DC Comics
PAT McCALLUM Executive Editor, DC Comics

DIANE NELSON President
DAN DiDIO Publisher
JIM LEE Publisher
GEOFF JOHNS President & Chief Creative Officer
AMIT DESAI Executive VP – Business & Marketing Strategy, Direct to Consumer & Global Franchise Management
SAM ADES Senior VP & General Manager, Digital Services
BOBBIE CHASE VP & Executive Editor, Young Reader & Talent Development
MARK CHIARELLO Senior VP – Art, Design & Collected Editions
JOHN CUNNINGHAM Senior VP – Sales & Trade Marketing
ANNE DePIES Senior VP – Business Strategy, Finance & Administration
DON FALLETTI VP – Manufacturing Operations
LAWRENCE GANEM VP – Editorial Administration & Talent Relations
ALISON GILL Senior VP – Manufacturing & Operations
HANK KANALZ Senior VP – Editorial Strategy & Administration
JAY KOGAN VP – Legal Affairs
JACK MAHAN VP – Business Affairs
NICK J. NAPOLITANO VP – Manufacturing Administration
EDDIE SCANNELL VP – Consumer Marketing
COURTNEY SIMMONS Senior VP – Publicity & Communications
JIM (SKI) SOKOLOWSKI VP – Comic Book Specialty Sales & Trade Marketing
NANCY SPEARS VP – Mass, Book, Digital Sales & Trade Marketing
MICHELE R. WELLS VP – Content Strategy

Color Reconstruction by MIKE SELLERS

BATMAN ARKHAM: HUGO STRANGE

DC COMICS, 2900 WEST ALAMEDA AVE., BURBANK, CA 91505
PRINTED BY LSC COMMUNICATIONS, KENDALLVILLE, IN, USA. 3/16/18. FIRST PRINTING.
ISBN: 978-1-4012-7470-2

LIBRARY OF CONGRESS CATALOGING-IN-PUBLICATION DATA IS AVAILABLE.

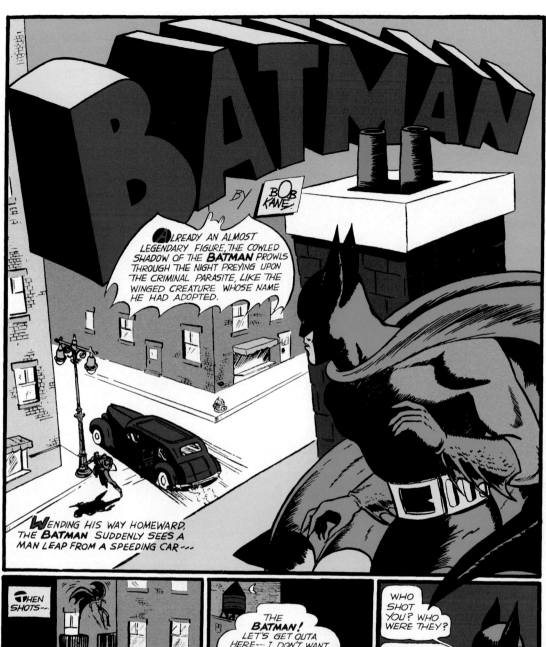

BATMAN

BY BOB KANE

Already an almost legendary figure, the cowled shadow of the BATMAN prowls through the night preying upon the criminal parasite, like the winged creature whose name he had adopted.

Wending his way homeward, the BATMAN suddenly sees a man leap from a speeding car---

Then shots---

THE BATMAN! LET'S GET OUTA HERE--- I DON'T WANT TO FOOL AROUND WITH HIM!

WHO SHOT YOU? WHO WERE THEY?

---FOG--FOG-- STRANGE--FOG-- STRANGE--AHHH

HE'S DEAD! PERHAPS THERE IS SOMETHING IN HIS POCKETS THAT MIGHT TELL ME SOMETHING!
HERE'S SOMETHING! A NOTEBOOK WI... POLICE!
THE BATMAN!
HE'S KILLED SOMEONE! SHOOT HIM DOWN!
THE BATMAN RUNS DOWN AN ALLEY---
--- EASILY CLEARS A SIX FOOT FENCE---
SO YOU WANT TO PLAY COPS 'N' ROBBERS, EH?
--- AND DISAPPEARS INTO THE BLACK NIGHT!
WELL, HE'S GONE, NO USE CHASING HIM ANY FURTHER, WE CAN'T SEE HIM IN THE DARK ANYWAY!
YOU MIGHT AS WELL CHASE A GHOST!
LATER, THE "GHOST," ALIAS THE BATMAN, ALIAS BRUCE WAYNE, SITS AT HOME PUZZLING OVER THE WORDS OF THE DEAD MAN---
THE WORDS OF THAT MAN HAVE GOT ME STUMPED. HE KEPT MUTTERING ABOUT A 'FOG', A "STRANGE" "FOG"--- MM... 'FOG'... 'STRANGE'... 'FOG'...
'FOG'--- 'STRANGE'--- 'STRANGE'--- OF COURSE! HE DIDN'T MEAN A STRANGE FOG, HE MEANT A "FOG" HAD SOMETHING TO DO WITH A PERSON NAMED 'STRANGE'--- PROFESSOR HUGO 'STRANGE'!
PROFESSOR HUGO STRANGE. THE MOST DANGEROUS MAN IN THE WORLD! SCIENTIST, PHILOSOPHER AND A CRIMINAL GENIUS--- LITTLE IS KNOWN OF HIM, YET THIS MAN IS UNDOUBTEDLY THE GREATEST ORGANIZER OF CRIME IN THE WORLD---
2
---MAYBE THAT LITTLE BLACK BOOK I FOUND CAN TELL ME MORE ABOUT HIM AND THE 'FOG'! MMM-- ALL THE PAGES ARE BLANK EXCEPT THIS ONE. WHY, IT'S A LIST OF BANKS AND OTHER PLACES! WHAT'S THIS ON THE BOTTOM--- THE F.B.I.--- THEN THAT MAN WAS A G.MAN!
State Trust Co
If this book is found please notify the F.B.I. John Davis

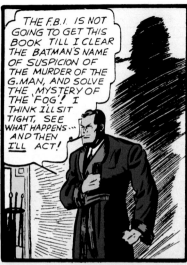

THE F.B.I. IS NOT GOING TO GET THIS BOOK TILL I CLEAR THE BATMAN'S NAME OF SUSPICION OF THE MURDER OF THE G. MAN, AND SOLVE THE MYSTERY OF THE 'FOG'! I THINK I'LL SIT TIGHT, SEE WHAT HAPPENS... AND THEN I'LL ACT!

NOT FAR AWAY, A MAN SITS IN A DIMLY LIT ROOM AND GAZES INTO THE FIRE ~~~

A MALIGNANT 'SMILE' CROSSES HIS FACE AS HE BROODS OVER THE MANY EVIL SCHEMES THAT SURGE THROUGH HIS BRILLIANT BUT DISTORTED BRAIN ~~~

PROFESSOR STRANGE! THAT G. MAN WE WERE SUPPOSED TO TAKE FOR A RIDE ~~~

THE GUNMAN TELLS HIS STORY ~~~

YOU COWARDLY FOOL, YOU SHOULD HAVE SHOT HIM DOWN, TOO! THE BATMAN IS THE ONLY MAN WITH THE IMAGINATION TO SENSE THE EXACT NATURE OF OUR PLANS. HOWEVER, SINCE THE G. MAN IS DEAD, HE CAN GET NO INFORMATION FROM THAT QUARTER!

~~~ AND THEN WHEN I SAW THE BATMAN I PULLED AWAY FAST!

IN THAT CASE WE WILL PROCEED AS PLANNED. TO-MORROW NIGHT THE 'FOG' WILL STRIKE! AND THEN ~~~ HA-HA~~ AND THEN ~~HA~~ HA-HA~~HA!

THE NEXT NIGHT A QUEER THING HAPPENS. A FOG, A THICK FOG SUCH AS ONE WOULD FIND ONLY IN ENGLAND, BLANKETS THE ENTIRE CITY.

SOME FOG, EH, CLANCY? I AIN'T EVER SEEN THE LIKES OF IT BEFORE, AND DID YA NOTICE HOW HOT IT'S GOT SINCE THE FOG HIT US?

AYE, THAT I DID, AND IT STRIKES ME AS AN EVIL SIGN. WHY IF I WAS TO HAVE TO CHASE A CROOK, I WOULDN'T BE ABLE TO SEE HIM AT ALL IN THIS FOG. THIS FOG WILL BE A BAD THING FOR THE POLICE FORCE!

CLANCY'S WORDS PROVE PROPHETIC, THE TWO FOLLOWING NIGHTS SEE BANKS ROBBED AS THE BANDITS FLEE AND ARE SWALLOWED UP IN THE FOG

POLICE HEADQUARTERS...

— BUT COMMISSIONER, WE CAN'T HELP IT IF WE LOST THE BANDIT'S CAR. DON'T FORGET WE'RE NOT USED TO ANY FOG!

WELL, **GET** USED TO IT! IF THIS BLASTED FOG KEEPS UP, THIS CITY IS GOING TO HAVE A CRIME-WAVE SUCH AS IT'S NEVER SEEN BEFORE!

THE HOME OF BRUCE WAYNE

~FLASH! THE CASE NATIONAL BANK REPORTS A LOSS OF $250,000, AND THE BOND EXCHANGE BANK $100,000... ~FLASH! HENRY JENKINS, THE MISSING ELECTRICAL ENGINEER, HAS NOT YET BEEN HEARD FROM. NO CLUES HAVE...

AN ELECTRICAL ENGINEER DISAPPEARS... AN UNUSUAL "FOG" COVERS THE CITY... THE FIRST NAMES ON THE LITTLE BOOK'S LIST ARE ROBBED... AND A DYING MAN UTTERS THE SINISTER NAME OF PROFESSOR HUGO STRANGE... HMM...

THAT NIGHT AS THE DENSE FOG AGAIN COVERS THE CITY, A MOVING VAN PULLS UP IN FRONT OF THE STERLING SILVER CO.

OPEN UP IN NAME OF THE LAW! I'M A DETECTIVE

STERLING SILVER COMPANY WAREHOUSE

MOVING VAN

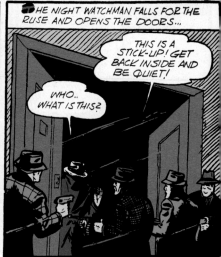

THE NIGHT WATCHMAN FALLS FOR THE RUSE AND OPENS THE DOORS...

THIS IS A STICK-UP! GET BACK INSIDE AND BE QUIET!

WHO.. WHAT IS THIS?

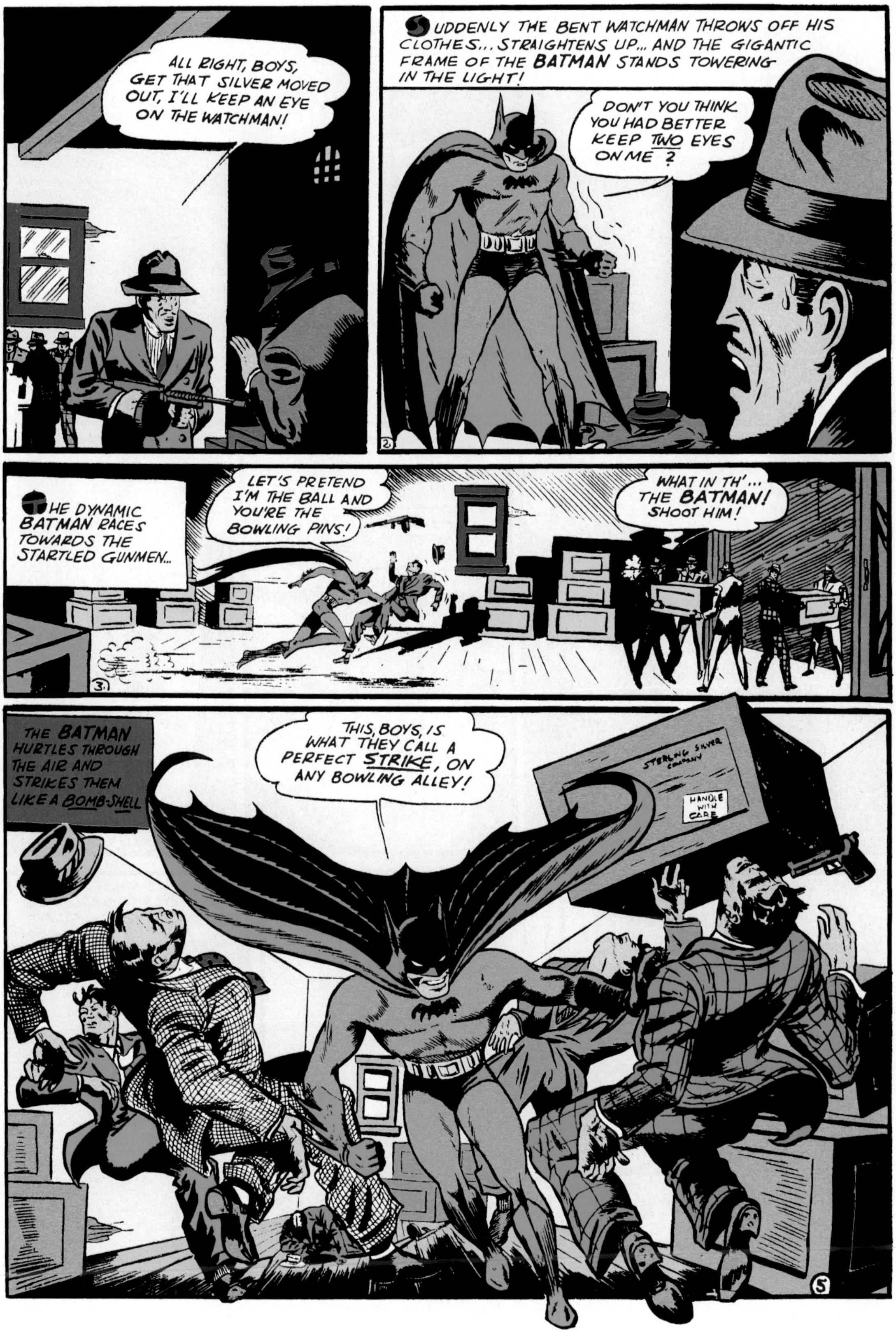
ALL RIGHT, BOYS, GET THAT SILVER MOVED OUT, I'LL KEEP AN EYE ON THE WATCHMAN!
SUDDENLY THE BENT WATCHMAN THROWS OFF HIS CLOTHES... STRAIGHTENS UP... AND THE GIGANTIC FRAME OF THE BATMAN STANDS TOWERING IN THE LIGHT!
DON'T YOU THINK YOU HAD BETTER KEEP TWO EYES ON ME ?
THE DYNAMIC BATMAN RACES TOWARDS THE STARTLED GUNMEN...
LET'S PRETEND I'M THE BALL AND YOU'RE THE BOWLING PINS!
WHAT IN TH'... THE BATMAN! SHOOT HIM!
THE BATMAN HURTLES THROUGH THE AIR AND STRIKES THEM LIKE A BOMB-SHELL
THIS, BOYS, IS WHAT THEY CALL A PERFECT STRIKE, ON ANY BOWLING ALLEY!
HANDLE WITH CARE

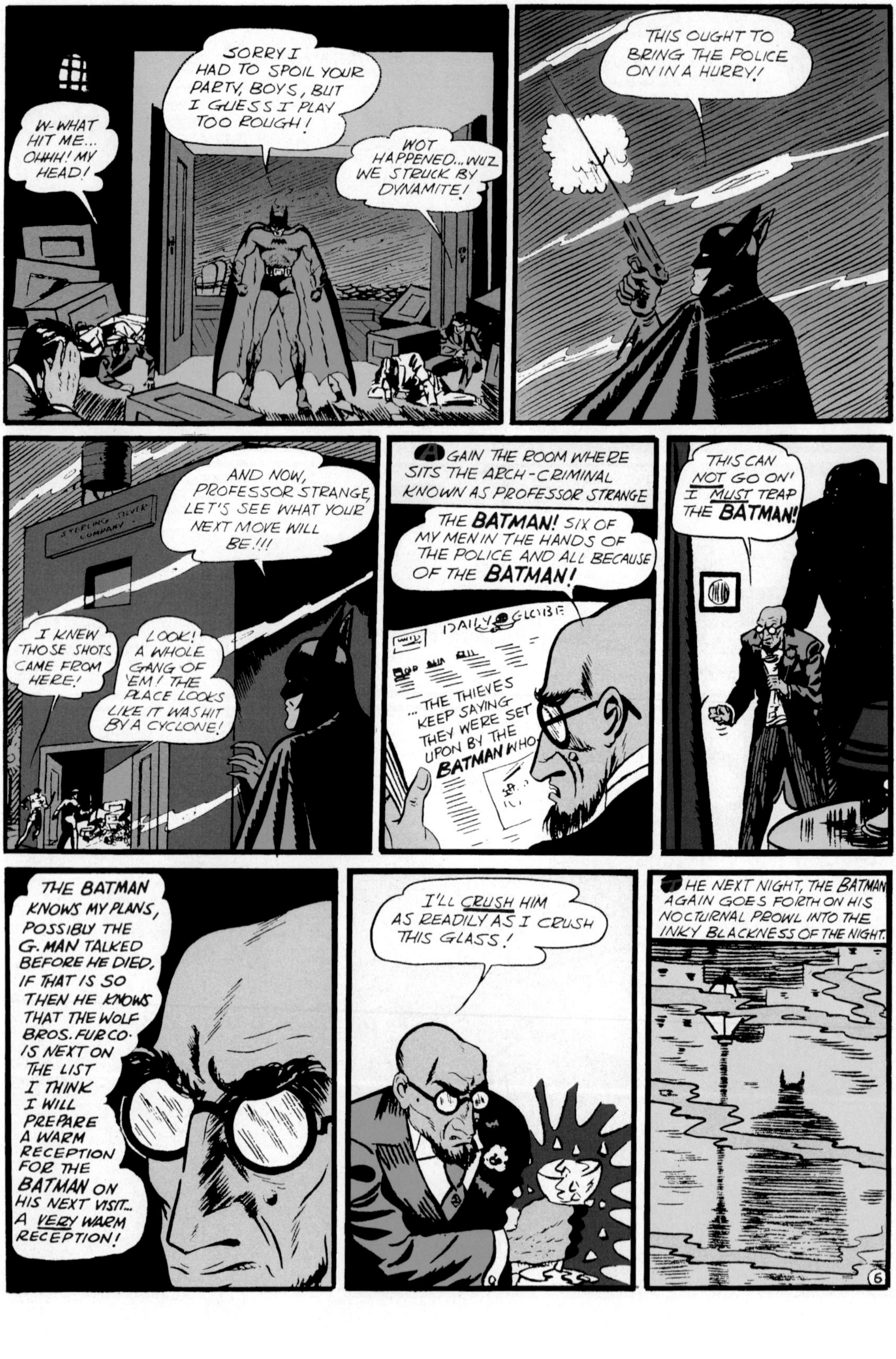
W-WHAT HIT ME... OHHH! MY HEAD!
SORRY I HAD TO SPOIL YOUR PARTY, BOYS, BUT I GUESS I PLAY TOO ROUGH!
WOT HAPPENED...WUZ WE STRUCK BY DYNAMITE!
THIS OUGHT TO BRING THE POLICE ON IN A HURRY!
AND NOW, PROFESSOR STRANGE, LET'S SEE WHAT YOUR NEXT MOVE WILL BE!!!
STERLING SILVER COMPANY
I KNEW THOSE SHOTS CAME FROM HERE!
LOOK! A WHOLE GANG OF 'EM! THE PLACE LOOKS LIKE IT WAS HIT BY A CYCLONE!
AGAIN THE ROOM WHERE SITS THE ARCH-CRIMINAL KNOWN AS PROFESSOR STRANGE
THE BATMAN! SIX OF MY MEN IN THE HANDS OF THE POLICE AND ALL BECAUSE OF THE BATMAN!
DAILY GLOBE
... THE THIEVES KEEP SAYING THEY WERE SET UPON BY THE BATMAN WHO-
THIS CAN NOT GO ON! I MUST TRAP THE BATMAN!
THE BATMAN KNOWS MY PLANS, POSSIBLY THE G. MAN TALKED BEFORE HE DIED, IF THAT IS SO THEN HE KNOWS THAT THE WOLF BROS. FUR CO. IS NEXT ON THE LIST I THINK I WILL PREPARE A WARM RECEPTION FOR THE BATMAN ON HIS NEXT VISIT... A VERY WARM RECEPTION!
I'LL CRUSH HIM AS READILY AS I CRUSH THIS GLASS!
THE NEXT NIGHT, THE BATMAN AGAIN GOES FORTH ON HIS NOCTURNAL PROWL INTO THE INKY BLACKNESS OF THE NIGHT.
6

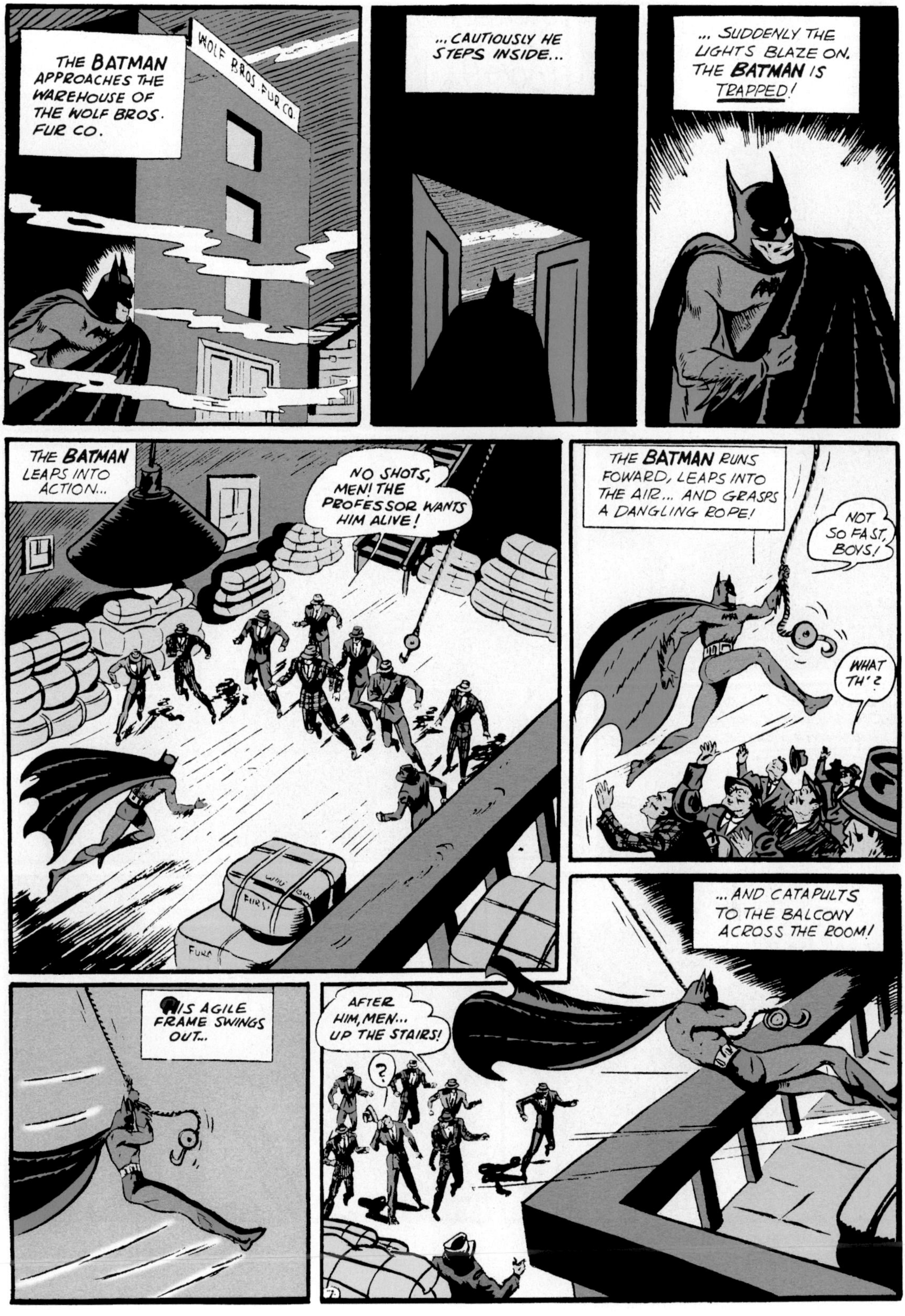
WOLF BROS. FUR CO.
THE BATMAN APPROACHES THE WAREHOUSE OF THE WOLF BROS. FUR CO.
...CAUTIOUSLY HE STEPS INSIDE...
...SUDDENLY THE LIGHTS BLAZE ON. THE BATMAN IS TRAPPED!
THE BATMAN LEAPS INTO ACTION...
NO SHOTS, MEN! THE PROFESSOR WANTS HIM ALIVE!
FURS
THE BATMAN RUNS FOWARD, LEAPS INTO THE AIR... AND GRASPS A DANGLING ROPE!
NOT SO FAST, BOYS!
WHAT TH'?
...AND CATAPULTS TO THE BALCONY ACROSS THE ROOM!
HIS AGILE FRAME SWINGS OUT...
AFTER HIM, MEN... UP THE STAIRS!
?

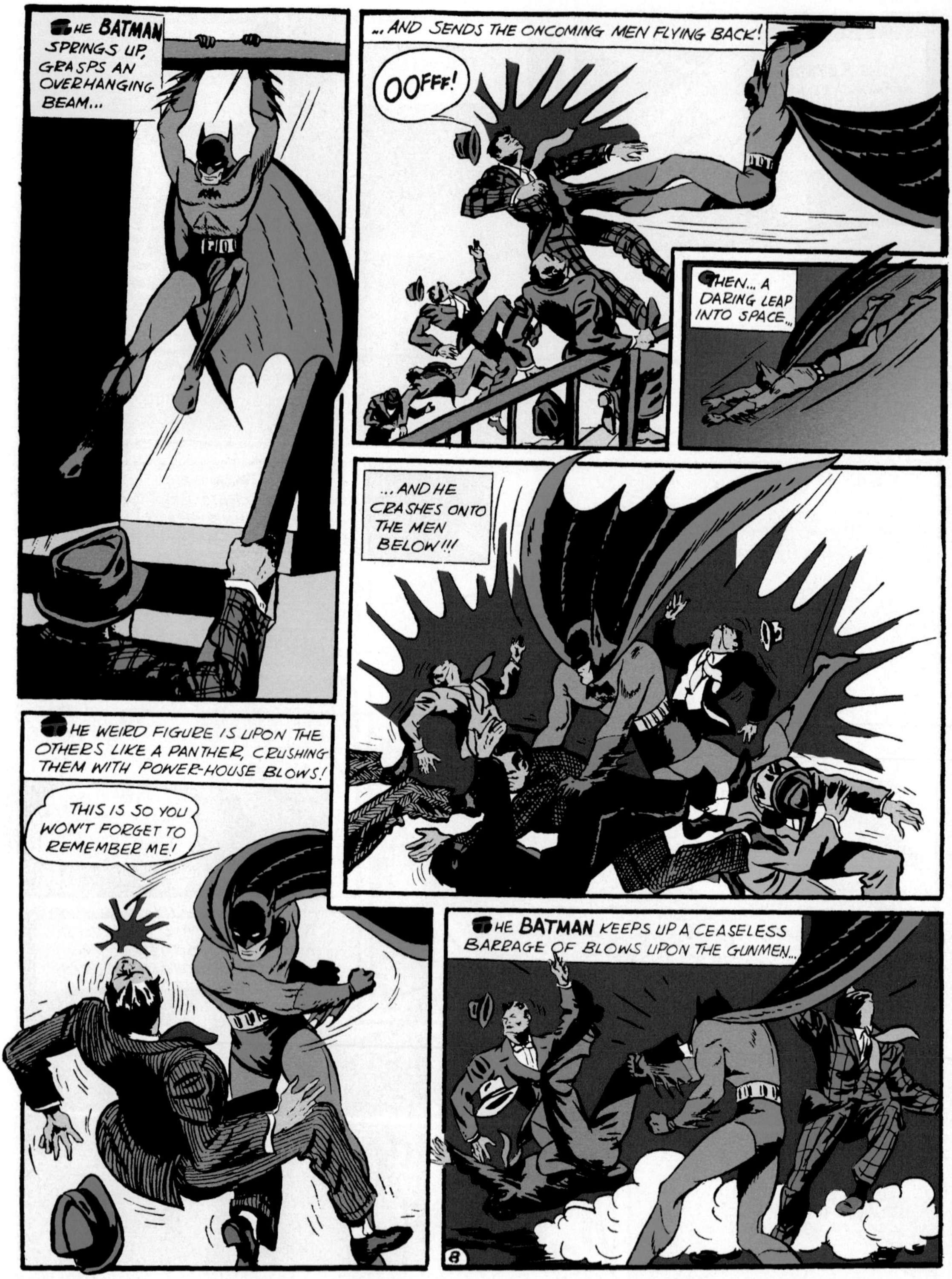
THE BATMAN SPRINGS UP, GRASPS AN OVERHANGING BEAM...
...AND SENDS THE ONCOMING MEN FLYING BACK!
OOFFF!
THEN... A DARING LEAP INTO SPACE...
...AND HE CRASHES ONTO THE MEN BELOW!!!
THE WEIRD FIGURE IS UPON THE OTHERS LIKE A PANTHER, CRUSHING THEM WITH POWER-HOUSE BLOWS!
THIS IS SO YOU WON'T FORGET TO REMEMBER ME!
THE BATMAN KEEPS UP A CEASELESS BARRAGE OF BLOWS UPON THE GUNMEN...
8

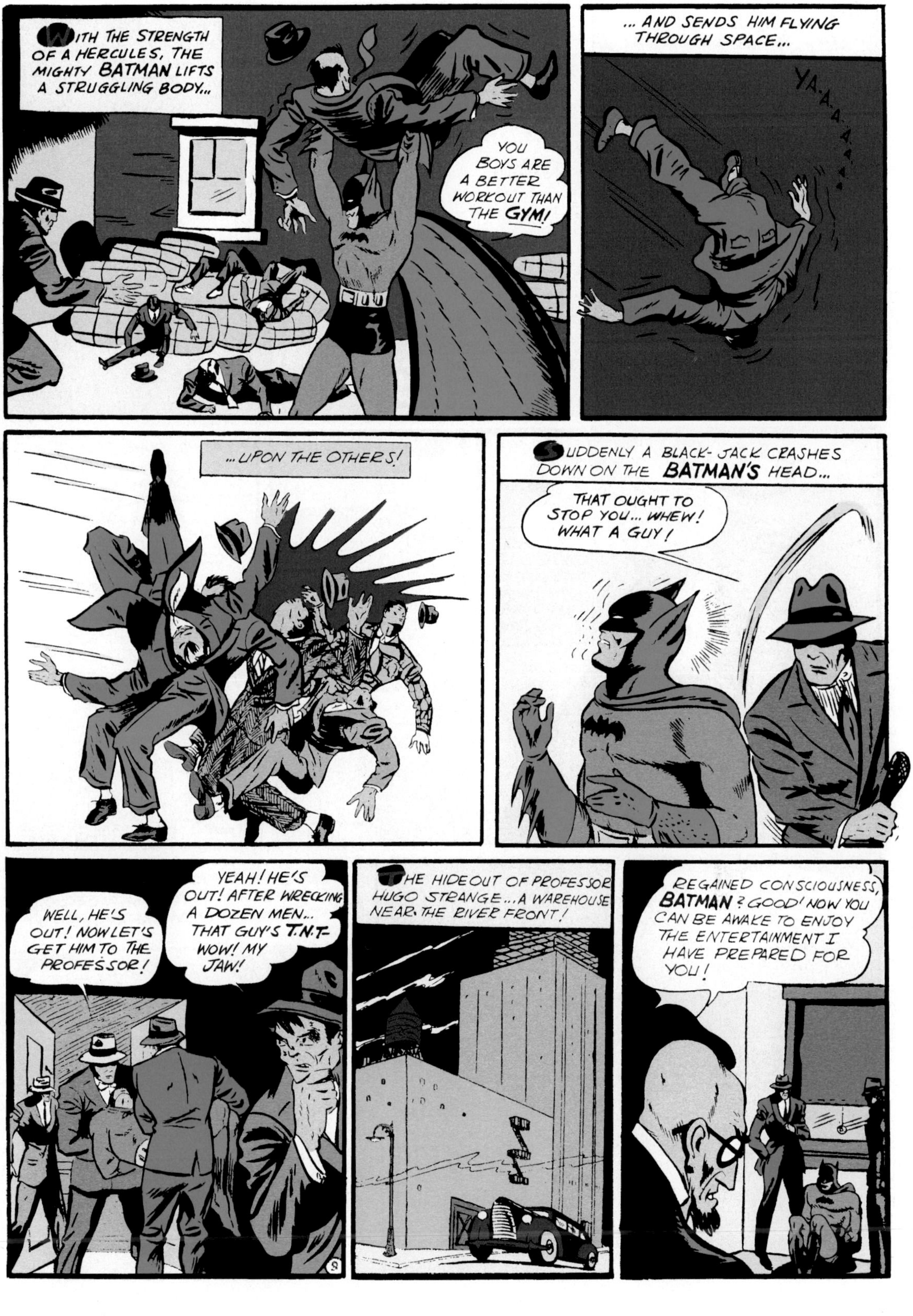
WITH THE STRENGTH OF A HERCULES, THE MIGHTY BATMAN LIFTS A STRUGGLING BODY...
YOU BOYS ARE A BETTER WORKOUT THAN THE GYM!
...AND SENDS HIM FLYING THROUGH SPACE...
YA-A-A-A-A-A
...UPON THE OTHERS!
SUDDENLY A BLACK-JACK CRASHES DOWN ON THE BATMAN'S HEAD...
THAT OUGHT TO STOP YOU... WHEW! WHAT A GUY!
WELL, HE'S OUT! NOW LET'S GET HIM TO THE PROFESSOR!
YEAH! HE'S OUT! AFTER WRECKING A DOZEN MEN... THAT GUY'S T.N.T.- WOW! MY JAW!
THE HIDEOUT OF PROFESSOR HUGO STRANGE... A WAREHOUSE NEAR THE RIVER FRONT!
REGAINED CONSCIOUSNESS, BATMAN? GOOD! NOW YOU CAN BE AWAKE TO ENJOY THE ENTERTAINMENT I HAVE PREPARED FOR YOU!

I HAVE BROUGHT YOU HERE _ALIVE_, SO THAT YOU MAY KNOW WHAT IT MEANS TO INTERFERE WITH PROFESSOR STRANGE!

THE BATMAN IS MADE READY FOR THE LASH!

I'LL TEACH YOU... WITH A TASTE OF THE LASH!

THE WHIP CRACKS DOWN ON THE MASSIVE FIGURE...

WHOSE STEEL MUSCLES SUDDENLY SURGE WITH STRENGTH AND SNAP HIS BONDS!

QUICKLY, HE DRAWS FORTH A GLASS PELLET...

...AS HE SLAMS IT TO THE FLOOR, A GAS EMANATES, OVERCOMING THE MEN!

SLEEPING GAS (COUGH) WELL, _THAT_ WON'T GET ME!

GAS!

MAYBE THE GAS WON'T, BUT _I_ WILL!

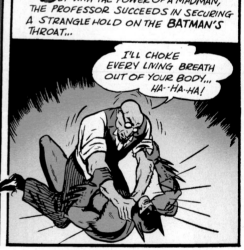

BUT WITH THE POWER OF A MADMAN, THE PROFESSOR SUCCEEDS IN SECURING A STRANGLE HOLD ON THE BATMAN'S THROAT...

I'LL CHOKE EVERY LIVING BREATH OUT OF YOUR BODY... HA--HA--HA!

10

14

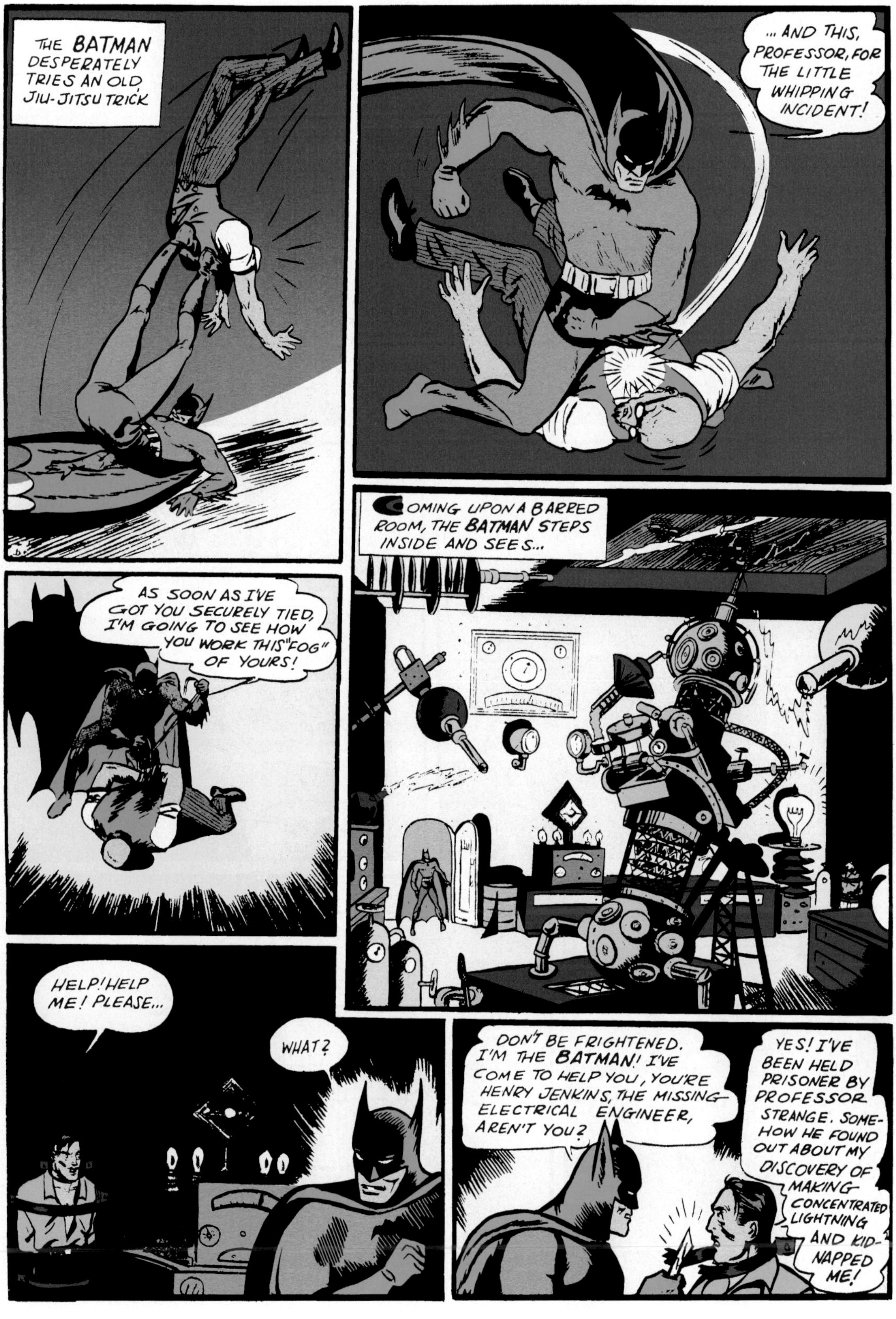
THE BATMAN DESPERATELY TRIES AN OLD JIU-JITSU TRICK
... AND THIS, PROFESSOR, FOR THE LITTLE WHIPPING INCIDENT!
AS SOON AS I'VE GOT YOU SECURELY TIED, I'M GOING TO SEE HOW YOU WORK THIS "FOG" OF YOURS!
COMING UPON A BARRED ROOM, THE BATMAN STEPS INSIDE AND SEES...
HELP! HELP ME! PLEASE...
WHAT?
DON'T BE FRIGHTENED. I'M THE BATMAN! I'VE COME TO HELP YOU, YOU'RE HENRY JENKINS, THE MISSING ELECTRICAL ENGINEER, AREN'T YOU?
YES! I'VE BEEN HELD PRISONER BY PROFESSOR STRANGE. SOMEHOW HE FOUND OUT ABOUT MY DISCOVERY OF MAKING CONCENTRATED LIGHTNING AND KIDNAPPED ME!

HE FOUND OUT THAT HOT LIGHTNING CAUSED CONDENSED STEAM IN THE AIR, LIKE A SORT OF UN-NATURAL FOG IN THE AIR HE FORCED ME TO MAKE THIS MACHINE FOR HIM, BUT FOR WHAT PURPOSE I DO NOT KNOW?

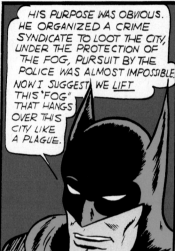

HIS PURPOSE WAS OBVIOUS. HE ORGANIZED A CRIME SYNDICATE TO LOOT THE CITY, UNDER THE PROTECTION OF THE FOG, PURSUIT BY THE POLICE WAS ALMOST IMPOSSIBLE. NOW I SUGGEST WE LIFT THIS "FOG" THAT HANGS OVER THIS CITY LIKE A PLAGUE.

THE TWO MEN SPRING TO THE CONTROLS OF THE GIGANTIC MACHINE...

...AND SOON...

AH! THE FOG IS LIFTING! 'TIS A FINE THING F'R THE POLICE FORCE!

IT'S NICE TO SEE A CLEAR MOON AGAIN!

WHO IS THE BATMAN, DADDY?

A GREAT MAN, SON, A GREAT MAN!

RADIO

...AND SO WE CITIZENS OF THIS CITY OWE OUR THANKS TO ONE MAN, THE BATMAN! BECAUSE OF HIM AN ARCH-CRIMINAL IS AT LAST CAPTURED! THERE IS...

BACK AT HIS HOME, BRUCE WAYNE, ALIAS THE BATMAN, LISTENS TO THE BROADCAST...

...THERE IS NO DOUBT THAT PROFESSOR HUGO STRANGE IS PUT AWAY FOR A LONG TIME TO COME.

I WONDER... I WONDER...

AT THE STATE PENITENTIARY...

THEY CAN'T KEEP ME HERE, CAGED LIKE SOME WILD BEAST! I'LL ESCAPE... AND WHEN I DO, I SHALL DEVOTE THE REST OF MY LIFE IN REVENGING MYSELF UPON THE BATMAN!

FINIS

THE Sensational BATMAN! AMERICA'S MOST EXCITING MYSTERY, ACTION, ADVENTURE STRIP...

Detective COMICS

APPEARS ONLY IN DETECTIVE COMICS! A NEW THRILLING EPISODE NEXT MONTH....

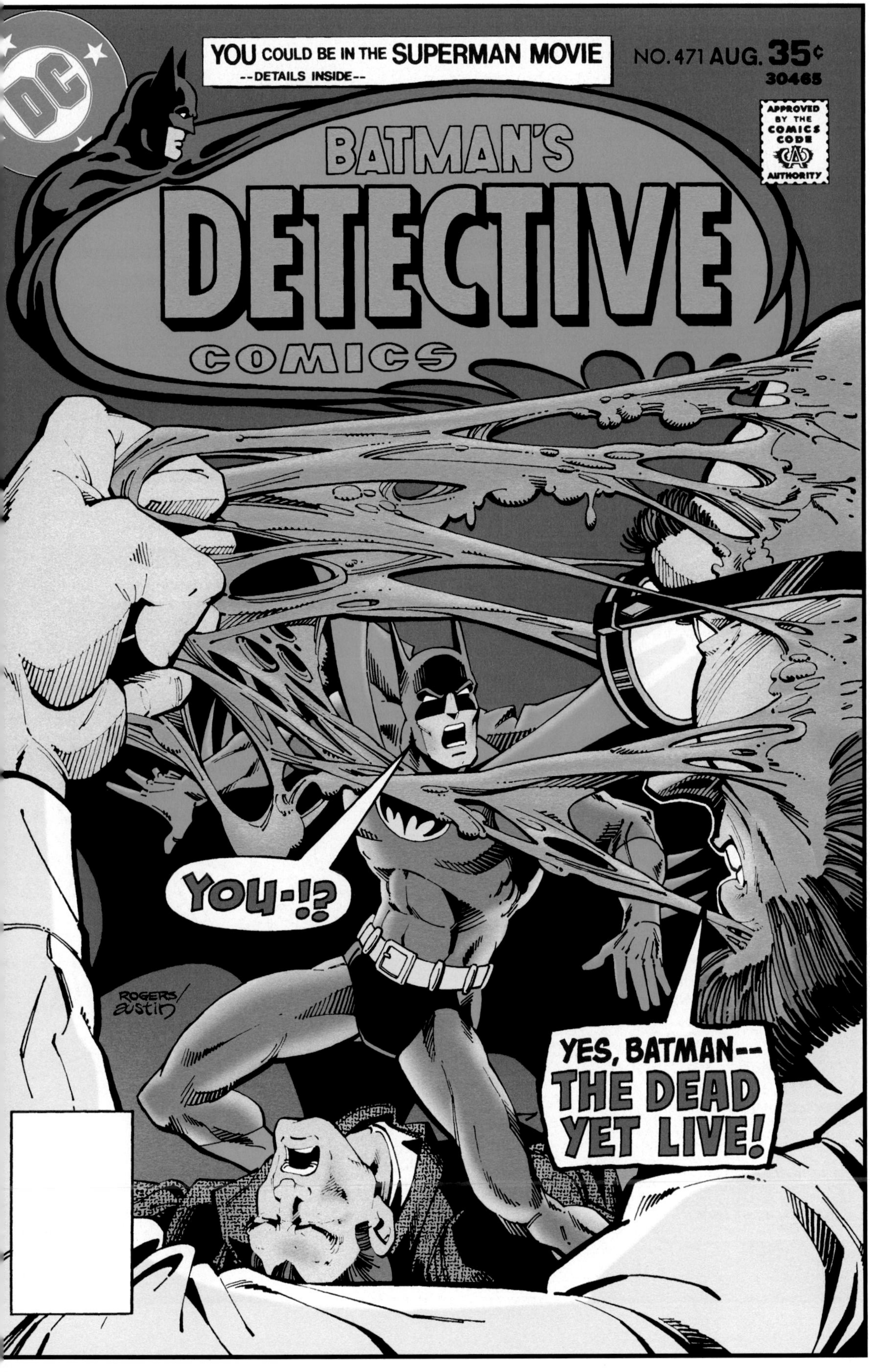

YOU COULD BE IN THE SUPERMAN MOVIE
--DETAILS INSIDE--
NO. 471 AUG. 35¢
30465
APPROVED BY THE COMICS CODE AUTHORITY
BATMAN'S
DETECTIVE
COMICS
YOU-!?
ROGERS/ AUSTIN
YES, BATMAN-- THE DEAD YET LIVE!

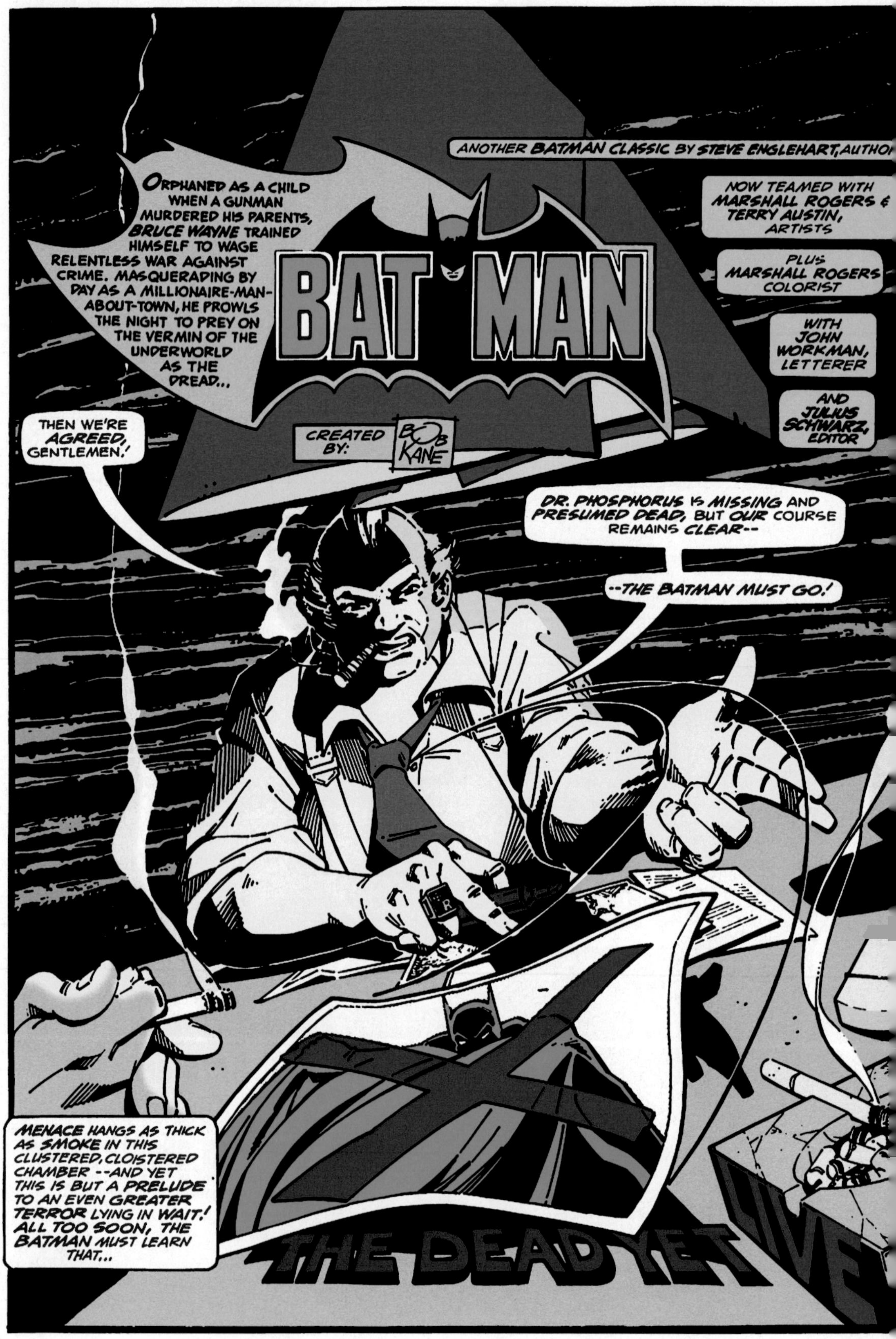
ANOTHER BATMAN CLASSIC BY STEVE ENGLEHART, AUTHOR
ORPHANED AS A CHILD WHEN A GUNMAN MURDERED HIS PARENTS, BRUCE WAYNE TRAINED HIMSELF TO WAGE RELENTLESS WAR AGAINST CRIME. MASQUERADING BY DAY AS A MILLIONAIRE-MAN-ABOUT-TOWN, HE PROWLS THE NIGHT TO PREY ON THE VERMIN OF THE UNDERWORLD AS THE DREAD...
BATMAN
CREATED BY: BOB KANE
NOW TEAMED WITH MARSHALL ROGERS & TERRY AUSTIN, ARTISTS
PLUS MARSHALL ROGERS COLORIST
WITH JOHN WORKMAN, LETTERER
AND JULIUS SCHWARZ, EDITOR
THEN WE'RE AGREED, GENTLEMEN!
DR. PHOSPHORUS IS MISSING AND PRESUMED DEAD, BUT OUR COURSE REMAINS CLEAR--
--THE BATMAN MUST GO!
MENACE HANGS AS THICK AS SMOKE IN THIS CLUSTERED, CLOISTERED CHAMBER --AND YET THIS IS BUT A PRELUDE TO AN EVEN GREATER TERROR LYING IN WAIT! ALL TOO SOON, THE BATMAN MUST LEARN THAT...
THE DEAD YET LIVE

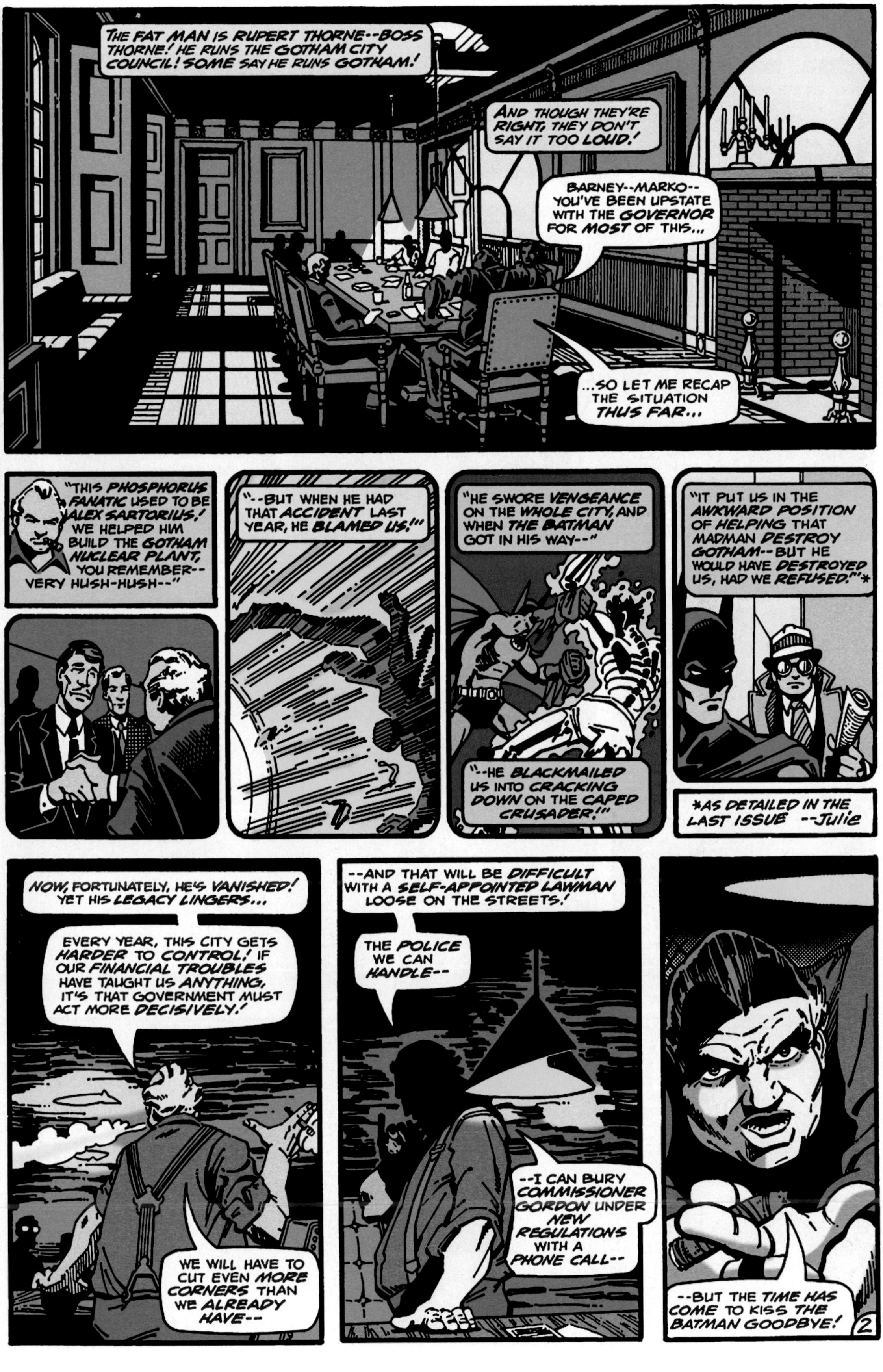
THE FAT MAN IS RUPERT THORNE--BOSS THORNE! HE RUNS THE GOTHAM CITY COUNCIL! SOME SAY HE RUNS GOTHAM!
AND THOUGH THEY'RE RIGHT, THEY DON'T SAY IT TOO LOUD!
BARNEY--MARKO--YOU'VE BEEN UPSTATE WITH THE GOVERNOR FOR MOST OF THIS...
...SO LET ME RECAP THE SITUATION THUS FAR...
"THIS PHOSPHORUS FANATIC USED TO BE ALEX SARTORIUS! WE HELPED HIM BUILD THE GOTHAM NUCLEAR PLANT, YOU REMEMBER--VERY HUSH-HUSH--"
"--BUT WHEN HE HAD THAT ACCIDENT LAST YEAR, HE BLAMED US!"
"HE SWORE VENGEANCE ON THE WHOLE CITY, AND WHEN THE BATMAN GOT IN HIS WAY--"
"--HE BLACKMAILED US INTO CRACKING DOWN ON THE CAPED CRUSADER!"
"IT PUT US IN THE AWKWARD POSITION OF HELPING THAT MADMAN DESTROY GOTHAM--BUT HE WOULD HAVE DESTROYED US, HAD WE REFUSED!"*
*AS DETAILED IN THE LAST ISSUE --Julie
NOW, FORTUNATELY, HE'S VANISHED! YET HIS LEGACY LINGERS...
EVERY YEAR, THIS CITY GETS HARDER TO CONTROL! IF OUR FINANCIAL TROUBLES HAVE TAUGHT US ANYTHING, IT'S THAT GOVERNMENT MUST ACT MORE DECISIVELY!
WE WILL HAVE TO CUT EVEN MORE CORNERS THAN WE ALREADY HAVE--
--AND THAT WILL BE DIFFICULT WITH A SELF-APPOINTED LAWMAN LOOSE ON THE STREETS!
THE POLICE WE CAN HANDLE--
--I CAN BURY COMMISSIONER GORDON UNDER NEW REGULATIONS WITH A PHONE CALL--
--BUT THE TIME HAS COME TO KISS THE BATMAN GOODBYE!
2

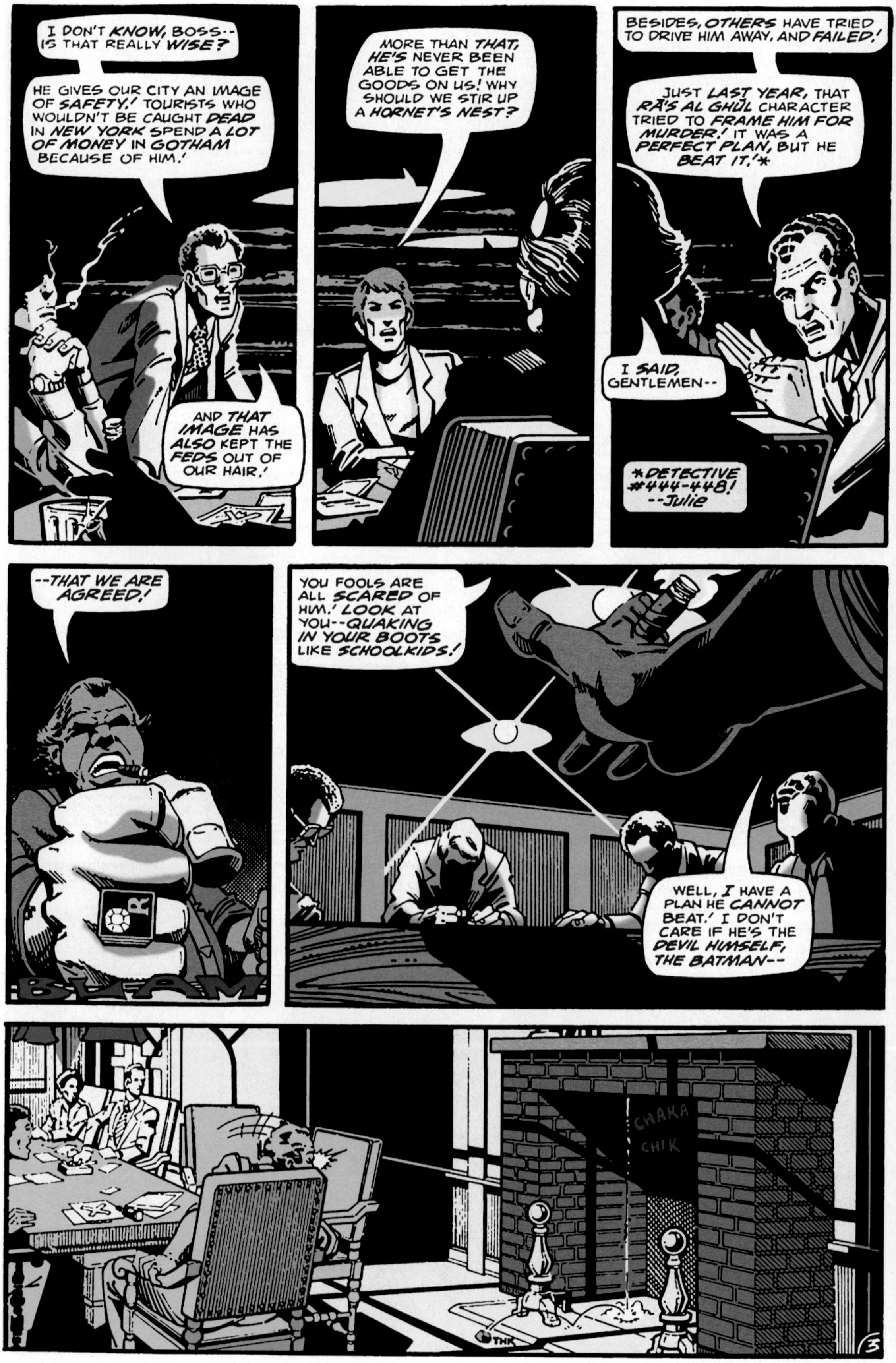
I DON'T KNOW, BOSS--IS THAT REALLY WISE?
HE GIVES OUR CITY AN IMAGE OF SAFETY! TOURISTS WHO WOULDN'T BE CAUGHT DEAD IN NEW YORK SPEND A LOT OF MONEY IN GOTHAM BECAUSE OF HIM!
AND THAT IMAGE HAS ALSO KEPT THE FEDS OUT OF OUR HAIR!
MORE THAN THAT, HE'S NEVER BEEN ABLE TO GET THE GOODS ON US! WHY SHOULD WE STIR UP A HORNET'S NEST?
BESIDES, OTHERS HAVE TRIED TO DRIVE HIM AWAY, AND FAILED!
JUST LAST YEAR, THAT RA'S AL GHUL CHARACTER TRIED TO FRAME HIM FOR MURDER! IT WAS A PERFECT PLAN, BUT HE BEAT IT!*
I SAID, GENTLEMEN--
*DETECTIVE #444-448! --Julie
--THAT WE ARE AGREED!
BLAM
YOU FOOLS ARE ALL SCARED OF HIM! LOOK AT YOU--QUAKING IN YOUR BOOTS LIKE SCHOOLKIDS!
WELL, I HAVE A PLAN HE CANNOT BEAT! I DON'T CARE IF HE'S THE DEVIL HIMSELF, THE BATMAN--
CHAKA
CHIK
THK
3

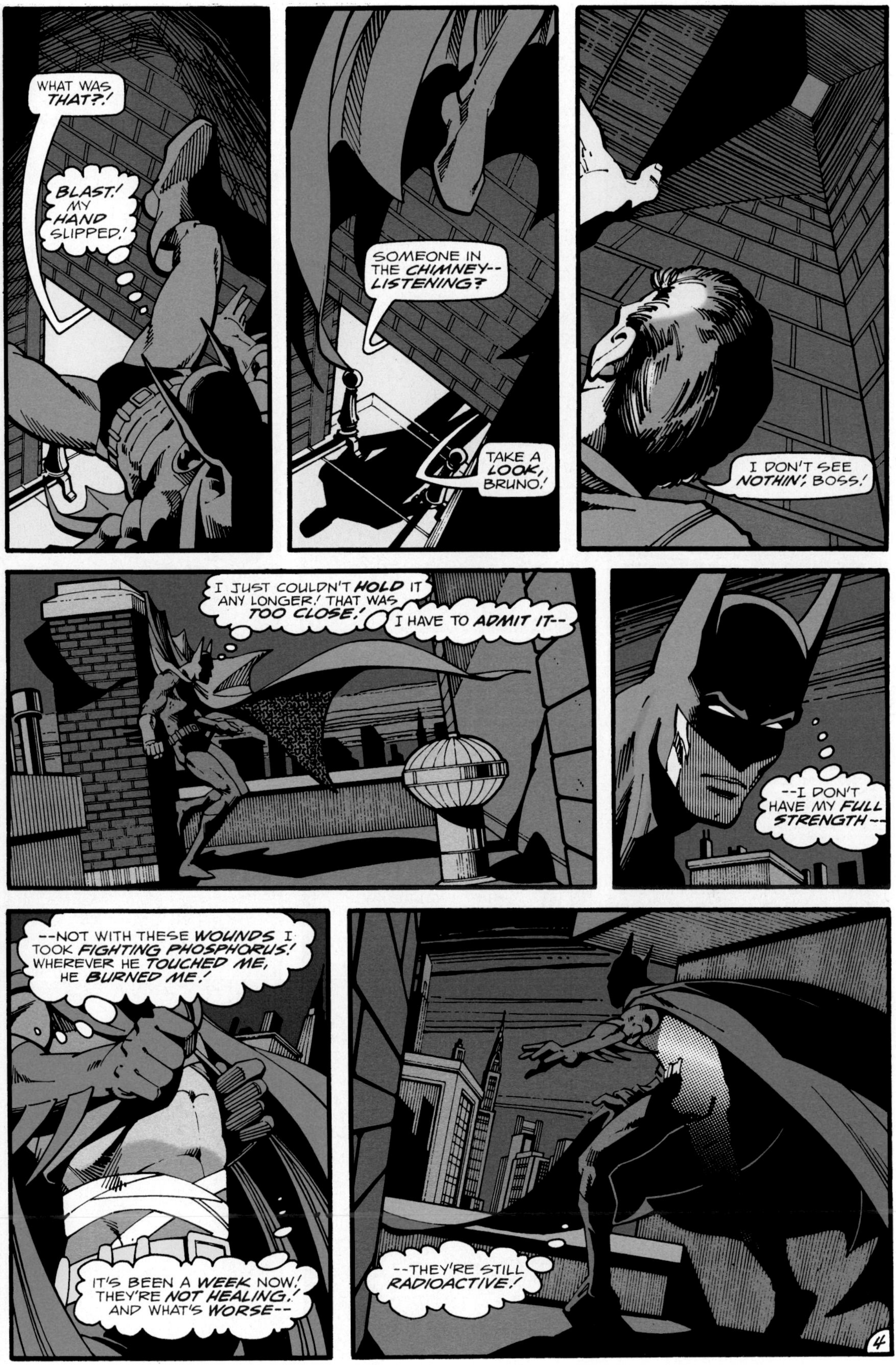
WHAT WAS THAT?!
BLAST! MY HAND SLIPPED!
SOMEONE IN THE CHIMNEY--LISTENING?
TAKE A LOOK, BRUNO!
I DON'T SEE NOTHIN', BOSS!
I JUST COULDN'T HOLD IT ANY LONGER! THAT WAS TOO CLOSE!
I HAVE TO ADMIT IT--
--I DON'T HAVE MY FULL STRENGTH--
--NOT WITH THESE WOUNDS I TOOK FIGHTING PHOSPHORUS! WHEREVER HE TOUCHED ME, HE BURNED ME!
IT'S BEEN A WEEK NOW! THEY'RE NOT HEALING! AND WHAT'S WORSE--
--THEY'RE STILL RADIOACTIVE!
4

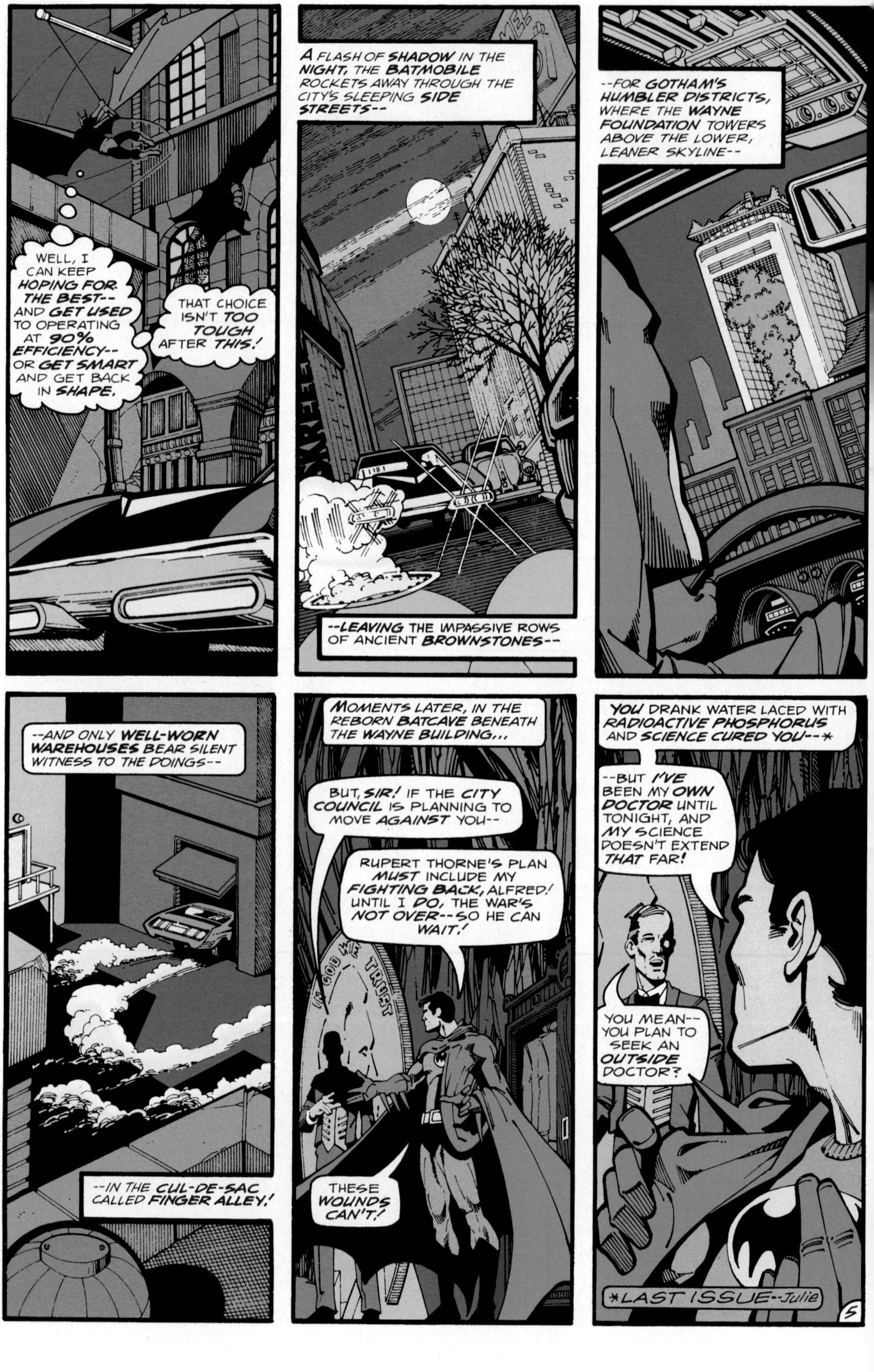

WELL, I CAN KEEP HOPING FOR THE BEST-- AND GET USED TO OPERATING AT 90% EFFICIENCY-- OR GET SMART AND GET BACK IN SHAPE.
THAT CHOICE ISN'T TOO TOUGH AFTER THIS!
A FLASH OF SHADOW IN THE NIGHT, THE BATMOBILE ROCKETS AWAY THROUGH THE CITY'S SLEEPING SIDE STREETS--
--LEAVING THE IMPASSIVE ROWS OF ANCIENT BROWNSTONES--
--FOR GOTHAM'S HUMBLER DISTRICTS, WHERE THE WAYNE FOUNDATION TOWERS ABOVE THE LOWER, LEANER SKYLINE--
--AND ONLY WELL-WORN WAREHOUSES BEAR SILENT WITNESS TO THE DOINGS--
--IN THE CUL-DE-SAC CALLED FINGER ALLEY!
MOMENTS LATER, IN THE REBORN BATCAVE BENEATH THE WAYNE BUILDING...
BUT, SIR! IF THE CITY COUNCIL IS PLANNING TO MOVE AGAINST YOU--
RUPERT THORNE'S PLAN MUST INCLUDE MY FIGHTING BACK, ALFRED! UNTIL I DO, THE WAR'S NOT OVER--SO HE CAN WAIT!
THESE WOUNDS CAN'T!
YOU DRANK WATER LACED WITH RADIOACTIVE PHOSPHORUS AND SCIENCE CURED YOU--*
--BUT I'VE BEEN MY OWN DOCTOR UNTIL TONIGHT, AND MY SCIENCE DOESN'T EXTEND THAT FAR!
YOU MEAN-- YOU PLAN TO SEEK AN OUTSIDE DOCTOR?
*LAST ISSUE--Julie
5

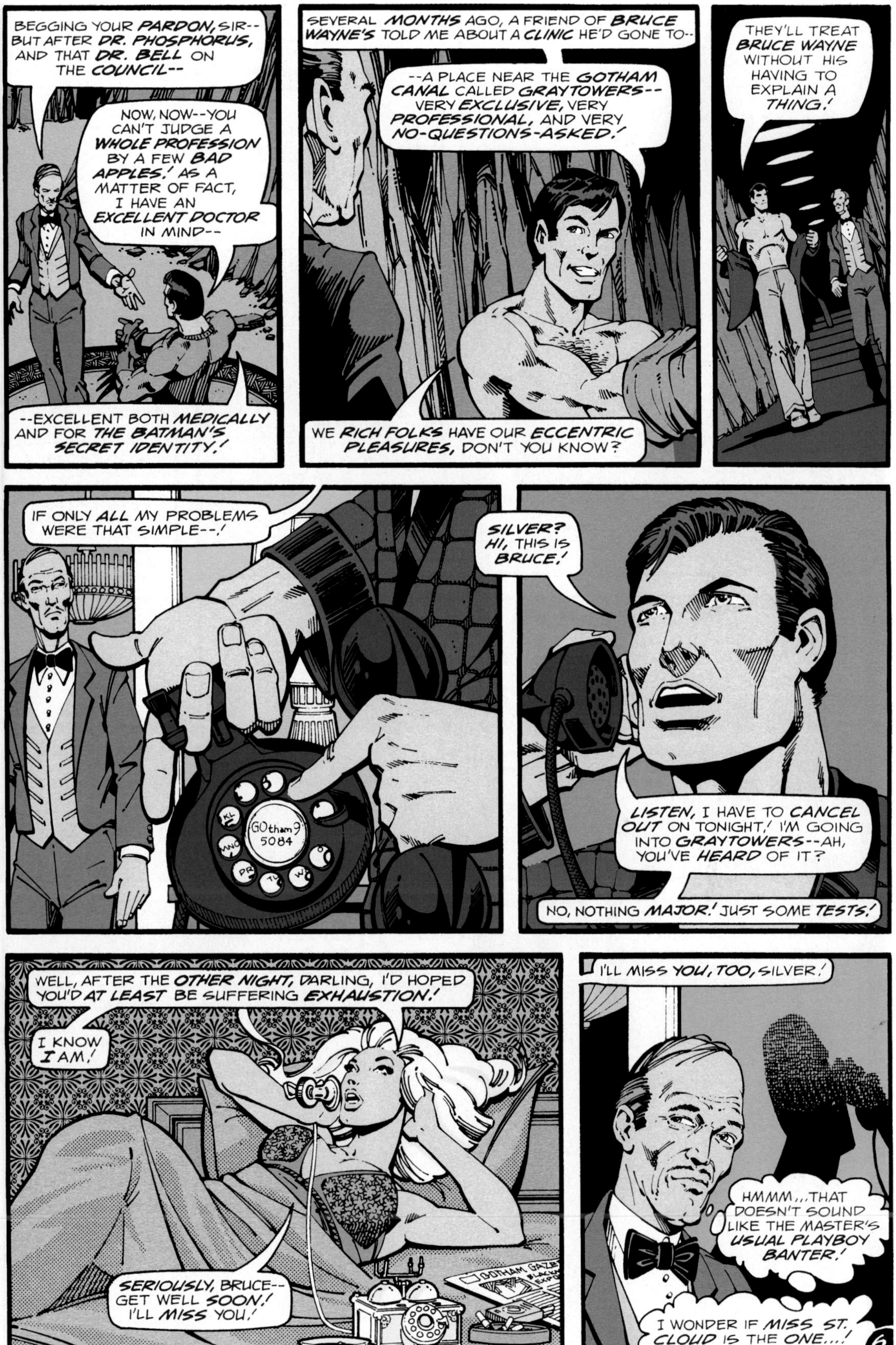
BEGGING YOUR PARDON, SIR-- BUT AFTER DR. PHOSPHORUS, AND THAT DR. BELL ON THE COUNCIL--
NOW, NOW--YOU CAN'T JUDGE A WHOLE PROFESSION BY A FEW BAD APPLES! AS A MATTER OF FACT, I HAVE AN EXCELLENT DOCTOR IN MIND--
--EXCELLENT BOTH MEDICALLY AND FOR THE BATMAN'S SECRET IDENTITY!
SEVERAL MONTHS AGO, A FRIEND OF BRUCE WAYNE'S TOLD ME ABOUT A CLINIC HE'D GONE TO--
--A PLACE NEAR THE GOTHAM CANAL CALLED GRAYTOWERS-- VERY EXCLUSIVE, VERY PROFESSIONAL, AND VERY NO-QUESTIONS-ASKED!
WE RICH FOLKS HAVE OUR ECCENTRIC PLEASURES, DON'T YOU KNOW?
THEY'LL TREAT BRUCE WAYNE WITHOUT HIS HAVING TO EXPLAIN A THING!
IF ONLY ALL MY PROBLEMS WERE THAT SIMPLE--!
GOtham 9 5084
SILVER? HI, THIS IS BRUCE!
LISTEN, I HAVE TO CANCEL OUT ON TONIGHT! I'M GOING INTO GRAYTOWERS--AH, YOU'VE HEARD OF IT?
NO, NOTHING MAJOR! JUST SOME TESTS!
WELL, AFTER THE OTHER NIGHT, DARLING, I'D HOPED YOU'D AT LEAST BE SUFFERING EXHAUSTION!
I KNOW I AM!
SERIOUSLY, BRUCE-- GET WELL SOON! I'LL MISS YOU!
I'LL MISS YOU, TOO, SILVER!
HMMM... THAT DOESN'T SOUND LIKE THE MASTER'S USUAL PLAYBOY BANTER!
I WONDER IF MISS ST. CLOUD IS THE ONE...!
6

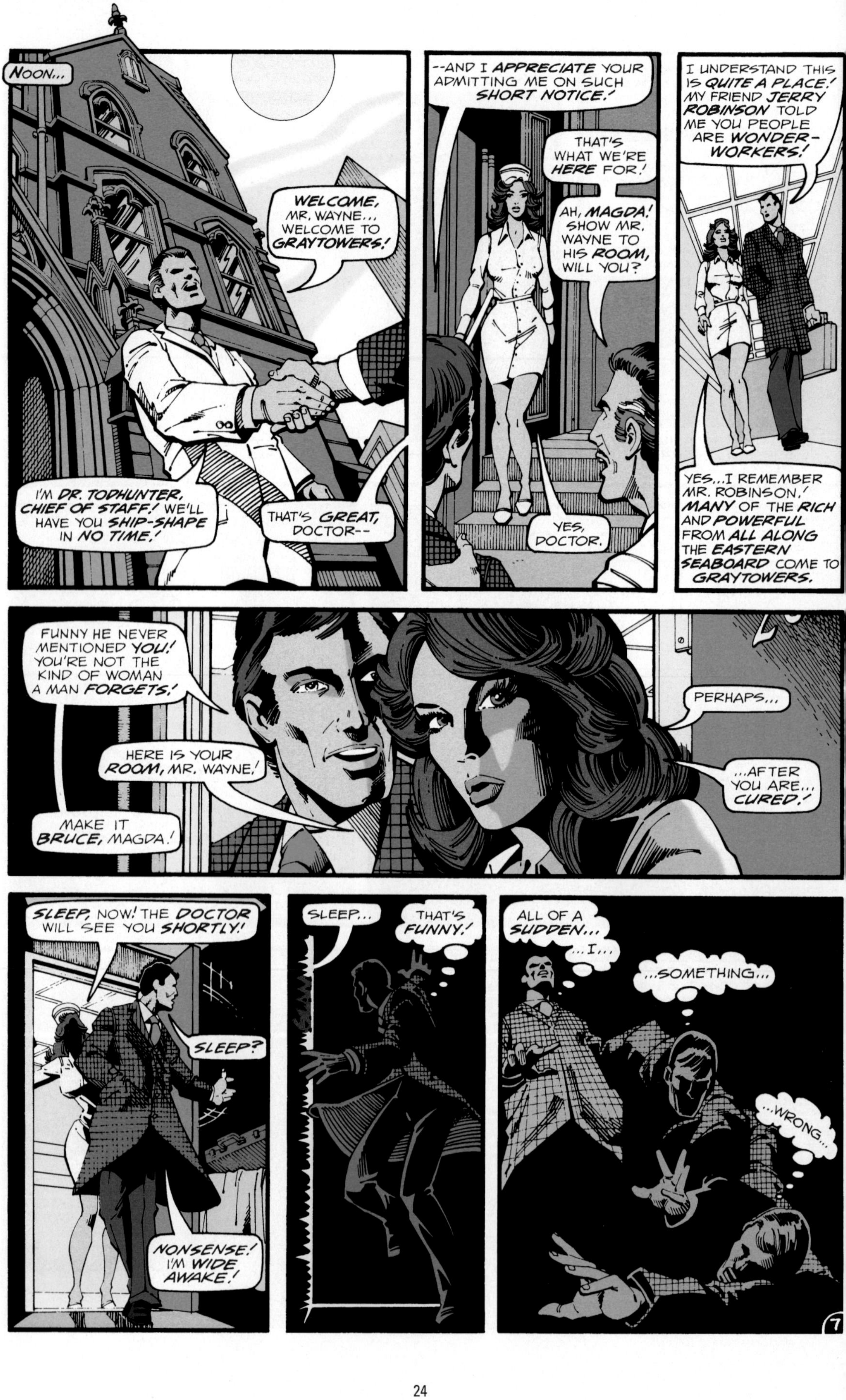
NOON...
WELCOME, MR. WAYNE... WELCOME TO GRAYTOWERS!
I'M DR. TODHUNTER, CHIEF OF STAFF! WE'LL HAVE YOU SHIP-SHAPE IN NO TIME!
THAT'S GREAT, DOCTOR--
--AND I APPRECIATE YOUR ADMITTING ME ON SUCH SHORT NOTICE!
THAT'S WHAT WE'RE HERE FOR!
AH, MAGDA! SHOW MR. WAYNE TO HIS ROOM, WILL YOU?
YES, DOCTOR.
I UNDERSTAND THIS IS QUITE A PLACE! MY FRIEND JERRY ROBINSON TOLD ME YOU PEOPLE ARE WONDER-WORKERS!
YES... I REMEMBER MR. ROBINSON! MANY OF THE RICH AND POWERFUL FROM ALL ALONG THE EASTERN SEABOARD COME TO GRAYTOWERS.
FUNNY HE NEVER MENTIONED YOU! YOU'RE NOT THE KIND OF WOMAN A MAN FORGETS!
PERHAPS...
...AFTER YOU ARE... CURED!
HERE IS YOUR ROOM, MR. WAYNE!
MAKE IT BRUCE, MAGDA!
SLEEP, NOW! THE DOCTOR WILL SEE YOU SHORTLY!
SLEEP?
NONSENSE! I'M WIDE AWAKE!
SLEEP...
THAT'S FUNNY!
ALL OF A SUDDEN...
...I...
...SOMETHING...
...WRONG...
7

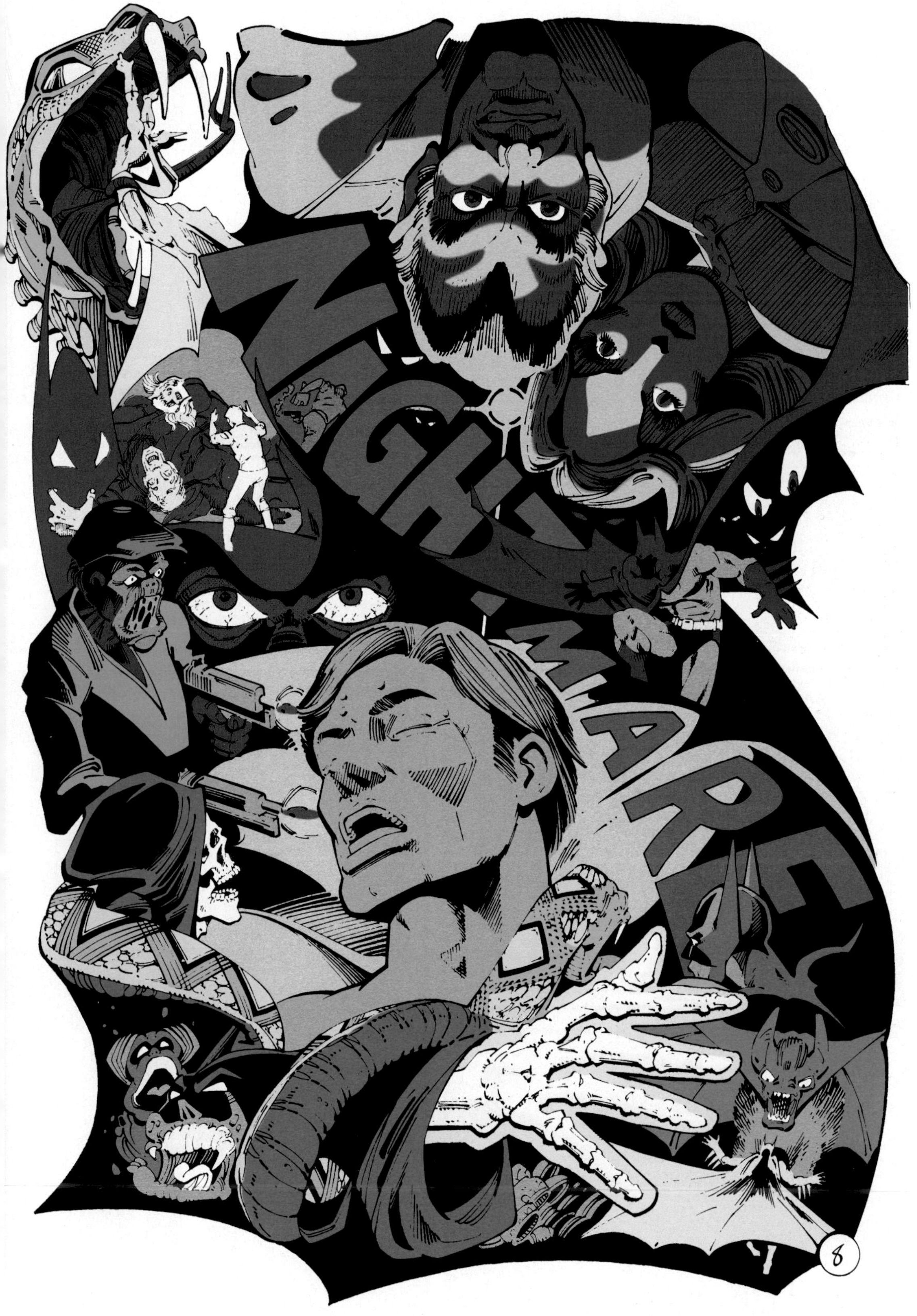

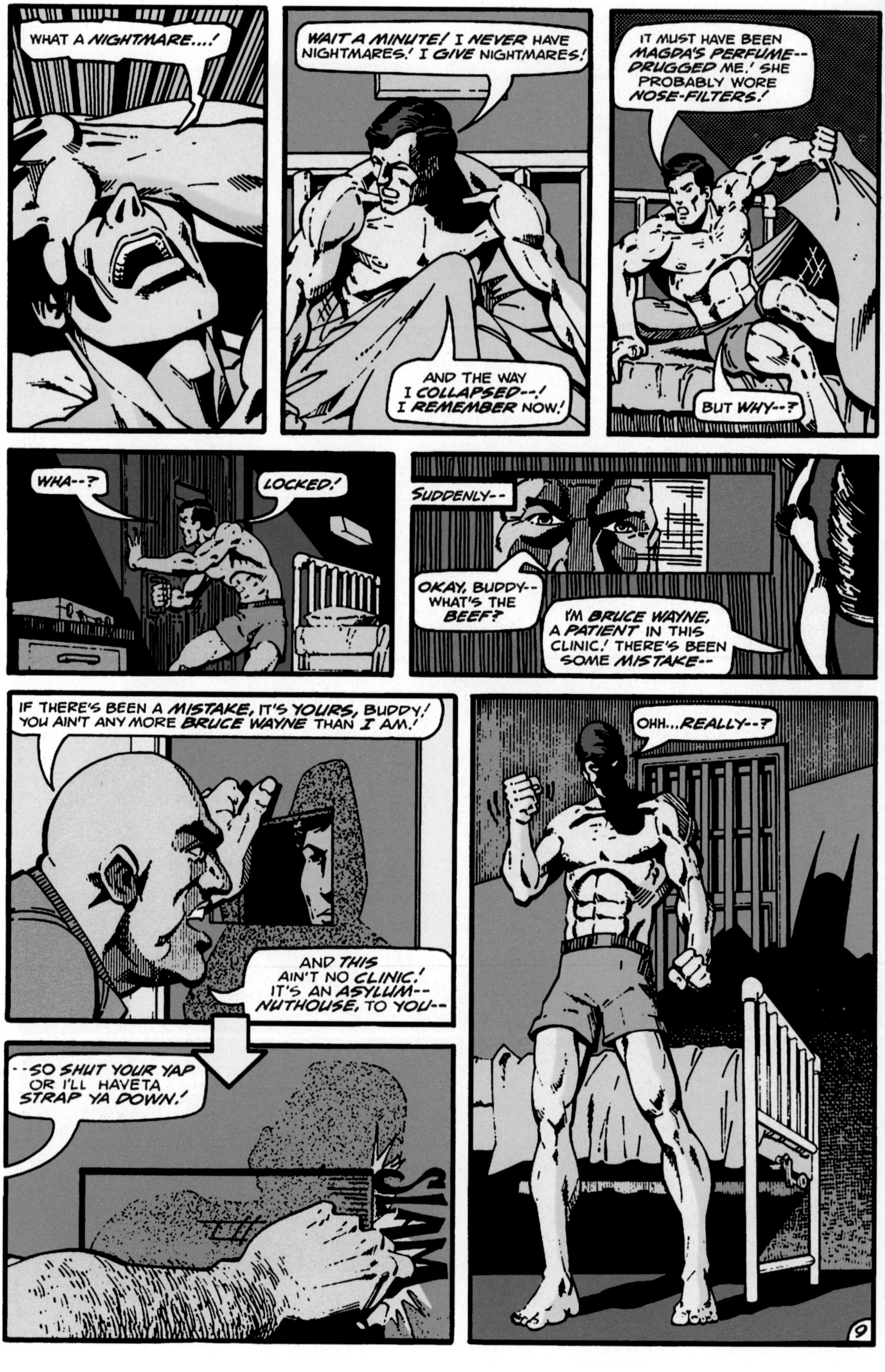
WHAT A NIGHTMARE...!
WAIT A MINUTE! I NEVER HAVE NIGHTMARES! I GIVE NIGHTMARES!
AND THE WAY I COLLAPSED--! I REMEMBER NOW!
IT MUST HAVE BEEN MAGDA'S PERFUME--DRUGGED ME! SHE PROBABLY WORE NOSE-FILTERS!
BUT WHY--?
WHA--?
LOCKED!
SUDDENLY--
OKAY, BUDDY--WHAT'S THE BEEF?
I'M BRUCE WAYNE, A PATIENT IN THIS CLINIC! THERE'S BEEN SOME MISTAKE--
IF THERE'S BEEN A MISTAKE, IT'S YOURS, BUDDY! YOU AIN'T ANY MORE BRUCE WAYNE THAN I AM!
AND THIS AIN'T NO CLINIC! IT'S AN ASYLUM--NUTHOUSE, TO YOU--
--SO SHUT YOUR YAP OR I'LL HAVETA STRAP YA DOWN!
OHH...REALLY--?
9

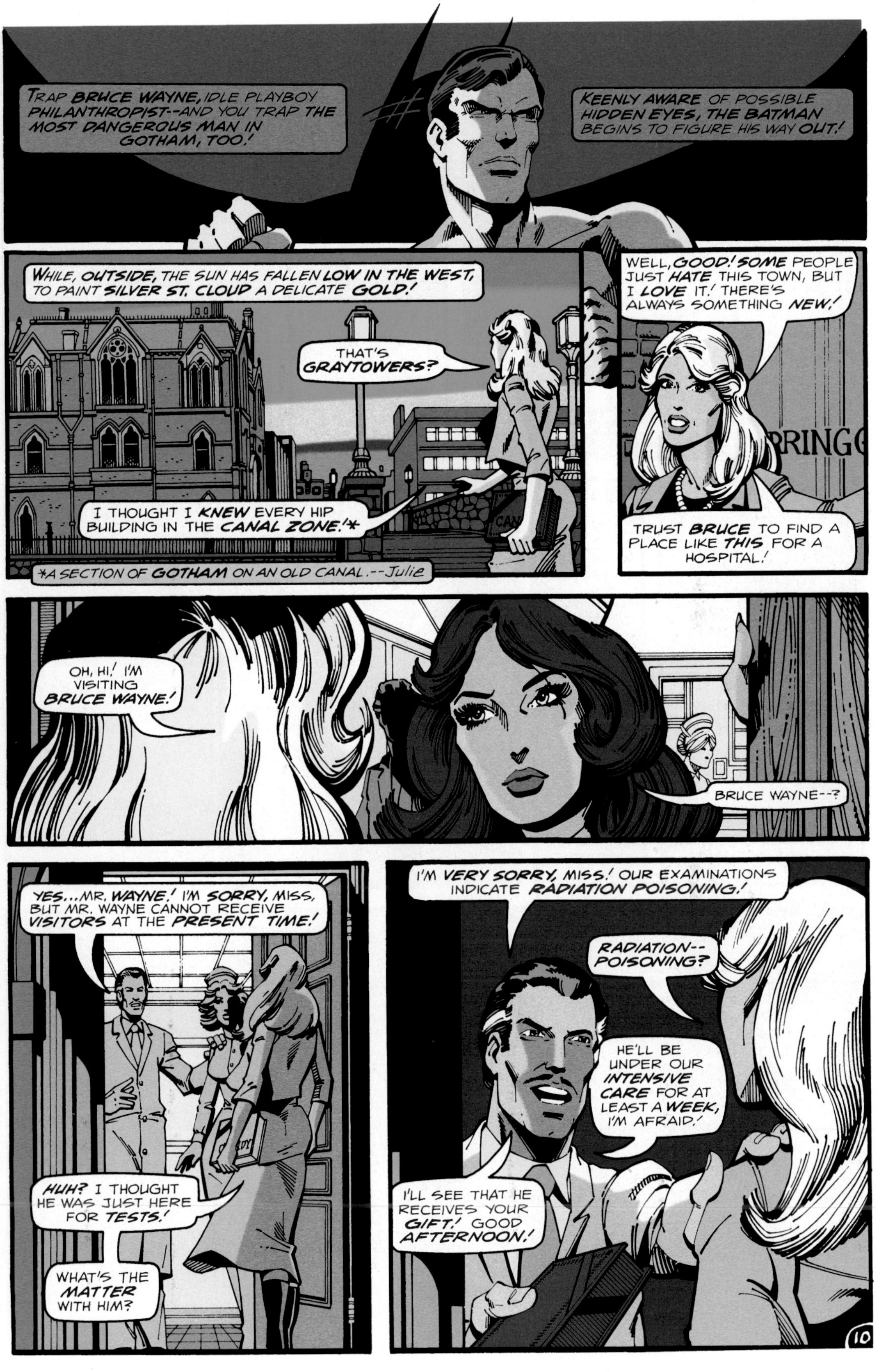
TRAP BRUCE WAYNE, IDLE PLAYBOY PHILANTHROPIST--AND YOU TRAP THE MOST DANGEROUS MAN IN GOTHAM, TOO!
KEENLY AWARE OF POSSIBLE HIDDEN EYES, THE BATMAN BEGINS TO FIGURE HIS WAY OUT!
WHILE, OUTSIDE, THE SUN HAS FALLEN LOW IN THE WEST, TO PAINT SILVER ST. CLOUD A DELICATE GOLD!
THAT'S GRAYTOWERS?
I THOUGHT I KNEW EVERY HIP BUILDING IN THE CANAL ZONE!*
*A SECTION OF GOTHAM ON AN OLD CANAL.--Julie
WELL, GOOD! SOME PEOPLE JUST HATE THIS TOWN, BUT I LOVE IT! THERE'S ALWAYS SOMETHING NEW!
TRUST BRUCE TO FIND A PLACE LIKE THIS FOR A HOSPITAL!
OH, HI! I'M VISITING BRUCE WAYNE!
BRUCE WAYNE--?
YES...MR. WAYNE! I'M SORRY, MISS, BUT MR. WAYNE CANNOT RECEIVE VISITORS AT THE PRESENT TIME!
HUH? I THOUGHT HE WAS JUST HERE FOR TESTS!
WHAT'S THE MATTER WITH HIM?
I'M VERY SORRY, MISS! OUR EXAMINATIONS INDICATE RADIATION POISONING!
RADIATION-- POISONING?
HE'LL BE UNDER OUR INTENSIVE CARE FOR AT LEAST A WEEK, I'M AFRAID!
I'LL SEE THAT HE RECEIVES YOUR GIFT! GOOD AFTERNOON!
10

IN THE NEXT **TWO HOURS**, THE DAY-WORLD DIES, AND THE NIGHT-WORLD FLOWS IN WITH ITS NEONS, SATINS, AND SABLES...

NOW, THE BATMAN IS READY!

HERE, HANDSOME! THE **REST** OF THIS **SWILL** IS FOR **YOU!**

AWRIGHT! CRACK WISE! BUT IF I HEAR A **PEEP** OUTA YOU TONIGHT, I'LL CRACK **YOU** IN **TWO!**

SLEEP, NOW! JUST LIE DOWN AND **SLEEP!**

MY FRIEND, IF YOU THINK I **REALLY** DRANK YOUR **DRUGGED SLOP,** YOU'RE EVEN **DUMBER** THAN YOU **LOOK!**

WITH A HOLLOW **BOOM,** THE **BOLT** SLAMS **SHUT** OUTSIDE--MASKING THE **POP** OF A **SECRET PANEL** IN THE LID OF A STYLISH **SUITCASE...**

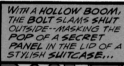

I HAVEN'T SPOTTED ANY **CAMERAS**--SO LET'S **ROLL THE DICE!**

COULDN'T WEAR THIS TO A **MEDICAL EXAM,** BUT IT'S **ALWAYS AROUND!**

AND THUS IS BORN THIS **WEIRD FIGURE OF THE DARK**-- THIS **AVENGER OF EVIL**--

THE BATMAN

11

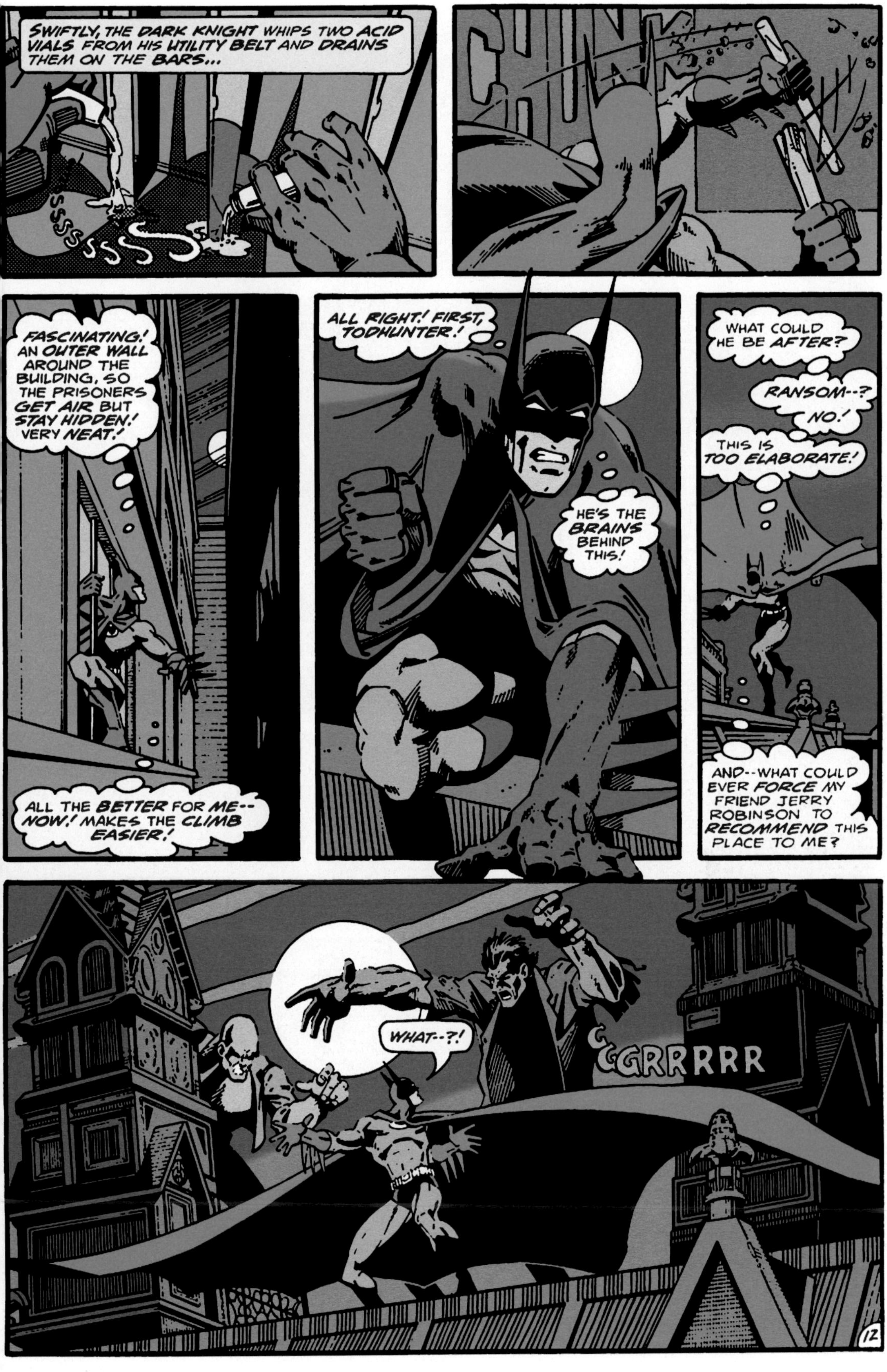
SWIFTLY, THE DARK KNIGHT WHIPS TWO ACID VIALS FROM HIS UTILITY BELT AND DRAINS THEM ON THE BARS...
SSSSSSSS
CHUNK
FASCINATING! AN OUTER WALL AROUND THE BUILDING, SO THE PRISONERS GET AIR BUT STAY HIDDEN! VERY NEAT!
ALL THE BETTER FOR ME--NOW! MAKES THE CLIMB EASIER!
ALL RIGHT! FIRST, TODHUNTER!
HE'S THE BRAINS BEHIND THIS!
WHAT COULD HE BE AFTER?
RANSOM--?
NO!
THIS IS TOO ELABORATE!
AND--WHAT COULD EVER FORCE MY FRIEND JERRY ROBINSON TO RECOMMEND THIS PLACE TO ME?
WHAT--?!
GGRRRRRR
12

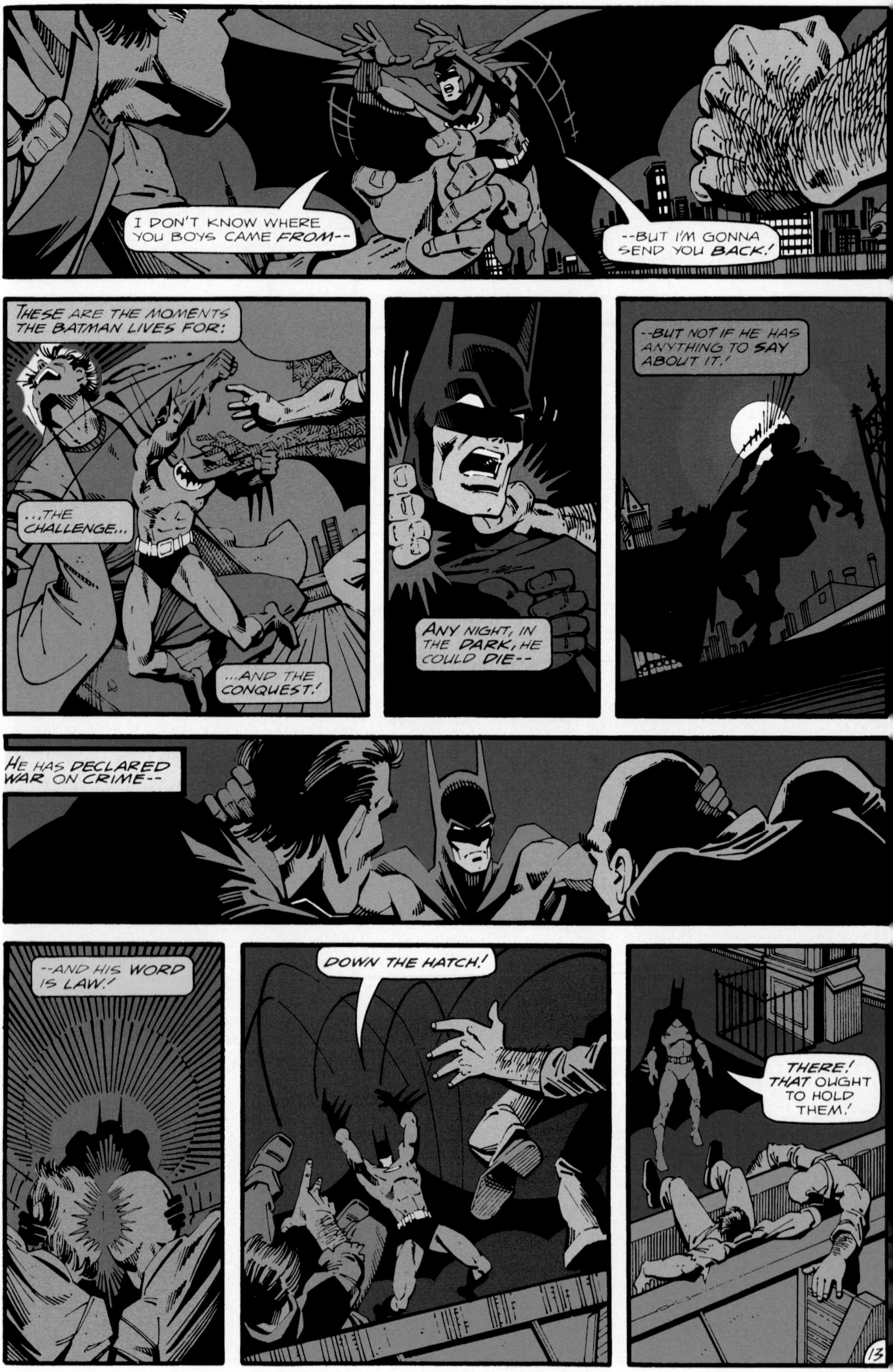
I DON'T KNOW WHERE YOU BOYS CAME FROM--
--BUT I'M GONNA SEND YOU BACK!
THESE ARE THE MOMENTS THE BATMAN LIVES FOR:
...THE CHALLENGE...
...AND THE CONQUEST!
ANY NIGHT, IN THE DARK, HE COULD DIE--
--BUT NOT IF HE HAS ANYTHING TO SAY ABOUT IT!
HE HAS DECLARED WAR ON CRIME--
--AND HIS WORD IS LAW!
DOWN THE HATCH!
THERE! THAT OUGHT TO HOLD THEM!
13

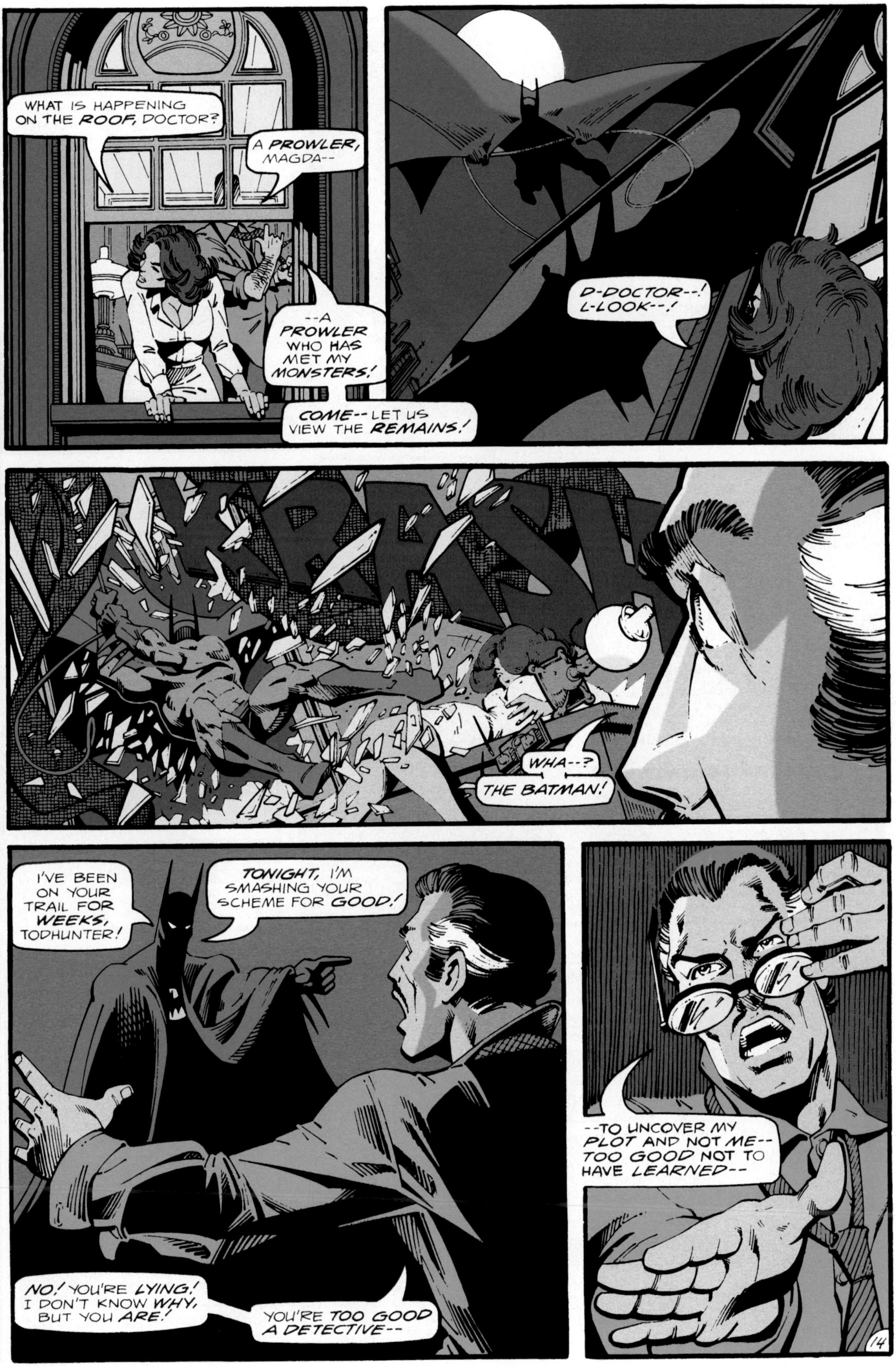

WHAT IS HAPPENING ON THE ROOF, DOCTOR?
A PROWLER, MAGDA--
--A PROWLER WHO HAS MET MY MONSTERS!
COME-- LET US VIEW THE REMAINS!
D-DOCTOR--! L-LOOK--!
WHA--? THE BATMAN!
I'VE BEEN ON YOUR TRAIL FOR WEEKS, TODHUNTER!
TONIGHT, I'M SMASHING YOUR SCHEME FOR GOOD!
NO! YOU'RE LYING! I DON'T KNOW WHY, BUT YOU ARE!
YOU'RE TOO GOOD A DETECTIVE--
--TO UNCOVER MY PLOT AND NOT ME-- TOO GOOD NOT TO HAVE LEARNED--
14

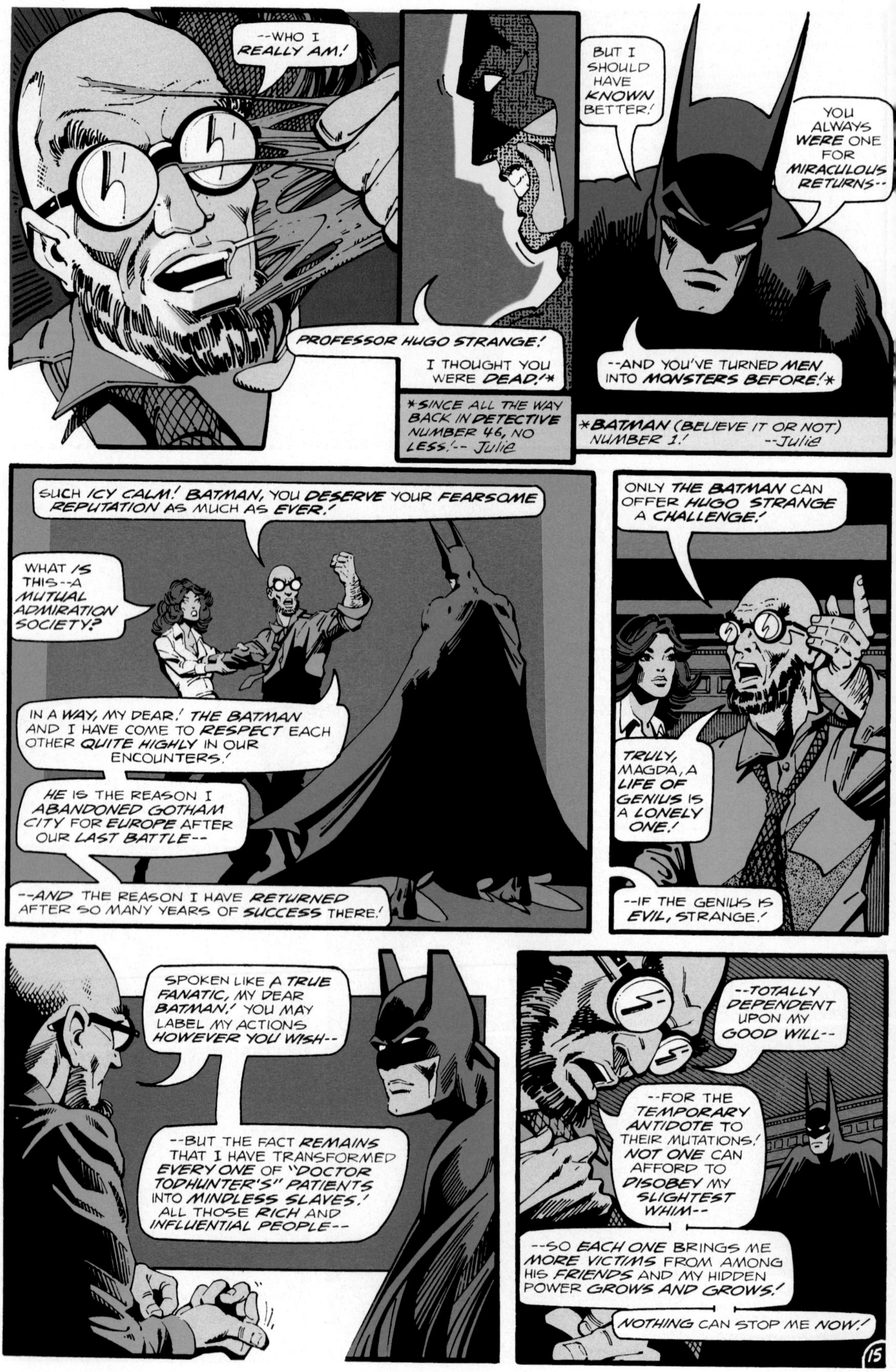
--WHO I REALLY AM!
PROFESSOR HUGO STRANGE!
I THOUGHT YOU WERE DEAD!*
*SINCE ALL THE WAY BACK IN DETECTIVE NUMBER 46, NO LESS!-- Julie
BUT I SHOULD HAVE KNOWN BETTER!
YOU ALWAYS WERE ONE FOR MIRACULOUS RETURNS--
--AND YOU'VE TURNED MEN INTO MONSTERS BEFORE!*
*BATMAN (BELIEVE IT OR NOT) NUMBER 1! --Julie
SUCH ICY CALM! BATMAN, YOU DESERVE YOUR FEARSOME REPUTATION AS MUCH AS EVER!
WHAT IS THIS--A MUTUAL ADMIRATION SOCIETY?
IN A WAY, MY DEAR! THE BATMAN AND I HAVE COME TO RESPECT EACH OTHER QUITE HIGHLY IN OUR ENCOUNTERS!
HE IS THE REASON I ABANDONED GOTHAM CITY FOR EUROPE AFTER OUR LAST BATTLE--
--AND THE REASON I HAVE RETURNED AFTER SO MANY YEARS OF SUCCESS THERE!
ONLY THE BATMAN CAN OFFER HUGO STRANGE A CHALLENGE!
TRULY, MAGDA, A LIFE OF GENIUS IS A LONELY ONE!
--IF THE GENIUS IS EVIL, STRANGE!
SPOKEN LIKE A TRUE FANATIC, MY DEAR BATMAN! YOU MAY LABEL MY ACTIONS HOWEVER YOU WISH--
--BUT THE FACT REMAINS THAT I HAVE TRANSFORMED EVERY ONE OF "DOCTOR TODHUNTER'S" PATIENTS INTO MINDLESS SLAVES! ALL THOSE RICH AND INFLUENTIAL PEOPLE--
--TOTALLY DEPENDENT UPON MY GOOD WILL--
--FOR THE TEMPORARY ANTIDOTE TO THEIR MUTATIONS! NOT ONE CAN AFFORD TO DISOBEY MY SLIGHTEST WHIM--
--SO EACH ONE BRINGS ME MORE VICTIMS FROM AMONG HIS FRIENDS AND MY HIDDEN POWER GROWS AND GROWS!
NOTHING CAN STOP ME NOW!
15

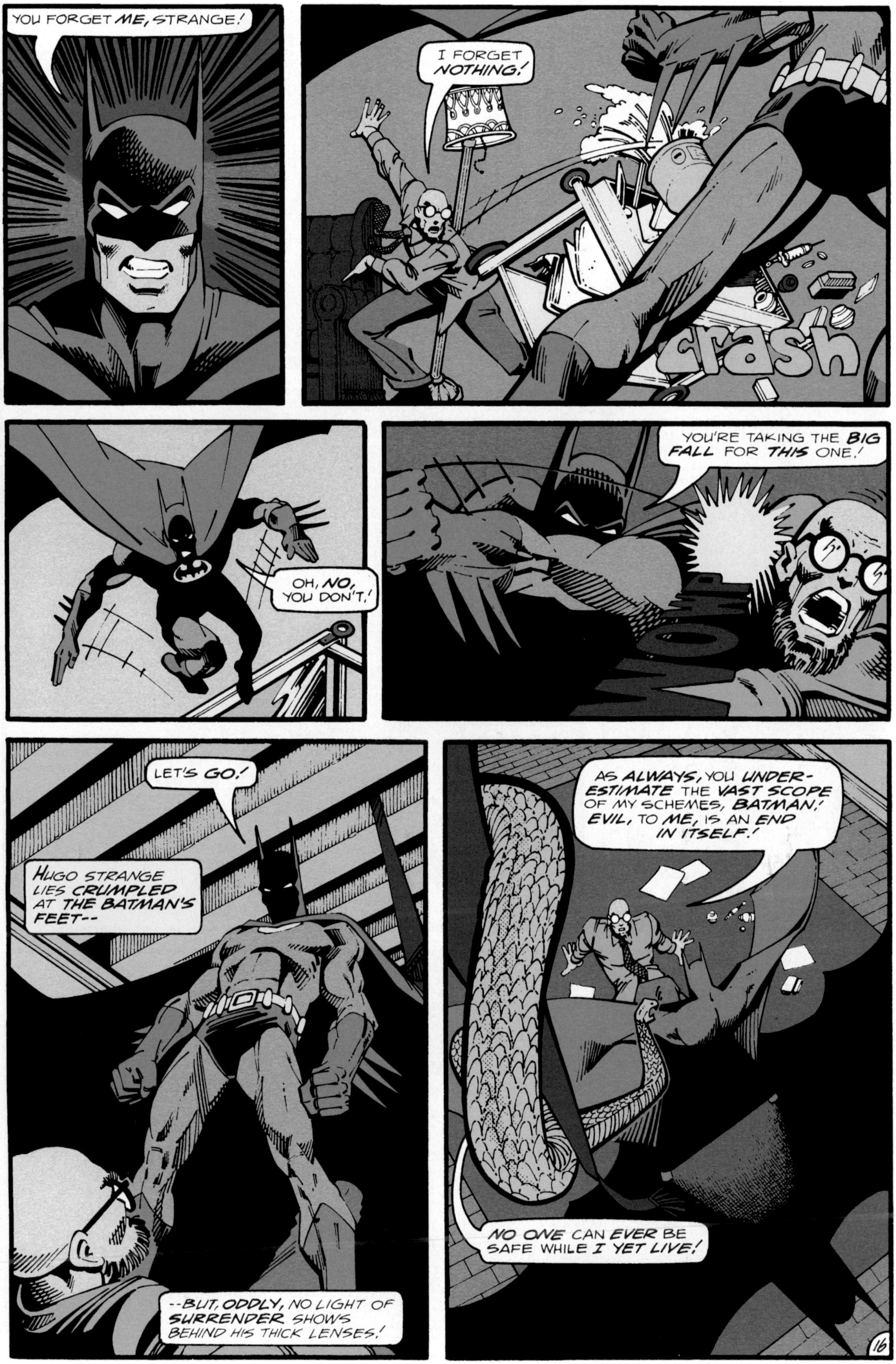
YOU FORGET ME, STRANGE!
I FORGET NOTHING!
CRASH
OH, NO, YOU DON'T!
YOU'RE TAKING THE BIG FALL FOR THIS ONE!
LET'S GO!
HUGO STRANGE LIES CRUMPLED AT THE BATMAN'S FEET--
--BUT, ODDLY, NO LIGHT OF SURRENDER SHOWS BEHIND HIS THICK LENSES!
AS ALWAYS, YOU UNDER-ESTIMATE THE VAST SCOPE OF MY SCHEMES, BATMAN! EVIL, TO ME, IS AN END IN ITSELF!
NO ONE CAN EVER BE SAFE WHILE I YET LIVE!
16

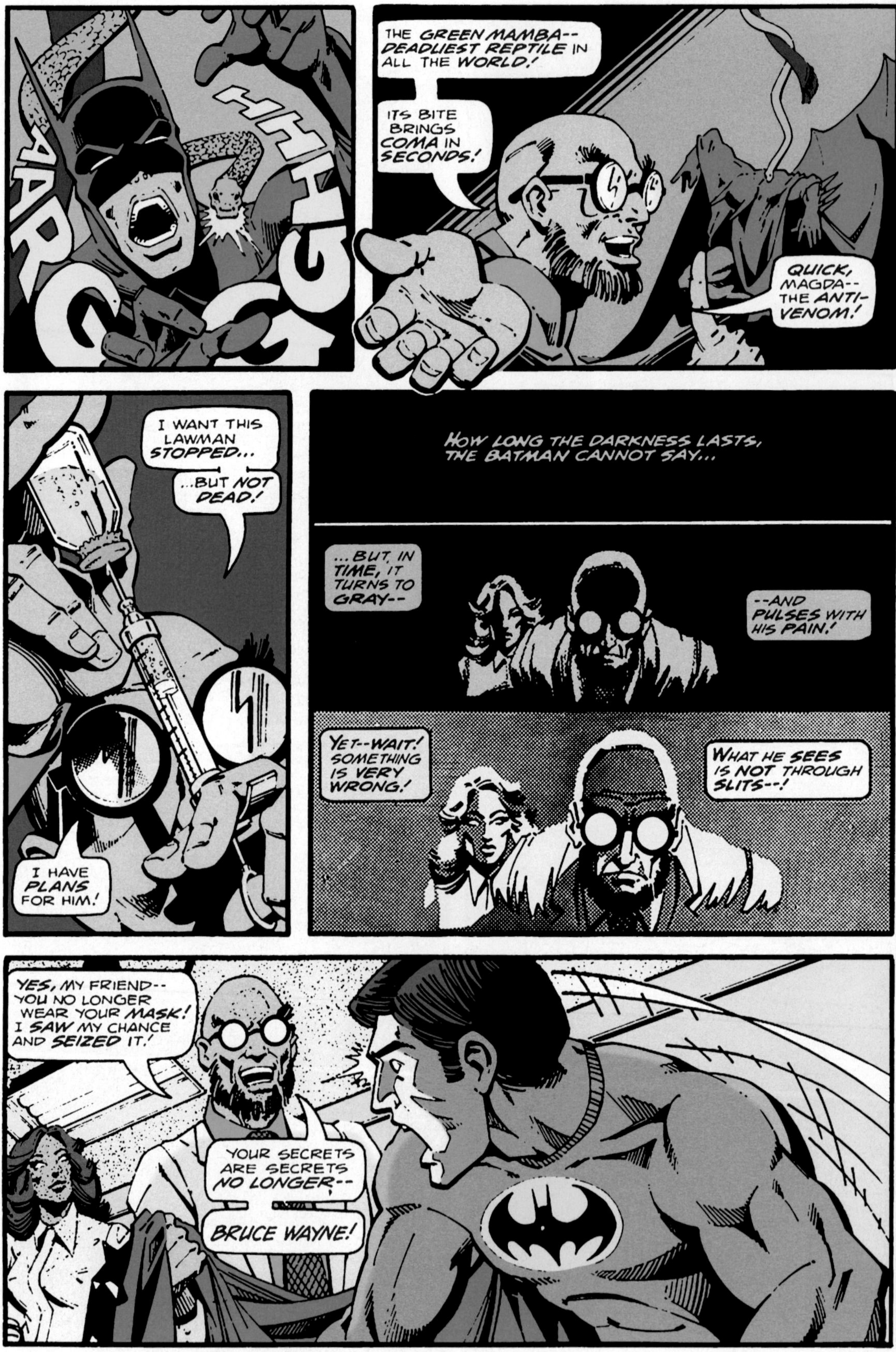

ARGGHH
THE GREEN MAMBA-- DEADLIEST REPTILE IN ALL THE WORLD!
ITS BITE BRINGS COMA IN SECONDS!
QUICK, MAGDA-- THE ANTI-VENOM!
I WANT THIS LAWMAN STOPPED...
...BUT NOT DEAD!
I HAVE PLANS FOR HIM!
HOW LONG THE DARKNESS LASTS, THE BATMAN CANNOT SAY...
...BUT, IN TIME, IT TURNS TO GRAY--
--AND PULSES WITH HIS PAIN!
YET--WAIT! SOMETHING IS VERY WRONG!
WHAT HE SEES IS NOT THROUGH SLITS--!
YES, MY FRIEND-- YOU NO LONGER WEAR YOUR MASK! I SAW MY CHANCE AND SEIZED IT!
YOUR SECRETS ARE SECRETS NO LONGER--
BRUCE WAYNE!

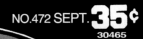

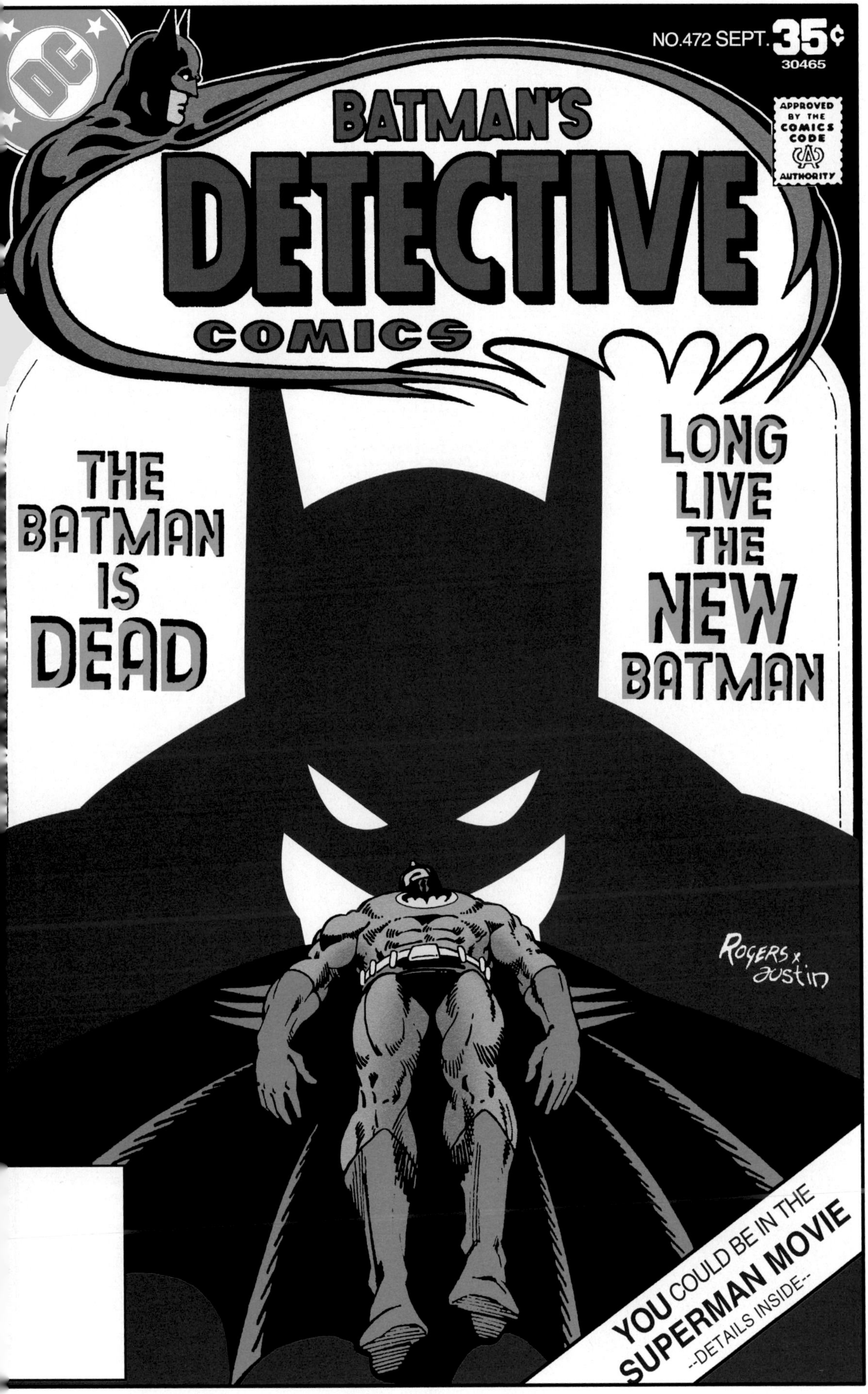

DC

NO.472 SEPT. **35**¢
30465

APPROVED
BY THE
COMICS
CODE
AUTHORITY

# BATMAN'S
# DETECTIVE
## COMICS

THE
BATMAN
IS
DEAD

LONG
LIVE
THE
NEW
BATMAN

Rogers x
austin

YOU COULD BE IN THE
SUPERMAN MOVIE
--DETAILS INSIDE--

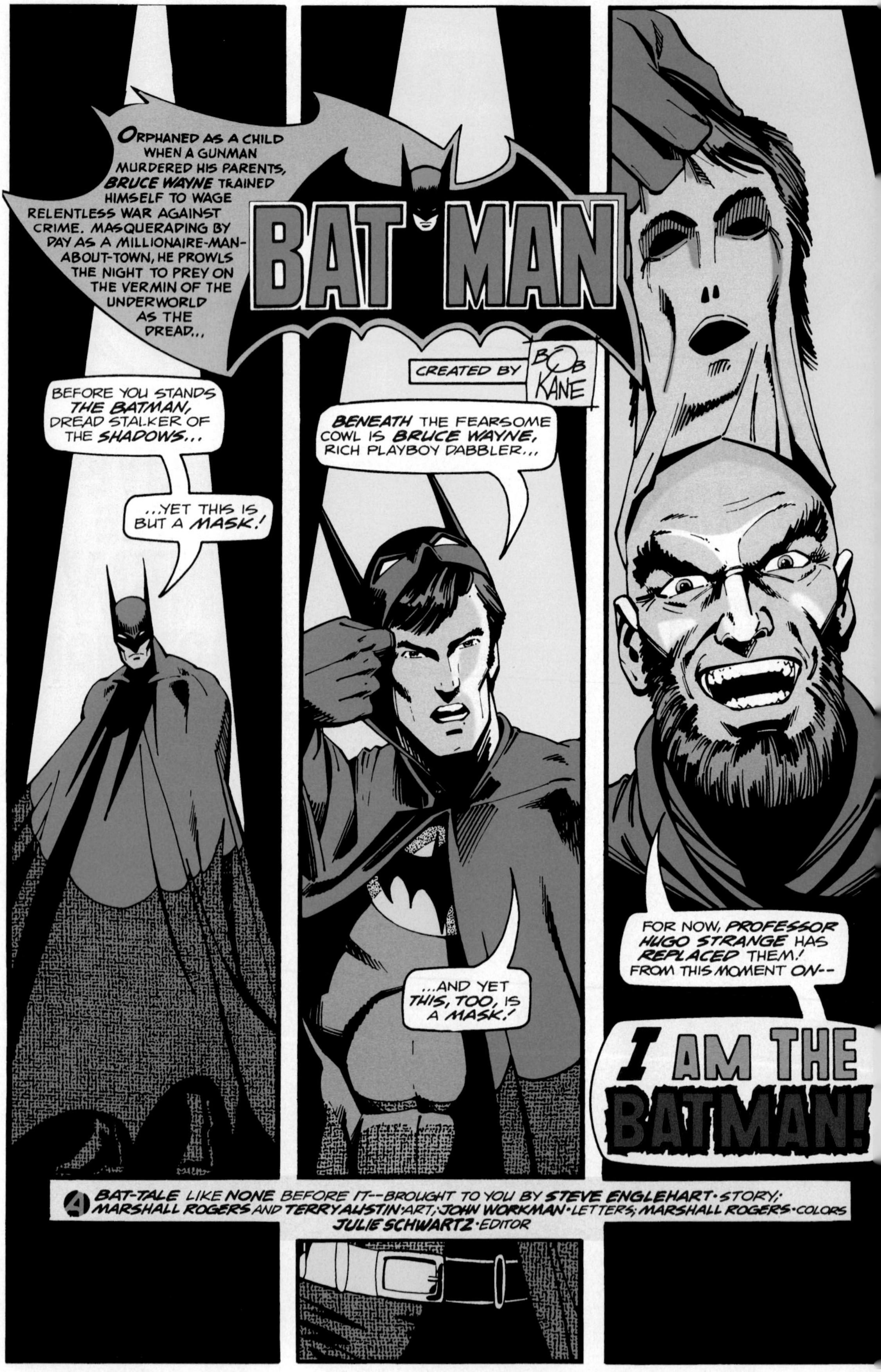

ORPHANED AS A CHILD WHEN A GUNMAN MURDERED HIS PARENTS, BRUCE WAYNE TRAINED HIMSELF TO WAGE RELENTLESS WAR AGAINST CRIME. MASQUERADING BY DAY AS A MILLIONAIRE-MAN-ABOUT-TOWN, HE PROWLS THE NIGHT TO PREY ON THE VERMIN OF THE UNDERWORLD AS THE DREAD...
BATMAN
CREATED BY BOB KANE
BEFORE YOU STANDS THE BATMAN, DREAD STALKER OF THE SHADOWS...
...YET THIS IS BUT A MASK!
BENEATH THE FEARSOME COWL IS BRUCE WAYNE, RICH PLAYBOY DABBLER...
...AND YET THIS, TOO, IS A MASK!
FOR NOW, PROFESSOR HUGO STRANGE HAS REPLACED THEM! FROM THIS MOMENT ON--
I AM THE BATMAN!
A BAT-TALE LIKE NONE BEFORE IT--BROUGHT TO YOU BY STEVE ENGLEHART·STORY; MARSHALL ROGERS AND TERRY AUSTIN·ART; JOHN WORKMAN·LETTERS; MARSHALL ROGERS·COLORS
JULIE SCHWARTZ·EDITOR

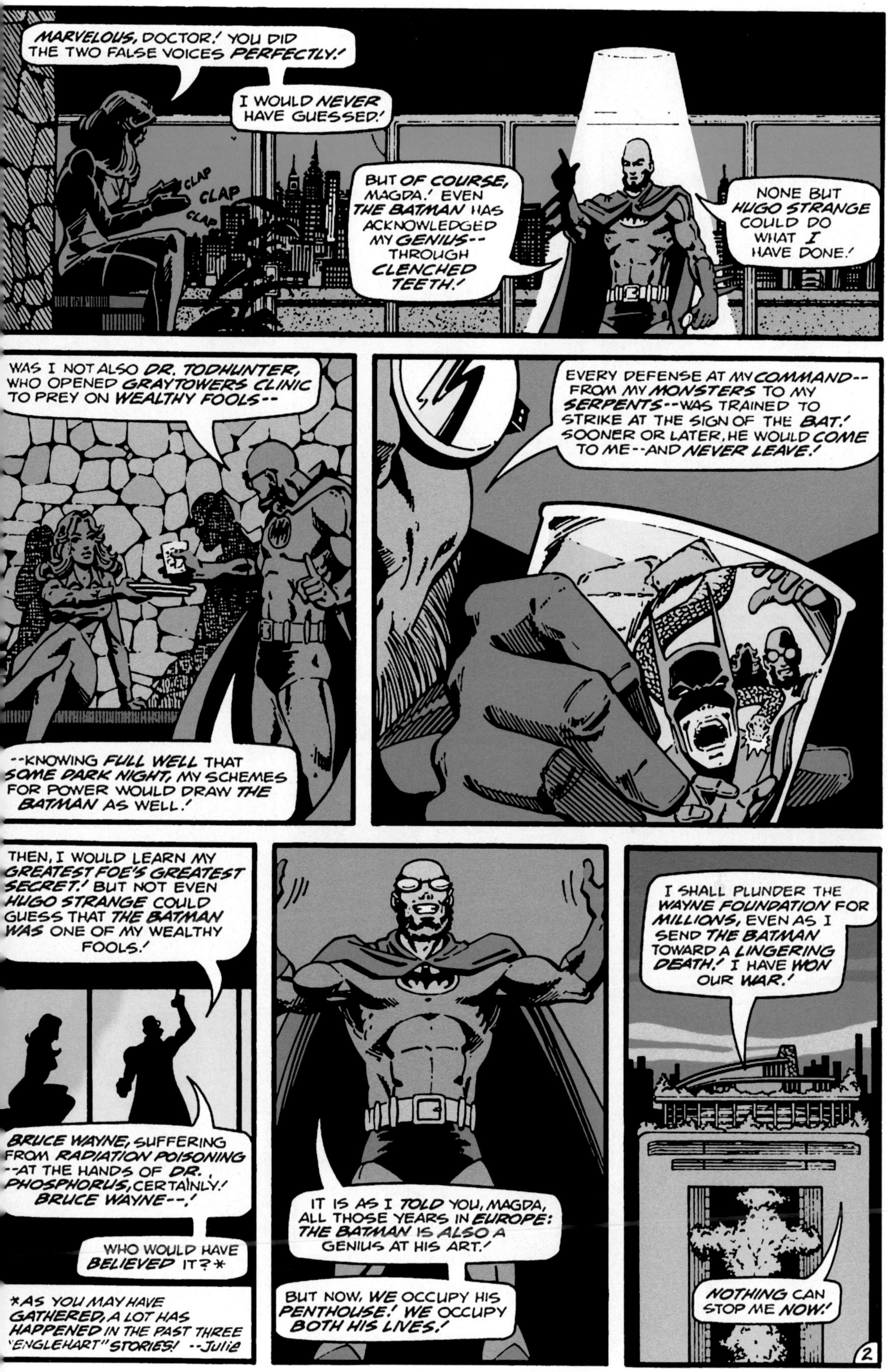
MARVELOUS, DOCTOR! YOU DID THE TWO FALSE VOICES PERFECTLY!
I WOULD NEVER HAVE GUESSED!
CLAP CLAP CLAP
BUT OF COURSE, MAGDA! EVEN THE BATMAN HAS ACKNOWLEDGED MY GENIUS--THROUGH CLENCHED TEETH!
NONE BUT HUGO STRANGE COULD DO WHAT I HAVE DONE!
WAS I NOT ALSO DR. TODHUNTER, WHO OPENED GRAYTOWERS CLINIC TO PREY ON WEALTHY FOOLS--
--KNOWING FULL WELL THAT SOME DARK NIGHT, MY SCHEMES FOR POWER WOULD DRAW THE BATMAN AS WELL!
EVERY DEFENSE AT MY COMMAND--FROM MY MONSTERS TO MY SERPENTS--WAS TRAINED TO STRIKE AT THE SIGN OF THE BAT! SOONER OR LATER, HE WOULD COME TO ME--AND NEVER LEAVE!
THEN, I WOULD LEARN MY GREATEST FOE'S GREATEST SECRET! BUT NOT EVEN HUGO STRANGE COULD GUESS THAT THE BATMAN WAS ONE OF MY WEALTHY FOOLS!
BRUCE WAYNE, SUFFERING FROM RADIATION POISONING--AT THE HANDS OF DR. PHOSPHORUS, CERTAINLY! BRUCE WAYNE--!
WHO WOULD HAVE BELIEVED IT?*
*AS YOU MAY HAVE GATHERED, A LOT HAS HAPPENED IN THE PAST THREE "ENGLEHART" STORIES! --Julie
IT IS AS I TOLD YOU, MAGDA, ALL THOSE YEARS IN EUROPE: THE BATMAN IS ALSO A GENIUS AT HIS ART!
BUT NOW, WE OCCUPY HIS PENTHOUSE! WE OCCUPY BOTH HIS LIVES!
I SHALL PLUNDER THE WAYNE FOUNDATION FOR MILLIONS, EVEN AS I SEND THE BATMAN TOWARD A LINGERING DEATH! I HAVE WON OUR WAR!
NOTHING CAN STOP ME NOW!
2

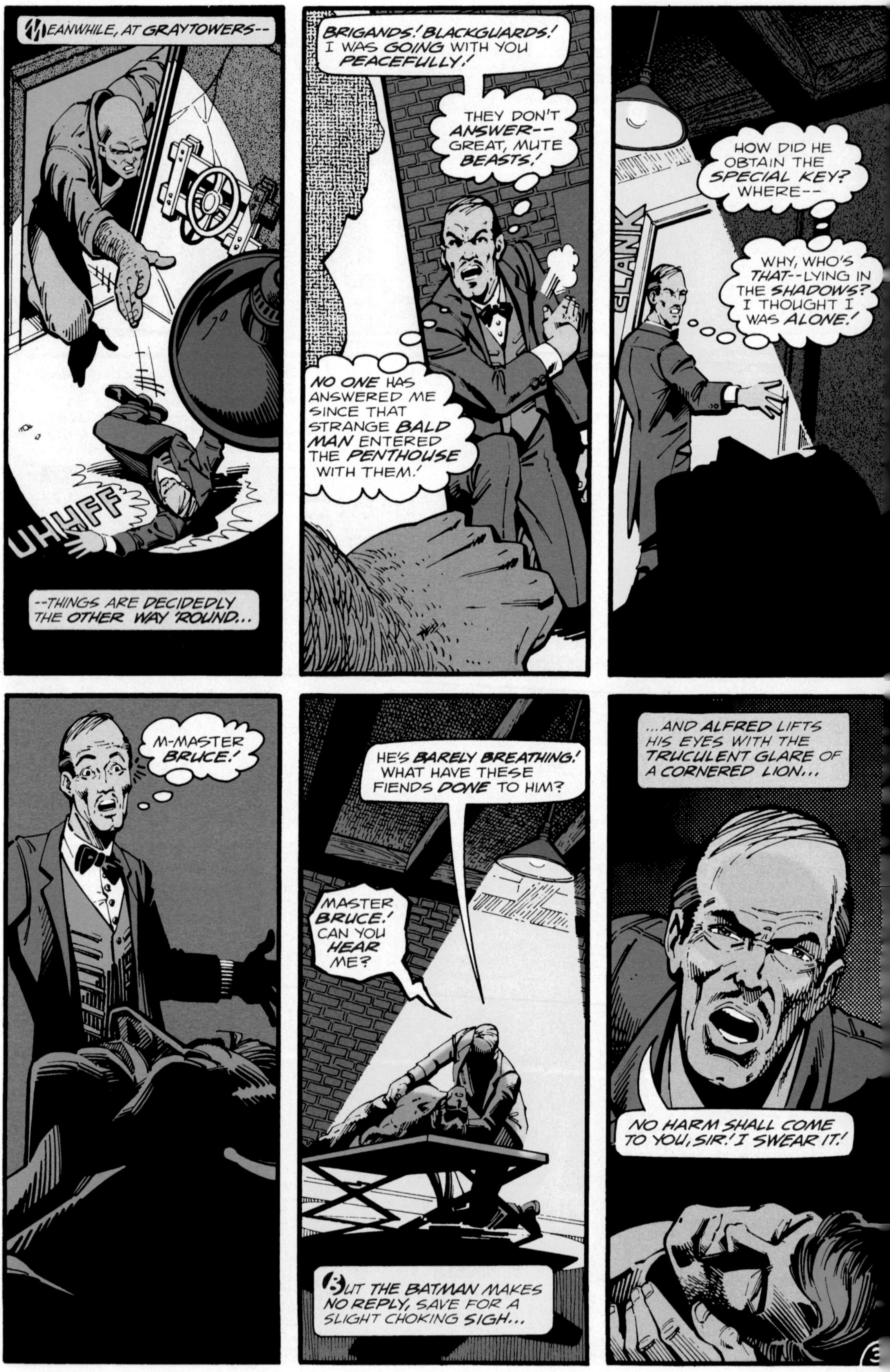
MEANWHILE, AT GRAYTOWERS--
UHHFF
--THINGS ARE DECIDEDLY THE OTHER WAY 'ROUND...
BRIGANDS! BLACKGUARDS! I WAS GOING WITH YOU PEACEFULLY!
THEY DON'T ANSWER-- GREAT, MUTE BEASTS!
NO ONE HAS ANSWERED ME SINCE THAT STRANGE BALD MAN ENTERED THE PENTHOUSE WITH THEM!
CLANK
HOW DID HE OBTAIN THE SPECIAL KEY? WHERE--
WHY, WHO'S THAT--LYING IN THE SHADOWS? I THOUGHT I WAS ALONE!
M-MASTER BRUCE!
HE'S BARELY BREATHING! WHAT HAVE THESE FIENDS DONE TO HIM?
MASTER BRUCE! CAN YOU HEAR ME?
BUT THE BATMAN MAKES NO REPLY, SAVE FOR A SLIGHT CHOKING SIGH...
...AND ALFRED LIFTS HIS EYES WITH THE TRUCULENT GLARE OF A CORNERED LION...
NO HARM SHALL COME TO YOU, SIR! I SWEAR IT!

BUT ALL THIS MAY BE TOO LITTLE AND TOO LATE! IN THE FOLLOWING DAYS, HUGO STRANGE MOVES TO MAKE GOOD ON HIS VOW--

--FIRST, RETREATING FROM PUBLIC VIEW IN A MANNER TO RIVAL HOWARD HUGHES...

I'M SORRY, MR. GOULD! MR. WAYNE HAS CANCELLED ALL HIS APPOINTMENTS FOR THE WEEK!

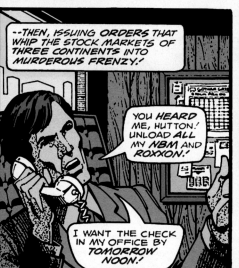

--THEN, ISSUING ORDERS THAT WHIP THE STOCK MARKETS OF THREE CONTINENTS INTO MURDEROUS FRENZY!

YOU HEARD ME, HUTTON! UNLOAD ALL MY NBM AND ROXXON!

I WANT THE CHECK IN MY OFFICE BY TOMORROW NOON!

NO ONE QUESTIONS BRUCE WAYNE--AND, WITH ALL THE FINANCIERS WHO SOUGHT HELP AT GRAYTOWERS NEEDING THE ANTIDOTE TO MY MONSTER SERUM AND FORCED TO BACK MY PLAY--

--I'LL BANKRUPT THIS FOUNDATION IN TWO WEEKS-- THEN LIVE IN LUXURY FOR THE REST OF MY LIFE!

MAGDA! HOW FARES OUR COMATOSE CAPTIVE?

THE SAME, DOCTOR! HIS BUTLER CARES FOR HIM CONTINUALLY!

GOOD! HE MUST BE PRESERVED UNTIL I HAVE FINISHED HERE! THEN--

SURPRISE, DARLING!

NAME OF THE DEVIL! IT'S THE GIRL WHO CAME TO VISIT WAYNE AT THE CLINIC!

YOU DIDN'T TELL ME YOU WERE HOME, BRUCE! I WASN'T EXPECTING YOU BACK FOR A WEEK!

IF YOU WEREN'T CREATING SUCH A STIR ON WALL STREET, I'D STILL BE PINING AWAY!

4

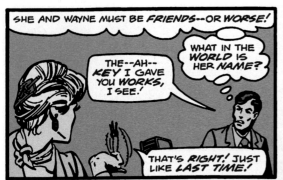

SHE AND WAYNE MUST BE *FRIENDS*--OR *WORSE!*

WHAT IN THE *WORLD* IS HER *NAME?*

THE--AH-- *KEY* I GAVE YOU *WORKS,* I SEE!

THAT'S *RIGHT!* JUST LIKE *LAST TIME!*

OH, *SURE!*

WELL, BUT--I REALLY *HAVE* TO GET BACK TO *WORK!* I STAND TO CLOSE THE *BIGGEST DEAL OF MY LIFE* IF I CAN RAISE THE *MONEY* IN TIME!

I'LL CALL YOU ON *SATURDAY!* HOW'S *THAT?*

EYES NARROWING, SILVER ST. CLOUD LEANS LOW ACROSS THE DESK...

THAT'S NOT *TOO GOOD,* BRUCE! WHAT'S *GOING ON?*

YOU *ARE* DIRECT, AREN'T YOU? WELL, TO BE *EQUALLY* BLUNT, I'M *BREAKING IT OFF!* WE'RE *FINISHED!*

SO THAT'S IT? SO LONG, SILVER-- IT'S BEEN LAUGHS?

*SILVER!*

WHY, YOU BIG *HAM!* WHO DO YOU THINK YOU *ARE?*

*SLAP*

NOW, SILVER....!

NOT *ANOTHER WORD!* I'VE HEARD ALL I *WANT* TO HEAR FROM *YOU!*

SWAK

I JUST HOPE THE *NEXT GIRL* BELIEVES YOUR *PLAYBOY REPUTATION*--

--INSTEAD OF YOUR *LYING EYES!*

WELL! THAT WAS *UNPLEASANT!* BUT IT *SERVED* ITS *PURPOSE!*

SHE WON'T *BOTHER* ME *AGAIN!* WONDER HOW MANY *MORE* KEYS WAYNE GAVE OUT?

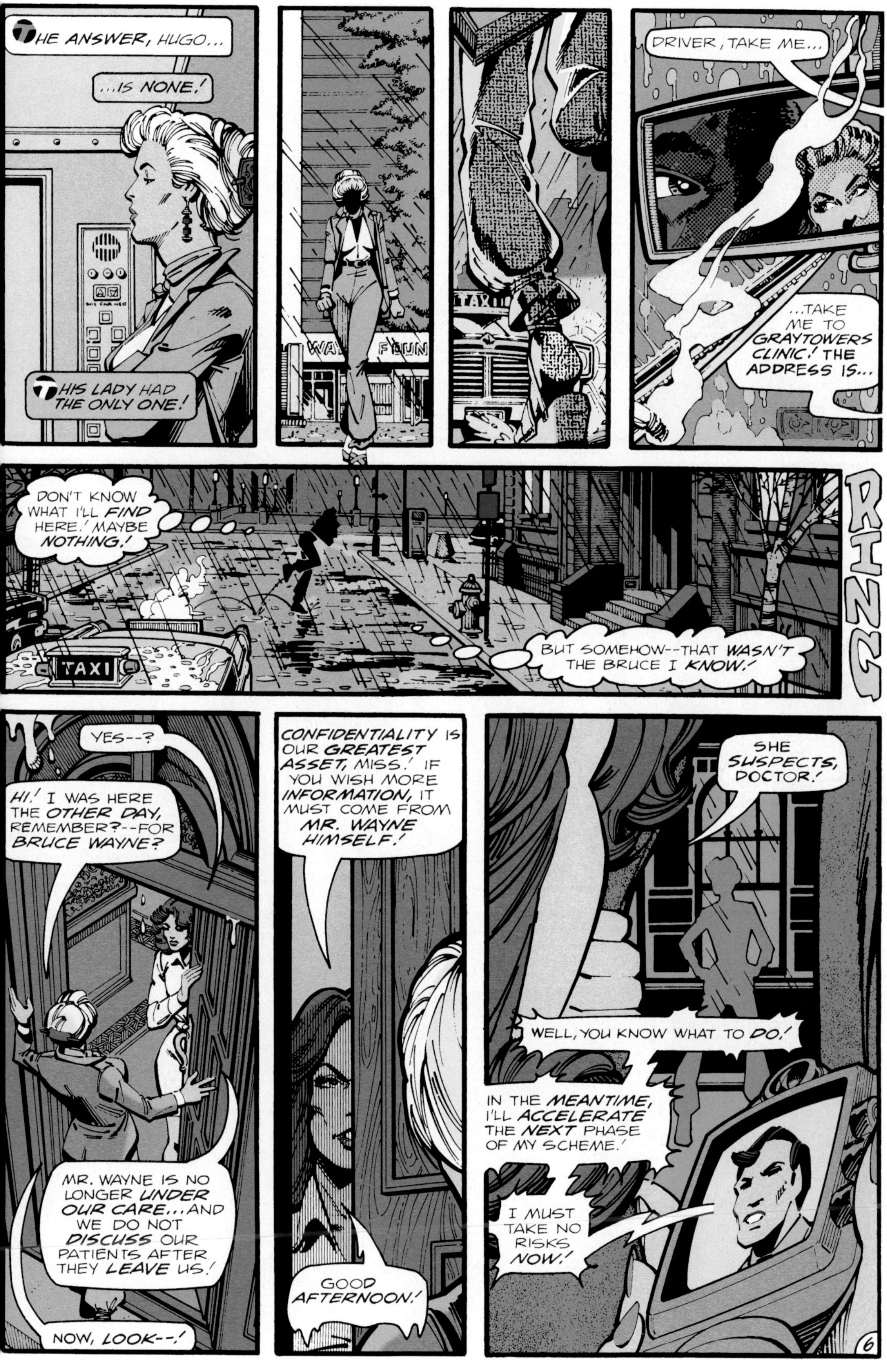
THE ANSWER, HUGO...
...IS NONE!
THIS LADY HAD THE ONLY ONE!
DRIVER, TAKE ME...
...TAKE ME TO GRAYTOWERS CLINIC! THE ADDRESS IS...
DON'T KNOW WHAT I'LL FIND HERE! MAYBE NOTHING!
BUT SOMEHOW--THAT WASN'T THE BRUCE I KNOW!
RING
YES--?
HI! I WAS HERE THE OTHER DAY, REMEMBER?--FOR BRUCE WAYNE?
MR. WAYNE IS NO LONGER UNDER OUR CARE... AND WE DO NOT DISCUSS OUR PATIENTS AFTER THEY LEAVE US!
NOW, LOOK--!
CONFIDENTIALITY IS OUR GREATEST ASSET, MISS! IF YOU WISH MORE INFORMATION, IT MUST COME FROM MR. WAYNE HIMSELF!
GOOD AFTERNOON!
SHE SUSPECTS, DOCTOR!
WELL, YOU KNOW WHAT TO DO!
IN THE MEANTIME, I'LL ACCELERATE THE NEXT PHASE OF MY SCHEME!
I MUST TAKE NO RISKS NOW!
6

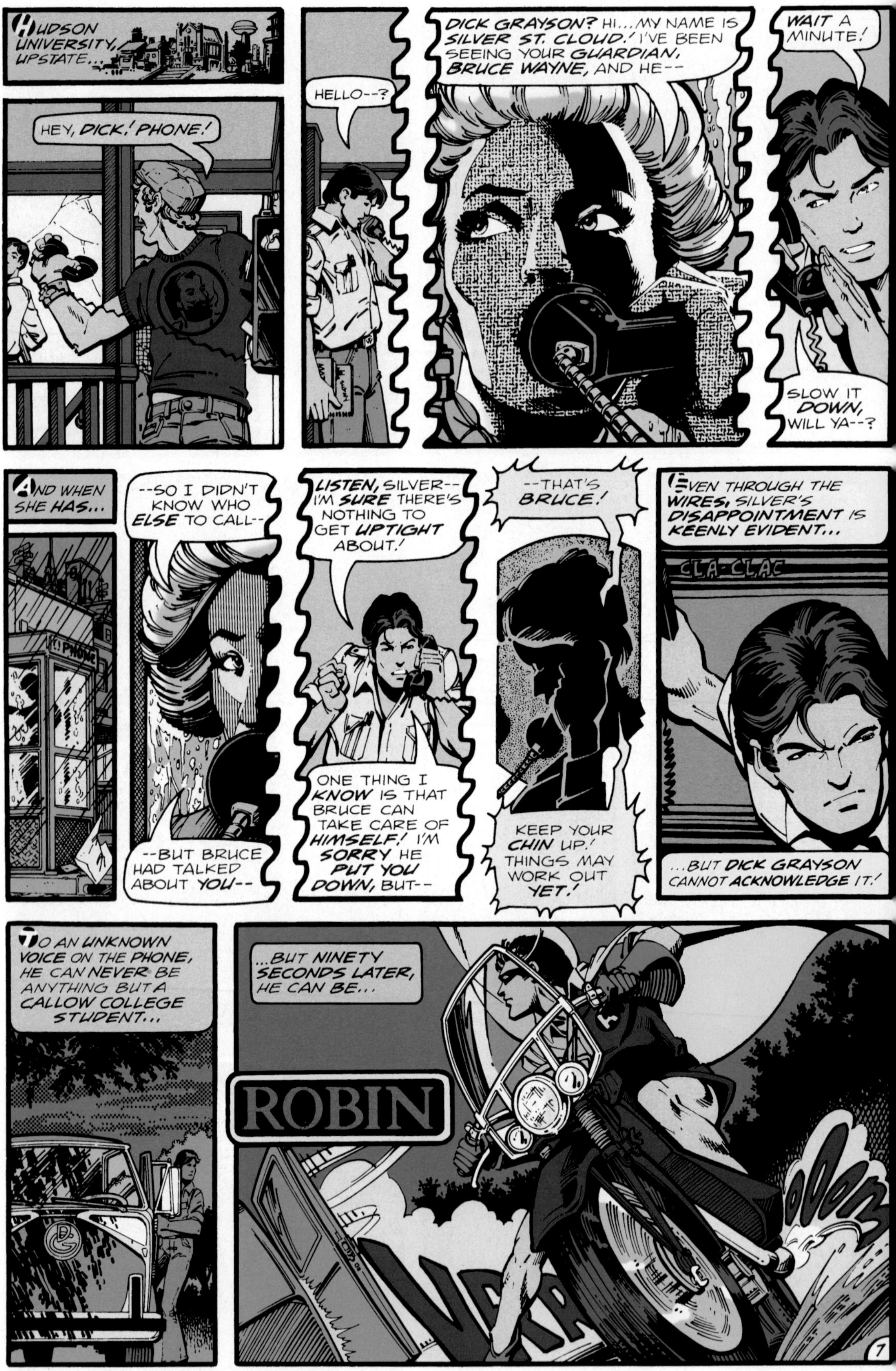
HUDSON UNIVERSITY, UPSTATE...
HEY, DICK! PHONE!
HELLO--?
DICK GRAYSON? HI... MY NAME IS SILVER ST. CLOUD! I'VE BEEN SEEING YOUR GUARDIAN, BRUCE WAYNE, AND HE--
WAIT A MINUTE!
SLOW IT DOWN, WILL YA--?
AND WHEN SHE HAS...
PHONE
--SO I DIDN'T KNOW WHO ELSE TO CALL--
--BUT BRUCE HAD TALKED ABOUT YOU--
LISTEN, SILVER-- I'M SURE THERE'S NOTHING TO GET UPTIGHT ABOUT!
ONE THING I KNOW IS THAT BRUCE CAN TAKE CARE OF HIMSELF! I'M SORRY HE PUT YOU DOWN, BUT--
--THAT'S BRUCE!
KEEP YOUR CHIN UP! THINGS MAY WORK OUT YET!
EVEN THROUGH THE WIRES, SILVER'S DISAPPOINTMENT IS KEENLY EVIDENT...
CLA-CLAC
...BUT DICK GRAYSON CANNOT ACKNOWLEDGE IT!
TO AN UNKNOWN VOICE ON THE PHONE, HE CAN NEVER BE ANYTHING BUT A CALLOW COLLEGE STUDENT...
...BUT NINETY SECONDS LATER, HE CAN BE...
ROBIN
VRRR
WOOOM
7

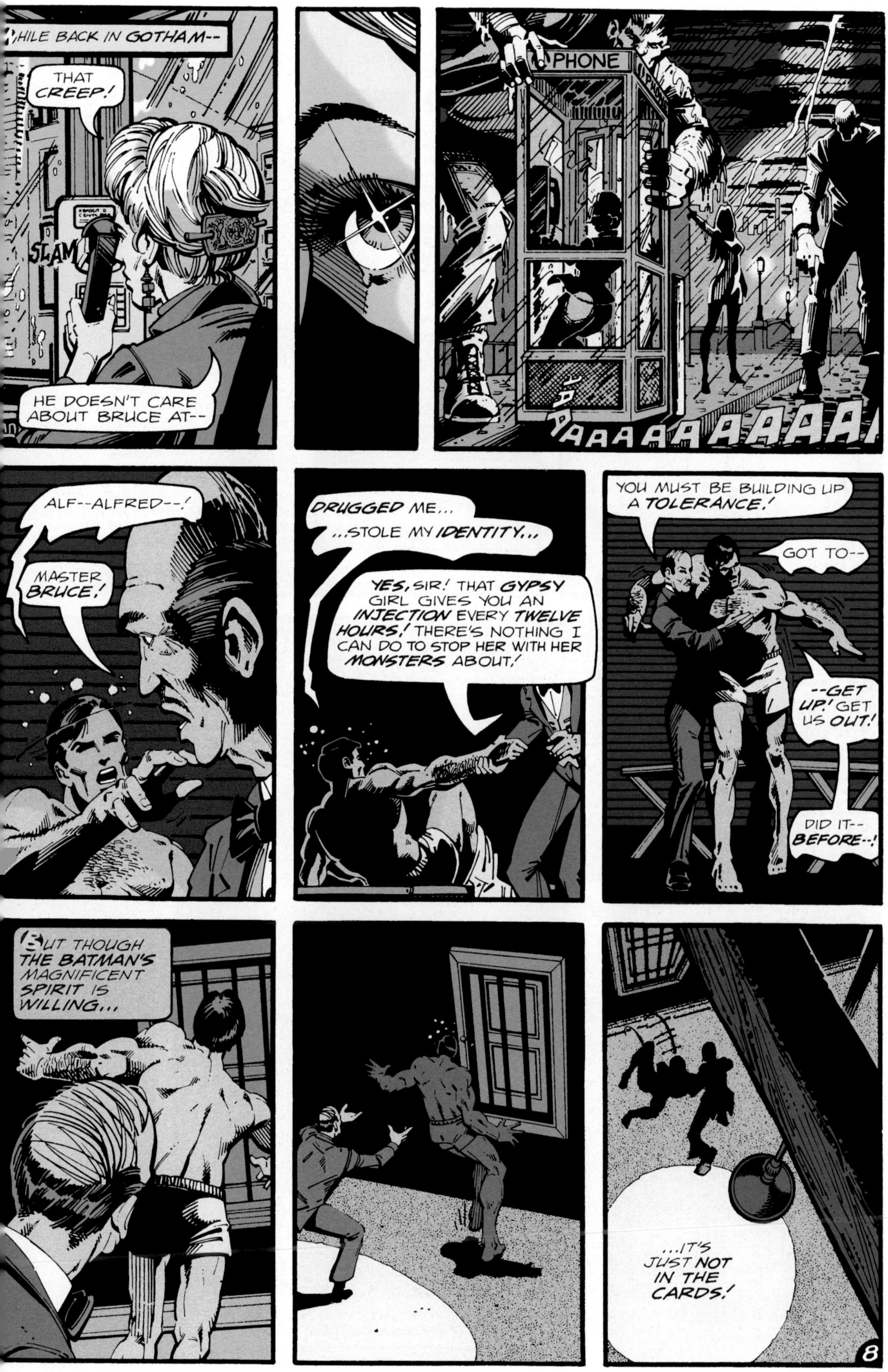
WHILE BACK IN GOTHAM--
THAT CREEP!
SLAM
HE DOESN'T CARE ABOUT BRUCE AT--
PHONE
AAAAAAAAAAAA!
ALF--ALFRED--!
MASTER BRUCE!
DRUGGED ME...
...STOLE MY IDENTITY...
YES, SIR! THAT GYPSY GIRL GIVES YOU AN INJECTION EVERY TWELVE HOURS! THERE'S NOTHING I CAN DO TO STOP HER WITH HER MONSTERS ABOUT!
YOU MUST BE BUILDING UP A TOLERANCE!
GOT TO--
--GET UP! GET US OUT!
DID IT--BEFORE--!
BUT THOUGH THE BATMAN'S MAGNIFICENT SPIRIT IS WILLING...
...IT'S JUST NOT IN THE CARDS!
8

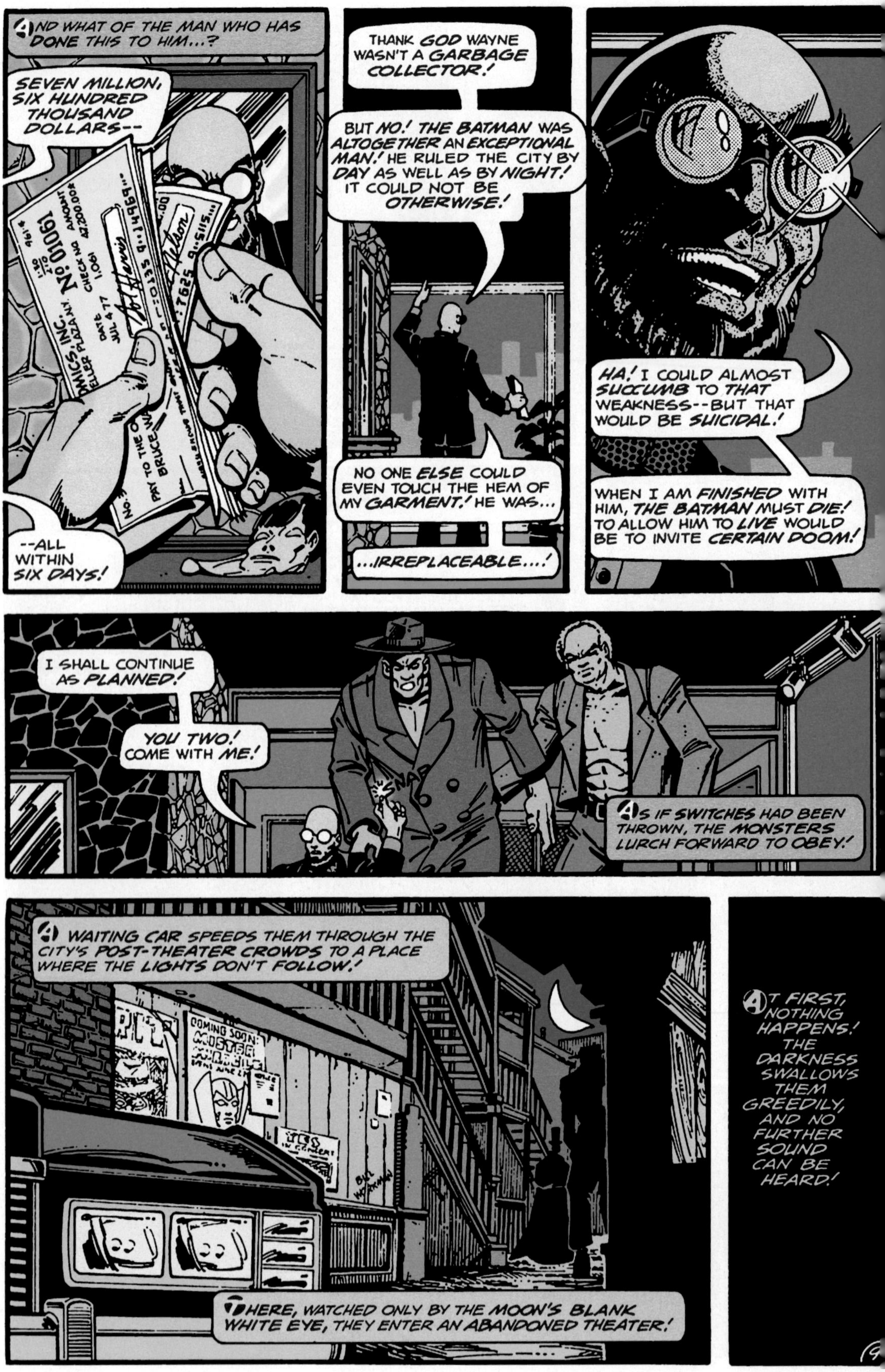
AND WHAT OF THE MAN WHO HAS DONE THIS TO HIM...?
SEVEN MILLION, SIX HUNDRED THOUSAND DOLLARS--
--ALL WITHIN SIX DAYS!
THANK GOD WAYNE WASN'T A GARBAGE COLLECTOR!
BUT NO! THE BATMAN WAS ALTOGETHER AN EXCEPTIONAL MAN! HE RULED THE CITY BY DAY AS WELL AS BY NIGHT! IT COULD NOT BE OTHERWISE!
NO ONE ELSE COULD EVEN TOUCH THE HEM OF MY GARMENT! HE WAS...
...IRREPLACEABLE...!
HA! I COULD ALMOST SUCCUMB TO THAT WEAKNESS--BUT THAT WOULD BE SUICIDAL!
WHEN I AM FINISHED WITH HIM, THE BATMAN MUST DIE! TO ALLOW HIM TO LIVE WOULD BE TO INVITE CERTAIN DOOM!
I SHALL CONTINUE AS PLANNED!
YOU TWO! COME WITH ME!
SNAP
AS IF SWITCHES HAD BEEN THROWN, THE MONSTERS LURCH FORWARD TO OBEY!
A WAITING CAR SPEEDS THEM THROUGH THE CITY'S POST-THEATER CROWDS TO A PLACE WHERE THE LIGHTS DON'T FOLLOW!
THERE, WATCHED ONLY BY THE MOON'S BLANK WHITE EYE, THEY ENTER AN ABANDONED THEATER!
AT FIRST, NOTHING HAPPENS! THE DARKNESS SWALLOWS THEM GREEDILY, AND NO FURTHER SOUND CAN BE HEARD!

BUT THEN...

IT IS PRECISELY MIDNIGHT!

I AM HUGO STRANGE, AND I AM HERE, AS ANNOUNCED THROUGH THE UNDERWORLD GRAPEVINE--TO SELL THE SECRET OF THE AGES--

--THE SECRET OF THE BATMAN'S IDENTITY!

I WARN YOU, PREPARATIONS FOR THIS MEETING HAVE BEEN VERY CAREFULLY MADE! A BULLET-PROOF SCREEN SEPARATES US--

--AND THOUGH I SHOW MYSELF AS A GESTURE OF GOOD FAITH, I AM INVULNERABLE!

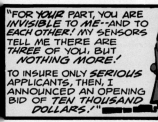

"FOR YOUR PART, YOU ARE INVISIBLE TO ME--AND TO EACH OTHER! MY SENSORS TELL ME THERE ARE THREE OF YOU, BUT NOTHING MORE!

TO INSURE ONLY SERIOUS APPLICANTS, THEN, I ANNOUNCED AN OPENING BID OF TEN THOUSAND DOLLARS!"

:CLICK!:

"PLEASE THROW THESE BIDS INTO THE SPOTLIGHT-- NOW!"

AND FROM THE SILENT SHADOWS...

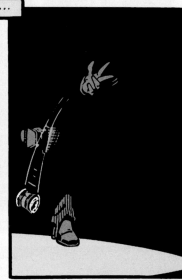

EXCELLENT! BIDDING WILL BEGIN TOMORROW MIDNIGHT! THE MINIMUM BID IS ONE MILLION! PLEASE PLAN YOUR STRATEGIES CAREFULLY!

10

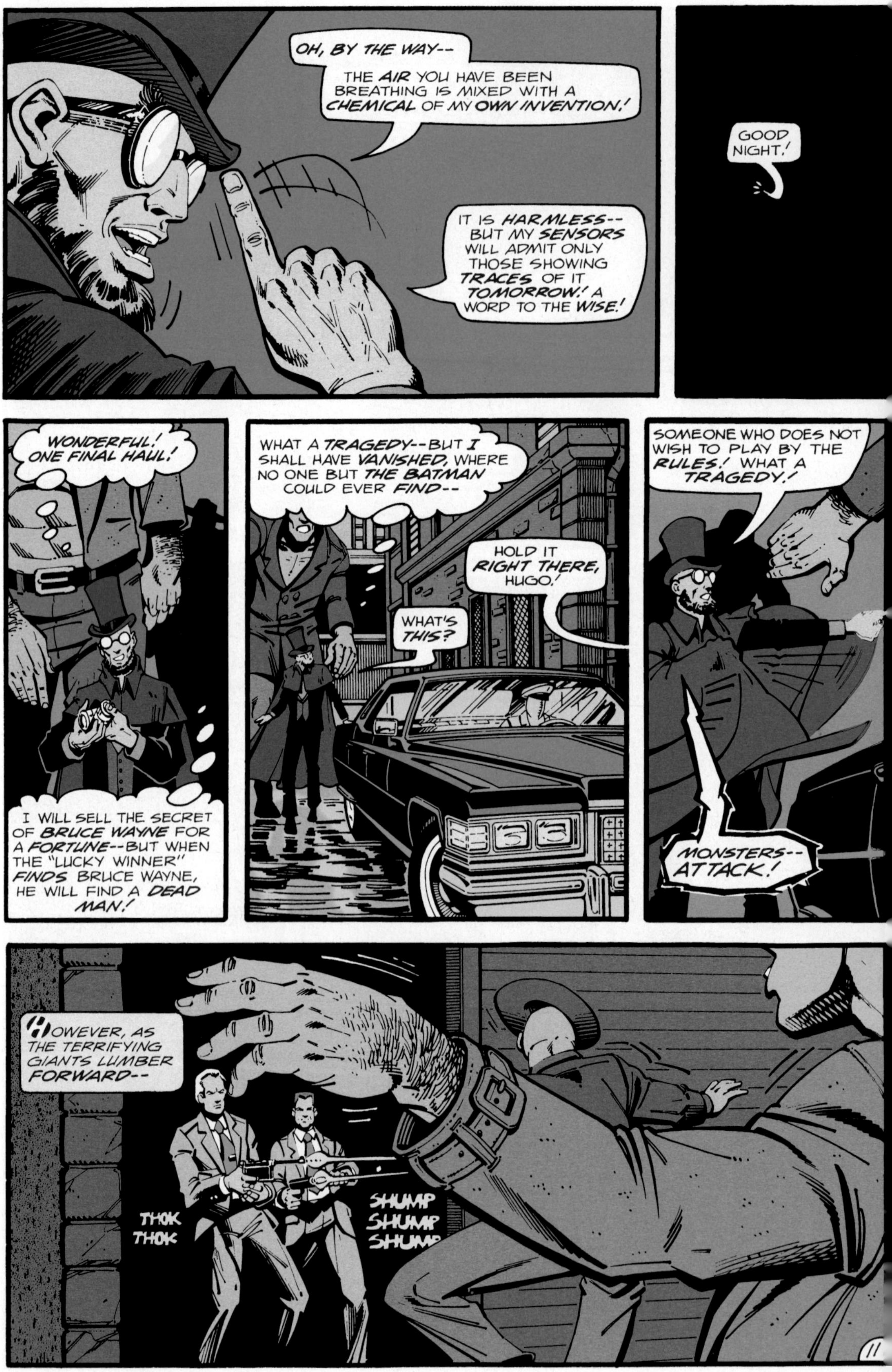
OH, BY THE WAY--
THE AIR YOU HAVE BEEN BREATHING IS MIXED WITH A CHEMICAL OF MY OWN INVENTION!
IT IS HARMLESS-- BUT MY SENSORS WILL ADMIT ONLY THOSE SHOWING TRACES OF IT TOMORROW! A WORD TO THE WISE!
GOOD NIGHT!
WONDERFUL! ONE FINAL HAUL!
I WILL SELL THE SECRET OF BRUCE WAYNE FOR A FORTUNE--BUT WHEN THE "LUCKY WINNER" FINDS BRUCE WAYNE, HE WILL FIND A DEAD MAN!
WHAT A TRAGEDY--BUT I SHALL HAVE VANISHED, WHERE NO ONE BUT THE BATMAN COULD EVER FIND--
HOLD IT RIGHT THERE, HUGO!
WHAT'S THIS?
SOMEONE WHO DOES NOT WISH TO PLAY BY THE RULES! WHAT A TRAGEDY!
MONSTERS-- ATTACK!
HOWEVER, AS THE TERRIFYING GIANTS LUMBER FORWARD--
THOK THOK
SHUMP SHUMP SHUMP
11

TRANQUILIZER GUNS, HUGO! MY BOYS AND I CAME PREPARED FOR *ANYTHING!*

YOUR *OTHER* BADDIES CAN *WAIT* TILL TOMORROW NIGHT, MAYBE--BUT *RUPERT THORNE* DON'T *PLAY* THAT WAY!

CRASH

EEAGHH

HOLD HIM!

HE'S GOT *HIDDEN WEAPONS!*

TOUGH LITTLE MONKEY, AREN'T YA? WE'LL *SEE* JUST HOW TOUGH YOU *ARE,* HUGO!

WE'LL SEE HOW *LONG* IT TAKES YOU TO TELL ME WHAT I WANT TO *KNOW!*

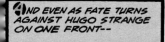

AND EVEN AS FATE TURNS AGAINST HUGO STRANGE ON ONE FRONT--

HSST! ALFRED!

UM! UH-- WHAT?

MASTER ROBIN!

THE GIRL WAS TELLING THE *TRUTH* ABOUT THIS PLACE, HUH? I'VE BEEN PROWLING SO *LONG,* I WAS ABOUT TO *GIVE UP!*

HOW ARE YOU *DOING?* HOW'S *BRUCE?*

THEY'VE KEPT HIM *DRUGGED* FOR A *WEEK,* BUT I'VE LOOKED *AFTER* HIM!

GOOD! JUST *HANG TIGHT!*

12

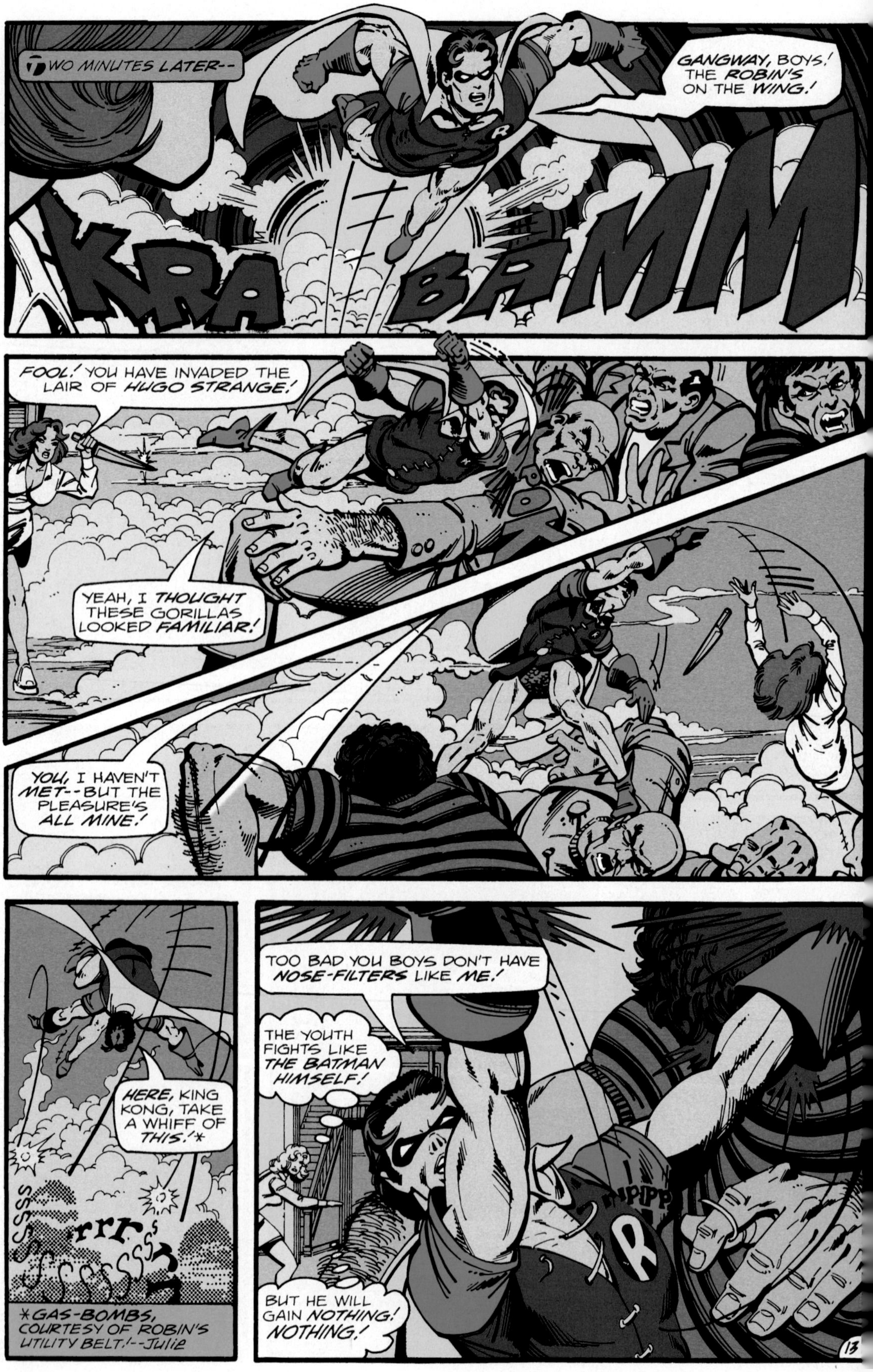
TWO MINUTES LATER--
GANGWAY, BOYS! THE ROBIN'S ON THE WING!
KRA BAMMM
FOOL! YOU HAVE INVADED THE LAIR OF HUGO STRANGE!
YEAH, I THOUGHT THESE GORILLAS LOOKED FAMILIAR!
YOU, I HAVEN'T MET--BUT THE PLEASURE'S ALL MINE!
HERE, KING KONG, TAKE A WHIFF OF THIS!*
*GAS-BOMBS, COURTESY OF ROBIN'S UTILITY BELT!--Julie
TOO BAD YOU BOYS DON'T HAVE NOSE-FILTERS LIKE ME!
THE YOUTH FIGHTS LIKE THE BATMAN HIMSELF!
BUT HE WILL GAIN NOTHING! NOTHING!
13

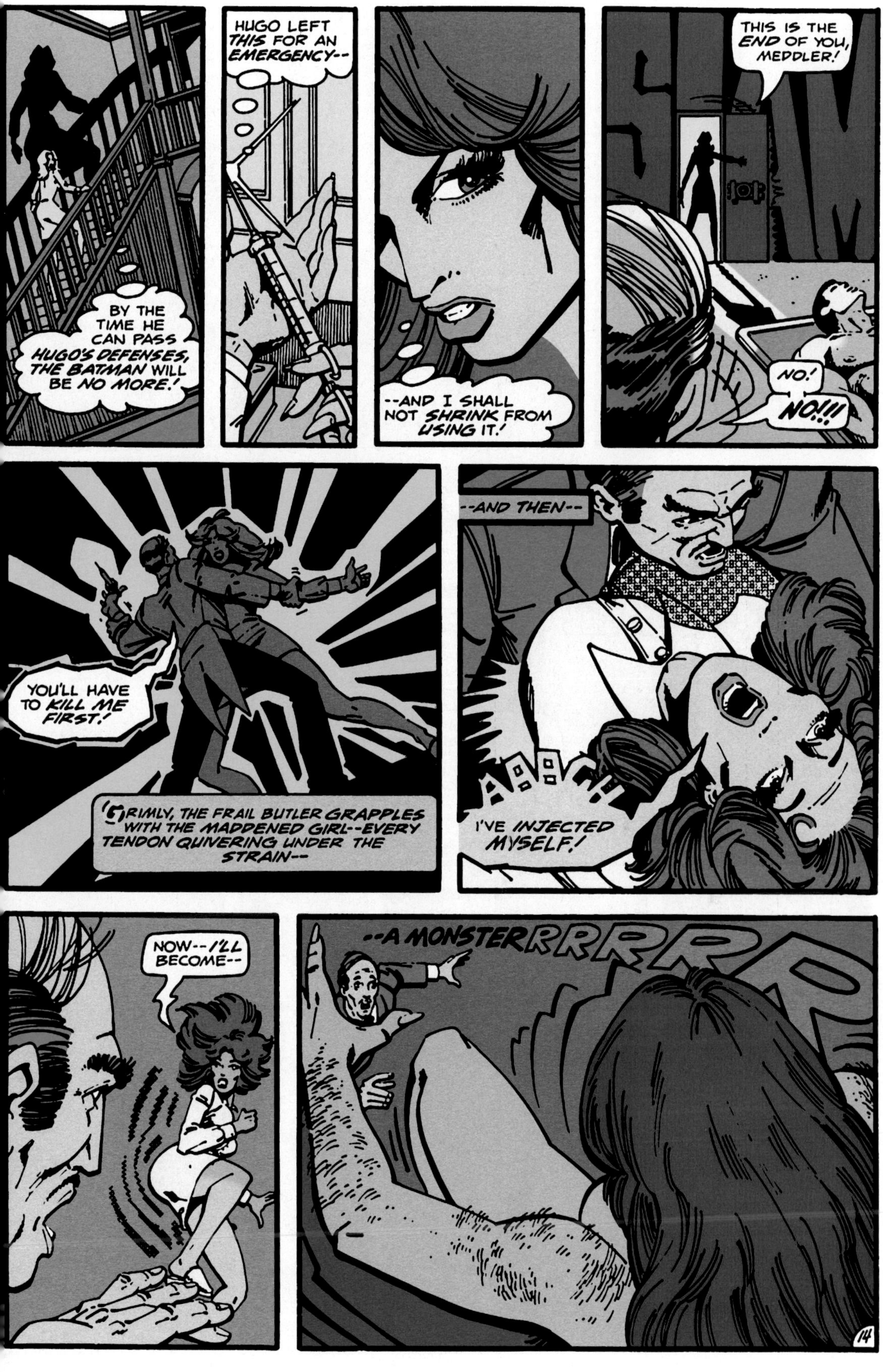
BY THE TIME HE CAN PASS HUGO'S DEFENSES, THE BATMAN WILL BE NO MORE!
HUGO LEFT THIS FOR AN EMERGENCY--
--AND I SHALL NOT SHRINK FROM USING IT!
THIS IS THE END OF YOU, MEDDLER!
NO!
NO!!!
YOU'LL HAVE TO KILL ME FIRST!
GRIMLY, THE FRAIL BUTLER GRAPPLES WITH THE MADDENED GIRL--EVERY TENDON QUIVERING UNDER THE STRAIN--
--AND THEN--
I'VE INJECTED MYSELF!
NOW--I'LL BECOME--
--A MONSTERRRRRR
14

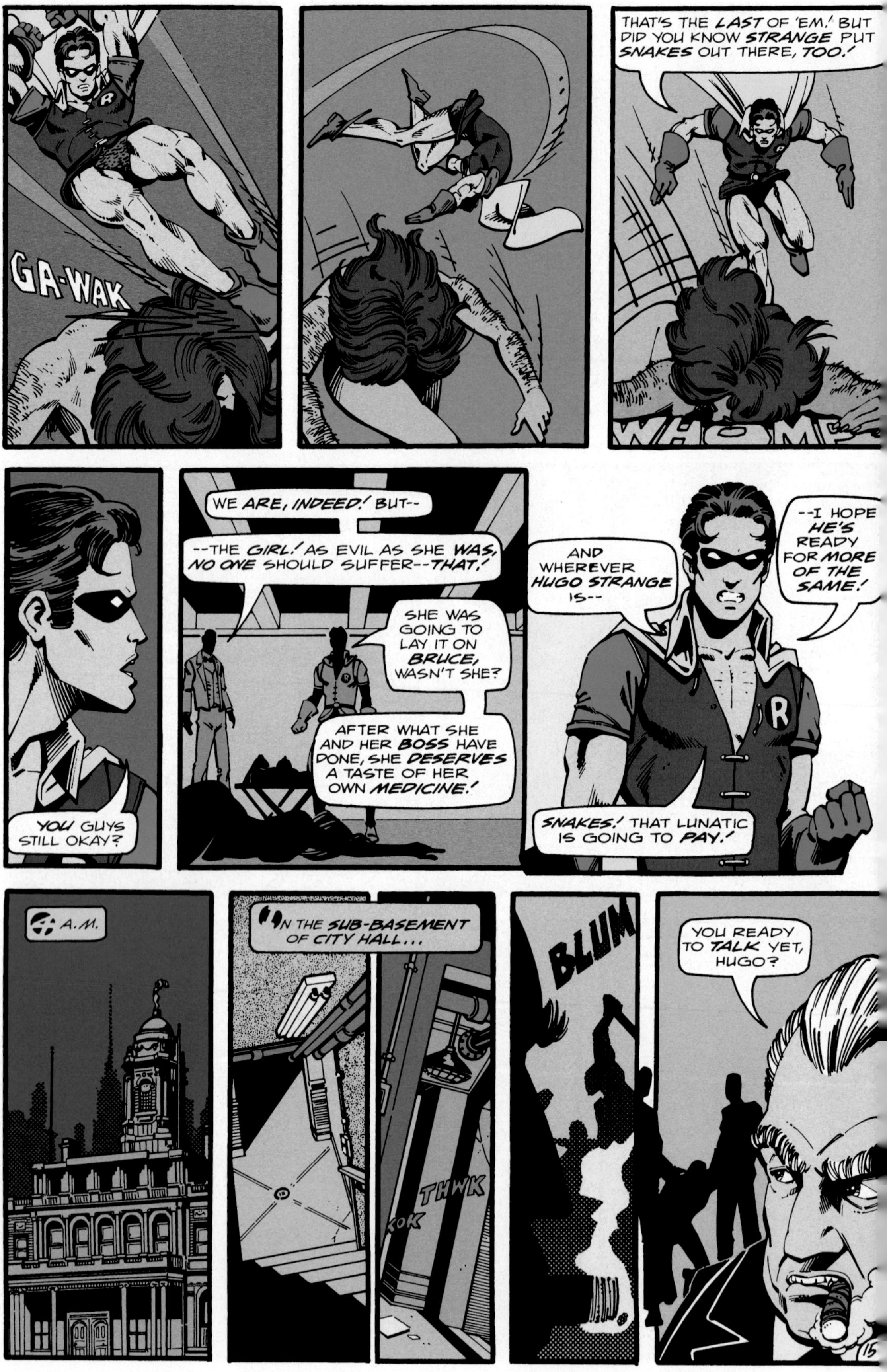
GA-WAK
THAT'S THE LAST OF 'EM! BUT DID YOU KNOW STRANGE PUT SNAKES OUT THERE, TOO!
WHOMP
YOU GUYS STILL OKAY?
WE ARE, INDEED! BUT--
--THE GIRL! AS EVIL AS SHE WAS, NO ONE SHOULD SUFFER--THAT!
SHE WAS GOING TO LAY IT ON BRUCE, WASN'T SHE?
AFTER WHAT SHE AND HER BOSS HAVE DONE, SHE DESERVES A TASTE OF HER OWN MEDICINE!
AND WHEREVER HUGO STRANGE IS--
--I HOPE HE'S READY FOR MORE OF THE SAME!
SNAKES! THAT LUNATIC IS GOING TO PAY!
4 A.M.
IN THE SUB-BASEMENT OF CITY HALL...
THWK
KOK
BLUM
YOU READY TO TALK YET, HUGO?
15

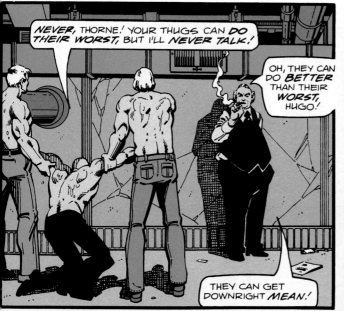

NEVER, THORNE! YOUR THUGS CAN *DO* THEIR *WORST*, BUT I'LL *NEVER TALK*!

OH, THEY CAN DO *BETTER* THAN THEIR *WORST*, HUGO!

THEY CAN GET DOWNRIGHT *MEAN*!

FOOL! THREATS MEAN *NOTHING* TO *HUGO STRANGE*! *YOU* MEAN NOTHING TO *HUGO STRANGE*!

TAKE HIM *BACK*, BOYS!

KLOMP

THWACK

THOMP

WUMP

CRACK

YOU READY TO *TALK* YET, HUGO?

N-NEVER!

YOU WON'T STEAL--THE FRUITS OF MY--*GENIUS*!

I--AND *I ALONE*--LEARNED THE *SECRET OF THE CENTURY*!

SUCH TREASURE--MUST BE *EARNED*--THORNE! I WILL *NEVER--GIVE* IT AWAY!

TAKE HIM *BACK*, BOYS!

16

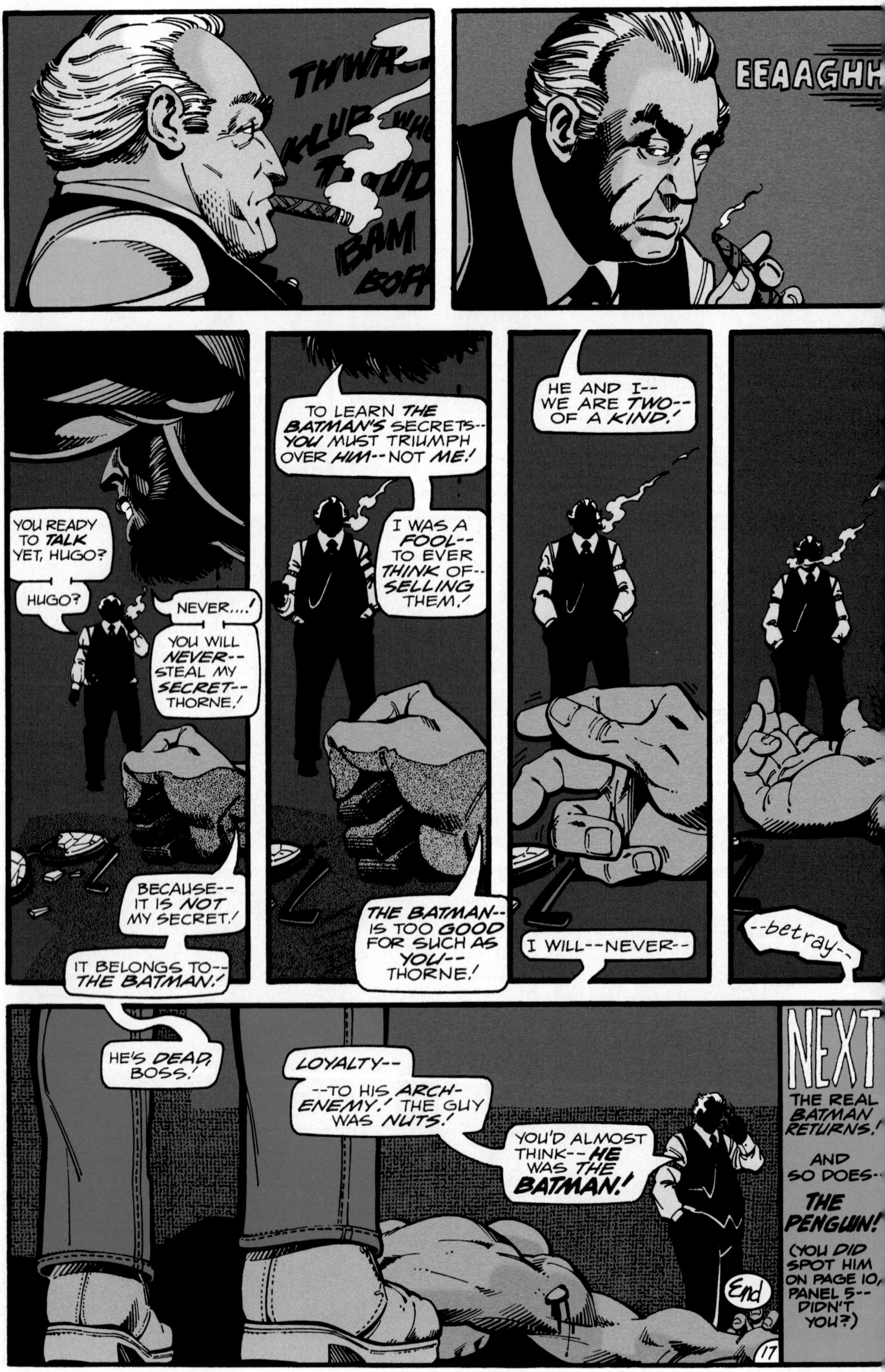
BAM
EEAAGHH
YOU READY TO TALK YET, HUGO?
HUGO?
NEVER....!
YOU WILL NEVER-- STEAL MY SECRET-- THORNE.!
BECAUSE-- IT IS NOT MY SECRET.!
IT BELONGS TO-- THE BATMAN.!
TO LEARN THE BATMAN'S SECRETS-- YOU MUST TRIUMPH OVER HIM--NOT ME.!
I WAS A FOOL-- TO EVER THINK OF-- SELLING THEM.!
THE BATMAN-- IS TOO GOOD FOR SUCH AS YOU-- THORNE.!
HE AND I-- WE ARE TWO-- OF A KIND.!
I WILL--NEVER--
--betray--
HE'S DEAD, BOSS.!
LOYALTY--
--TO HIS ARCH-ENEMY.! THE GUY WAS NUTS.!
YOU'D ALMOST THINK--HE WAS THE BATMAN.!
End
17
NEXT
THE REAL BATMAN RETURNS.!
AND SO DOES-- THE PENGUIN!
(YOU DID SPOT HIM ON PAGE 10, PANEL 5-- DIDN'T YOU?)

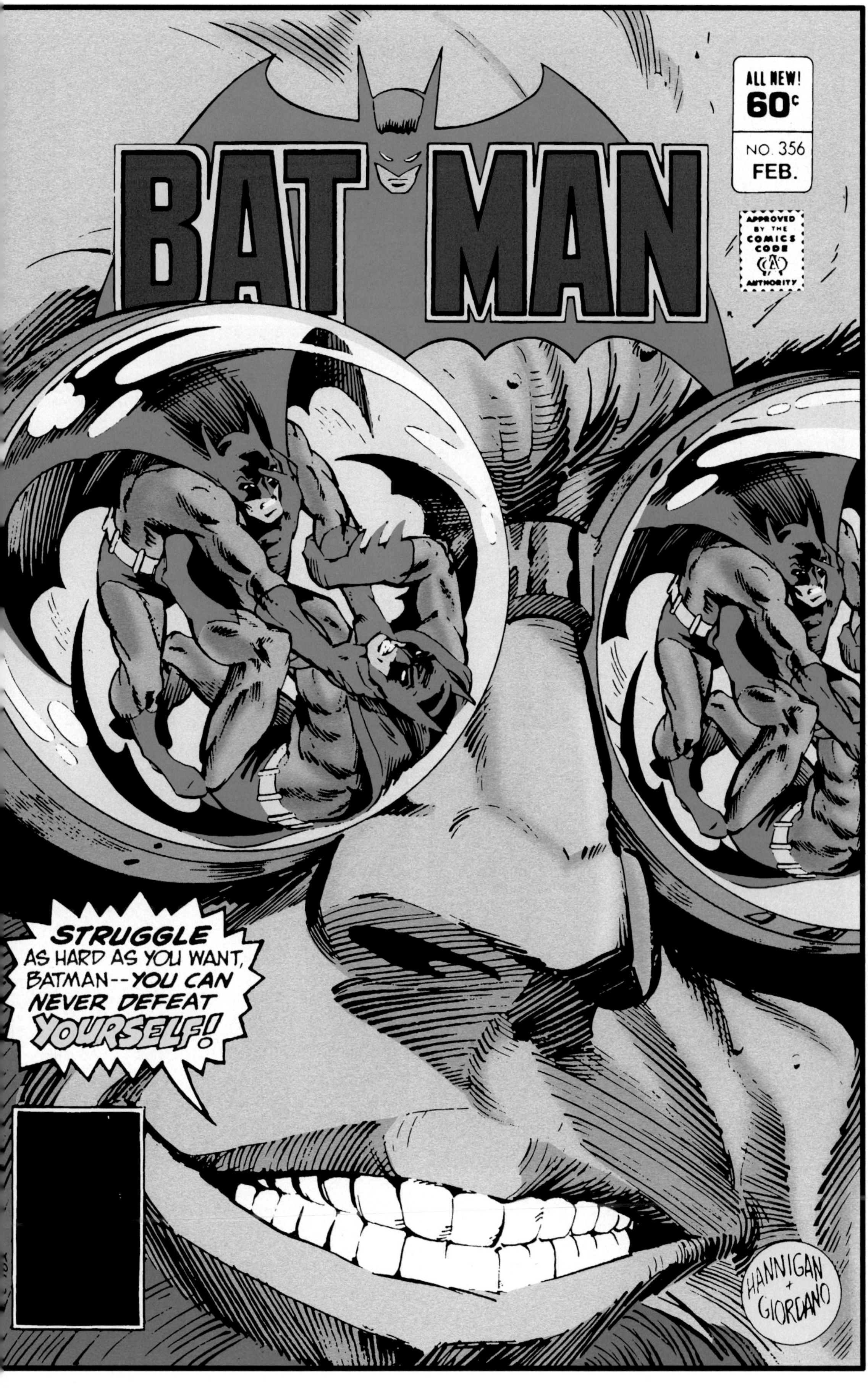
BATMAN
ALL NEW! 60¢
NO. 356 FEB.
APPROVED BY THE COMICS CODE AUTHORITY
STRUGGLE AS HARD AS YOU WANT, BATMAN--YOU CAN NEVER DEFEAT YOURSELF!
HANNIGAN + GIORDANO

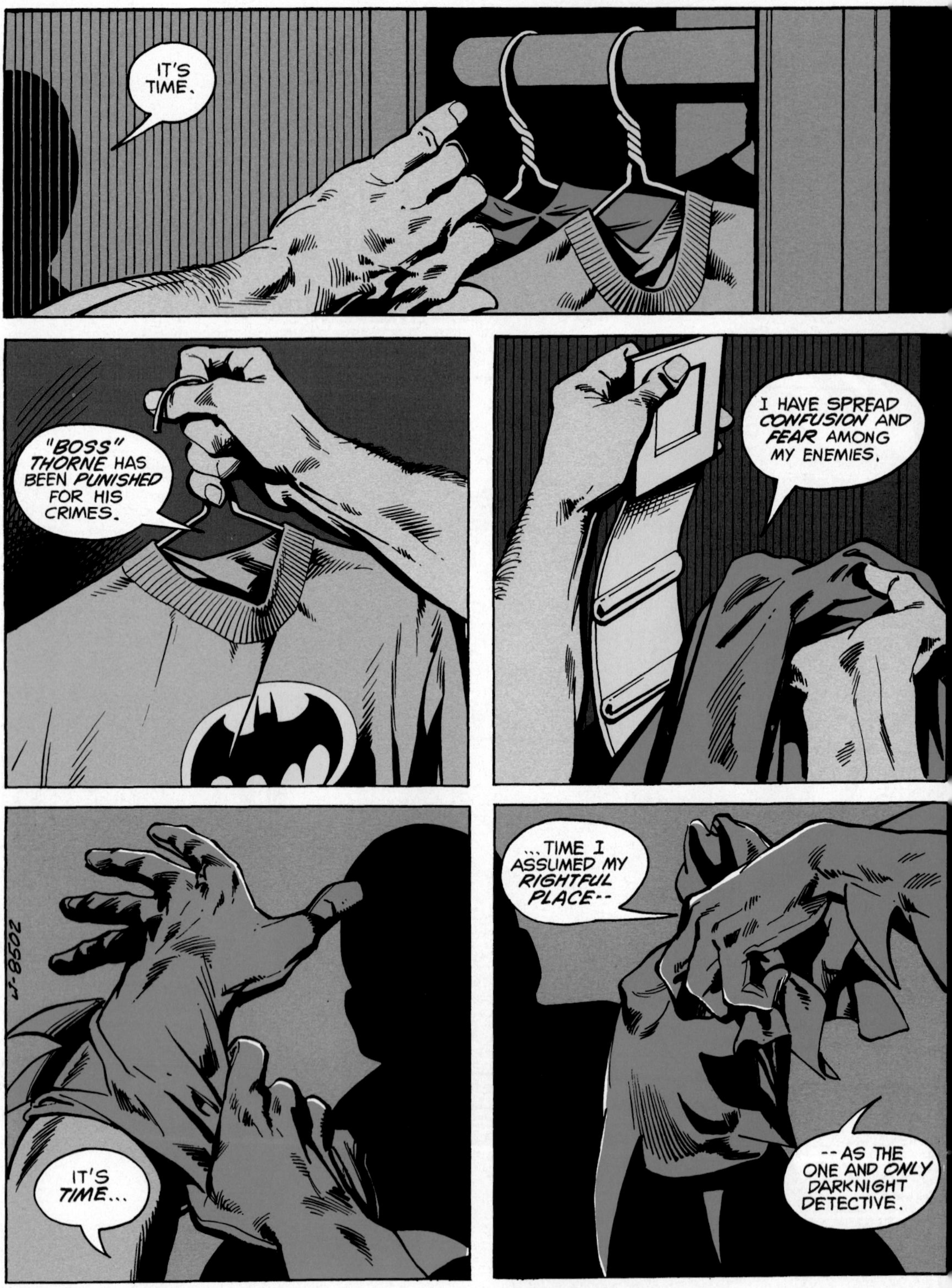
IT'S TIME.
"BOSS" THORNE HAS BEEN PUNISHED FOR HIS CRIMES.
I HAVE SPREAD CONFUSION AND FEAR AMONG MY ENEMIES.
IT'S TIME...
...TIME I ASSUMED MY RIGHTFUL PLACE--
--AS THE ONE AND ONLY DARKNIGHT DETECTIVE.

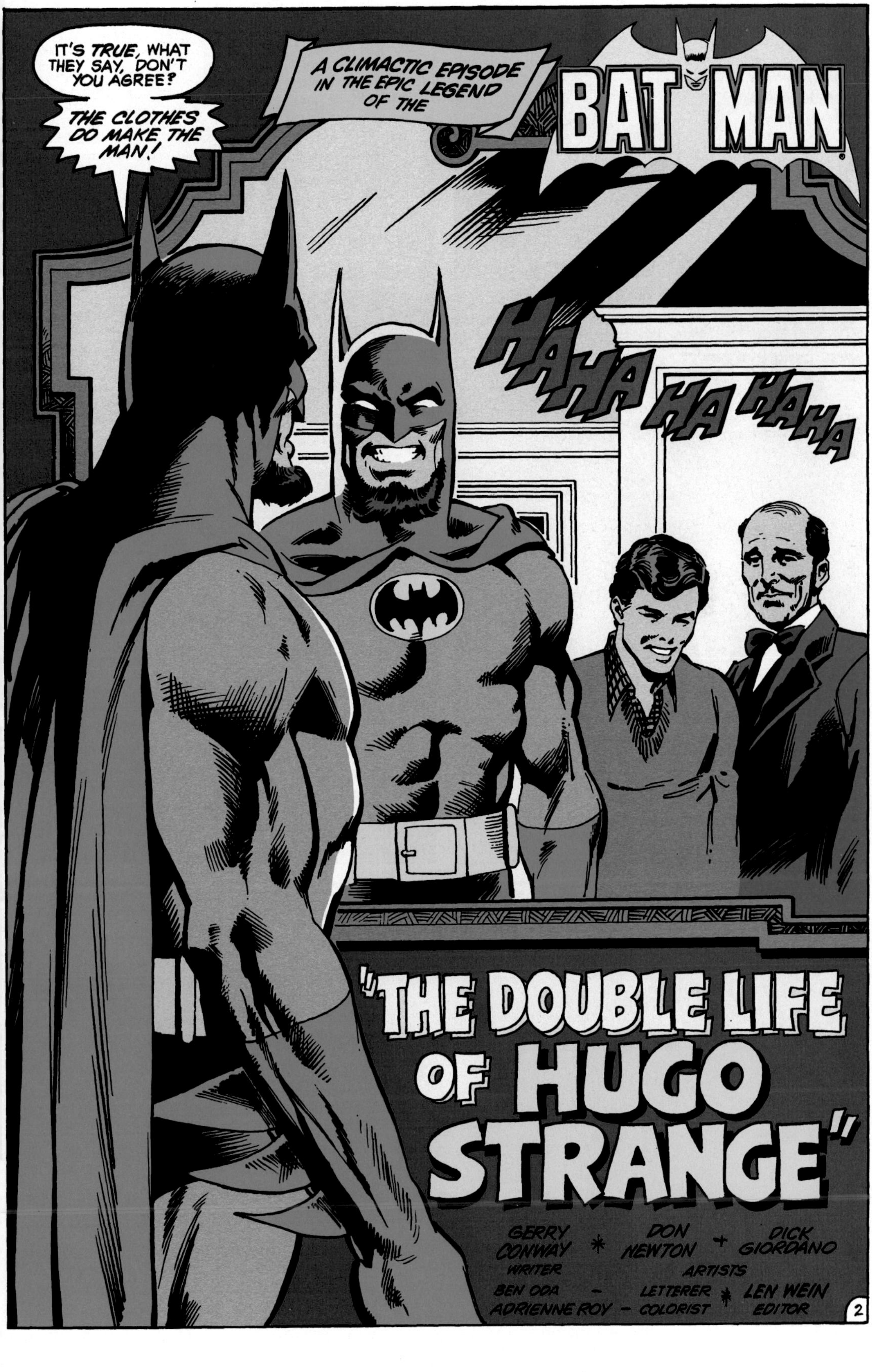

IT'S TRUE, WHAT THEY SAY, DON'T YOU AGREE?
THE CLOTHES DO MAKE THE MAN!
A CLIMACTIC EPISODE IN THE EPIC LEGEND OF THE
BATMAN
HAHAHA HA HAHAHA
"THE DOUBLE LIFE OF HUGO STRANGE"
GERRY CONWAY WRITER
DON NEWTON + DICK GIORDANO ARTISTS
BEN ODA - LETTERER
ADRIENNE ROY - COLORIST
LEN WEIN EDITOR
2

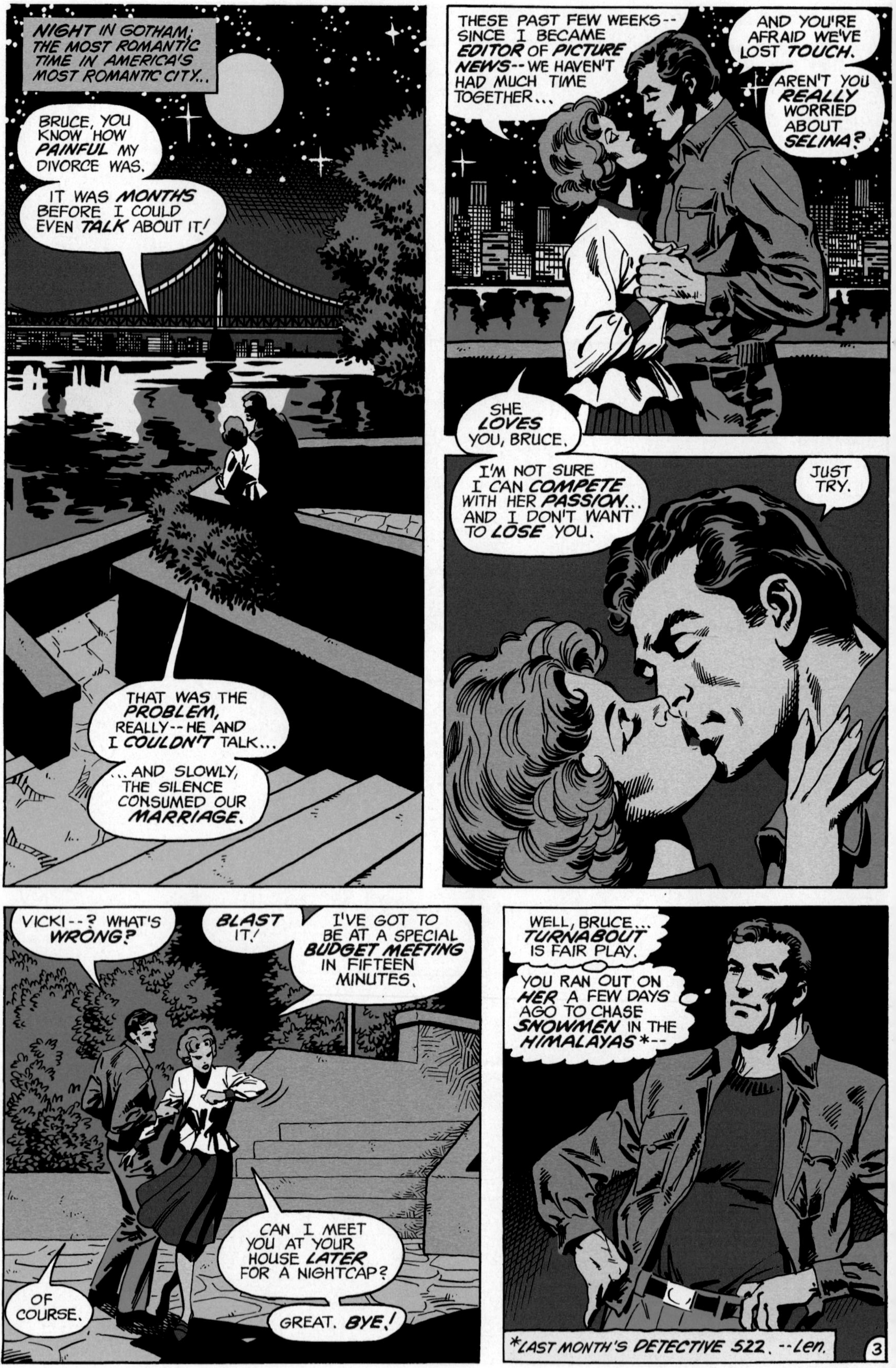
NIGHT IN GOTHAM: THE MOST ROMANTIC TIME IN AMERICA'S MOST ROMANTIC CITY...
BRUCE, YOU KNOW HOW PAINFUL MY DIVORCE WAS.
IT WAS MONTHS BEFORE I COULD EVEN TALK ABOUT IT!
THAT WAS THE PROBLEM, REALLY--HE AND I COULDN'T TALK...
...AND SLOWLY, THE SILENCE CONSUMED OUR MARRIAGE.
THESE PAST FEW WEEKS--SINCE I BECAME EDITOR OF PICTURE NEWS--WE HAVEN'T HAD MUCH TIME TOGETHER...
AND YOU'RE AFRAID WE'VE LOST TOUCH.
AREN'T YOU REALLY WORRIED ABOUT SELINA?
SHE LOVES YOU, BRUCE.
I'M NOT SURE I CAN COMPETE WITH HER PASSION... AND I DON'T WANT TO LOSE YOU.
JUST TRY.
VICKI--? WHAT'S WRONG?
BLAST IT!
I'VE GOT TO BE AT A SPECIAL BUDGET MEETING IN FIFTEEN MINUTES.
CAN I MEET YOU AT YOUR HOUSE LATER FOR A NIGHTCAP?
OF COURSE.
GREAT. BYE!
WELL, BRUCE... TURNABOUT IS FAIR PLAY.
YOU RAN OUT ON HER A FEW DAYS AGO TO CHASE SNOWMEN IN THE HIMALAYAS*--
*LAST MONTH'S DETECTIVE 522. --Len.
3

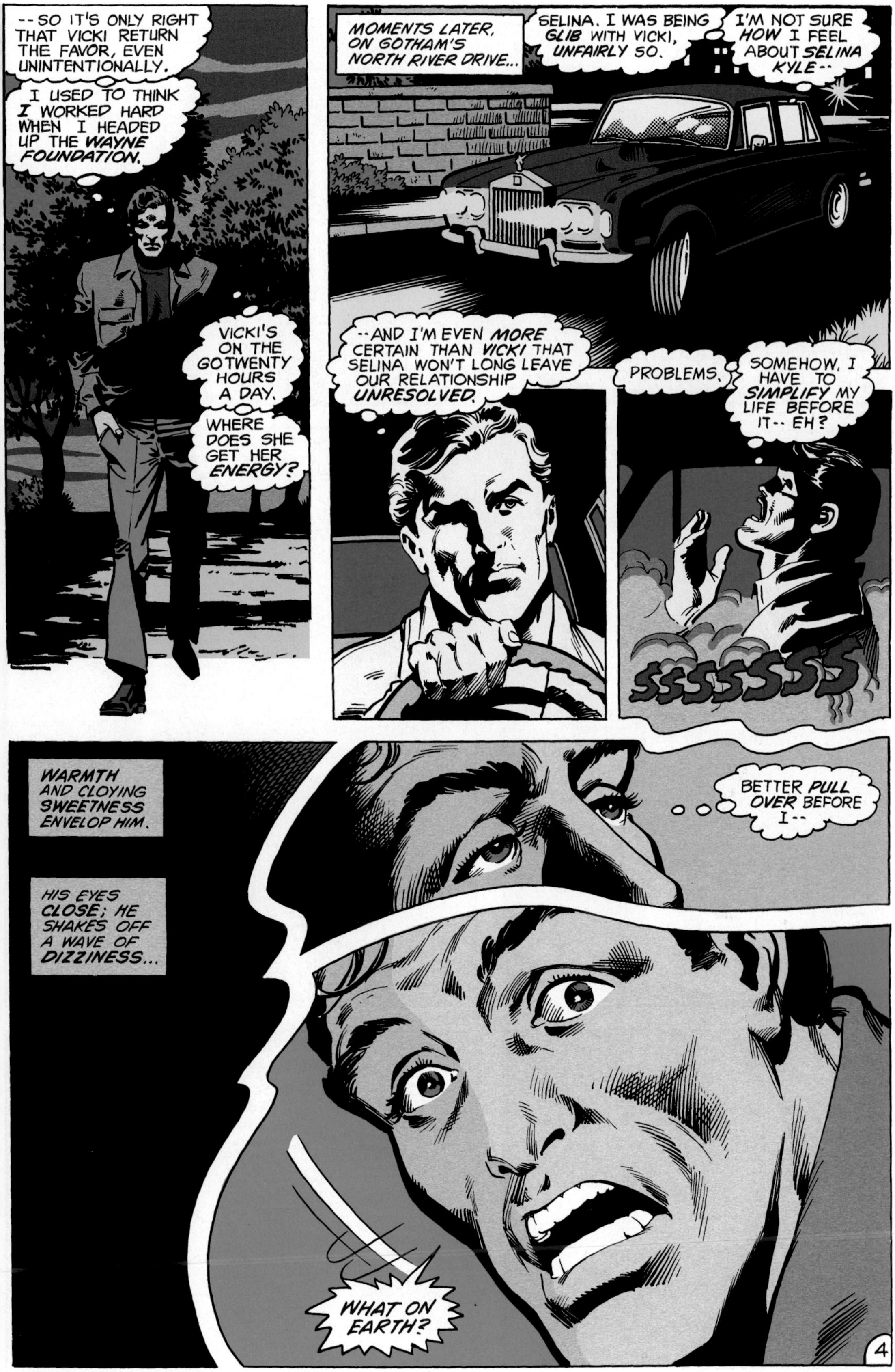
-- SO IT'S ONLY RIGHT THAT VICKI RETURN THE FAVOR, EVEN UNINTENTIONALLY.
I USED TO THINK I WORKED HARD WHEN I HEADED UP THE WAYNE FOUNDATION.
VICKI'S ON THE GO TWENTY HOURS A DAY.
WHERE DOES SHE GET HER ENERGY?
MOMENTS LATER, ON GOTHAM'S NORTH RIVER DRIVE...
SELINA. I WAS BEING GLIB WITH VICKI, UNFAIRLY SO.
I'M NOT SURE HOW I FEEL ABOUT SELINA KYLE --
-- AND I'M EVEN MORE CERTAIN THAN VICKI THAT SELINA WON'T LONG LEAVE OUR RELATIONSHIP UNRESOLVED.
PROBLEMS.
SOMEHOW, I HAVE TO SIMPLIFY MY LIFE BEFORE IT -- EH?
SSSSSSSS
WARMTH AND CLOYING SWEETNESS ENVELOP HIM.
HIS EYES CLOSE; HE SHAKES OFF A WAVE OF DIZZINESS...
BETTER PULL OVER BEFORE I --
WHAT ON EARTH?
4

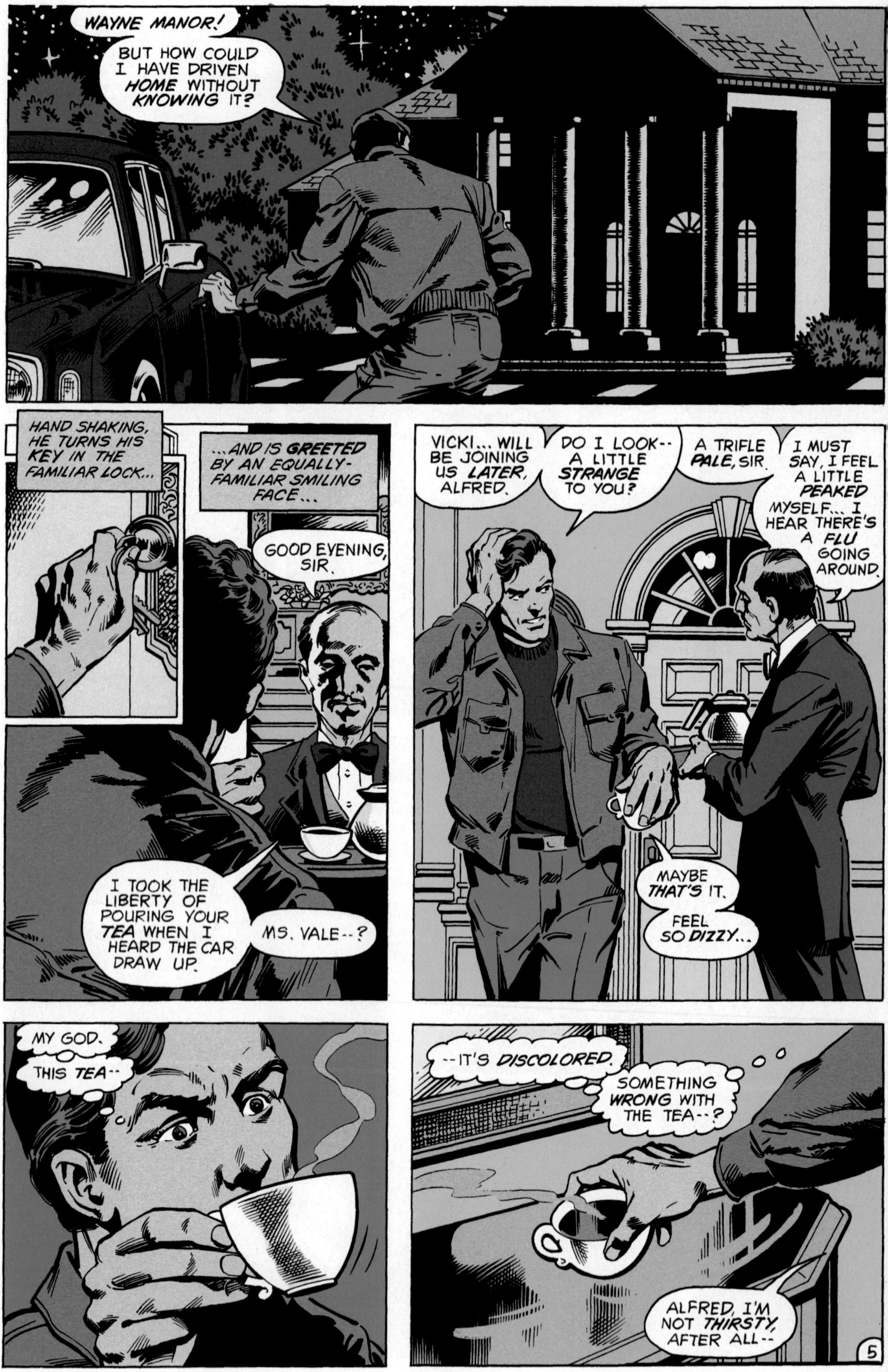
WAYNE MANOR!
BUT HOW COULD I HAVE DRIVEN HOME WITHOUT KNOWING IT?
HAND SHAKING, HE TURNS HIS KEY IN THE FAMILIAR LOCK...
...AND IS GREETED BY AN EQUALLY-FAMILIAR SMILING FACE...
GOOD EVENING, SIR.
I TOOK THE LIBERTY OF POURING YOUR TEA WHEN I HEARD THE CAR DRAW UP.
MS. VALE--?
VICKI... WILL BE JOINING US LATER, ALFRED.
DO I LOOK-- A LITTLE STRANGE TO YOU?
A TRIFLE PALE, SIR.
I MUST SAY, I FEEL A LITTLE PEAKED MYSELF... I HEAR THERE'S A FLU GOING AROUND.
MAYBE THAT'S IT.
FEEL SO DIZZY...
MY GOD.
THIS TEA--
--IT'S DISCOLORED.
SOMETHING WRONG WITH THE TEA--?
ALFRED, I'M NOT THIRSTY, AFTER ALL--
5

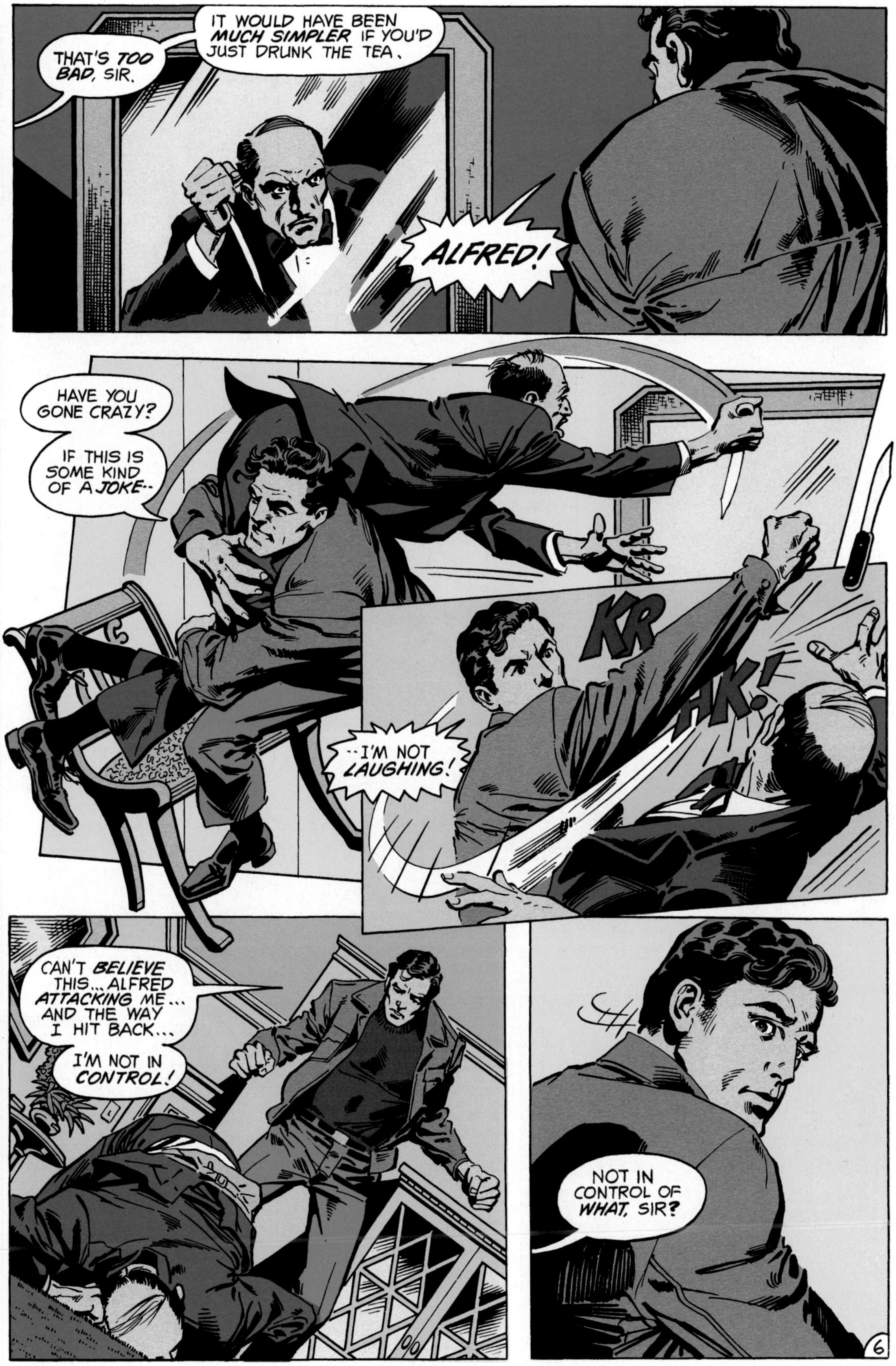
IT WOULD HAVE BEEN MUCH SIMPLER IF YOU'D JUST DRUNK THE TEA.
THAT'S TOO BAD, SIR.
ALFRED!
HAVE YOU GONE CRAZY?
IF THIS IS SOME KIND OF A JOKE--
KR AK!
--I'M NOT LAUGHING!
CAN'T BELIEVE THIS... ALFRED ATTACKING ME... AND THE WAY I HIT BACK...
I'M NOT IN CONTROL!
NOT IN CONTROL OF WHAT, SIR?
6

FORGIVE ME FOR NOT MEETING YOU AT THE *DOOR*.

I WAS IN THE *KITCHEN*--

--FIXING A SPOT OF *TEA*.

BUT--

IS ANYTHING *WRONG*, MASTER BRUCE?

YOU LOOK A TRIFLE *PALE*.

THIS IS *SURREAL*! AM I HAVING *BLACKOUTS*?

THAT *MUST* BE IT-- SOME KIND OF *DELAYED STRESS REACTION* TO TENSION.

EXCELLENT *EARL GREY*, ALFRED...AS USUAL.

I THINK I'LL GO *UPSTAIRS* NOW ...TAKE A *SHOWER* ...BEFORE VICKI ARRIVES...

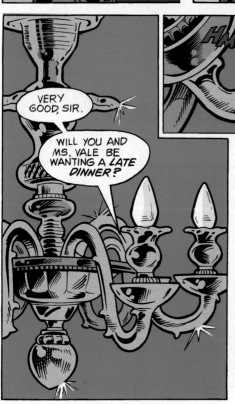

VERY GOOD, SIR.

WILL YOU AND MS. VALE BE WANTING A *LATE* DINNER?

*HMMM-CLICK*

NO...JUST PUT OUT THE *TATTINGER '59* TO CHILL...

...AND SET SOME LOGS ON THE FIRE IN THE DRAWING ROOM.

7

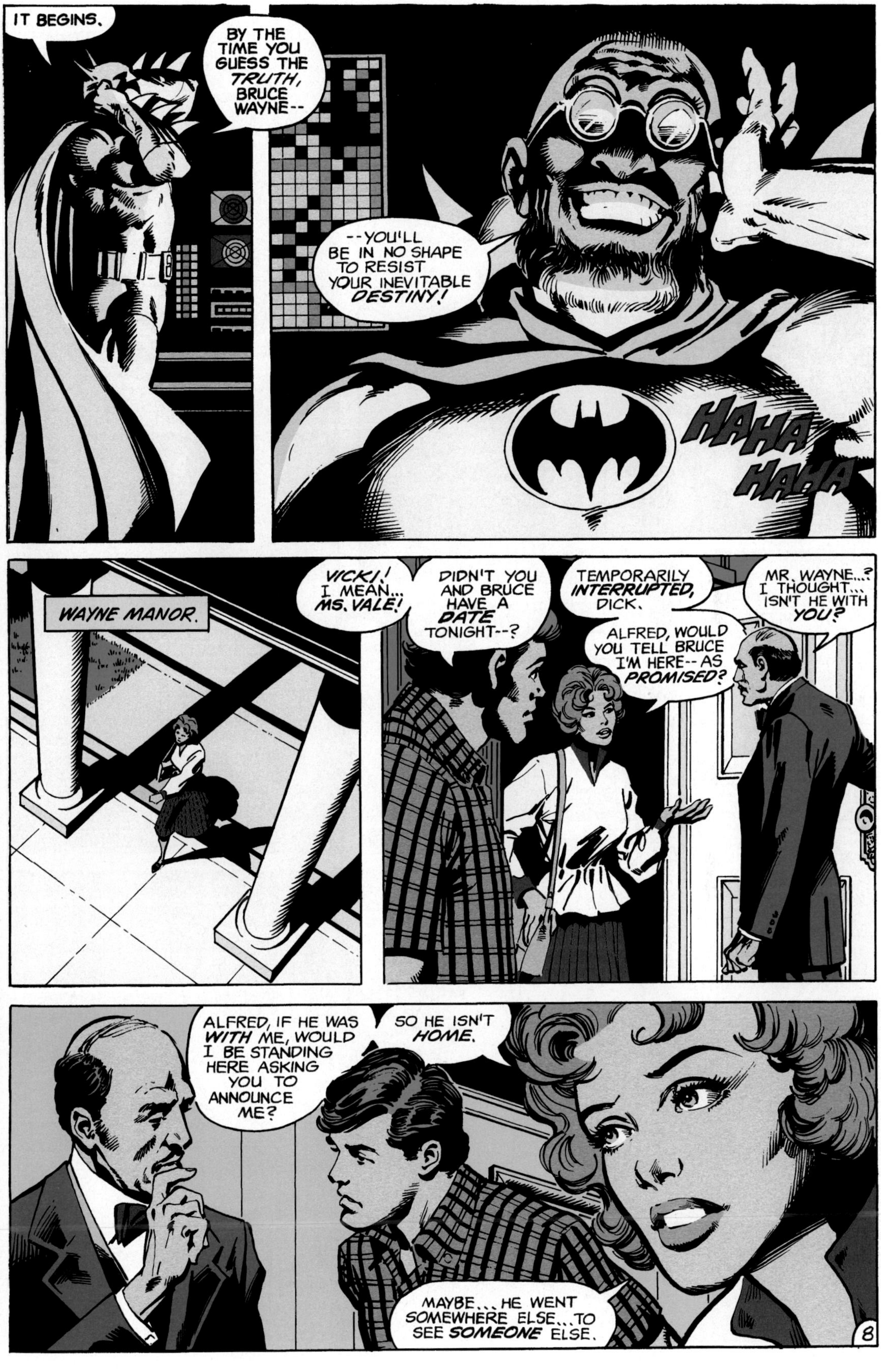
IT BEGINS.
BY THE TIME YOU GUESS THE TRUTH, BRUCE WAYNE--
--YOU'LL BE IN NO SHAPE TO RESIST YOUR INEVITABLE DESTINY!
HAHA HAHA
WAYNE MANOR.
VICKI! I MEAN... MS. VALE!
DIDN'T YOU AND BRUCE HAVE A DATE TONIGHT--?
TEMPORARILY INTERRUPTED, DICK.
ALFRED, WOULD YOU TELL BRUCE I'M HERE-- AS PROMISED?
MR. WAYNE...? I THOUGHT... ISN'T HE WITH YOU?
ALFRED, IF HE WAS WITH ME, WOULD I BE STANDING HERE ASKING YOU TO ANNOUNCE ME?
SO HE ISN'T HOME.
MAYBE... HE WENT SOMEWHERE ELSE...TO SEE SOMEONE ELSE.
8

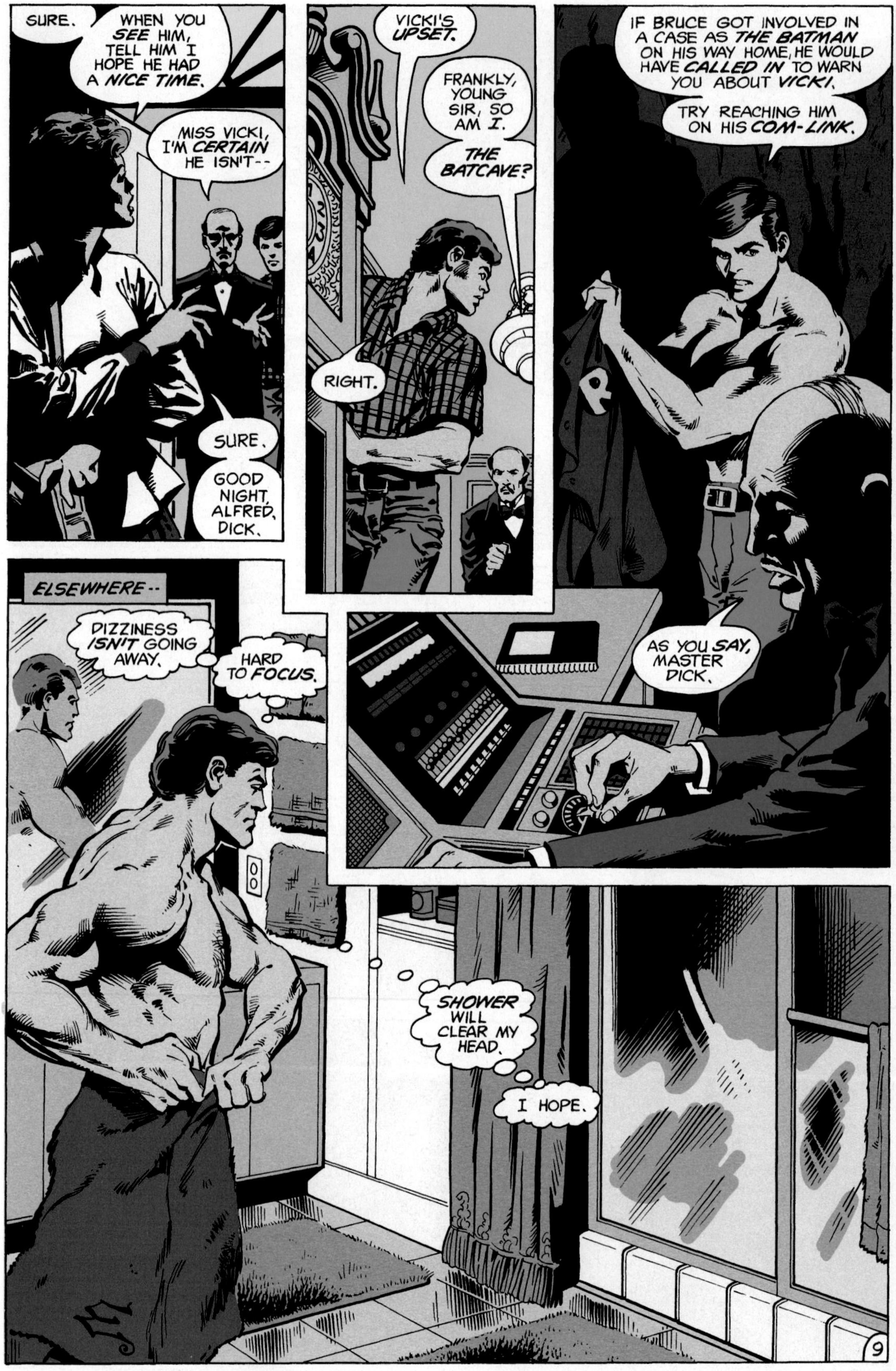
SURE.
WHEN YOU SEE HIM, TELL HIM I HOPE HE HAD A NICE TIME.
MISS VICKI, I'M CERTAIN HE ISN'T--
SURE.
GOOD NIGHT, ALFRED, DICK.
VICKI'S UPSET.
FRANKLY, YOUNG SIR, SO AM I.
THE BATCAVE?
RIGHT.
IF BRUCE GOT INVOLVED IN A CASE AS THE BATMAN ON HIS WAY HOME, HE WOULD HAVE CALLED IN TO WARN YOU ABOUT VICKI.
TRY REACHING HIM ON HIS COM-LINK.
AS YOU SAY, MASTER DICK.
ELSEWHERE--
DIZZINESS ISN'T GOING AWAY.
HARD TO FOCUS.
SHOWER WILL CLEAR MY HEAD.
I HOPE.
9

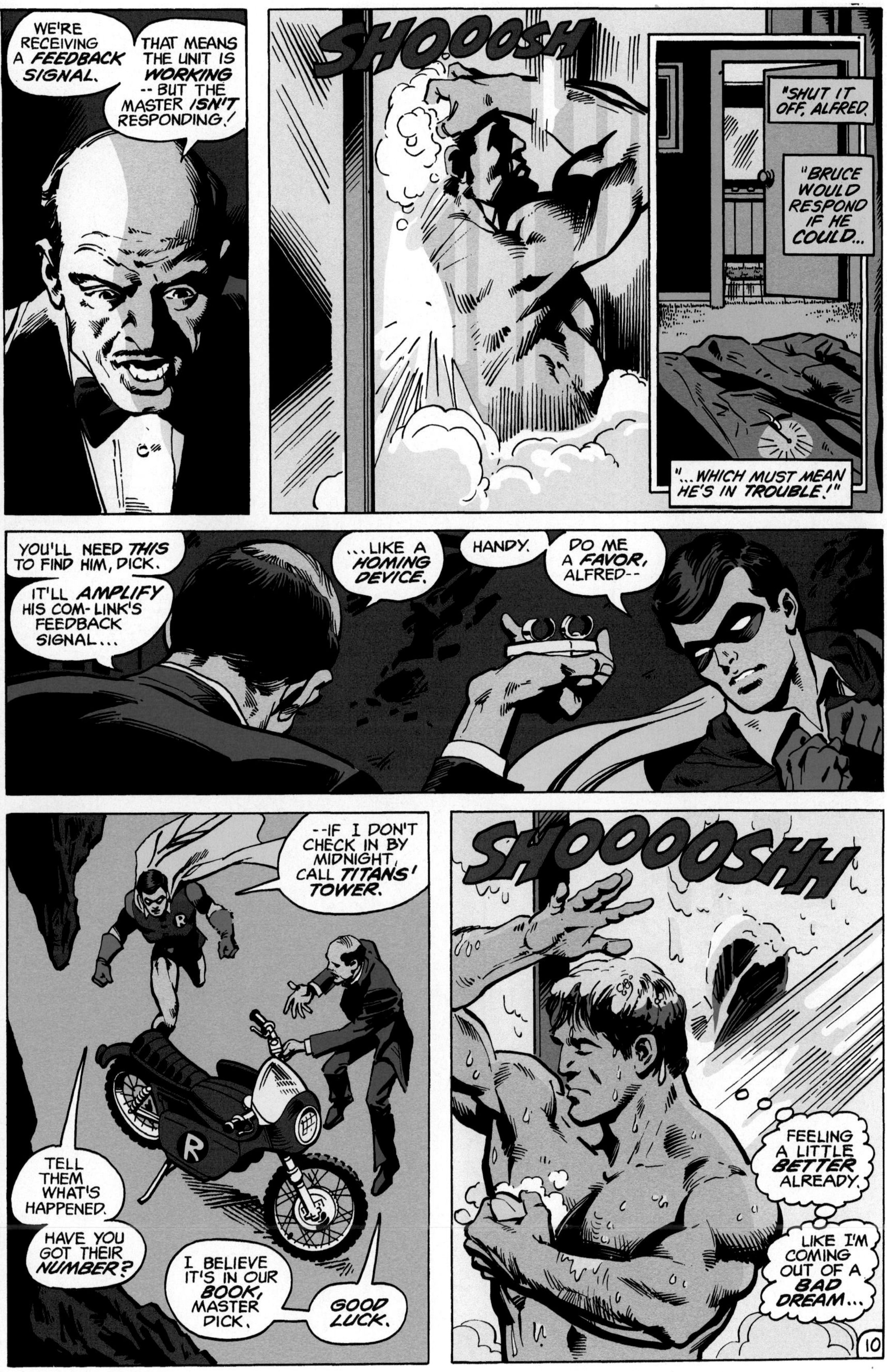
WE'RE RECEIVING A FEEDBACK SIGNAL.
THAT MEANS THE UNIT IS WORKING -- BUT THE MASTER ISN'T RESPONDING!
SHOOOSH
"SHUT IT OFF, ALFRED.
"BRUCE WOULD RESPOND IF HE COULD...
"...WHICH MUST MEAN HE'S IN TROUBLE!"
YOU'LL NEED THIS TO FIND HIM, DICK.
IT'LL AMPLIFY HIS COM-LINK'S FEEDBACK SIGNAL...
...LIKE A HOMING DEVICE.
HANDY.
DO ME A FAVOR, ALFRED--
--IF I DON'T CHECK IN BY MIDNIGHT, CALL TITANS' TOWER.
TELL THEM WHAT'S HAPPENED.
HAVE YOU GOT THEIR NUMBER?
I BELIEVE IT'S IN OUR BOOK, MASTER DICK.
GOOD LUCK.
SHOOOOSHH
FEELING A LITTLE BETTER ALREADY.
LIKE I'M COMING OUT OF A BAD DREAM...
10

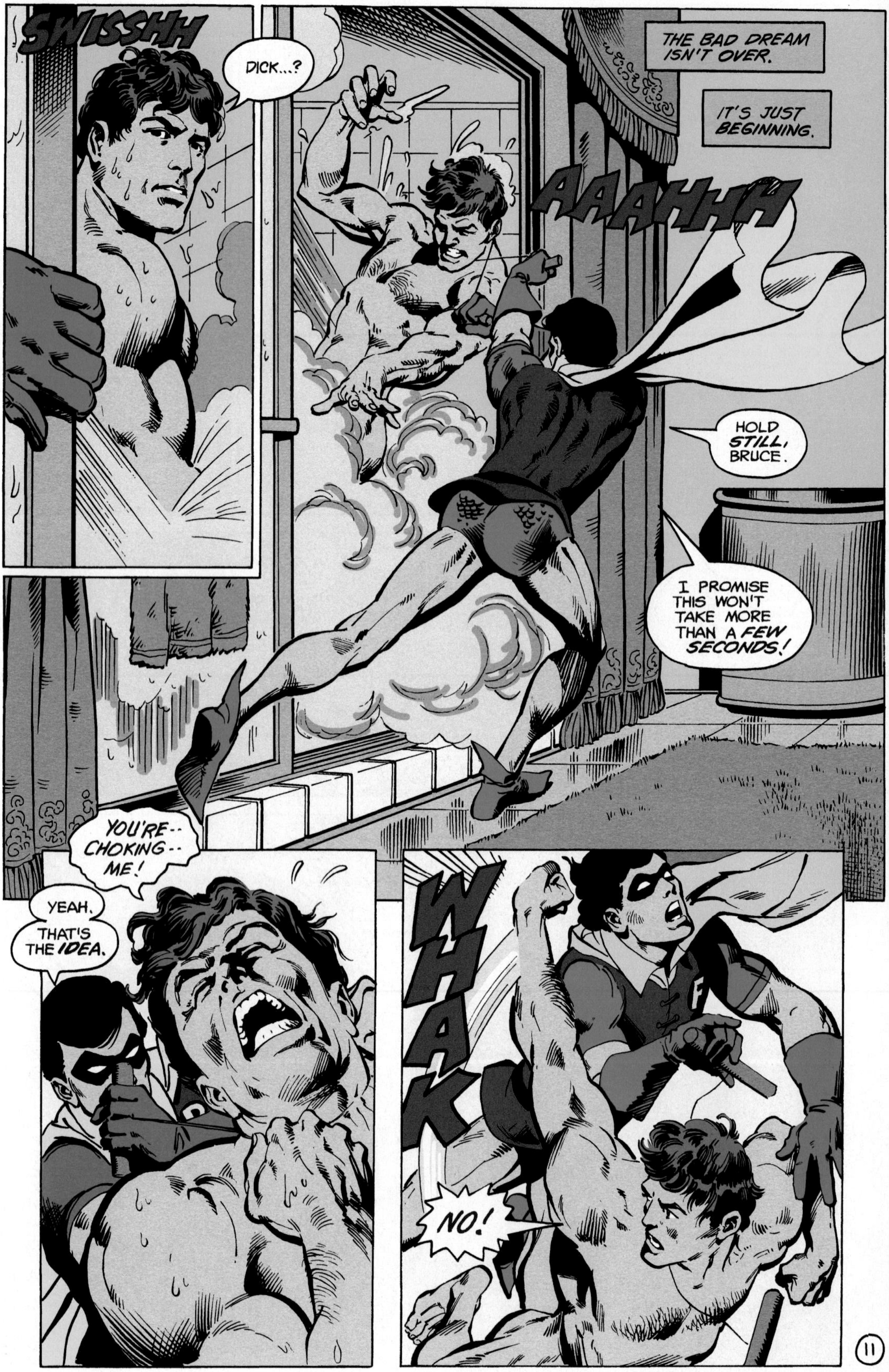
SWISSHH
DICK...?
THE BAD DREAM ISN'T OVER.
IT'S JUST BEGINNING.
AAAHHH
HOLD STILL, BRUCE.
I PROMISE THIS WON'T TAKE MORE THAN A FEW SECONDS!
YOU'RE-- CHOKING-- ME!
YEAH, THAT'S THE IDEA.
WHAK
NO!
11

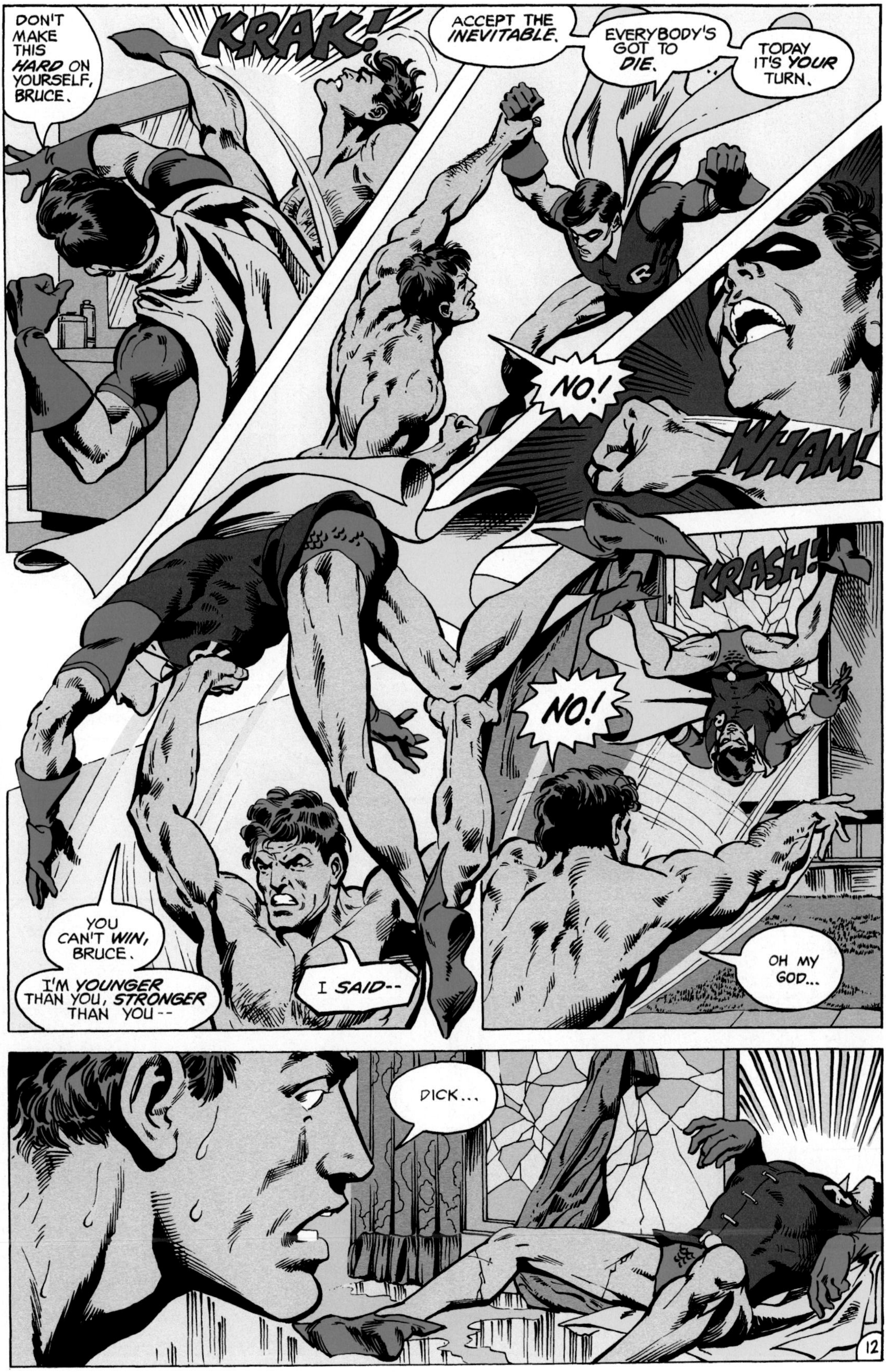
DON'T MAKE THIS HARD ON YOURSELF, BRUCE.
KRAK!
ACCEPT THE INEVITABLE.
EVERYBODY'S GOT TO DIE.
TODAY IT'S YOUR TURN.
NO!
WHAM!
KRASH!
NO!
YOU CAN'T WIN, BRUCE.
I'M YOUNGER THAN YOU, STRONGER THAN YOU--
I SAID--
OH MY GOD...
DICK...
12

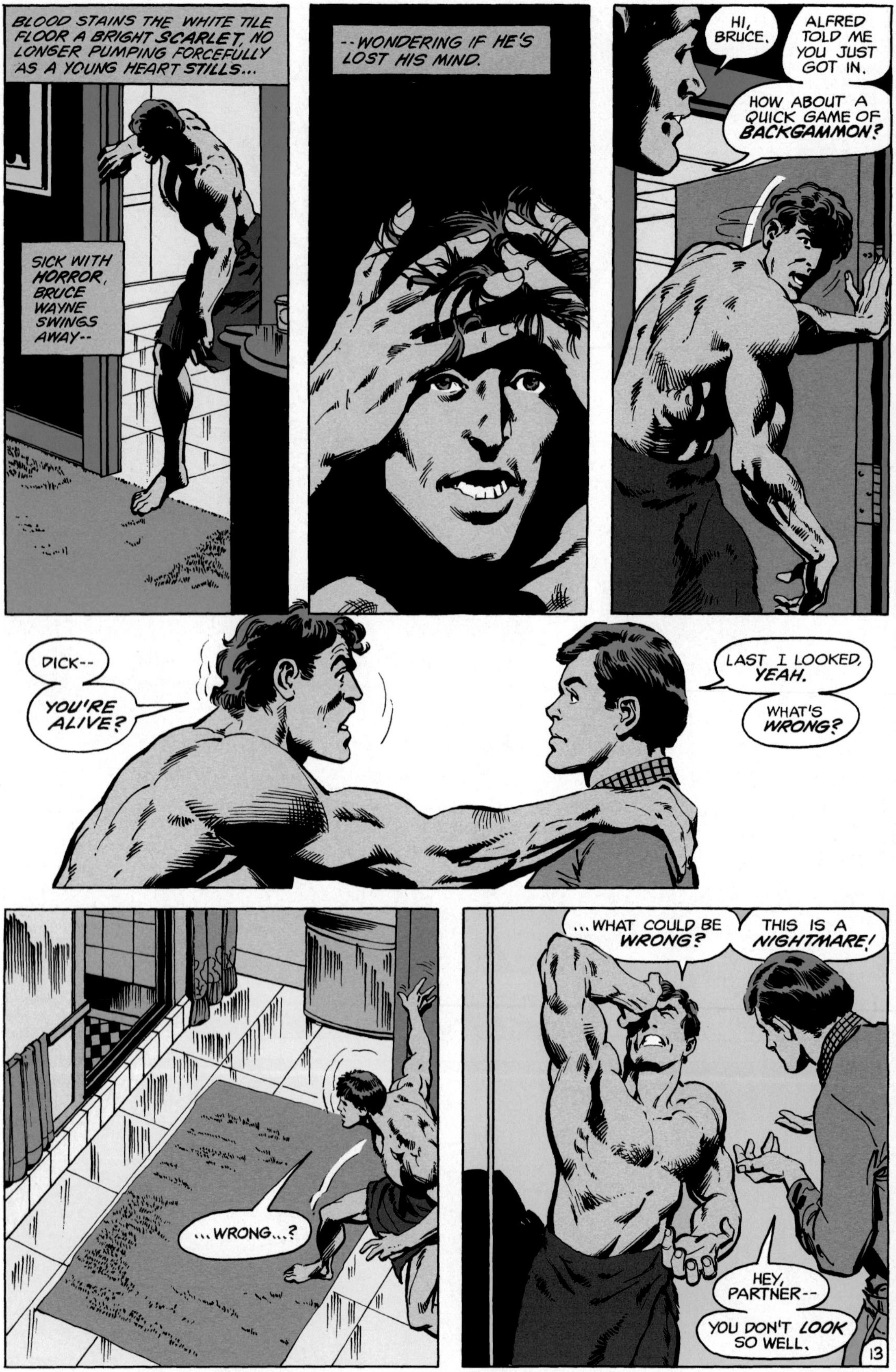
BLOOD STAINS THE WHITE TILE FLOOR A BRIGHT SCARLET, NO LONGER PUMPING FORCEFULLY AS A YOUNG HEART STILLS...
SICK WITH HORROR, BRUCE WAYNE SWINGS AWAY--
--WONDERING IF HE'S LOST HIS MIND.
HI, BRUCE.
ALFRED TOLD ME YOU JUST GOT IN.
HOW ABOUT A QUICK GAME OF BACKGAMMON?
DICK--
YOU'RE ALIVE?
LAST I LOOKED, YEAH.
WHAT'S WRONG?
...WRONG...?
...WHAT COULD BE WRONG?
THIS IS A NIGHTMARE!
HEY, PARTNER--
YOU DON'T LOOK SO WELL.
13

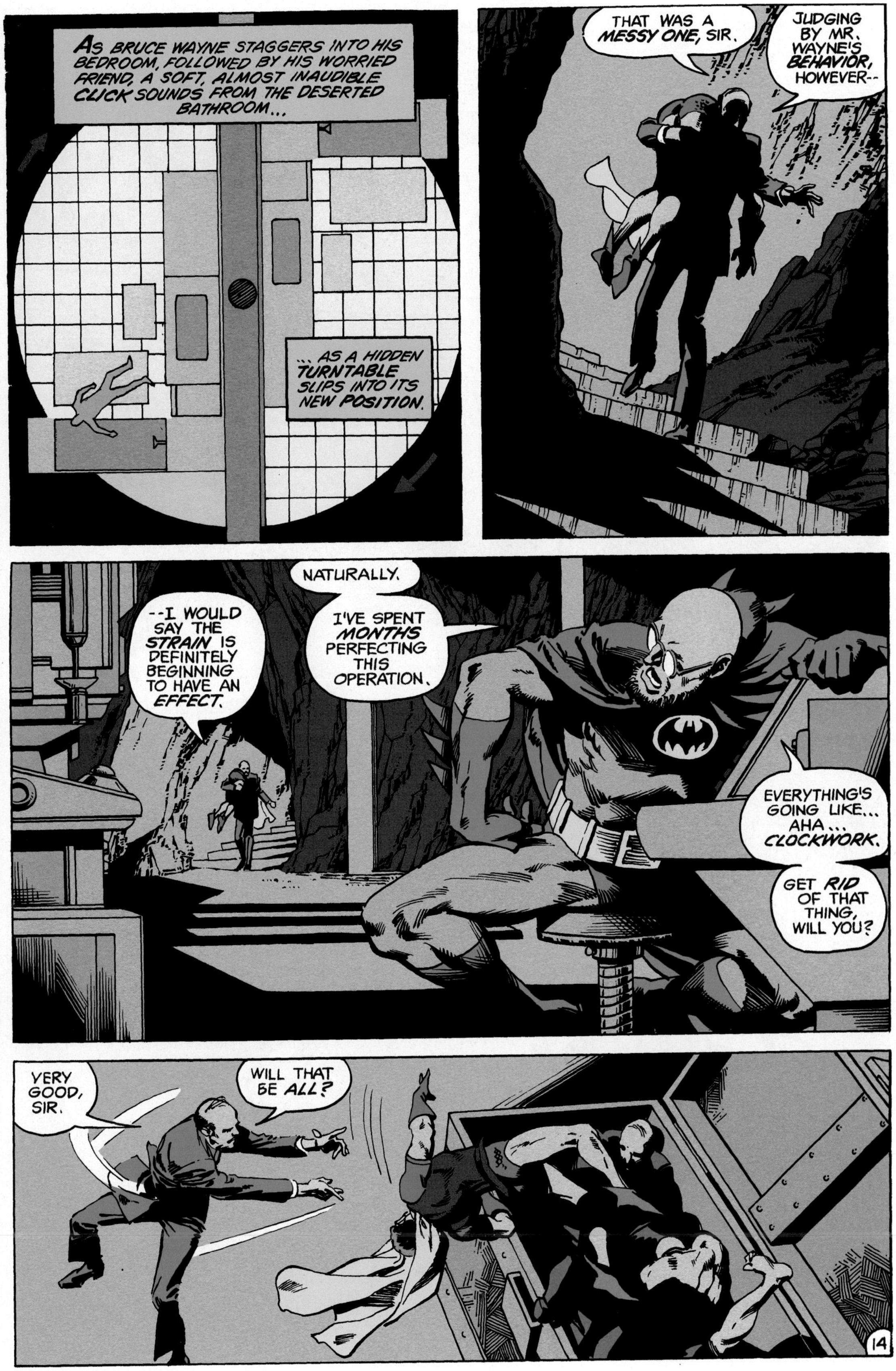
AS BRUCE WAYNE STAGGERS INTO HIS BEDROOM, FOLLOWED BY HIS WORRIED FRIEND, A SOFT, ALMOST INAUDIBLE CLICK SOUNDS FROM THE DESERTED BATHROOM...
... AS A HIDDEN TURNTABLE SLIPS INTO ITS NEW POSITION.
THAT WAS A MESSY ONE, SIR.
JUDGING BY MR. WAYNE'S BEHAVIOR, HOWEVER--
--I WOULD SAY THE STRAIN IS DEFINITELY BEGINNING TO HAVE AN EFFECT.
NATURALLY.
I'VE SPENT MONTHS PERFECTING THIS OPERATION.
EVERYTHING'S GOING LIKE... AHA... CLOCKWORK.
GET RID OF THAT THING, WILL YOU?
VERY GOOD, SIR.
WILL THAT BE ALL?
14

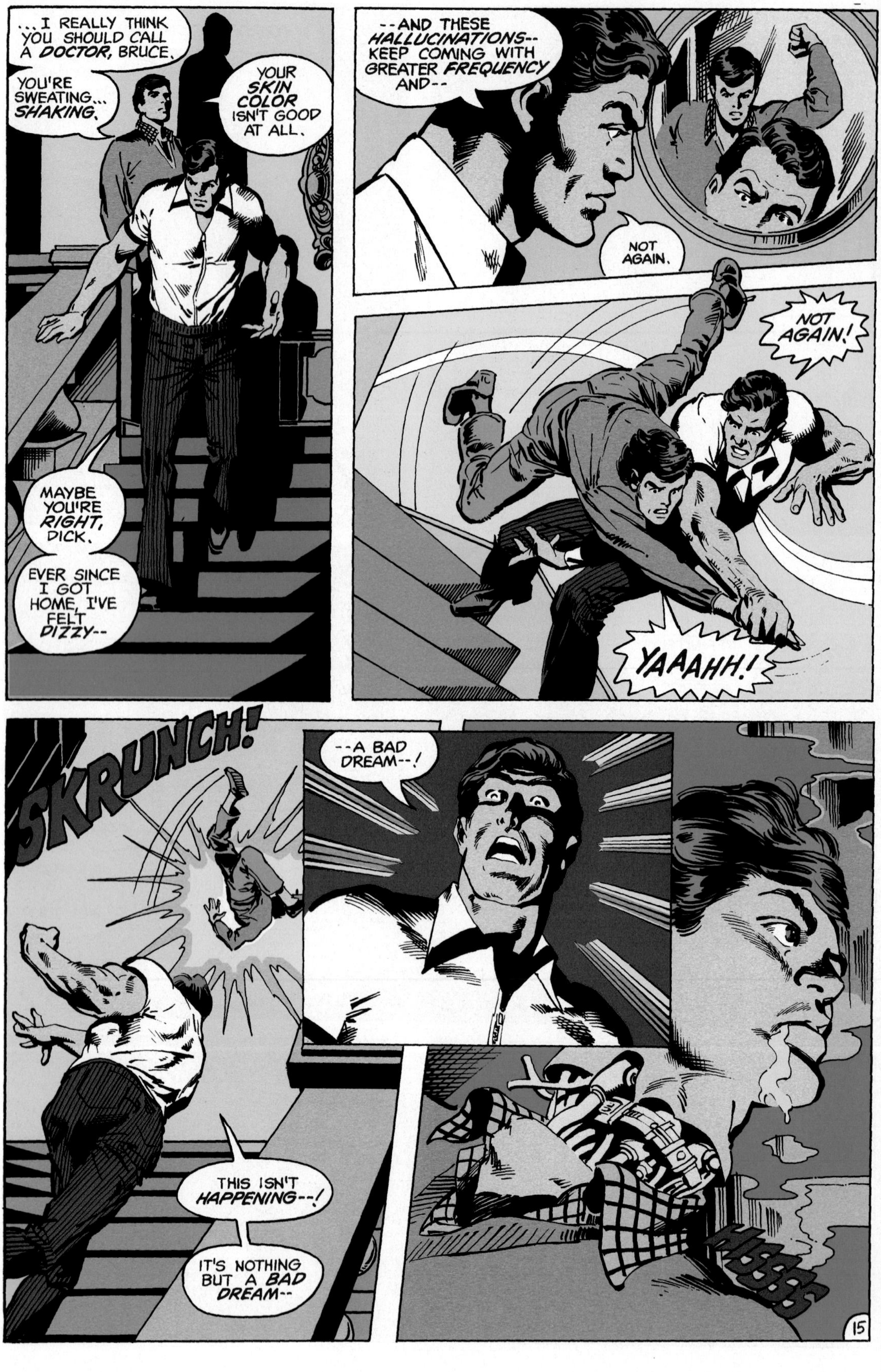
...I REALLY THINK YOU SHOULD CALL A DOCTOR, BRUCE.
YOU'RE SWEATING... SHAKING.
YOUR SKIN COLOR ISN'T GOOD AT ALL.
MAYBE YOU'RE RIGHT, DICK.
EVER SINCE I GOT HOME, I'VE FELT DIZZY--
--AND THESE HALLUCINATIONS--KEEP COMING WITH GREATER FREQUENCY AND--
NOT AGAIN.
NOT AGAIN!
YAAAHH!
SKRUNCH!
THIS ISN'T HAPPENING--!
IT'S NOTHING BUT A BAD DREAM--
--A BAD DREAM--!
HISSSS
15

OF COURSE...

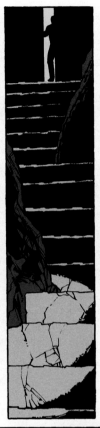

COME IN, MISTER WAYNE.

I WAS *WONDERING* WHEN YOU'D FINALLY SEEK ME OUT.

WELCOME TO *MY* BATCAVE.

IF YOU'LL GET *DRESSED,* WE'LL *BEGIN.*

THIS *ISN'T* THE BATCAVE... AND THAT HOUSE UP THERE *ISN'T* WAYNE MANOR.

I KNOW YOUR *VOICE*--

16

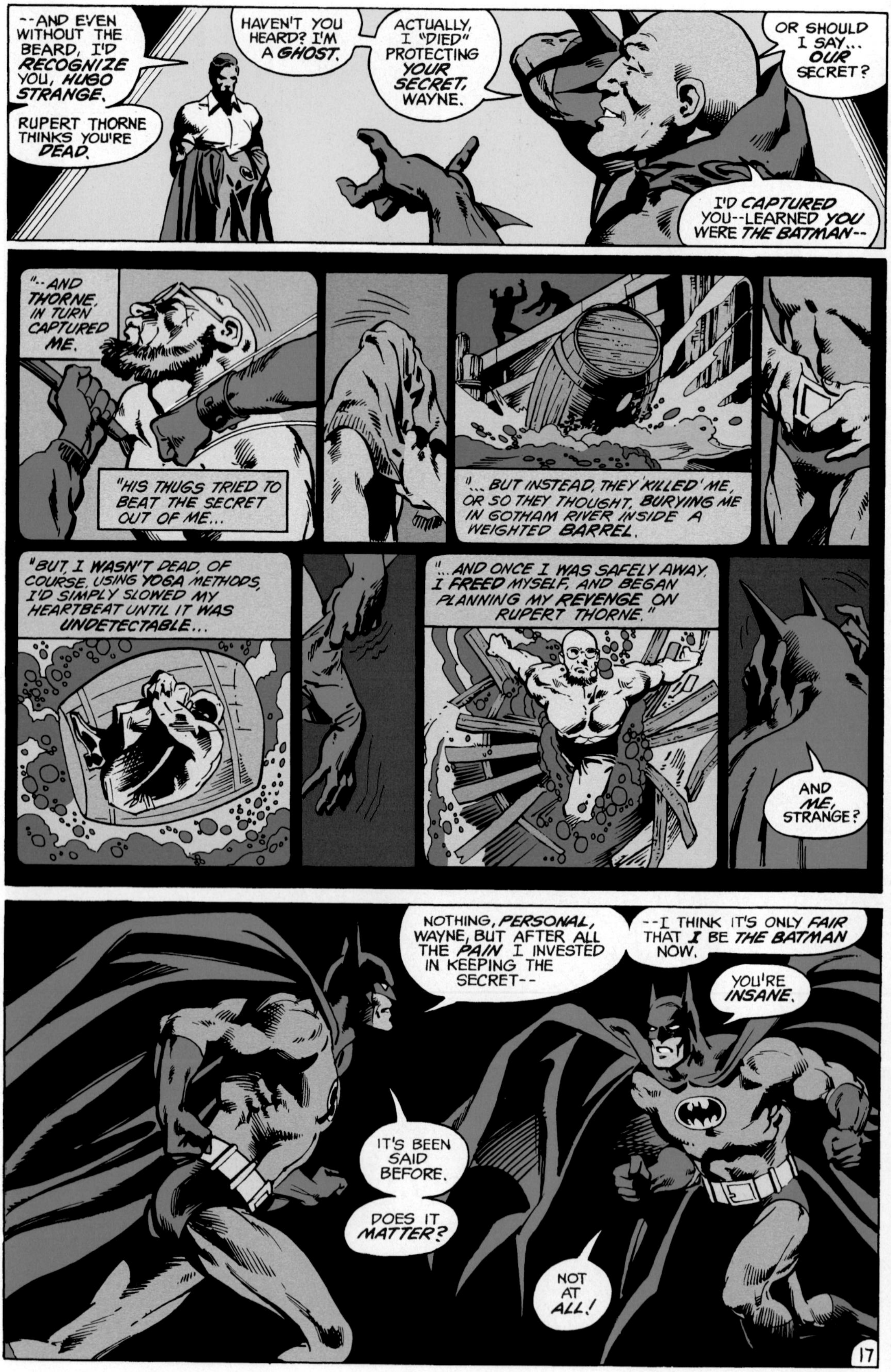
--AND EVEN WITHOUT THE BEARD, I'D RECOGNIZE YOU, HUGO STRANGE.
RUPERT THORNE THINKS YOU'RE DEAD.
HAVEN'T YOU HEARD? I'M A GHOST.
ACTUALLY, I "DIED" PROTECTING YOUR SECRET, WAYNE.
OR SHOULD I SAY... OUR SECRET?
I'D CAPTURED YOU--LEARNED YOU WERE THE BATMAN--
"--AND THORNE, IN TURN CAPTURED ME.
"HIS THUGS TRIED TO BEAT THE SECRET OUT OF ME...
"... BUT INSTEAD, THEY 'KILLED' ME, OR SO THEY THOUGHT, BURYING ME IN GOTHAM RIVER INSIDE A WEIGHTED BARREL.
"BUT, I WASN'T DEAD, OF COURSE. USING YOGA METHODS, I'D SIMPLY SLOWED MY HEARTBEAT UNTIL IT WAS UNDETECTABLE...
"... AND ONCE I WAS SAFELY AWAY, I FREED MYSELF, AND BEGAN PLANNING MY REVENGE ON RUPERT THORNE."
AND ME, STRANGE?
NOTHING PERSONAL, WAYNE, BUT AFTER ALL THE PAIN I INVESTED IN KEEPING THE SECRET--
--I THINK IT'S ONLY FAIR THAT I BE THE BATMAN NOW.
YOU'RE INSANE.
IT'S BEEN SAID BEFORE.
DOES IT MATTER?
NOT AT ALL!
17

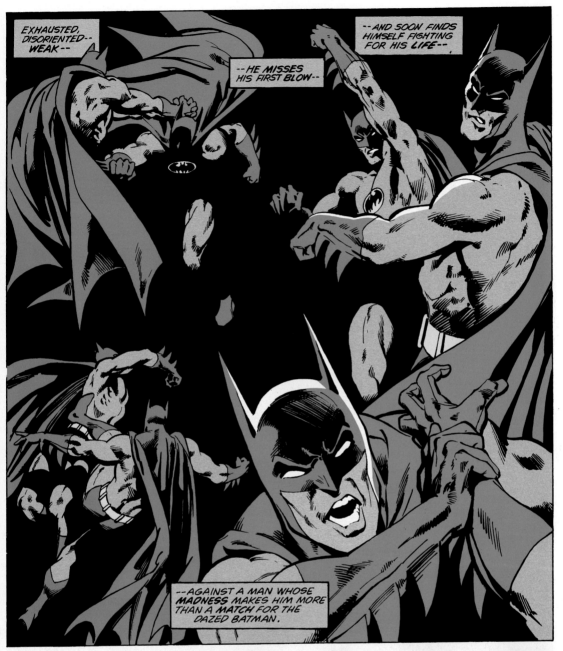

EXHAUSTED, DISORIENTED-- WEAK--

--HE MISSES HIS FIRST BLOW--

--AND SOON FINDS HIMSELF FIGHTING FOR HIS *LIFE*--.

--AGAINST A MAN WHOSE *MADNESS* MAKES HIM MORE THAN A MATCH FOR THE DAZED BATMAN.

SIMULTANEOUSLY, ABOVE...

HOMING SIGNAL COMING IN *LOUD* AND *CLEAR!*

SHOULD BE AROUND THIS *CURVE*--

HUH?

WAYNE MANOR--?

OR-- AN EXACT COPY!?

18

71

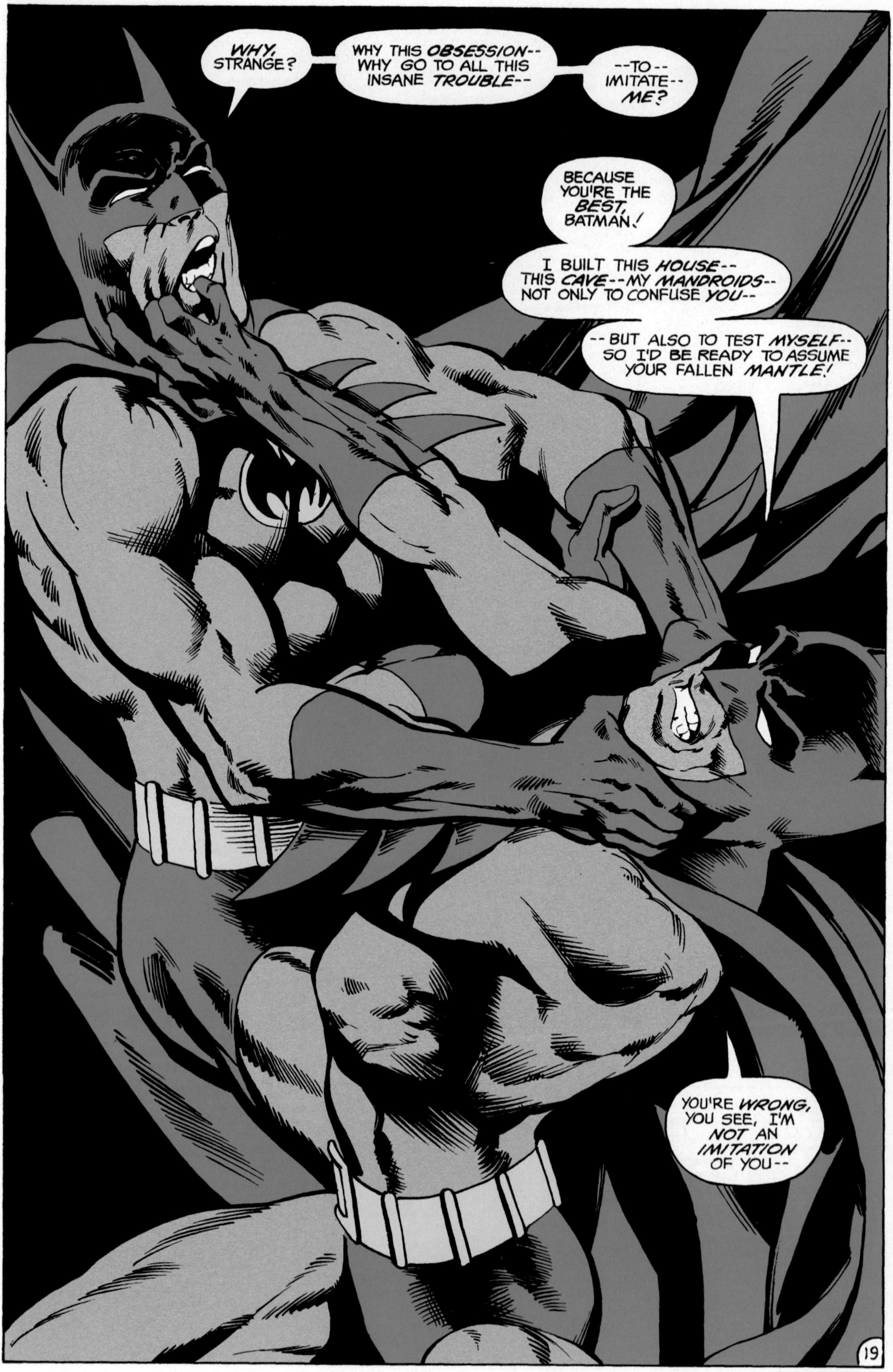
WHY, STRANGE?
WHY THIS OBSESSION-- WHY GO TO ALL THIS INSANE TROUBLE--
--TO-- IMITATE-- ME?
BECAUSE YOU'RE THE BEST, BATMAN!
I BUILT THIS HOUSE-- THIS CAVE--MY MANDROIDS-- NOT ONLY TO CONFUSE YOU--
--BUT ALSO TO TEST MYSELF-- SO I'D BE READY TO ASSUME YOUR FALLEN MANTLE!
YOU'RE WRONG, YOU SEE, I'M NOT AN IMITATION OF YOU--
19

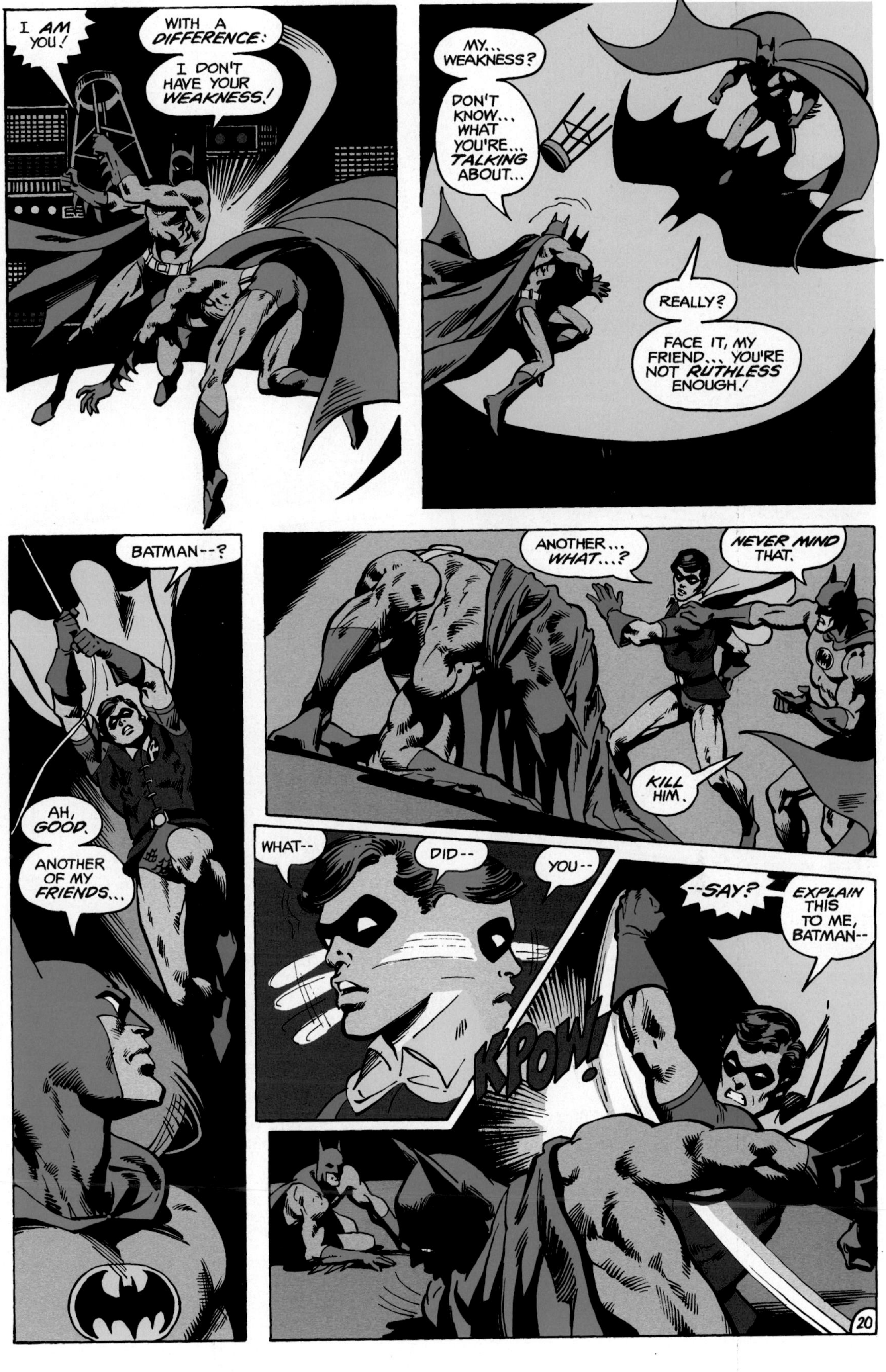
I AM YOU!
WITH A DIFFERENCE:
I DON'T HAVE YOUR WEAKNESS!
MY... WEAKNESS?
DON'T KNOW... WHAT YOU'RE... TALKING ABOUT...
REALLY?
FACE IT, MY FRIEND... YOU'RE NOT RUTHLESS ENOUGH!
BATMAN--?
AH, GOOD.
ANOTHER OF MY FRIENDS...
ANOTHER... WHAT...?
NEVER MIND THAT.
KILL HIM.
WHAT--
DID--
YOU--
--SAY?
EXPLAIN THIS TO ME, BATMAN--
KPOW!
20

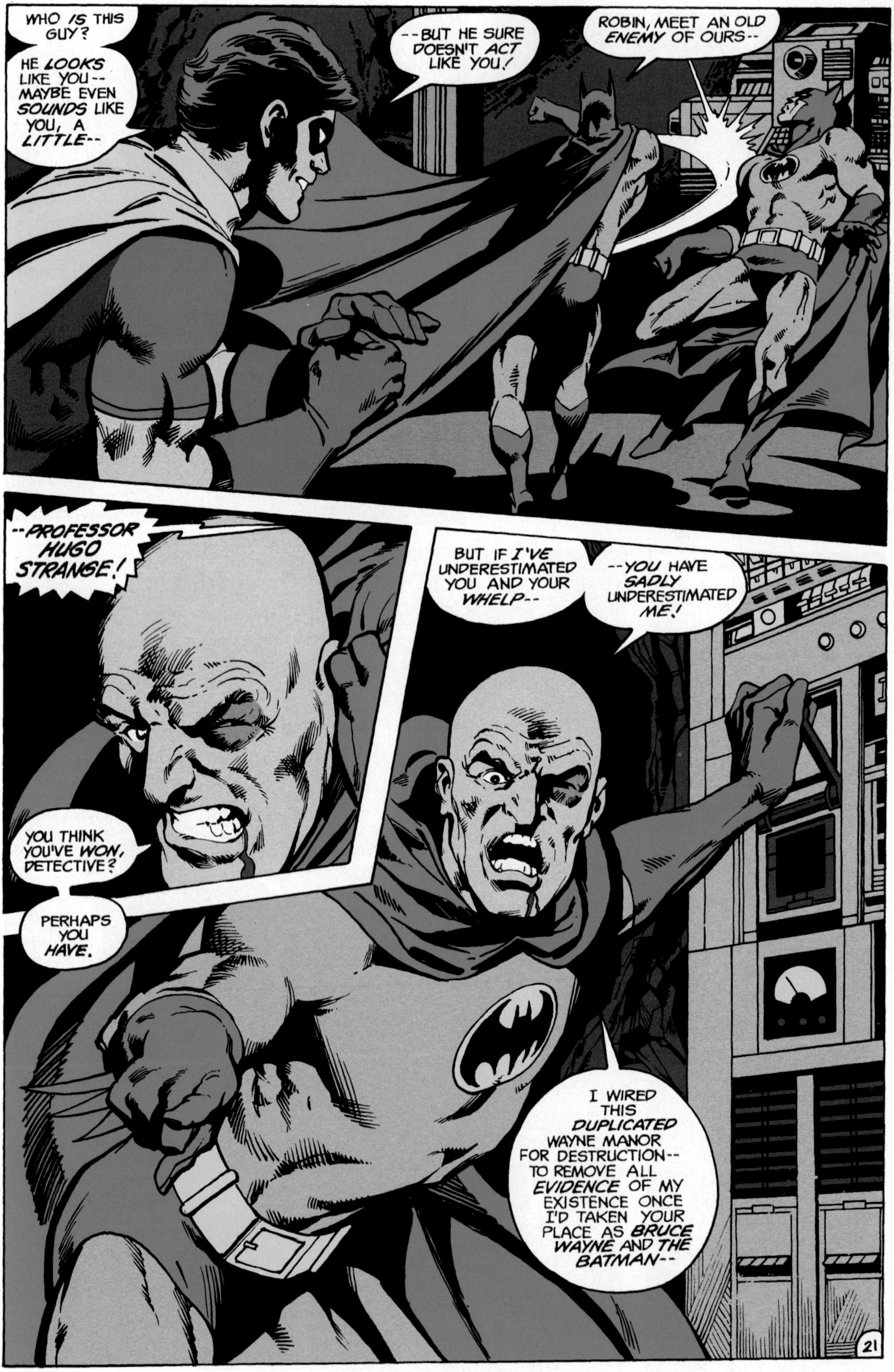
WHO IS THIS GUY?
HE LOOKS LIKE YOU-- MAYBE EVEN SOUNDS LIKE YOU, A LITTLE--
--BUT HE SURE DOESN'T ACT LIKE YOU!
ROBIN, MEET AN OLD ENEMY OF OURS--
--PROFESSOR HUGO STRANGE!
YOU THINK YOU'VE WON, DETECTIVE?
PERHAPS YOU HAVE.
BUT IF I'VE UNDERESTIMATED YOU AND YOUR WHELP--
--YOU HAVE SADLY UNDERESTIMATED ME!
I WIRED THIS DUPLICATED WAYNE MANOR FOR DESTRUCTION-- TO REMOVE ALL EVIDENCE OF MY EXISTENCE ONCE I'D TAKEN YOUR PLACE AS BRUCE WAYNE AND THE BATMAN--
21

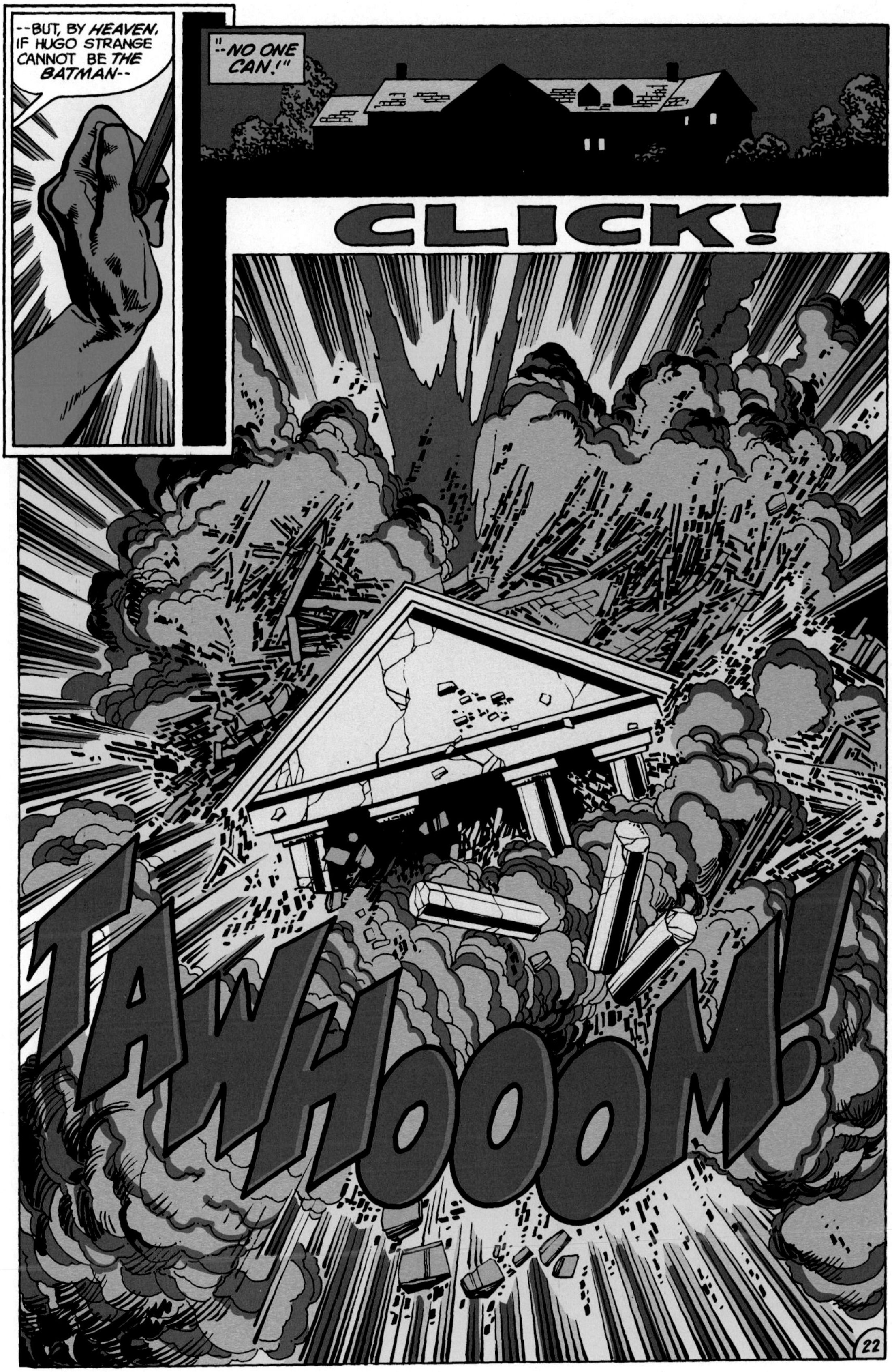
--BUT, BY HEAVEN, IF HUGO STRANGE CANNOT BE THE BATMAN--
"--NO ONE CAN!"
CLICK!
TAWHOOOM!
22

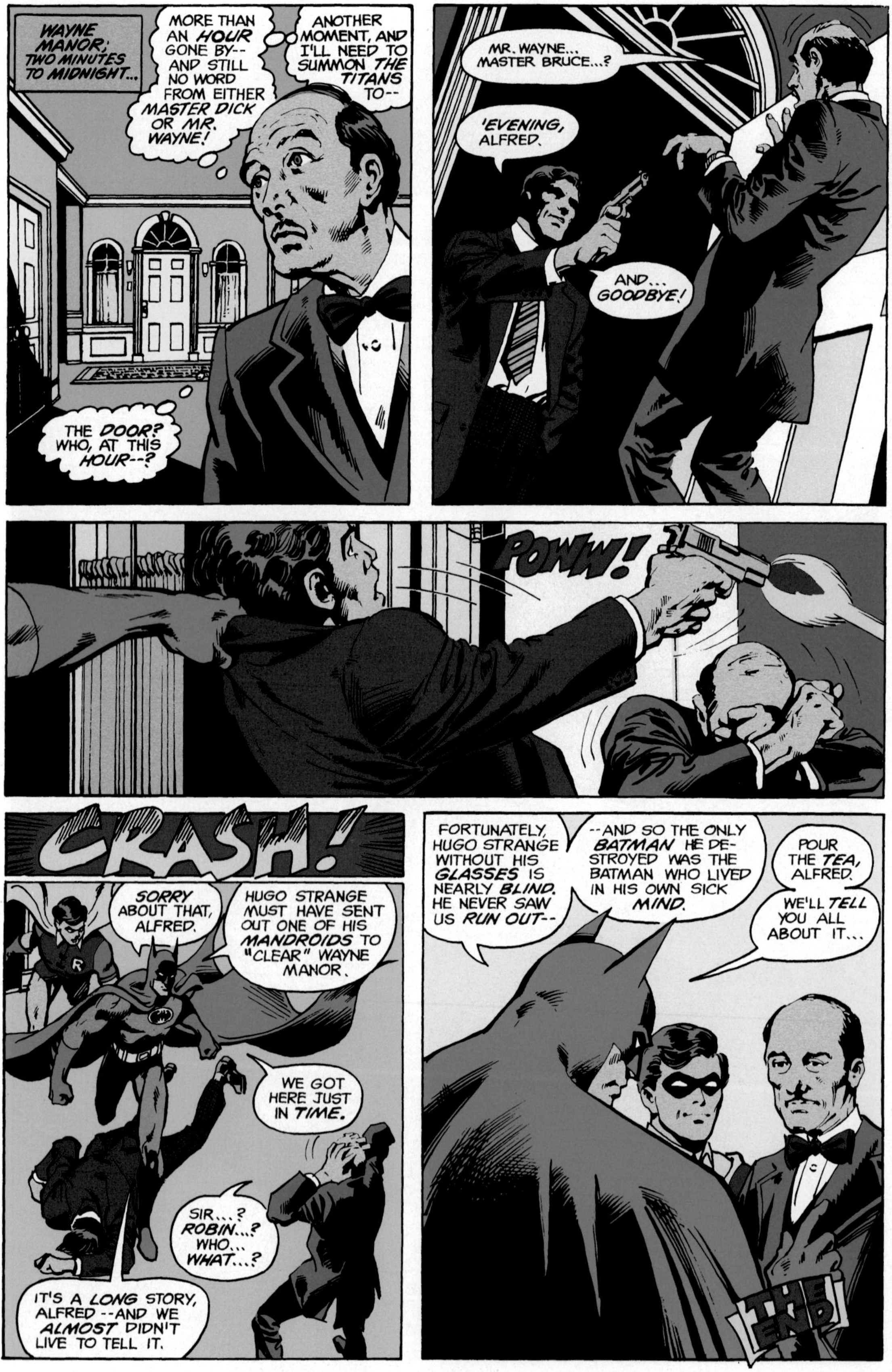
WAYNE MANOR; TWO MINUTES TO MIDNIGHT...
MORE THAN AN HOUR GONE BY-- AND STILL NO WORD FROM EITHER MASTER DICK OR MR. WAYNE!
ANOTHER MOMENT, AND I'LL NEED TO SUMMON THE TITANS TO--
THE DOOR? WHO, AT THIS HOUR--?
MR. WAYNE... MASTER BRUCE...?
'EVENING, ALFRED.
AND... GOODBYE!
POWW!
CRASH!
SORRY ABOUT THAT, ALFRED.
HUGO STRANGE MUST HAVE SENT OUT ONE OF HIS MANDROIDS TO "CLEAR" WAYNE MANOR.
WE GOT HERE JUST IN TIME.
SIR...? ROBIN...? WHO... WHAT...?
IT'S A LONG STORY, ALFRED --AND WE ALMOST DIDN'T LIVE TO TELL IT.
FORTUNATELY, HUGO STRANGE WITHOUT HIS GLASSES IS NEARLY BLIND. HE NEVER SAW US RUN OUT--
--AND SO THE ONLY BATMAN HE DESTROYED WAS THE BATMAN WHO LIVED IN HIS OWN SICK MIND.
POUR THE TEA, ALFRED.
WE'LL TELL YOU ALL ABOUT IT...
THE END

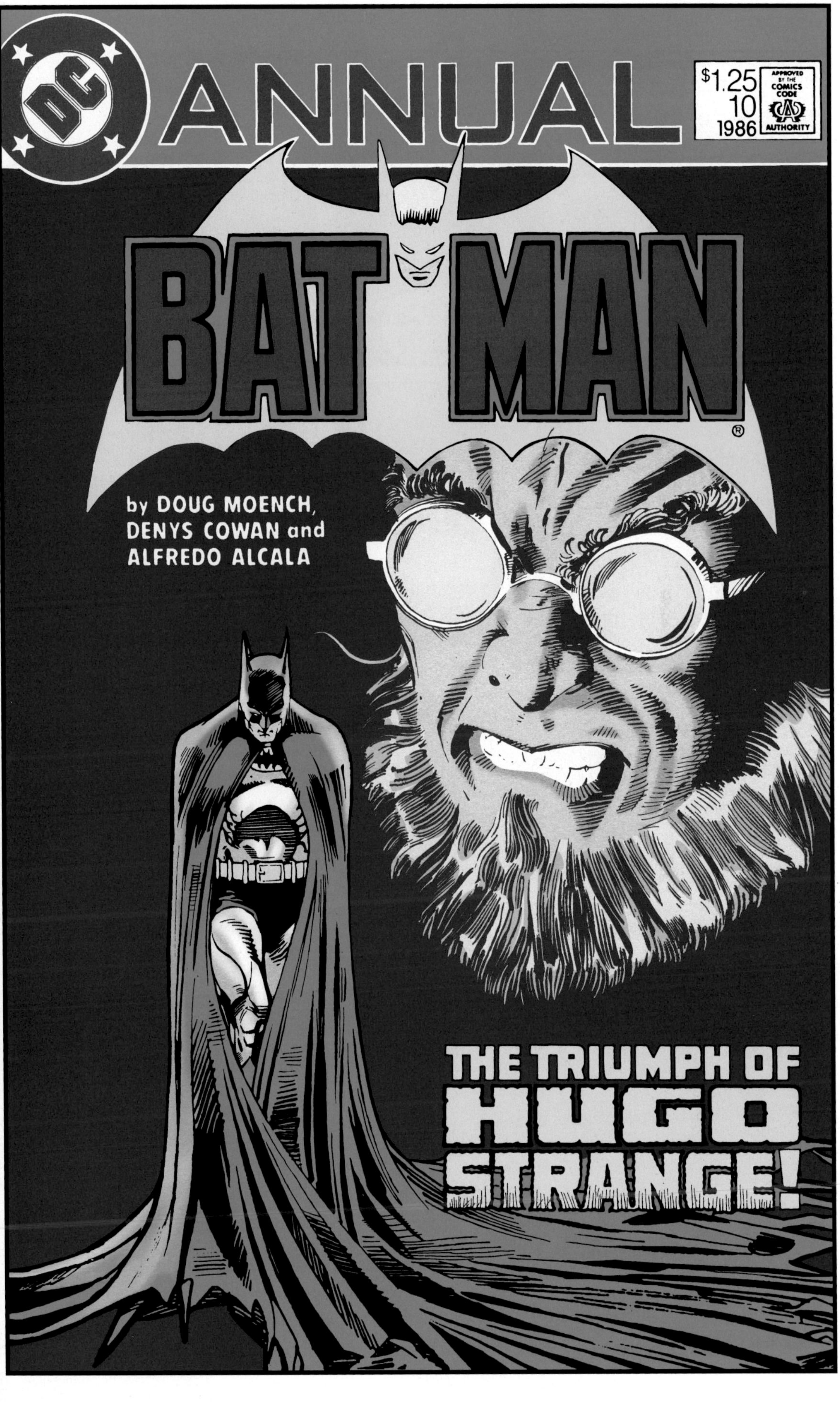
DC
ANNUAL
$1.25
10
1986
APPROVED BY THE COMICS CODE AUTHORITY
BATMAN
by DOUG MOENCH,
DENYS COWAN and
ALFREDO ALCALA
THE TRIUMPH OF
HUGO
STRANGE!

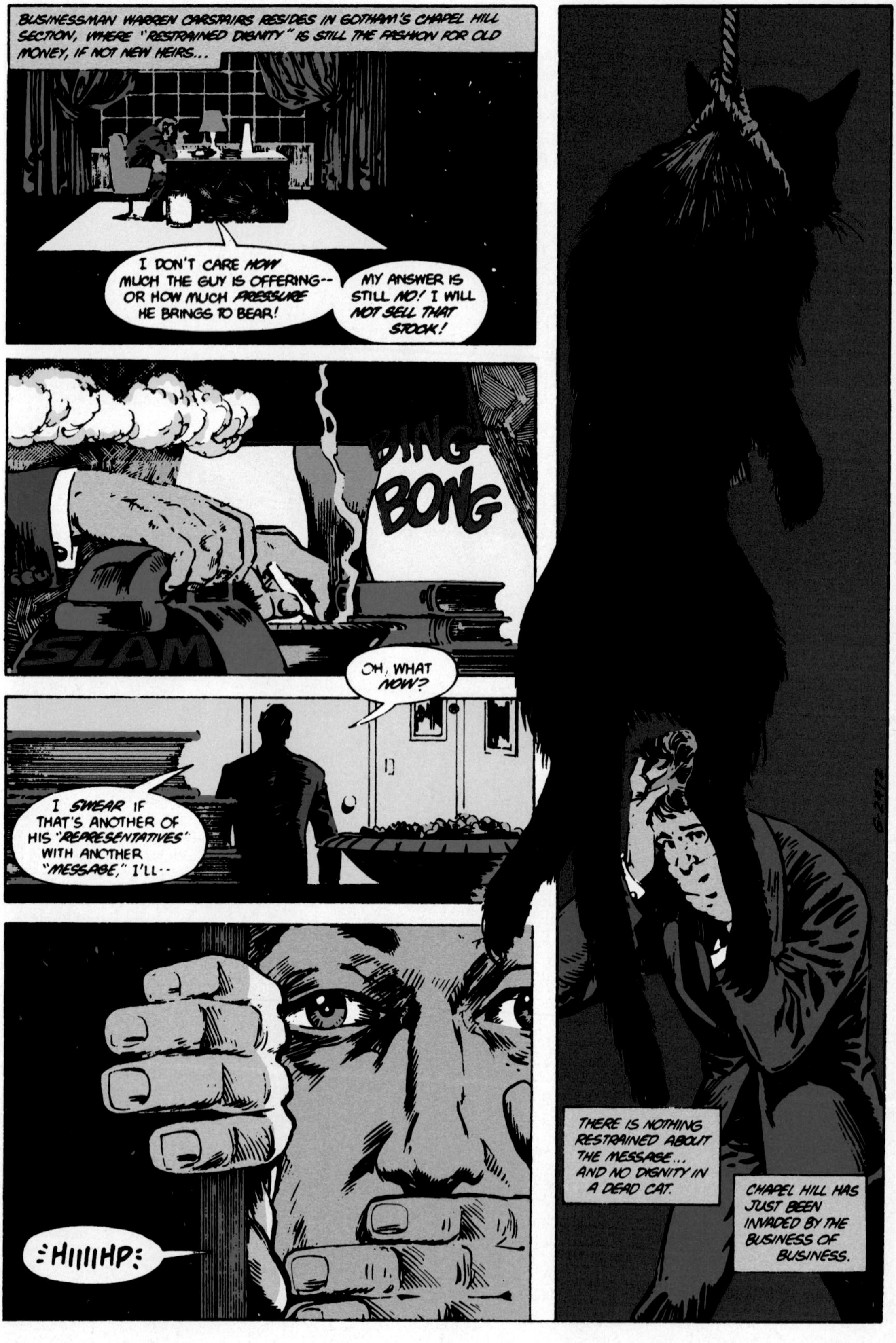

BUSINESSMAN WARREN CARSTAIRS RESIDES IN GOTHAM'S CHAPEL HILL SECTION, WHERE "RESTRAINED DIGNITY" IS STILL THE FASHION FOR OLD MONEY, IF NOT NEW HEIRS...
I DON'T CARE HOW MUCH THE GUY IS OFFERING-- OR HOW MUCH PRESSURE HE BRINGS TO BEAR!
MY ANSWER IS STILL NO! I WILL NOT SELL THAT STOCK!
SLAM
BING BONG
OH, WHAT NOW?
I SWEAR IF THAT'S ANOTHER OF HIS "REPRESENTATIVES" WITH ANOTHER "MESSAGE," I'LL--
:HIIIIHP:
THERE IS NOTHING RESTRAINED ABOUT THE MESSAGE... AND NO DIGNITY IN A DEAD CAT.
CHAPEL HILL HAS JUST BEEN INVADED BY THE BUSINESS OF BUSINESS.

MIDTOWN: BUT YOU MUST *ADMIT*, FRANKLIN, IT PICKED UP IN THE *THIRD* ACT...

I WOULDN'T KNOW-- I FELL *ASLEEP*.

THEN AT LEAST IT TOOK YOUR MIND OFF THAT ATTEMPTED STOCK--

--GRAB?

*;MMPHH!;*

*FRANKLIN!!*

STOP IT! YOU'RE HURTING HIM! POLICE!!

WUMP WUMP

WE GOT SOME *ADVICE* FOR YOU, MR. FRANKLIN HERSCH...

*SELL.*

AND THE NORTH GOTHAM STUDY OF ERIC HAMMOND MAKES *THREE*.

HMM... A *VERY* ATTRACTIVE SECOND OFFER... ALMOST *DOUBLE* THE *FIRST*...

...BUT I STILL *THINK NOT*.

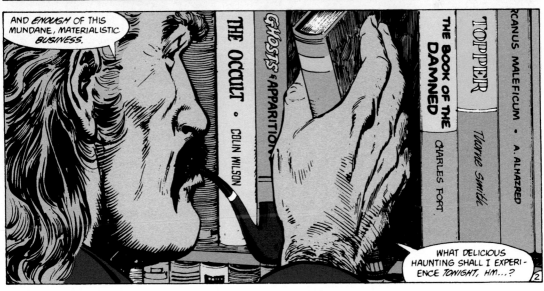

AND *ENOUGH* OF THIS MUNDANE, MATERIALISTIC BUSINESS.

THE OCCULT • COLIN WILSON

GHOSTS & APPARITIONS

TOPPER • Thorne Smith

THE BOOK OF THE DAMNED • CHARLES FORT

RCANUS MALEFICUM • A. ALHAZRED

WHAT DELICIOUS HAUNTING SHALL I EXPERIENCE *TONIGHT*, HM...?

2

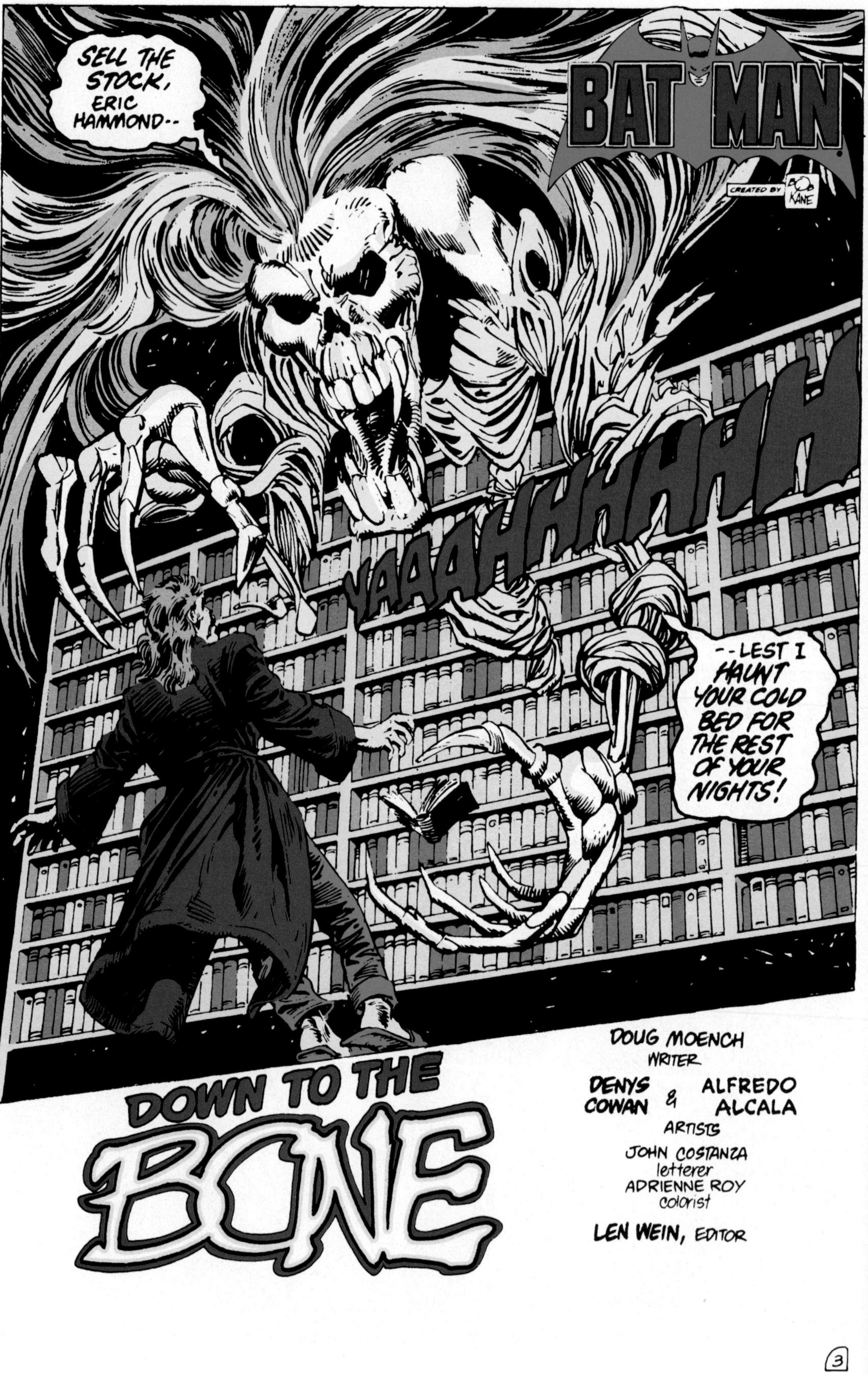
BATMAN
CREATED BY BOB KANE
SELL THE STOCK, ERIC HAMMOND--
YAAAHHHHHHH
--LEST I HAUNT YOUR COLD BED FOR THE REST OF YOUR NIGHTS!
DOWN TO THE BONE
DOUG MOENCH WRITER
DENYS COWAN & ALFREDO ALCALA ARTISTS
JOHN COSTANZA letterer
ADRIENNE ROY colorist
LEN WEIN, EDITOR
3

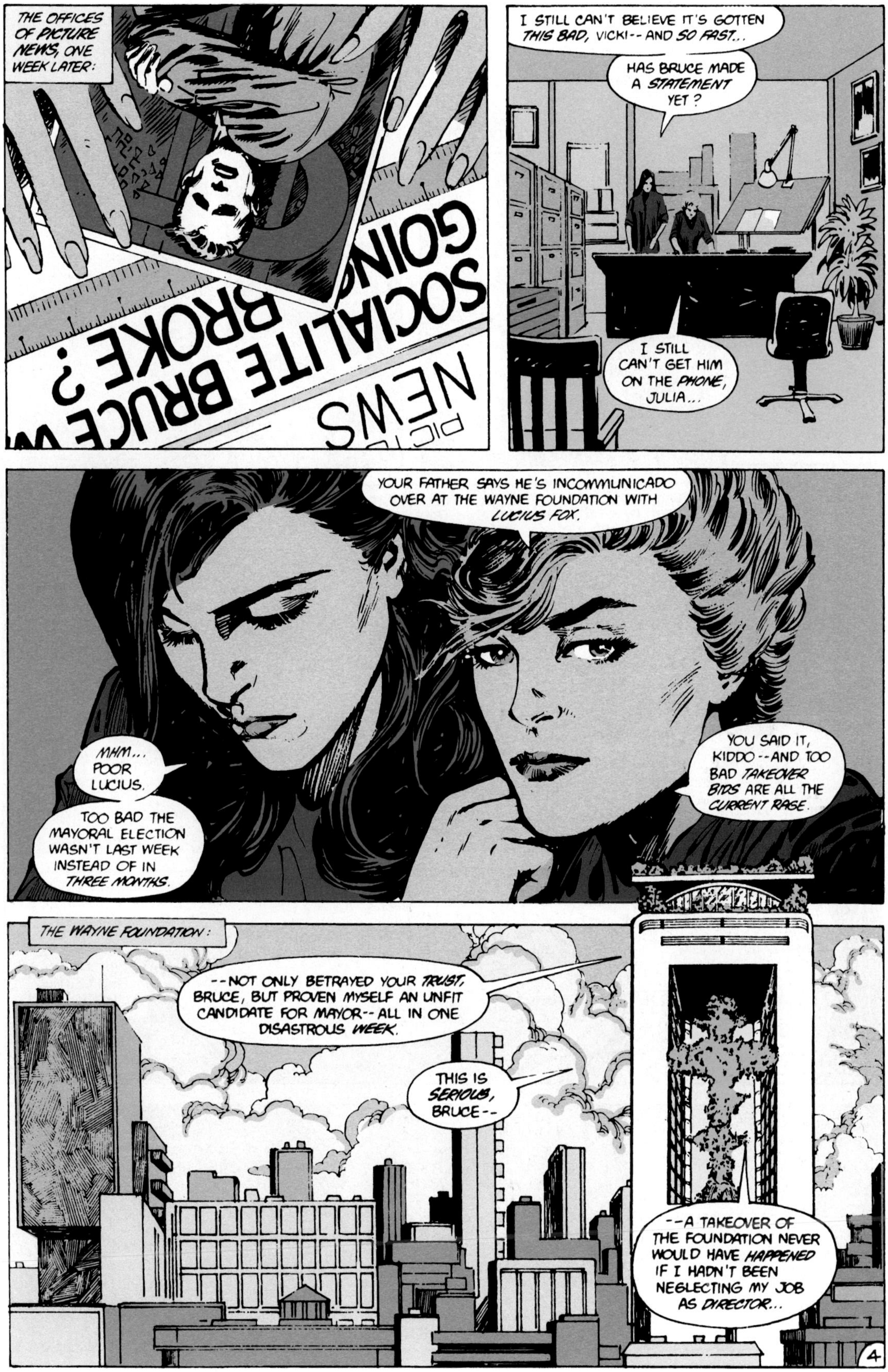

THE OFFICES OF PICTURE NEWS, ONE WEEK LATER:
NEWS
SOCIALITE BRUCE
BROKE ?
I STILL CAN'T BELIEVE IT'S GOTTEN THIS BAD, VICKI-- AND SO FAST...
HAS BRUCE MADE A STATEMENT YET ?
I STILL CAN'T GET HIM ON THE PHONE, JULIA...
YOUR FATHER SAYS HE'S INCOMMUNICADO OVER AT THE WAYNE FOUNDATION WITH LUCIUS FOX.
MHM... POOR LUCIUS.
TOO BAD THE MAYORAL ELECTION WASN'T LAST WEEK INSTEAD OF IN THREE MONTHS.
YOU SAID IT, KIDDO--AND TOO BAD TAKEOVER BIDS ARE ALL THE CURRENT RAGE.
THE WAYNE FOUNDATION:
--NOT ONLY BETRAYED YOUR TRUST, BRUCE, BUT PROVEN MYSELF AN UNFIT CANDIDATE FOR MAYOR-- ALL IN ONE DISASTROUS WEEK.
THIS IS SERIOUS, BRUCE--
--A TAKEOVER OF THE FOUNDATION NEVER WOULD HAVE HAPPENED IF I HADN'T BEEN NEGLECTING MY JOB AS DIRECTOR...
4

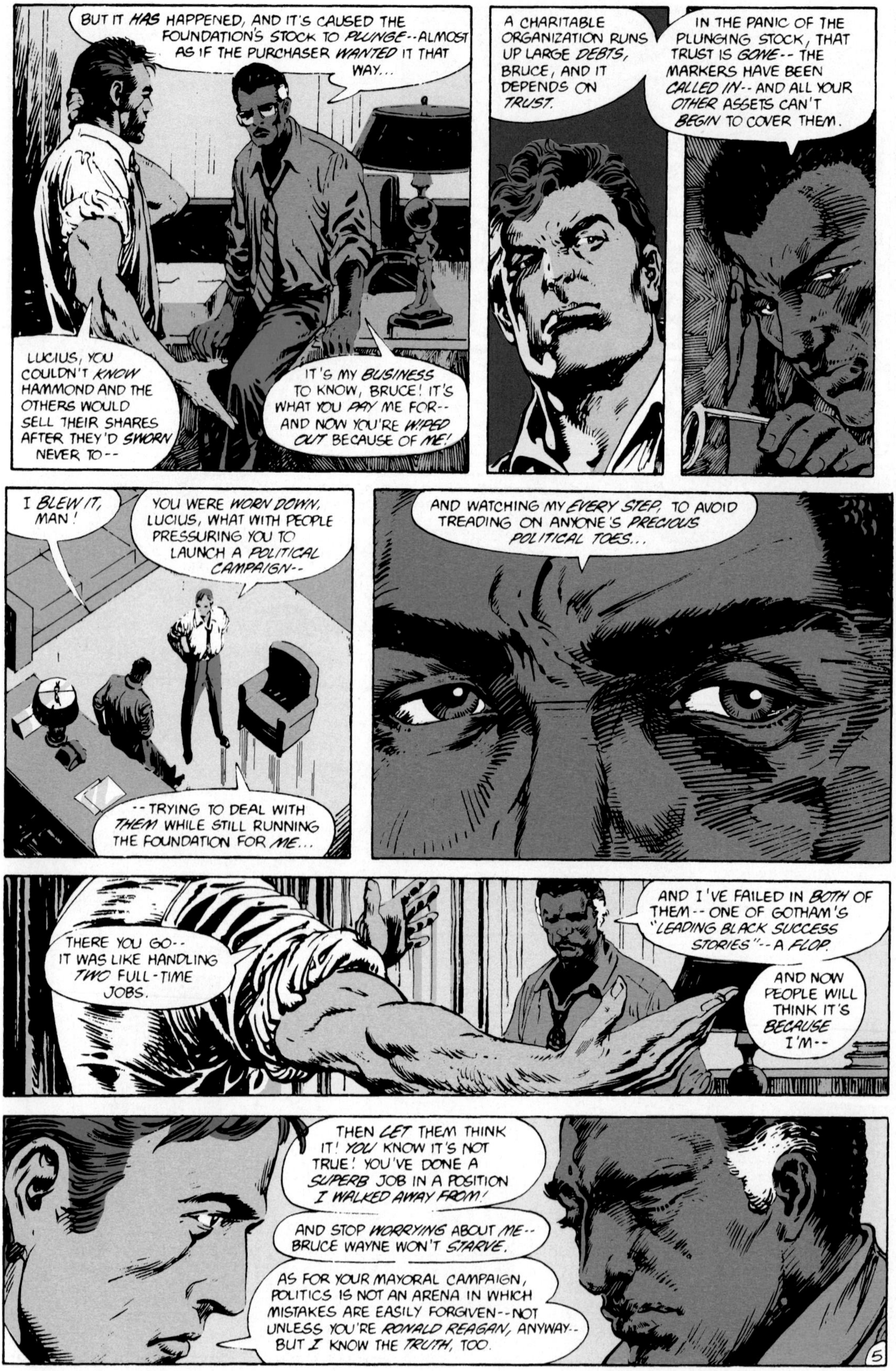

BUT IT HAS HAPPENED, AND IT'S CAUSED THE FOUNDATION'S STOCK TO PLUNGE--ALMOST AS IF THE PURCHASER WANTED IT THAT WAY...
LUCIUS, YOU COULDN'T KNOW HAMMOND AND THE OTHERS WOULD SELL THEIR SHARES AFTER THEY'D SWORN NEVER TO--
IT'S MY BUSINESS TO KNOW, BRUCE! IT'S WHAT YOU PAY ME FOR--AND NOW YOU'RE WIPED OUT BECAUSE OF ME!
A CHARITABLE ORGANIZATION RUNS UP LARGE DEBTS, BRUCE, AND IT DEPENDS ON TRUST.
IN THE PANIC OF THE PLUNGING STOCK, THAT TRUST IS GONE-- THE MARKERS HAVE BEEN CALLED IN-- AND ALL YOUR OTHER ASSETS CAN'T BEGIN TO COVER THEM.
I BLEW IT, MAN!
YOU WERE WORN DOWN, LUCIUS, WHAT WITH PEOPLE PRESSURING YOU TO LAUNCH A POLITICAL CAMPAIGN--
--TRYING TO DEAL WITH THEM WHILE STILL RUNNING THE FOUNDATION FOR ME...
AND WATCHING MY EVERY STEP, TO AVOID TREADING ON ANYONE'S PRECIOUS POLITICAL TOES...
THERE YOU GO-- IT WAS LIKE HANDLING TWO FULL-TIME JOBS.
AND I'VE FAILED IN BOTH OF THEM-- ONE OF GOTHAM'S "LEADING BLACK SUCCESS STORIES"--A FLOP.
AND NOW PEOPLE WILL THINK IT'S BECAUSE I'M--
THEN LET THEM THINK IT! YOU KNOW IT'S NOT TRUE! YOU'VE DONE A SUPERB JOB IN A POSITION I WALKED AWAY FROM!
AND STOP WORRYING ABOUT ME-- BRUCE WAYNE WON'T STARVE.
AS FOR YOUR MAYORAL CAMPAIGN, POLITICS IS NOT AN ARENA IN WHICH MISTAKES ARE EASILY FORGIVEN--NOT UNLESS YOU'RE RONALD REAGAN, ANYWAY-- BUT I KNOW THE TRUTH, TOO.
5

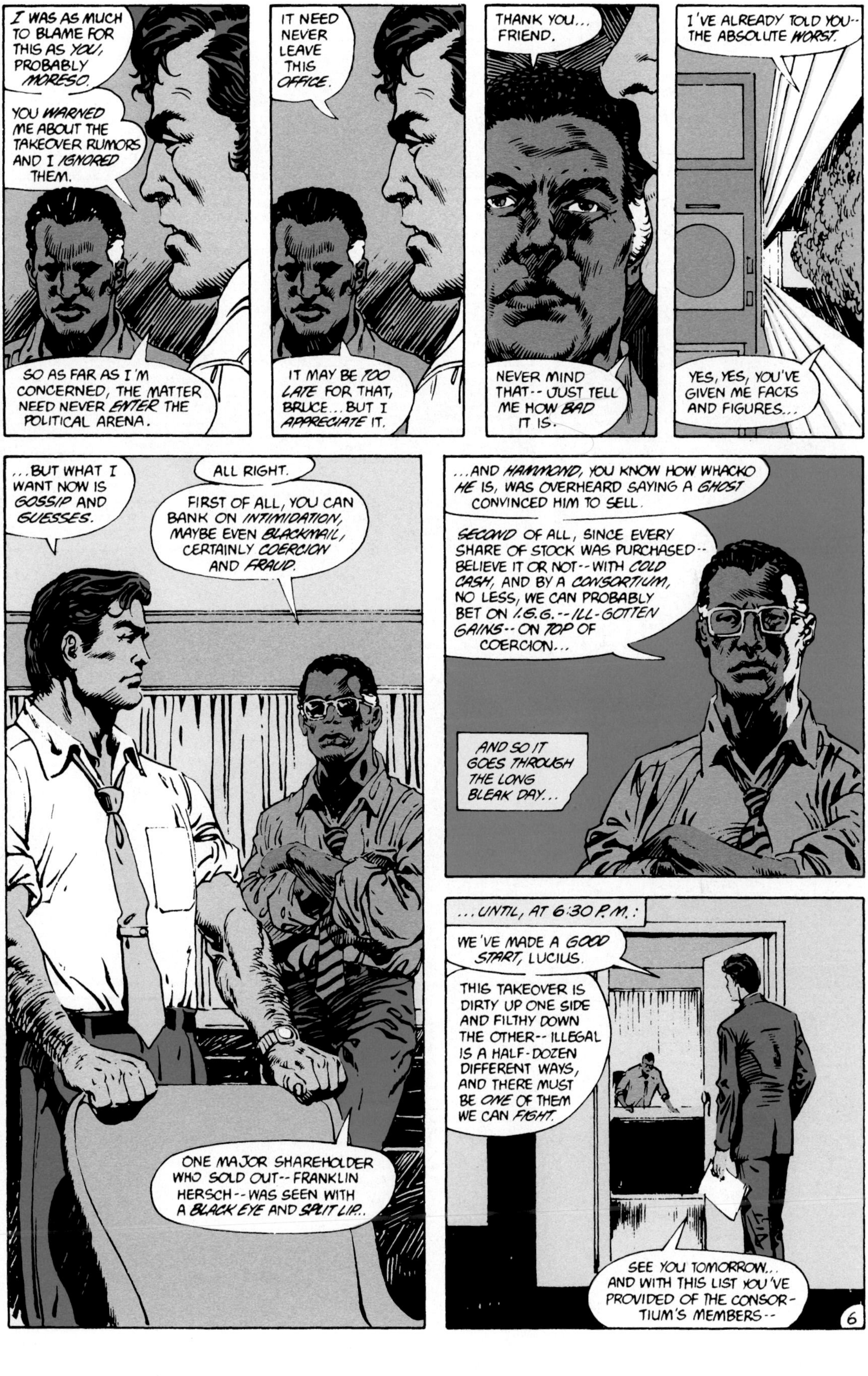
I WAS AS MUCH TO BLAME FOR THIS AS YOU, PROBABLY MORESO.
YOU WARNED ME ABOUT THE TAKEOVER RUMORS AND I IGNORED THEM.
SO AS FAR AS I'M CONCERNED, THE MATTER NEED NEVER ENTER THE POLITICAL ARENA.
IT NEED NEVER LEAVE THIS OFFICE.
IT MAY BE TOO LATE FOR THAT, BRUCE... BUT I APPRECIATE IT.
THANK YOU... FRIEND.
NEVER MIND THAT-- JUST TELL ME HOW BAD IT IS.
I'VE ALREADY TOLD YOU-- THE ABSOLUTE WORST.
YES, YES, YOU'VE GIVEN ME FACTS AND FIGURES...
...BUT WHAT I WANT NOW IS GOSSIP AND GUESSES.
ALL RIGHT.
FIRST OF ALL, YOU CAN BANK ON INTIMIDATION, MAYBE EVEN BLACKMAIL, CERTAINLY COERCION AND FRAUD.
ONE MAJOR SHAREHOLDER WHO SOLD OUT-- FRANKLIN HERSCH-- WAS SEEN WITH A BLACK EYE AND SPLIT LIP..
...AND HAMMOND, YOU KNOW HOW WHACKO HE IS, WAS OVERHEARD SAYING A GHOST CONVINCED HIM TO SELL.
SECOND OF ALL, SINCE EVERY SHARE OF STOCK WAS PURCHASED-- BELIEVE IT OR NOT-- WITH COLD CASH, AND BY A CONSORTIUM, NO LESS, WE CAN PROBABLY BET ON I.G.G.-- ILL-GOTTEN GAINS-- ON TOP OF COERCION...
AND SO IT GOES THROUGH THE LONG BLEAK DAY...
...UNTIL, AT 6:30 P.M.:
WE'VE MADE A GOOD START, LUCIUS.
THIS TAKEOVER IS DIRTY UP ONE SIDE AND FILTHY DOWN THE OTHER-- ILLEGAL IS A HALF-DOZEN DIFFERENT WAYS, AND THERE MUST BE ONE OF THEM WE CAN FIGHT.
SEE YOU TOMORROW... AND WITH THIS LIST YOU'VE PROVIDED OF THE CONSORTIUM'S MEMBERS--
6

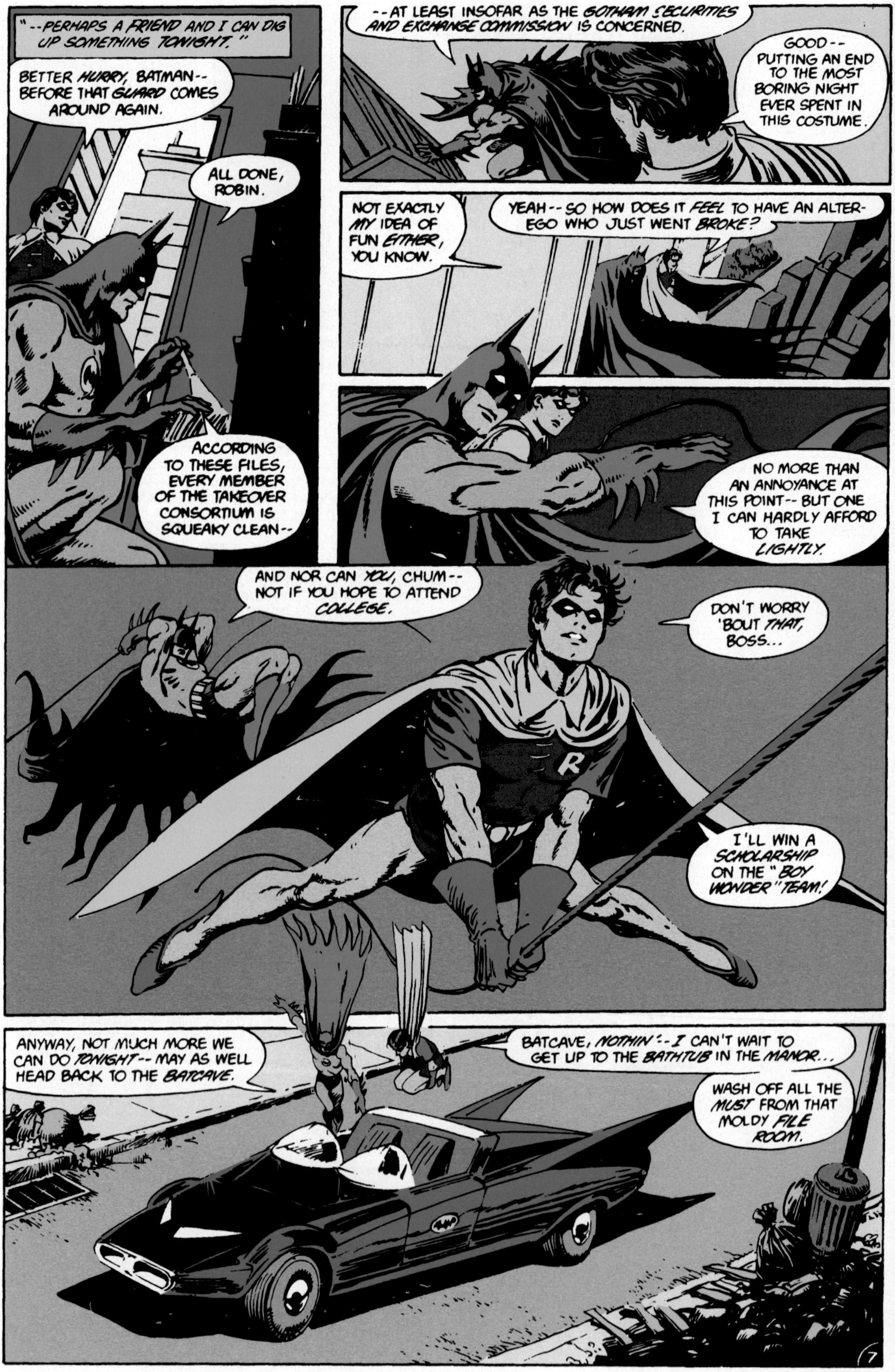

"--PERHAPS A FRIEND AND I CAN DIG UP SOMETHING TONIGHT."
BETTER HURRY, BATMAN-- BEFORE THAT GUARD COMES AROUND AGAIN.
ALL DONE, ROBIN.
ACCORDING TO THESE FILES, EVERY MEMBER OF THE TAKEOVER CONSORTIUM IS SQUEAKY CLEAN--
--AT LEAST INSOFAR AS THE GOTHAM SECURITIES AND EXCHANGE COMMISSION IS CONCERNED.
GOOD-- PUTTING AN END TO THE MOST BORING NIGHT EVER SPENT IN THIS COSTUME.
NOT EXACTLY MY IDEA OF FUN EITHER, YOU KNOW.
YEAH--SO HOW DOES IT FEEL TO HAVE AN ALTER-EGO WHO JUST WENT BROKE?
NO MORE THAN AN ANNOYANCE AT THIS POINT-- BUT ONE I CAN HARDLY AFFORD TO TAKE LIGHTLY.
AND NOR CAN YOU, CHUM-- NOT IF YOU HOPE TO ATTEND COLLEGE.
DON'T WORRY 'BOUT THAT, BOSS...
I'LL WIN A SCHOLARSHIP ON THE "BOY WONDER" TEAM!
ANYWAY, NOT MUCH MORE WE CAN DO TONIGHT-- MAY AS WELL HEAD BACK TO THE BATCAVE.
BATCAVE, NOTHIN'--I CAN'T WAIT TO GET UP TO THE BATHTUB IN THE MANOR...
WASH OFF ALL THE MUST FROM THAT MOLDY FILE ROOM.
7

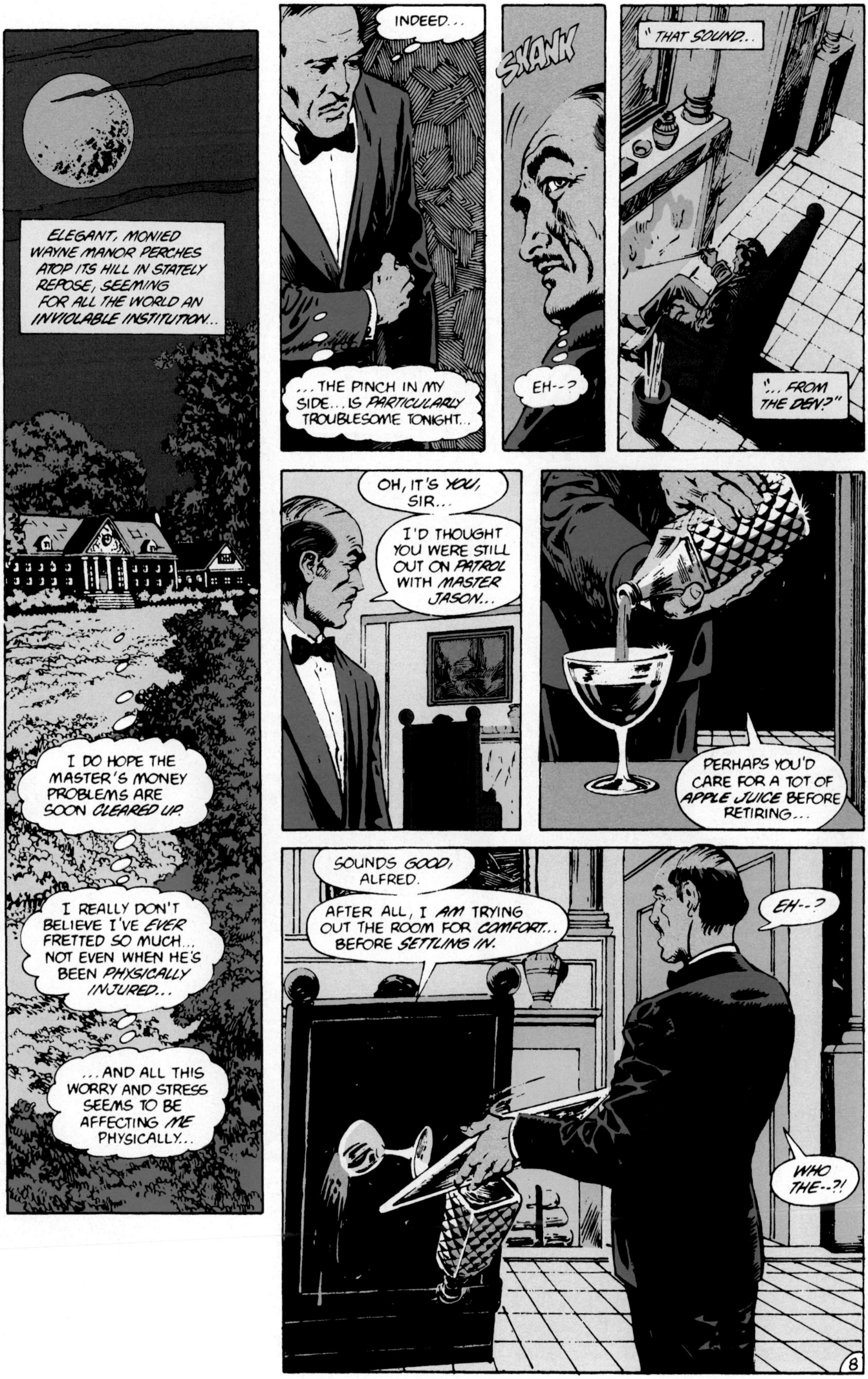
ELEGANT, MONIED WAYNE MANOR PERCHES ATOP ITS HILL IN STATELY REPOSE, SEEMING FOR ALL THE WORLD AN INVIOLABLE INSTITUTION...
I DO HOPE THE MASTER'S MONEY PROBLEMS ARE SOON CLEARED UP.
I REALLY DON'T BELIEVE I'VE EVER FRETTED SO MUCH... NOT EVEN WHEN HE'S BEEN PHYSICALLY INJURED...
...AND ALL THIS WORRY AND STRESS SEEMS TO BE AFFECTING ME PHYSICALLY...
INDEED...
...THE PINCH IN MY SIDE... IS PARTICULARLY TROUBLESOME TONIGHT...
SKANK
EH--?
"THAT SOUND...
"...FROM THE DEN?"
OH, IT'S YOU, SIR...
I'D THOUGHT YOU WERE STILL OUT ON PATROL WITH MASTER JASON...
PERHAPS YOU'D CARE FOR A TOT OF APPLE JUICE BEFORE RETIRING...
SOUNDS GOOD, ALFRED.
AFTER ALL, I AM TRYING OUT THE ROOM FOR COMFORT... BEFORE SETTLING IN.
EH--?
WHO THE--?!
8

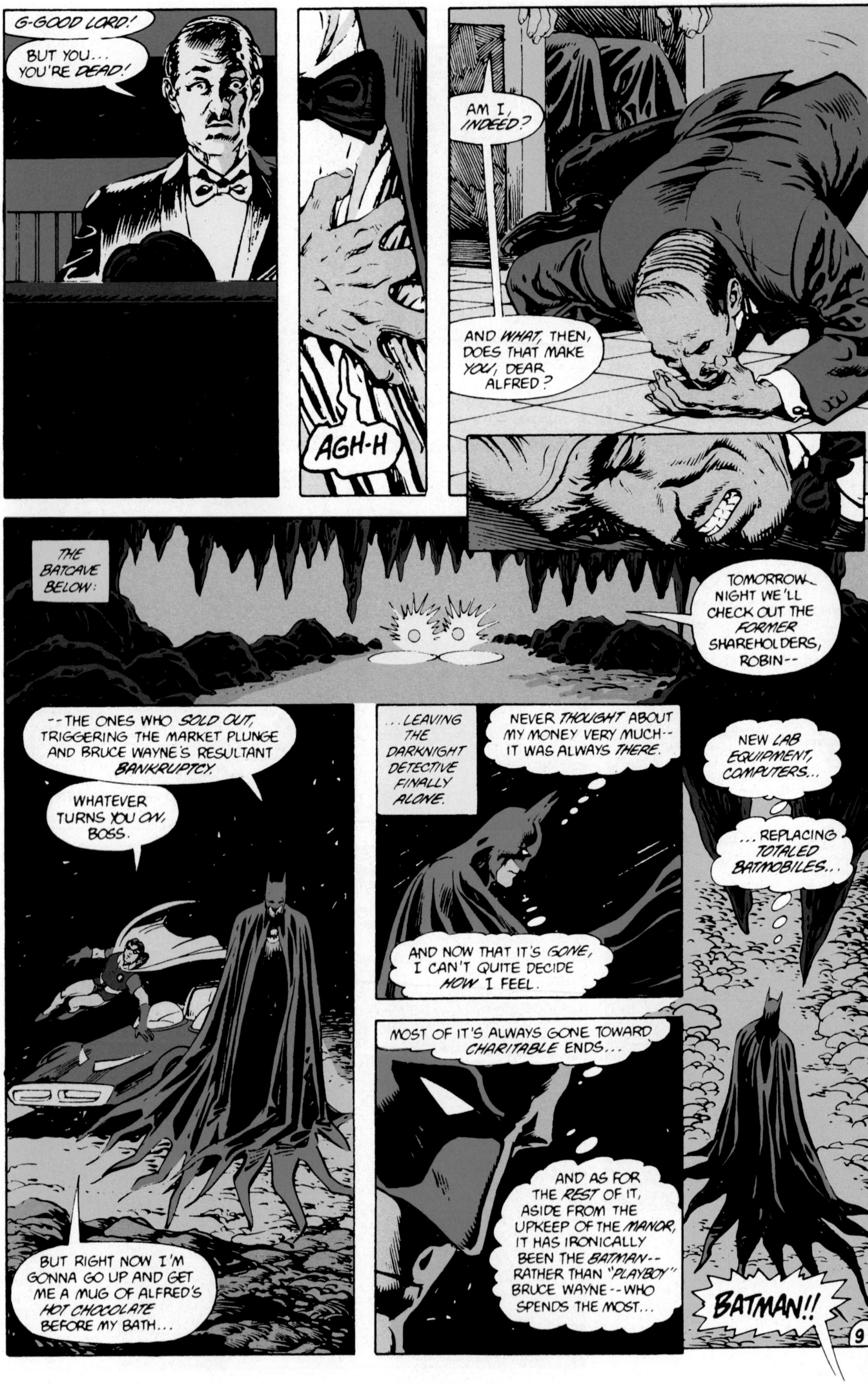
G-GOOD LORD!
BUT YOU... YOU'RE DEAD!
AGH-H
AM I, INDEED?
AND WHAT, THEN, DOES THAT MAKE YOU, DEAR ALFRED?
THE BATCAVE BELOW:
TOMORROW NIGHT WE'LL CHECK OUT THE FORMER SHAREHOLDERS, ROBIN--
--THE ONES WHO SOLD OUT, TRIGGERING THE MARKET PLUNGE AND BRUCE WAYNE'S RESULTANT BANKRUPTCY.
WHATEVER TURNS YOU ON, BOSS.
BUT RIGHT NOW I'M GONNA GO UP AND GET ME A MUG OF ALFRED'S HOT CHOCOLATE BEFORE MY BATH...
...LEAVING THE DARKNIGHT DETECTIVE FINALLY ALONE.
NEVER THOUGHT ABOUT MY MONEY VERY MUCH-- IT WAS ALWAYS THERE.
AND NOW THAT IT'S GONE, I CAN'T QUITE DECIDE HOW I FEEL.
NEW LAB EQUIPMENT, COMPUTERS...
...REPLACING TOTALED BATMOBILES...
MOST OF IT'S ALWAYS GONE TOWARD CHARITABLE ENDS...
AND AS FOR THE REST OF IT, ASIDE FROM THE UPKEEP OF THE MANOR, IT HAS IRONICALLY BEEN THE BATMAN-- RATHER THAN "PLAYBOY" BRUCE WAYNE--WHO SPENDS THE MOST...
BATMAN!!
9

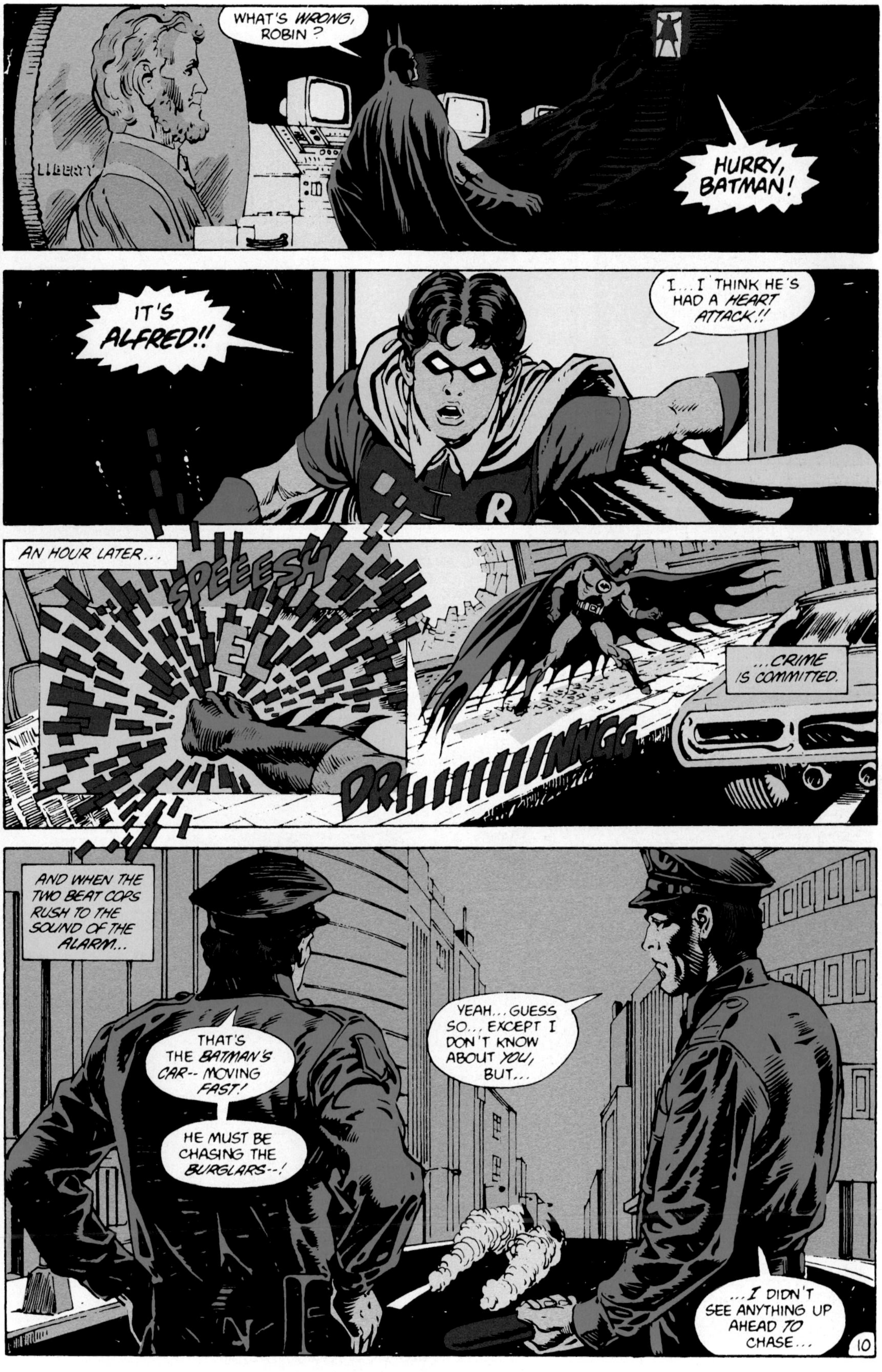
WHAT'S WRONG, ROBIN?
HURRY, BATMAN!
IT'S ALFRED!!
I... I THINK HE'S HAD A HEART ATTACK!!
AN HOUR LATER...
SPEEESH
...CRIME IS COMMITTED.
DRIIIIIIIINNGG
AND WHEN THE TWO BEAT COPS RUSH TO THE SOUND OF THE ALARM...
THAT'S THE BATMAN'S CAR-- MOVING FAST!
HE MUST BE CHASING THE BURGLARS--!
YEAH... GUESS SO... EXCEPT I DON'T KNOW ABOUT YOU, BUT...
...I DIDN'T SEE ANYTHING UP AHEAD TO CHASE...
10

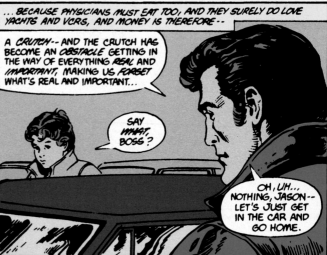

GOTHAM GENERAL HOSPITAL:

I'M AFRAID MR. PENNYWORTH HAS SUFFERED A STROKE, BUT A VERY *MILD* ONE, AND WITH ANY LUCK WE MAY EXPECT *FULL RECOVERY...*

OH, THANK GOD.

HOWEVER, MR. WAYNE, I ADVISE A FULL WEEK'S STAY FOR *OBSERVATION.*

WHATEVER IT *TAKES,* DOCTOR.

I WANT ALFRED TO RECEIVE THE *BEST MEDICAL ATTENTION POSSIBLE,* AND *MONEY* IS NO...

UH... THAT IS...

YES, MR. WAYNE?

UH... *NOTHING,* DOCTOR.

I... I WAS JUST SAYING THAT MONEY IS... *NO OBJECT.*

BUT THAT, OF COURSE, IS PRECISELY WHAT IT *IS.* IN *THIS* MODERN WORLD, OBJECTIVE AND SUBJECTIVE ARE ONE AND THE SAME, INEXTRICABLY MERGED, THE *SYMBOL SUPPLANTING REALITY.*

MONEY IS NOT JUST YACHTS AND VCRS--IT IS FOOD AND SHELTER AND EVEN THE LIFE-SUSTAINING CARE WHICH *SHOULD* COME FROM LOVE AND CONCERN...

...BUT WHICH *ACTUALLY* DERIVES FROM THE *GOAL* OF A PHYSICIAN'S *PAYCHECK...*

...BECAUSE PHYSICIANS MUST EAT TOO, AND THEY SURELY DO LOVE YACHTS AND VCRS, AND MONEY IS THEREFORE--

A *CRUTCH*-- AND THE CRUTCH HAS BECOME AN *OBSTACLE* GETTING IN THE WAY OF EVERYTHING *REAL* AND *IMPORTANT,* MAKING US *FORGET* WHAT'S REAL AND IMPORTANT...

SAY *WHAT,* BOSS?

OH, UH... NOTHING, JASON-- LET'S JUST GET IN THE CAR AND GO HOME.

SO... GREAT NEWS ABOUT *ALFIE,* HUH, BRUCE?

YES... YES, JASON... THE BEST NEWS POSSIBLE...

LOSING ALL THE MONEY IN THE WORLD IS NOTHING, *NOTHING...* IN THE FACE OF ALMOST LOSING SUCH A *FRIEND.*

RIGHT. UH... MIND IF I JUICE THE *RADIO?*

BRUCE SHRUGS, AS IF NEVER HAVING *HEARD* OF SUCH A THING AS A "RADIO," LET ALONE THE $3000 CUSTOMIZED SOUND SYSTEM INSTALLED WITHIN *THESE* WHEELS...

11

KLIK

--BRAZEN JEWELRY STORE BURGLARY IN DOWNTOWN GOTHAM. THE BATMOBILE WAS SEEN SPEEDING AWAY FROM THE SCENE, APPARENTLY IN PURSUIT OF THE THIEF OR THIEVES...

THE BATMOBILE?

OBVIOUSLY A MISTAKEN WITNESS.

YES -- SOME ITALIAN SPORTSCAR.. GLIMPSED IN THE DARK...

AND LET'S LET THE POLICE DEAL WITH THIS ONE, HUH?

AFTER THE SHOCK OF FINDING ALFRED IN THE DEN LIKE THAT, I'M WHIPPED TILL DAWN AT LEAST.

AGREED -- THERE ARE BIG DAYS AHEAD FOR BRUCE WAYNE... AND BIGGER NIGHTS FOR THE BATMAN

TRUER WORDS WERE NEVER BREATHED.

HA HA    HA HA HA

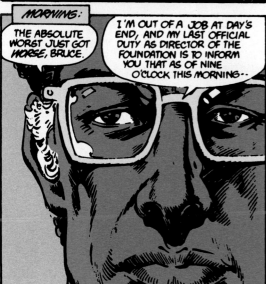

MORNING:

THE ABSOLUTE WORST JUST GOT WORSE, BRUCE.

I'M OUT OF A JOB AT DAY'S END, AND MY LAST OFFICIAL DUTY AS DIRECTOR OF THE FOUNDATION IS TO INFORM YOU THAT AS OF NINE O'CLOCK THIS MORNING--

--YOU HAVE BEEN EVICTED FROM THE PROPERTY FORMERLY KNOWN AS WAYNE MANOR.

WHAAAT?!

YOUR HOUSE AND ALL ITS CONTENTS -- INCLUDING THE GARAGE AND CARS -- HAVE BEEN SEIZED FOR AUCTION TO PAY OFF YOUR DEBTS, BRUCE.

BUT...BUT THAT'S GOT TO BE ILLEGAL, LUCIUS!

12

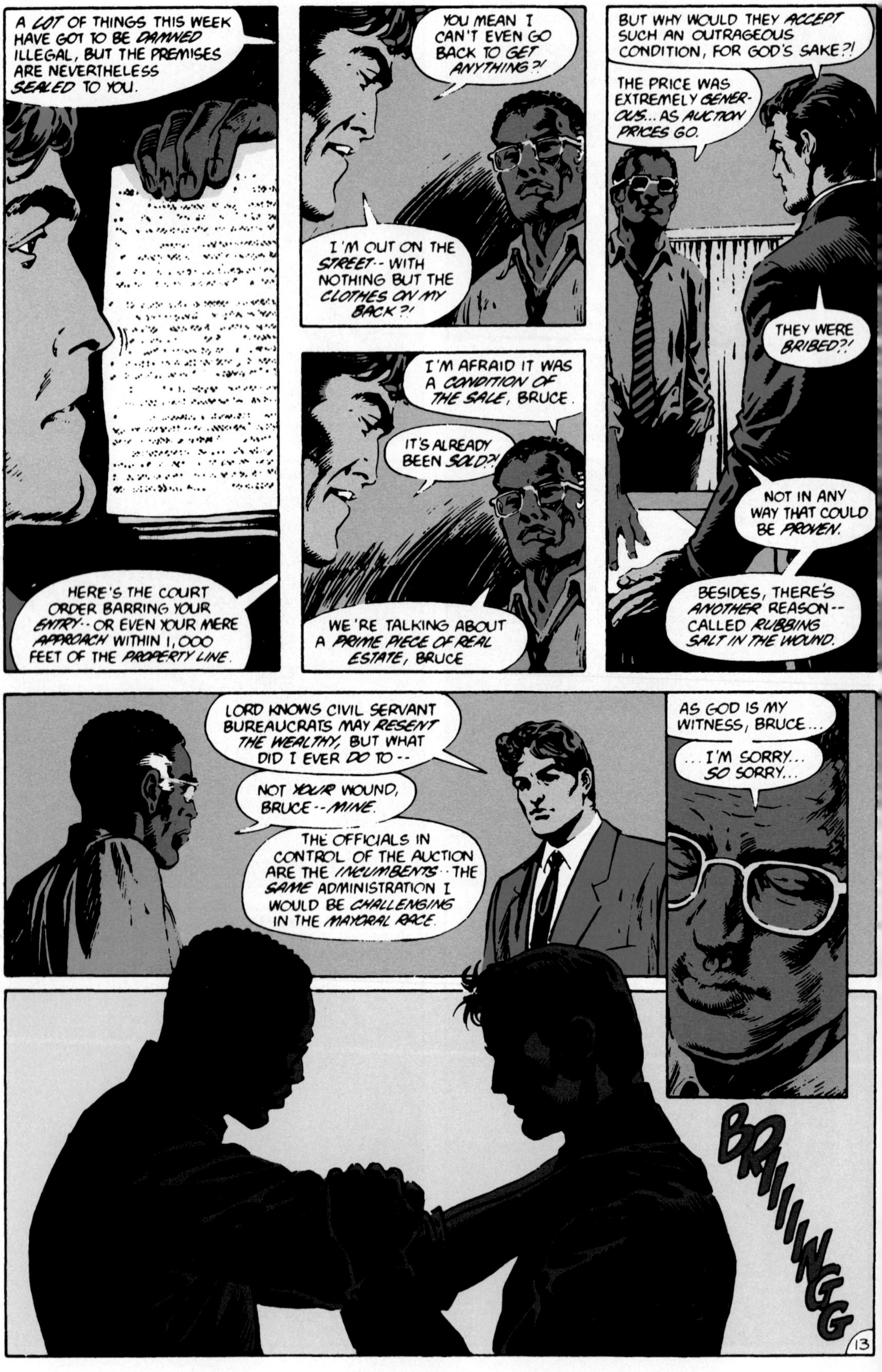
A LOT OF THINGS THIS WEEK HAVE GOT TO BE DAMNED ILLEGAL, BUT THE PREMISES ARE NEVERTHELESS SEALED TO YOU.
HERE'S THE COURT ORDER BARRING YOUR ENTRY-- OR EVEN YOUR MERE APPROACH WITHIN 1,000 FEET OF THE PROPERTY LINE.
YOU MEAN I CAN'T EVEN GO BACK TO GET ANYTHING?!
I'M OUT ON THE STREET-- WITH NOTHING BUT THE CLOTHES ON MY BACK?!
I'M AFRAID IT WAS A CONDITION OF THE SALE, BRUCE.
IT'S ALREADY BEEN SOLD?!
WE'RE TALKING ABOUT A PRIME PIECE OF REAL ESTATE, BRUCE
BUT WHY WOULD THEY ACCEPT SUCH AN OUTRAGEOUS CONDITION, FOR GOD'S SAKE?!
THE PRICE WAS EXTREMELY GENER-OUS... AS AUCTION PRICES GO.
THEY WERE BRIBED?!
NOT IN ANY WAY THAT COULD BE PROVEN.
BESIDES, THERE'S ANOTHER REASON-- CALLED RUBBING SALT IN THE WOUND.
LORD KNOWS CIVIL SERVANT BUREAUCRATS MAY RESENT THE WEALTHY, BUT WHAT DID I EVER DO TO--
NOT YOUR WOUND, BRUCE--MINE.
THE OFFICIALS IN CONTROL OF THE AUCTION ARE THE INCUMBENTS-- THE SAME ADMINISTRATION I WOULD BE CHALLENGING IN THE MAYORAL RACE.
AS GOD IS MY WITNESS, BRUCE...
...I'M SORRY... SO SORRY...
BRIIIINGG
13

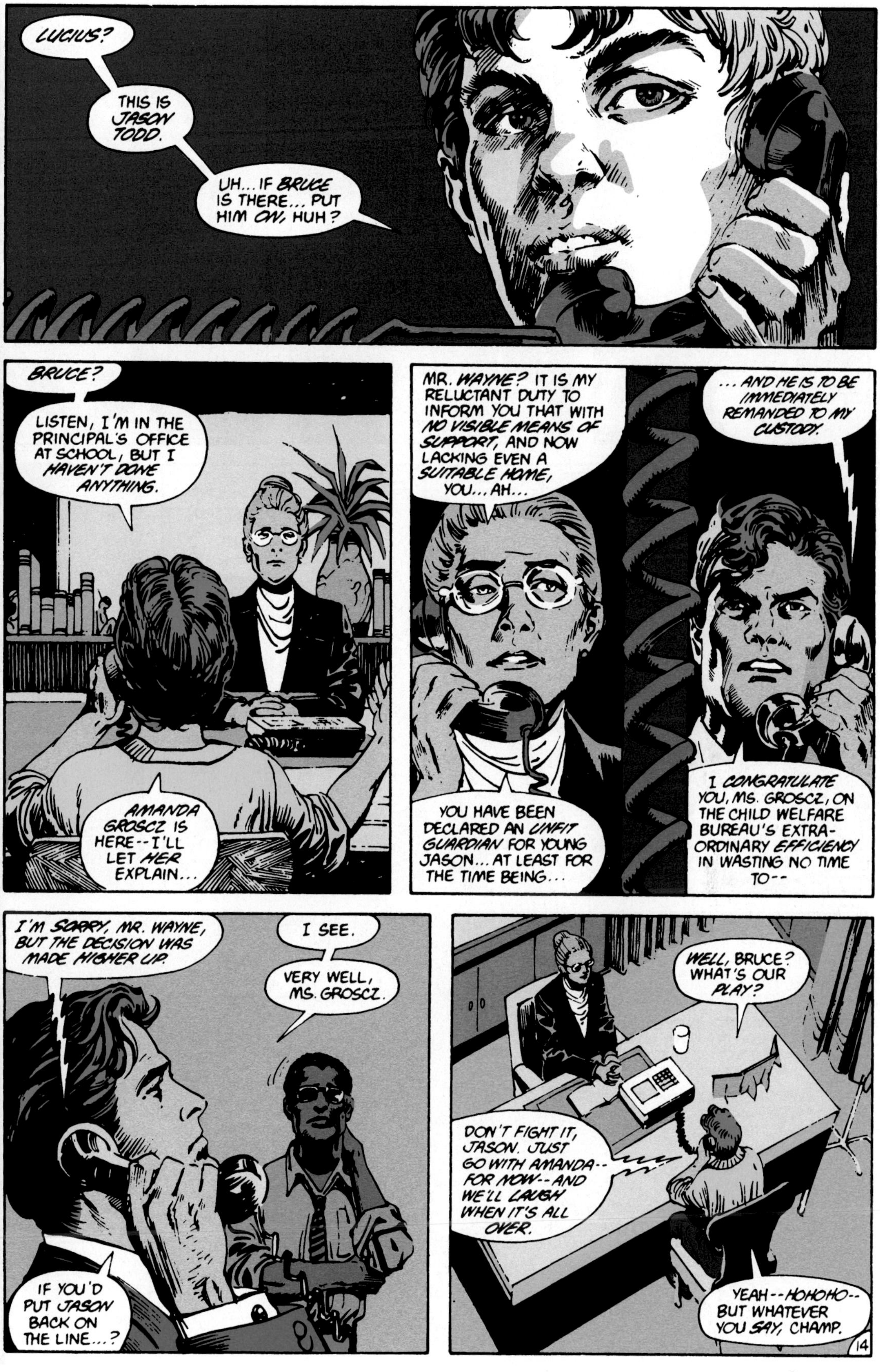
LUCIUS?
THIS IS JASON TODD.
UH... IF BRUCE IS THERE... PUT HIM ON, HUH?
BRUCE?
LISTEN, I'M IN THE PRINCIPAL'S OFFICE AT SCHOOL, BUT I HAVEN'T DONE ANYTHING.
AMANDA GROSCZ IS HERE--I'LL LET HER EXPLAIN...
MR. WAYNE? IT IS MY RELUCTANT DUTY TO INFORM YOU THAT WITH NO VISIBLE MEANS OF SUPPORT, AND NOW LACKING EVEN A SUITABLE HOME, YOU... AH...
YOU HAVE BEEN DECLARED AN UNFIT GUARDIAN FOR YOUNG JASON... AT LEAST FOR THE TIME BEING...
... AND HE IS TO BE IMMEDIATELY REMANDED TO MY CUSTODY.
I CONGRATULATE YOU, MS. GROSCZ, ON THE CHILD WELFARE BUREAU'S EXTRAORDINARY EFFICIENCY IN WASTING NO TIME TO--
I'M SORRY, MR. WAYNE, BUT THE DECISION WAS MADE HIGHER UP.
I SEE.
VERY WELL, MS. GROSCZ.
IF YOU'D PUT JASON BACK ON THE LINE...?
WELL, BRUCE? WHAT'S OUR PLAY?
DON'T FIGHT IT, JASON. JUST GO WITH AMANDA--FOR NOW--AND WE'LL LAUGH WHEN IT'S ALL OVER.
YEAH--HOHOHO--BUT WHATEVER YOU SAY, CHAMP.
14

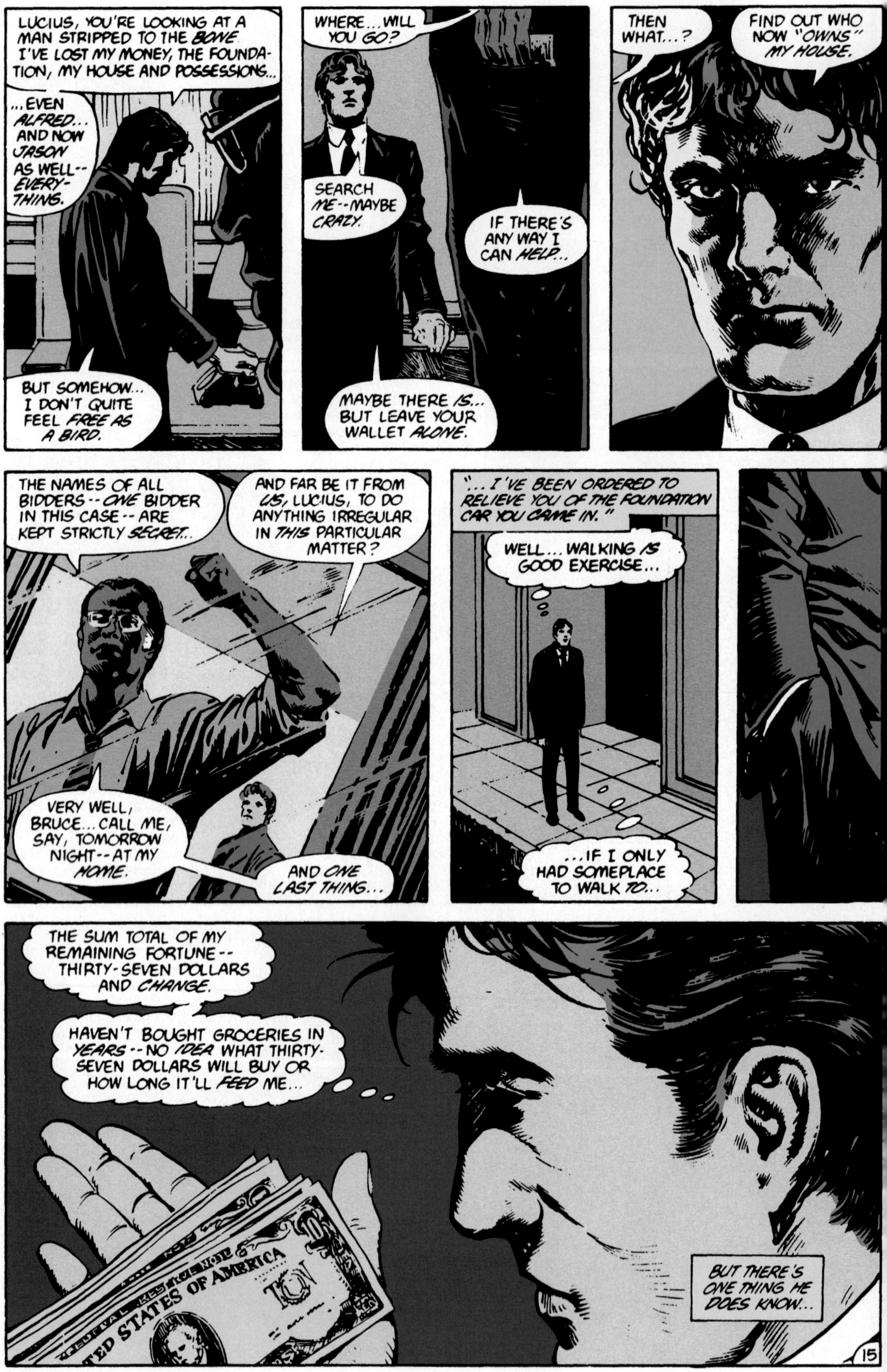
LUCIUS, YOU'RE LOOKING AT A MAN STRIPPED TO THE BONE. I'VE LOST MY MONEY, THE FOUNDATION, MY HOUSE AND POSSESSIONS...
...EVEN ALFRED... AND NOW JASON AS WELL--EVERYTHING.
BUT SOMEHOW... I DON'T QUITE FEEL FREE AS A BIRD.
WHERE... WILL YOU GO?
SEARCH ME--MAYBE CRAZY.
IF THERE'S ANY WAY I CAN HELP...
MAYBE THERE IS... BUT LEAVE YOUR WALLET ALONE.
THEN WHAT...?
FIND OUT WHO NOW "OWNS" MY HOUSE.
THE NAMES OF ALL BIDDERS--ONE BIDDER IN THIS CASE--ARE KEPT STRICTLY SECRET...
AND FAR BE IT FROM US, LUCIUS, TO DO ANYTHING IRREGULAR IN THIS PARTICULAR MATTER?
VERY WELL, BRUCE... CALL ME, SAY, TOMORROW NIGHT--AT MY HOME.
AND ONE LAST THING...
"...I'VE BEEN ORDERED TO RELIEVE YOU OF THE FOUNDATION CAR YOU CAME IN."
WELL... WALKING IS GOOD EXERCISE...
...IF I ONLY HAD SOMEPLACE TO WALK TO...
THE SUM TOTAL OF MY REMAINING FORTUNE--THIRTY-SEVEN DOLLARS AND CHANGE.
HAVEN'T BOUGHT GROCERIES IN YEARS--NO IDEA WHAT THIRTY-SEVEN DOLLARS WILL BUY OR HOW LONG IT'LL FEED ME...
UNITED STATES OF AMERICA
BUT THERE'S ONE THING HE DOES KNOW...
15

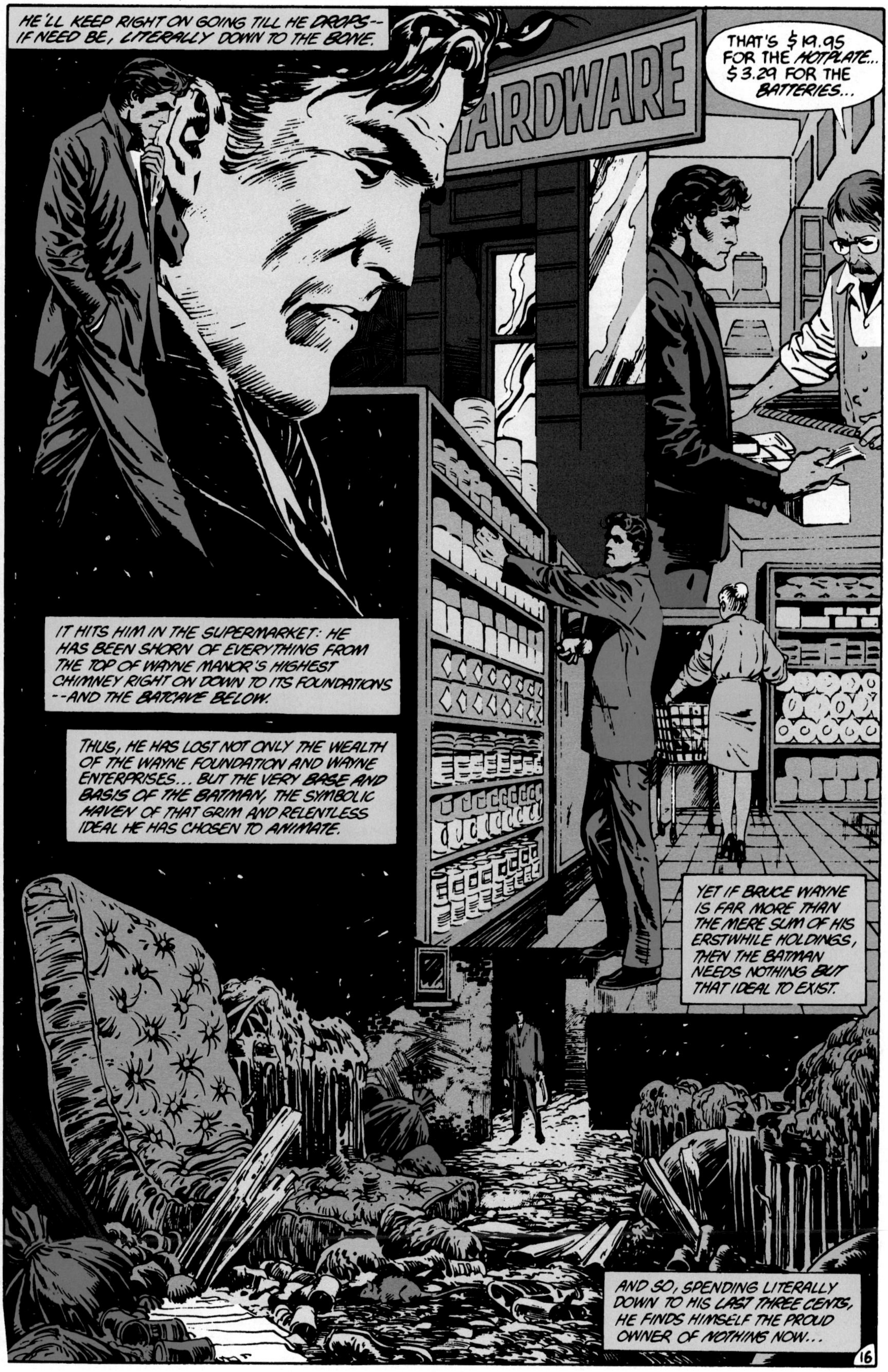
HE'LL KEEP RIGHT ON GOING TILL HE DROPS-- IF NEED BE, LITERALLY DOWN TO THE BONE.
HARDWARE
THAT'S $19.95 FOR THE HOTPLATE... $3.29 FOR THE BATTERIES...
IT HITS HIM IN THE SUPERMARKET: HE HAS BEEN SHORN OF EVERYTHING FROM THE TOP OF WAYNE MANOR'S HIGHEST CHIMNEY RIGHT ON DOWN TO ITS FOUNDATIONS --AND THE BATCAVE BELOW.
THUS, HE HAS LOST NOT ONLY THE WEALTH OF THE WAYNE FOUNDATION AND WAYNE ENTERPRISES... BUT THE VERY BASE AND BASIS OF THE BATMAN, THE SYMBOLIC HAVEN OF THAT GRIM AND RELENTLESS IDEAL HE HAS CHOSEN TO ANIMATE.
YET IF BRUCE WAYNE IS FAR MORE THAN THE MERE SUM OF HIS ERSTWHILE HOLDINGS, THEN THE BATMAN NEEDS NOTHING BUT THAT IDEAL TO EXIST.
AND SO, SPENDING LITERALLY DOWN TO HIS LAST THREE CENTS, HE FINDS HIMSELF THE PROUD OWNER OF NOTHING NOW...
16

NOTHING BUT THE SECOND SKIN OF HIS COSTUME, AND THE ULTIMATE BOY SCOUT FANTASY OF HIS *UTILITY BELT*, AND HIS STRENGTH AND HIS WILL.

AND THESE HE WILL *USE* TO REGAIN EVERYTHING *ELSE...AND TO PUNISH* WHOMEVER HAS MADE THE EFFORT NECESSARY.

NOT BECAUSE HE *NEEDS* EVERYTHING ELSE, BUT BECAUSE IT HAS BEEN *STOLEN*.

AND IN THE *MEANTIME*--

HARDLY THE *HIGH RENT DISTRICT...* BUT AT THE MOMENT, *JUST MY SPEED.*

A *BAT* IN A *BELFRY.*

GUESS I *HAVE* GONE CRAZY...

...BUT WITH THE HEADFUL OF THOUGHTS *I'VE* GOT...IT'S *ALLOWED.*

THOUGHT *NUMBER ONE*: WHAT HAPPENS IF THE NEW OWNER OF WAYNE MANOR DECIDES TO *REPLACE* THE GRANDFATHER *CLOCK?*

THOUGHT NUMBER *TWO*:

WHAT HAPPENS IF SAID NEW OWNER *THEN* DECIDES TO OPEN THE SECRET DOORWAY FORMERLY *CONCEALED* BY THE GRANDFATHER CLOCK--

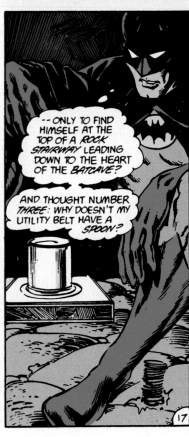

--ONLY TO FIND HIMSELF AT THE TOP OF A *ROCK* STAIRWAY LEADING DOWN TO THE HEART OF THE *BATCAVE?*

AND THOUGHT NUMBER *THREE*: WHY DOESN'T MY UTILITY BELT HAVE A *SPOON?*

17

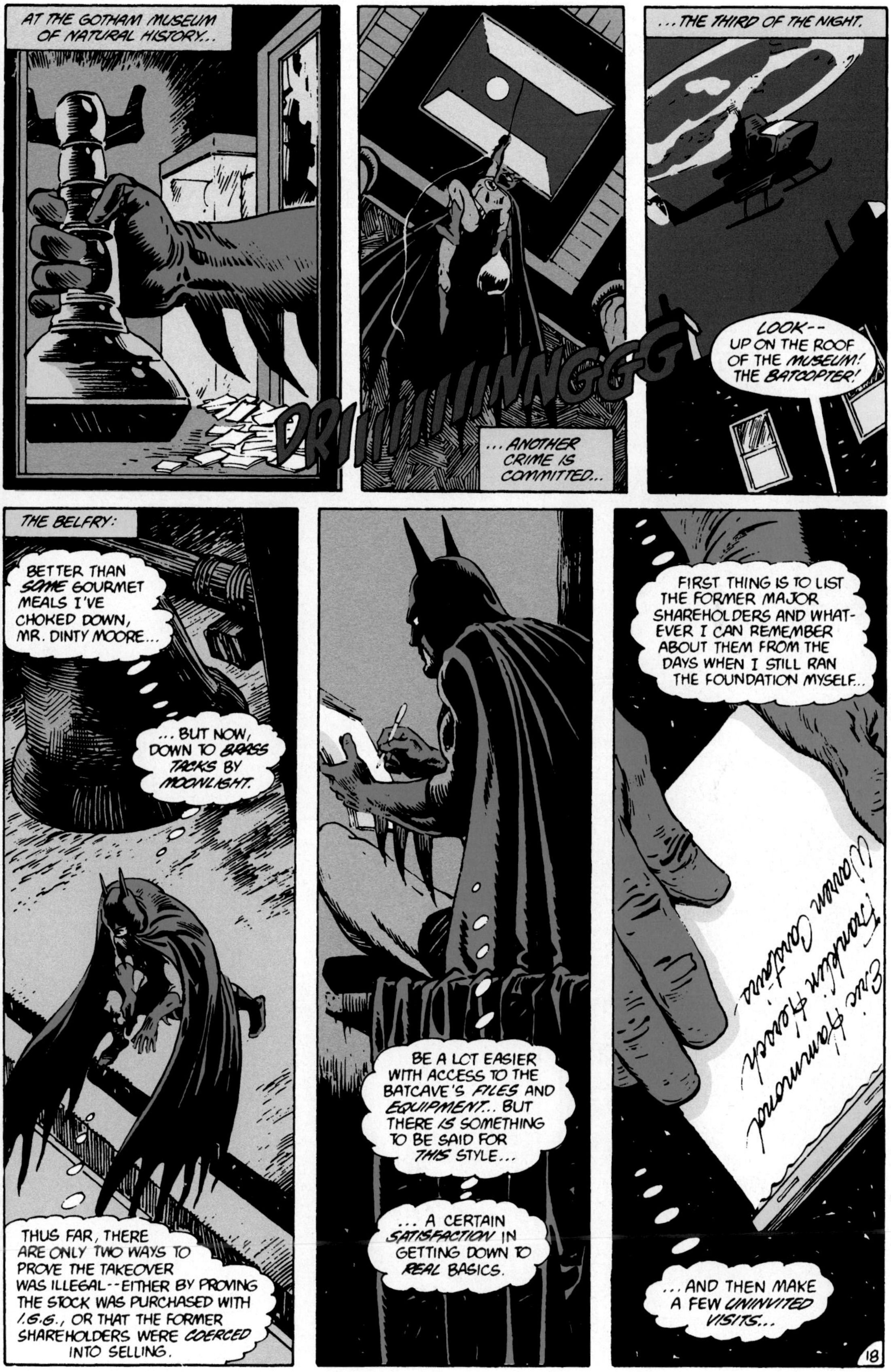
AT THE GOTHAM MUSEUM OF NATURAL HISTORY...
DRIIIIIIIINNGGG
...ANOTHER CRIME IS COMMITTED...
...THE THIRD OF THE NIGHT.
LOOK-- UP ON THE ROOF OF THE MUSEUM! THE BATCOPTER!
THE BELFRY:
BETTER THAN SOME GOURMET MEALS I'VE CHOKED DOWN, MR. DINTY MOORE...
...BUT NOW, DOWN TO BRASS TACKS BY MOONLIGHT.
THUS FAR, THERE ARE ONLY TWO WAYS TO PROVE THE TAKEOVER WAS ILLEGAL--EITHER BY PROVING THE STOCK WAS PURCHASED WITH I.G.G., OR THAT THE FORMER SHAREHOLDERS WERE COERCED INTO SELLING.
BE A LOT EASIER WITH ACCESS TO THE BATCAVE'S FILES AND EQUIPMENT... BUT THERE IS SOMETHING TO BE SAID FOR THIS STYLE...
...A CERTAIN SATISFACTION IN GETTING DOWN TO REAL BASICS.
FIRST THING IS TO LIST THE FORMER MAJOR SHAREHOLDERS AND WHATEVER I CAN REMEMBER ABOUT THEM FROM THE DAYS WHEN I STILL RAN THE FOUNDATION MYSELF...
...AND THEN MAKE A FEW UNINVITED VISITS...
18

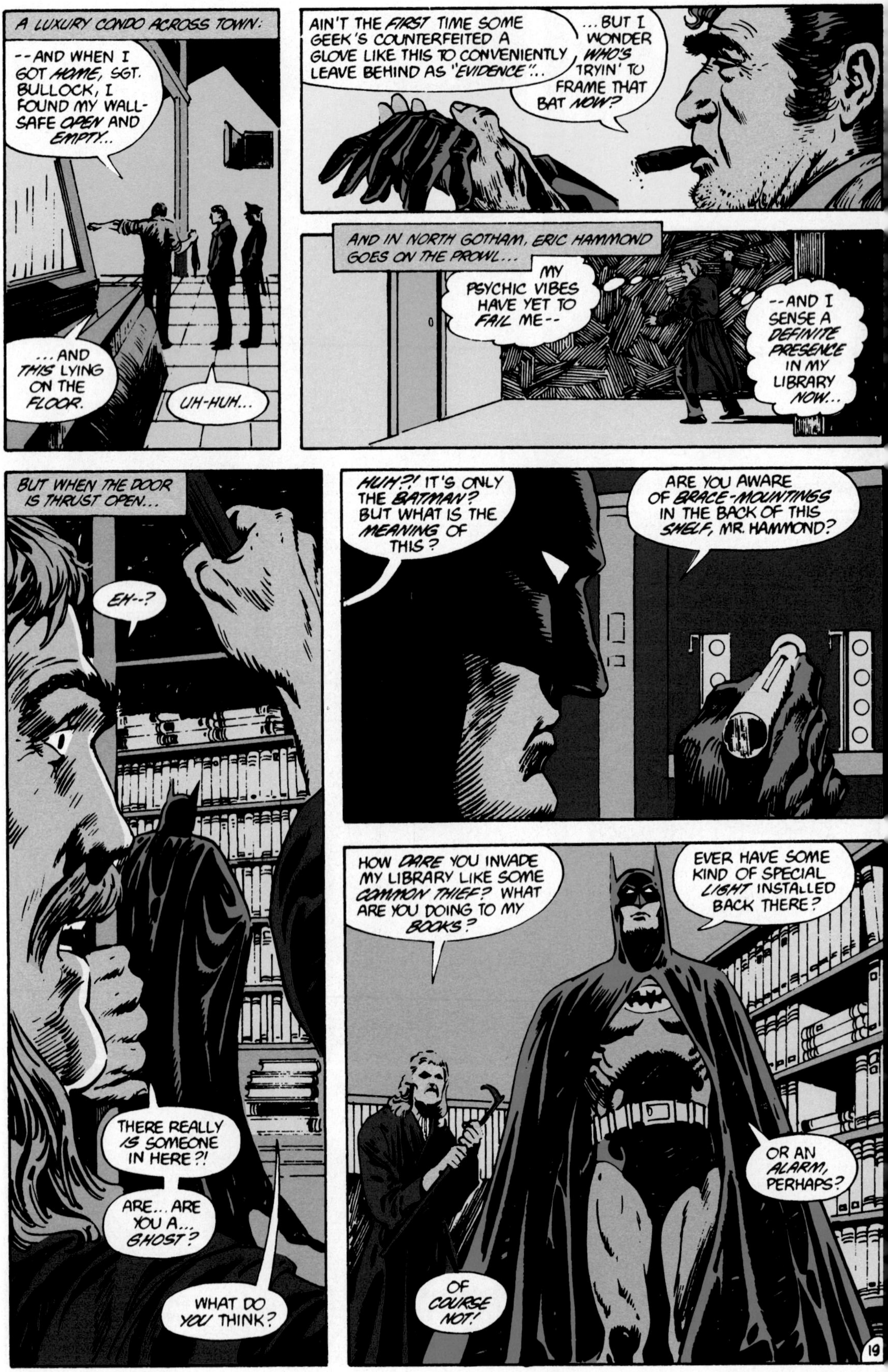
A LUXURY CONDO ACROSS TOWN:
--AND WHEN I GOT HOME, SGT. BULLOCK, I FOUND MY WALL-SAFE OPEN AND EMPTY...
...AND THIS LYING ON THE FLOOR.
UH-HUH...
AIN'T THE FIRST TIME SOME GEEK'S COUNTERFEITED A GLOVE LIKE THIS TO CONVENIENTLY LEAVE BEHIND AS "EVIDENCE"...
...BUT I WONDER WHO'S TRYIN' TO FRAME THAT BAT NOW?
AND IN NORTH GOTHAM, ERIC HAMMOND GOES ON THE PROWL...
MY PSYCHIC VIBES HAVE YET TO FAIL ME--
--AND I SENSE A DEFINITE PRESENCE IN MY LIBRARY NOW...
BUT WHEN THE DOOR IS THRUST OPEN...
EH--?
THERE REALLY IS SOMEONE IN HERE?!
ARE... ARE YOU A... GHOST?
WHAT DO YOU THINK?
HUH?! IT'S ONLY THE BATMAN? BUT WHAT IS THE MEANING OF THIS?
ARE YOU AWARE OF BRACE-MOUNTINGS IN THE BACK OF THIS SHELF, MR. HAMMOND?
HOW DARE YOU INVADE MY LIBRARY LIKE SOME COMMON THIEF? WHAT ARE YOU DOING TO MY BOOKS?
EVER HAVE SOME KIND OF SPECIAL LIGHT INSTALLED BACK THERE?
OR AN ALARM, PERHAPS?
OF COURSE NOT!
19

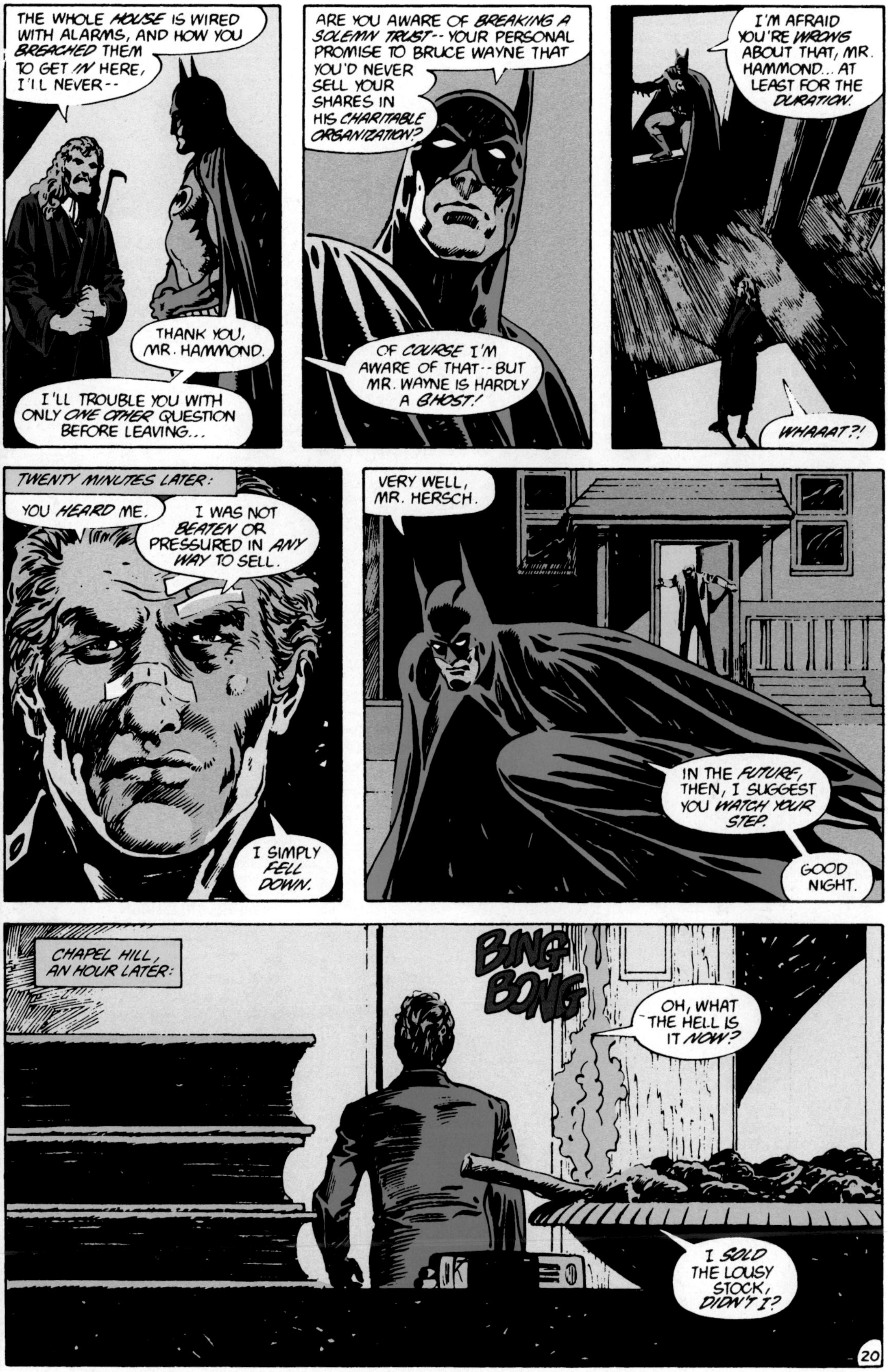
THE WHOLE HOUSE IS WIRED WITH ALARMS, AND HOW YOU BREACHED THEM TO GET IN HERE, I'LL NEVER--
THANK YOU, MR. HAMMOND.
I'LL TROUBLE YOU WITH ONLY ONE OTHER QUESTION BEFORE LEAVING...
ARE YOU AWARE OF BREAKING A SOLEMN TRUST-- YOUR PERSONAL PROMISE TO BRUCE WAYNE THAT YOU'D NEVER SELL YOUR SHARES IN HIS CHARITABLE ORGANIZATION?
OF COURSE I'M AWARE OF THAT--BUT MR. WAYNE IS HARDLY A GHOST!
I'M AFRAID YOU'RE WRONG ABOUT THAT, MR. HAMMOND... AT LEAST FOR THE DURATION.
WHAAAT?!
TWENTY MINUTES LATER:
YOU HEARD ME.
I WAS NOT BEATEN OR PRESSURED IN ANY WAY TO SELL.
I SIMPLY FELL DOWN.
VERY WELL, MR. HERSCH.
IN THE FUTURE, THEN, I SUGGEST YOU WATCH YOUR STEP.
GOOD NIGHT.
CHAPEL HILL, AN HOUR LATER:
BING BONG
OH, WHAT THE HELL IS IT NOW?
I SOLD THE LOUSY STOCK, DIDN'T I?
20

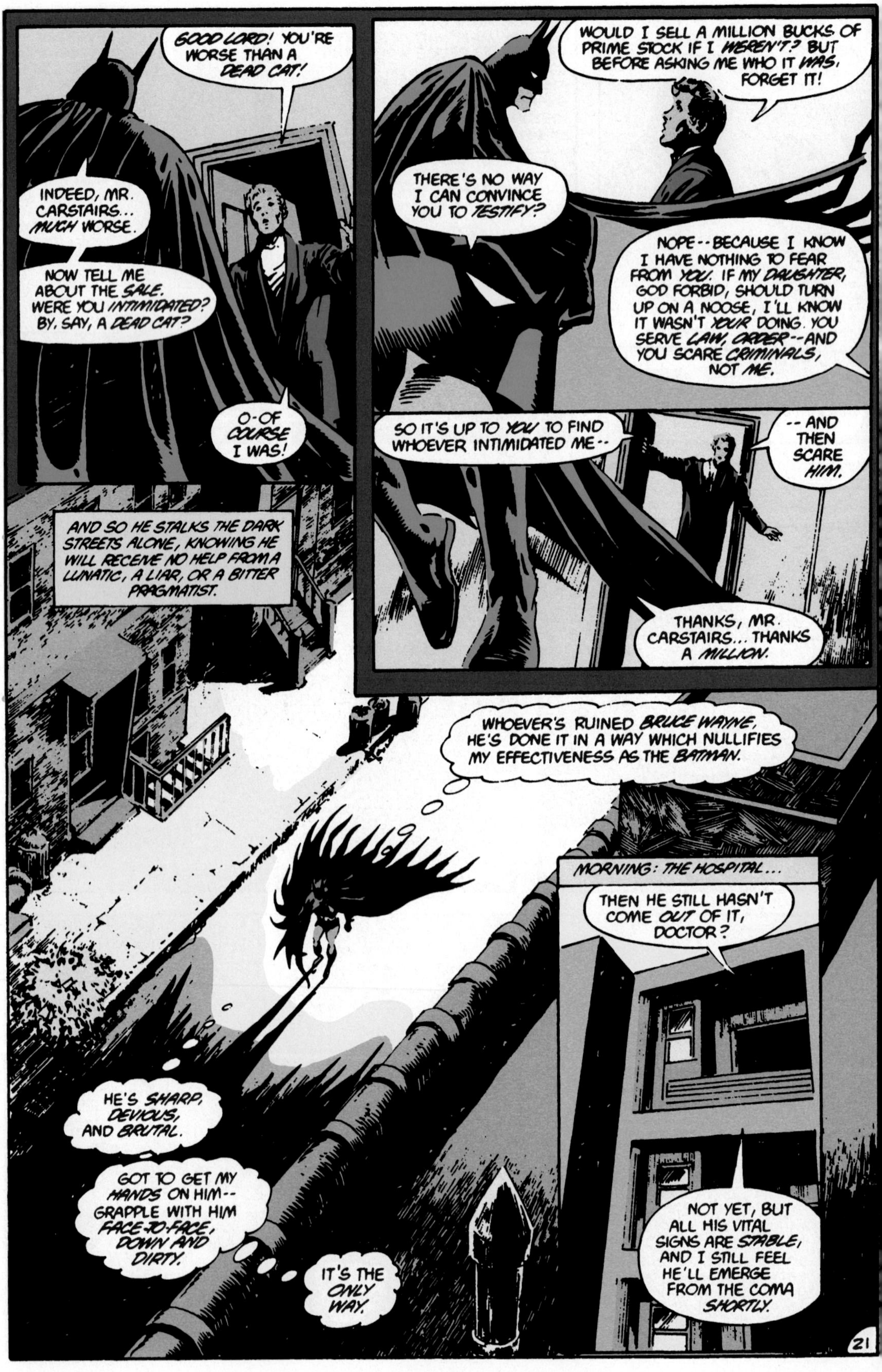
GOOD LORD! YOU'RE WORSE THAN A DEAD CAT!
INDEED, MR. CARSTAIRS... MUCH WORSE.
NOW TELL ME ABOUT THE SALE. WERE YOU INTIMIDATED? BY, SAY, A DEAD CAT?
O-OF COURSE I WAS!
WOULD I SELL A MILLION BUCKS OF PRIME STOCK IF I WEREN'T? BUT BEFORE ASKING ME WHO IT WAS, FORGET IT!
THERE'S NO WAY I CAN CONVINCE YOU TO TESTIFY?
NOPE--BECAUSE I KNOW I HAVE NOTHING TO FEAR FROM YOU. IF MY DAUGHTER, GOD FORBID, SHOULD TURN UP ON A NOOSE, I'LL KNOW IT WASN'T YOUR DOING. YOU SERVE LAW, ORDER--AND YOU SCARE CRIMINALS, NOT ME.
SO IT'S UP TO YOU TO FIND WHOEVER INTIMIDATED ME--
--AND THEN SCARE HIM.
THANKS, MR. CARSTAIRS... THANKS A MILLION.
AND SO HE STALKS THE DARK STREETS ALONE, KNOWING HE WILL RECEIVE NO HELP FROM A LUNATIC, A LIAR, OR A BITTER PRAGMATIST.
WHOEVER'S RUINED BRUCE WAYNE, HE'S DONE IT IN A WAY WHICH NULLIFIES MY EFFECTIVENESS AS THE BATMAN.
HE'S SHARP, DEVIOUS, AND BRUTAL.
GOT TO GET MY HANDS ON HIM--GRAPPLE WITH HIM FACE-TO-FACE, DOWN AND DIRTY.
IT'S THE ONLY WAY.
MORNING: THE HOSPITAL...
THEN HE STILL HASN'T COME OUT OF IT, DOCTOR?
NOT YET, BUT ALL HIS VITAL SIGNS ARE STABLE, AND I STILL FEEL HE'LL EMERGE FROM THE COMA SHORTLY.
21

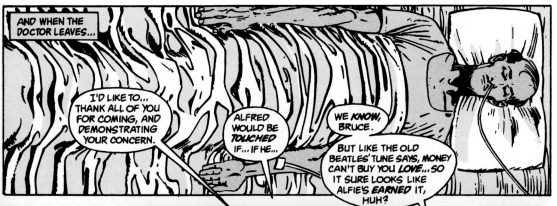

AND WHEN THE DOCTOR LEAVES...

I'D LIKE TO... THANK ALL OF YOU FOR COMING, AND DEMONSTRATING YOUR CONCERN.

ALFRED WOULD BE *TOUCHED* IF... IF HE...

WE *KNOW,* BRUCE.

BUT LIKE THE OLD BEATLES' TUNE SAYS, MONEY CAN'T BUY YOU *LOVE...* SO IT SURE LOOKS LIKE ALFIE'S *EARNED* IT, HUH?

WHY DON'T THE REST OF YOU GO FOR COFFEE?

I'LL STAY HERE WITH DAD.

AND I'LL KEEP YOU *COMPANY,* JULIA--I'VE HAD ENOUGH COFFEE FOR A *WEEK.*

POOR BRUCE...IF ONLY HE'D ASK FOR *HELP,* OR AT LEAST LET US *OFFER* IT.

*NEVER,* KIDDO. I'VE KNOWN HIM LONGER THAN YOU, AND HE'S JUST NOT THAT KIND OF *MAN.*

WELL, I GOTTA GET BACK TO HEADQUARTERS AN' TAKE CARE OF--

THAT *HEADLINE--!*

YEAH--SOMEONE'S *FRAMIN'* THE BATMAN AGAIN--AN' THE PRESS HAS *POUNCED* ON IT, BABY, WITH *DOUBLE-OOMPH.*

AIN'TCHA BEEN LISTENIN' TO YER *RADIO,* WAYNE?

AH...NO, SGT. BULLOCK.

I *HAVEN'T* BEEN LISTENING... TO MY RADIO...

22

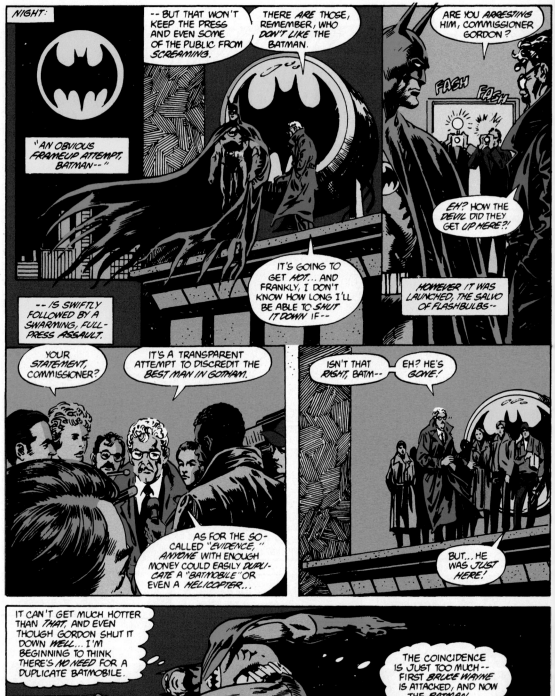

NIGHT:

"AN OBVIOUS FRAMEUP ATTEMPT, BATMAN--"

-- BUT THAT WON'T KEEP THE PRESS AND EVEN SOME OF THE PUBLIC FROM SCREAMING.

THERE *ARE* THOSE, REMEMBER, WHO *DON'T LIKE* THE BATMAN.

ARE YOU *ARRESTING* HIM, COMMISSIONER GORDON?

-- IS SWIFTLY FOLLOWED BY A SWARMING, FULL-PRESS ASSAULT.

IT'S GOING TO GET *HOT* ... AND FRANKLY, I DON'T KNOW HOW LONG I'LL BE ABLE TO *SHUT IT DOWN* IF --

EH? HOW THE *DEVIL* DID THEY GET *UP HERE?!*

*HOWEVER* IT WAS LAUNCHED, THE SALVO OF FLASHBULBS--

YOUR *STATEMENT,* COMMISSIONER?

IT'S A TRANSPARENT ATTEMPT TO DISCREDIT THE *BEST MAN IN GOTHAM.*

AS FOR THE SO-CALLED *"EVIDENCE,"* *ANYONE* WITH ENOUGH MONEY COULD EASILY *DUPLI-CATE* A *"BATMOBILE"* OR EVEN A *HELICOPTER* ...

ISN'T THAT *RIGHT,* BATM--

EH? HE'S *GONE!*

BUT... HE WAS *JUST HERE!*

IT CAN'T GET MUCH HOTTER THAN *THAT,* AND EVEN THOUGH GORDON SHUT IT DOWN *WELL* ... I'M BEGINNING TO THINK THERE'S *NO NEED* FOR A DUPLICATE BATMOBILE.

THE COINCIDENCE IS JUST TOO MUCH -- FIRST *BRUCE WAYNE* IS ATTACKED, AND NOW THE *BATMAN* ...

I'D BETTER PHONE *LUCIUS* ...

23

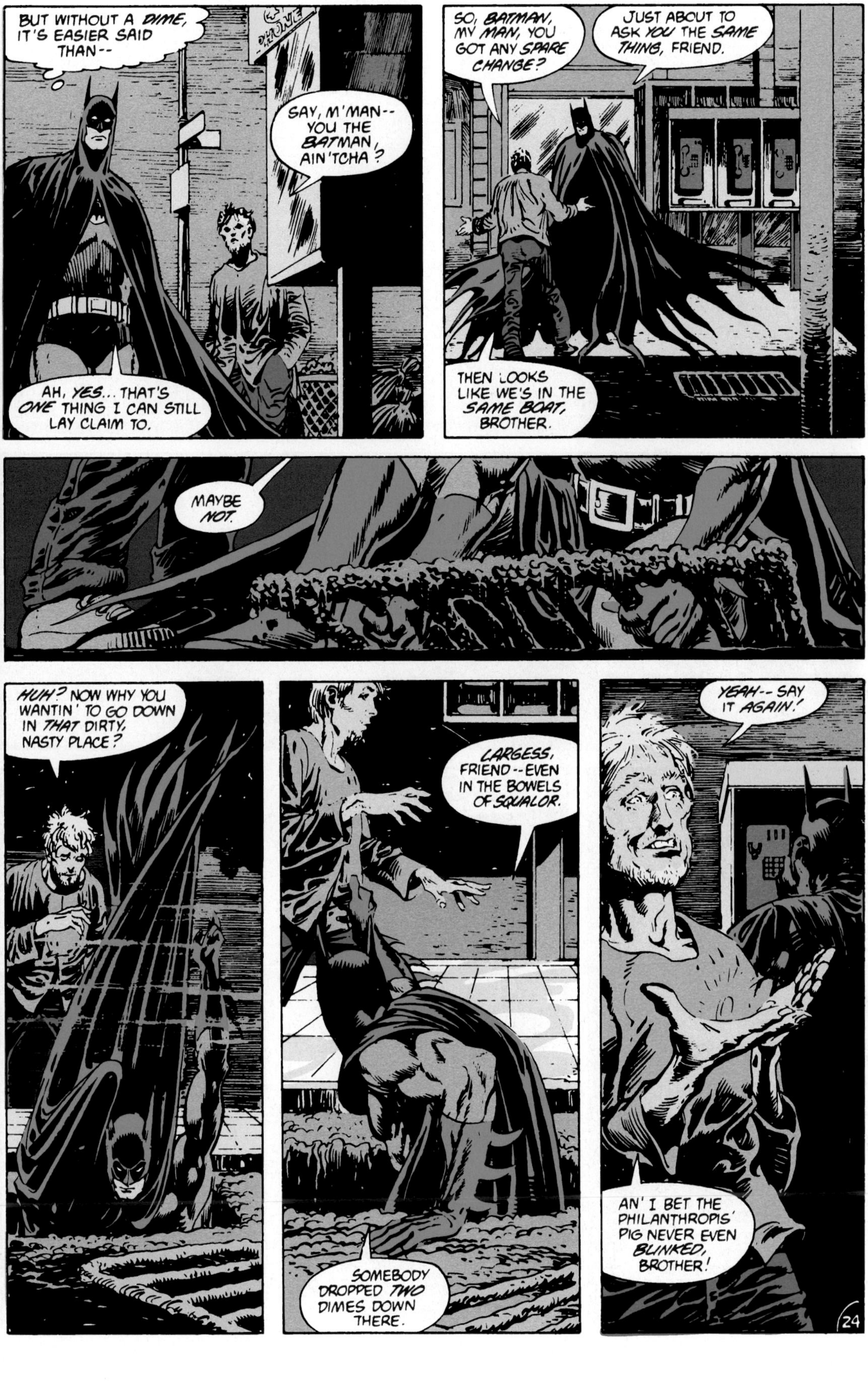
BUT WITHOUT A DIME, IT'S EASIER SAID THAN--
SAY, M'MAN-- YOU THE BATMAN, AIN'TCHA?
AH, YES... THAT'S ONE THING I CAN STILL LAY CLAIM TO.
SO, BATMAN, MY MAN, YOU GOT ANY SPARE CHANGE?
JUST ABOUT TO ASK YOU THE SAME THING, FRIEND.
THEN LOOKS LIKE WE'S IN THE SAME BOAT, BROTHER.
MAYBE NOT.
HUH? NOW WHY YOU WANTIN' TO GO DOWN IN THAT DIRTY, NASTY PLACE?
LARGESS, FRIEND--EVEN IN THE BOWELS OF SQUALOR.
SOMEBODY DROPPED TWO DIMES DOWN THERE.
YEAH-- SAY IT AGAIN!
AN' I BET THE PHILANTHROPIS' PIG NEVER EVEN BLINKED, BROTHER!
24

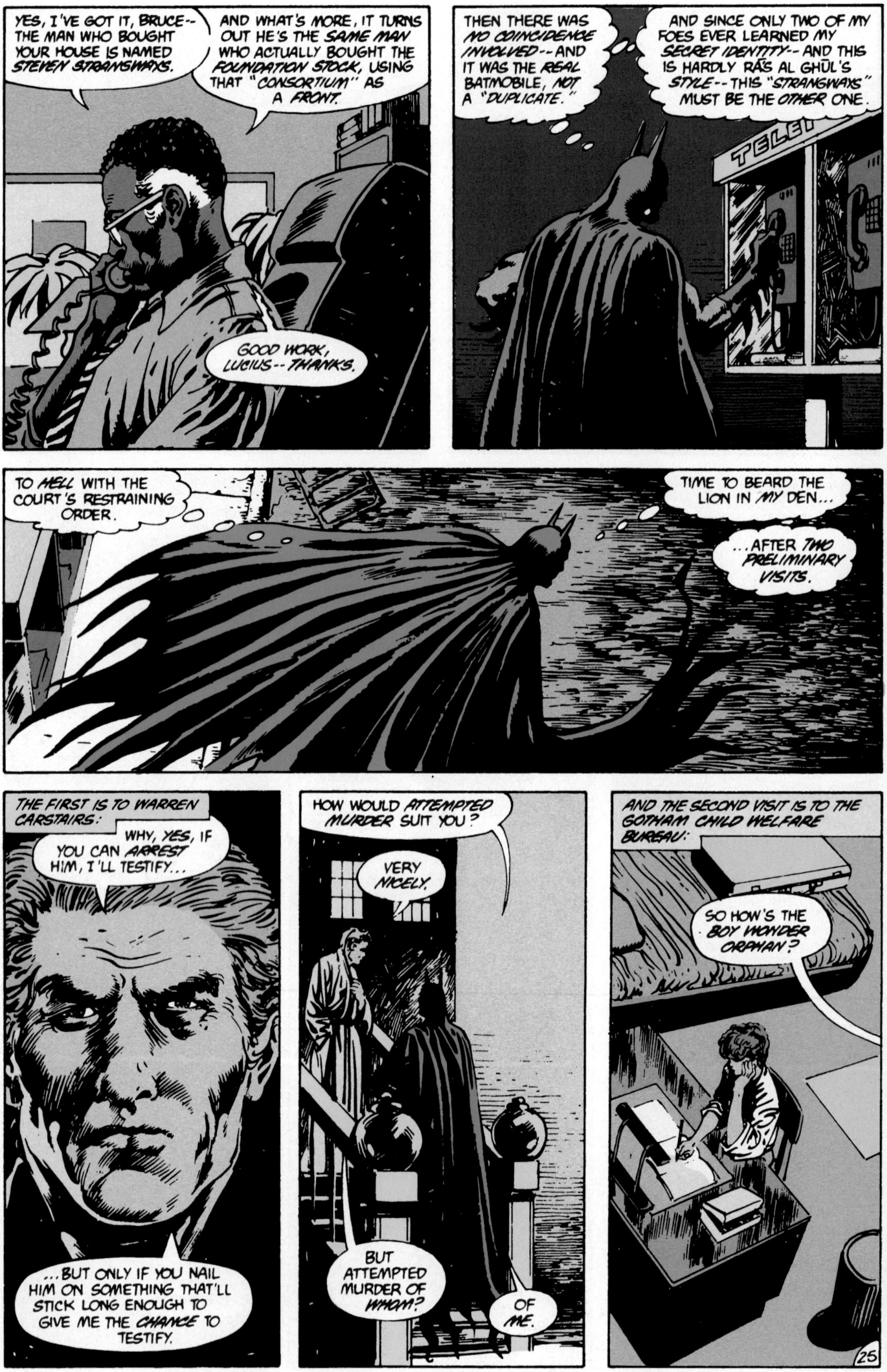
YES, I'VE GOT IT, BRUCE-- THE MAN WHO BOUGHT YOUR HOUSE IS NAMED STEVEN STRANGWAYS.
AND WHAT'S MORE, IT TURNS OUT HE'S THE SAME MAN WHO ACTUALLY BOUGHT THE FOUNDATION STOCK, USING THAT "CONSORTIUM" AS A FRONT.
GOOD WORK, LUCIUS--THANKS.
THEN THERE WAS NO COINCIDENCE INVOLVED--AND IT WAS THE REAL BATMOBILE, NOT A "DUPLICATE."
AND SINCE ONLY TWO OF MY FOES EVER LEARNED MY SECRET IDENTITY-- AND THIS IS HARDLY RA'S AL GHUL'S STYLE--THIS "STRANGWAYS" MUST BE THE OTHER ONE.
TELE
TO HELL WITH THE COURT'S RESTRAINING ORDER.
TIME TO BEARD THE LION IN MY DEN...
...AFTER TWO PRELIMINARY VISITS.
THE FIRST IS TO WARREN CARSTAIRS:
WHY, YES, IF YOU CAN ARREST HIM, I'LL TESTIFY...
...BUT ONLY IF YOU NAIL HIM ON SOMETHING THAT'LL STICK LONG ENOUGH TO GIVE ME THE CHANCE TO TESTIFY.
HOW WOULD ATTEMPTED MURDER SUIT YOU?
VERY NICELY.
BUT ATTEMPTED MURDER OF WHOM?
OF ME.
AND THE SECOND VISIT IS TO THE GOTHAM CHILD WELFARE BUREAU:
SO HOW'S THE BOY WONDER ORPHAN?
25

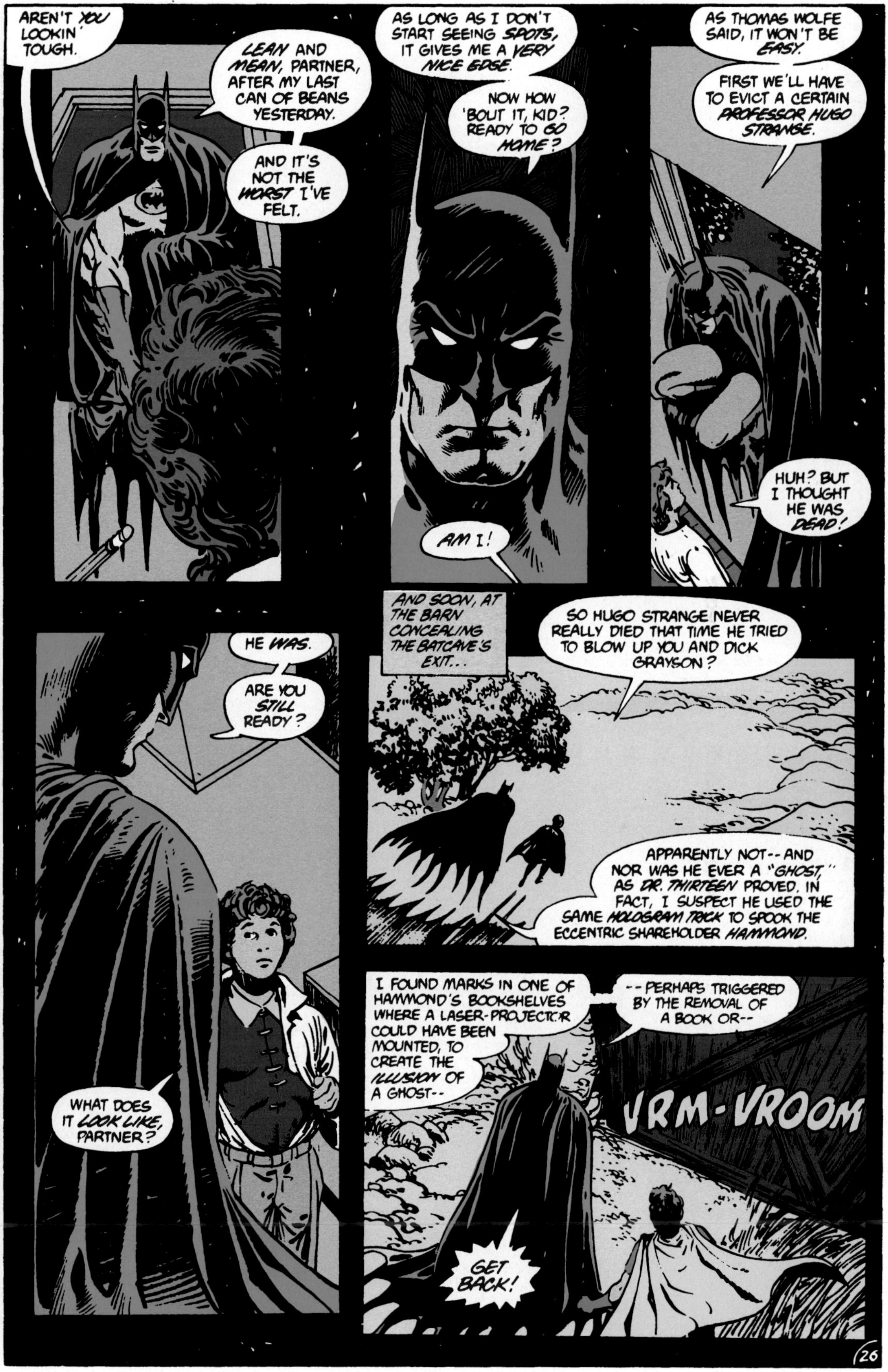
AREN'T YOU LOOKIN' TOUGH.
LEAN AND MEAN, PARTNER, AFTER MY LAST CAN OF BEANS YESTERDAY.
AND IT'S NOT THE WORST I'VE FELT.
AS LONG AS I DON'T START SEEING SPOTS, IT GIVES ME A VERY NICE EDGE.
NOW HOW 'BOUT IT, KID? READY TO GO HOME?
AM I!
AS THOMAS WOLFE SAID, IT WON'T BE EASY.
FIRST WE'LL HAVE TO EVICT A CERTAIN PROFESSOR HUGO STRANGE.
HUH? BUT I THOUGHT HE WAS DEAD!
HE WAS.
ARE YOU STILL READY?
WHAT DOES IT LOOK LIKE, PARTNER?
AND SOON, AT THE BARN CONCEALING THE BATCAVE'S EXIT...
SO HUGO STRANGE NEVER REALLY DIED THAT TIME HE TRIED TO BLOW UP YOU AND DICK GRAYSON?
APPARENTLY NOT-- AND NOR WAS HE EVER A "GHOST," AS DR. THIRTEEN PROVED. IN FACT, I SUSPECT HE USED THE SAME HOLOGRAM TRICK TO SPOOK THE ECCENTRIC SHAREHOLDER HAMMOND.
I FOUND MARKS IN ONE OF HAMMOND'S BOOKSHELVES WHERE A LASER-PROJECTOR COULD HAVE BEEN MOUNTED, TO CREATE THE ILLUSION OF A GHOST--
--PERHAPS TRIGGERED BY THE REMOVAL OF A BOOK OR--
VRM-VROOM
GET BACK!
26

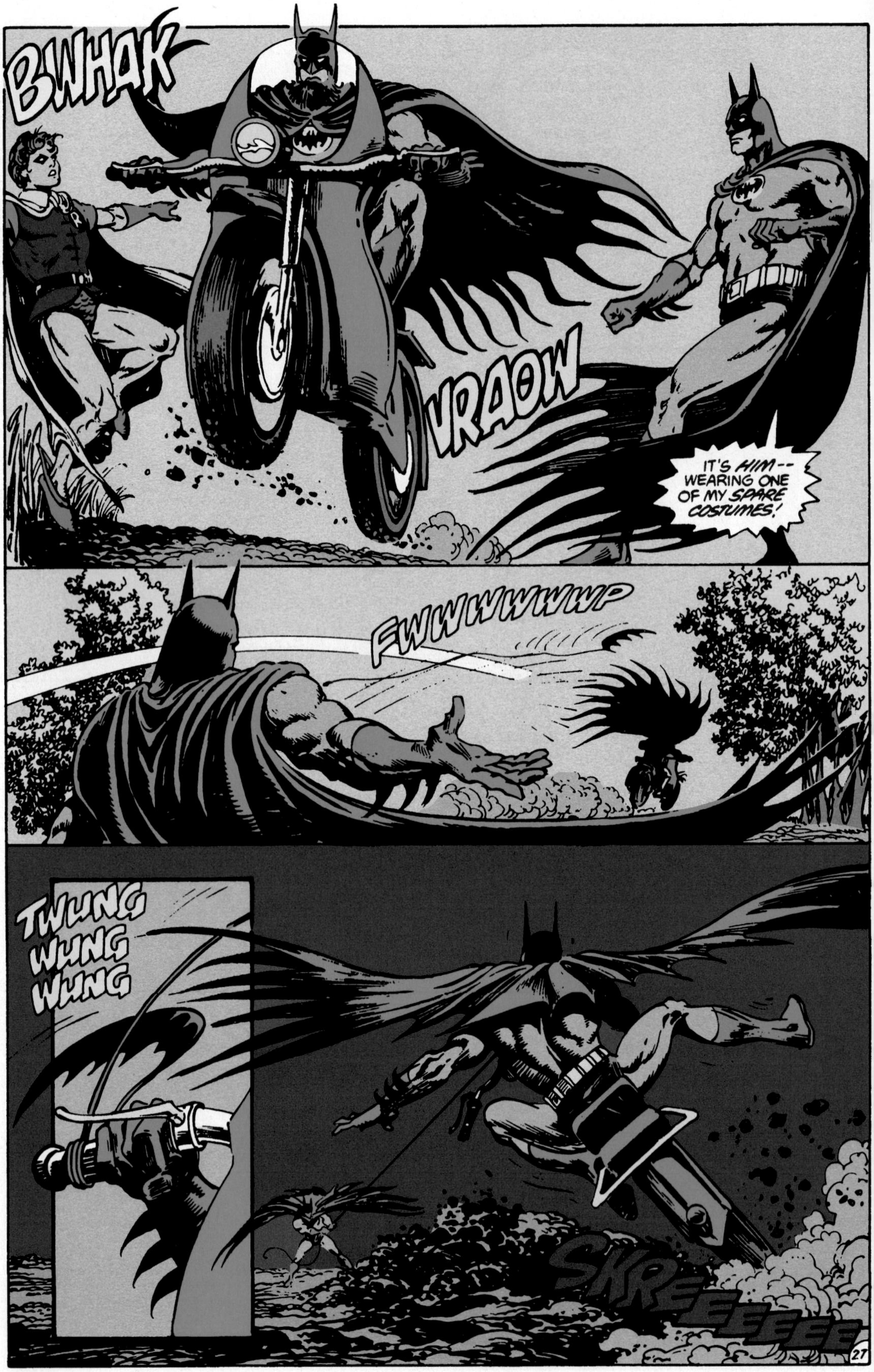
BWHAK
VRAOW
IT'S HIM -- WEARING ONE OF MY SPARE COSTUMES!
FWWWWWWP
TWUNG WUNG WUNG
SKREEEEEEEE
27

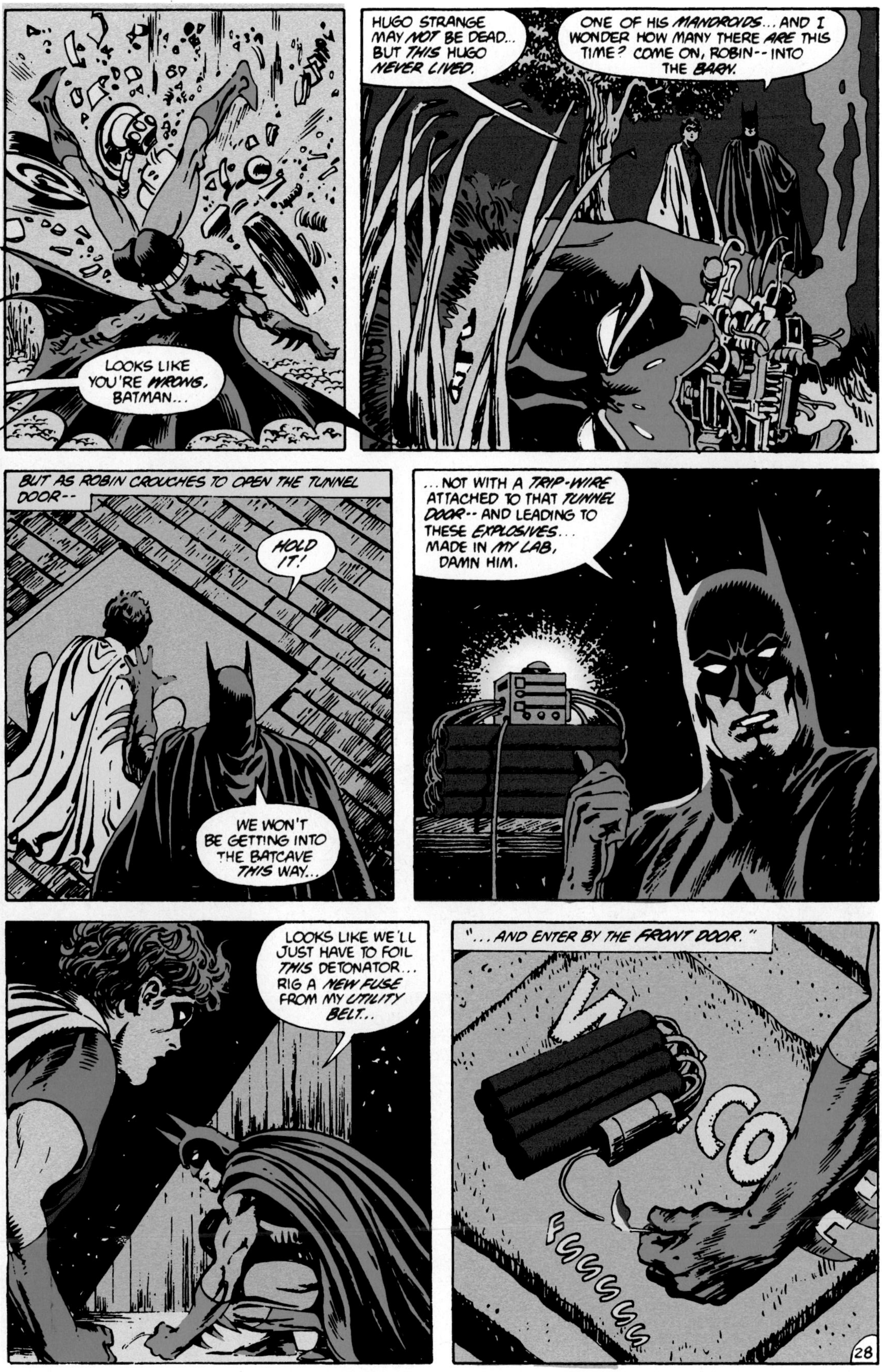
LOOKS LIKE YOU'RE WRONG, BATMAN...
HUGO STRANGE MAY NOT BE DEAD... BUT THIS HUGO NEVER LIVED.
ONE OF HIS MANDROIDS... AND I WONDER HOW MANY THERE ARE THIS TIME? COME ON, ROBIN-- INTO THE BARN.
BUT AS ROBIN CROUCHES TO OPEN THE TUNNEL DOOR--
HOLD IT!
WE WON'T BE GETTING INTO THE BATCAVE THIS WAY...
...NOT WITH A TRIP-WIRE ATTACHED TO THAT TUNNEL DOOR-- AND LEADING TO THESE EXPLOSIVES... MADE IN MY LAB, DAMN HIM.
LOOKS LIKE WE'LL JUST HAVE TO FOIL THIS DETONATOR... RIG A NEW FUSE FROM MY UTILITY BELT...
"...AND ENTER BY THE FRONT DOOR."
FSSSSSS
28

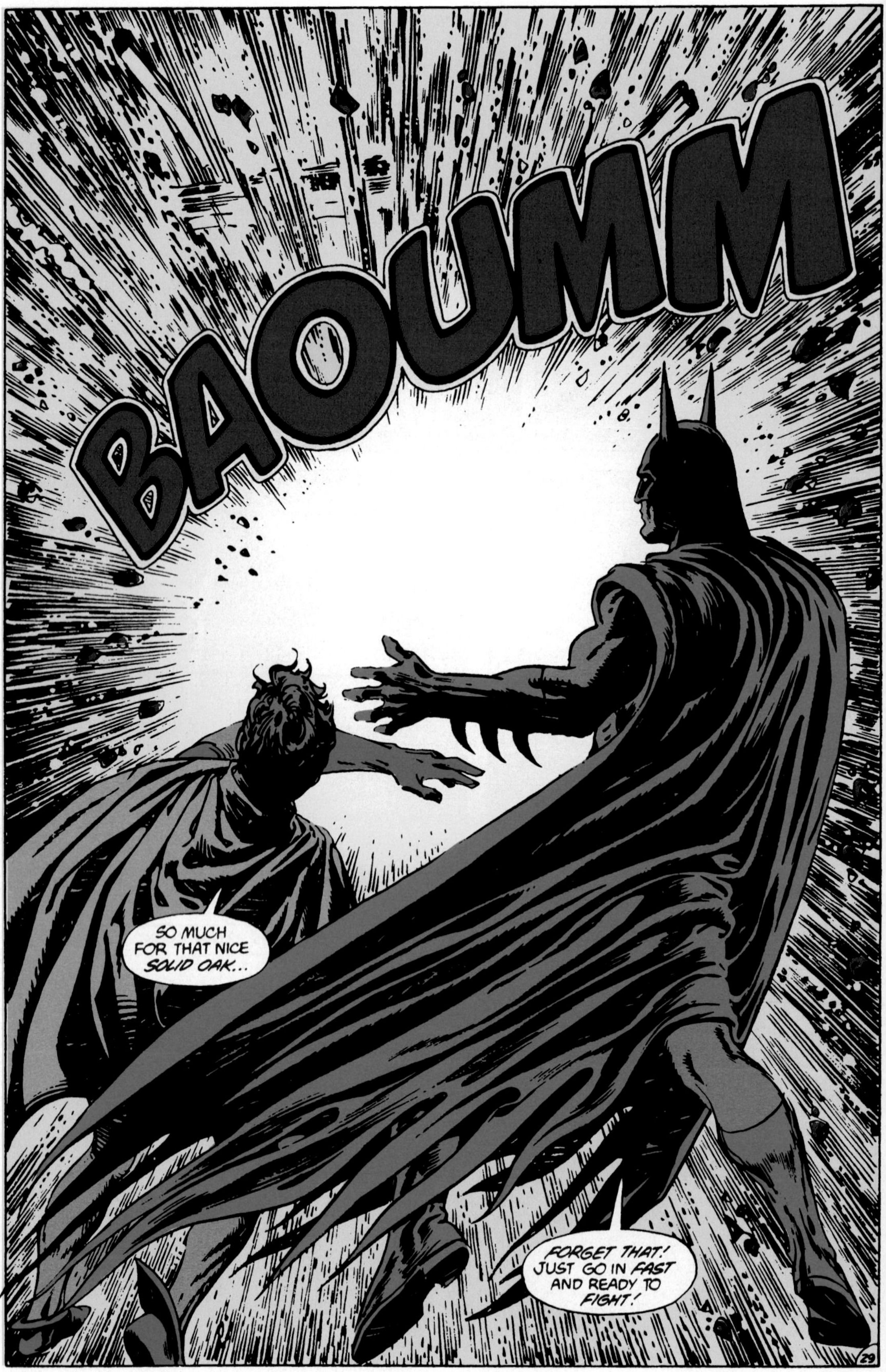
BAOUMM
SO MUCH FOR THAT NICE *SOLID OAK*...
*FORGET THAT!* JUST GO IN *FAST* AND READY TO *FIGHT!*
29

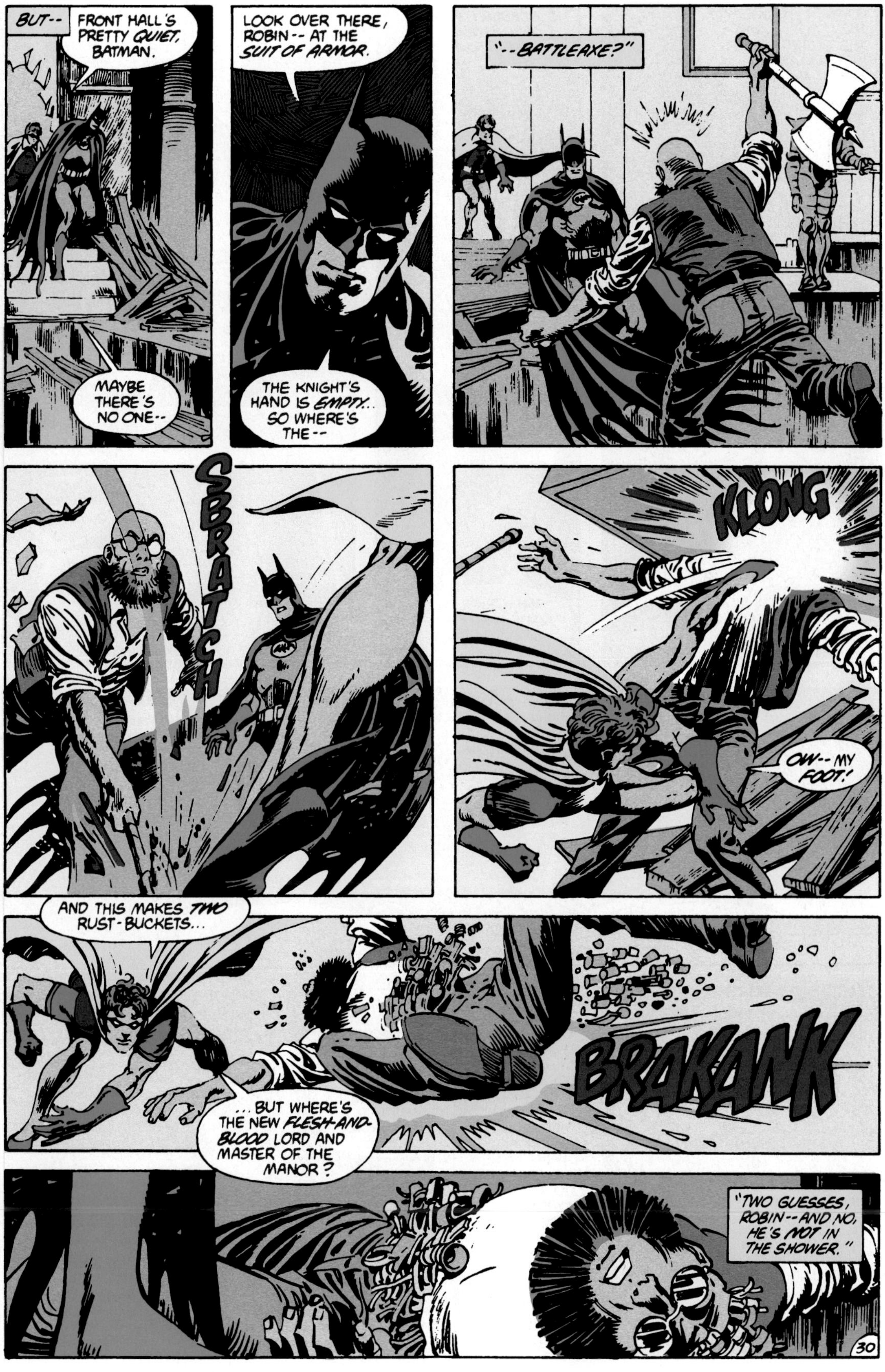
BUT--
FRONT HALL'S PRETTY QUIET, BATMAN.
MAYBE THERE'S NO ONE--
LOOK OVER THERE, ROBIN-- AT THE SUIT OF ARMOR.
THE KNIGHT'S HAND IS EMPTY.. SO WHERE'S THE--
"--BATTLEAXE?"
SBRATCH
KLONG
OW-- MY FOOT!
AND THIS MAKES TWO RUST-BUCKETS...
BRAKANK
...BUT WHERE'S THE NEW FLESH-AND-BLOOD LORD AND MASTER OF THE MANOR?
"TWO GUESSES, ROBIN--AND NO, HE'S NOT IN THE SHOWER."
30

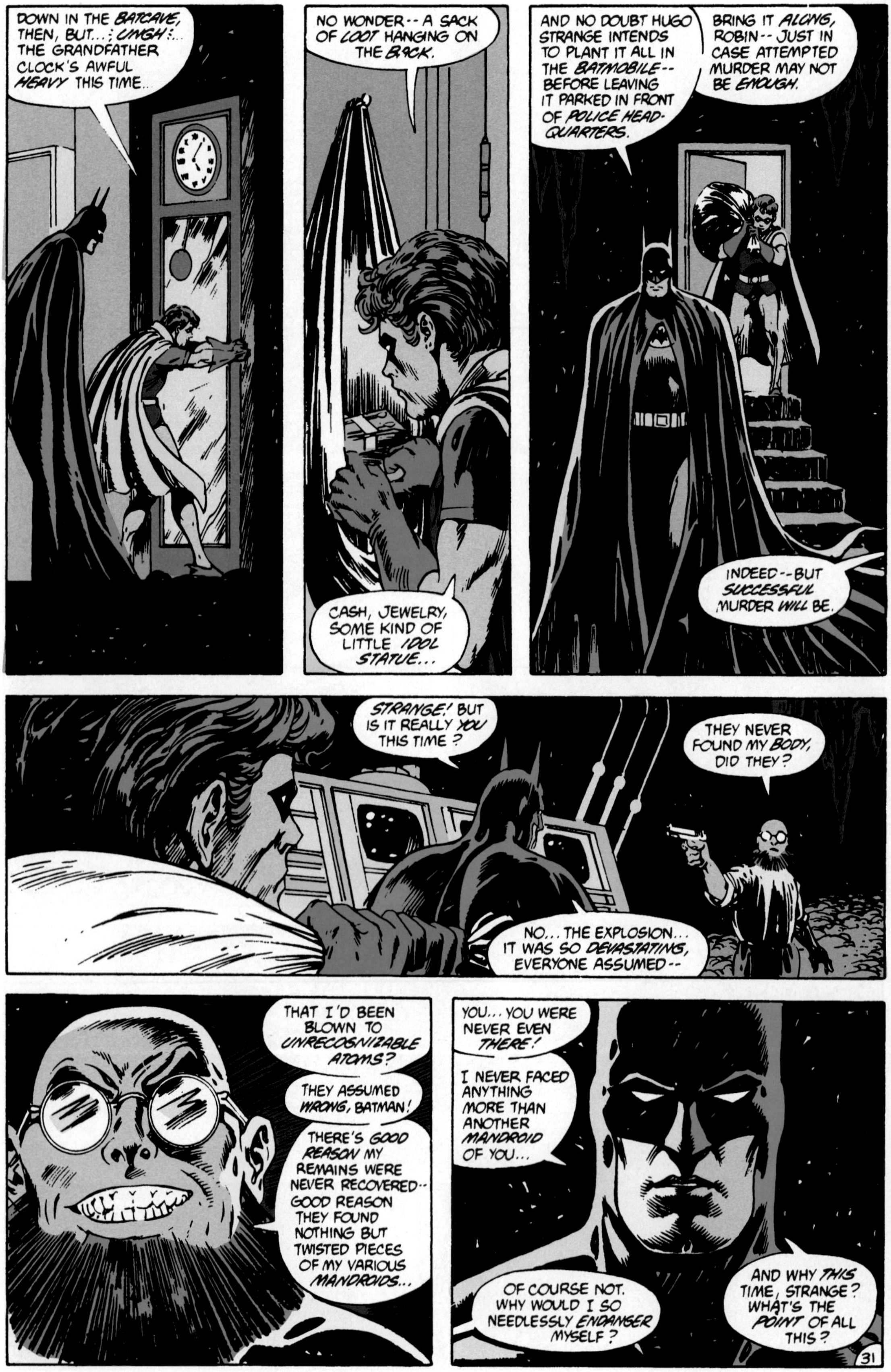

DOWN IN THE BATCAVE, THEN, BUT... ; UNGH ;... THE GRANDFATHER CLOCK'S AWFUL HEAVY THIS TIME...
NO WONDER -- A SACK OF LOOT HANGING ON THE BACK.
CASH, JEWELRY, SOME KIND OF LITTLE IDOL STATUE...
AND NO DOUBT HUGO STRANGE INTENDS TO PLANT IT ALL IN THE BATMOBILE -- BEFORE LEAVING IT PARKED IN FRONT OF POLICE HEADQUARTERS.
BRING IT ALONG, ROBIN -- JUST IN CASE ATTEMPTED MURDER MAY NOT BE ENOUGH.
INDEED -- BUT SUCCESSFUL MURDER WILL BE.
STRANGE! BUT IS IT REALLY YOU THIS TIME?
THEY NEVER FOUND MY BODY, DID THEY?
NO... THE EXPLOSION... IT WAS SO DEVASTATING, EVERYONE ASSUMED --
THAT I'D BEEN BLOWN TO UNRECOGNIZABLE ATOMS?
THEY ASSUMED WRONG, BATMAN!
THERE'S GOOD REASON MY REMAINS WERE NEVER RECOVERED -- GOOD REASON THEY FOUND NOTHING BUT TWISTED PIECES OF MY VARIOUS MANDROIDS...
YOU... YOU WERE NEVER EVEN THERE!
I NEVER FACED ANYTHING MORE THAN ANOTHER MANDROID OF YOU...
OF COURSE NOT. WHY WOULD I SO NEEDLESSLY ENDANGER MYSELF?
AND WHY THIS TIME, STRANGE? WHAT'S THE POINT OF ALL THIS?
31

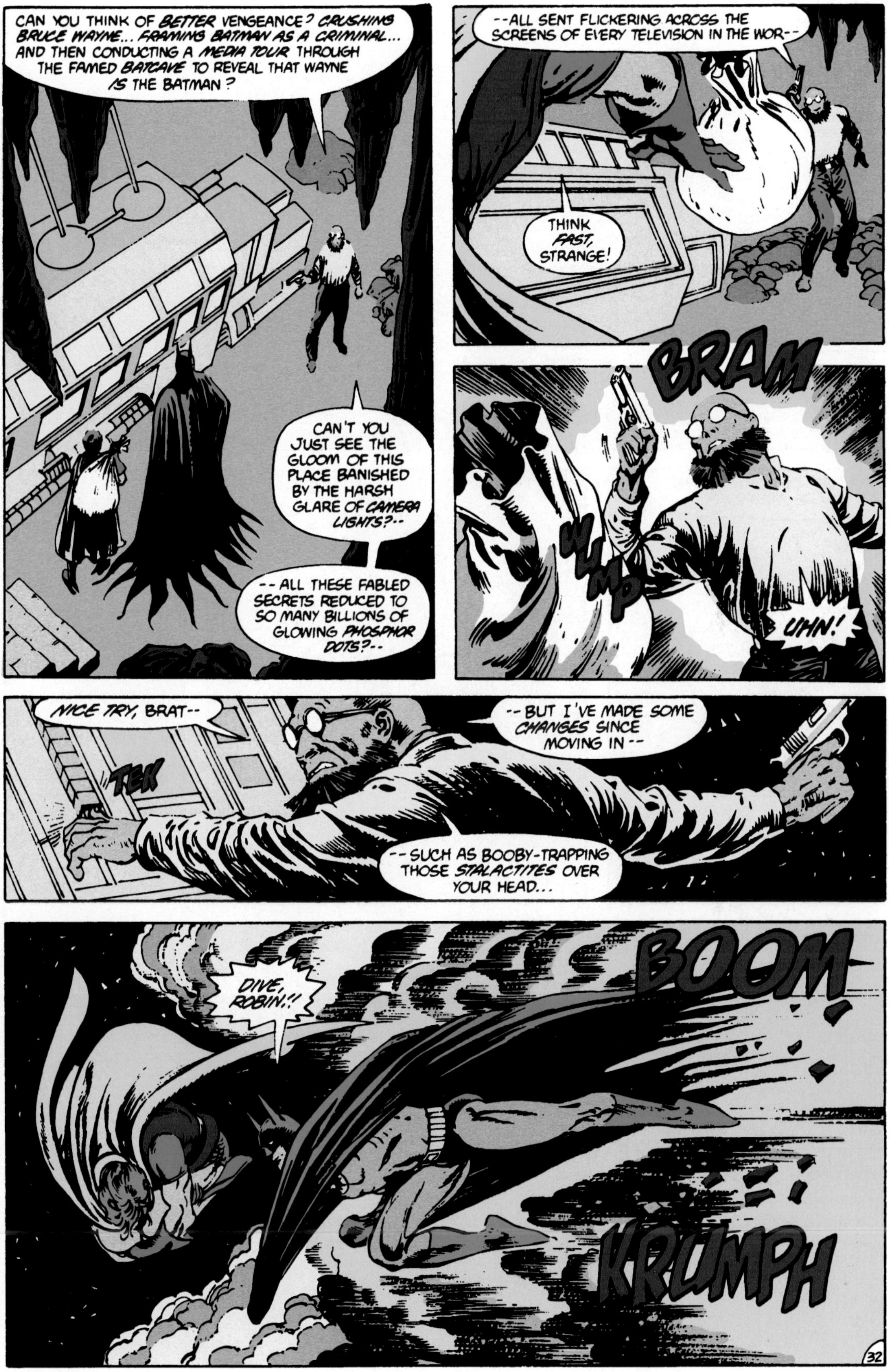
CAN YOU THINK OF BETTER VENGEANCE? CRUSHING BRUCE WAYNE... FRAMING BATMAN AS A CRIMINAL... AND THEN CONDUCTING A MEDIA TOUR THROUGH THE FAMED BATCAVE TO REVEAL THAT WAYNE IS THE BATMAN?
CAN'T YOU JUST SEE THE GLOOM OF THIS PLACE BANISHED BY THE HARSH GLARE OF CAMERA LIGHTS?--
--ALL THESE FABLED SECRETS REDUCED TO SO MANY BILLIONS OF GLOWING PHOSPHOR DOTS?--
--ALL SENT FLICKERING ACROSS THE SCREENS OF EVERY TELEVISION IN THE WOR--
THINK FAST, STRANGE!
BRAM
WUMP
UHN!
NICE TRY, BRAT--
TEK
--BUT I'VE MADE SOME CHANGES SINCE MOVING IN--
--SUCH AS BOOBY-TRAPPING THOSE STALACTITES OVER YOUR HEAD...
BOOM
DIVE, ROBIN!!
KRUMPH
32

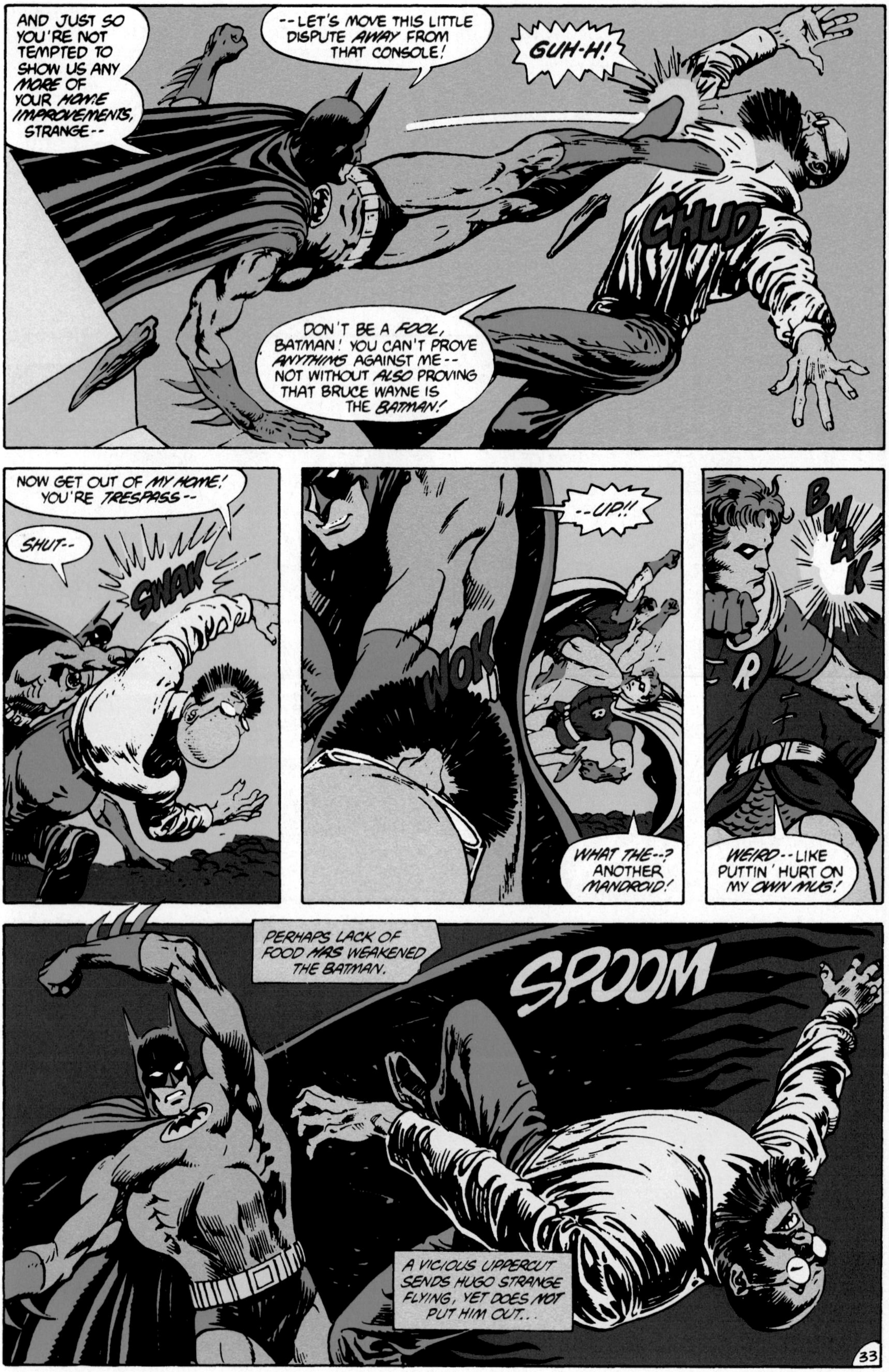
AND JUST SO YOU'RE NOT TEMPTED TO SHOW US ANY MORE OF YOUR HOME IMPROVEMENTS, STRANGE--
--LET'S MOVE THIS LITTLE DISPUTE AWAY FROM THAT CONSOLE!
GUH-H!
CHUD
DON'T BE A FOOL, BATMAN! YOU CAN'T PROVE ANYTHING AGAINST ME--NOT WITHOUT ALSO PROVING THAT BRUCE WAYNE IS THE BATMAN!
NOW GET OUT OF MY HOME! YOU'RE TRESPASS--
SHUT--
SWAK
--UP!!
WOK
WHAT THE--? ANOTHER MANDROID!
BWAK
WEIRD--LIKE PUTTIN' HURT ON MY OWN MUG!
PERHAPS LACK OF FOOD HAS WEAKENED THE BATMAN.
SPOOM
A VICIOUS UPPERCUT SENDS HUGO STRANGE FLYING, YET DOES NOT PUT HIM OUT...
33

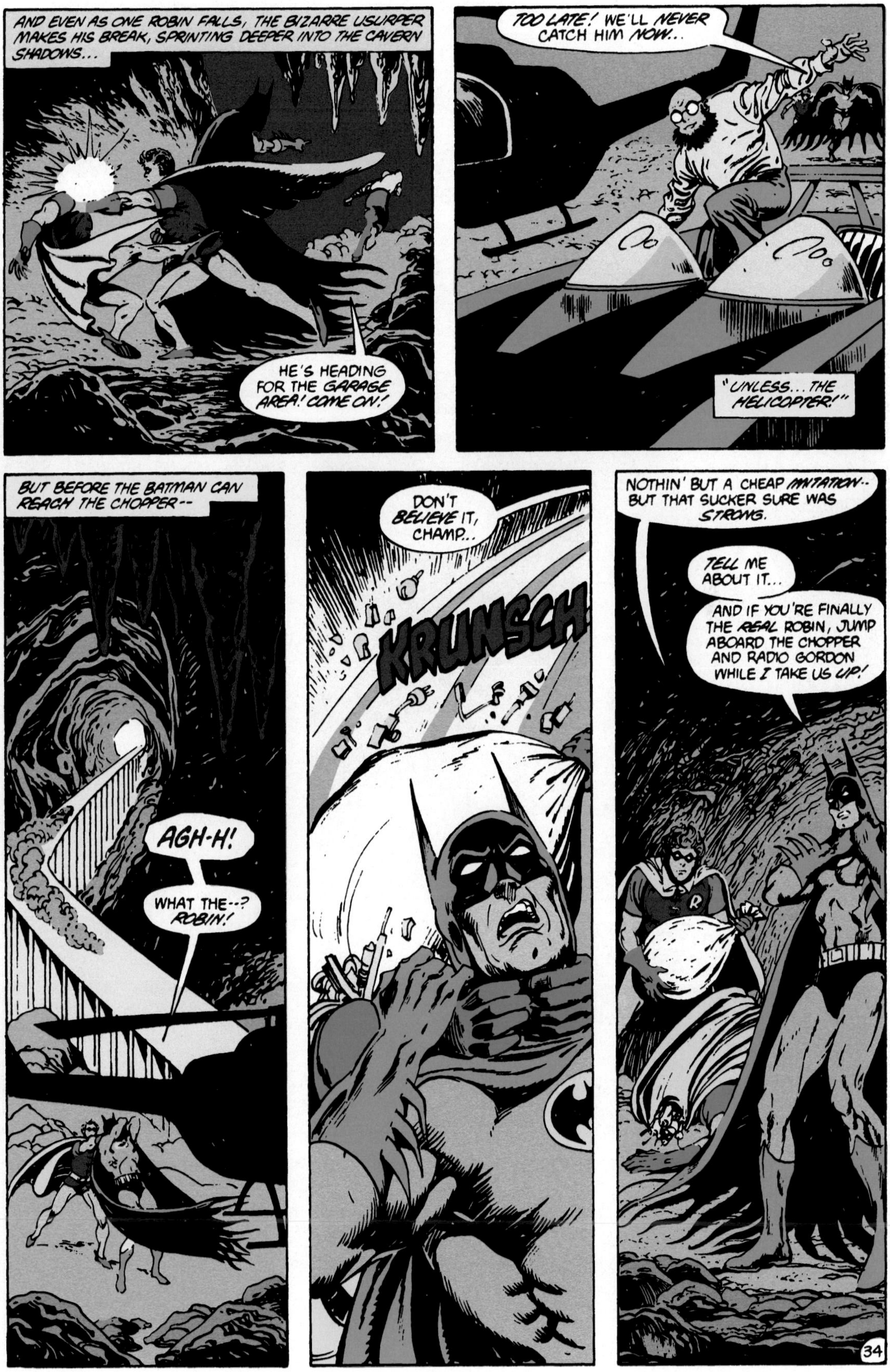
AND EVEN AS ONE ROBIN FALLS, THE BIZARRE USURPER MAKES HIS BREAK, SPRINTING DEEPER INTO THE CAVERN SHADOWS...
HE'S HEADING FOR THE GARAGE AREA! COME ON!
TOO LATE! WE'LL NEVER CATCH HIM NOW..
"UNLESS... THE HELICOPTER!"
BUT BEFORE THE BATMAN CAN REACH THE CHOPPER--
AGH-H!
WHAT THE--? ROBIN!
DON'T BELIEVE IT, CHAMP..
KRUNSCH
NOTHIN' BUT A CHEAP IMITATION.. BUT THAT SUCKER SURE WAS STRONG.
TELL ME ABOUT IT...
AND IF YOU'RE FINALLY THE REAL ROBIN, JUMP ABOARD THE CHOPPER AND RADIO GORDON WHILE I TAKE US UP!
34

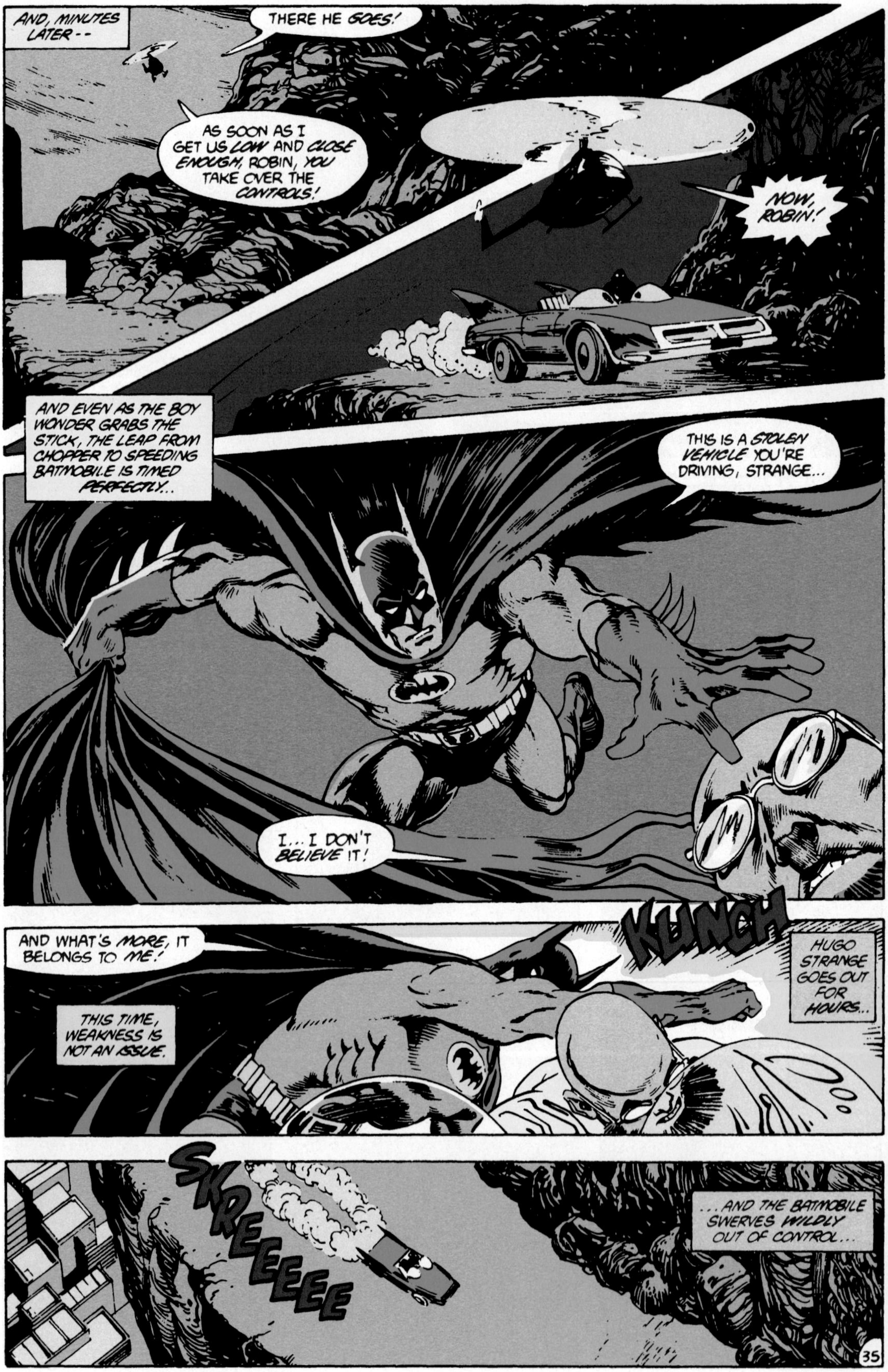
AND, MINUTES LATER--
THERE HE GOES!
AS SOON AS I GET US LOW AND CLOSE ENOUGH, ROBIN, YOU TAKE OVER THE CONTROLS!
NOW, ROBIN!
AND EVEN AS THE BOY WONDER GRABS THE STICK, THE LEAP FROM CHOPPER TO SPEEDING BATMOBILE IS TIMED PERFECTLY...
THIS IS A STOLEN VEHICLE YOU'RE DRIVING, STRANGE...
I... I DON'T BELIEVE IT!
KLUNCH
AND WHAT'S MORE, IT BELONGS TO ME!
HUGO STRANGE GOES OUT FOR HOURS...
THIS TIME, WEAKNESS IS NOT AN ISSUE.
SKREEEEEEE
...AND THE BATMOBILE SWERVES WILDLY OUT OF CONTROL...
35

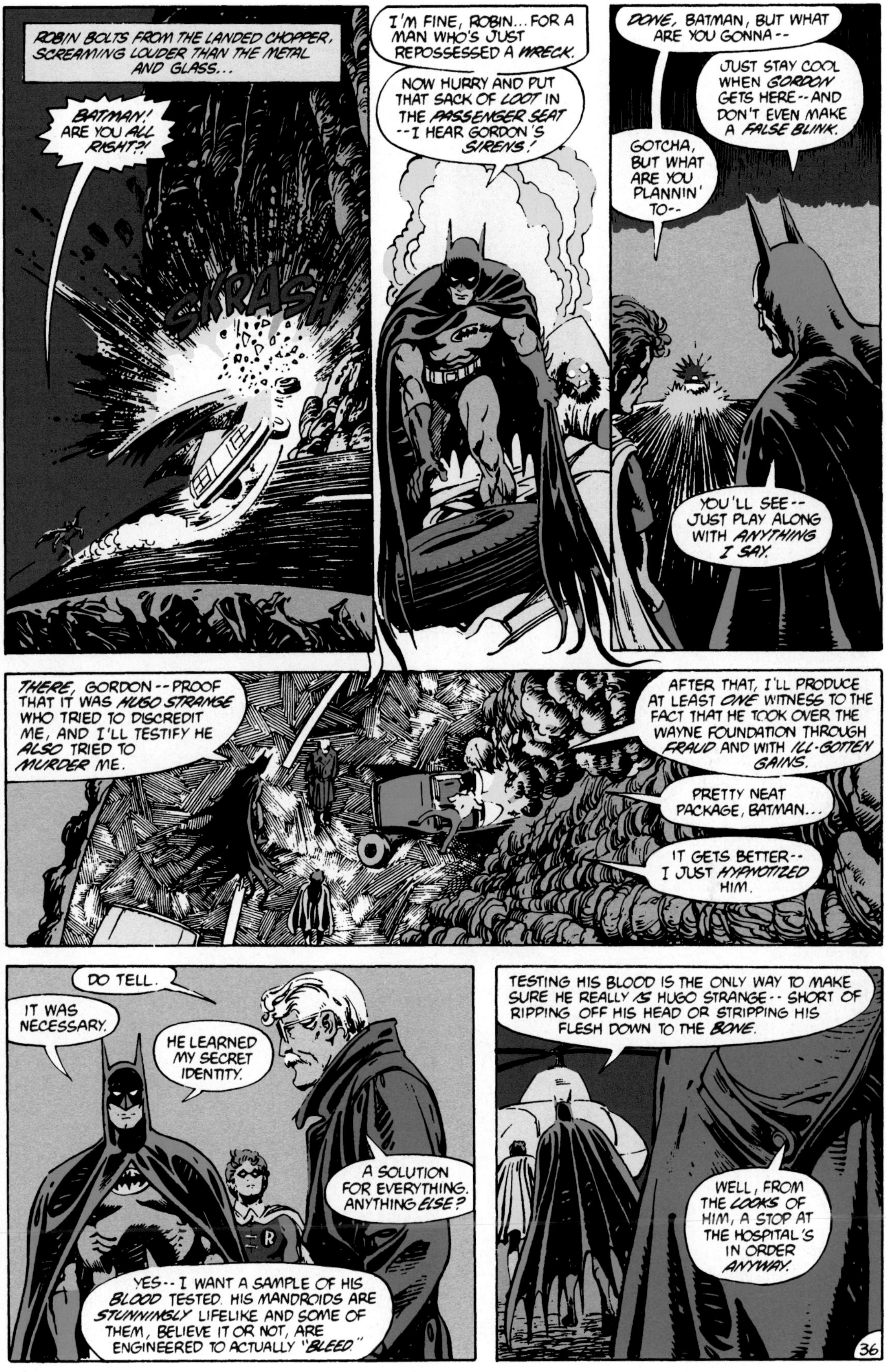
ROBIN BOLTS FROM THE LANDED CHOPPER, SCREAMING LOUDER THAN THE METAL AND GLASS...
BATMAN! ARE YOU ALL RIGHT?!
SKRASH
I'M FINE, ROBIN... FOR A MAN WHO'S JUST REPOSSESSED A WRECK.
NOW HURRY AND PUT THAT SACK OF LOOT IN THE PASSENGER SEAT --I HEAR GORDON'S SIRENS!
DONE, BATMAN, BUT WHAT ARE YOU GONNA--
JUST STAY COOL WHEN GORDON GETS HERE--AND DON'T EVEN MAKE A FALSE BLINK.
GOTCHA, BUT WHAT ARE YOU PLANNIN' TO--
YOU'LL SEE-- JUST PLAY ALONG WITH ANYTHING I SAY.
THERE, GORDON--PROOF THAT IT WAS HUGO STRANGE WHO TRIED TO DISCREDIT ME, AND I'LL TESTIFY HE ALSO TRIED TO MURDER ME.
AFTER THAT, I'LL PRODUCE AT LEAST ONE WITNESS TO THE FACT THAT HE TOOK OVER THE WAYNE FOUNDATION THROUGH FRAUD AND WITH ILL-GOTTEN GAINS.
PRETTY NEAT PACKAGE, BATMAN...
IT GETS BETTER-- I JUST HYPNOTIZED HIM.
DO TELL.
IT WAS NECESSARY.
HE LEARNED MY SECRET IDENTITY.
A SOLUTION FOR EVERYTHING. ANYTHING ELSE?
YES--I WANT A SAMPLE OF HIS BLOOD TESTED. HIS MANDROIDS ARE STUNNINGLY LIFELIKE AND SOME OF THEM, BELIEVE IT OR NOT, ARE ENGINEERED TO ACTUALLY "BLEED."
TESTING HIS BLOOD IS THE ONLY WAY TO MAKE SURE HE REALLY IS HUGO STRANGE-- SHORT OF RIPPING OFF HIS HEAD OR STRIPPING HIS FLESH DOWN TO THE BONE.
WELL, FROM THE LOOKS OF HIM, A STOP AT THE HOSPITAL'S IN ORDER ANYWAY.
36

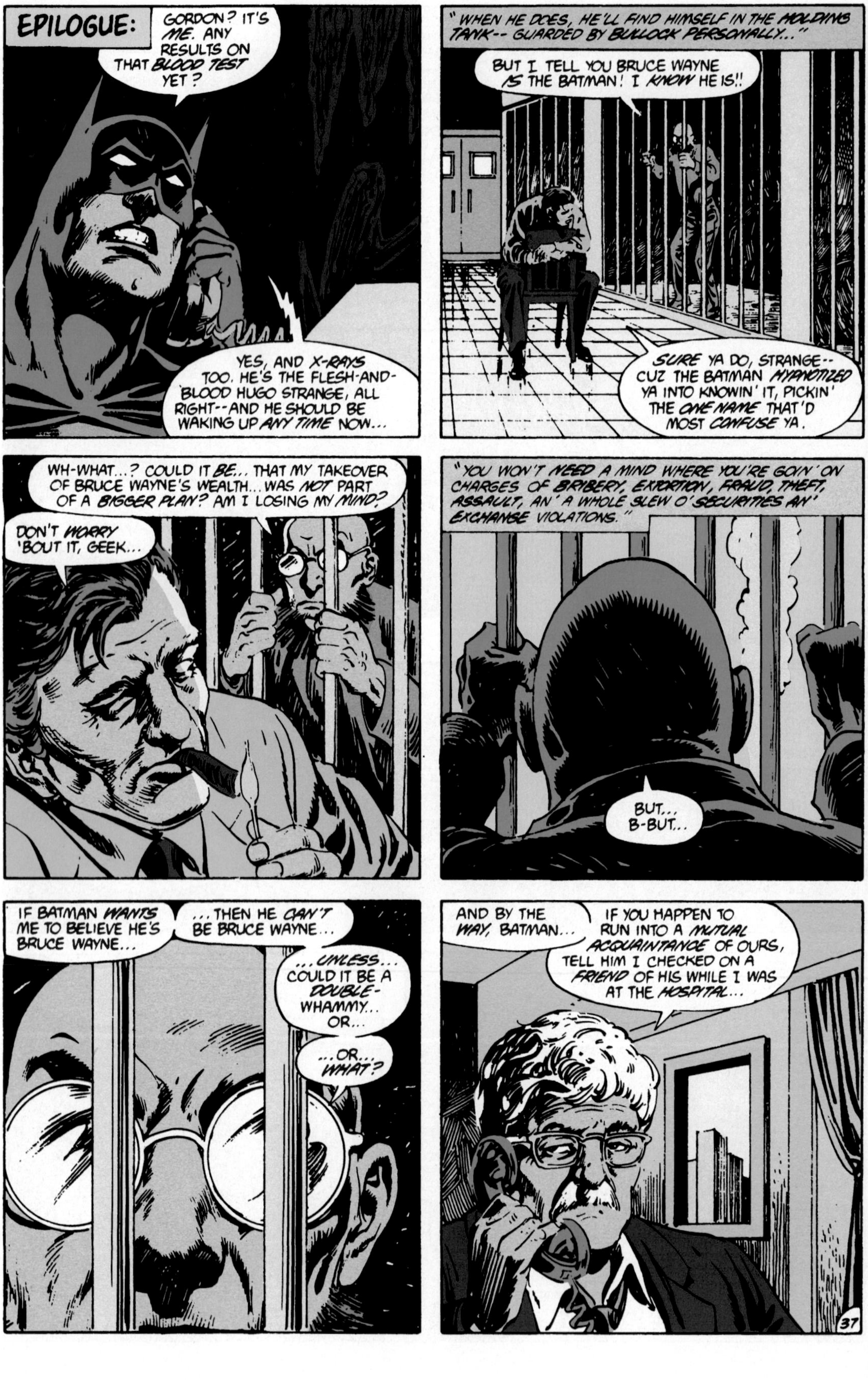
EPILOGUE:
GORDON? IT'S ME. ANY RESULTS ON THAT BLOOD TEST YET?
YES, AND X-RAYS TOO. HE'S THE FLESH-AND-BLOOD HUGO STRANGE, ALL RIGHT--AND HE SHOULD BE WAKING UP ANY TIME NOW...
"WHEN HE DOES, HE'LL FIND HIMSELF IN THE HOLDING TANK-- GUARDED BY BULLOCK PERSONALLY..."
BUT I TELL YOU BRUCE WAYNE IS THE BATMAN! I KNOW HE IS!!
SURE YA DO, STRANGE-- CUZ THE BATMAN HYPNOTIZED YA INTO KNOWIN' IT, PICKIN' THE ONE NAME THAT'D MOST CONFUSE YA.
WH-WHAT...? COULD IT BE... THAT MY TAKEOVER OF BRUCE WAYNE'S WEALTH... WAS NOT PART OF A BIGGER PLAN? AM I LOSING MY MIND?
DON'T WORRY 'BOUT IT, GEEK...
"YOU WON'T NEED A MIND WHERE YOU'RE GOIN' ON CHARGES OF BRIBERY, EXTORTION, FRAUD, THEFT, ASSAULT, AN' A WHOLE SLEW O' SECURITIES AN' EXCHANGE VIOLATIONS."
BUT... B-BUT...
IF BATMAN WANTS ME TO BELIEVE HE'S BRUCE WAYNE...
...THEN HE CAN'T BE BRUCE WAYNE...
...UNLESS... COULD IT BE A DOUBLE-WHAMMY... OR...
...OR... WHAT?
AND BY THE WAY, BATMAN...
IF YOU HAPPEN TO RUN INTO A MUTUAL ACQUAINTANCE OF OURS, TELL HIM I CHECKED ON A FRIEND OF HIS WHILE I WAS AT THE HOSPITAL...
37

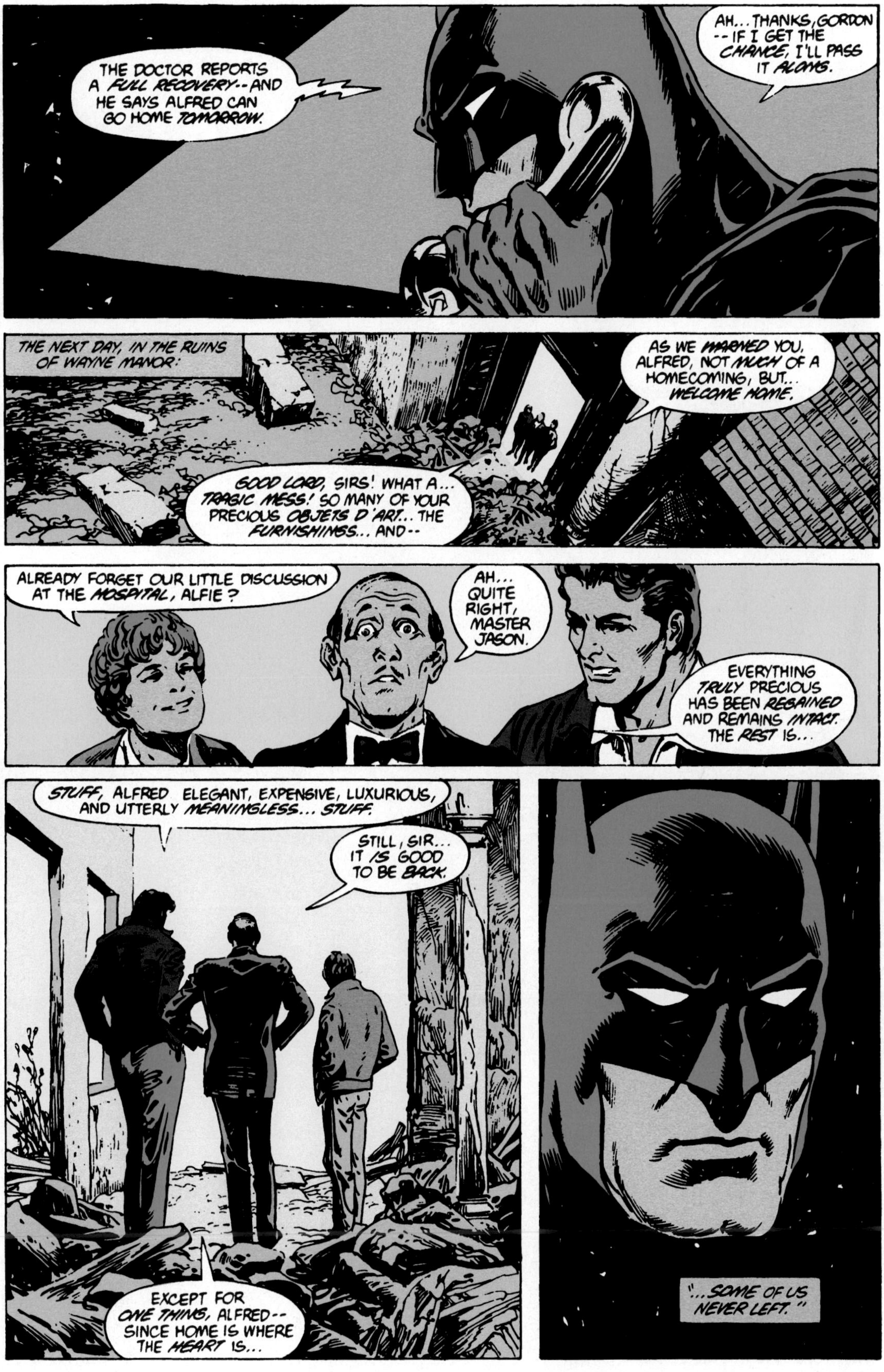
THE DOCTOR REPORTS A FULL RECOVERY--AND HE SAYS ALFRED CAN GO HOME TOMORROW.
AH... THANKS, GORDON --IF I GET THE CHANCE, I'LL PASS IT ALONG.
THE NEXT DAY, IN THE RUINS OF WAYNE MANOR:
AS WE WARNED YOU, ALFRED, NOT MUCH OF A HOMECOMING, BUT... WELCOME HOME.
GOOD LORD, SIRS! WHAT A... TRAGIC MESS! SO MANY OF YOUR PRECIOUS OBJETS D'ART... THE FURNISHINGS... AND--
ALREADY FORGET OUR LITTLE DISCUSSION AT THE HOSPITAL, ALFIE?
AH... QUITE RIGHT, MASTER JASON.
EVERYTHING TRULY PRECIOUS HAS BEEN REGAINED AND REMAINS INTACT. THE REST IS...
STUFF, ALFRED ELEGANT, EXPENSIVE, LUXURIOUS, AND UTTERLY MEANINGLESS... STUFF.
STILL, SIR... IT IS GOOD TO BE BACK.
EXCEPT FOR ONE THING, ALFRED-- SINCE HOME IS WHERE THE HEART IS...
"...SOME OF US NEVER LEFT."

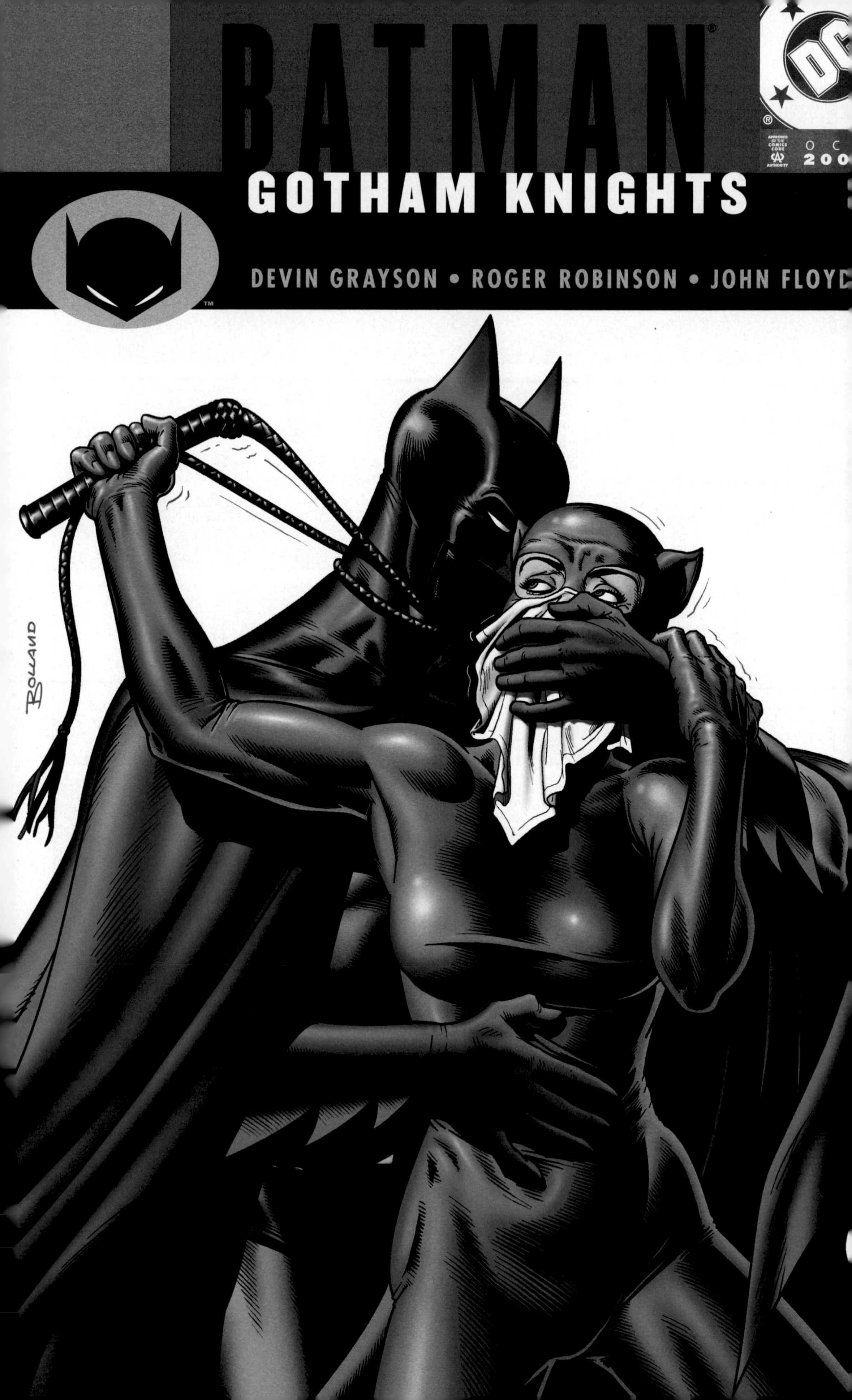
BATMAN
DC
APPROVED BY THE COMICS CODE AUTHORITY
GOTHAM KNIGHTS
DEVIN GRAYSON • ROGER ROBINSON • JOHN FLOY
BOLLAND

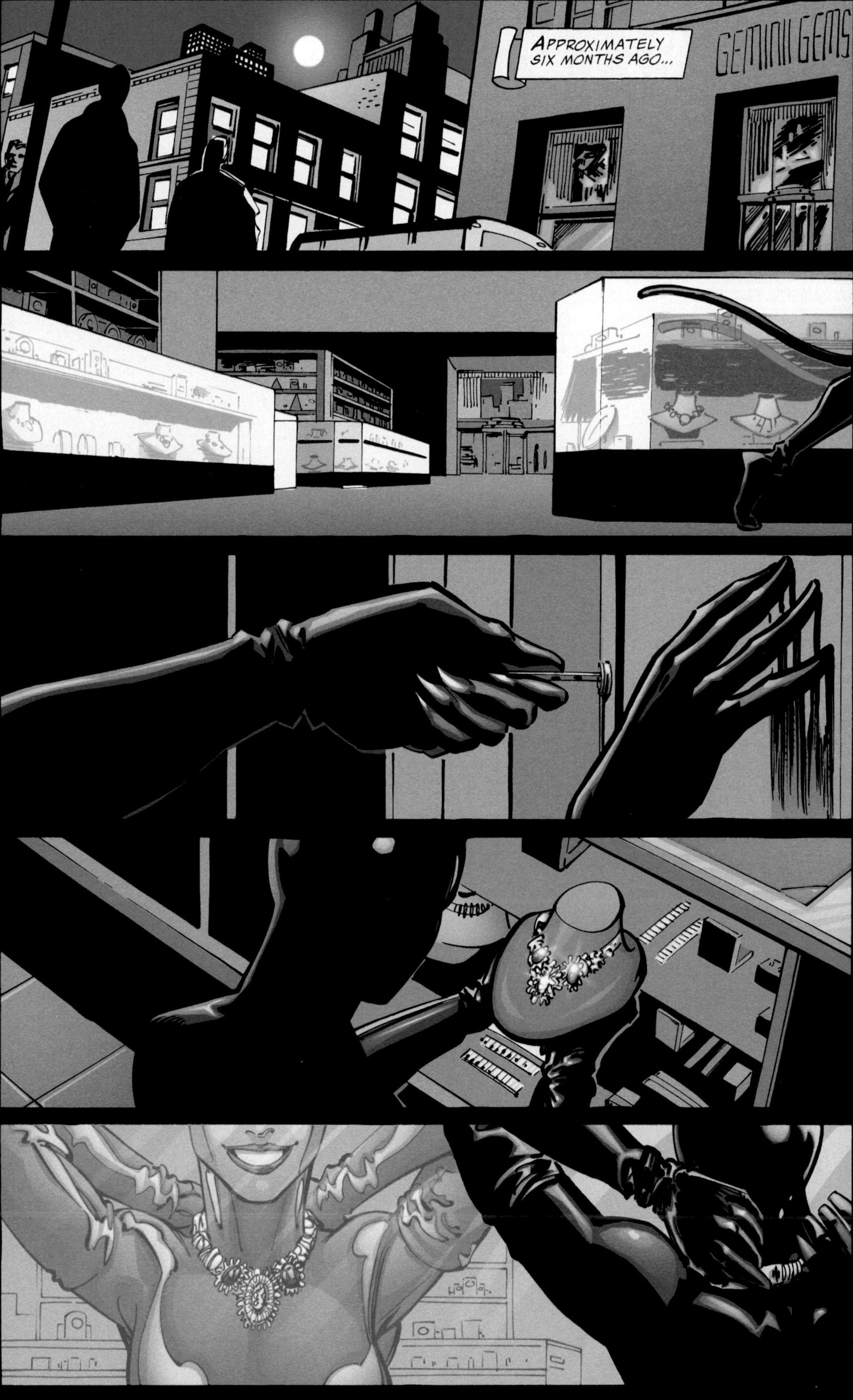
APPROXIMATELY SIX MONTHS AGO...
GEMINI GEMS

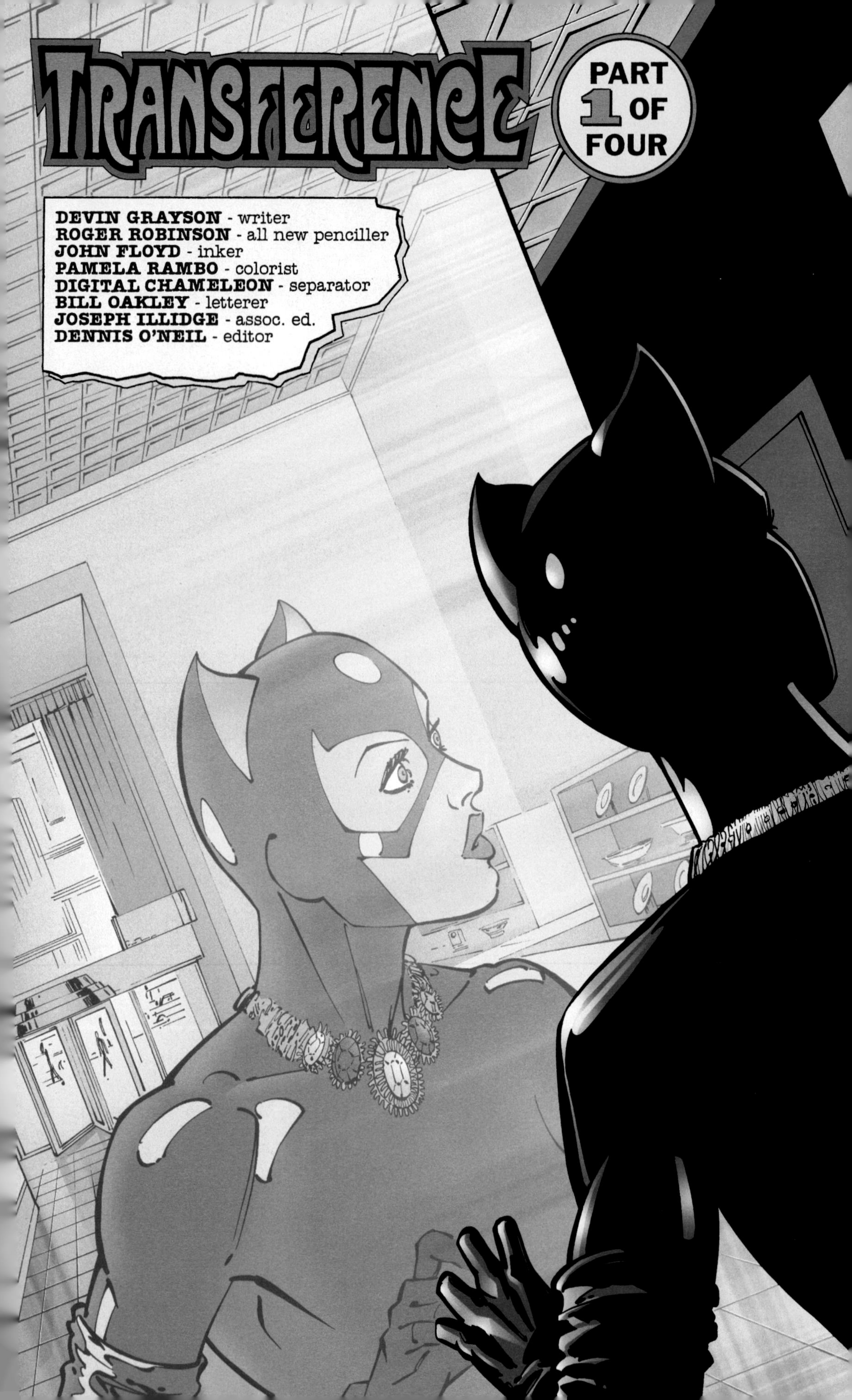
TRANSFERENCE
PART 1 OF FOUR
DEVIN GRAYSON - writer
ROGER ROBINSON - all new penciller
JOHN FLOYD - inker
PAMELA RAMBO - colorist
DIGITAL CHAMELEON - separator
BILL OAKLEY - letterer
JOSEPH ILLIDGE - assoc. ed.
DENNIS O'NEIL - editor

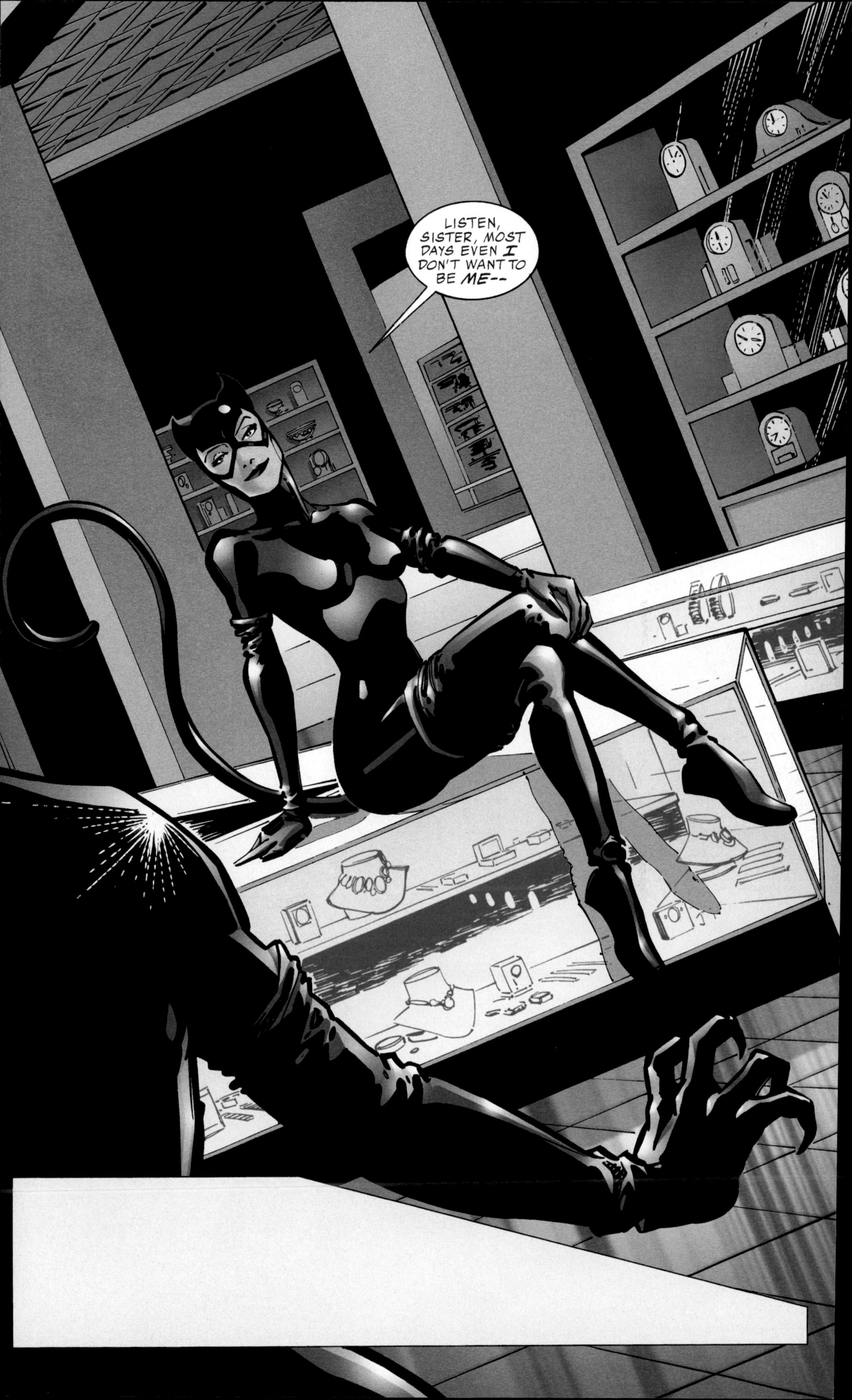
LISTEN, SISTER, MOST DAYS EVEN I DON'T WANT TO BE ME--

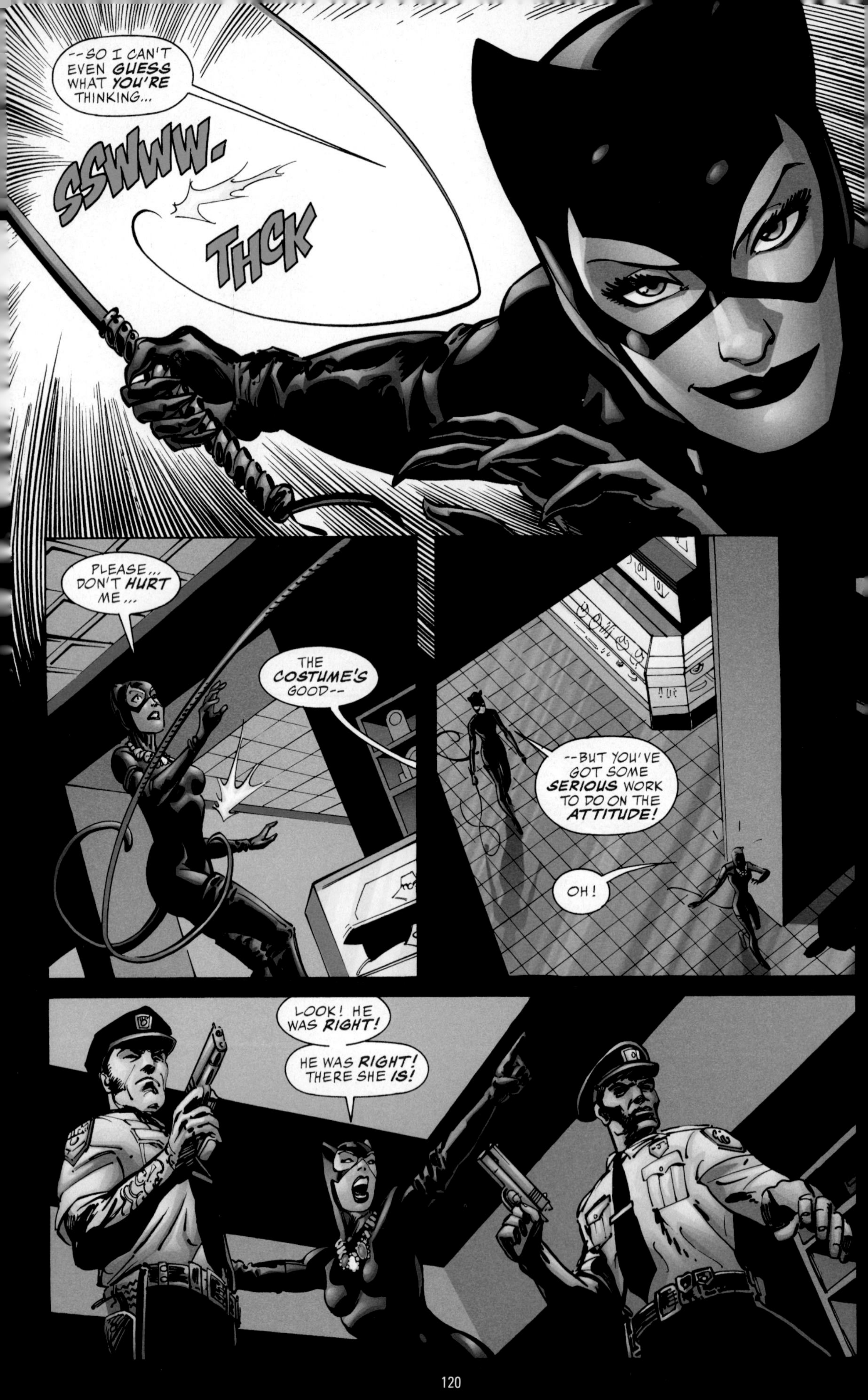
--SO I CAN'T EVEN GUESS WHAT YOU'RE THINKING...
SSWWW-
THCK
PLEASE... DON'T HURT ME...
THE COSTUME'S GOOD--
--BUT YOU'VE GOT SOME SERIOUS WORK TO DO ON THE ATTITUDE!
OH!
LOOK! HE WAS RIGHT!
HE WAS RIGHT! THERE SHE IS!

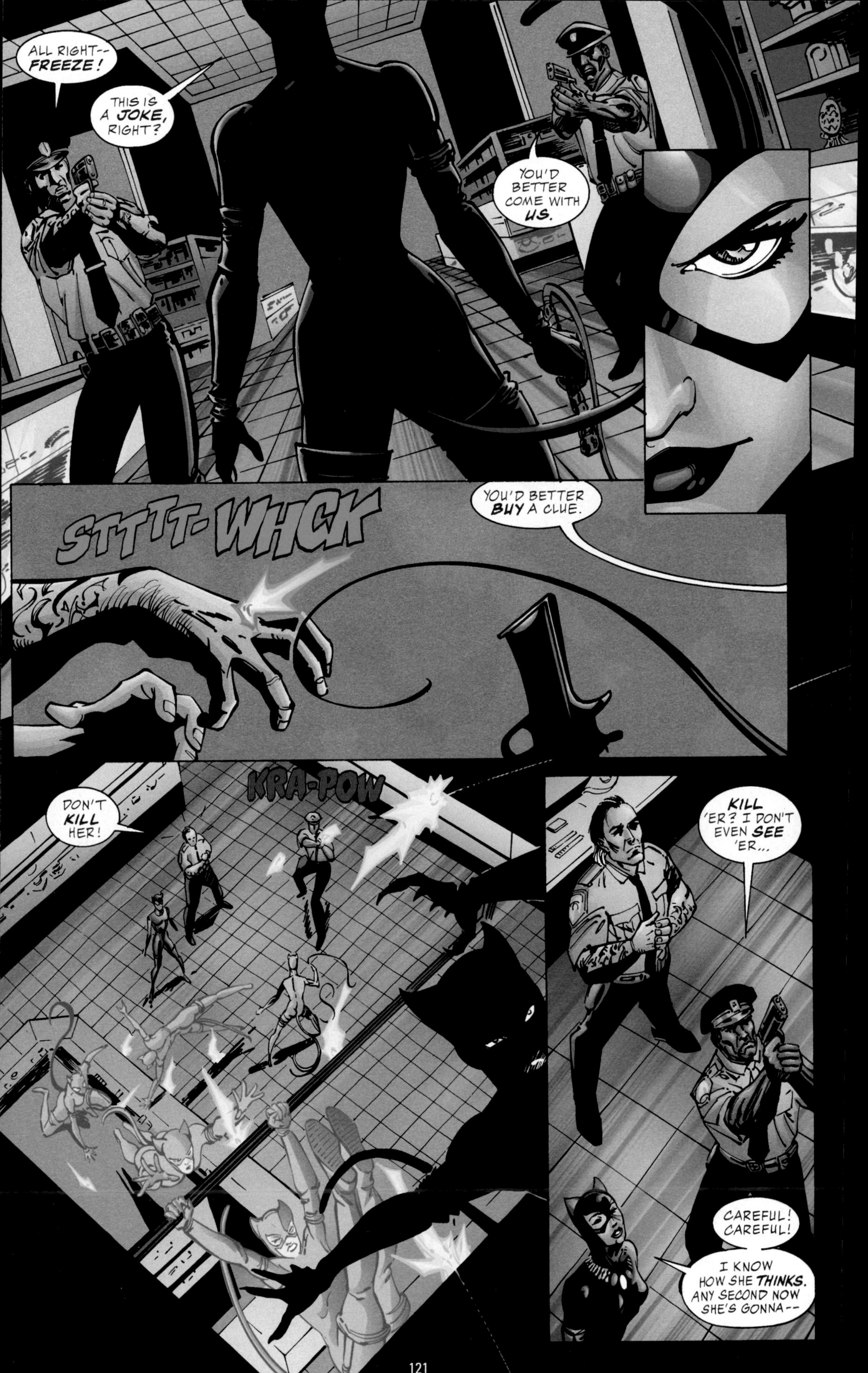
ALL RIGHT-- FREEZE!
THIS IS A JOKE, RIGHT?
YOU'D BETTER COME WITH US.
YOU'D BETTER BUY A CLUE.
STTTT-WHCK
KRA-POW
DON'T KILL HER!
KILL 'ER? I DON'T EVEN SEE 'ER...
CAREFUL! CAREFUL!
I KNOW HOW SHE THINKS. ANY SECOND NOW SHE'S GONNA--

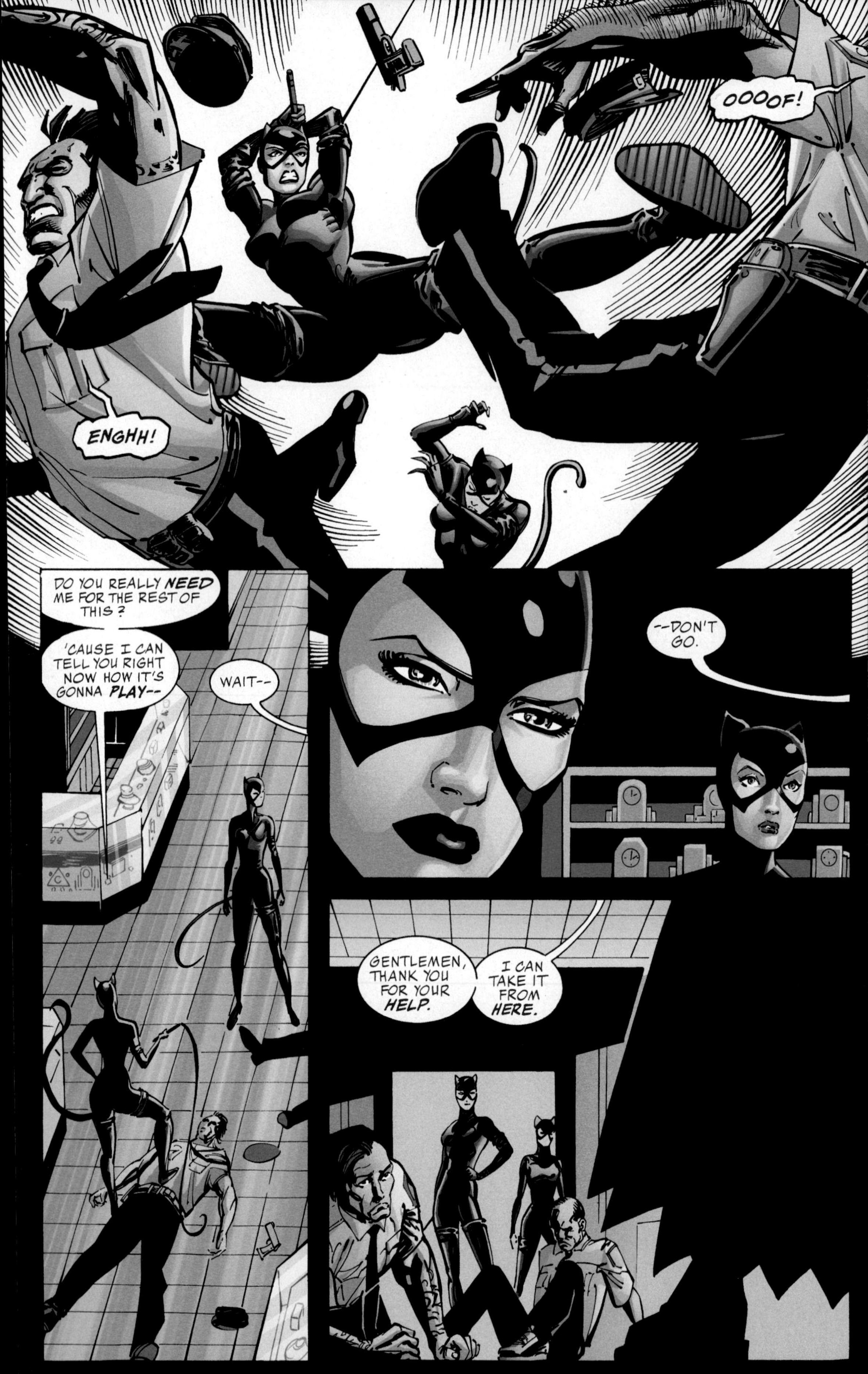
OOOOF!
ENGHH!
DO YOU REALLY NEED ME FOR THE REST OF THIS?
'CAUSE I CAN TELL YOU RIGHT NOW HOW IT'S GONNA PLAY--
WAIT--
--DON'T GO.
GENTLEMEN, THANK YOU FOR YOUR HELP.
I CAN TAKE IT FROM HERE.

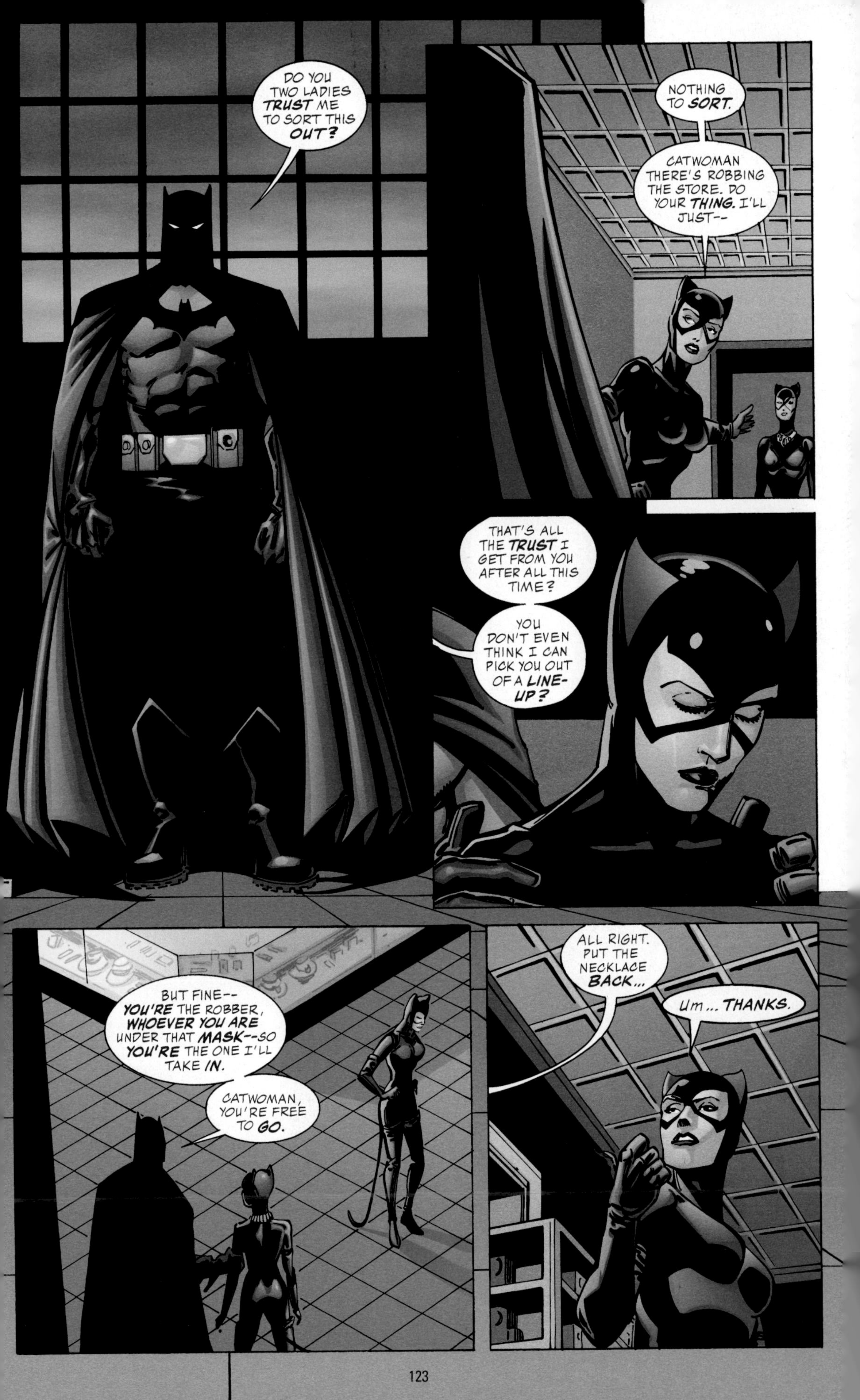
DO YOU TWO LADIES **TRUST** ME TO SORT THIS **OUT?**
NOTHING TO **SORT.**
CATWOMAN THERE'S ROBBING THE STORE. DO YOUR **THING.** I'LL JUST--
THAT'S ALL THE **TRUST** I GET FROM YOU AFTER ALL THIS TIME?
YOU DON'T EVEN THINK I CAN PICK YOU OUT OF A **LINE-UP?**
BUT FINE-- **YOU'RE** THE ROBBER, **WHOEVER YOU ARE** UNDER THAT **MASK**--SO **YOU'RE** THE ONE I'LL TAKE **IN.**
CATWOMAN, YOU'RE FREE TO **GO.**
ALL RIGHT. PUT THE NECKLACE **BACK...**
Um... **THANKS.**

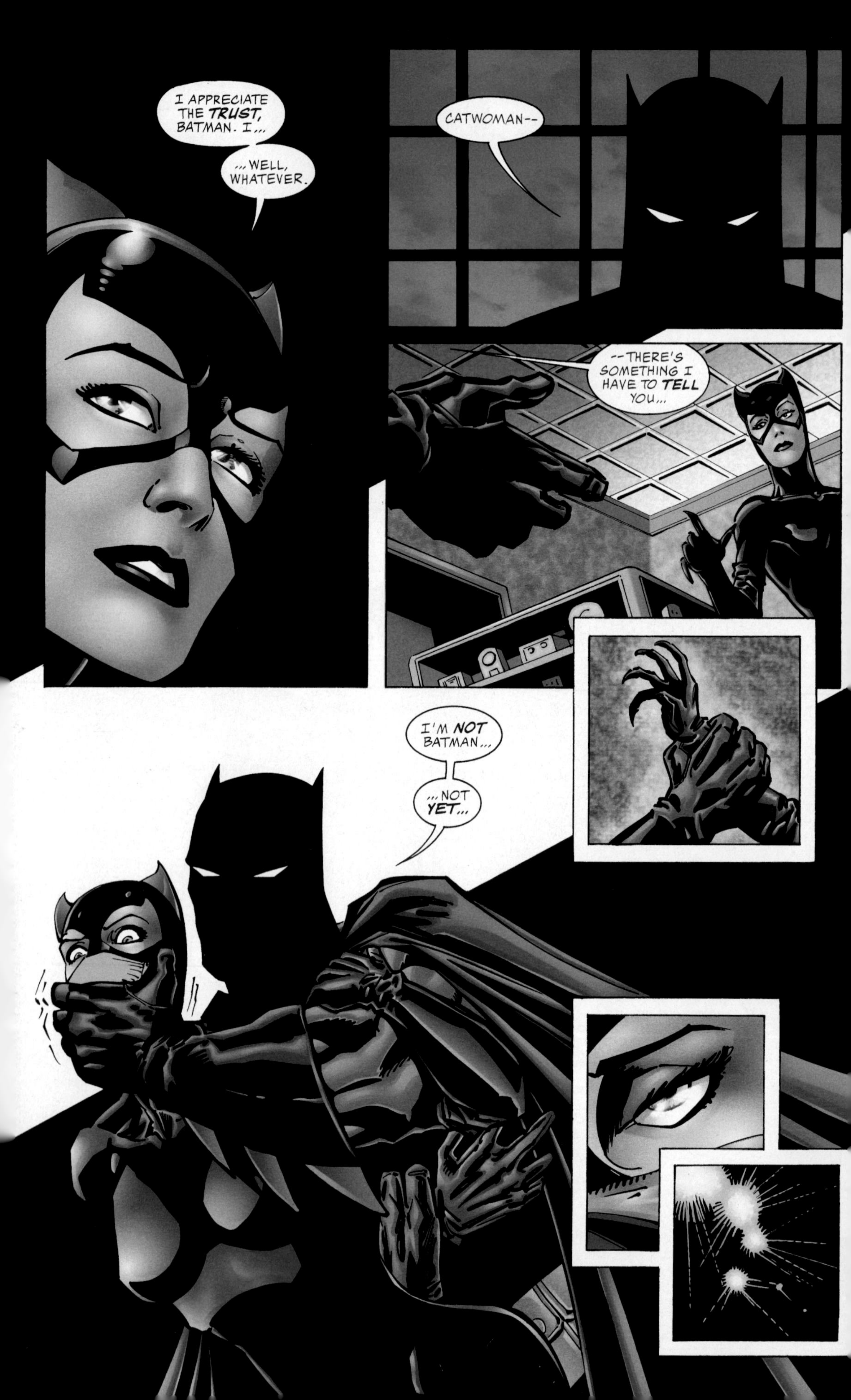
I APPRECIATE THE TRUST, BATMAN. I...
...WELL, WHATEVER.
CATWOMAN--
--THERE'S SOMETHING I HAVE TO TELL YOU...
I'M NOT BATMAN...
...NOT YET...

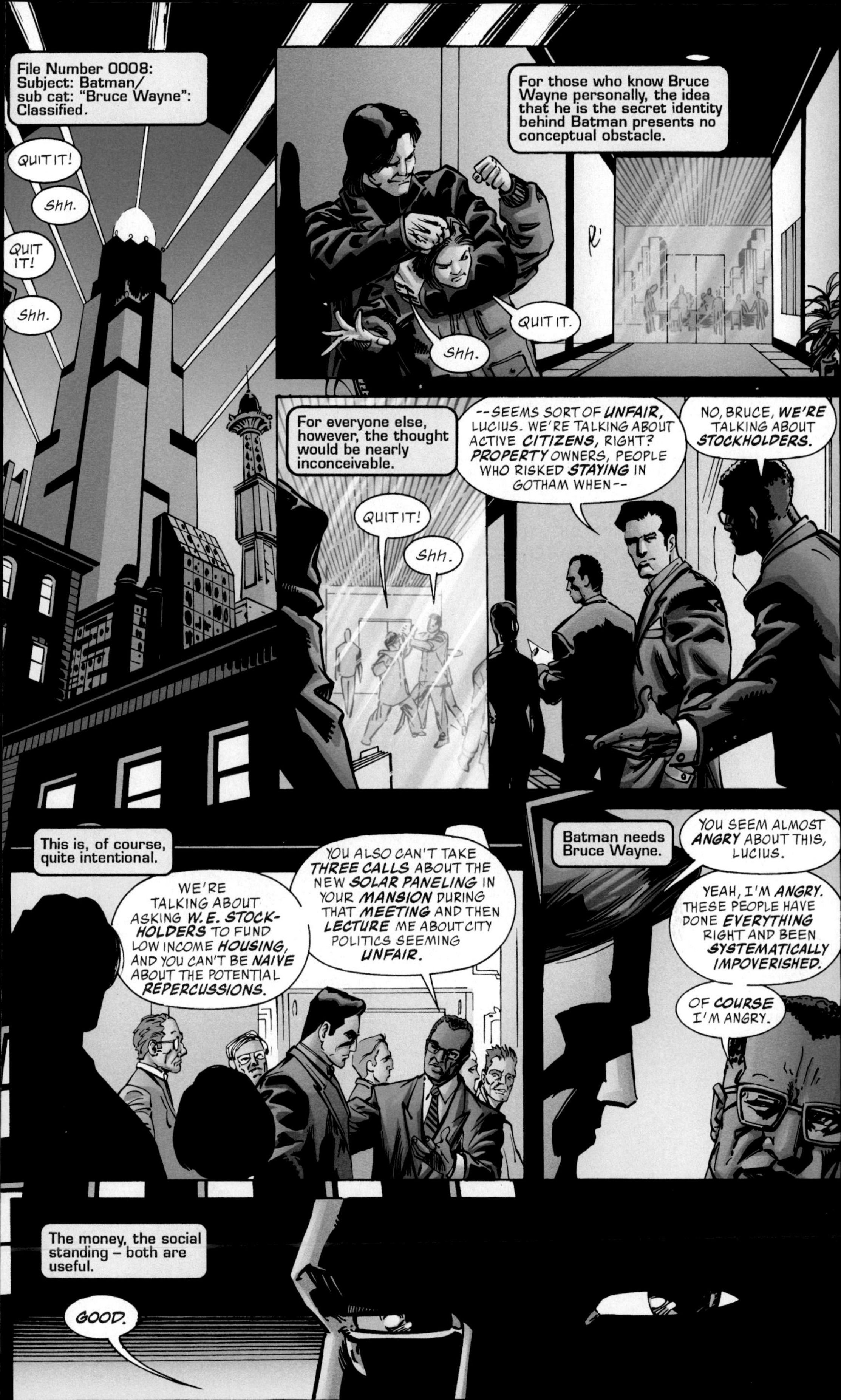

File Number 0008:
Subject: Batman/
sub cat: "Bruce Wayne":
Classified.
QUIT IT!
Shh.
QUIT IT!
Shh.
For those who know Bruce Wayne personally, the idea that he is the secret identity behind Batman presents no conceptual obstacle.
QUIT IT.
Shh.
For everyone else, however, the thought would be nearly inconceivable.
--SEEMS SORT OF UNFAIR, LUCIUS. WE'RE TALKING ABOUT ACTIVE CITIZENS, RIGHT? PROPERTY OWNERS, PEOPLE WHO RISKED STAYING IN GOTHAM WHEN--
NO, BRUCE, WE'RE TALKING ABOUT STOCKHOLDERS.
QUIT IT!
Shh.
This is, of course, quite intentional.
WE'RE TALKING ABOUT ASKING W.E. STOCK-HOLDERS TO FUND LOW INCOME HOUSING, AND YOU CAN'T BE NAIVE ABOUT THE POTENTIAL REPERCUSSIONS.
YOU ALSO CAN'T TAKE THREE CALLS ABOUT THE NEW SOLAR PANELING IN YOUR MANSION DURING THAT MEETING AND THEN LECTURE ME ABOUT CITY POLITICS SEEMING UNFAIR.
Batman needs Bruce Wayne.
YOU SEEM ALMOST ANGRY ABOUT THIS, LUCIUS.
YEAH, I'M ANGRY. THESE PEOPLE HAVE DONE EVERYTHING RIGHT AND BEEN SYSTEMATICALLY IMPOVERISHED.
OF COURSE I'M ANGRY.
The money, the social standing – both are useful.
GOOD.

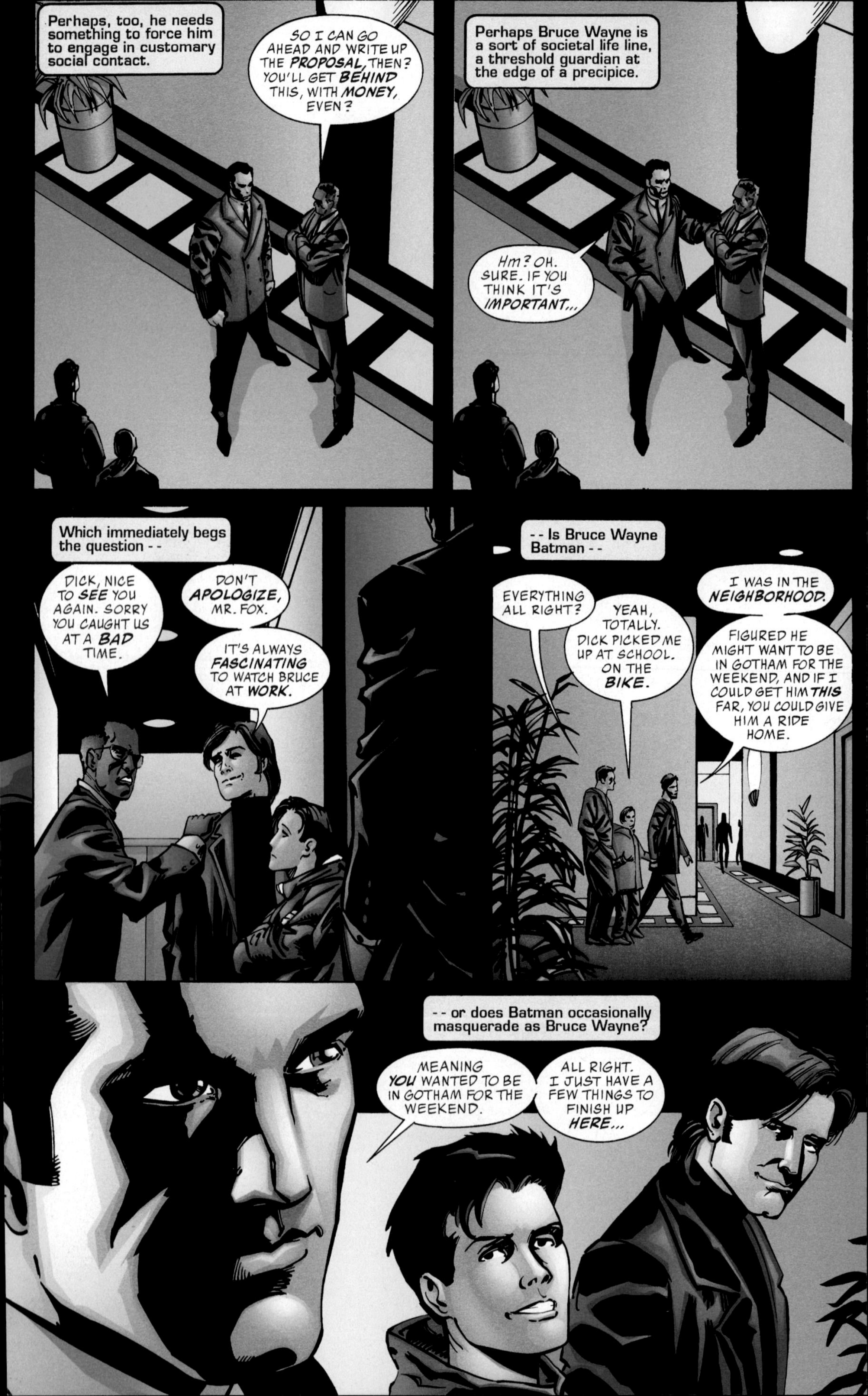
Perhaps, too, he needs something to force him to engage in customary social contact.
SO I CAN GO AHEAD AND WRITE UP THE PROPOSAL, THEN? YOU'LL GET BEHIND THIS, WITH MONEY, EVEN?
Perhaps Bruce Wayne is a sort of societal life line, a threshold guardian at the edge of a precipice.
Hm? OH. SURE. IF YOU THINK IT'S IMPORTANT...
Which immediately begs the question - -
DICK, NICE TO SEE YOU AGAIN. SORRY YOU CAUGHT US AT A BAD TIME.
DON'T APOLOGIZE, MR. FOX.
IT'S ALWAYS FASCINATING TO WATCH BRUCE AT WORK.
- - Is Bruce Wayne Batman - -
EVERYTHING ALL RIGHT?
YEAH, TOTALLY. DICK PICKED ME UP AT SCHOOL. ON THE BIKE.
I WAS IN THE NEIGHBORHOOD.
FIGURED HE MIGHT WANT TO BE IN GOTHAM FOR THE WEEKEND, AND IF I COULD GET HIM THIS FAR, YOU COULD GIVE HIM A RIDE HOME.
- - or does Batman occasionally masquerade as Bruce Wayne?
MEANING YOU WANTED TO BE IN GOTHAM FOR THE WEEKEND.
ALL RIGHT. I JUST HAVE A FEW THINGS TO FINISH UP HERE...

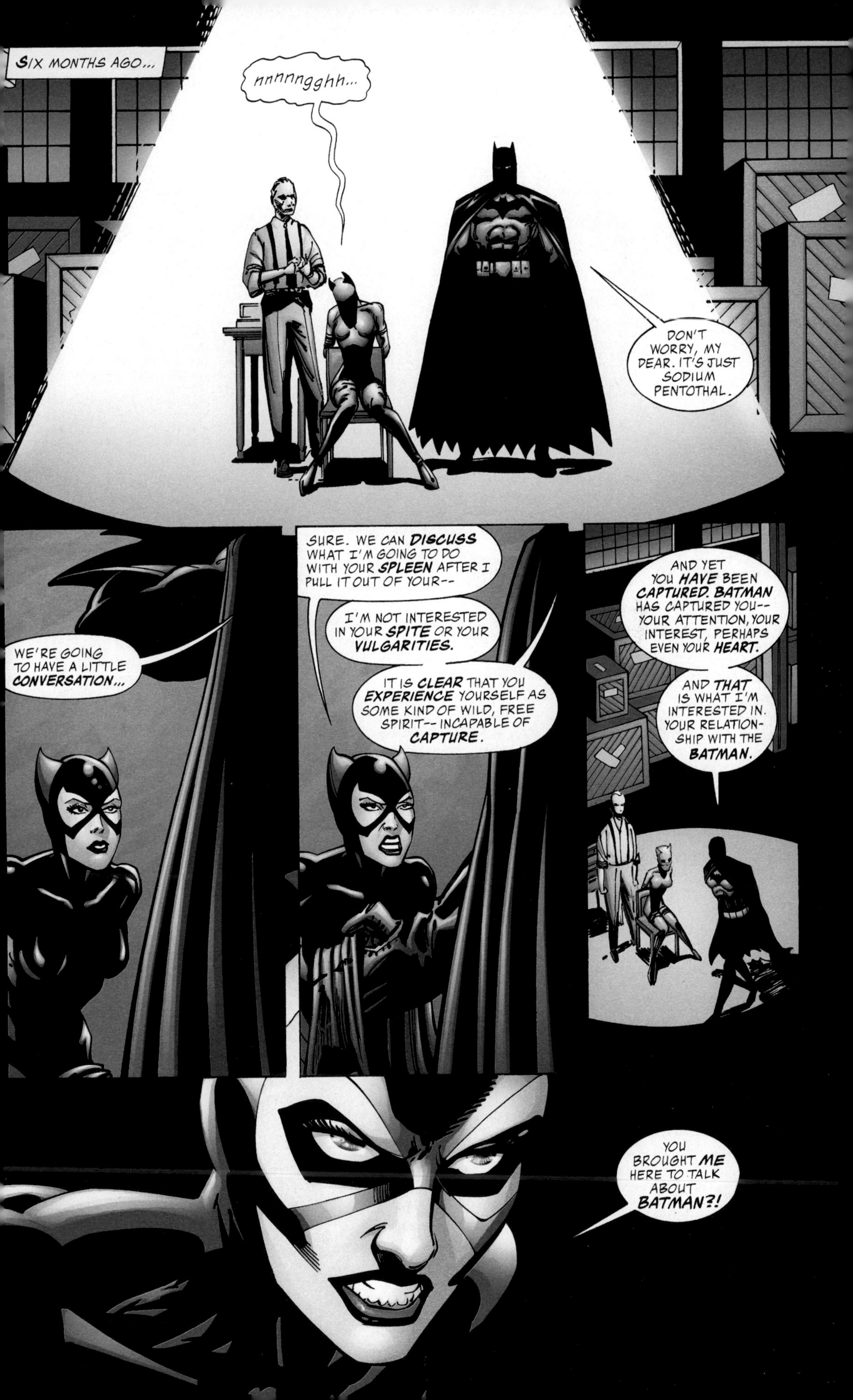
SIX MONTHS AGO...
nnnnngghh...
DON'T WORRY, MY DEAR. IT'S JUST SODIUM PENTOTHAL.
WE'RE GOING TO HAVE A LITTLE CONVERSATION...
SURE. WE CAN DISCUSS WHAT I'M GOING TO DO WITH YOUR SPLEEN AFTER I PULL IT OUT OF YOUR--
I'M NOT INTERESTED IN YOUR SPITE OR YOUR VULGARITIES.
IT IS CLEAR THAT YOU EXPERIENCE YOURSELF AS SOME KIND OF WILD, FREE SPIRIT-- INCAPABLE OF CAPTURE.
AND YET YOU HAVE BEEN CAPTURED. BATMAN HAS CAPTURED YOU-- YOUR ATTENTION, YOUR INTEREST, PERHAPS EVEN YOUR HEART.
AND THAT IS WHAT I'M INTERESTED IN. YOUR RELATIONSHIP WITH THE BATMAN.
YOU BROUGHT ME HERE TO TALK ABOUT BATMAN?!

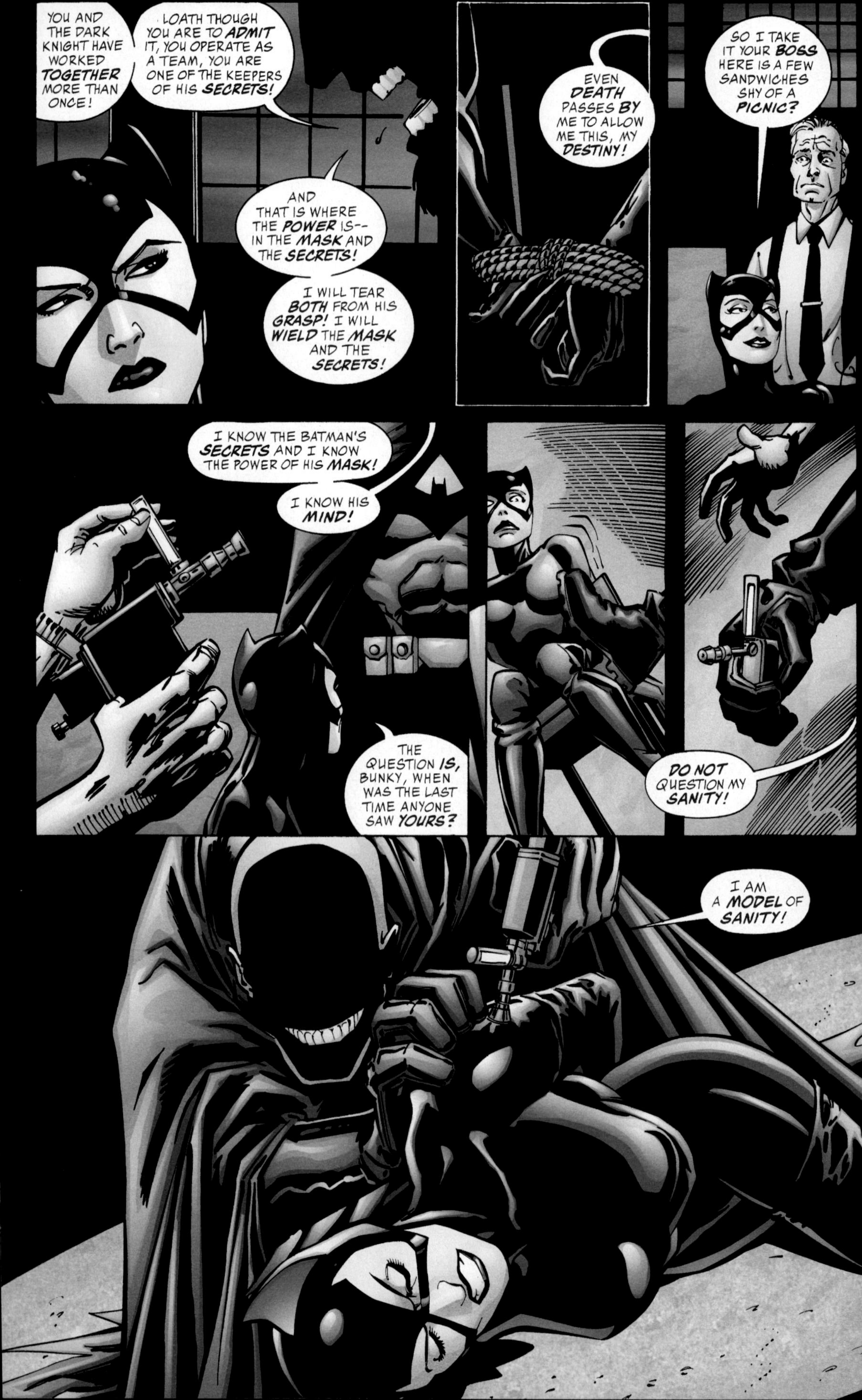
YOU AND THE DARK KNIGHT HAVE WORKED TOGETHER MORE THAN ONCE!
LOATH THOUGH YOU ARE TO ADMIT IT, YOU OPERATE AS A TEAM, YOU ARE ONE OF THE KEEPERS OF HIS SECRETS!
AND THAT IS WHERE THE POWER IS-- IN THE MASK AND THE SECRETS!
I WILL TEAR BOTH FROM HIS GRASP! I WILL WIELD THE MASK AND THE SECRETS!
EVEN DEATH PASSES BY ME TO ALLOW ME THIS, MY DESTINY!
SO I TAKE IT YOUR BOSS HERE IS A FEW SANDWICHES SHY OF A PICNIC?
I KNOW THE BATMAN'S SECRETS AND I KNOW THE POWER OF HIS MASK!
I KNOW HIS MIND!
THE QUESTION IS, BUNKY, WHEN WAS THE LAST TIME ANYONE SAW YOURS?
DO NOT QUESTION MY SANITY!
I AM A MODEL OF SANITY!

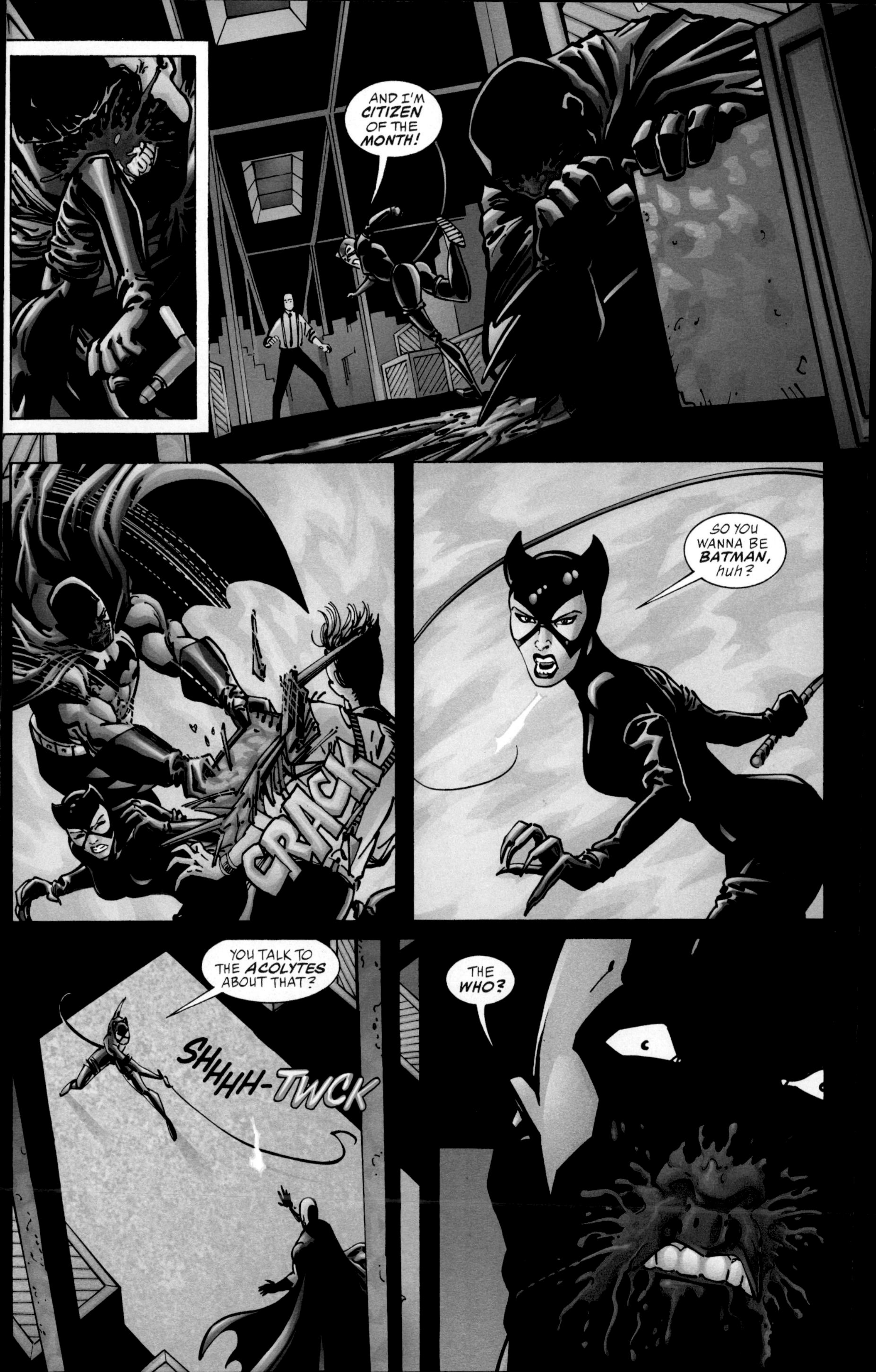
AND I'M CITIZEN OF THE MONTH!
CRACK
SO YOU WANNA BE BATMAN, huh?
YOU TALK TO THE ACOLYTES ABOUT THAT?
SHHHH-TWCK
THE WHO?

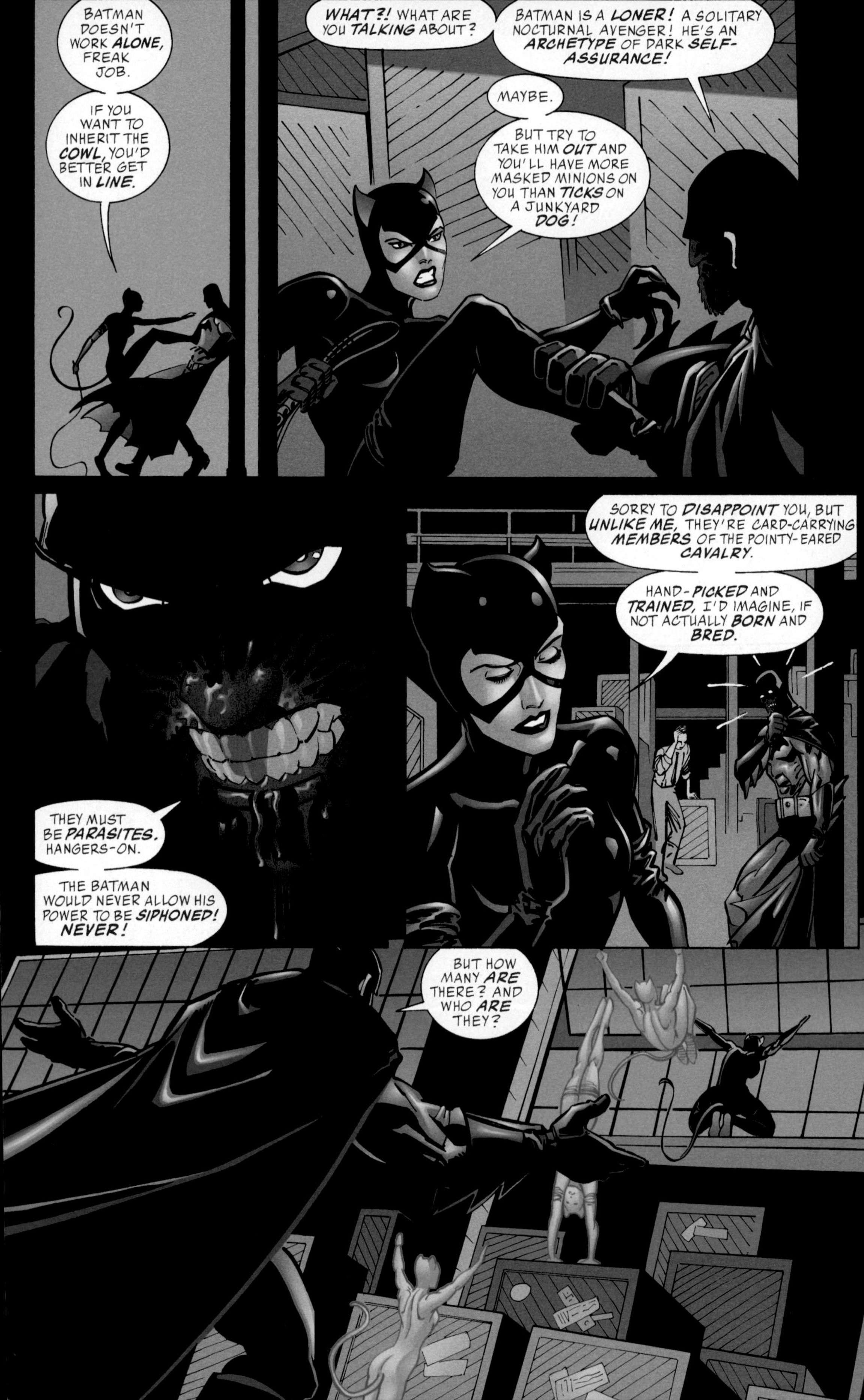
BATMAN DOESN'T WORK ALONE, FREAK JOB.
IF YOU WANT TO INHERIT THE COWL, YOU'D BETTER GET IN LINE.
WHAT?! WHAT ARE YOU TALKING ABOUT?
BATMAN IS A LONER! A SOLITARY NOCTURNAL AVENGER! HE'S AN ARCHETYPE OF DARK SELF-ASSURANCE!
MAYBE.
BUT TRY TO TAKE HIM OUT AND YOU'LL HAVE MORE MASKED MINIONS ON YOU THAN TICKS ON A JUNKYARD DOG!
SORRY TO DISAPPOINT YOU, BUT UNLIKE ME, THEY'RE CARD-CARRYING MEMBERS OF THE POINTY-EARED CAVALRY.
HAND-PICKED AND TRAINED, I'D IMAGINE, IF NOT ACTUALLY BORN AND BRED.
THEY MUST BE PARASITES. HANGERS-ON.
THE BATMAN WOULD NEVER ALLOW HIS POWER TO BE SIPHONED! NEVER!
BUT HOW MANY ARE THERE? AND WHO ARE THEY?

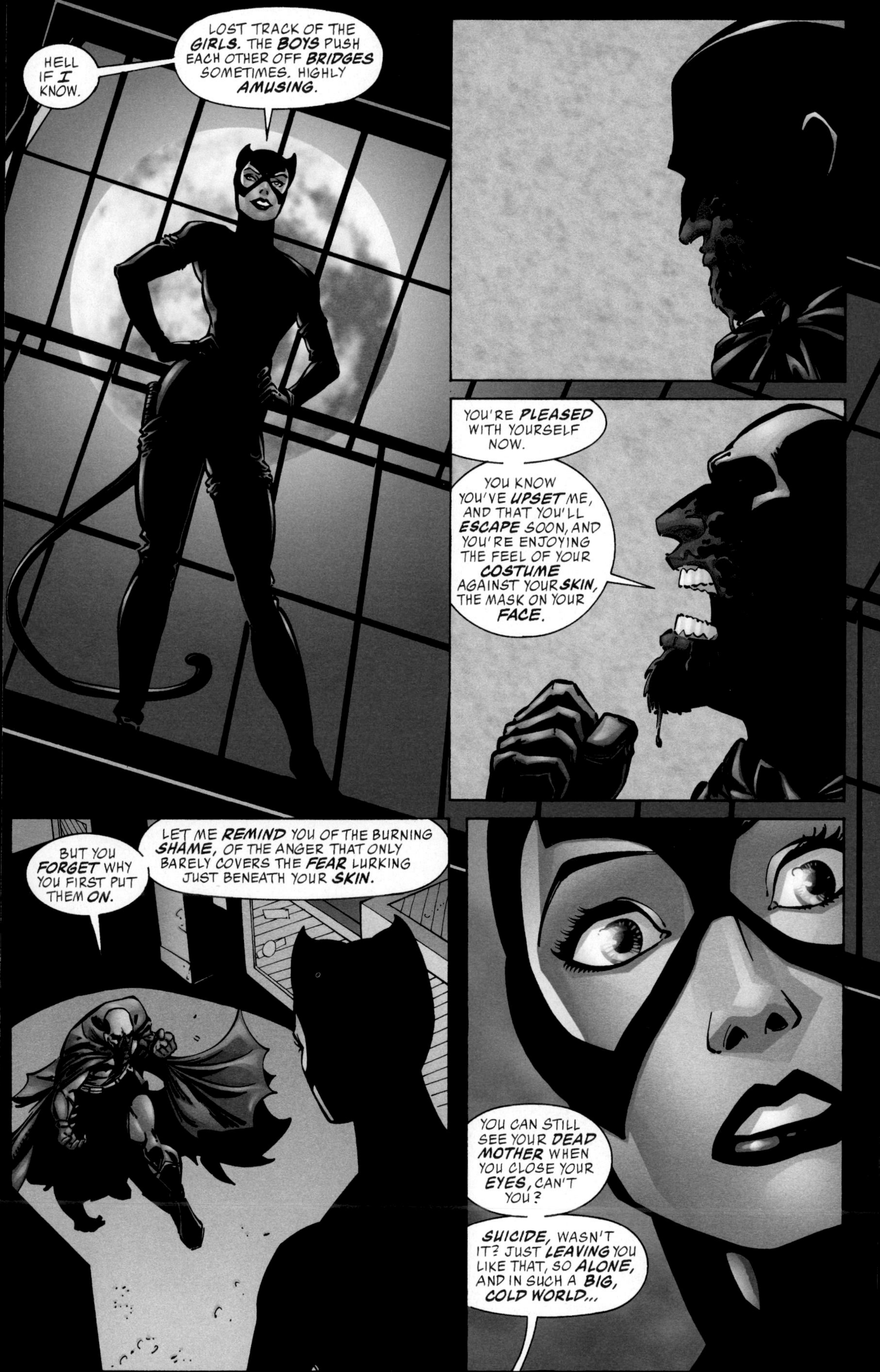
HELL IF I KNOW.
LOST TRACK OF THE GIRLS. THE BOYS PUSH EACH OTHER OFF BRIDGES SOMETIMES. HIGHLY AMUSING.
YOU'RE PLEASED WITH YOURSELF NOW.
YOU KNOW YOU'VE UPSET ME, AND THAT YOU'LL ESCAPE SOON, AND YOU'RE ENJOYING THE FEEL OF YOUR COSTUME AGAINST YOUR SKIN, THE MASK ON YOUR FACE.
BUT YOU FORGET WHY YOU FIRST PUT THEM ON.
LET ME REMIND YOU OF THE BURNING SHAME, OF THE ANGER THAT ONLY BARELY COVERS THE FEAR LURKING JUST BENEATH YOUR SKIN.
YOU CAN STILL SEE YOUR DEAD MOTHER WHEN YOU CLOSE YOUR EYES, CAN'T YOU?
SUICIDE, WASN'T IT? JUST LEAVING YOU LIKE THAT, SO ALONE, AND IN SUCH A BIG, COLD WORLD...

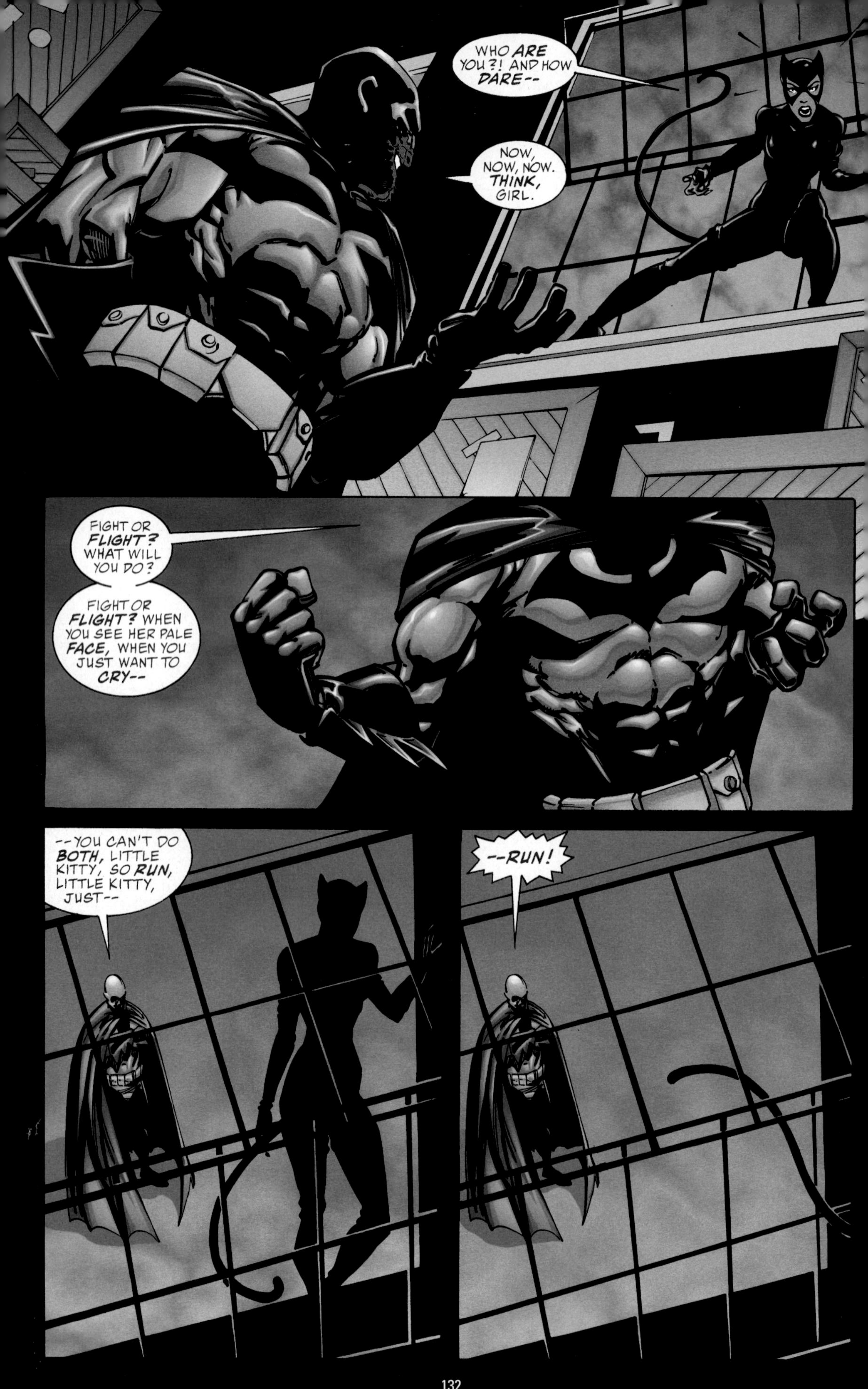
WHO ARE YOU?! AND HOW DARE--
NOW, NOW, NOW. THINK, GIRL.
FIGHT OR FLIGHT? WHAT WILL YOU DO?
FIGHT OR FLIGHT? WHEN YOU SEE HER PALE FACE, WHEN YOU JUST WANT TO CRY--
--YOU CAN'T DO BOTH, LITTLE KITTY, SO RUN, LITTLE KITTY, JUST--
--RUN!

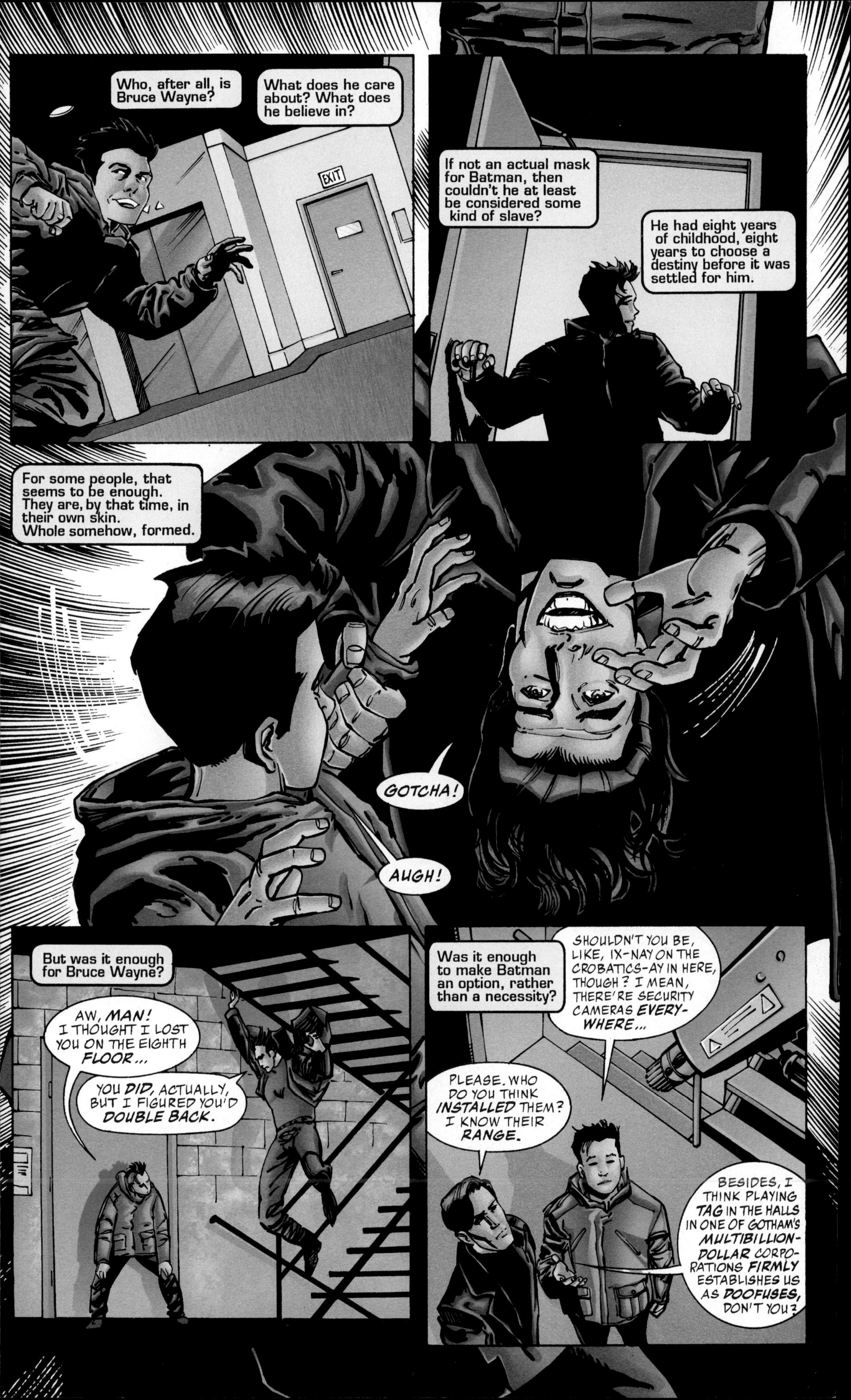

Who, after all, is Bruce Wayne?
What does he care about? What does he believe in?
EXIT
If not an actual mask for Batman, then couldn't he at least be considered some kind of slave?
He had eight years of childhood, eight years to choose a destiny before it was settled for him.
For some people, that seems to be enough. They are, by that time, in their own skin. Whole somehow, formed.
GOTCHA!
AUGH!
But was it enough for Bruce Wayne?
AW, MAN! I THOUGHT I LOST YOU ON THE EIGHTH FLOOR...
YOU DID, ACTUALLY, BUT I FIGURED YOU'D DOUBLE BACK.
Was it enough to make Batman an option, rather than a necessity?
SHOULDN'T YOU BE, LIKE, IX-NAY ON THE CROBATICS-AY IN HERE, THOUGH? I MEAN, THERE'RE SECURITY CAMERAS EVERY-WHERE...
PLEASE. WHO DO YOU THINK INSTALLED THEM? I KNOW THEIR RANGE.
BESIDES, I THINK PLAYING TAG IN THE HALLS IN ONE OF GOTHAM'S MULTIBILLION-DOLLAR CORPO-RATIONS FIRMLY ESTABLISHES US AS DOOFUSES, DON'T YOU?

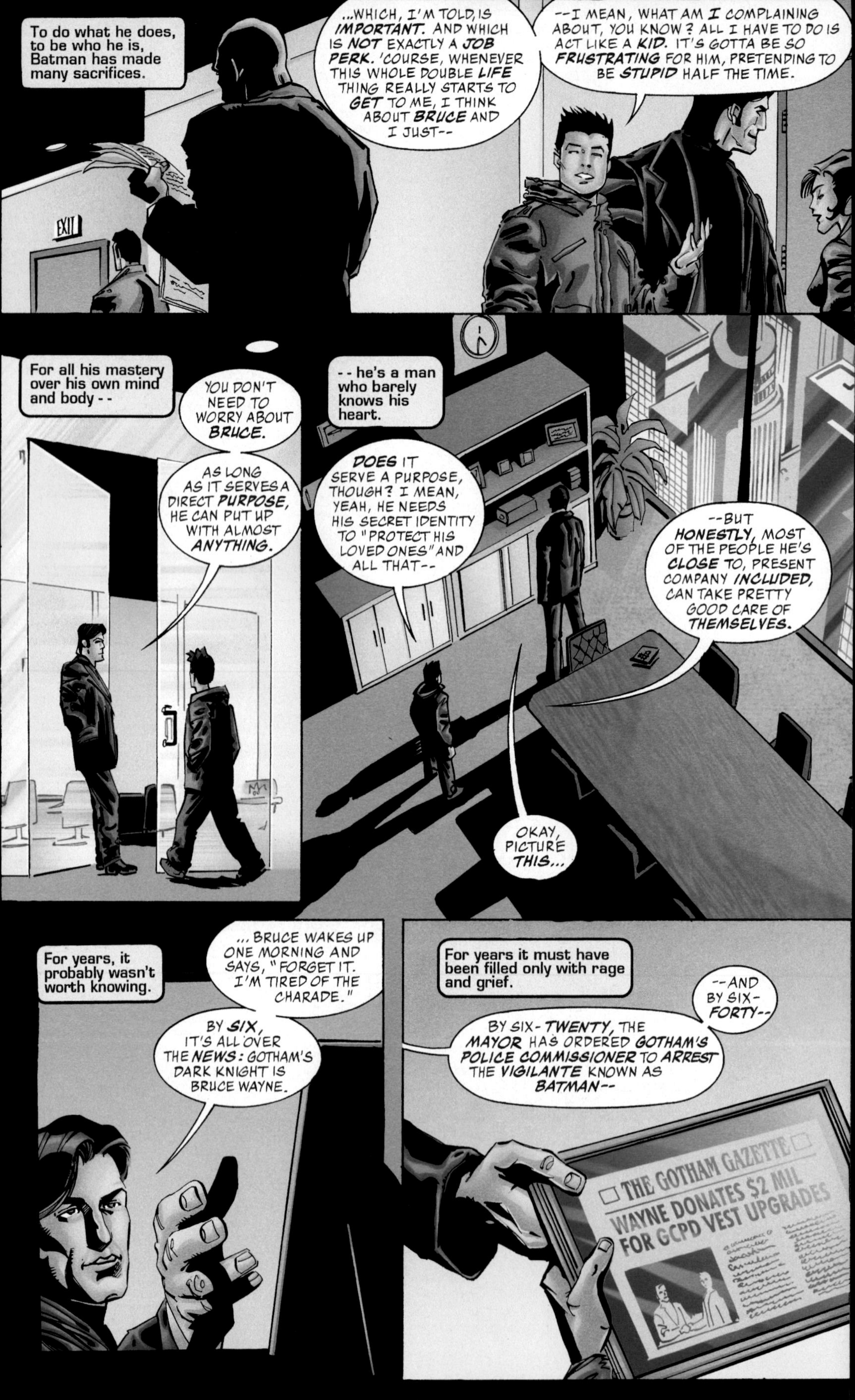
To do what he does, to be who he is, Batman has made many sacrifices.
...WHICH, I'M TOLD, IS IMPORTANT. AND WHICH IS NOT EXACTLY A JOB PERK. 'COURSE, WHENEVER THIS WHOLE DOUBLE LIFE THING REALLY STARTS TO GET TO ME, I THINK ABOUT BRUCE AND I JUST--
--I MEAN, WHAT AM I COMPLAINING ABOUT, YOU KNOW? ALL I HAVE TO DO IS ACT LIKE A KID. IT'S GOTTA BE SO FRUSTRATING FOR HIM, PRETENDING TO BE STUPID HALF THE TIME.
EXIT
For all his mastery over his own mind and body --
YOU DON'T NEED TO WORRY ABOUT BRUCE.
AS LONG AS IT SERVES A DIRECT PURPOSE, HE CAN PUT UP WITH ALMOST ANYTHING.
-- he's a man who barely knows his heart.
DOES IT SERVE A PURPOSE, THOUGH? I MEAN, YEAH, HE NEEDS HIS SECRET IDENTITY TO "PROTECT HIS LOVED ONES" AND ALL THAT--
--BUT HONESTLY, MOST OF THE PEOPLE HE'S CLOSE TO, PRESENT COMPANY INCLUDED, CAN TAKE PRETTY GOOD CARE OF THEMSELVES.
OKAY, PICTURE THIS...
For years, it probably wasn't worth knowing.
...BRUCE WAKES UP ONE MORNING AND SAYS, "FORGET IT. I'M TIRED OF THE CHARADE."
BY SIX, IT'S ALL OVER THE NEWS: GOTHAM'S DARK KNIGHT IS BRUCE WAYNE.
For years it must have been filled only with rage and grief.
BY SIX-TWENTY, THE MAYOR HAS ORDERED GOTHAM'S POLICE COMMISSIONER TO ARREST THE VIGILANTE KNOWN AS BATMAN--
--AND BY SIX-FORTY--
THE GOTHAM GAZETTE
WAYNE DONATES $2 MIL FOR GCPD VEST UPGRADES

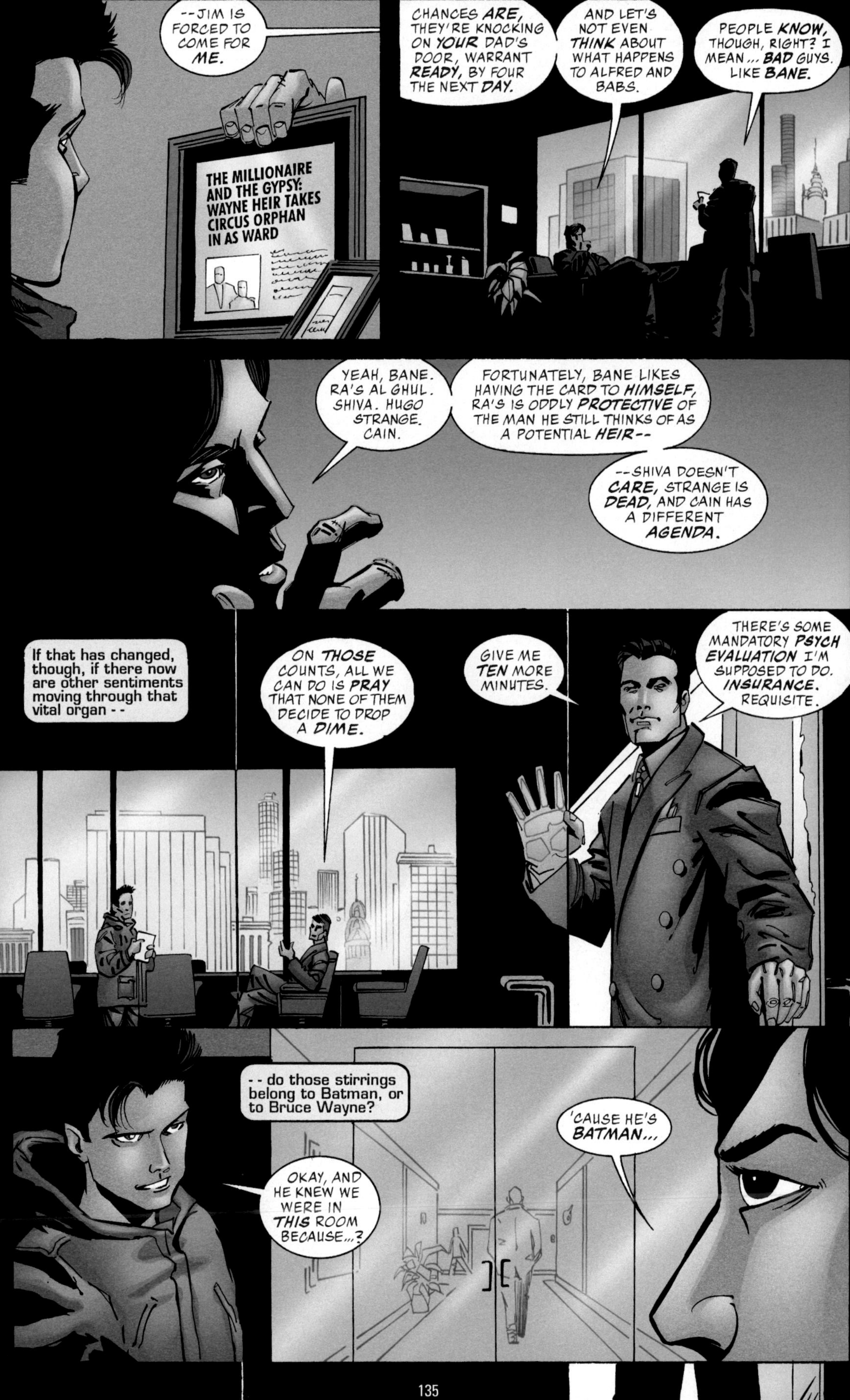
--JIM IS FORCED TO COME FOR ME.
THE MILLIONAIRE AND THE GYPSY: WAYNE HEIR TAKES CIRCUS ORPHAN IN AS WARD
CHANCES ARE, THEY'RE KNOCKING ON YOUR DAD'S DOOR, WARRANT READY, BY FOUR THE NEXT DAY.
AND LET'S NOT EVEN THINK ABOUT WHAT HAPPENS TO ALFRED AND BABS.
PEOPLE KNOW, THOUGH, RIGHT? I MEAN... BAD GUYS. LIKE BANE.
YEAH, BANE. RA'S AL GHUL. SHIVA. HUGO STRANGE. CAIN.
FORTUNATELY, BANE LIKES HAVING THE CARD TO HIMSELF, RA'S IS ODDLY PROTECTIVE OF THE MAN HE STILL THINKS OF AS A POTENTIAL HEIR--
--SHIVA DOESN'T CARE, STRANGE IS DEAD, AND CAIN HAS A DIFFERENT AGENDA.
If that has changed, though, if there now are other sentiments moving through that vital organ --
ON THOSE COUNTS, ALL WE CAN DO IS PRAY THAT NONE OF THEM DECIDE TO DROP A DIME.
GIVE ME TEN MORE MINUTES.
THERE'S SOME MANDATORY PSYCH EVALUATION I'M SUPPOSED TO DO. INSURANCE. REQUISITE.
-- do those stirrings belong to Batman, or to Bruce Wayne?
OKAY, AND HE KNEW WE WERE IN THIS ROOM BECAUSE...?
'CAUSE HE'S BATMAN...

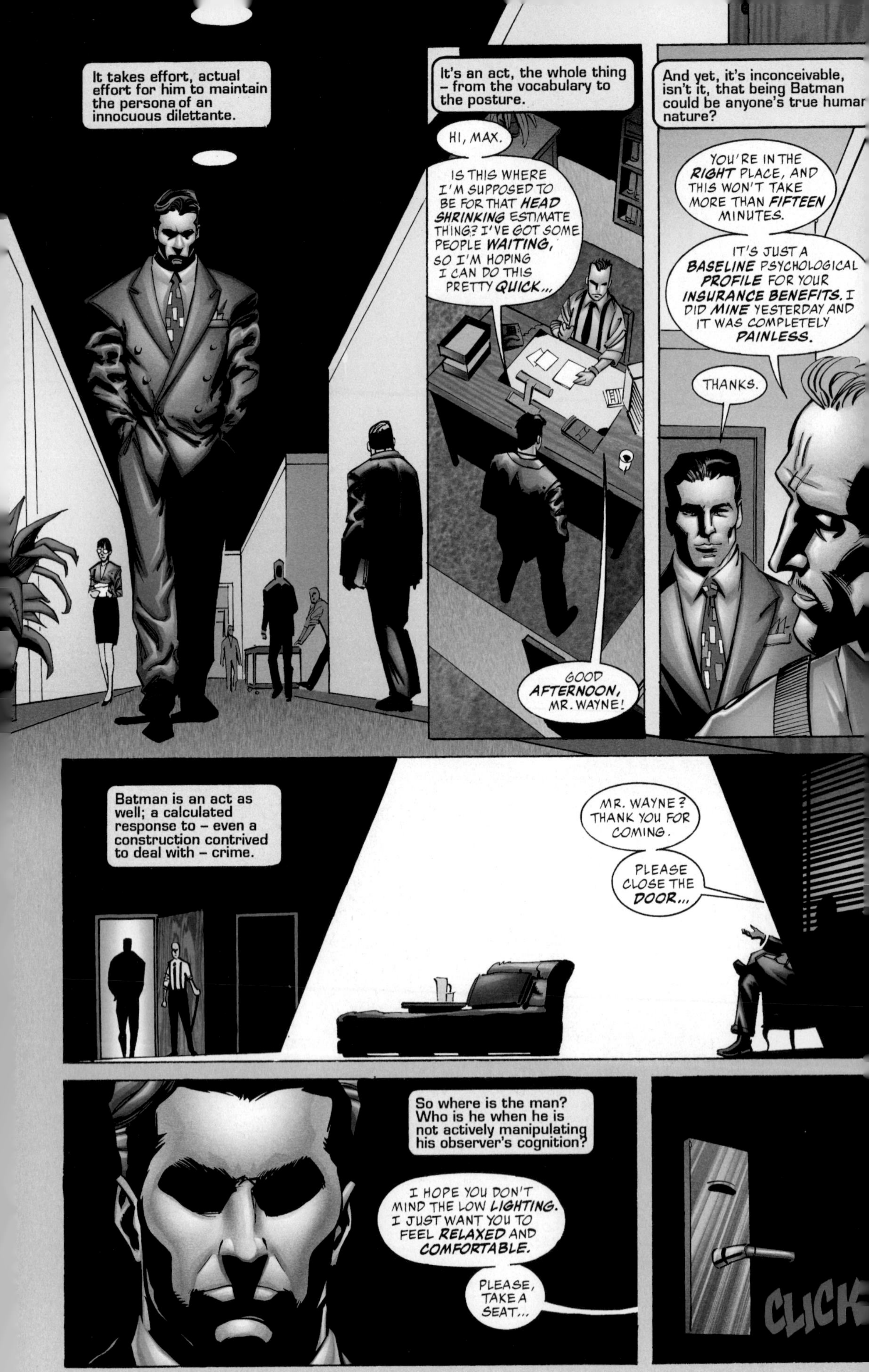

It takes effort, actual effort for him to maintain the persona of an innocuous dilettante.
It's an act, the whole thing – from the vocabulary to the posture.
HI, MAX.
IS THIS WHERE I'M SUPPOSED TO BE FOR THAT HEAD SHRINKING ESTIMATE THING? I'VE GOT SOME PEOPLE WAITING, SO I'M HOPING I CAN DO THIS PRETTY QUICK...
GOOD AFTERNOON, MR. WAYNE!
And yet, it's inconceivable, isn't it, that being Batman could be anyone's true human nature?
YOU'RE IN THE RIGHT PLACE, AND THIS WON'T TAKE MORE THAN FIFTEEN MINUTES.
IT'S JUST A BASELINE PSYCHOLOGICAL PROFILE FOR YOUR INSURANCE BENEFITS. I DID MINE YESTERDAY AND IT WAS COMPLETELY PAINLESS.
THANKS.
Batman is an act as well; a calculated response to – even a construction contrived to deal with – crime.
MR. WAYNE? THANK YOU FOR COMING.
PLEASE CLOSE THE DOOR...
So where is the man? Who is he when he is not actively manipulating his observer's cognition?
I HOPE YOU DON'T MIND THE LOW LIGHTING. I JUST WANT YOU TO FEEL RELAXED AND COMFORTABLE.
PLEASE, TAKE A SEAT...
CLICK

What does it mean about him if he himself does not know?

I'M GOING TO ASK YOU A SERIES OF QUESTIONS DESIGNED TO HELP EVALUATE YOUR *STRESS* LEVEL, MR. WAYNE, AND I WANT YOU TO ANSWER AS HONESTLY AS YOU *CAN*.

NONE OF THIS WILL AFFECT YOUR CURRENT *INSURANCE PLAN*, WE'RE JUST INTERESTED IN *MONITORING* AND *ASSUAGING* CORPORATE *TENSION*, ALL RIGHT?

MM-HMM.

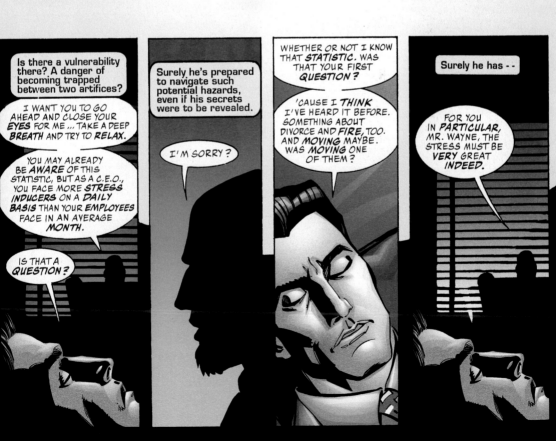

Is there a vulnerability there? A danger of becoming trapped between two artifices?

I WANT YOU TO GO AHEAD AND CLOSE YOUR *EYES* FOR ME ... TAKE A DEEP *BREATH* AND TRY TO *RELAX*.

YOU MAY ALREADY BE *AWARE* OF THIS STATISTIC, BUT AS A C.E.O., YOU FACE MORE *STRESS INDUCERS* ON A *DAILY BASIS* THAN YOUR *EMPLOYEES* FACE IN AN AVERAGE *MONTH*.

IS THAT A *QUESTION*?

Surely he's prepared to navigate such potential hazards, even if his secrets were to be revealed.

I'M SORRY?

WHETHER OR NOT I KNOW THAT *STATISTIC*. WAS THAT YOUR FIRST *QUESTION*?

'CAUSE I *THINK* I'VE HEARD IT BEFORE. SOMETHING ABOUT DIVORCE AND *FIRE*, TOO. AND *MOVING* MAYBE. WAS *MOVING* ONE OF THEM?

Surely he has --

FOR YOU IN *PARTICULAR*, MR. WAYNE, THE STRESS MUST BE *VERY GREAT INDEED*.

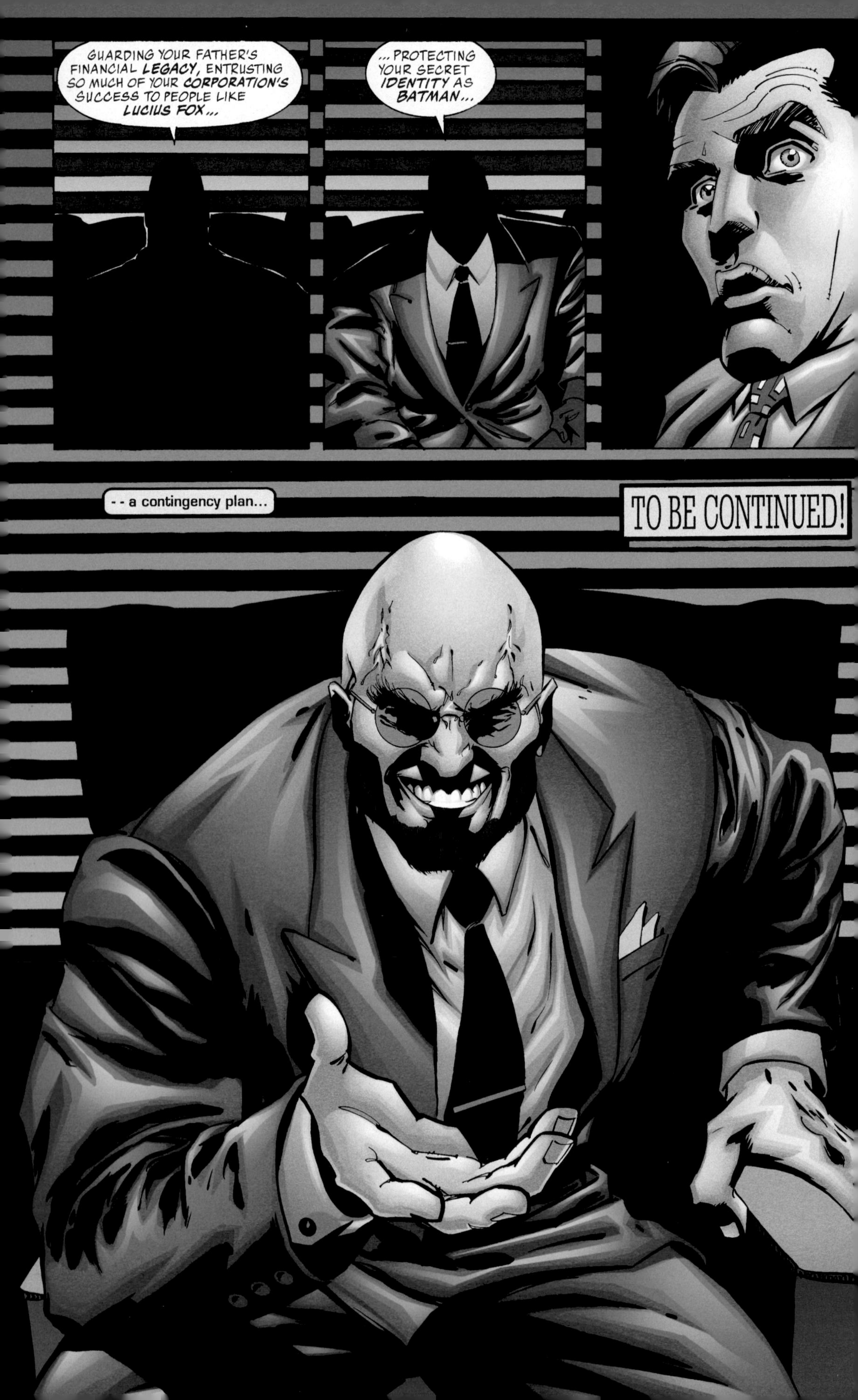
GUARDING YOUR FATHER'S FINANCIAL LEGACY, ENTRUSTING SO MUCH OF YOUR CORPORATION'S SUCCESS TO PEOPLE LIKE LUCIUS FOX...
...PROTECTING YOUR SECRET IDENTITY AS BATMAN...
--a contingency plan...
TO BE CONTINUED!

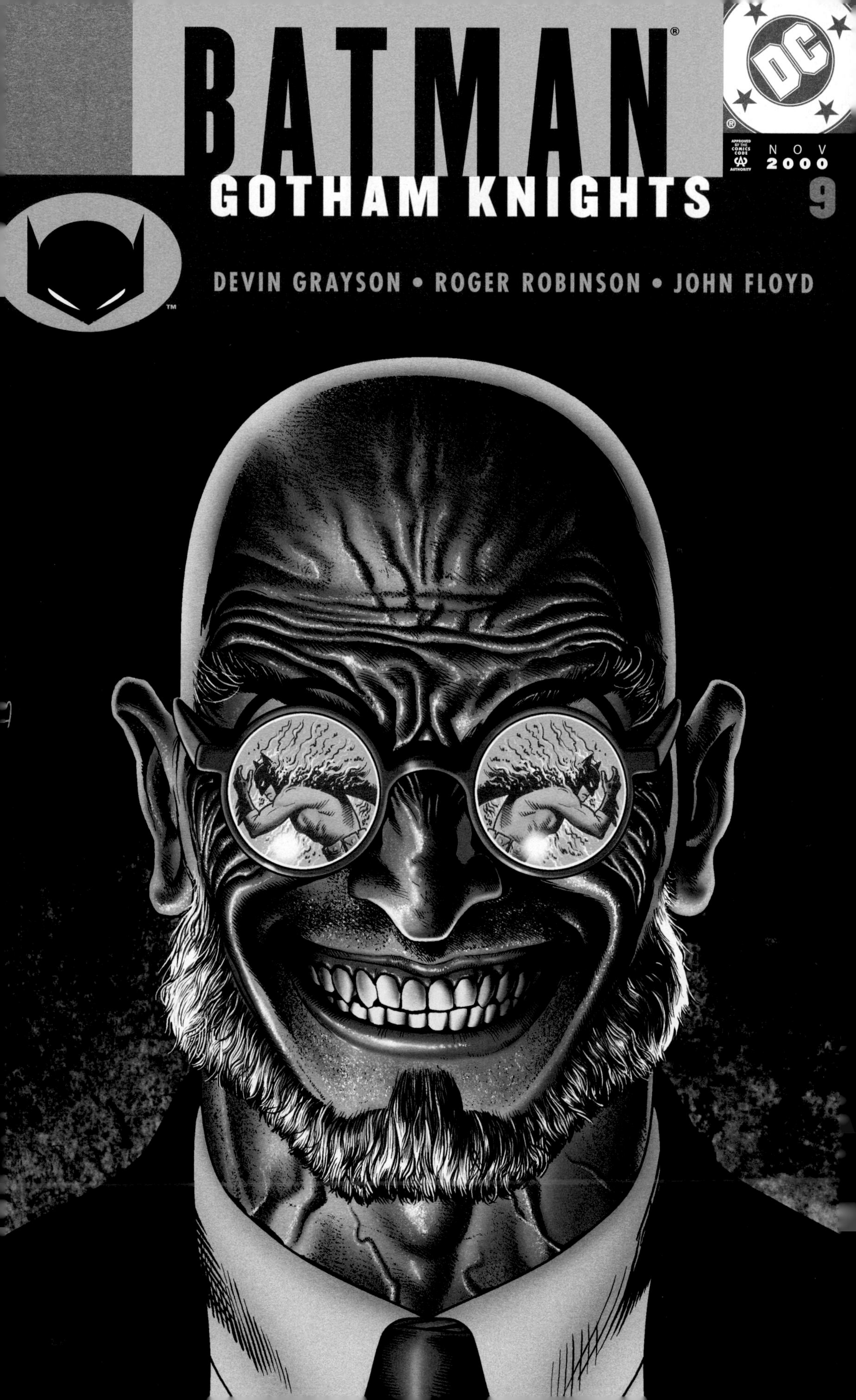
BATMAN®
GOTHAM KNIGHTS
DC
APPROVED BY THE COMICS CODE AUTHORITY
NOV 2000
9
DEVIN GRAYSON • ROGER ROBINSON • JOHN FLOYD

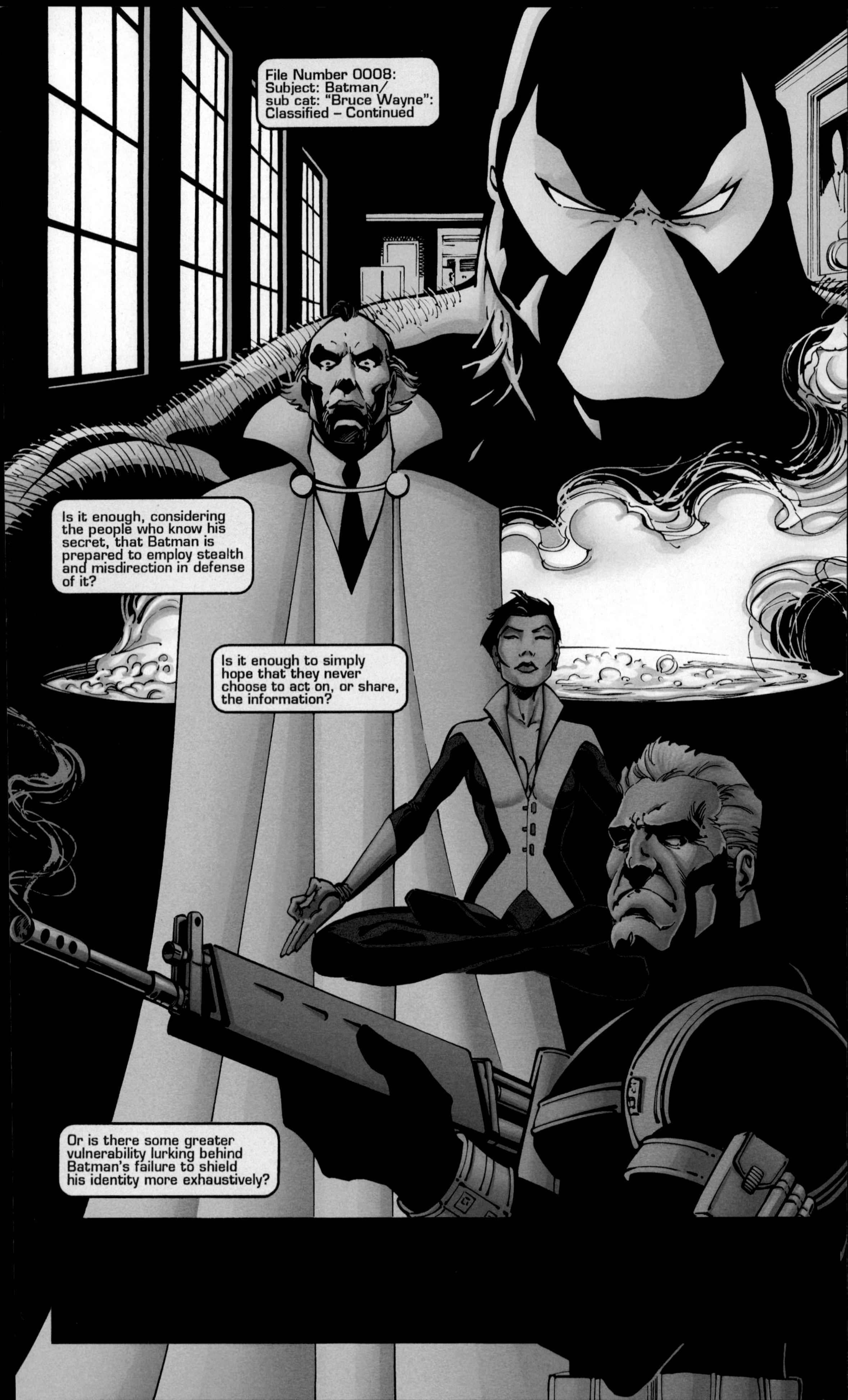
File Number 0008:
Subject: Batman/
sub cat: "Bruce Wayne":
Classified – Continued
Is it enough, considering the people who know his secret, that Batman is prepared to employ stealth and misdirection in defense of it?
Is it enough to simply hope that they never choose to act on, or share, the information?
Or is there some greater vulnerability lurking behind Batman's failure to shield his identity more exhaustively?

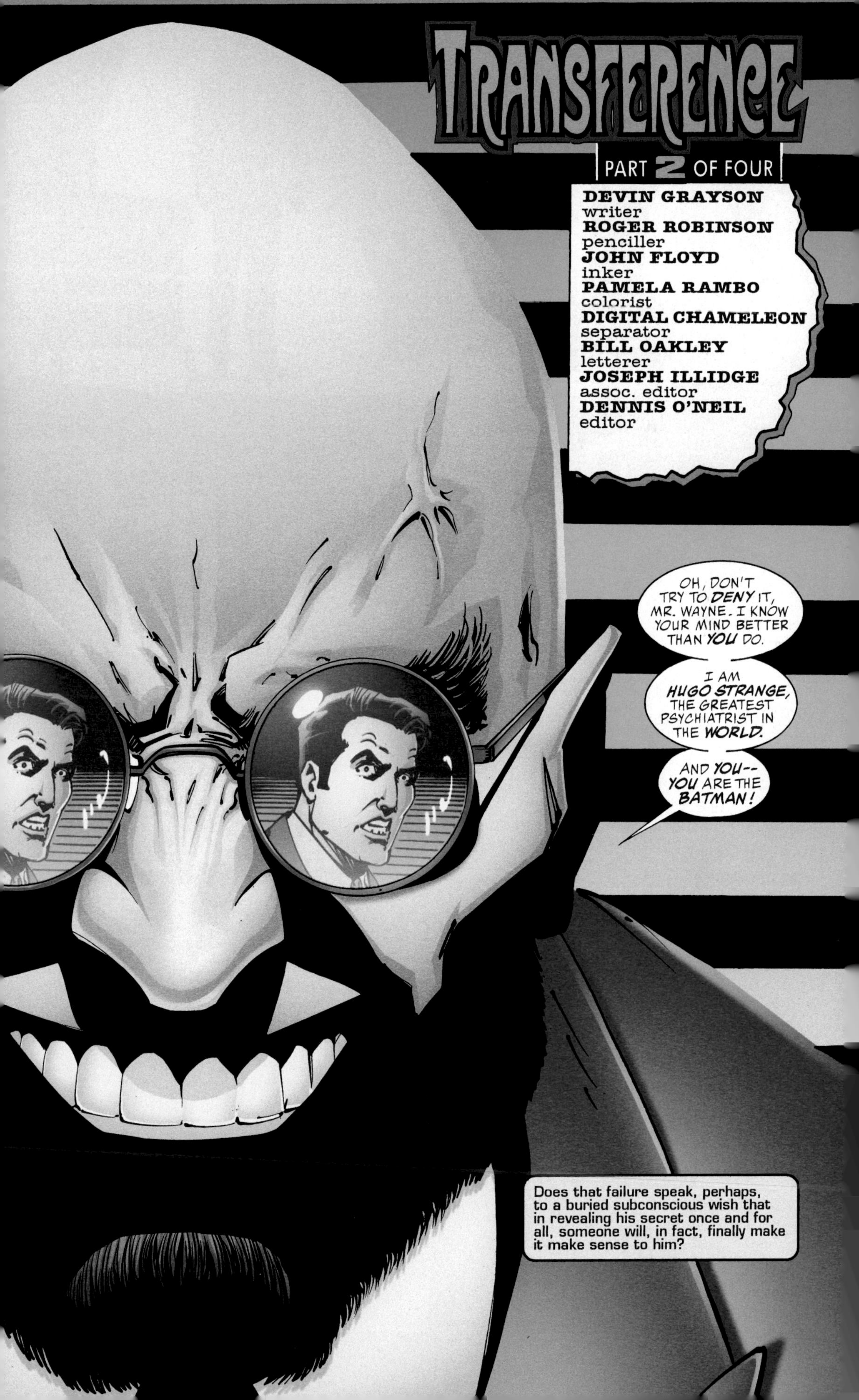

TRANSFERENCE
PART 2 OF FOUR
DEVIN GRAYSON writer
ROGER ROBINSON penciller
JOHN FLOYD inker
PAMELA RAMBO colorist
DIGITAL CHAMELEON separator
BILL OAKLEY letterer
JOSEPH ILLIDGE assoc. editor
DENNIS O'NEIL editor
OH, DON'T TRY TO DENY IT, MR. WAYNE. I KNOW YOUR MIND BETTER THAN YOU DO.
I AM HUGO STRANGE, THE GREATEST PSYCHIATRIST IN THE WORLD.
AND YOU-- YOU ARE THE BATMAN!
Does that failure speak, perhaps, to a buried subconscious wish that in revealing his secret once and for all, someone will, in fact, finally make it make sense to him?

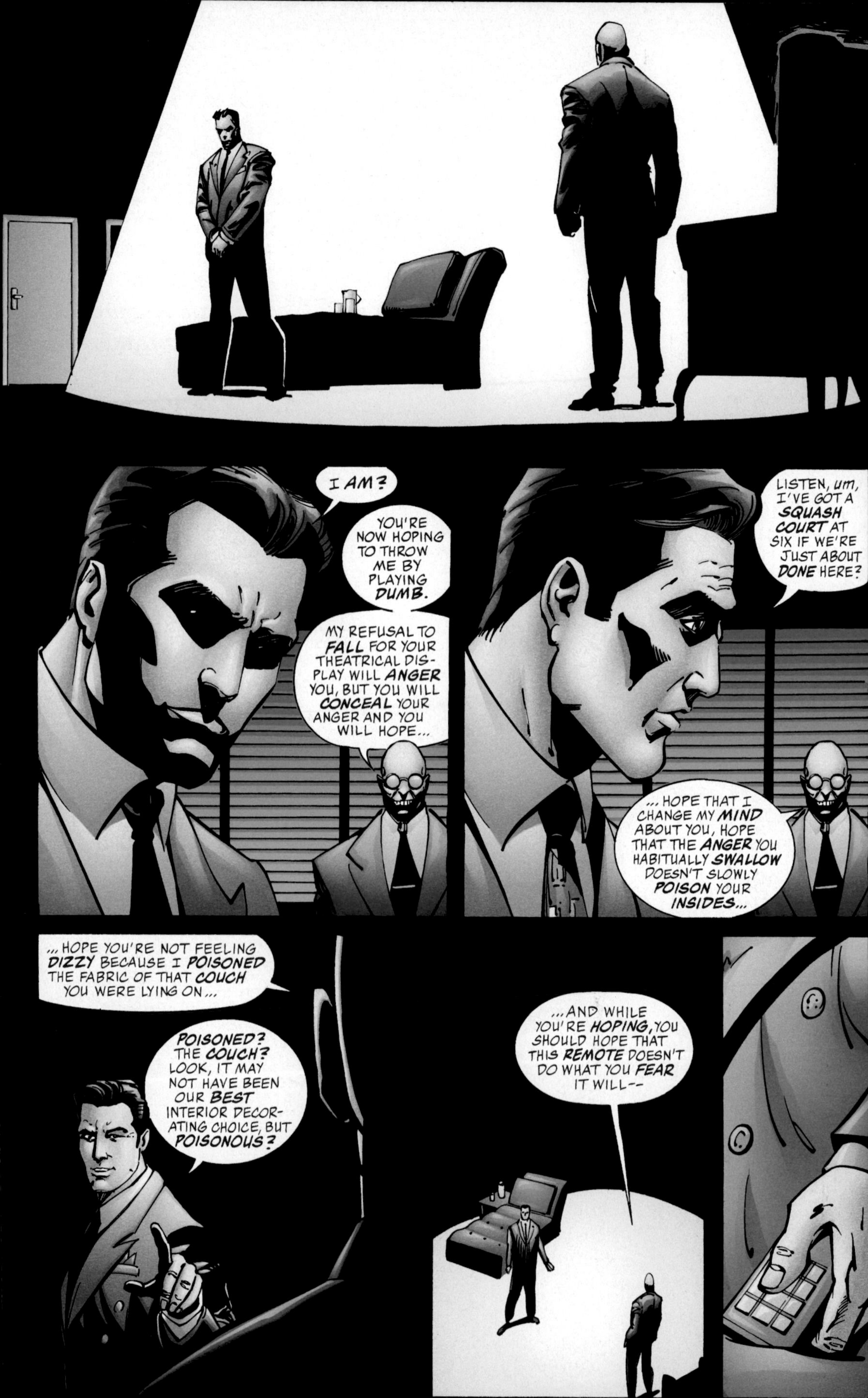
I AM?
YOU'RE NOW HOPING TO THROW ME BY PLAYING DUMB.
MY REFUSAL TO FALL FOR YOUR THEATRICAL DISPLAY WILL ANGER YOU, BUT YOU WILL CONCEAL YOUR ANGER AND YOU WILL HOPE...
LISTEN, um, I'VE GOT A SQUASH COURT AT SIX IF WE'RE JUST ABOUT DONE HERE?
...HOPE THAT I CHANGE MY MIND ABOUT YOU, HOPE THAT THE ANGER YOU HABITUALLY SWALLOW DOESN'T SLOWLY POISON YOUR INSIDES...
...HOPE YOU'RE NOT FEELING DIZZY BECAUSE I POISONED THE FABRIC OF THAT COUCH YOU WERE LYING ON...
POISONED? THE COUCH? LOOK, IT MAY NOT HAVE BEEN OUR BEST INTERIOR DECORATING CHOICE, BUT POISONOUS?
...AND WHILE YOU'RE HOPING, YOU SHOULD HOPE THAT THIS REMOTE DOESN'T DO WHAT YOU FEAR IT WILL--

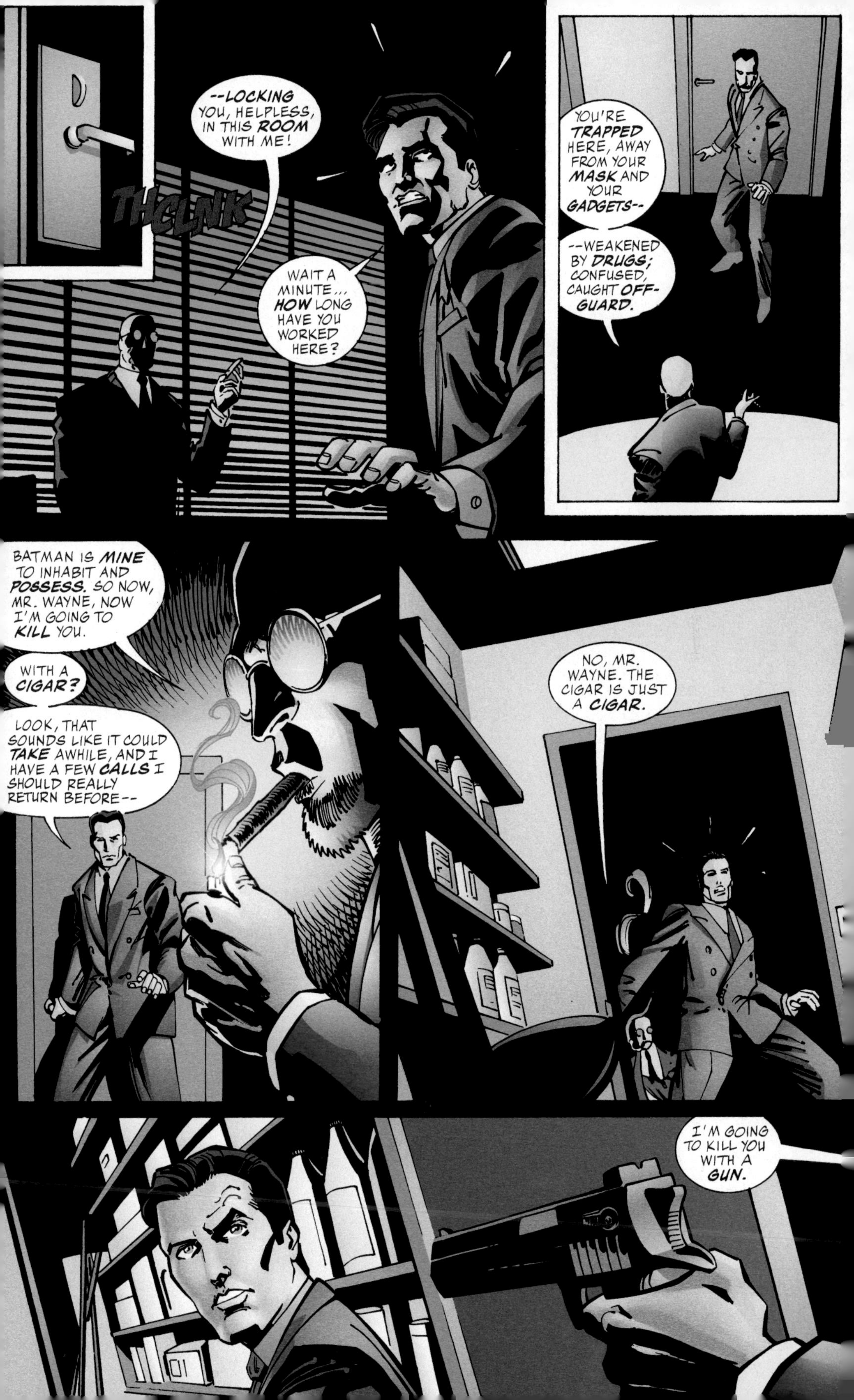
THCLNK
--LOCKING YOU, HELPLESS, IN THIS ROOM WITH ME!
WAIT A MINUTE... HOW LONG HAVE YOU WORKED HERE?
YOU'RE TRAPPED HERE, AWAY FROM YOUR MASK AND YOUR GADGETS--
--WEAKENED BY DRUGS; CONFUSED, CAUGHT OFF-GUARD.
BATMAN IS MINE TO INHABIT AND POSSESS. SO NOW, MR. WAYNE, NOW I'M GOING TO KILL YOU.
WITH A CIGAR?
LOOK, THAT SOUNDS LIKE IT COULD TAKE AWHILE, AND I HAVE A FEW CALLS I SHOULD REALLY RETURN BEFORE--
NO, MR. WAYNE. THE CIGAR IS JUST A CIGAR.
I'M GOING TO KILL YOU WITH A GUN.

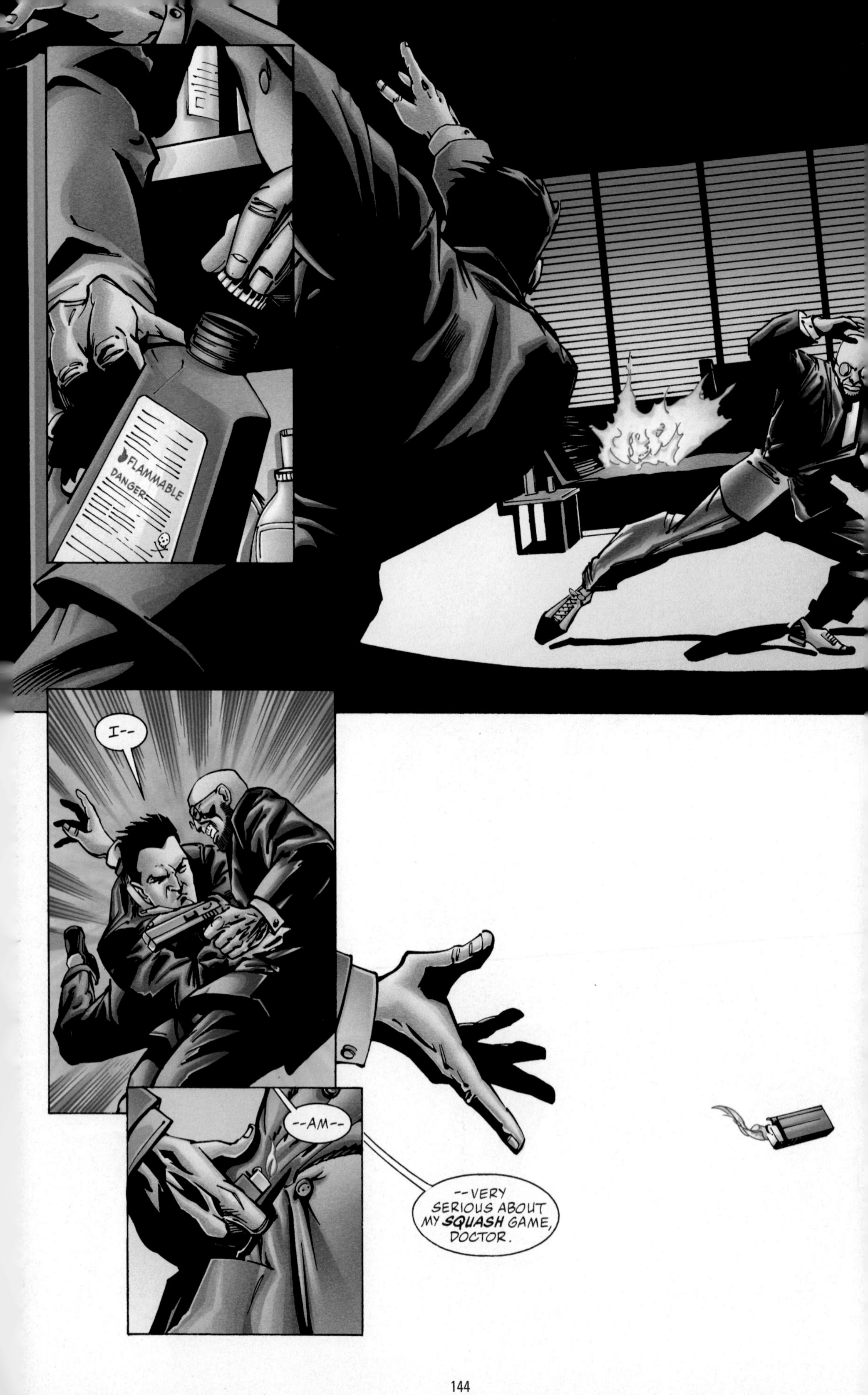
FLAMMABLE
DANGER
I--
--AM--
--VERY SERIOUS ABOUT MY SQUASH GAME, DOCTOR.

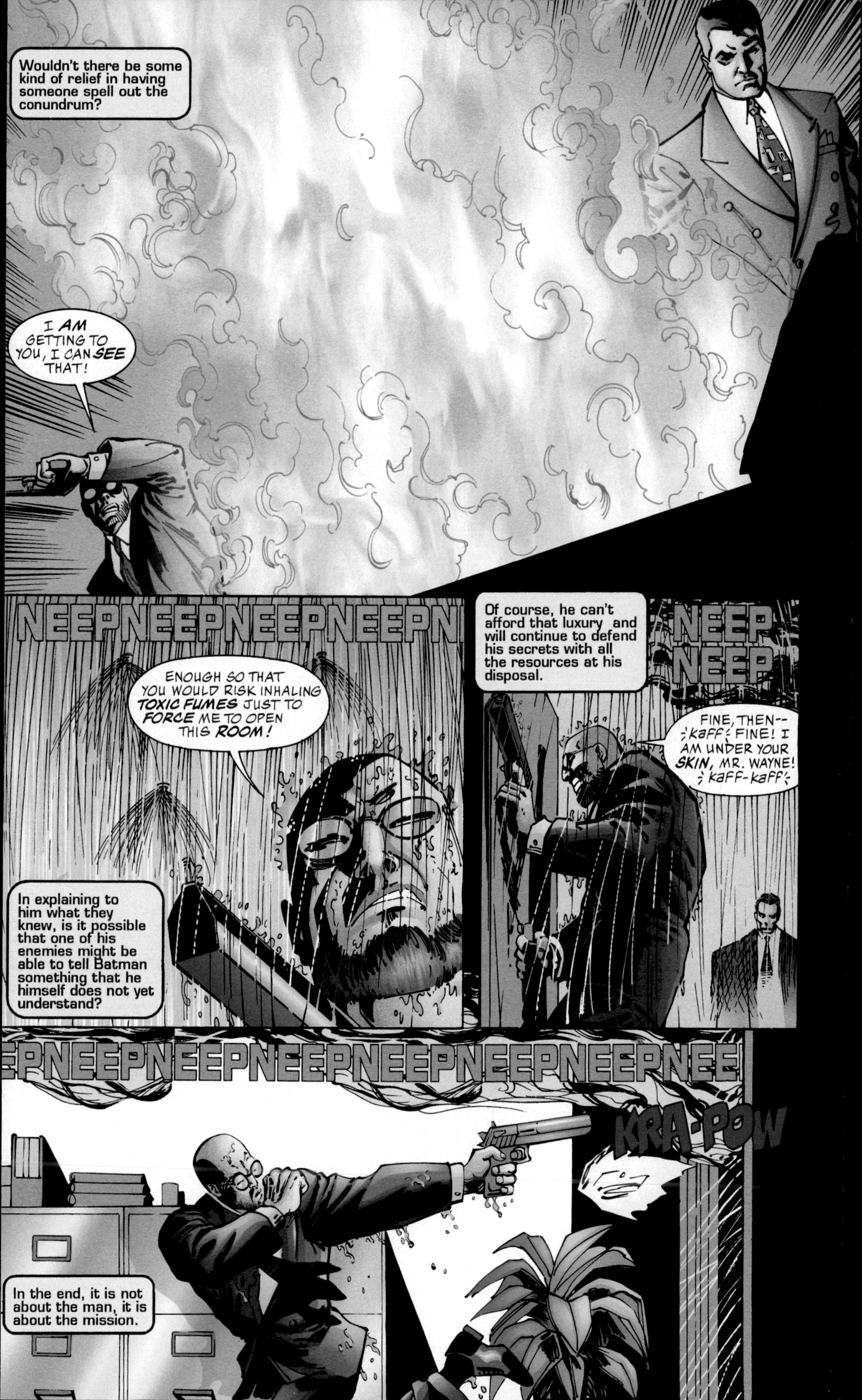

Wouldn't there be some kind of relief in having someone spell out the conundrum?
I AM GETTING TO YOU, I CAN SEE THAT!
NEEPNEEPNEEPNEEPNE
ENOUGH SO THAT YOU WOULD RISK INHALING TOXIC FUMES JUST TO FORCE ME TO OPEN THIS ROOM!
In explaining to him what they knew, is it possible that one of his enemies might be able to tell Batman something that he himself does not yet understand?
Of course, he can't afford that luxury and will continue to defend his secrets with all the resources at his disposal.
NEEP NEEP
FINE, THEN-- kaff FINE! I AM UNDER YOUR SKIN, MR. WAYNE! kaff-kaff
EPNEEPNEEPNEEPNEEPNEEPNEE
KRA-POW
In the end, it is not about the man, it is about the mission.

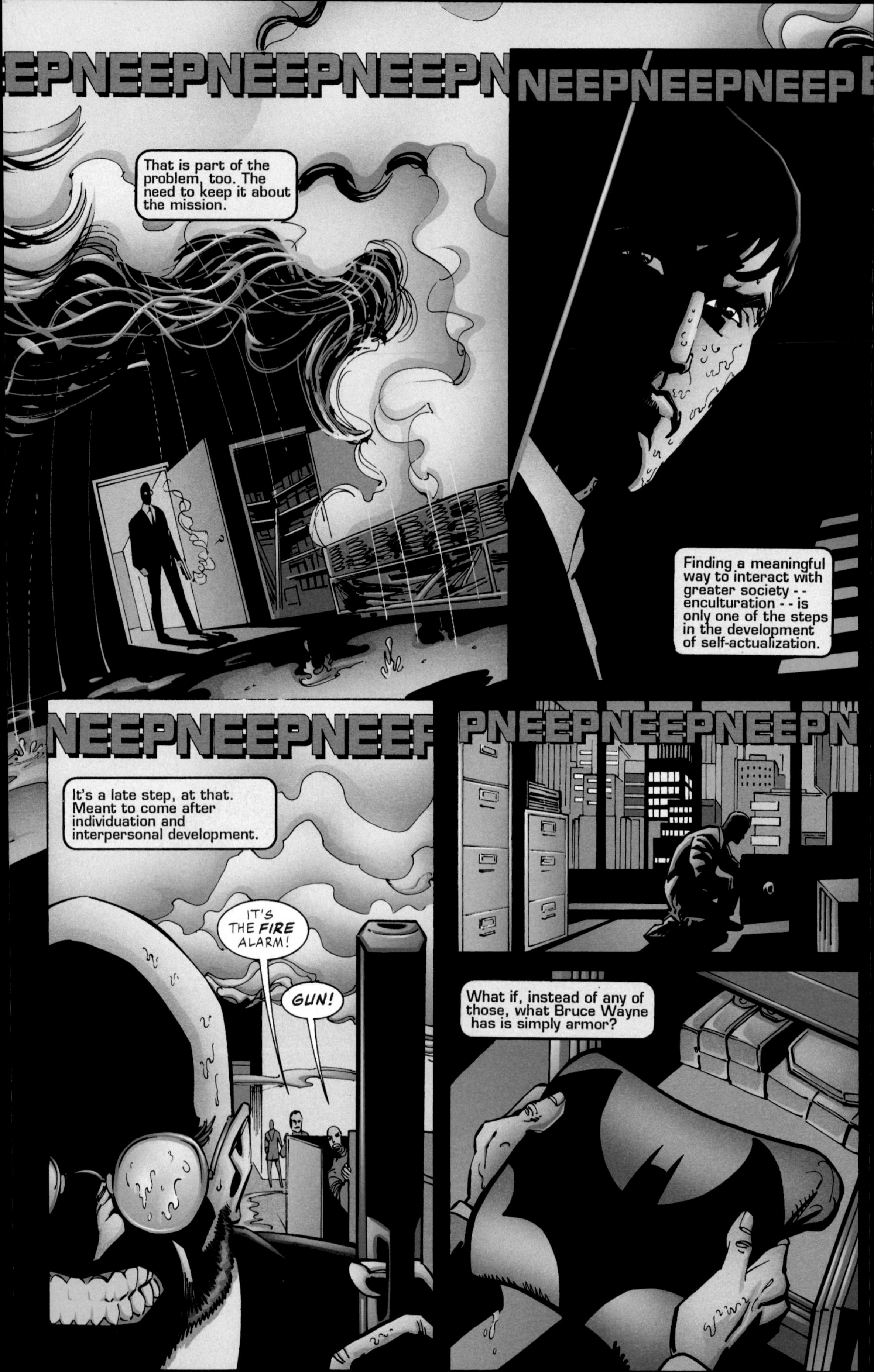
EPNEEPNEEPNEEPN
That is part of the problem, too. The need to keep it about the mission.
NEEPNEEPNEEP
Finding a meaningful way to interact with greater society - - enculturation - - is only one of the steps in the development of self-actualization.
NEEPNEEPNEEP
It's a late step, at that. Meant to come after individuation and interpersonal development.
IT'S THE FIRE ALARM!
GUN!
PNEEPNEEPNEEPN
What if, instead of any of those, what Bruce Wayne has is simply armor?

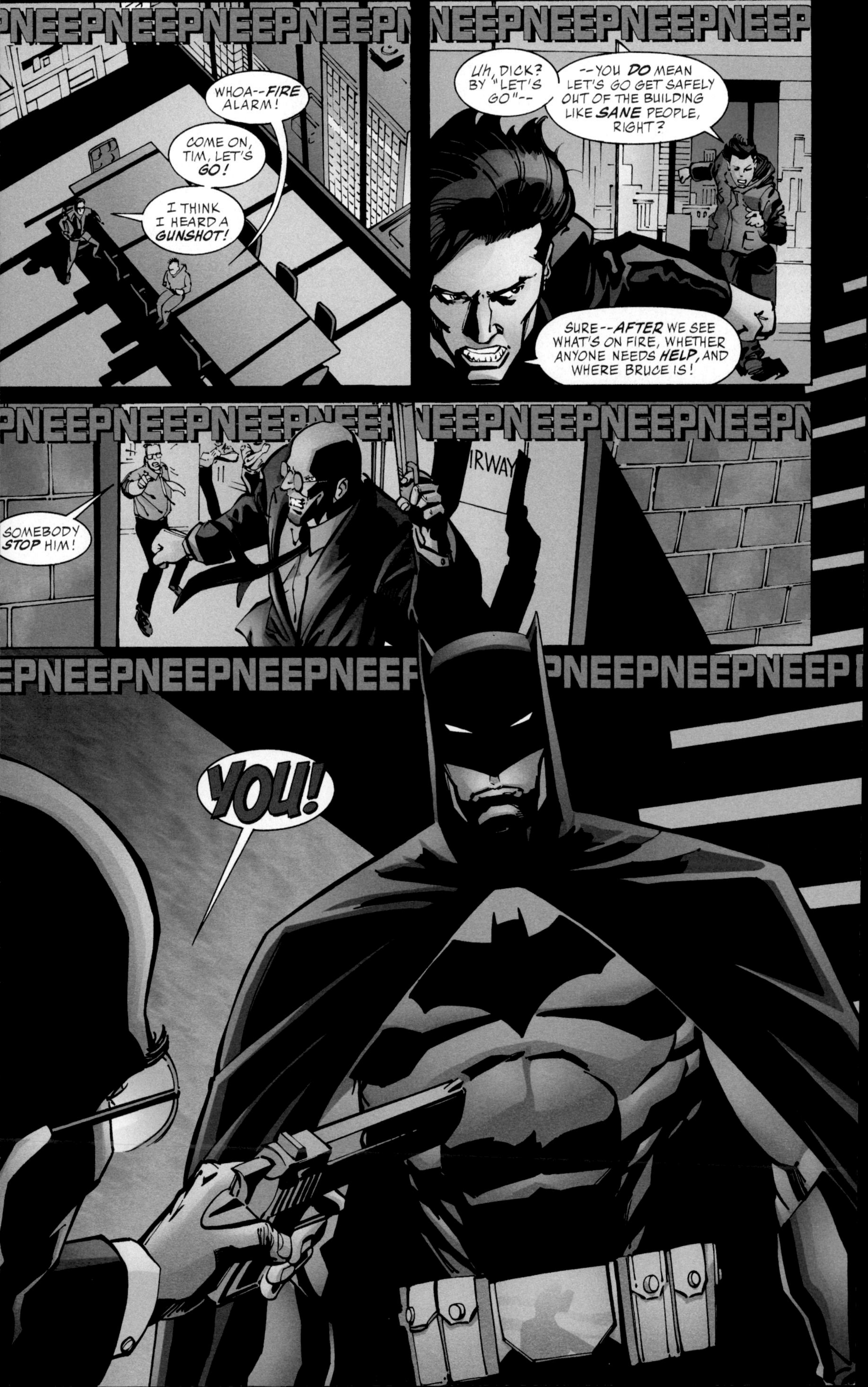
PNEEPNEEPNEEPNEEPN
NEEPNEEPNEEPNEEP
WHOA--FIRE ALARM!
COME ON, TIM, LET'S GO!
I THINK I HEARD A GUNSHOT!
Uh, DICK? BY "LET'S GO"--
--YOU DO MEAN LET'S GO GET SAFELY OUT OF THE BUILDING LIKE SANE PEOPLE, RIGHT?
SURE--AFTER WE SEE WHAT'S ON FIRE, WHETHER ANYONE NEEDS HELP, AND WHERE BRUCE IS!
PNEEPNEEPNEEPNEEPNEEPNEEPNEEPNEEPN
SOMEBODY STOP HIM!
IRWAY
EPNEEPNEEPNEEPNEEPNEEPNEEPNEEPNEEP
YOU!

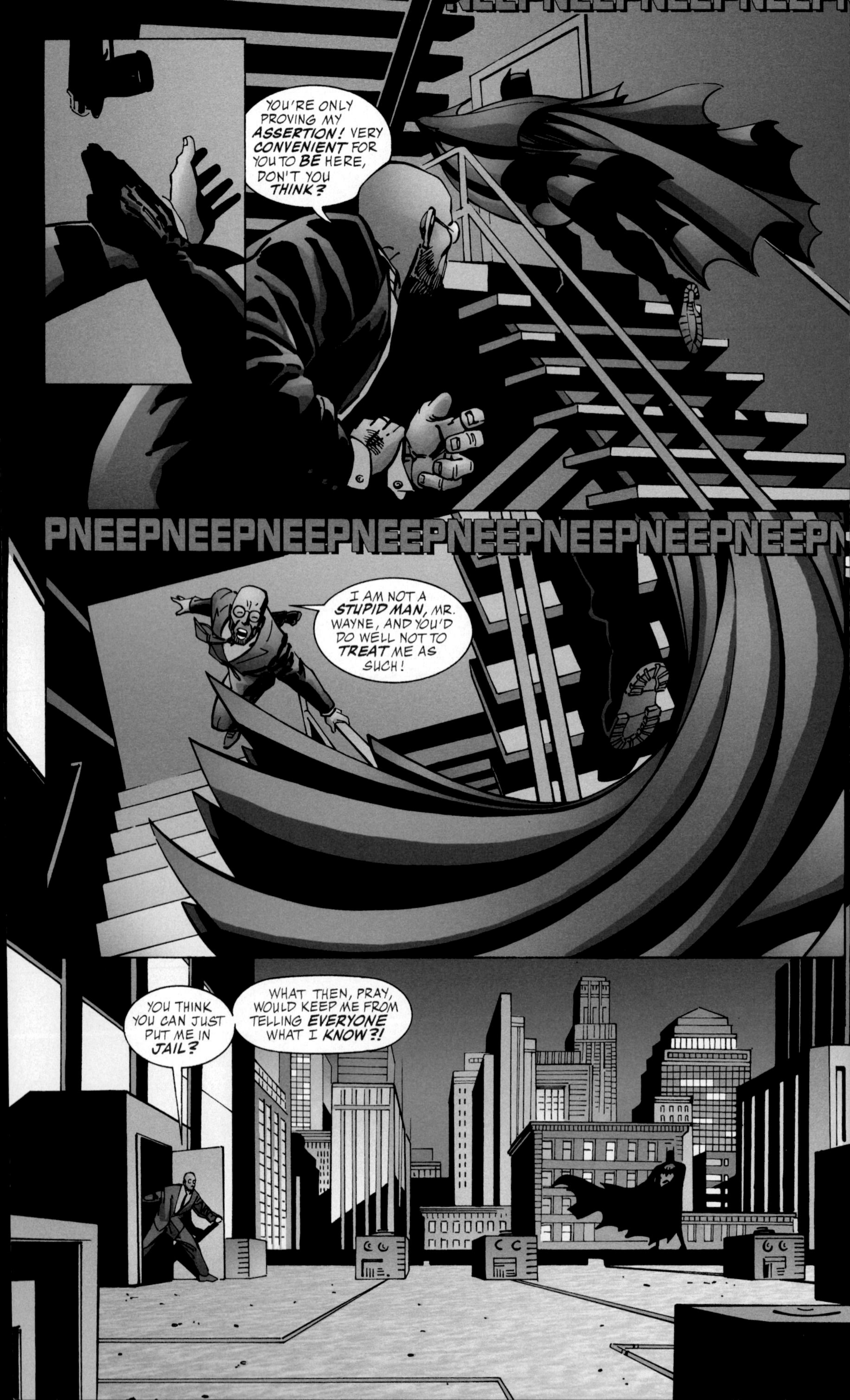
NEEPNEEPNEEPNEEP
YOU'RE ONLY PROVING MY ASSERTION! VERY CONVENIENT FOR YOU TO BE HERE, DON'T YOU THINK?
PNEEPNEEPNEEPNEEPNEEPNEEPNEEPNEEP
I AM NOT A STUPID MAN, MR. WAYNE, AND YOU'D DO WELL NOT TO TREAT ME AS SUCH!
YOU THINK YOU CAN JUST PUT ME IN JAIL?
WHAT THEN, PRAY, WOULD KEEP ME FROM TELLING EVERYONE WHAT I KNOW?!

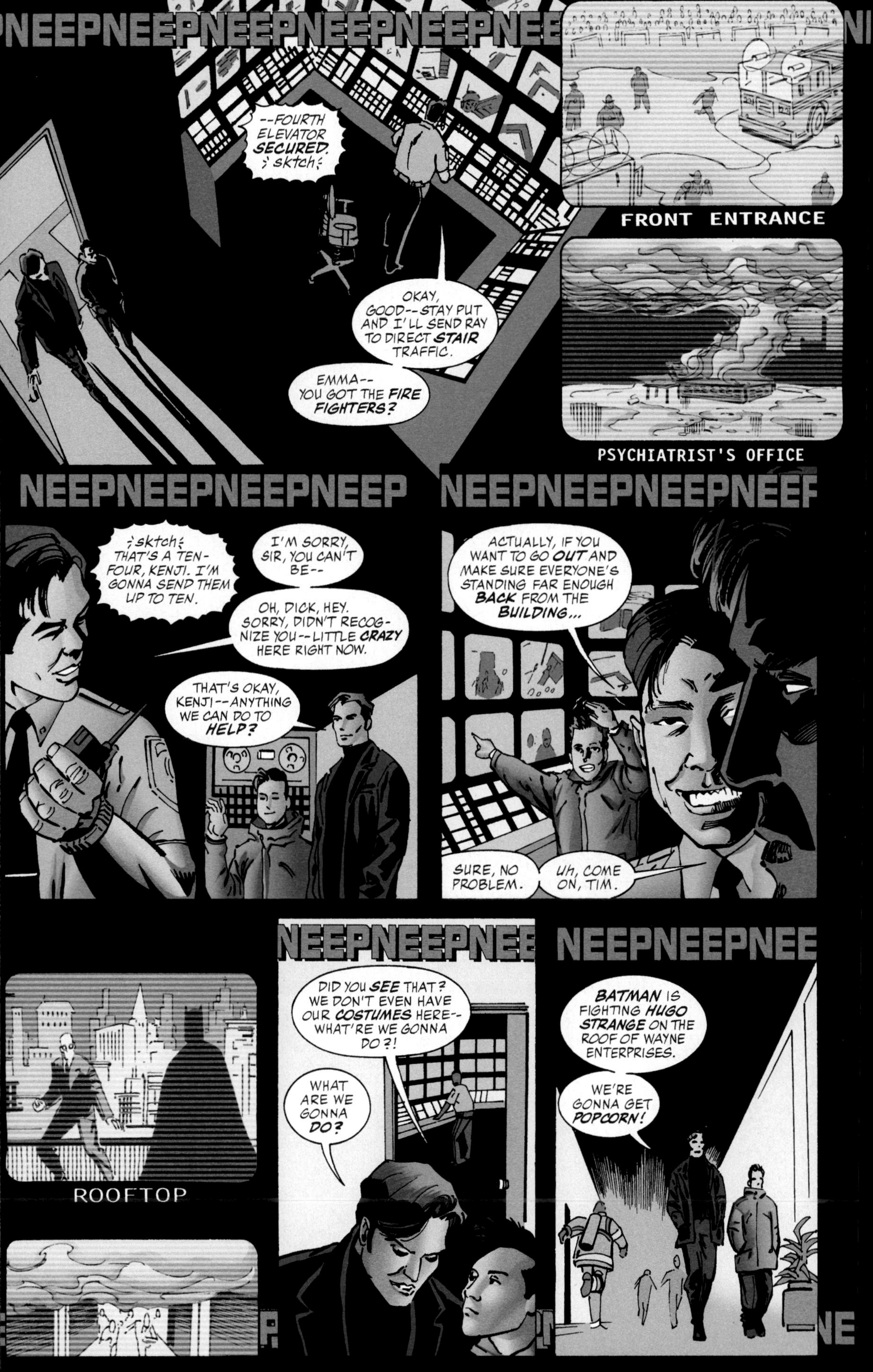
NEEPNEEPNEEPNEEPNEEPNEEPNEE
--FOURTH ELEVATOR SECURED. ;sktch;
FRONT ENTRANCE
OKAY, GOOD--STAY PUT AND I'LL SEND RAY TO DIRECT STAIR TRAFFIC.
EMMA--YOU GOT THE FIRE FIGHTERS?
PSYCHIATRIST'S OFFICE
NEEPNEEPNEEPNEEP
;sktch; THAT'S A TEN-FOUR, KENJI. I'M GONNA SEND THEM UP TO TEN.
I'M SORRY, SIR, YOU CAN'T BE--
OH, DICK, HEY. SORRY, DIDN'T RECOG-NIZE YOU--LITTLE CRAZY HERE RIGHT NOW.
THAT'S OKAY, KENJI--ANYTHING WE CAN DO TO HELP?
NEEPNEEPNEEPNEEF
ACTUALLY, IF YOU WANT TO GO OUT AND MAKE SURE EVERYONE'S STANDING FAR ENOUGH BACK FROM THE BUILDING...
SURE, NO PROBLEM.
UH, COME ON, TIM.
ROOFTOP
NEEPNEEPNEE
DID YOU SEE THAT? WE DON'T EVEN HAVE OUR COSTUMES HERE--WHAT'RE WE GONNA DO?!
WHAT ARE WE GONNA DO?
NEEPNEEPNEE
BATMAN IS FIGHTING HUGO STRANGE ON THE ROOF OF WAYNE ENTERPRISES.
WE'RE GONNA GET POPCORN!

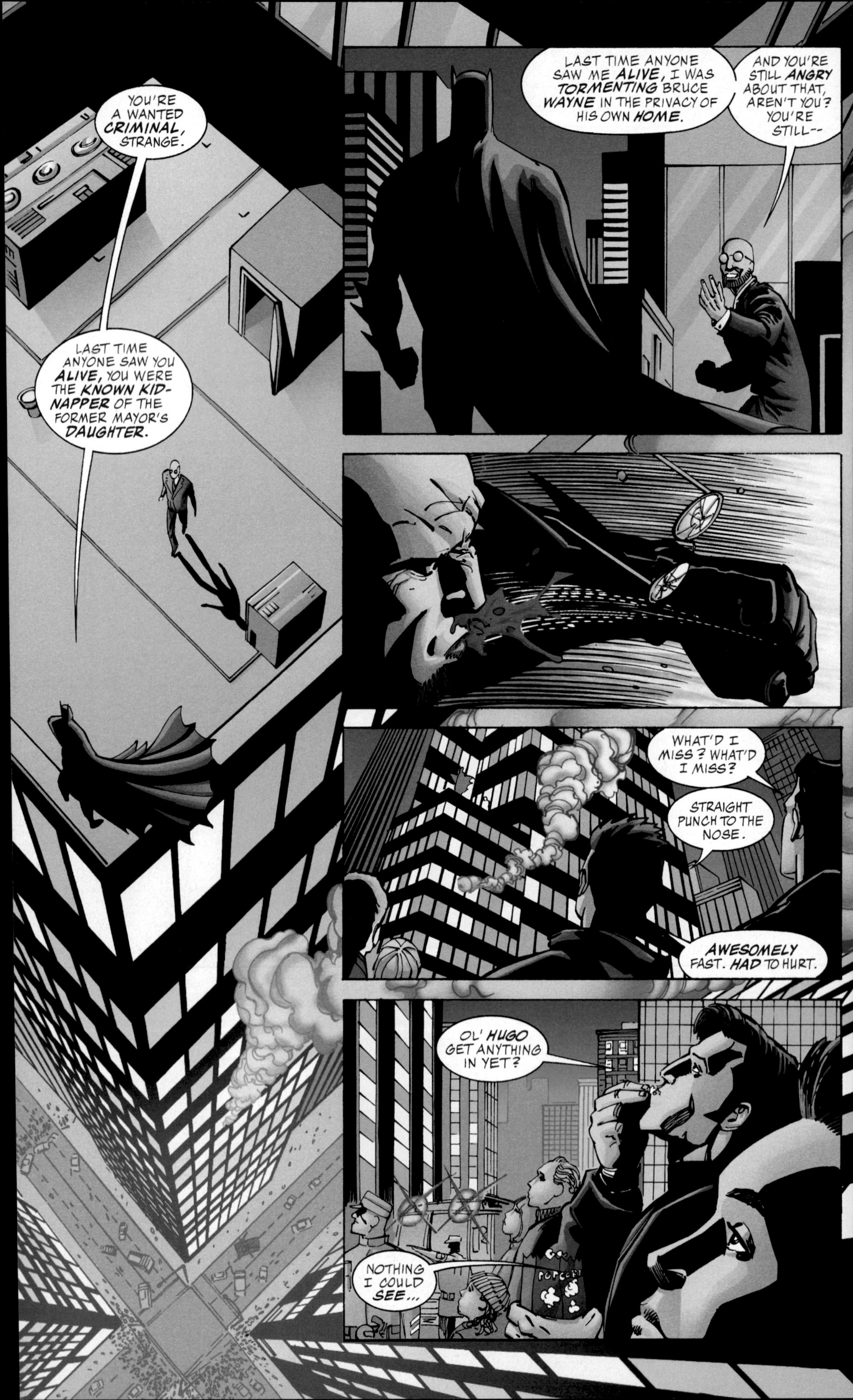
YOU'RE A WANTED CRIMINAL, STRANGE.
LAST TIME ANYONE SAW YOU ALIVE, YOU WERE THE KNOWN KID-NAPPER OF THE FORMER MAYOR'S DAUGHTER.
LAST TIME ANYONE SAW ME ALIVE, I WAS TORMENTING BRUCE WAYNE IN THE PRIVACY OF HIS OWN HOME.
AND YOU'RE STILL ANGRY ABOUT THAT, AREN'T YOU? YOU'RE STILL--
WHAT'D I MISS? WHAT'D I MISS?
STRAIGHT PUNCH TO THE NOSE.
AWESOMELY FAST. HAD TO HURT.
OL' HUGO GET ANYTHING IN YET?
NOTHING I COULD SEE...

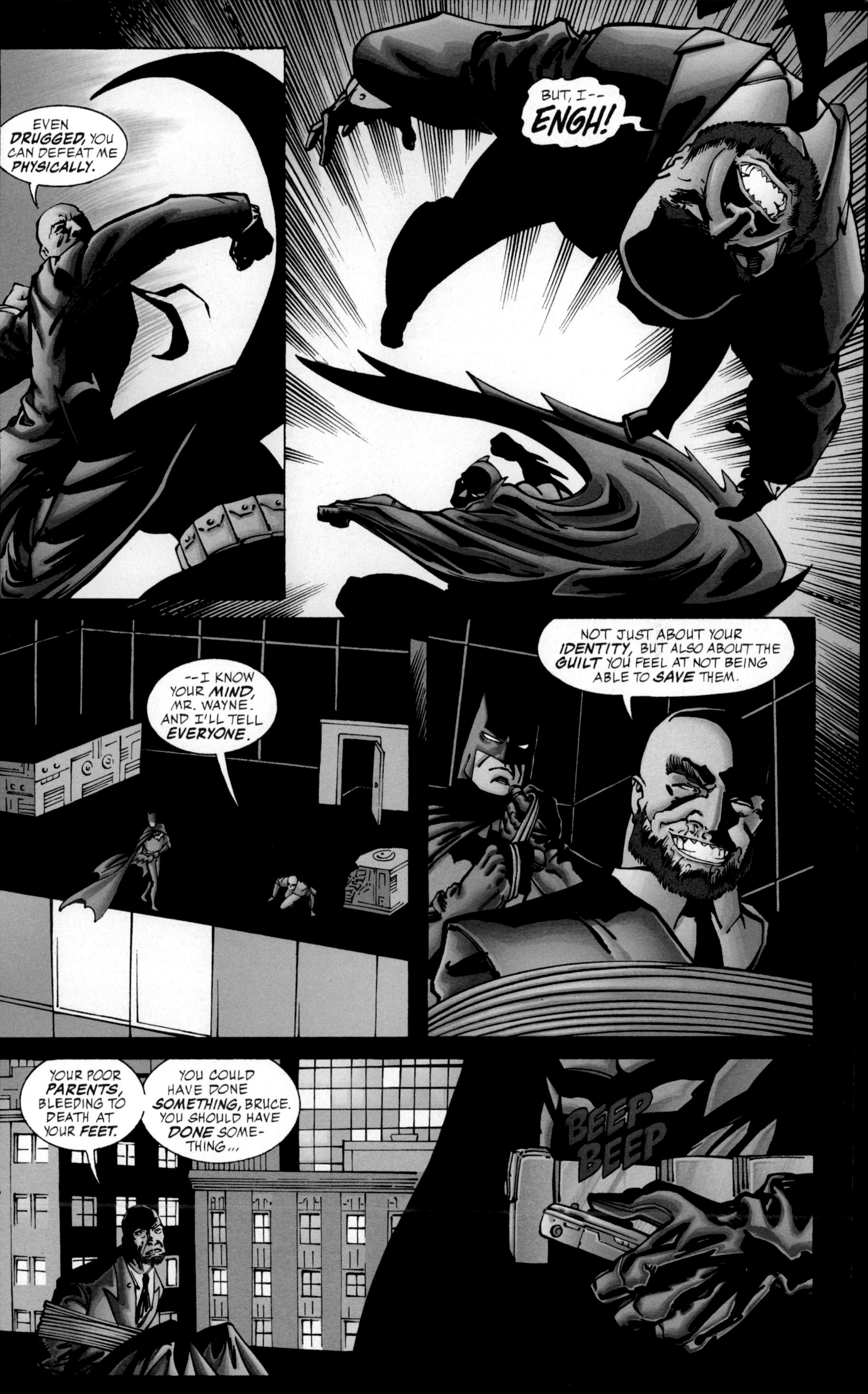
EVEN DRUGGED, YOU CAN DEFEAT ME PHYSICALLY.
BUT, I-- ENGH!
--I KNOW YOUR MIND, MR. WAYNE. AND I'LL TELL EVERYONE.
NOT JUST ABOUT YOUR IDENTITY, BUT ALSO ABOUT THE GUILT YOU FEEL AT NOT BEING ABLE TO SAVE THEM.
YOUR POOR PARENTS, BLEEDING TO DEATH AT YOUR FEET.
YOU COULD HAVE DONE SOMETHING, BRUCE. YOU SHOULD HAVE DONE SOME-THING...
BEEP BEEP

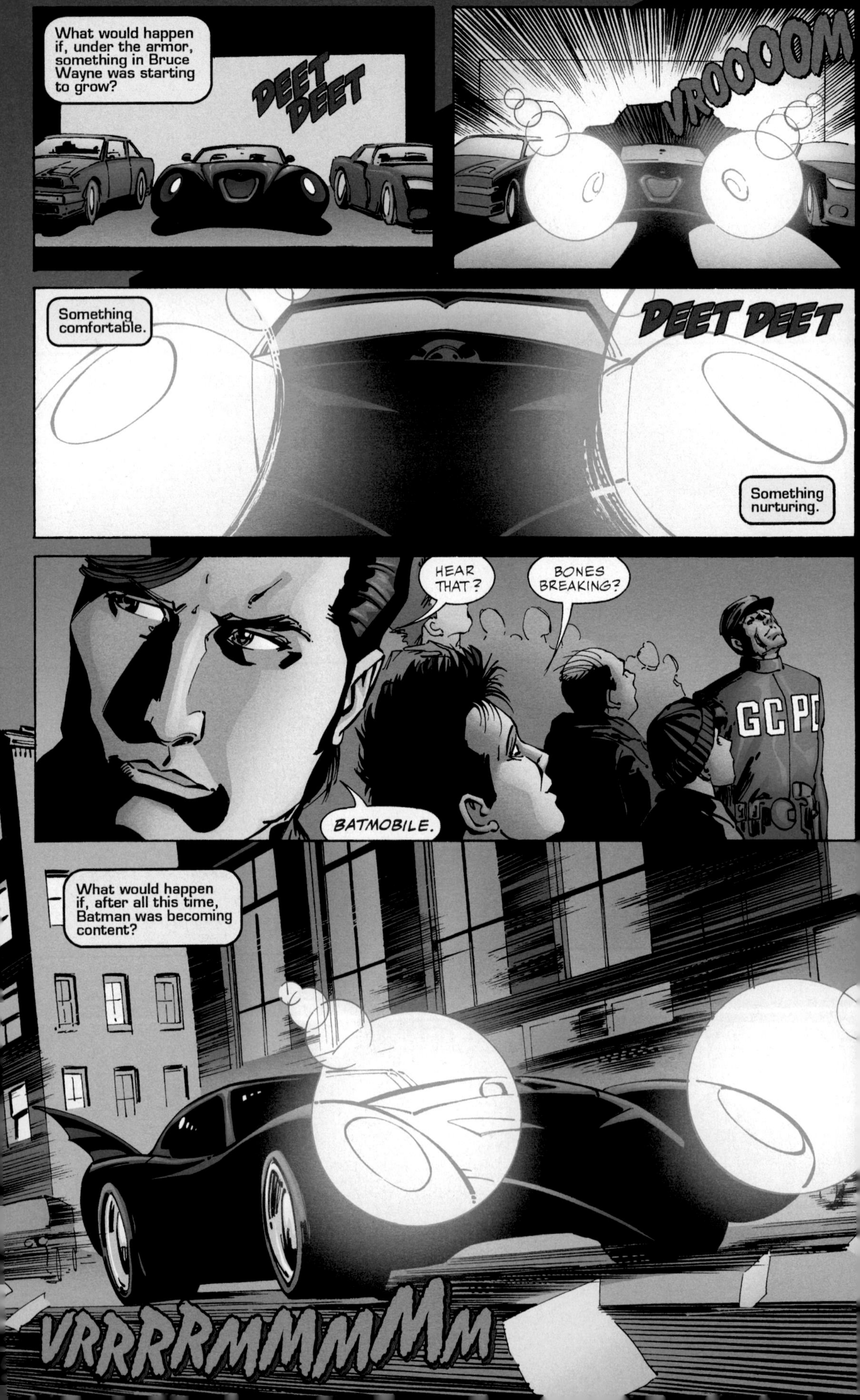
What would happen if, under the armor, something in Bruce Wayne was starting to grow?
DEET DEET
VROOOOM
Something comfortable.
DEET DEET
Something nurturing.
HEAR THAT?
BONES BREAKING?
GCPD
BATMOBILE.
What would happen if, after all this time, Batman was becoming content?
VRRRRMMMMMm

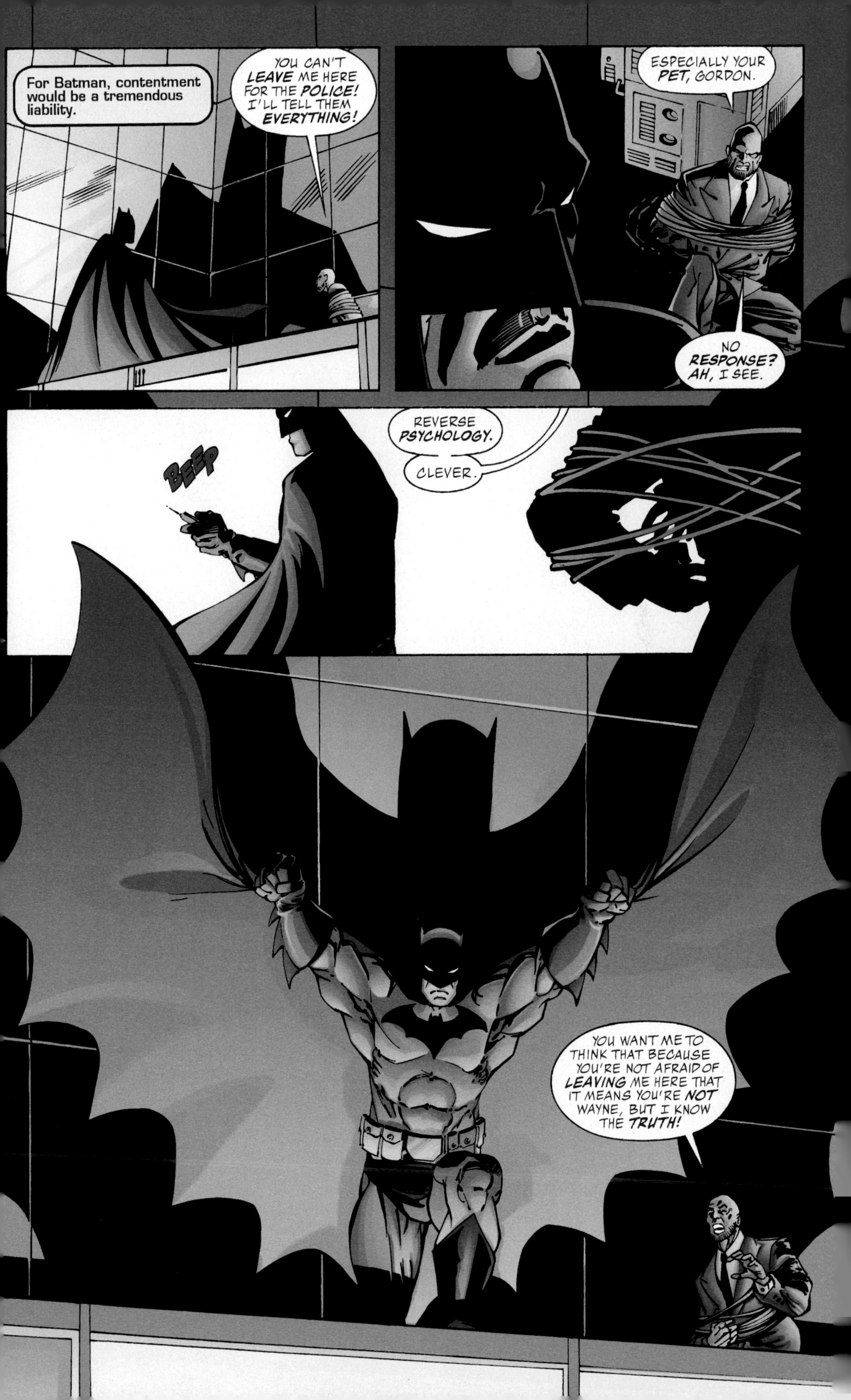
For Batman, contentment would be a tremendous liability.
YOU CAN'T LEAVE ME HERE FOR THE POLICE! I'LL TELL THEM EVERYTHING!
ESPECIALLY YOUR PET, GORDON.
NO RESPONSE? AH, I SEE.
REVERSE PSYCHOLOGY.
CLEVER.
BEEP
YOU WANT ME TO THINK THAT BECAUSE YOU'RE NOT AFRAID OF LEAVING ME HERE THAT IT MEANS YOU'RE NOT WAYNE, BUT I KNOW THE TRUTH!

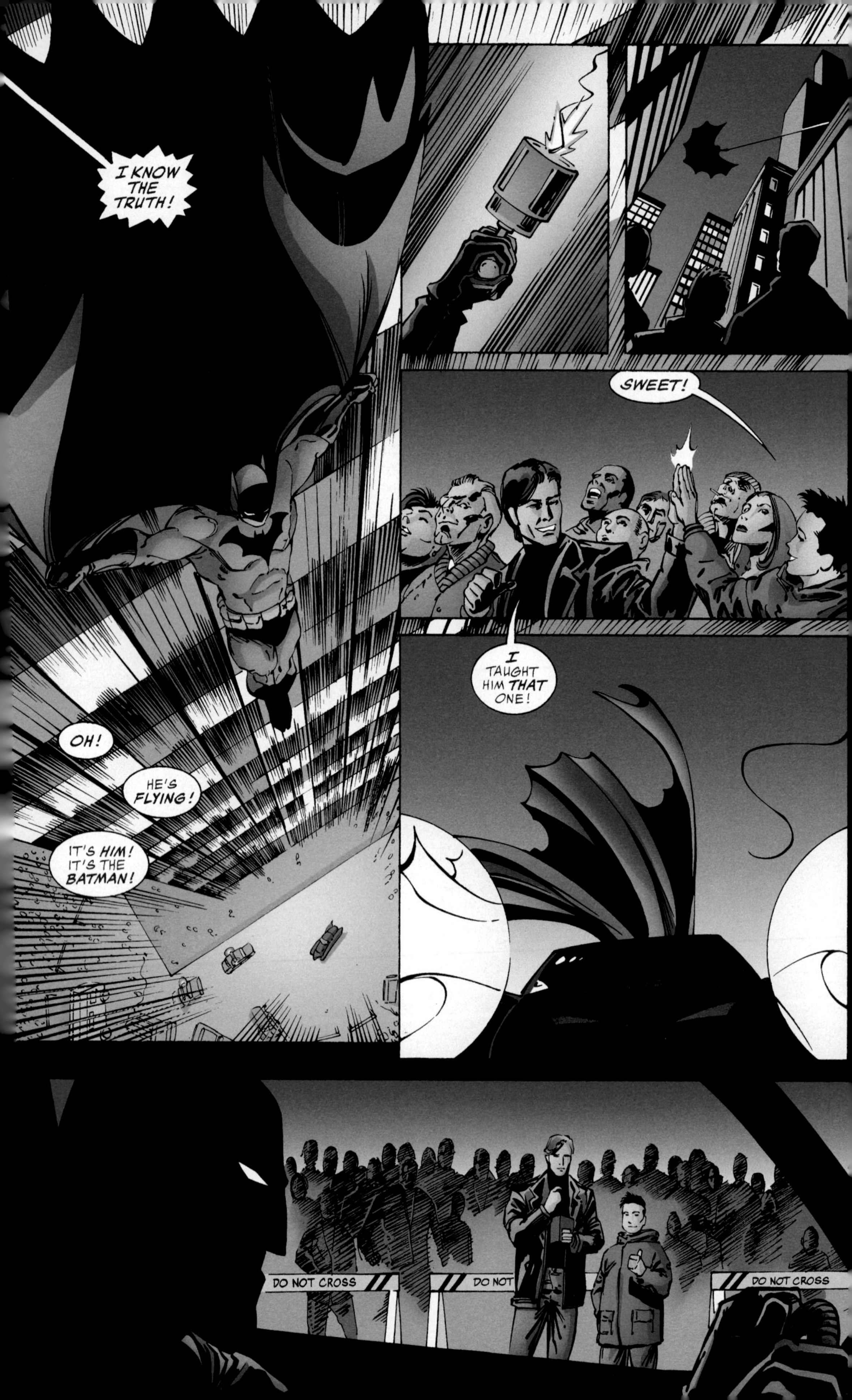
I KNOW THE TRUTH!
OH!
HE'S FLYING!
IT'S HIM! IT'S THE BATMAN!
SWEET!
I TAUGHT HIM THAT ONE!
DO NOT CROSS
DO NOT
DO NOT CROSS

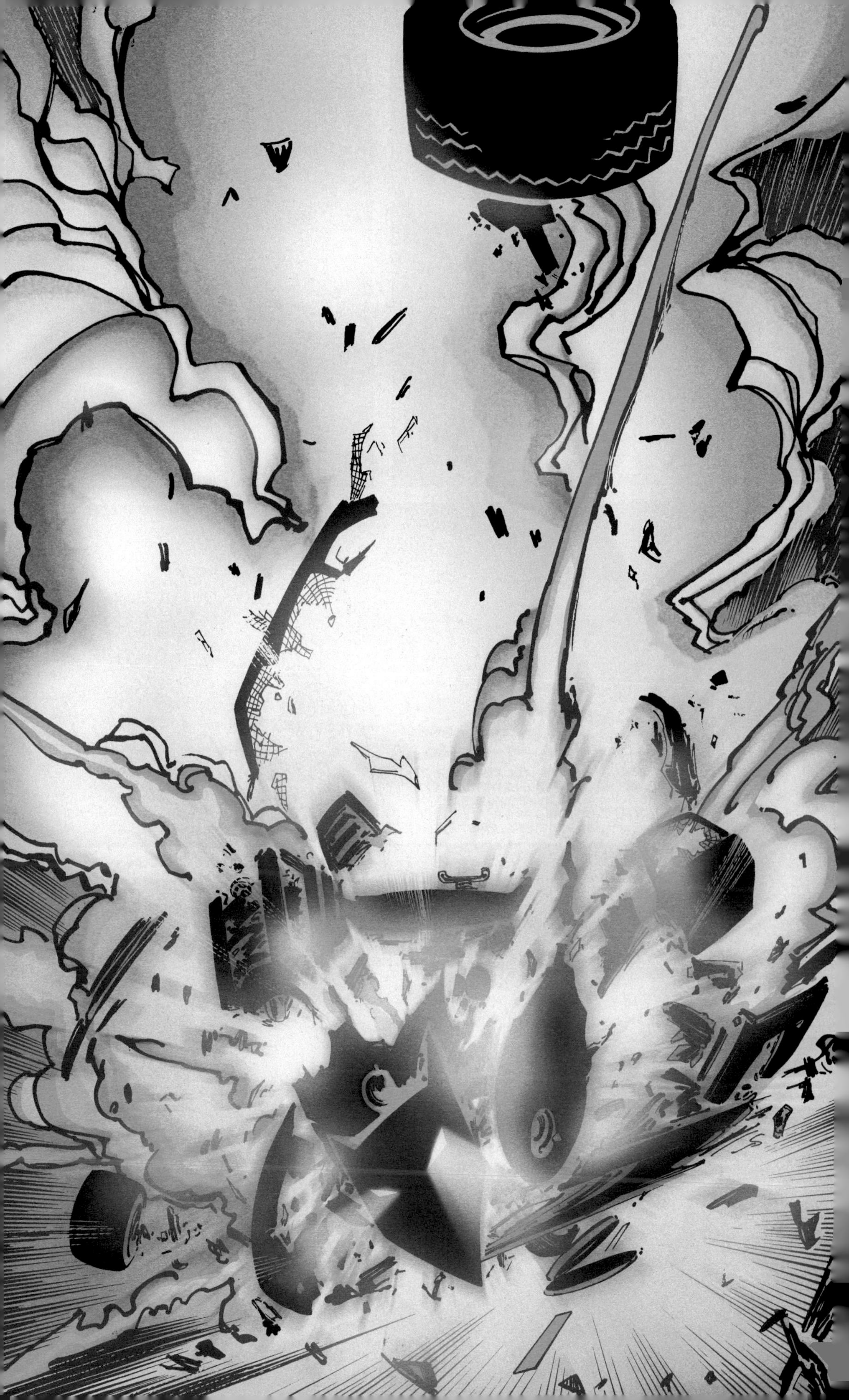

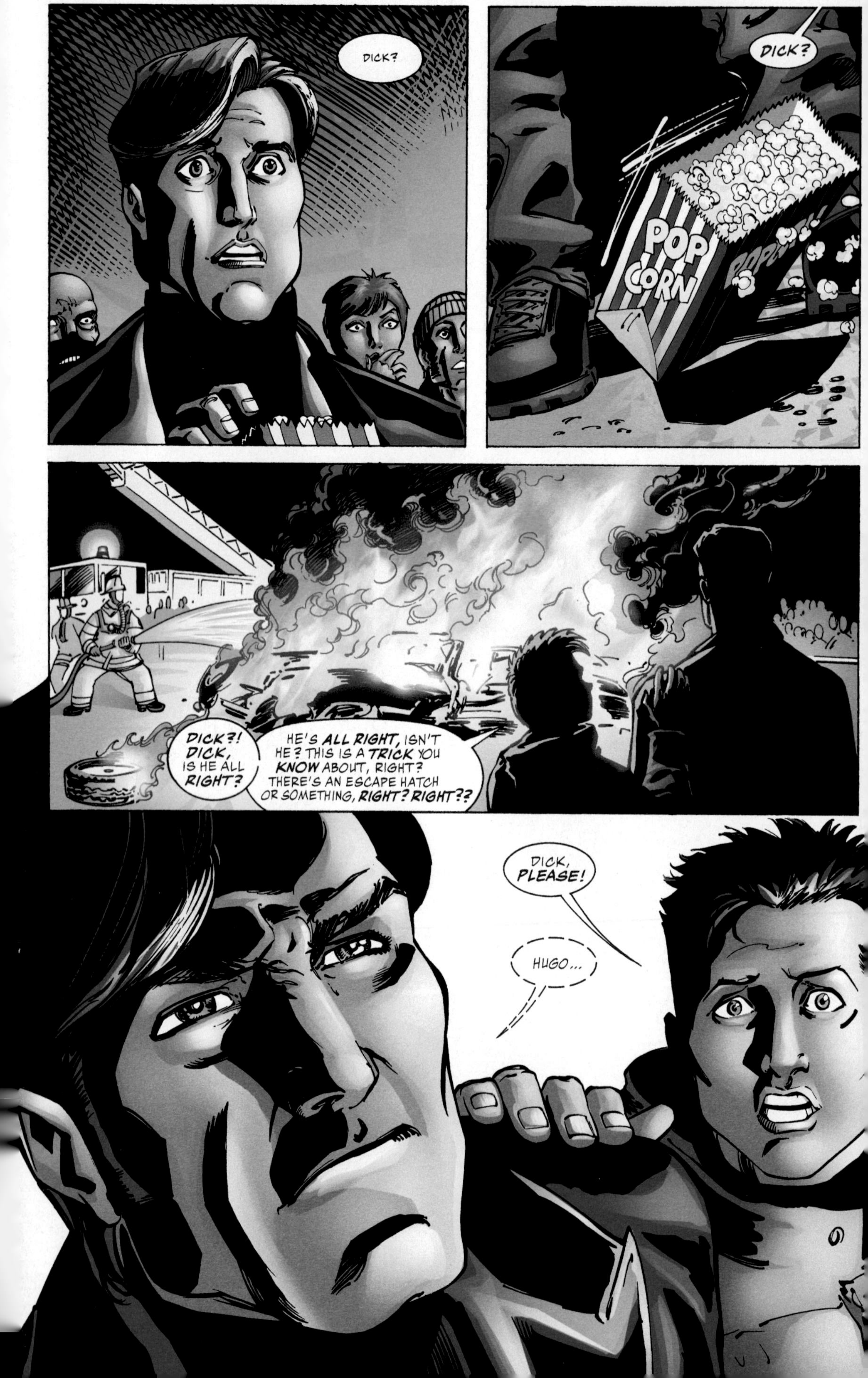
DICK?
DICK?
POP CORN
DICK?! DICK, IS HE ALL RIGHT?
HE'S ALL RIGHT, ISN'T HE? THIS IS A TRICK YOU KNOW ABOUT, RIGHT? THERE'S AN ESCAPE HATCH OR SOMETHING, RIGHT? RIGHT??
DICK, PLEASE!
HUGO...

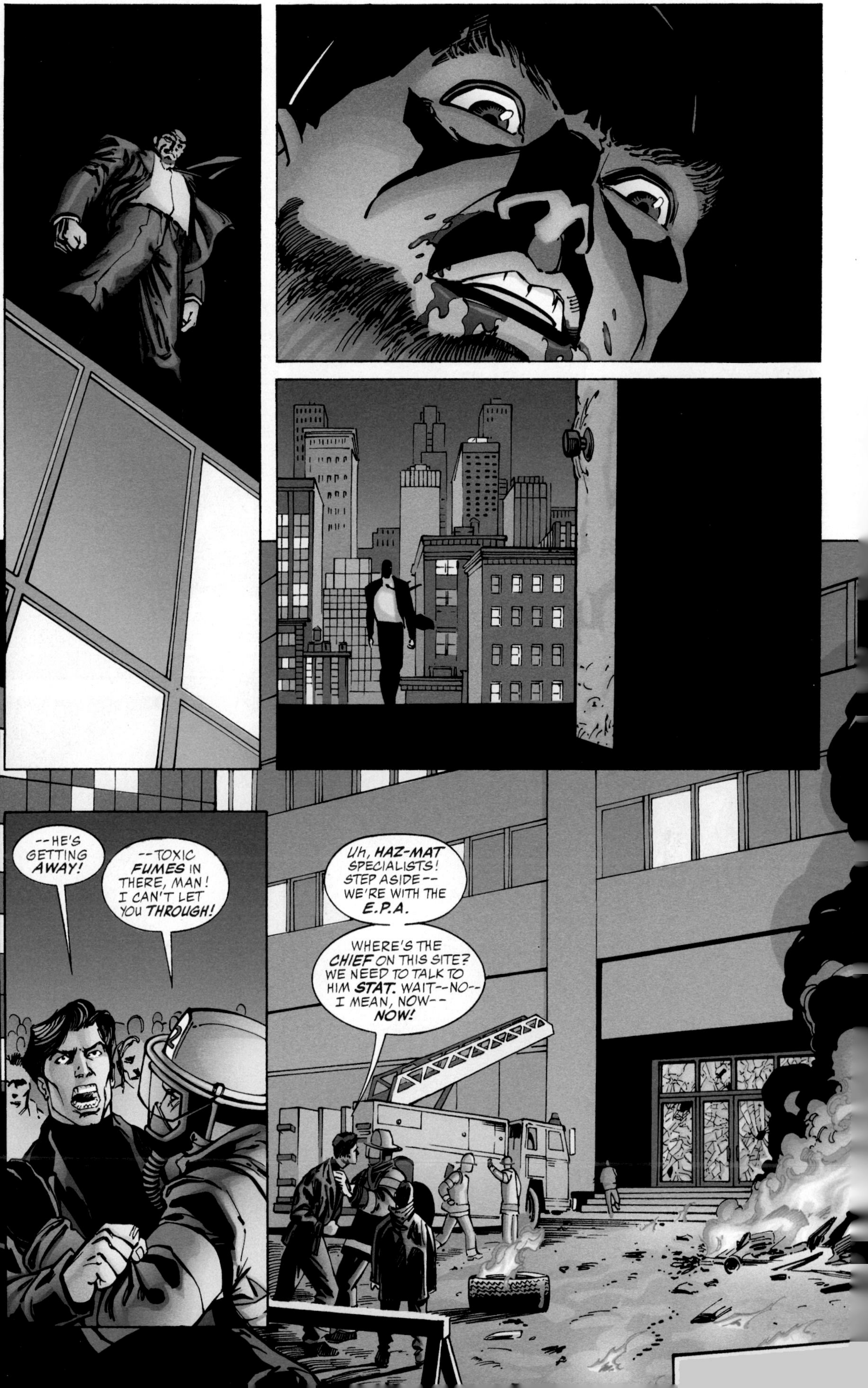
--HE'S GETTING AWAY!
--TOXIC FUMES IN THERE, MAN! I CAN'T LET YOU THROUGH!
Uh, HAZ-MAT SPECIALISTS! STEP ASIDE-- WE'RE WITH THE E.P.A.
WHERE'S THE CHIEF ON THIS SITE? WE NEED TO TALK TO HIM STAT. WAIT--NO-- I MEAN, NOW-- NOW!

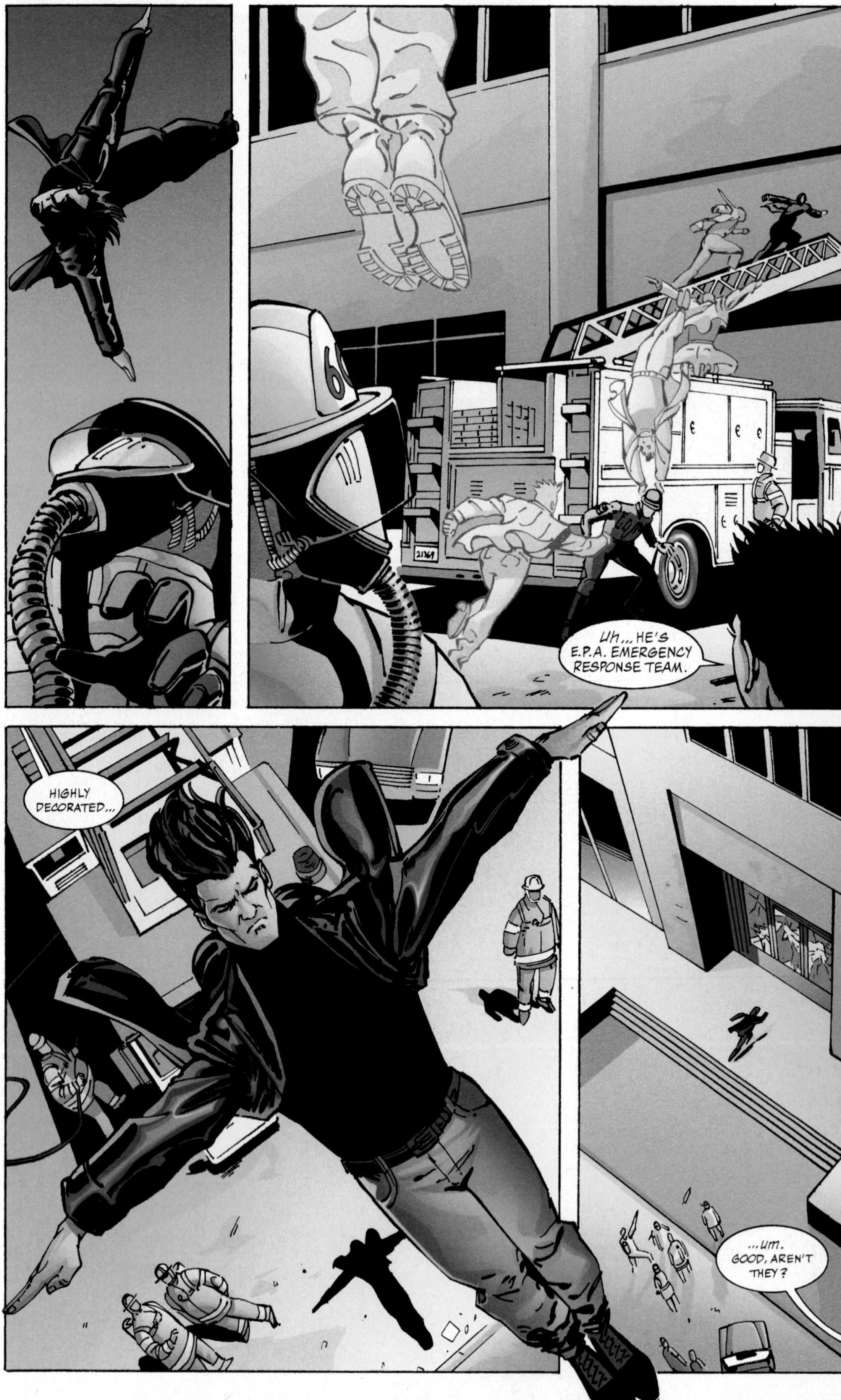

UH... HE'S
E.P.A. EMERGENCY
RESPONSE TEAM.
HIGHLY
DECORATED...
...UM.
GOOD, AREN'T
THEY?

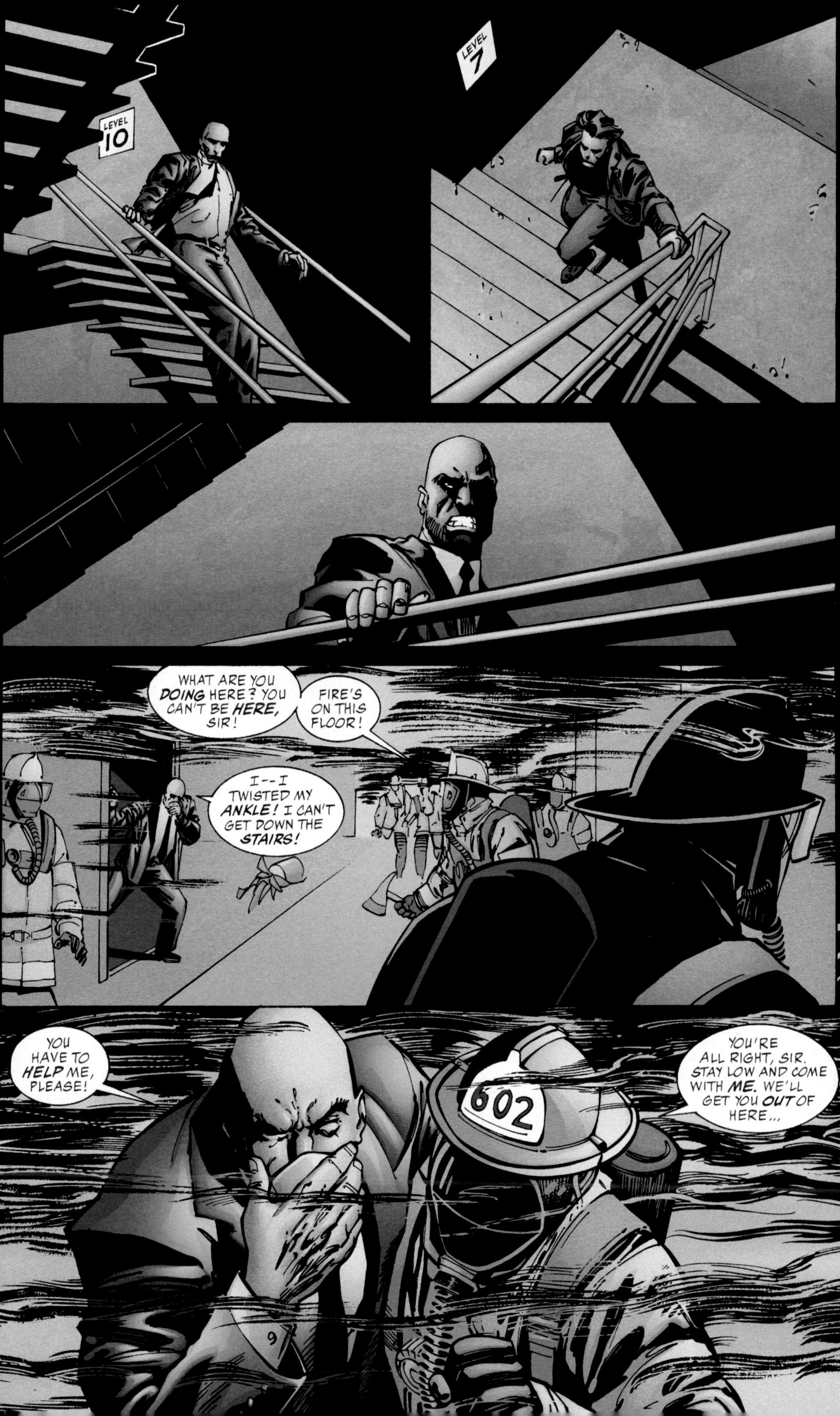
LEVEL 10
LEVEL 7
WHAT ARE YOU DOING HERE? YOU CAN'T BE HERE, SIR!
FIRE'S ON THIS FLOOR!
I--I TWISTED MY ANKLE! I CAN'T GET DOWN THE STAIRS!
YOU HAVE TO HELP ME, PLEASE!
602
YOU'RE ALL RIGHT, SIR. STAY LOW AND COME WITH ME. WE'LL GET YOU OUT OF HERE...

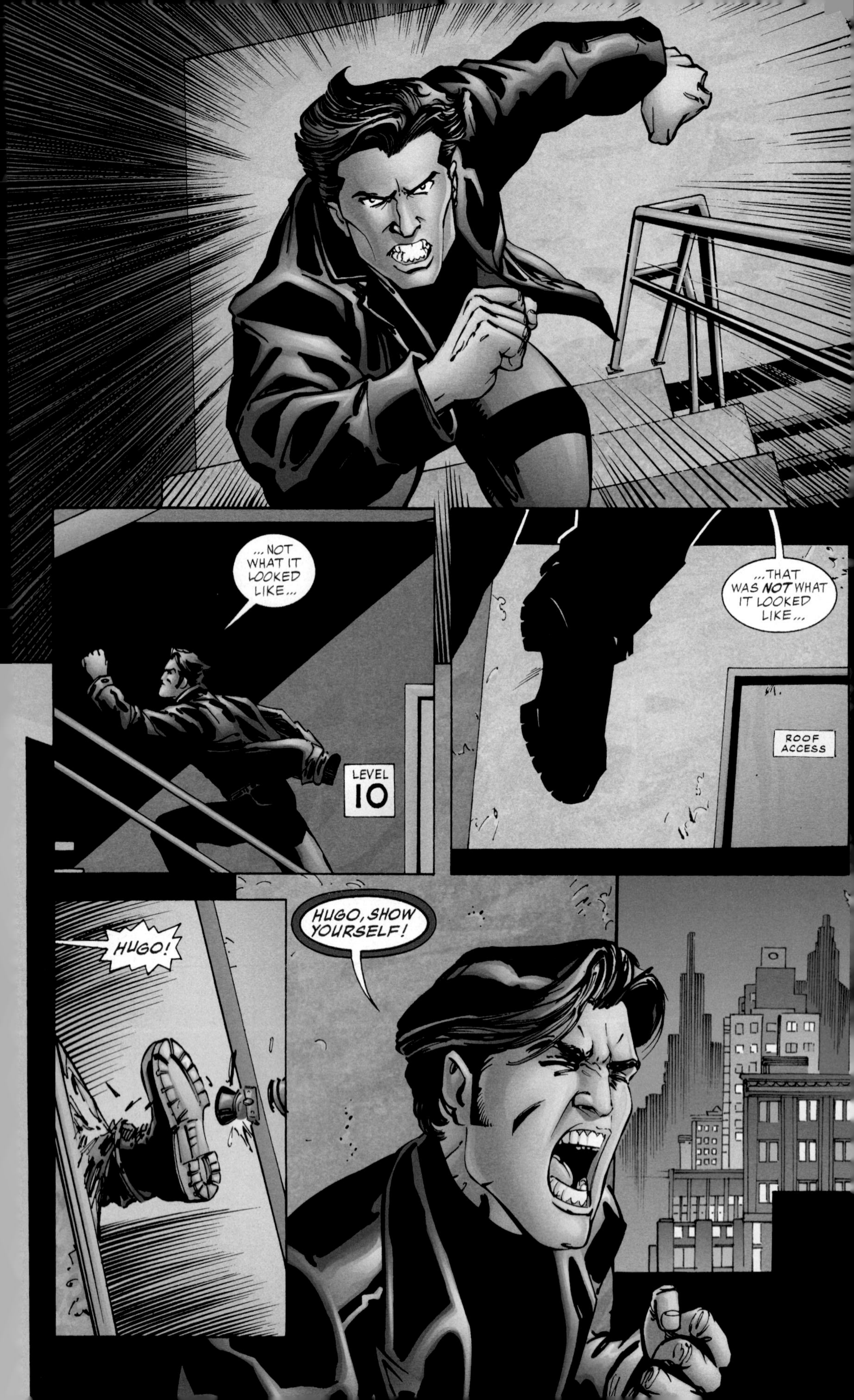
...NOT WHAT IT LOOKED LIKE...
LEVEL 10
...THAT WAS NOT WHAT IT LOOKED LIKE...
ROOF ACCESS
HUGO!
HUGO, SHOW YOURSELF!

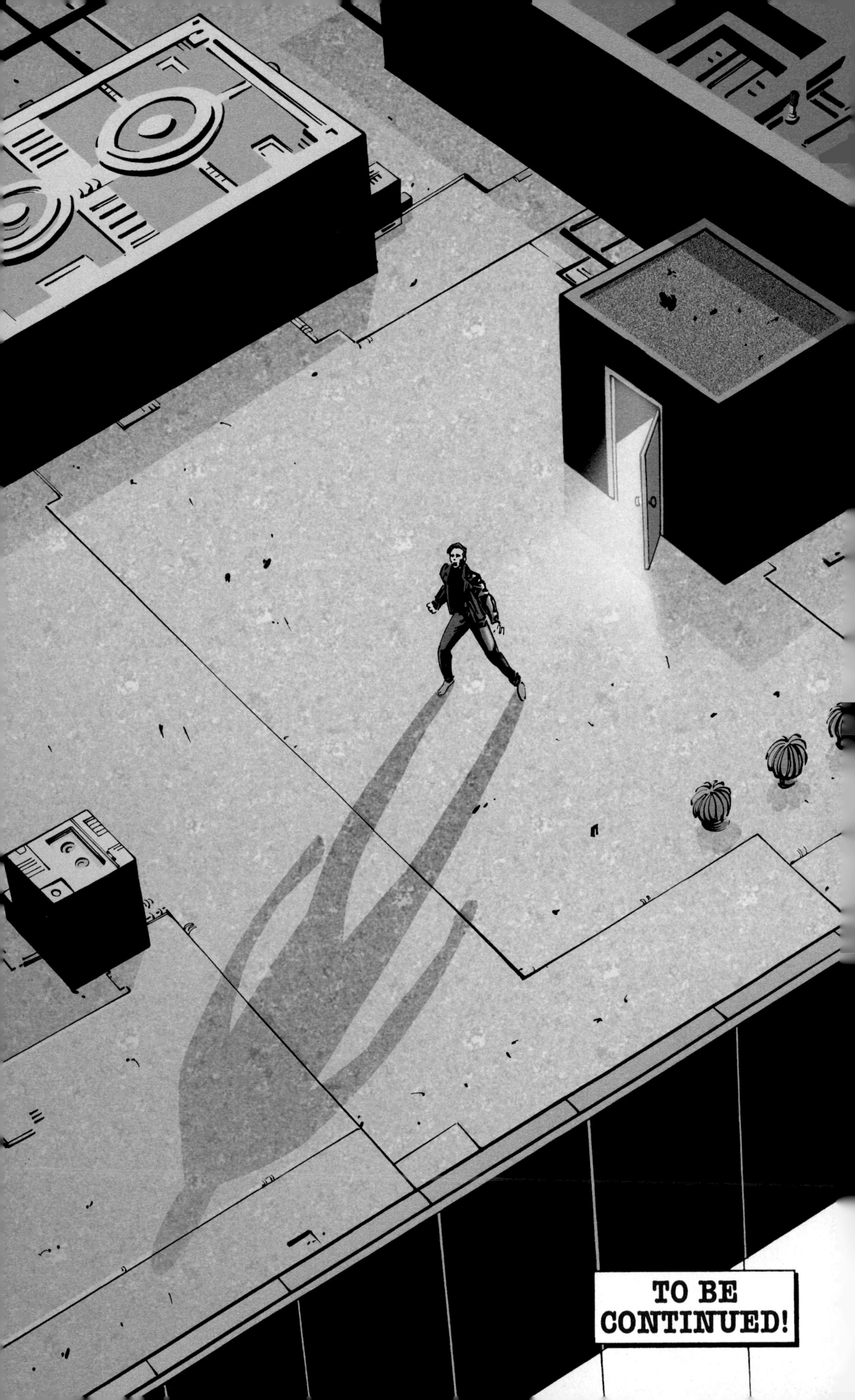
TO BE CONTINUED!

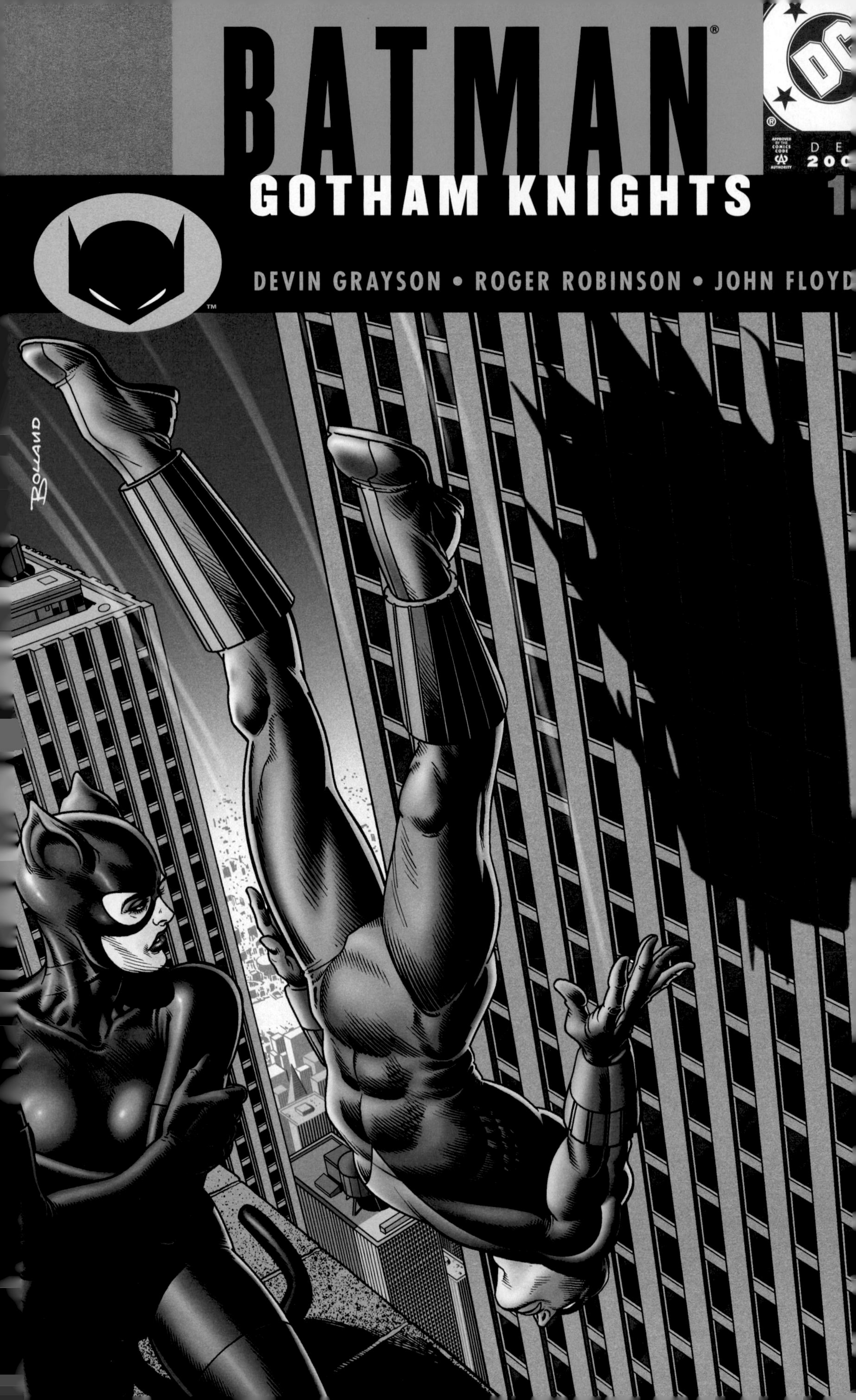
BATMAN®
GOTHAM KNIGHTS
DEVIN GRAYSON • ROGER ROBINSON • JOHN FLOYD
APPROVED BY THE COMICS CODE AUTHORITY
BOLLAND

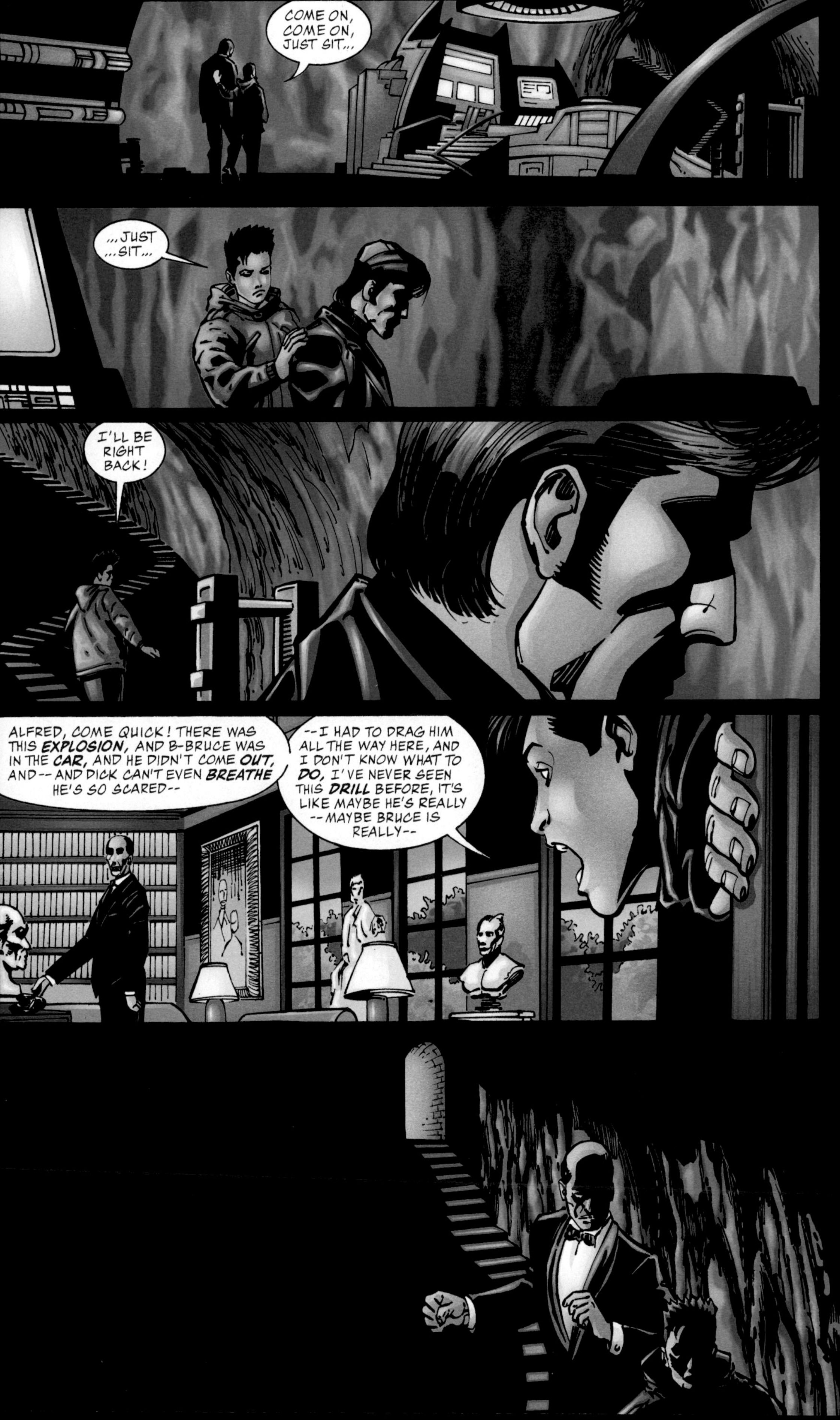
COME ON, COME ON, JUST SIT...
...JUST ...SIT...
I'LL BE RIGHT BACK!
ALFRED, COME QUICK! THERE WAS THIS EXPLOSION, AND B-BRUCE WAS IN THE CAR, AND HE DIDN'T COME OUT, AND-- AND DICK CAN'T EVEN BREATHE HE'S SO SCARED--
--I HAD TO DRAG HIM ALL THE WAY HERE, AND I DON'T KNOW WHAT TO DO, I'VE NEVER SEEN THIS DRILL BEFORE, IT'S LIKE MAYBE HE'S REALLY --MAYBE BRUCE IS REALLY--

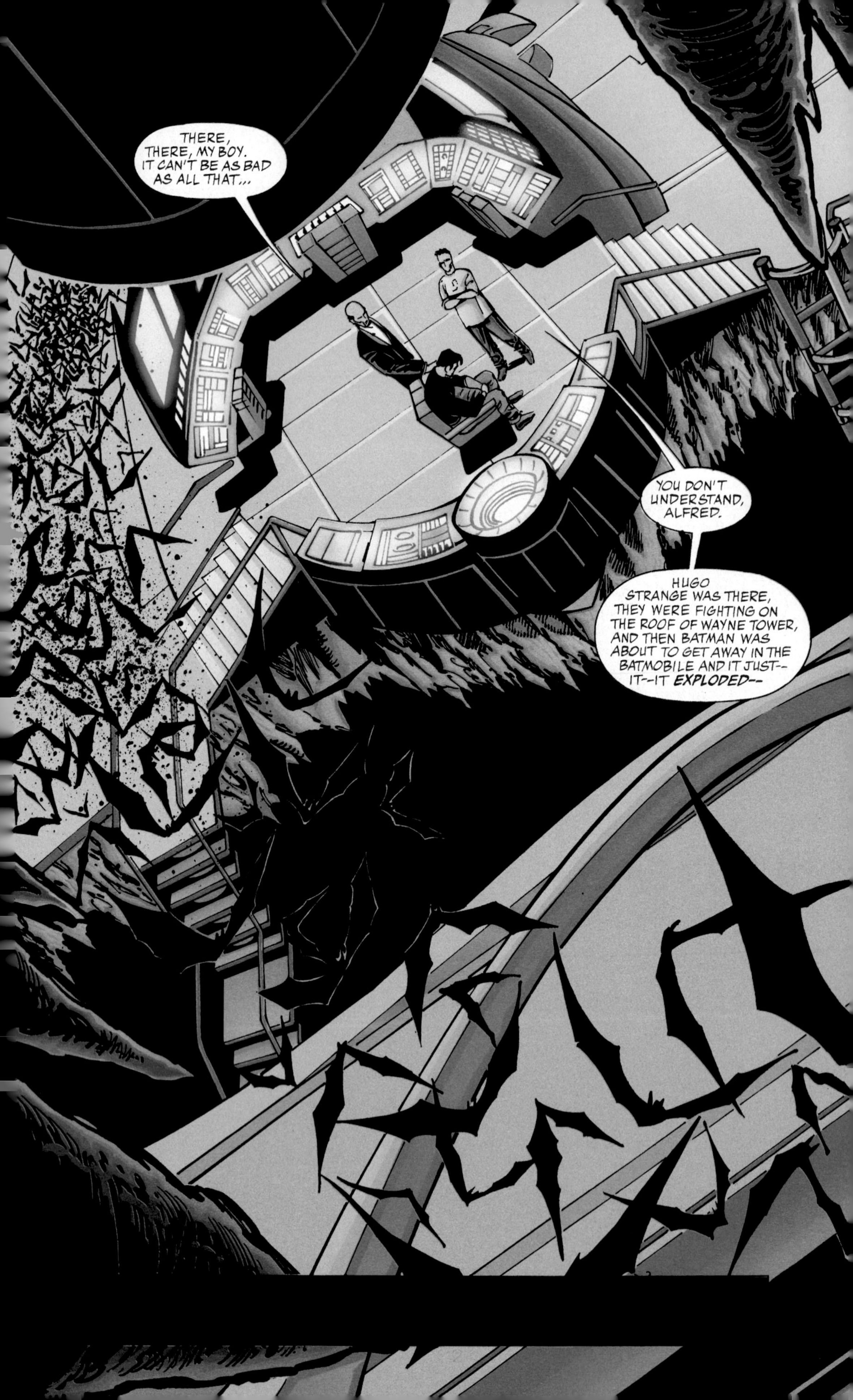
THERE, THERE, MY BOY. IT CAN'T BE AS BAD AS ALL THAT...
YOU DON'T UNDERSTAND, ALFRED.
HUGO STRANGE WAS THERE, THEY WERE FIGHTING ON THE ROOF OF WAYNE TOWER, AND THEN BATMAN WAS ABOUT TO GET AWAY IN THE BATMOBILE AND IT JUST-- IT--IT EXPLODED--

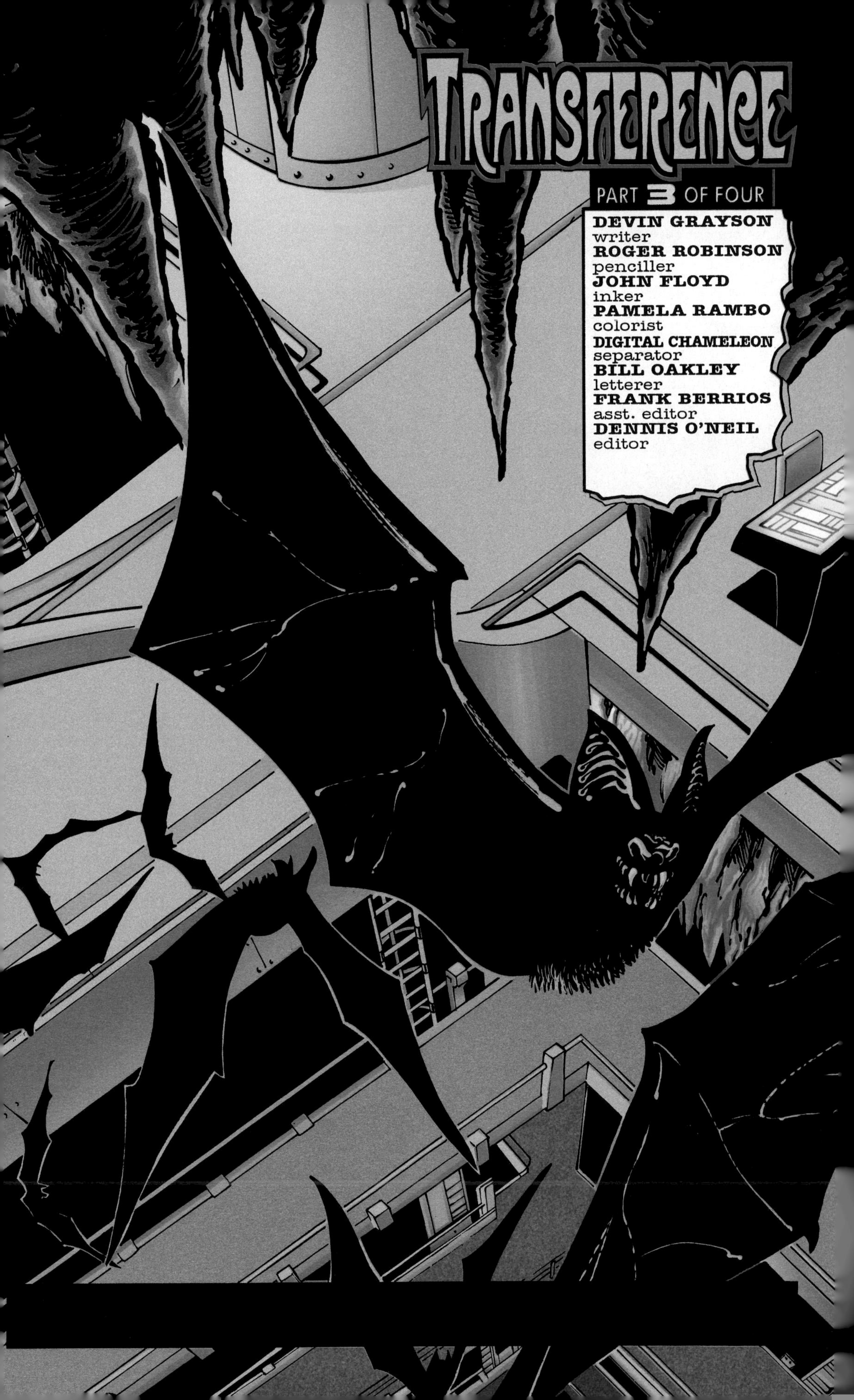
TRANSFERENCE
PART 3 OF FOUR
DEVIN GRAYSON writer
ROGER ROBINSON penciller
JOHN FLOYD inker
PAMELA RAMBO colorist
DIGITAL CHAMELEON separator
BILL OAKLEY letterer
FRANK BERRIOS asst. editor
DENNIS O'NEIL editor

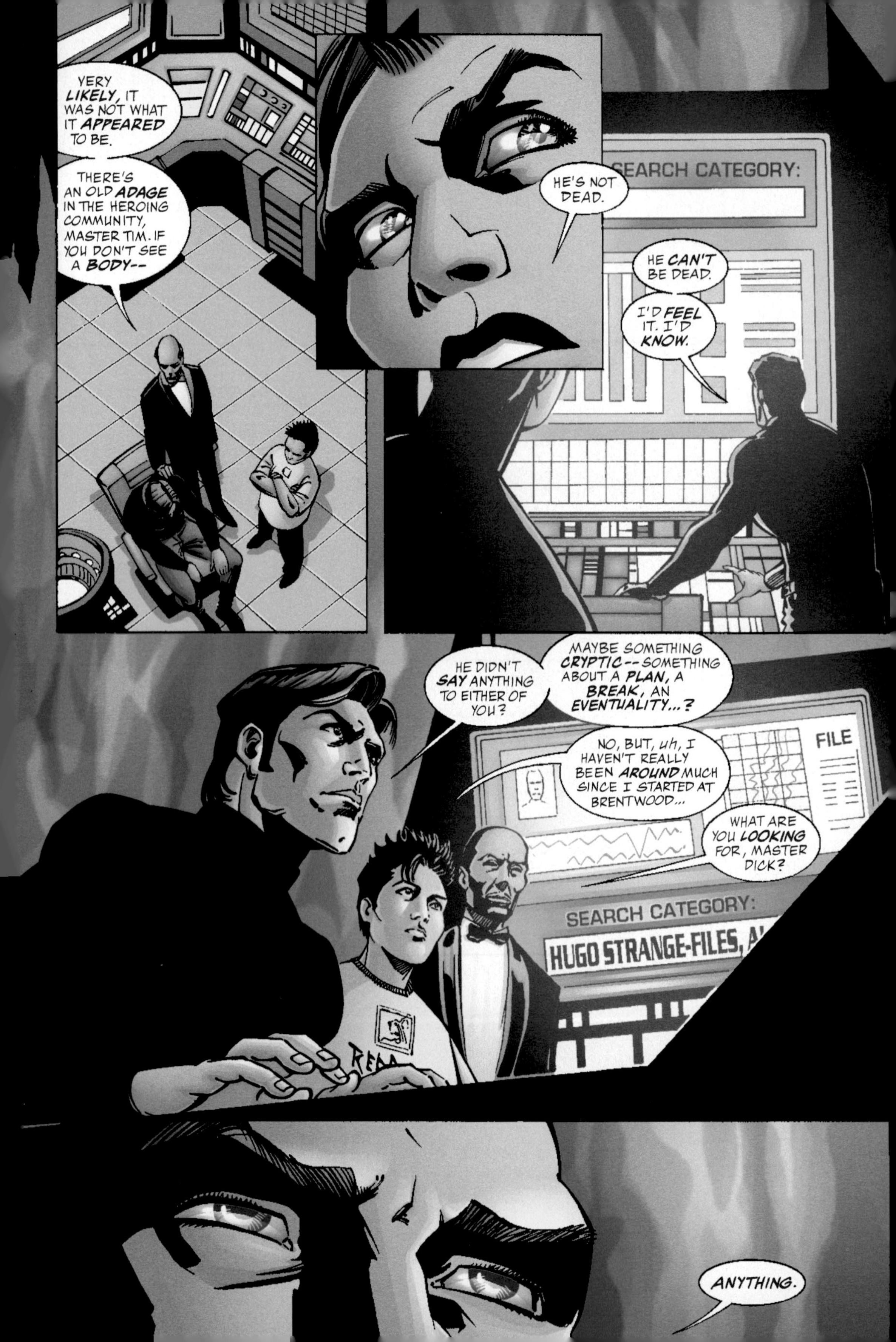

VERY LIKELY, IT WAS NOT WHAT IT APPEARED TO BE.
THERE'S AN OLD ADAGE IN THE HEROING COMMUNITY, MASTER TIM. IF YOU DON'T SEE A BODY--
HE'S NOT DEAD.
SEARCH CATEGORY:
HE CAN'T BE DEAD.
I'D FEEL IT. I'D KNOW.
HE DIDN'T SAY ANYTHING TO EITHER OF YOU?
MAYBE SOMETHING CRYPTIC--SOMETHING ABOUT A PLAN, A BREAK, AN EVENTUALITY...?
FILE
NO, BUT, uh, I HAVEN'T REALLY BEEN AROUND MUCH SINCE I STARTED AT BRENTWOOD...
WHAT ARE YOU LOOKING FOR, MASTER DICK?
SEARCH CATEGORY:
HUGO STRANGE-FILES, A
ANYTHING.

YEAH, GOOD. I DON'T HAVE THE *PATIENCE* FOR THIS.

NO *KIDDING*...

CALL IN *BABS* IF YOU NEED TO.

AND IF *HUGO* DOESN'T YIELD ANYTHING, CHECK ANY FILES WITH YOUR OR MY *NAME* IN THEM-- MAYBE HE LEFT US A *MESSAGE* SOMEWHERE.

AND WHERE ARE *YOU* GOING, MASTER DICK?

SEARCH CATEGORY:

## HUGO STRANGE-FILES, ALL

YIELDS 472 MATCHES
ENTER SORT PARAMETER?

AH, BRUCE, FOR CRYING OUT LOUD, YOU DON'T NEED TO WRITE DOWN *EVERYTHING*...

I CAN LOOK THROUGH THOSE *FOR* YOU IF YOU WANT...?

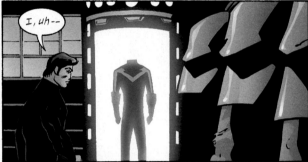

I, *uh*--

I'M GONNA GO CHECK THE *CRIME SCENE* AGAIN...

...MAYBE GET A CLUE AS TO WHERE BRUCE OR HUGO MIGHT HAVE *GONE*...

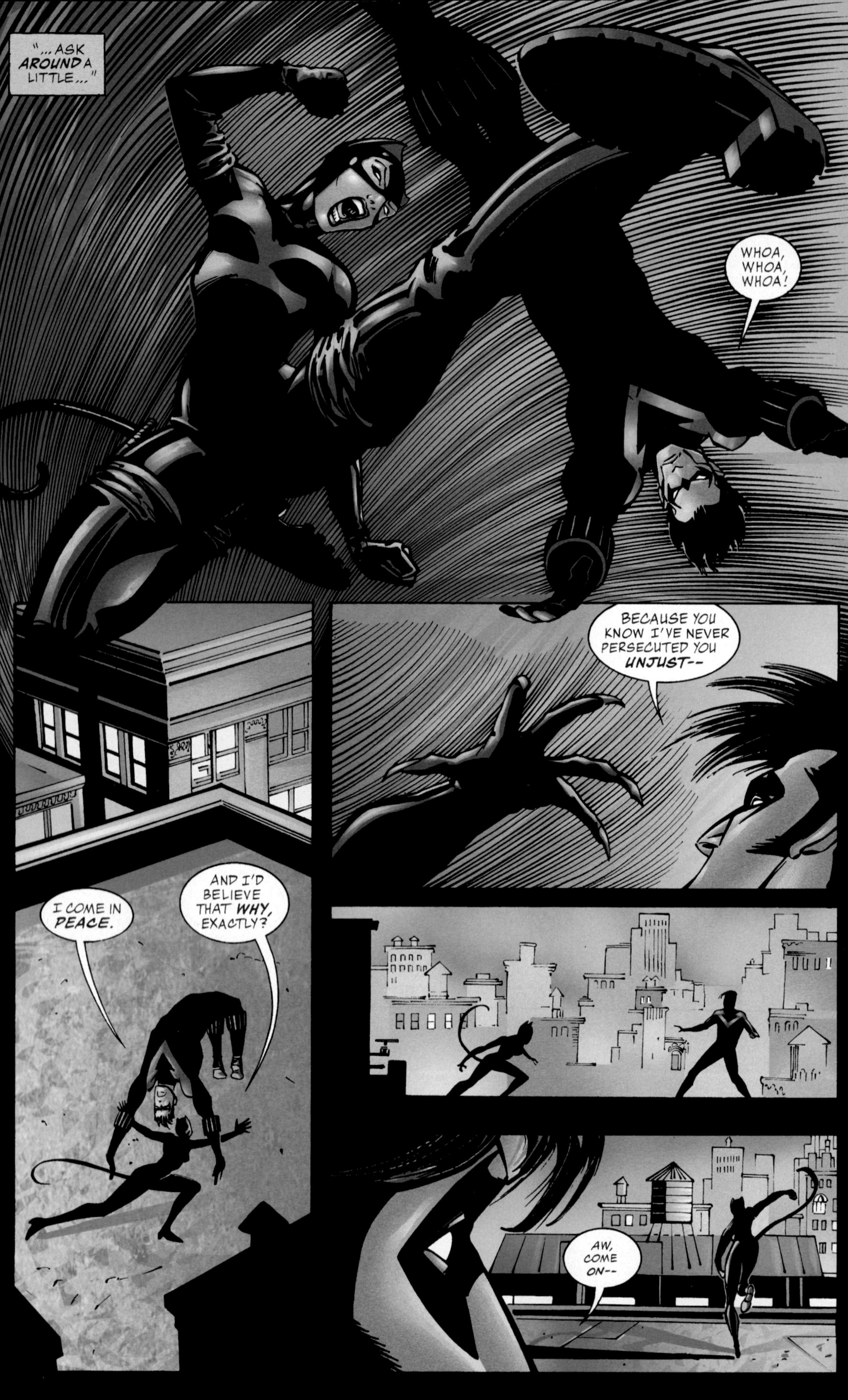
"...ASK AROUND A LITTLE..."
WHOA, WHOA, WHOA!
BECAUSE YOU KNOW I'VE NEVER PERSECUTED YOU UNJUST--
I COME IN PEACE.
AND I'D BELIEVE THAT WHY, EXACTLY?
AW, COME ON--

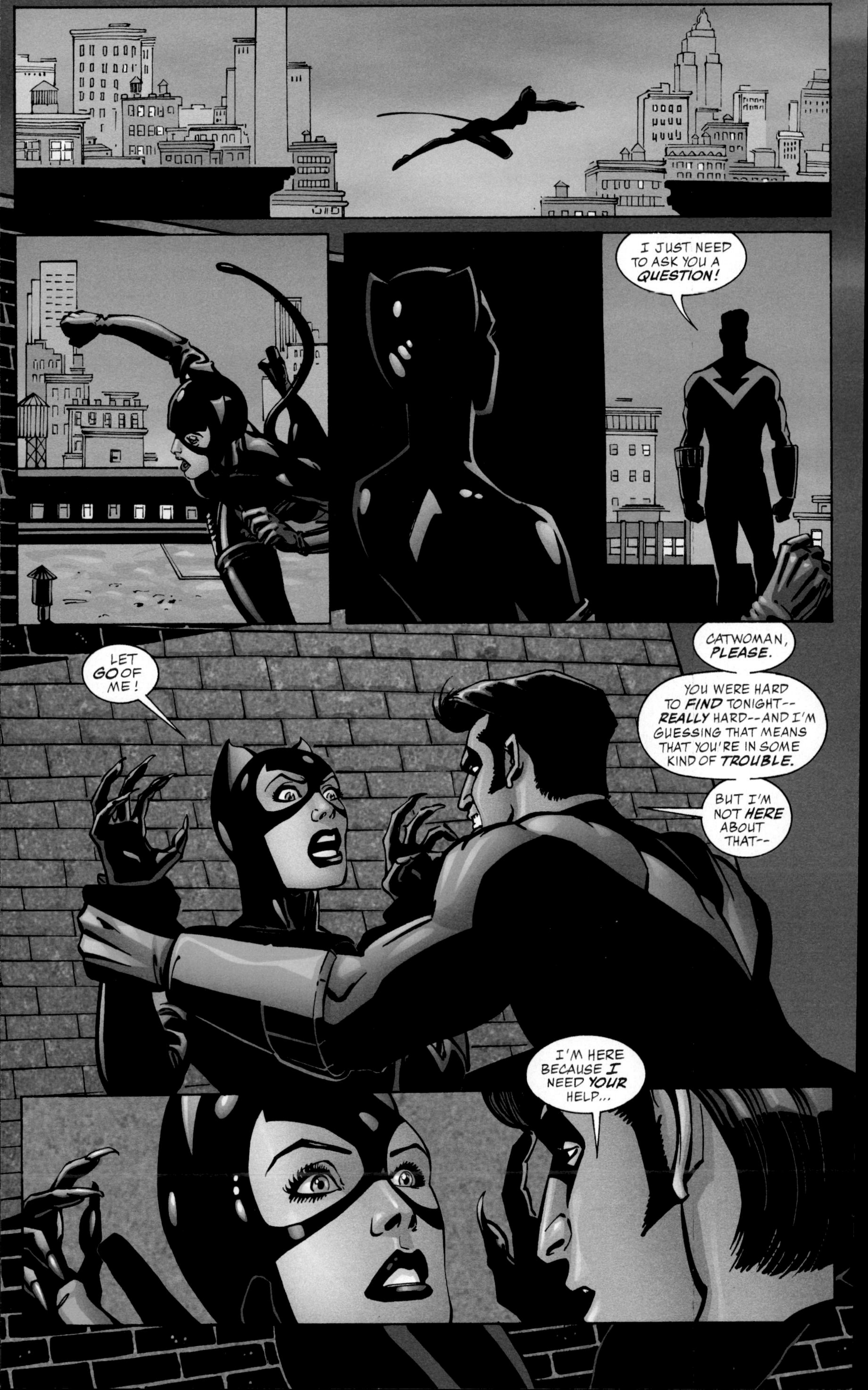
I JUST NEED TO ASK YOU A QUESTION!
LET GO OF ME!
CATWOMAN, PLEASE.
YOU WERE HARD TO FIND TONIGHT-- REALLY HARD--AND I'M GUESSING THAT MEANS THAT YOU'RE IN SOME KIND OF TROUBLE.
BUT I'M NOT HERE ABOUT THAT--
I'M HERE BECAUSE I NEED YOUR HELP...

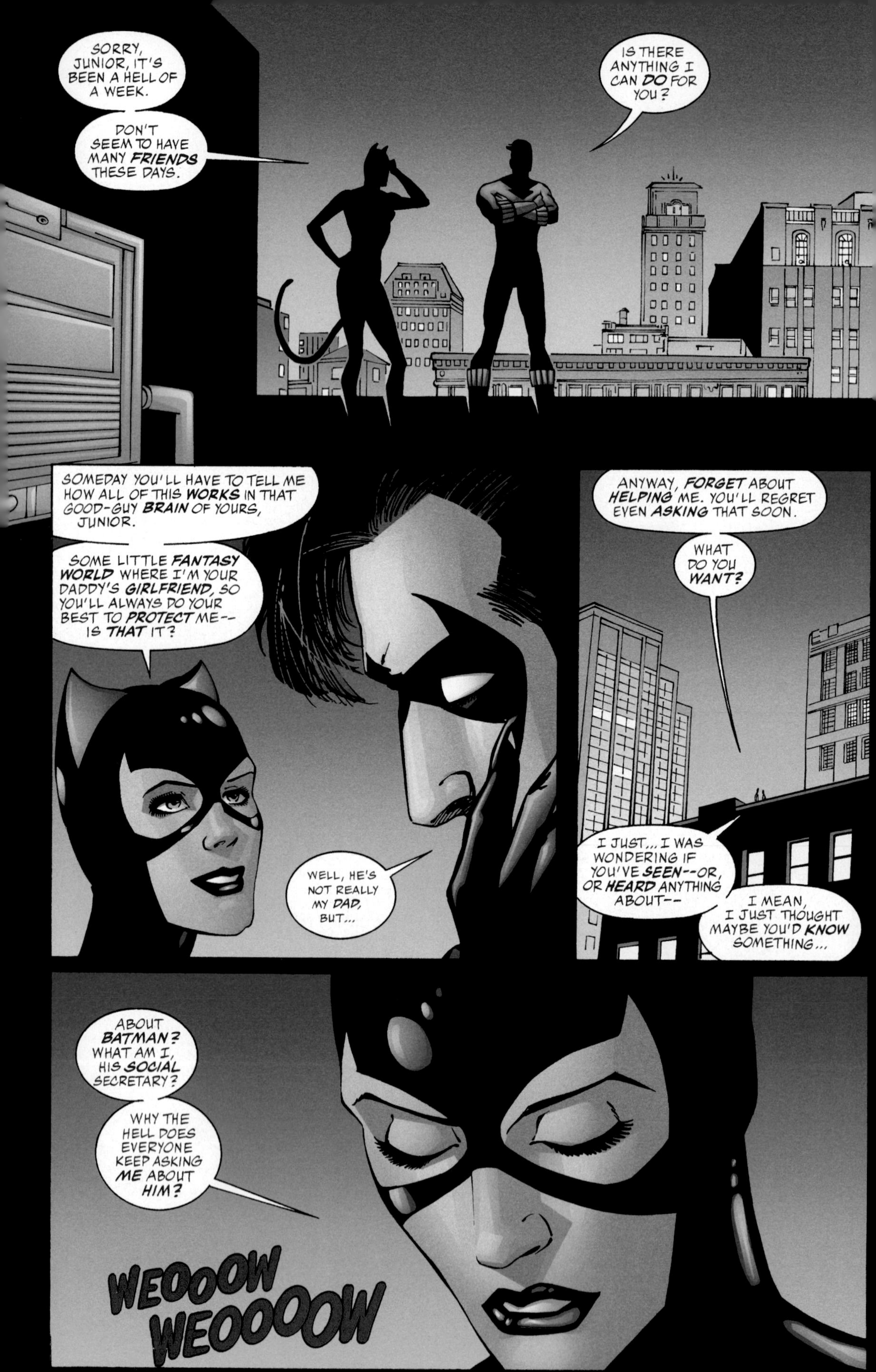
SORRY, JUNIOR, IT'S BEEN A HELL OF A WEEK.
DON'T SEEM TO HAVE MANY FRIENDS THESE DAYS.
IS THERE ANYTHING I CAN DO FOR YOU?
SOMEDAY YOU'LL HAVE TO TELL ME HOW ALL OF THIS WORKS IN THAT GOOD-GUY BRAIN OF YOURS, JUNIOR.
SOME LITTLE FANTASY WORLD WHERE I'M YOUR DADDY'S GIRLFRIEND, SO YOU'LL ALWAYS DO YOUR BEST TO PROTECT ME-- IS THAT IT?
WELL, HE'S NOT REALLY MY DAD, BUT...
ANYWAY, FORGET ABOUT HELPING ME. YOU'LL REGRET EVEN ASKING THAT SOON.
WHAT DO YOU WANT?
I JUST... I WAS WONDERING IF YOU'VE SEEN--OR, OR HEARD ANYTHING ABOUT--
I MEAN, I JUST THOUGHT MAYBE YOU'D KNOW SOMETHING...
ABOUT BATMAN? WHAT AM I, HIS SOCIAL SECRETARY?
WHY THE HELL DOES EVERYONE KEEP ASKING ME ABOUT HIM?
WEOOOW WEOOOOW

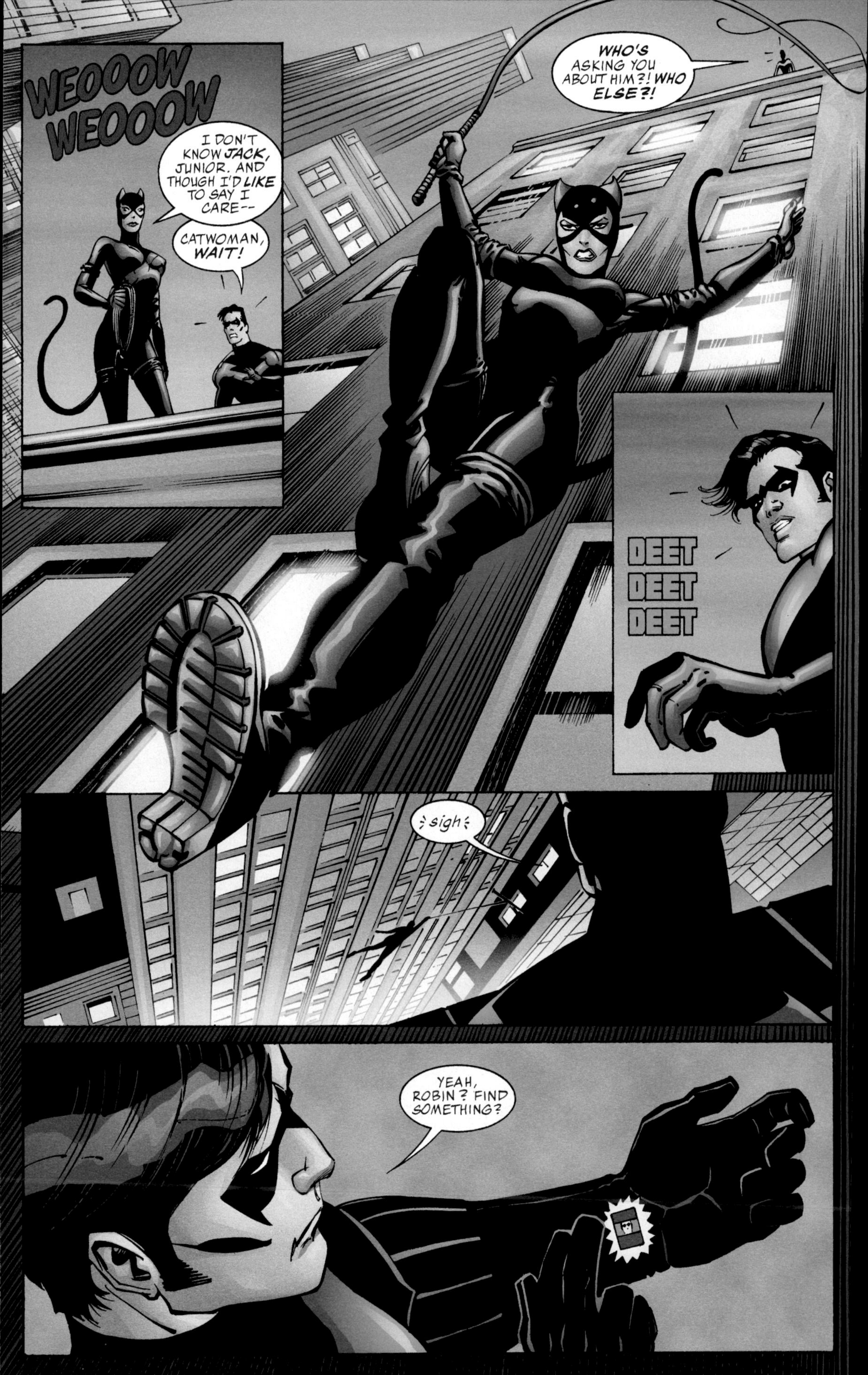
WEOOOW WEOOOW
I DON'T KNOW JACK, JUNIOR. AND THOUGH I'D LIKE TO SAY I CARE--
CATWOMAN, WAIT!
WHO'S ASKING YOU ABOUT HIM?! WHO ELSE?!
DEET DEET DEET
sigh
YEAH, ROBIN? FIND SOMETHING?

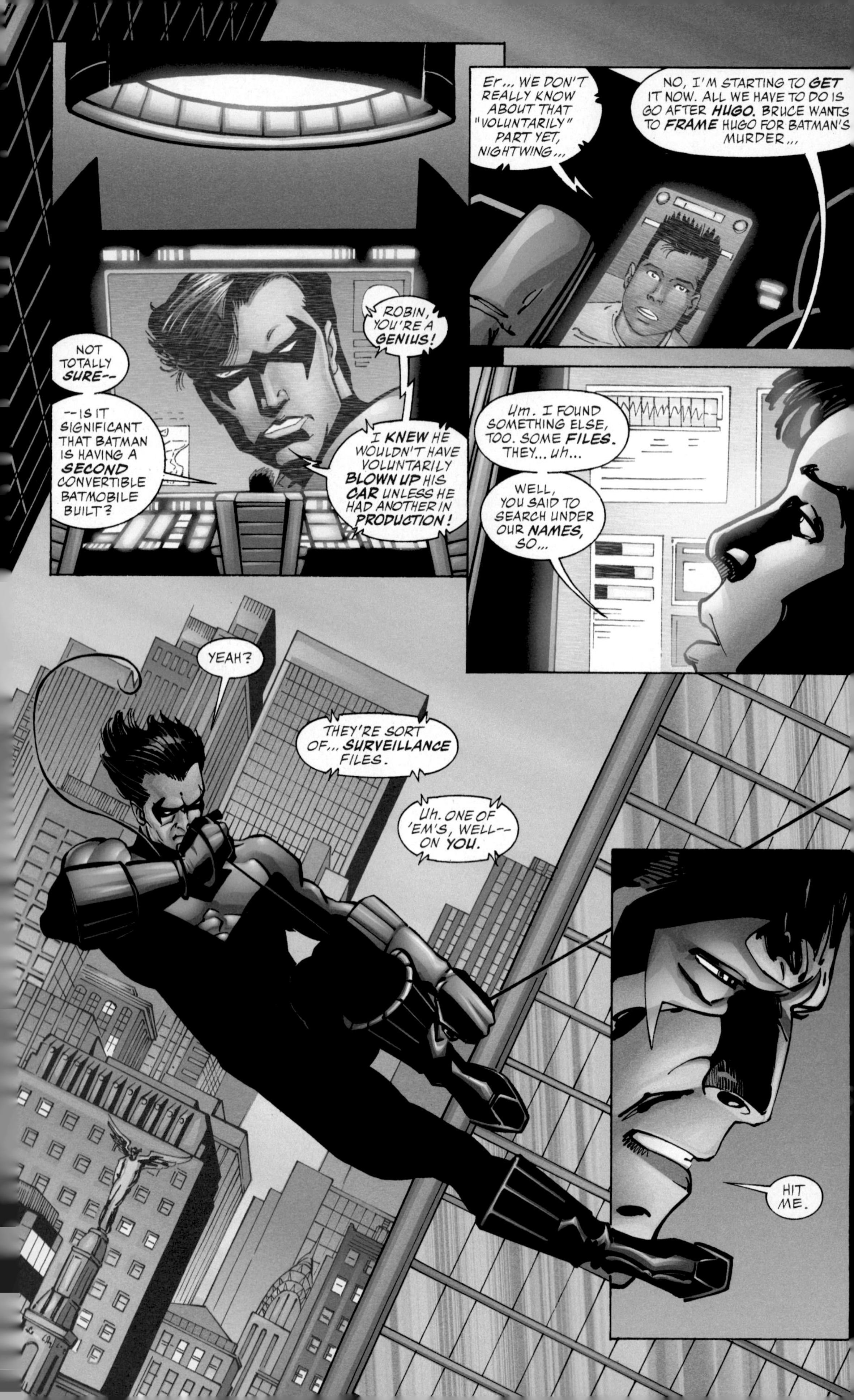
NOT TOTALLY SURE--
--IS IT SIGNIFICANT THAT BATMAN IS HAVING A SECOND CONVERTIBLE BATMOBILE BUILT?
ROBIN, YOU'RE A GENIUS!
I KNEW HE WOULDN'T HAVE VOLUNTARILY BLOWN UP HIS CAR UNLESS HE HAD ANOTHER IN PRODUCTION!
Er... WE DON'T REALLY KNOW ABOUT THAT "VOLUNTARILY" PART YET, NIGHTWING...
NO, I'M STARTING TO GET IT NOW. ALL WE HAVE TO DO IS GO AFTER HUGO. BRUCE WANTS TO FRAME HUGO FOR BATMAN'S MURDER...
Um. I FOUND SOMETHING ELSE, TOO. SOME FILES. THEY... uh...
WELL, YOU SAID TO SEARCH UNDER OUR NAMES, SO...
YEAH?
THEY'RE SORT OF... SURVEILLANCE FILES.
Uh. ONE OF 'EM'S, WELL-- ON YOU.
HIT ME.

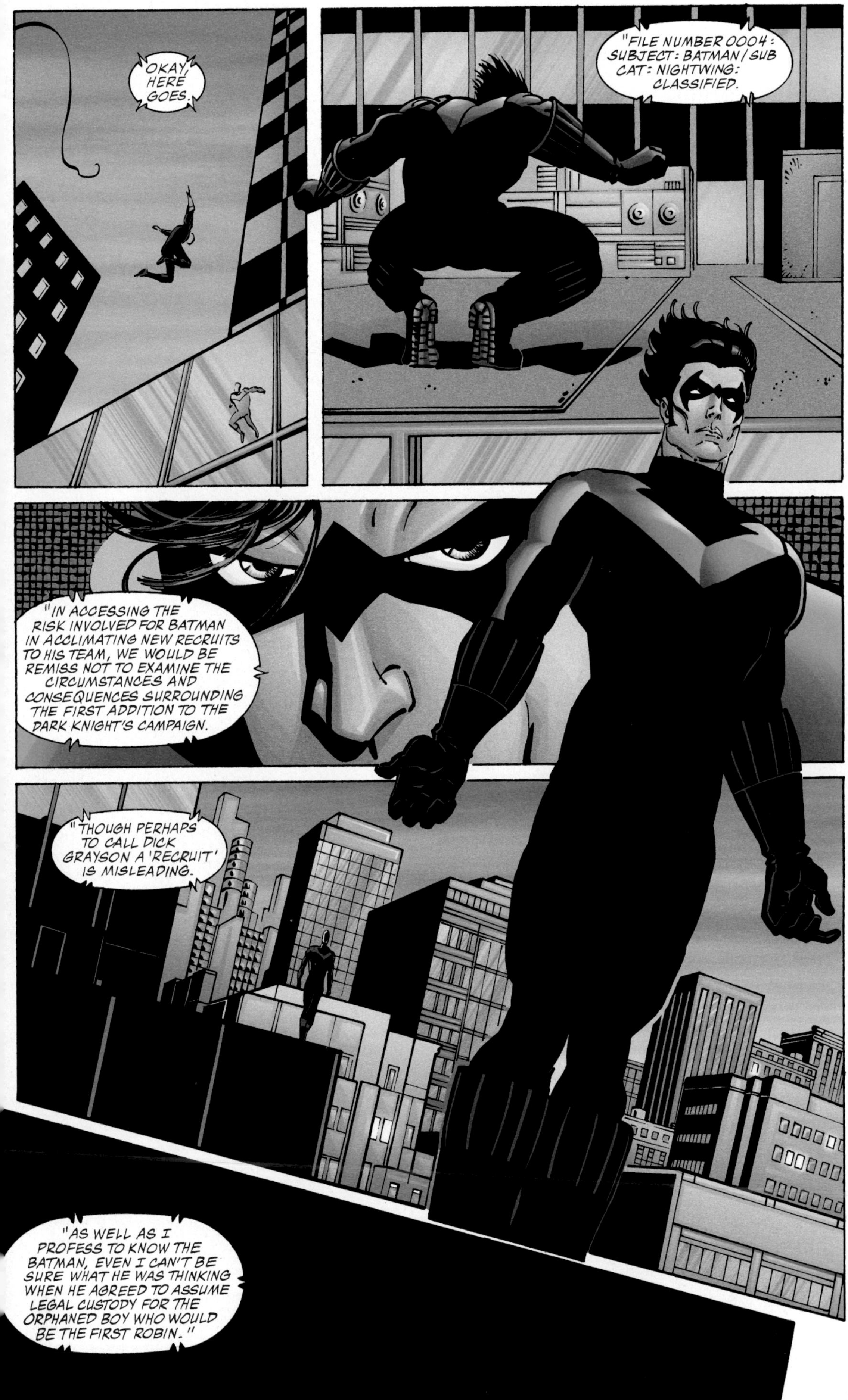
OKAY, HERE GOES.
"FILE NUMBER 0004: SUBJECT: BATMAN / SUB CAT: NIGHTWING: CLASSIFIED.
"IN ACCESSING THE RISK INVOLVED FOR BATMAN IN ACCLIMATING NEW RECRUITS TO HIS TEAM, WE WOULD BE REMISS NOT TO EXAMINE THE CIRCUMSTANCES AND CONSEQUENCES SURROUNDING THE FIRST ADDITION TO THE DARK KNIGHT'S CAMPAIGN.
"THOUGH PERHAPS TO CALL DICK GRAYSON A 'RECRUIT' IS MISLEADING.
"AS WELL AS I PROFESS TO KNOW THE BATMAN, EVEN I CAN'T BE SURE WHAT HE WAS THINKING WHEN HE AGREED TO ASSUME LEGAL CUSTODY FOR THE ORPHANED BOY WHO WOULD BE THE FIRST ROBIN."

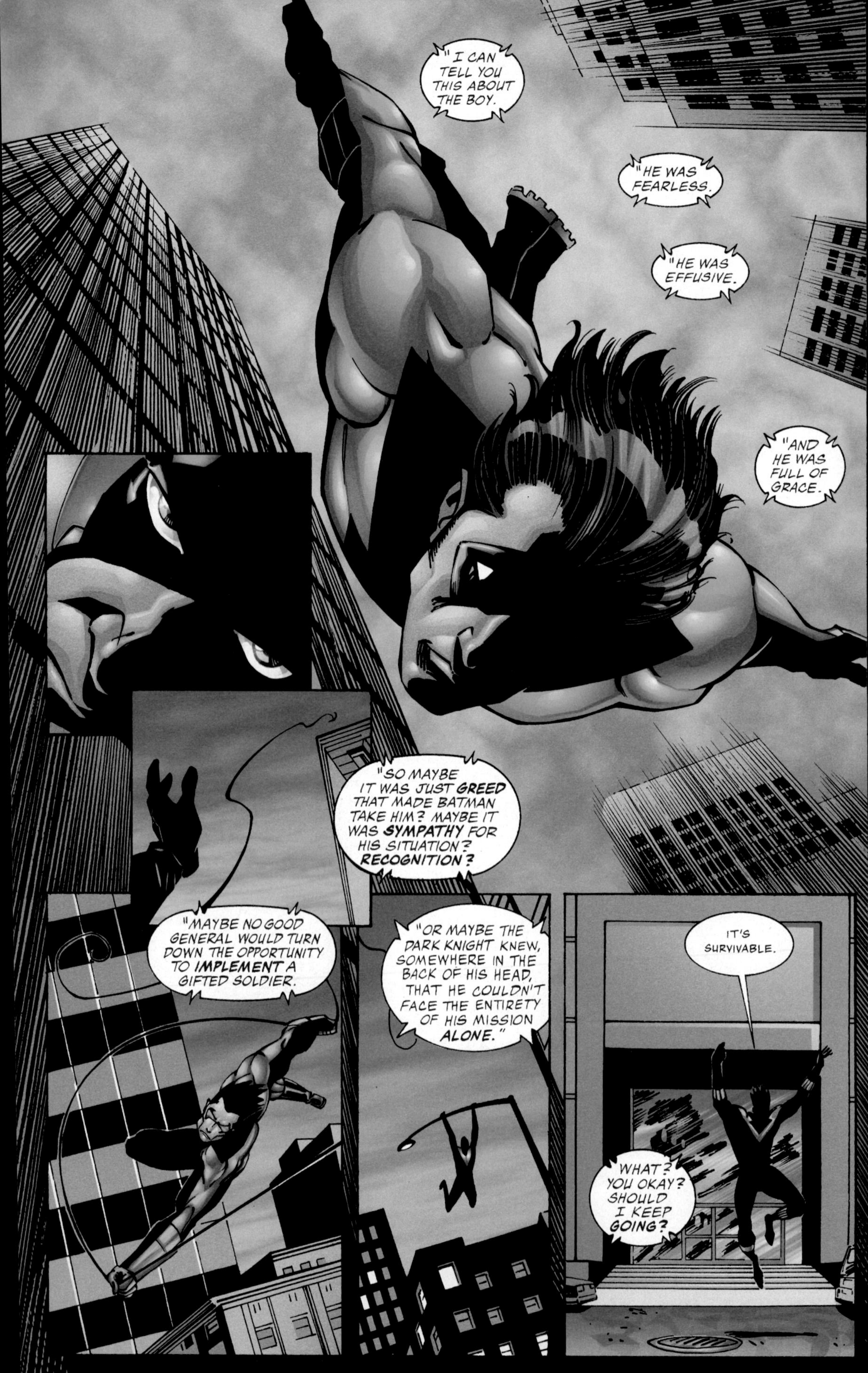
"I CAN TELL YOU THIS ABOUT THE BOY.
"HE WAS FEARLESS.
"HE WAS EFFUSIVE.
"AND HE WAS FULL OF GRACE.
"SO MAYBE IT WAS JUST GREED THAT MADE BATMAN TAKE HIM? MAYBE IT WAS SYMPATHY FOR HIS SITUATION? RECOGNITION?
"MAYBE NO GOOD GENERAL WOULD TURN DOWN THE OPPORTUNITY TO IMPLEMENT A GIFTED SOLDIER.
"OR MAYBE THE DARK KNIGHT KNEW, SOMEWHERE IN THE BACK OF HIS HEAD, THAT HE COULDN'T FACE THE ENTIRETY OF HIS MISSION ALONE."
IT'S SURVIVABLE.
WHAT? YOU OKAY? SHOULD I KEEP GOING?

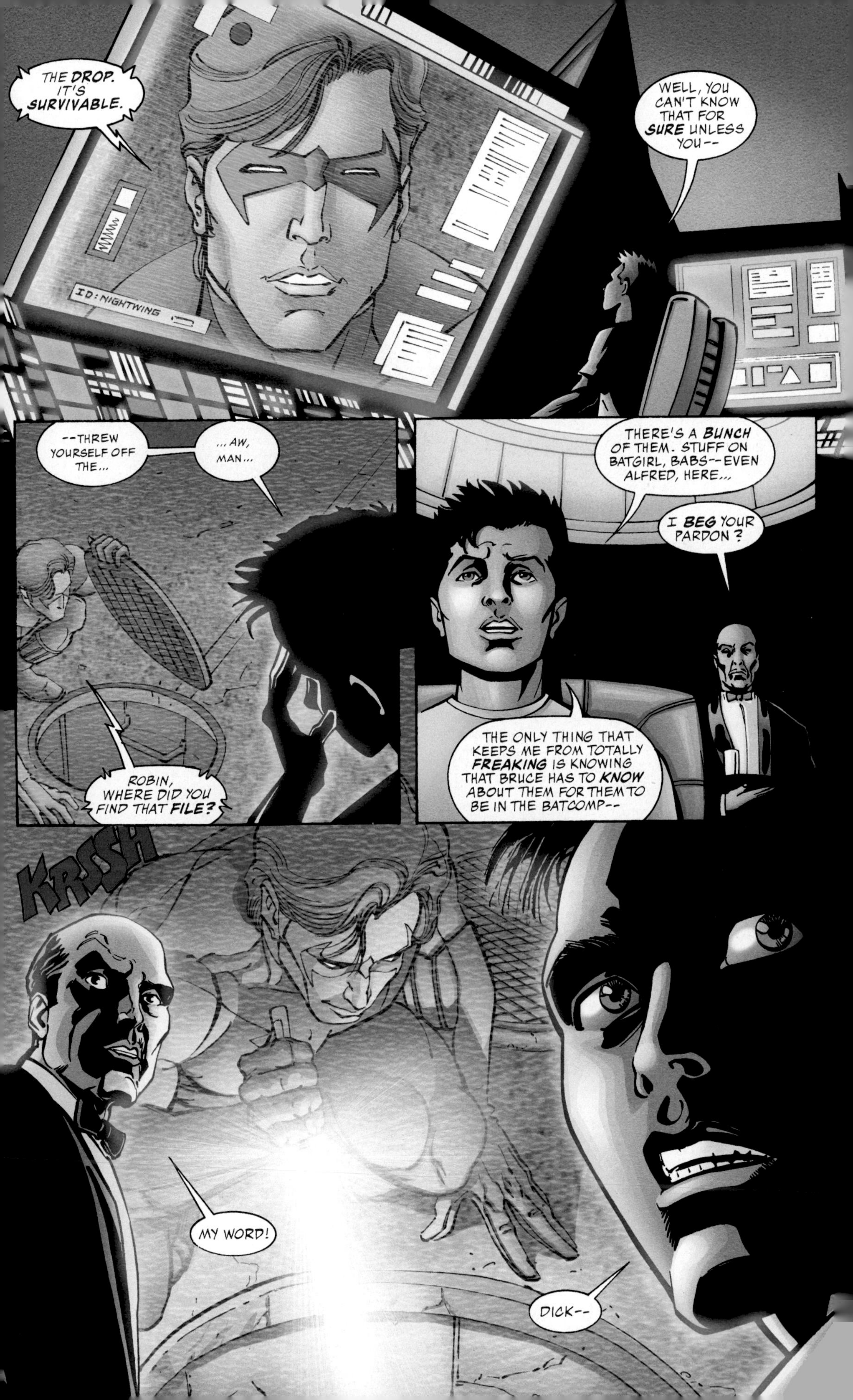
THE DROP. IT'S SURVIVABLE.
WELL, YOU CAN'T KNOW THAT FOR SURE UNLESS YOU--
ID: NIGHTWING
--THREW YOURSELF OFF THE...
...AW, MAN...
ROBIN, WHERE DID YOU FIND THAT FILE?
THERE'S A BUNCH OF THEM. STUFF ON BATGIRL, BABS--EVEN ALFRED, HERE...
I BEG YOUR PARDON?
THE ONLY THING THAT KEEPS ME FROM TOTALLY FREAKING IS KNOWING THAT BRUCE HAS TO KNOW ABOUT THEM FOR THEM TO BE IN THE BATCOMP--
KRSSH
MY WORD!
DICK--

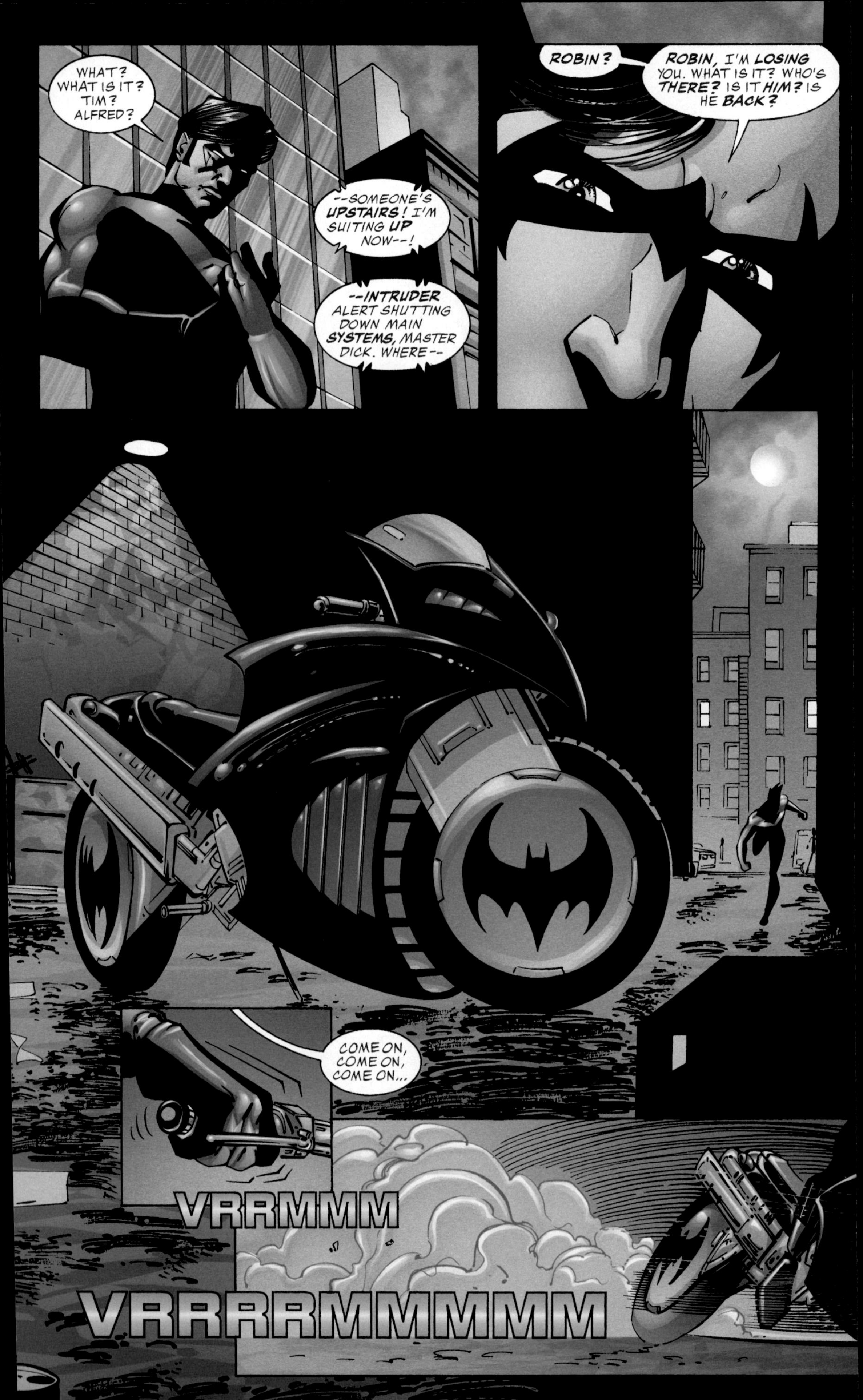
WHAT? WHAT IS IT? TIM? ALFRED?
--SOMEONE'S UPSTAIRS! I'M SUITING UP NOW--!
--INTRUDER ALERT SHUTTING DOWN MAIN SYSTEMS, MASTER DICK. WHERE--
ROBIN?
ROBIN, I'M LOSING YOU. WHAT IS IT? WHO'S THERE? IS IT HIM? IS HE BACK?
COME ON, COME ON, COME ON...
VRRMMM
VRRRRMMMMMM

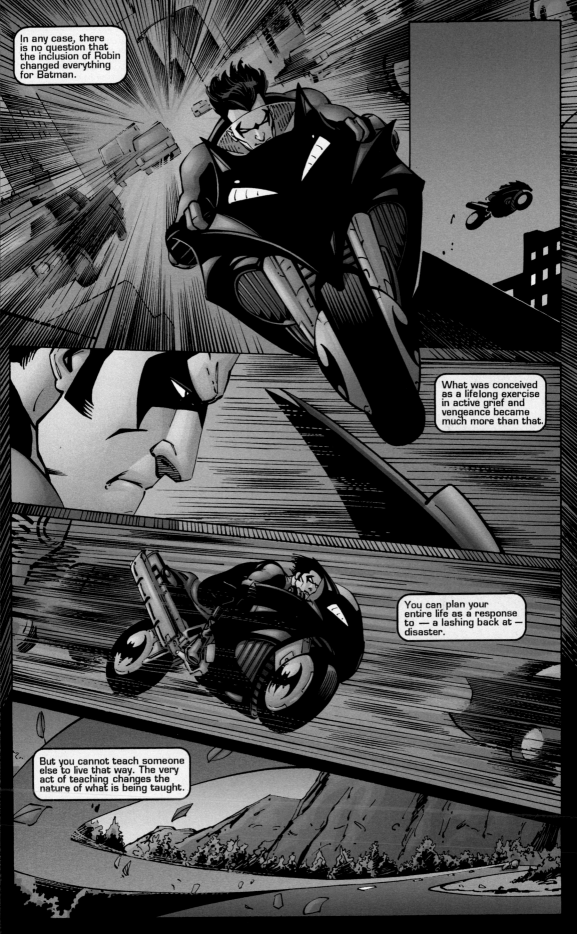

In any case, there is no question that the inclusion of Robin changed everything for Batman.

What was conceived as a lifelong exercise in active grief and vengeance became much more than that.

You can plan your entire life as a response to — a lashing back at — disaster.

But you cannot teach someone else to live that way. The very act of teaching changes the nature of what is being taught.

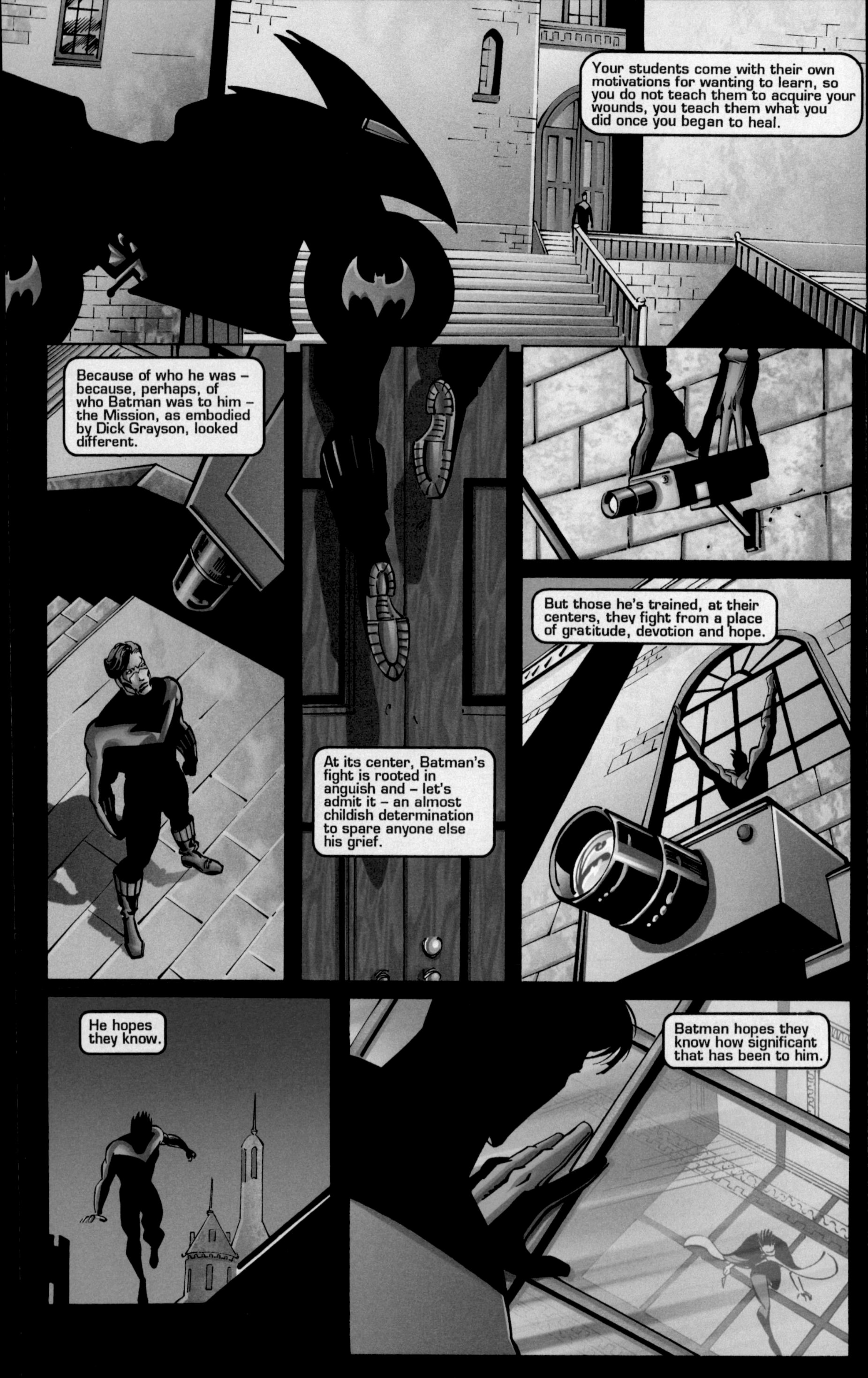
Your students come with their own motivations for wanting to learn, so you do not teach them to acquire your wounds, you teach them what you did once you began to heal.
Because of who he was – because, perhaps, of who Batman was to him – the Mission, as embodied by Dick Grayson, looked different.
At its center, Batman's fight is rooted in anguish and – let's admit it – an almost childish determination to spare anyone else his grief.
But those he's trained, at their centers, they fight from a place of gratitude, devotion and hope.
He hopes they know.
Batman hopes they know how significant that has been to him.

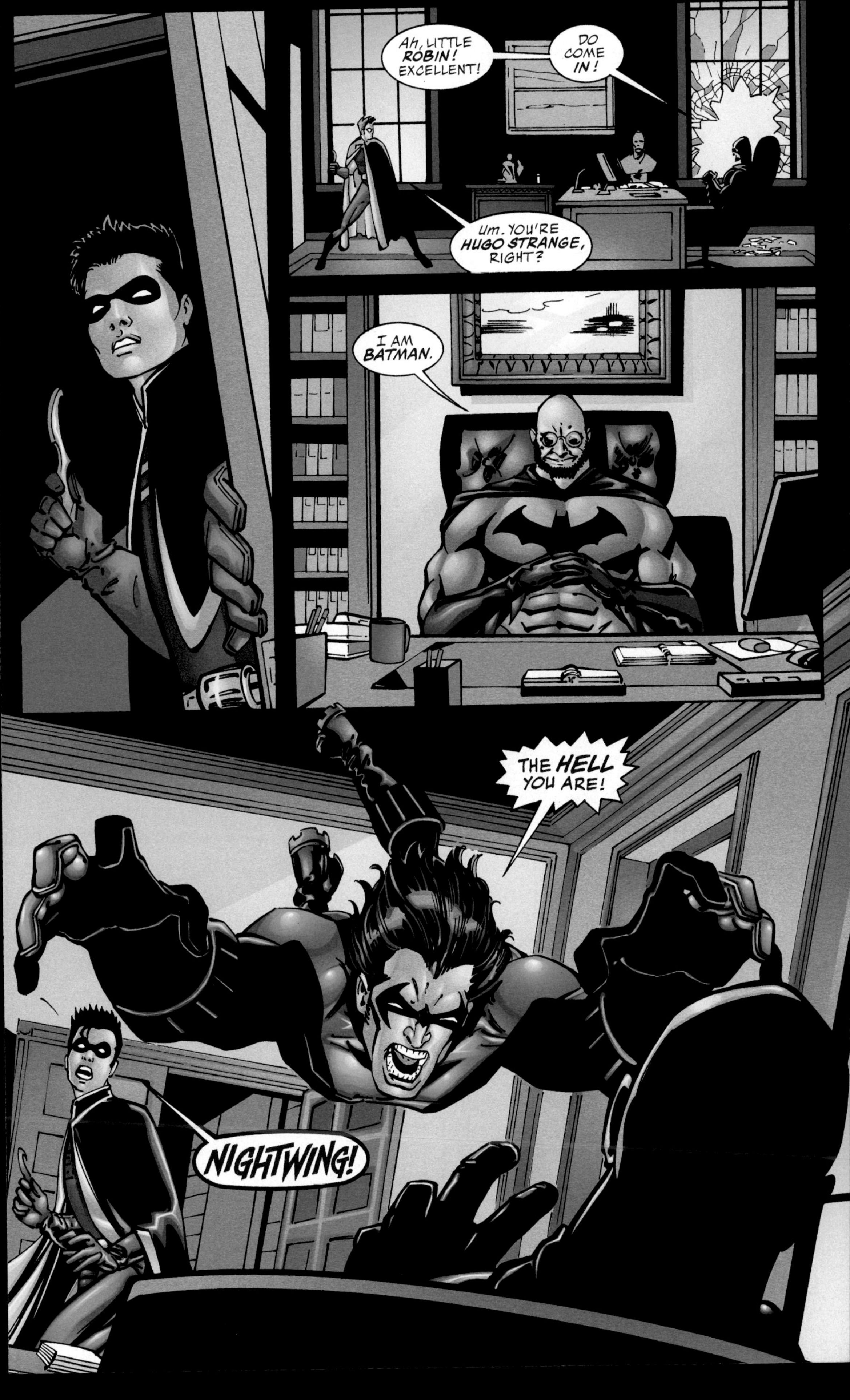
Ah, LITTLE ROBIN! EXCELLENT!
DO COME IN!
Um. YOU'RE HUGO STRANGE, RIGHT?
I AM BATMAN.
THE HELL YOU ARE!
NIGHTWING!

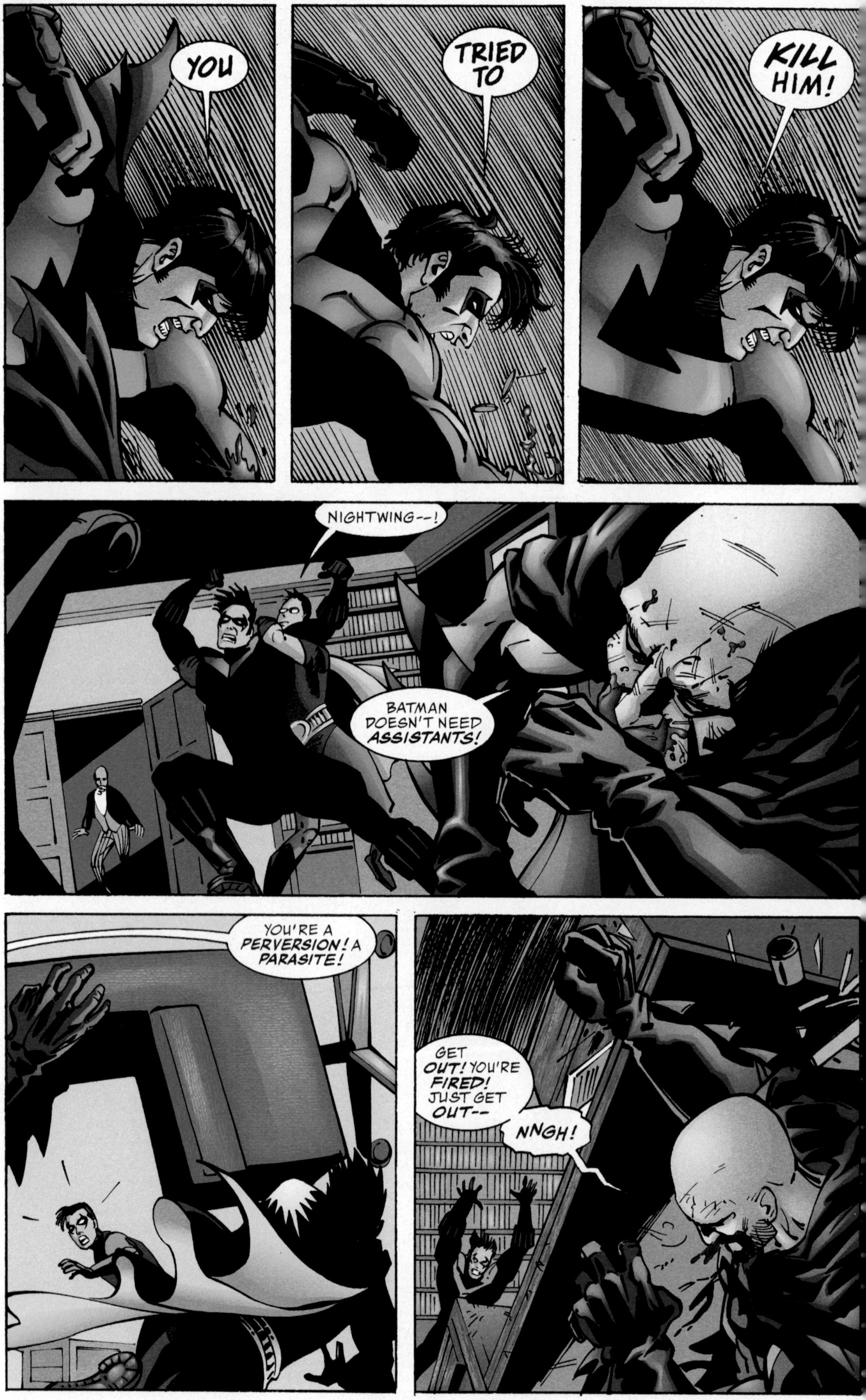
YOU
TRIED TO
KILL HIM!
NIGHTWING--!
BATMAN DOESN'T NEED ASSISTANTS!
YOU'RE A PERVERSION! A PARASITE!
GET OUT! YOU'RE FIRED! JUST GET OUT--
NNGH!

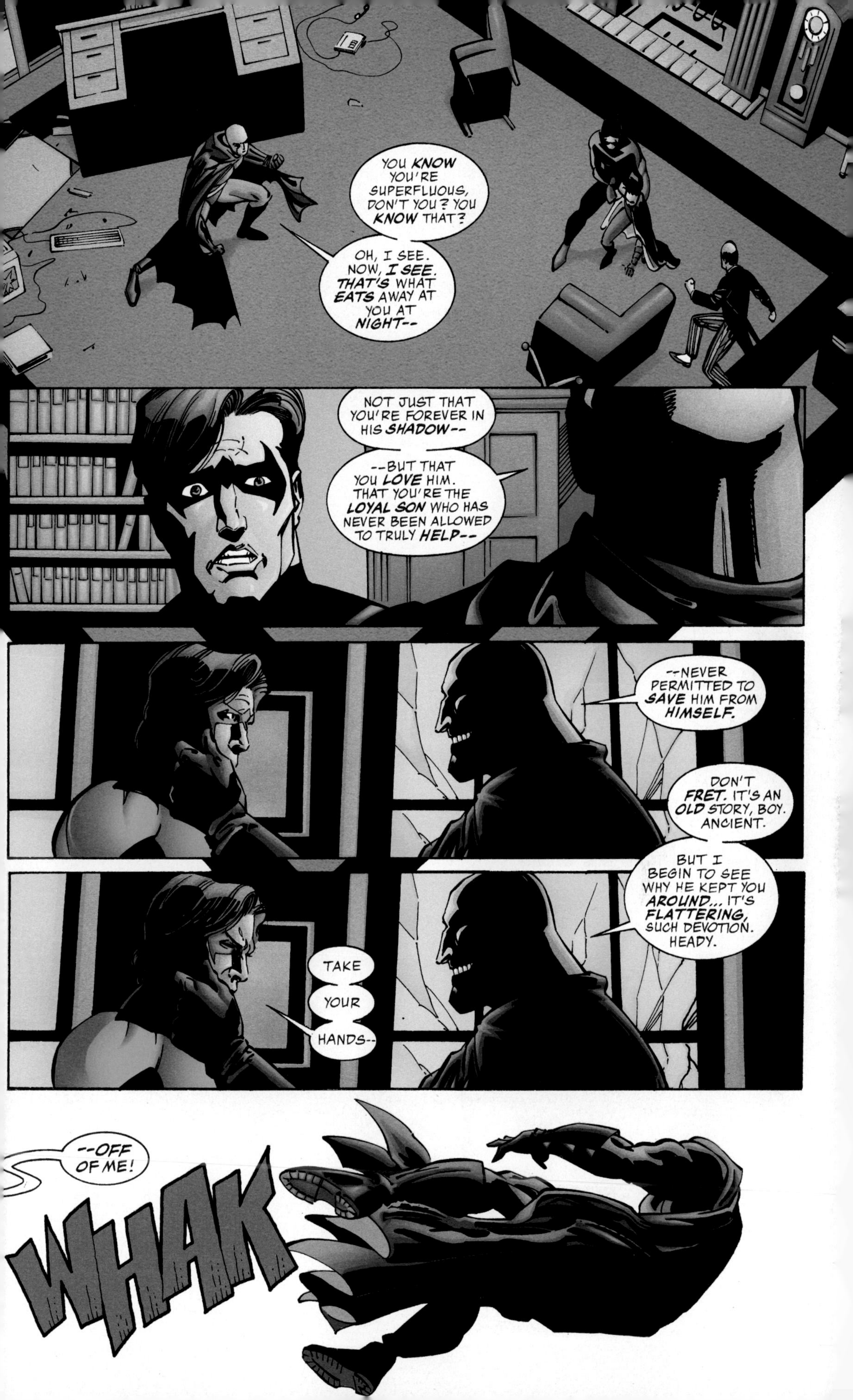

YOU KNOW YOU'RE SUPERFLUOUS, DON'T YOU? YOU KNOW THAT?
OH, I SEE. NOW, I SEE. THAT'S WHAT EATS AWAY AT YOU AT NIGHT--
NOT JUST THAT YOU'RE FOREVER IN HIS SHADOW--
--BUT THAT YOU LOVE HIM. THAT YOU'RE THE LOYAL SON WHO HAS NEVER BEEN ALLOWED TO TRULY HELP--
--NEVER PERMITTED TO SAVE HIM FROM HIMSELF.
DON'T FRET. IT'S AN OLD STORY, BOY. ANCIENT.
BUT I BEGIN TO SEE WHY HE KEPT YOU AROUND... IT'S FLATTERING, SUCH DEVOTION. HEADY.
TAKE
YOUR
HANDS--
--OFF OF ME!
WHAK

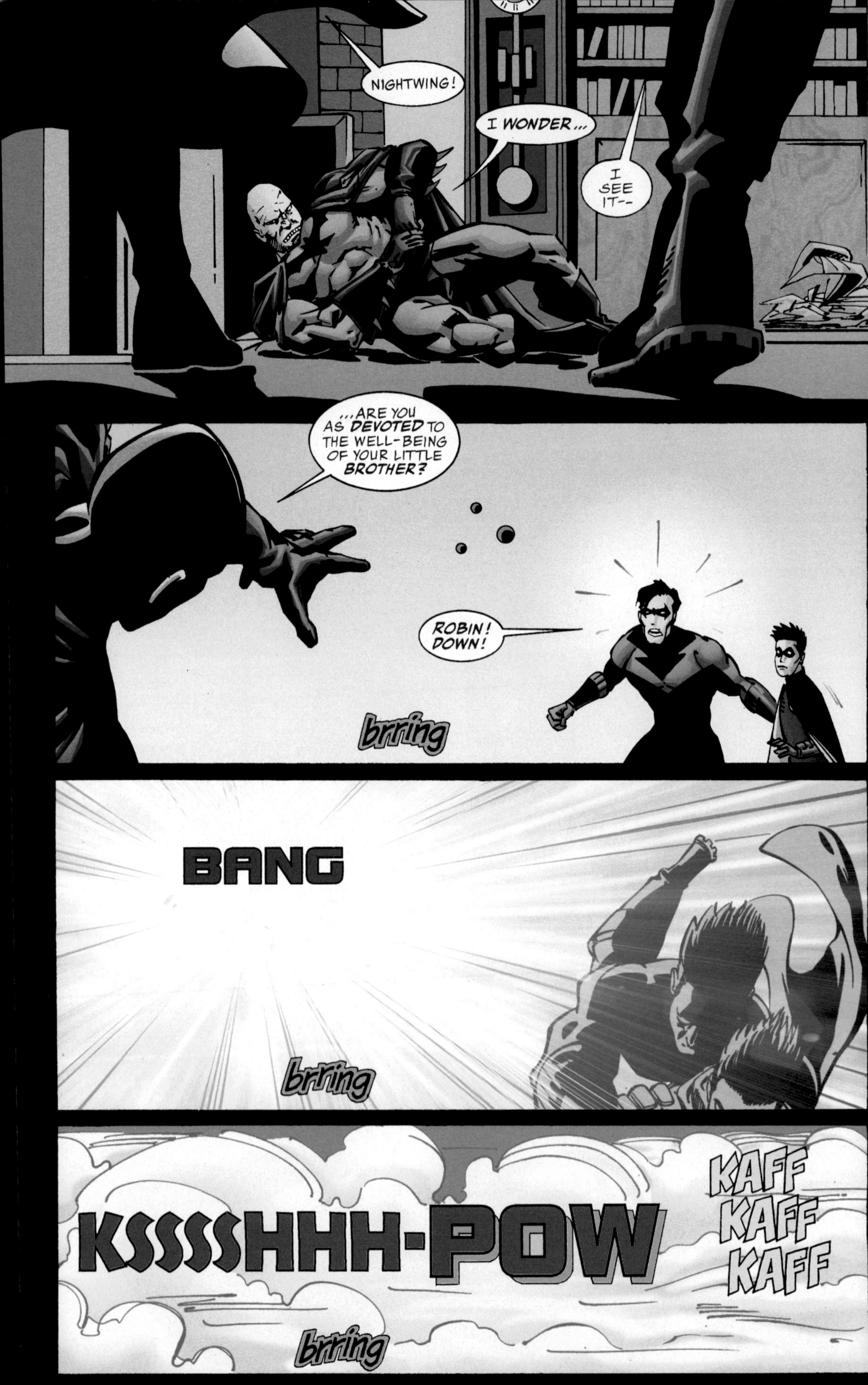
NIGHTWING!
I WONDER...
I SEE IT--
...ARE YOU AS DEVOTED TO THE WELL-BEING OF YOUR LITTLE BROTHER?
ROBIN! DOWN!
brrring
BANG
brrring
KSSSSHHH-POW
KAFF KAFF KAFF
brrring

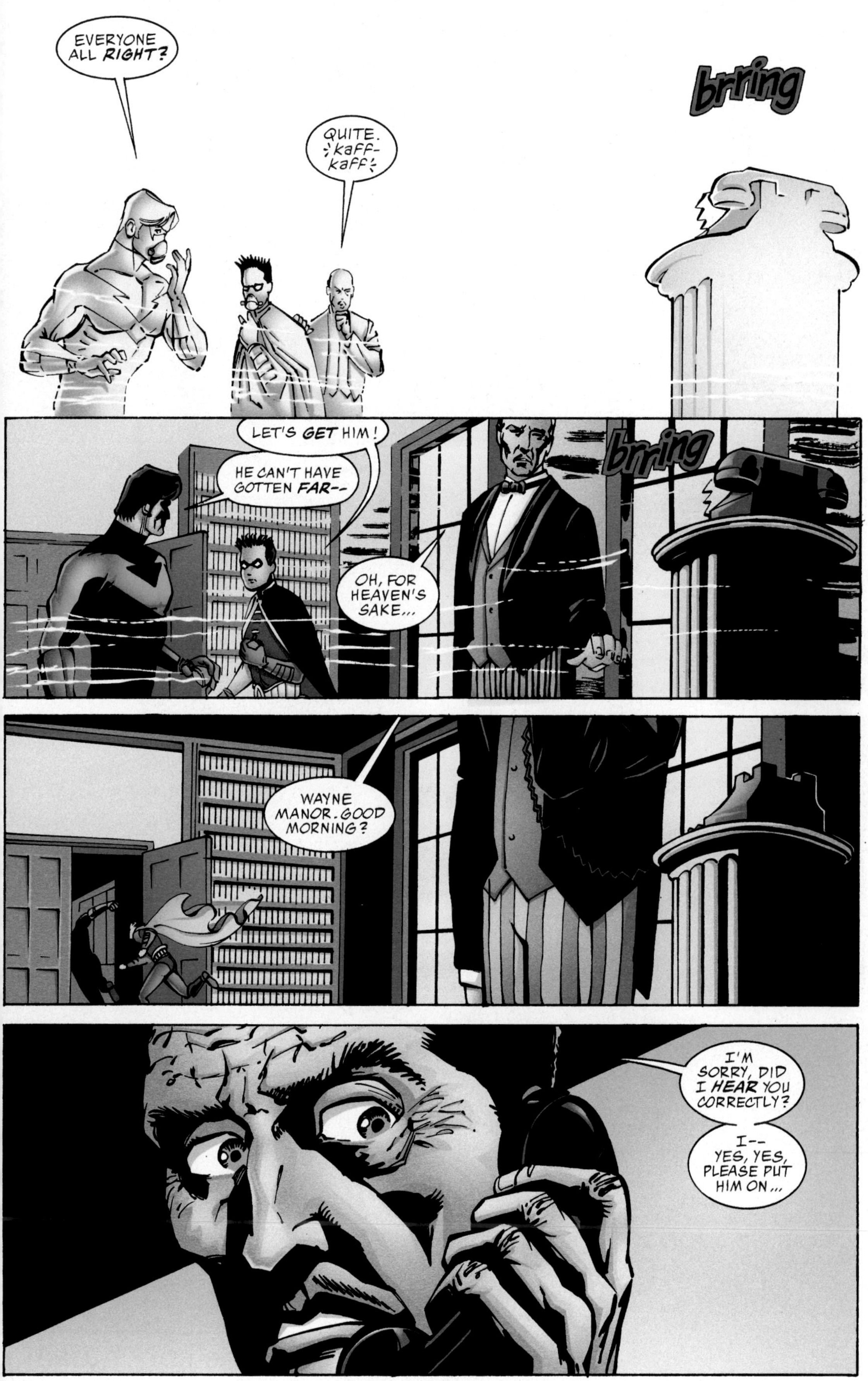
EVERYONE ALL RIGHT?
QUITE. kaff-kaff
brring
LET'S GET HIM!
HE CAN'T HAVE GOTTEN FAR--
brring
OH, FOR HEAVEN'S SAKE...
WAYNE MANOR. GOOD MORNING?
I'M SORRY, DID I HEAR YOU CORRECTLY?
I-- YES, YES, PLEASE PUT HIM ON...

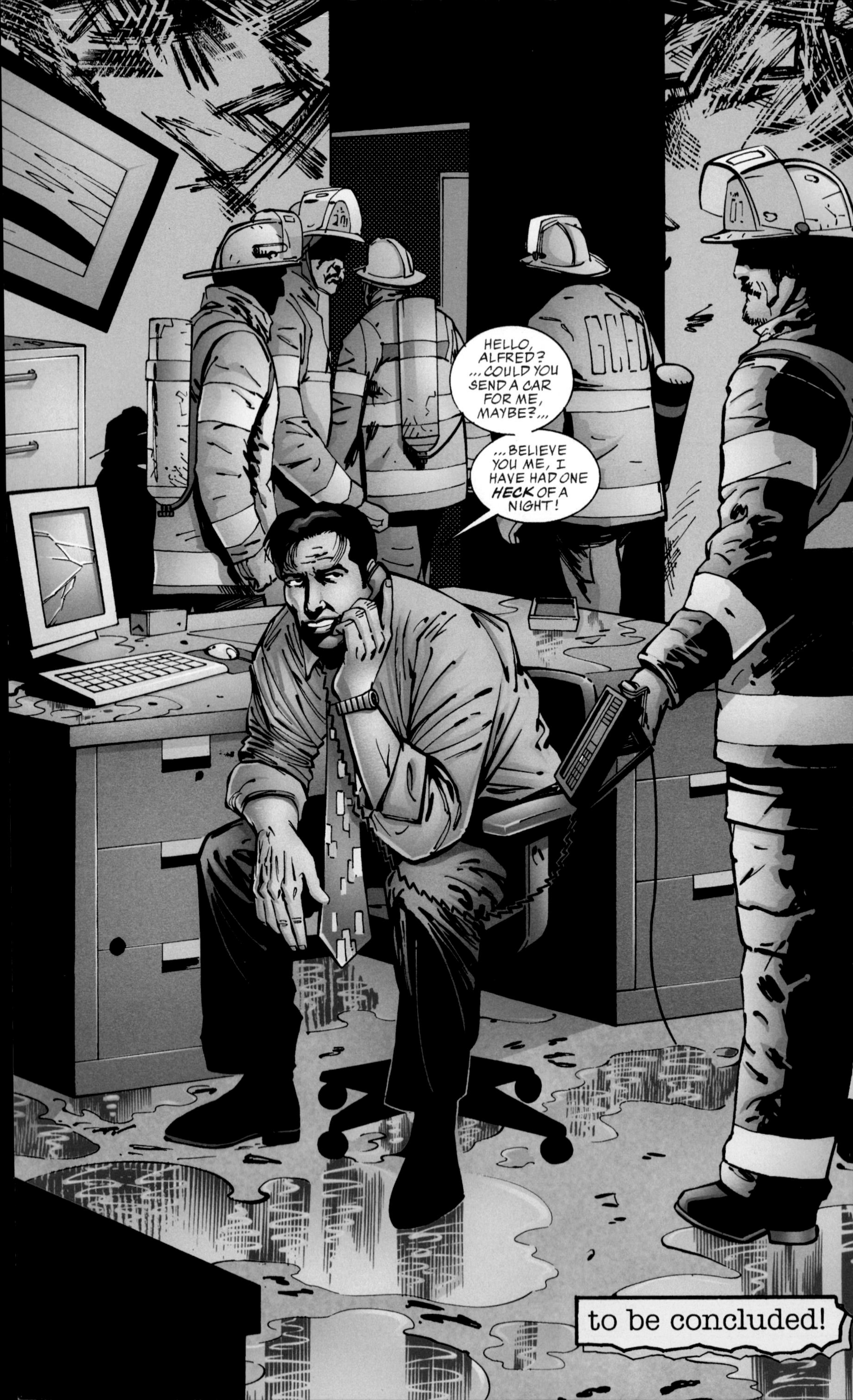
HELLO, ALFRED? ...COULD YOU SEND A CAR FOR ME, MAYBE?...
...BELIEVE YOU ME, I HAVE HAD ONE HECK OF A NIGHT!
to be concluded!

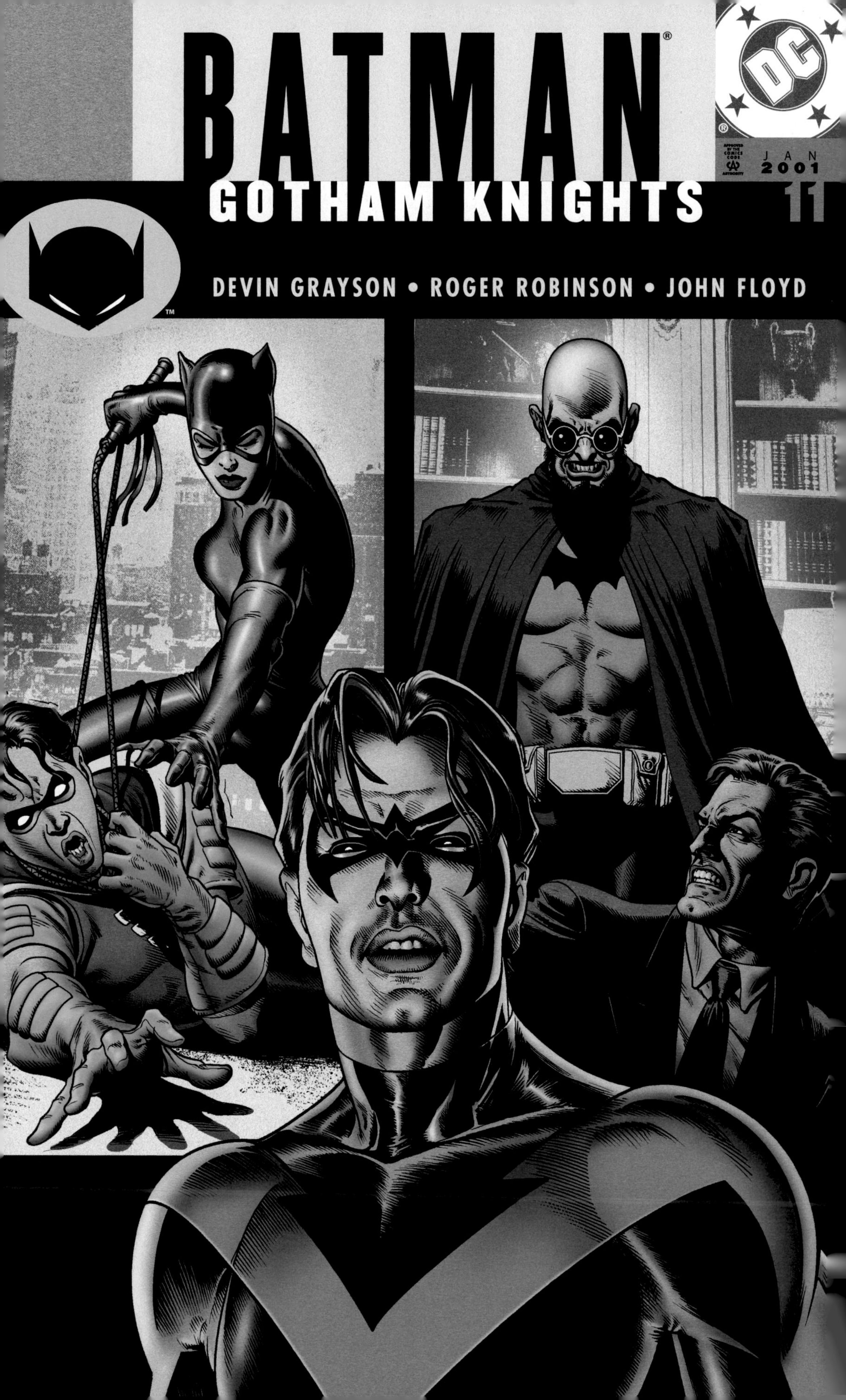
BATMAN®
GOTHAM KNIGHTS
11
JAN 2001
DC
DEVIN GRAYSON • ROGER ROBINSON • JOHN FLOYD

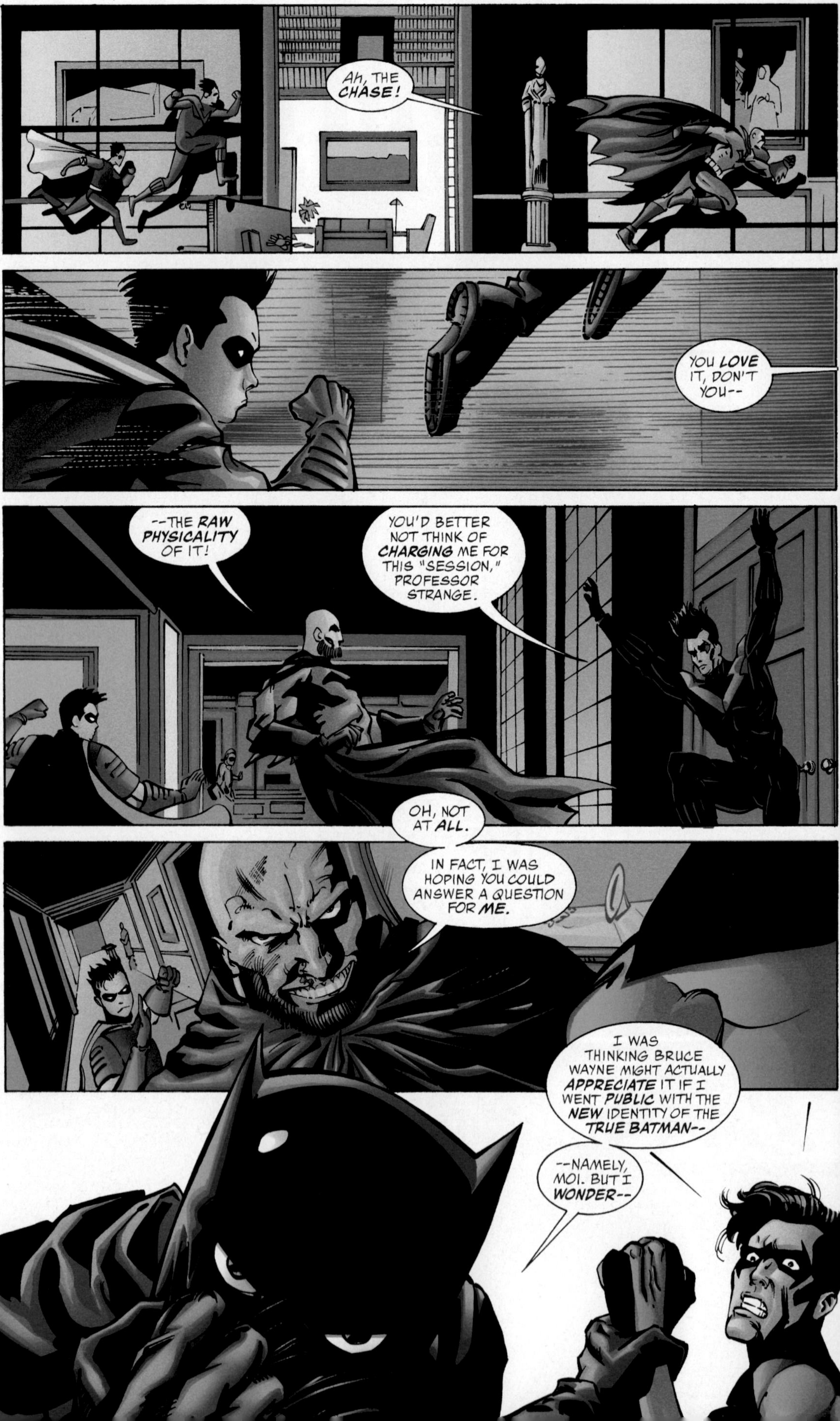
AH, THE CHASE!
YOU LOVE IT, DON'T YOU--
--THE RAW PHYSICALITY OF IT!
YOU'D BETTER NOT THINK OF CHARGING ME FOR THIS "SESSION," PROFESSOR STRANGE.
OH, NOT AT ALL.
IN FACT, I WAS HOPING YOU COULD ANSWER A QUESTION FOR ME.
I WAS THINKING BRUCE WAYNE MIGHT ACTUALLY APPRECIATE IT IF I WENT PUBLIC WITH THE NEW IDENTITY OF THE TRUE BATMAN--
--NAMELY, MOI. BUT I WONDER--

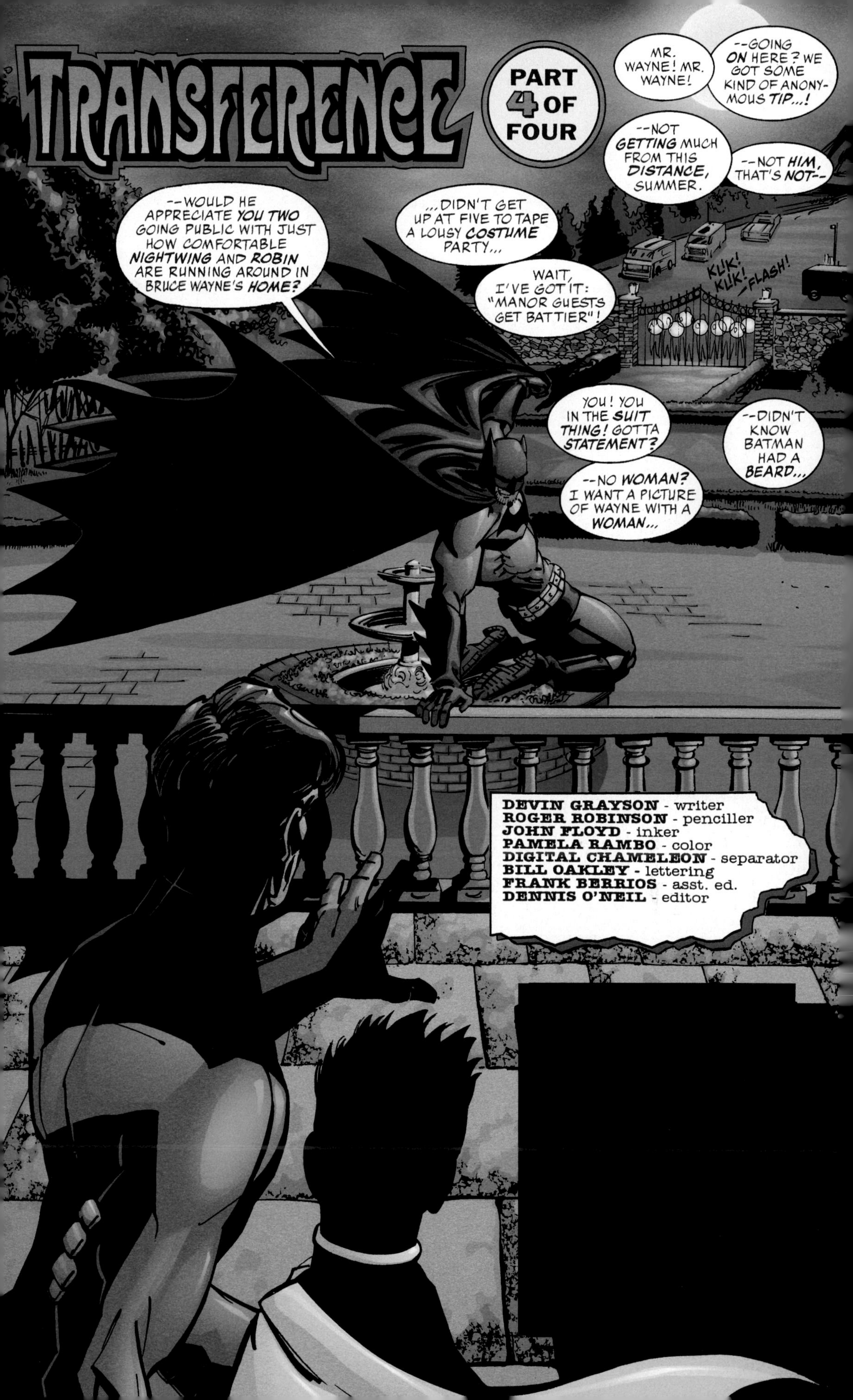
TRANSFERENCE
PART 4 OF FOUR
MR. WAYNE! MR. WAYNE!
--GOING ON HERE? WE GOT SOME KIND OF ANONY-MOUS TIP...!
--NOT GETTING MUCH FROM THIS DISTANCE, SUMMER.
--NOT HIM, THAT'S NOT--
--WOULD HE APPRECIATE YOU TWO GOING PUBLIC WITH JUST HOW COMFORTABLE NIGHTWING AND ROBIN ARE RUNNING AROUND IN BRUCE WAYNE'S HOME?
...DIDN'T GET UP AT FIVE TO TAPE A LOUSY COSTUME PARTY...
WAIT, I'VE GOT IT: "MANOR GUESTS GET BATTIER"!
KLIK! KLIK! FLASH!
YOU! YOU IN THE SUIT THING! GOTTA STATEMENT?
--DIDN'T KNOW BATMAN HAD A BEARD...
--NO WOMAN? I WANT A PICTURE OF WAYNE WITH A WOMAN...
DEVIN GRAYSON - writer
ROGER ROBINSON - penciller
JOHN FLOYD - inker
PAMELA RAMBO - color
DIGITAL CHAMELEON - separator
BILL OAKLEY - lettering
FRANK BERRIOS - asst. ed.
DENNIS O'NEIL - editor

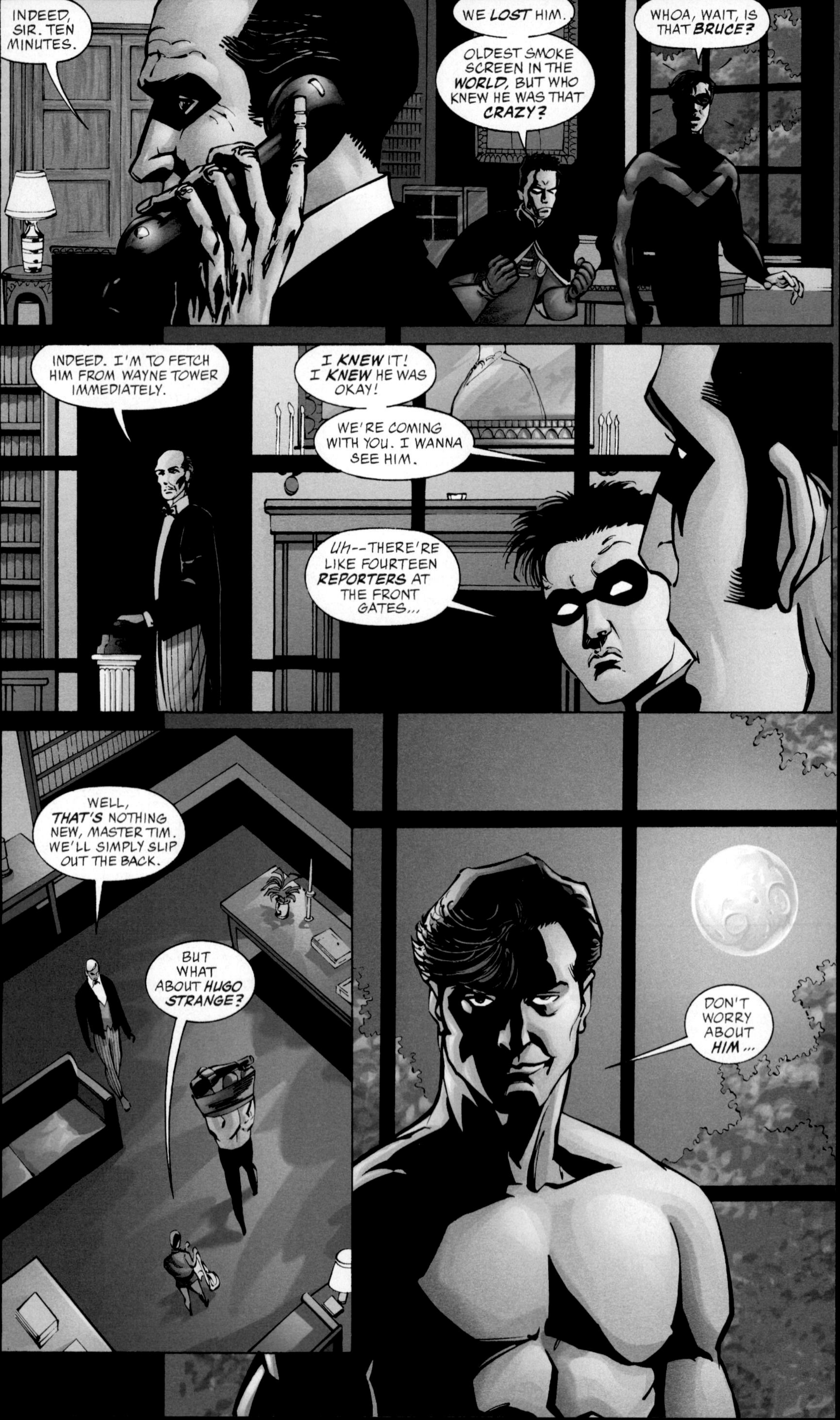
INDEED, SIR. TEN MINUTES.
WE LOST HIM.
OLDEST SMOKE SCREEN IN THE WORLD, BUT WHO KNEW HE WAS THAT CRAZY?
WHOA, WAIT, IS THAT BRUCE?
INDEED. I'M TO FETCH HIM FROM WAYNE TOWER IMMEDIATELY.
I KNEW IT! I KNEW HE WAS OKAY!
WE'RE COMING WITH YOU. I WANNA SEE HIM.
Uh--THERE'RE LIKE FOURTEEN REPORTERS AT THE FRONT GATES...
WELL, THAT'S NOTHING NEW, MASTER TIM. WE'LL SIMPLY SLIP OUT THE BACK.
BUT WHAT ABOUT HUGO STRANGE?
DON'T WORRY ABOUT HIM...

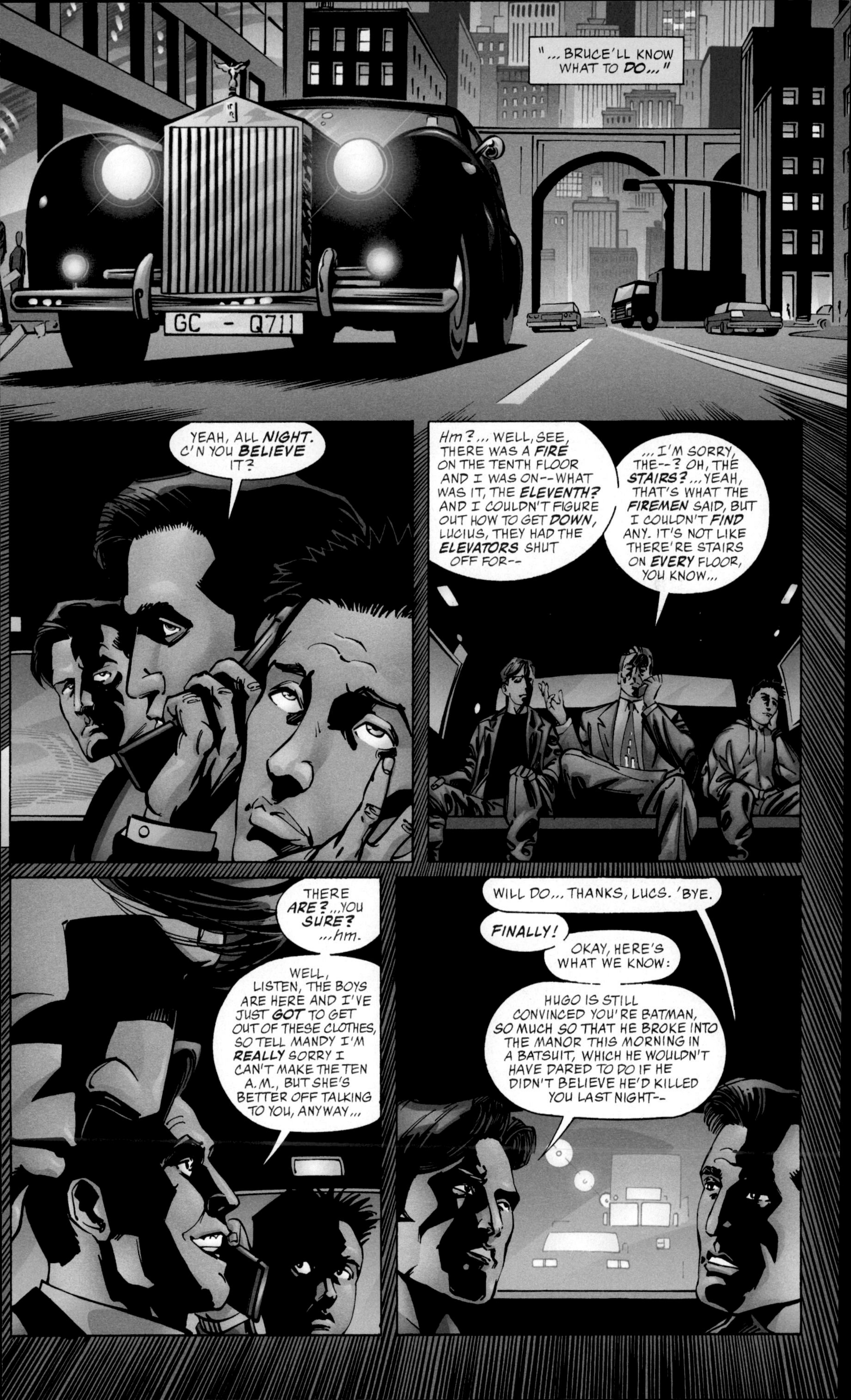
"...BRUCE'LL KNOW WHAT TO DO..."
GC - Q711
YEAH, ALL NIGHT. C'N YOU BELIEVE IT?
Hm?... WELL, SEE, THERE WAS A FIRE ON THE TENTH FLOOR AND I WAS ON--WHAT WAS IT, THE ELEVENTH? AND I COULDN'T FIGURE OUT HOW TO GET DOWN, LUCIUS, THEY HAD THE ELEVATORS SHUT OFF FOR--
...I'M SORRY, THE--? OH, THE STAIRS?...YEAH, THAT'S WHAT THE FIREMEN SAID, BUT I COULDN'T FIND ANY. IT'S NOT LIKE THERE'RE STAIRS ON EVERY FLOOR, YOU KNOW...
THERE ARE?...YOU SURE? ...hm.
WELL, LISTEN, THE BOYS ARE HERE AND I'VE JUST GOT TO GET OUT OF THESE CLOTHES, SO TELL MANDY I'M REALLY SORRY I CAN'T MAKE THE TEN A.M., BUT SHE'S BETTER OFF TALKING TO YOU, ANYWAY...
WILL DO... THANKS, LUCS. 'BYE.
FINALLY!
OKAY, HERE'S WHAT WE KNOW:
HUGO IS STILL CONVINCED YOU'RE BATMAN, SO MUCH SO THAT HE BROKE INTO THE MANOR THIS MORNING IN A BATSUIT, WHICH HE WOULDN'T HAVE DARED TO DO IF HE DIDN'T BELIEVE HE'D KILLED YOU LAST NIGHT--

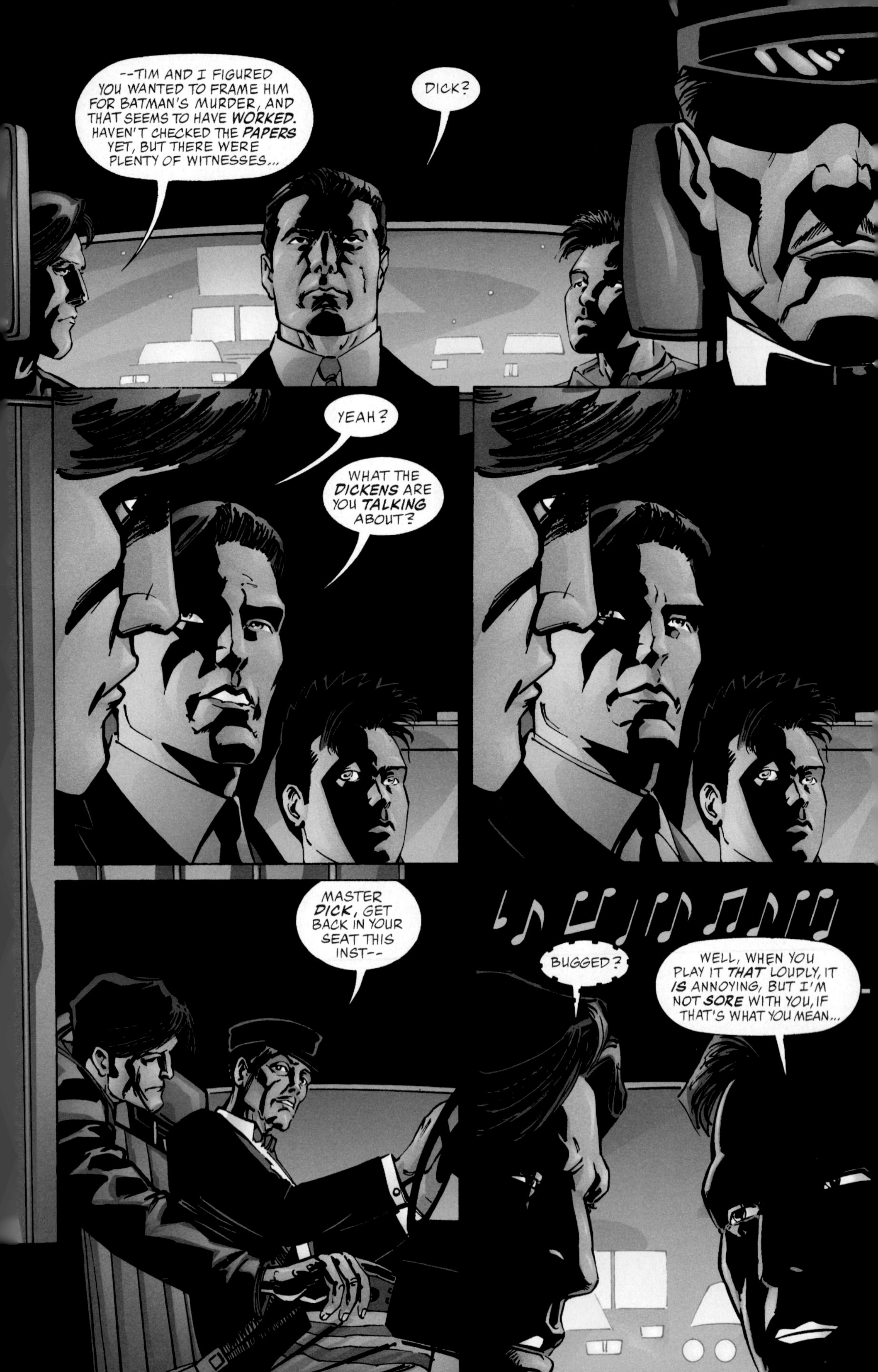
--TIM AND I FIGURED YOU WANTED TO FRAME HIM FOR BATMAN'S MURDER, AND THAT SEEMS TO HAVE WORKED. HAVEN'T CHECKED THE PAPERS YET, BUT THERE WERE PLENTY OF WITNESSES...
DICK?
YEAH?
WHAT THE DICKENS ARE YOU TALKING ABOUT?
MASTER DICK, GET BACK IN YOUR SEAT THIS INST--
BUGGED?
WELL, WHEN YOU PLAY IT THAT LOUDLY, IT IS ANNOYING, BUT I'M NOT SORE WITH YOU, IF THAT'S WHAT YOU MEAN...

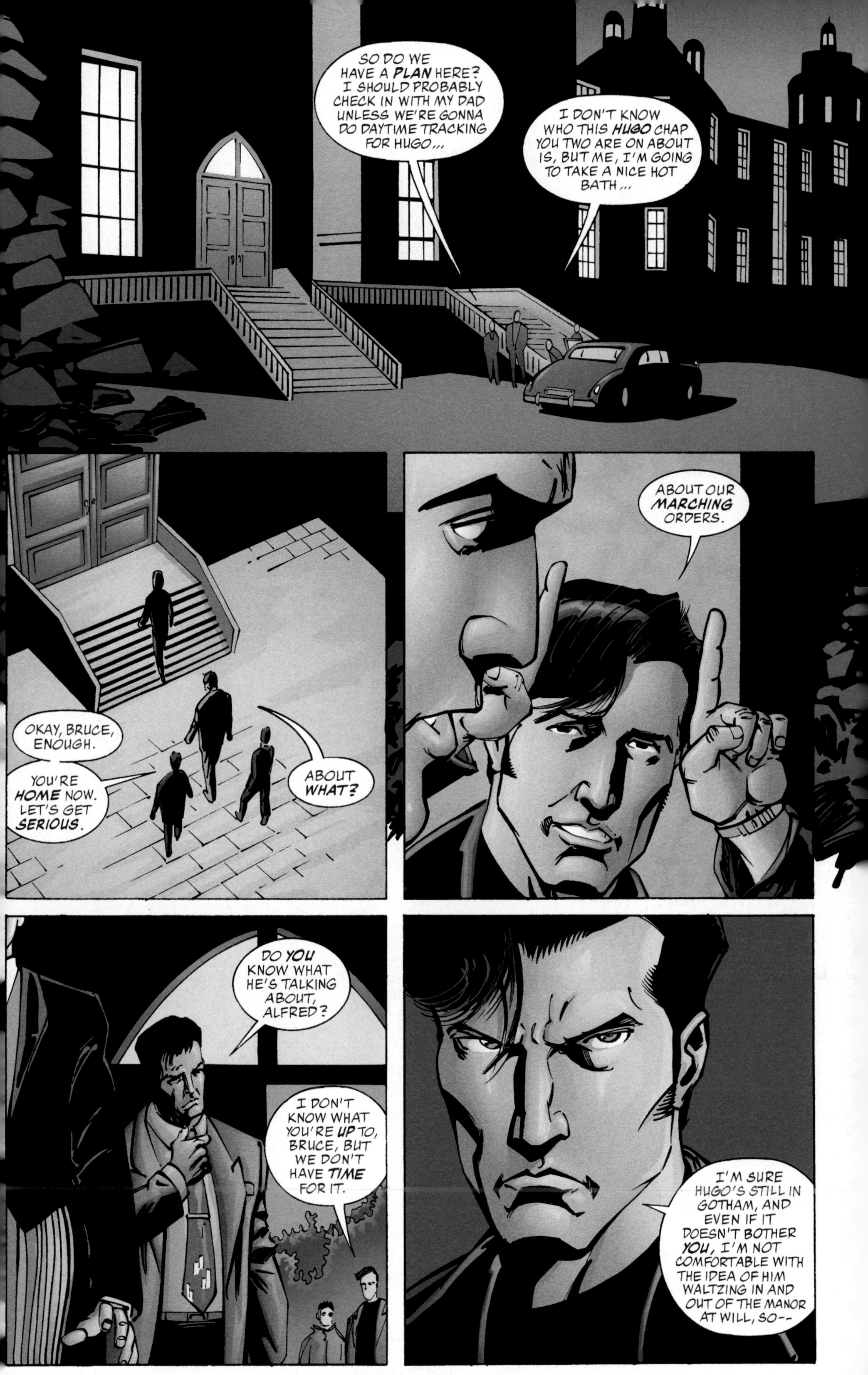
SO DO WE HAVE A PLAN HERE? I SHOULD PROBABLY CHECK IN WITH MY DAD UNLESS WE'RE GONNA DO DAYTIME TRACKING FOR HUGO...
I DON'T KNOW WHO THIS HUGO CHAP YOU TWO ARE ON ABOUT IS, BUT ME, I'M GOING TO TAKE A NICE HOT BATH...
OKAY, BRUCE, ENOUGH.
YOU'RE HOME NOW. LET'S GET SERIOUS.
ABOUT WHAT?
ABOUT OUR MARCHING ORDERS.
DO YOU KNOW WHAT HE'S TALKING ABOUT, ALFRED?
I DON'T KNOW WHAT YOU'RE UP TO, BRUCE, BUT WE DON'T HAVE TIME FOR IT.
I'M SURE HUGO'S STILL IN GOTHAM, AND EVEN IF IT DOESN'T BOTHER YOU, I'M NOT COMFORTABLE WITH THE IDEA OF HIM WALTZING IN AND OUT OF THE MANOR AT WILL, SO--

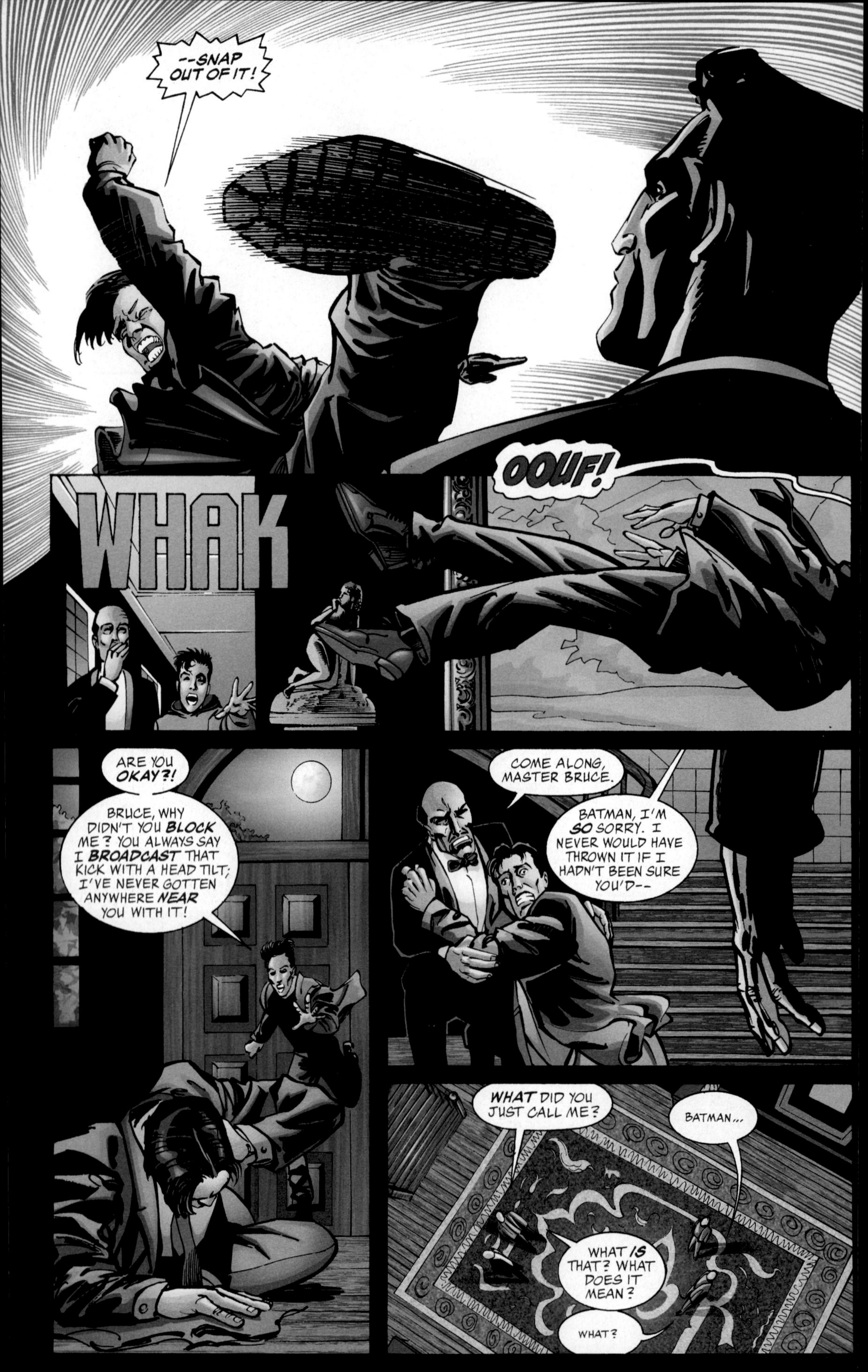
--SNAP OUT OF IT!
WHAK
OOUF!
ARE YOU OKAY?!
BRUCE, WHY DIDN'T YOU BLOCK ME? YOU ALWAYS SAY I BROADCAST THAT KICK WITH A HEAD TILT; I'VE NEVER GOTTEN ANYWHERE NEAR YOU WITH IT!
COME ALONG, MASTER BRUCE.
BATMAN, I'M SO SORRY. I NEVER WOULD HAVE THROWN IT IF I HADN'T BEEN SURE YOU'D--
WHAT DID YOU JUST CALL ME?
BATMAN...
WHAT IS THAT? WHAT DOES IT MEAN?
WHAT?

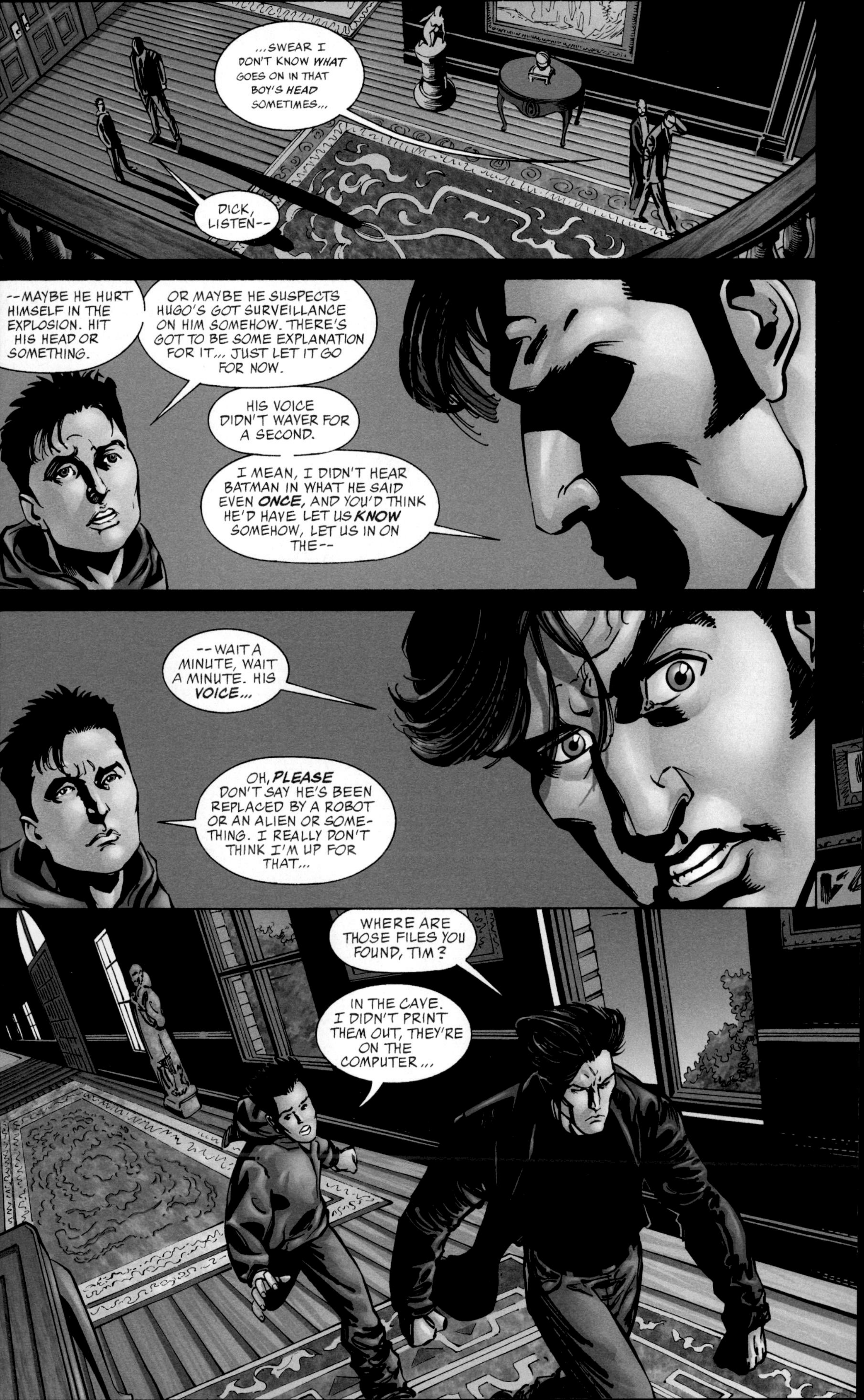
...SWEAR I DON'T KNOW WHAT GOES ON IN THAT BOY'S HEAD SOMETIMES...
DICK, LISTEN--
--MAYBE HE HURT HIMSELF IN THE EXPLOSION. HIT HIS HEAD OR SOMETHING.
OR MAYBE HE SUSPECTS HUGO'S GOT SURVEILLANCE ON HIM SOMEHOW. THERE'S GOT TO BE SOME EXPLANATION FOR IT... JUST LET IT GO FOR NOW.
HIS VOICE DIDN'T WAVER FOR A SECOND.
I MEAN, I DIDN'T HEAR BATMAN IN WHAT HE SAID EVEN ONCE, AND YOU'D THINK HE'D HAVE LET US KNOW SOMEHOW, LET US IN ON THE--
--WAIT A MINUTE, WAIT A MINUTE. HIS VOICE...
OH, PLEASE DON'T SAY HE'S BEEN REPLACED BY A ROBOT OR AN ALIEN OR SOMETHING. I REALLY DON'T THINK I'M UP FOR THAT...
WHERE ARE THOSE FILES YOU FOUND, TIM?
IN THE CAVE. I DIDN'T PRINT THEM OUT, THEY'RE ON THE COMPUTER...

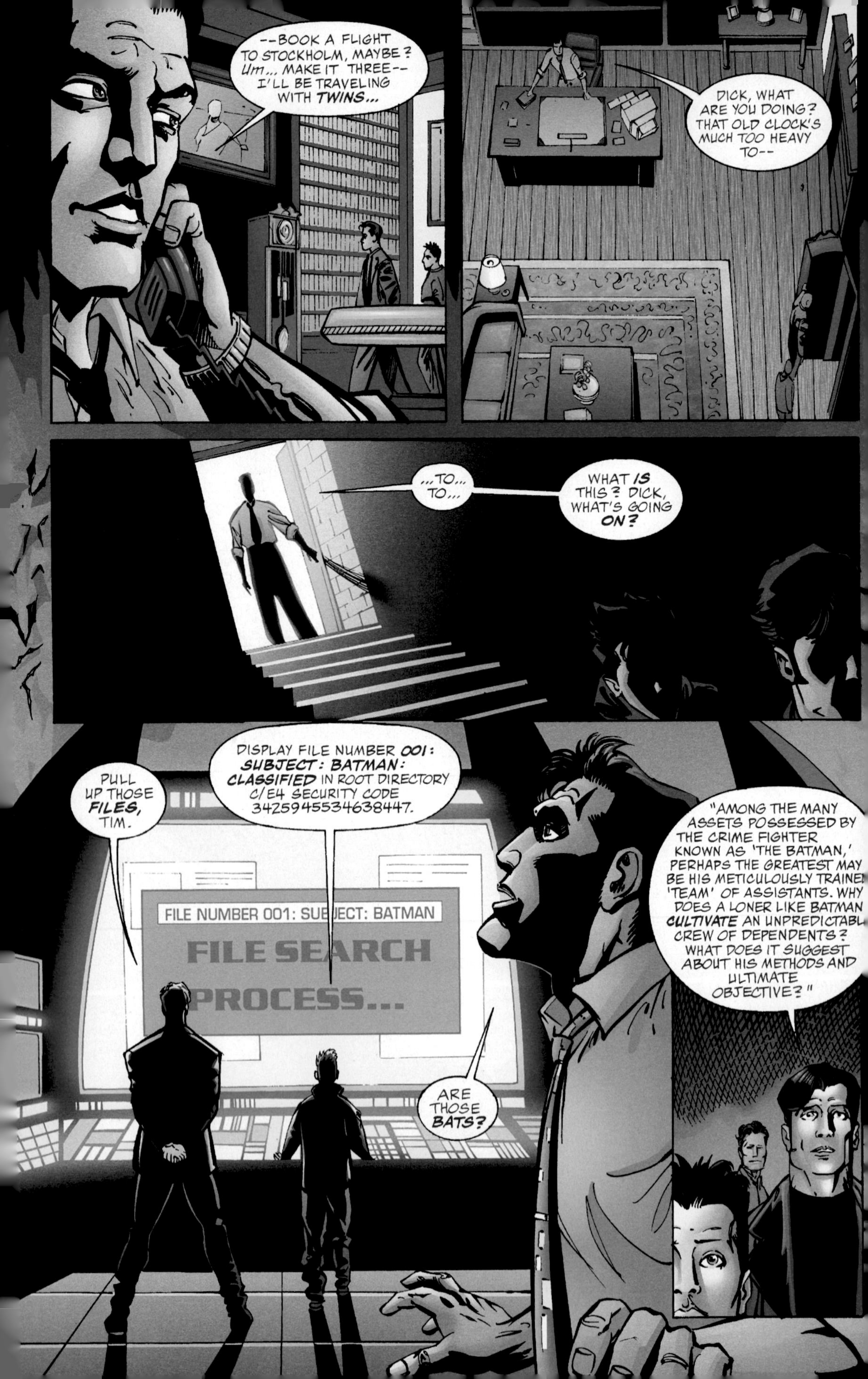
--BOOK A FLIGHT TO STOCKHOLM, MAYBE? UM... MAKE IT THREE-- I'LL BE TRAVELING WITH TWINS...
DICK, WHAT ARE YOU DOING? THAT OLD CLOCK'S MUCH TOO HEAVY TO--
...TO... TO...
WHAT IS THIS? DICK, WHAT'S GOING ON?
PULL UP THOSE FILES, TIM.
DISPLAY FILE NUMBER 001: SUBJECT: BATMAN: CLASSIFIED IN ROOT DIRECTORY C/E4 SECURITY CODE 34259455346384447.
FILE NUMBER 001: SUBJECT: BATMAN
FILE SEARCH PROCESS...
ARE THOSE BATS?
"AMONG THE MANY ASSETS POSSESSED BY THE CRIME FIGHTER KNOWN AS 'THE BATMAN,' PERHAPS THE GREATEST MAY BE HIS METICULOUSLY TRAINED 'TEAM' OF ASSISTANTS. WHY DOES A LONER LIKE BATMAN CULTIVATE AN UNPREDICTABLE CREW OF DEPENDENTS? WHAT DOES IT SUGGEST ABOUT HIS METHODS AND ULTIMATE OBJECTIVE?"

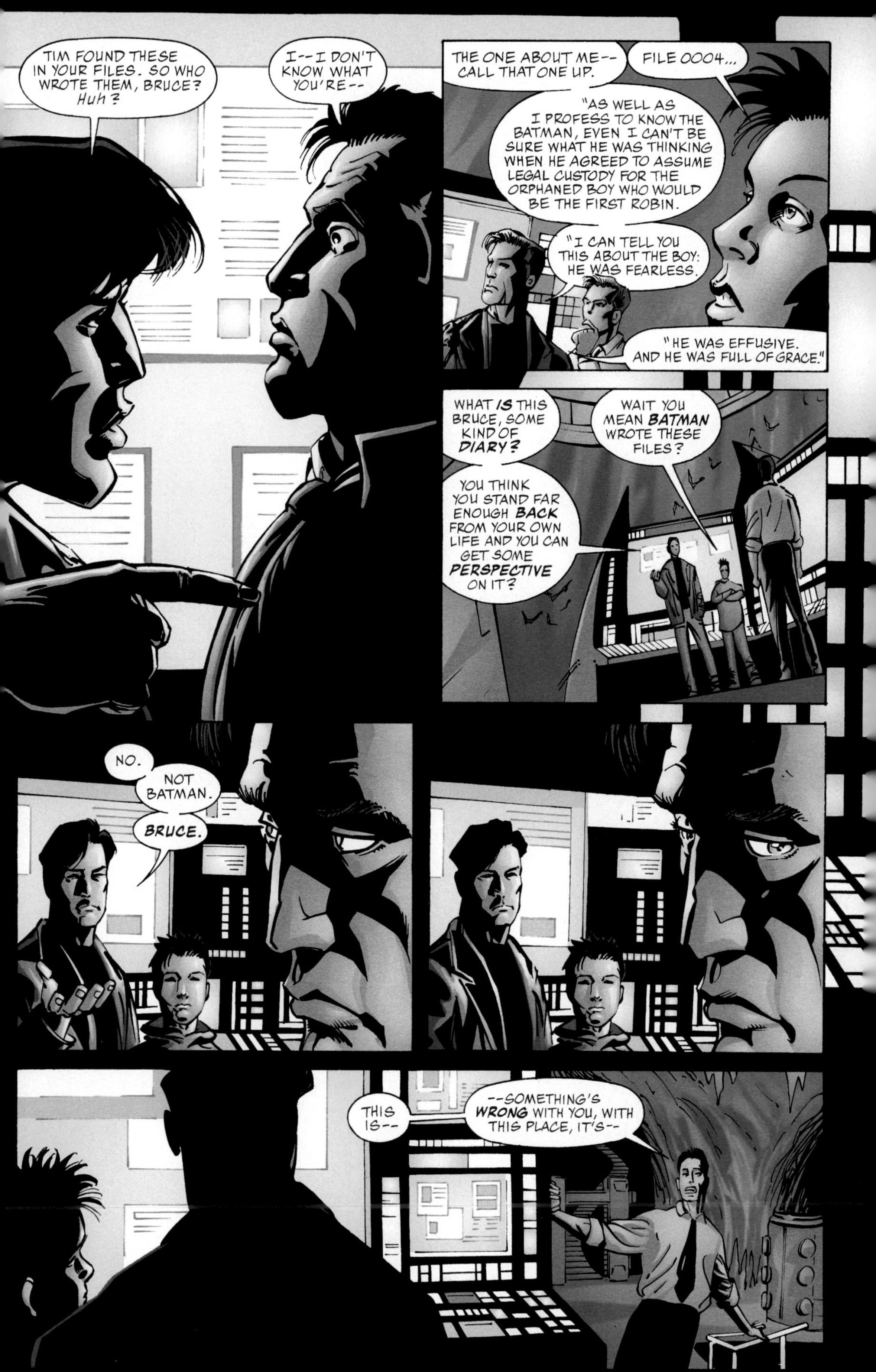

TIM FOUND THESE IN YOUR FILES. SO WHO WROTE THEM, BRUCE? Huh?
I--I DON'T KNOW WHAT YOU'RE--
THE ONE ABOUT ME--CALL THAT ONE UP.
FILE 0004...
"AS WELL AS I PROFESS TO KNOW THE BATMAN, EVEN I CAN'T BE SURE WHAT HE WAS THINKING WHEN HE AGREED TO ASSUME LEGAL CUSTODY FOR THE ORPHANED BOY WHO WOULD BE THE FIRST ROBIN.
"I CAN TELL YOU THIS ABOUT THE BOY: HE WAS FEARLESS.
"HE WAS EFFUSIVE. AND HE WAS FULL OF GRACE."
WHAT IS THIS BRUCE, SOME KIND OF DIARY?
WAIT YOU MEAN BATMAN WROTE THESE FILES?
YOU THINK YOU STAND FAR ENOUGH BACK FROM YOUR OWN LIFE AND YOU CAN GET SOME PERSPECTIVE ON IT?
NO.
NOT BATMAN.
BRUCE.
THIS IS--
--SOMETHING'S WRONG WITH YOU, WITH THIS PLACE, IT'S--

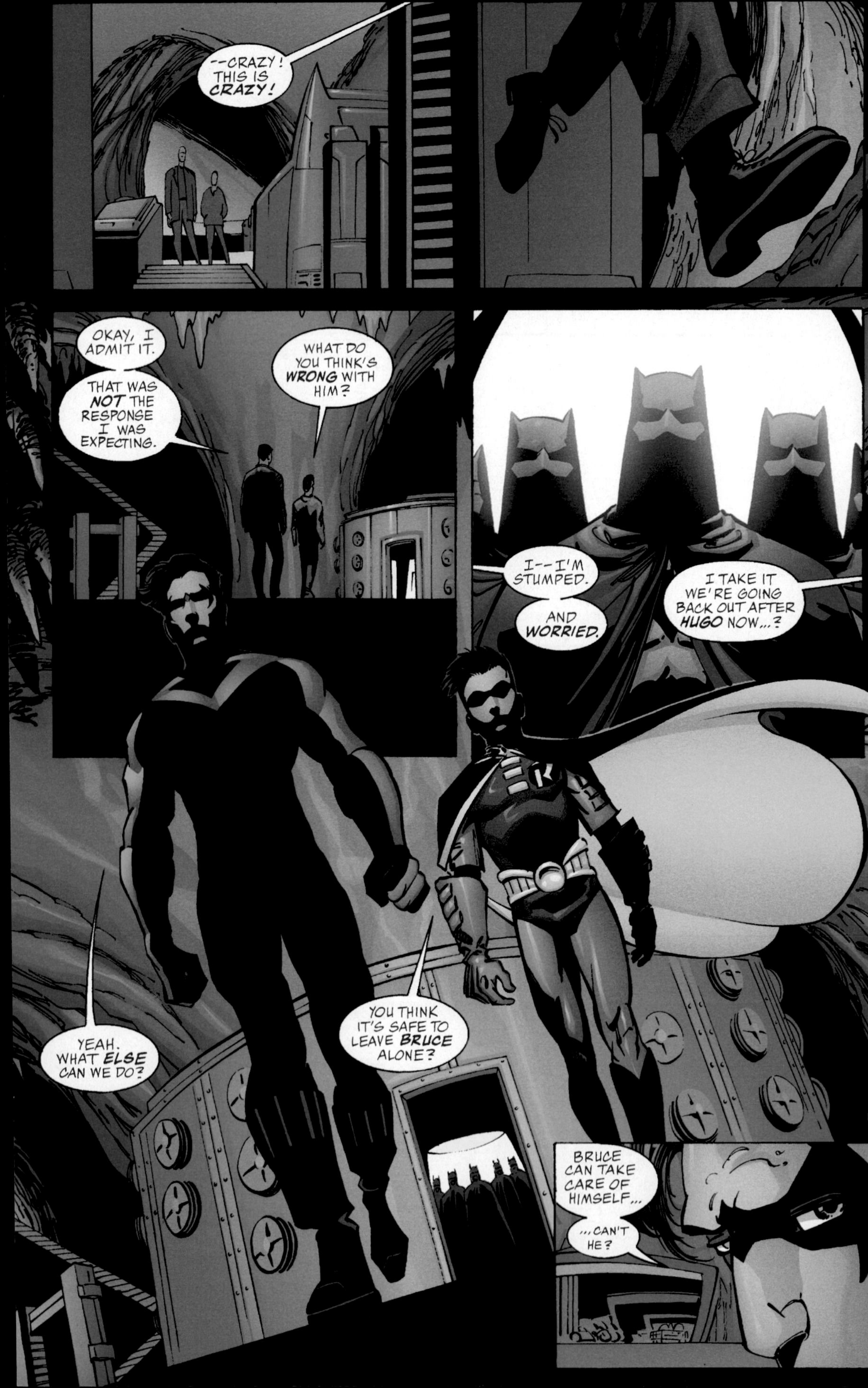
--CRAZY! THIS IS CRAZY!
OKAY, I ADMIT IT.
THAT WAS NOT THE RESPONSE I WAS EXPECTING.
WHAT DO YOU THINK'S WRONG WITH HIM?
I--I'M STUMPED.
AND WORRIED.
I TAKE IT WE'RE GOING BACK OUT AFTER HUGO NOW...?
YEAH. WHAT ELSE CAN WE DO?
YOU THINK IT'S SAFE TO LEAVE BRUCE ALONE?
BRUCE CAN TAKE CARE OF HIMSELF...
...CAN'T HE?

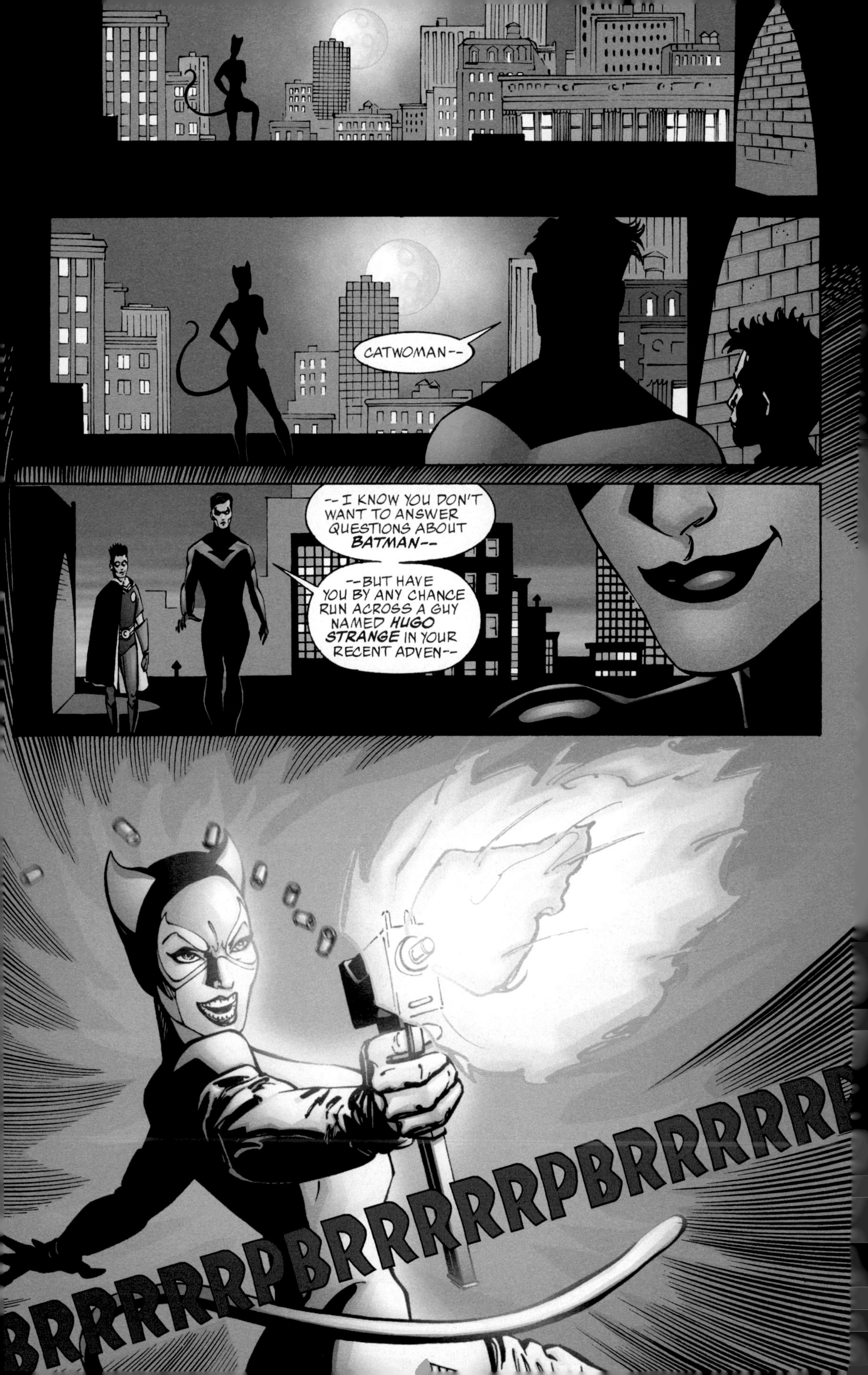
CATWOMAN--
--I KNOW YOU DON'T WANT TO ANSWER QUESTIONS ABOUT BATMAN--
--BUT HAVE YOU BY ANY CHANCE RUN ACROSS A GUY NAMED HUGO STRANGE IN YOUR RECENT ADVEN--
BRRRRRRPBRRRRRRRPBRRRRRRR

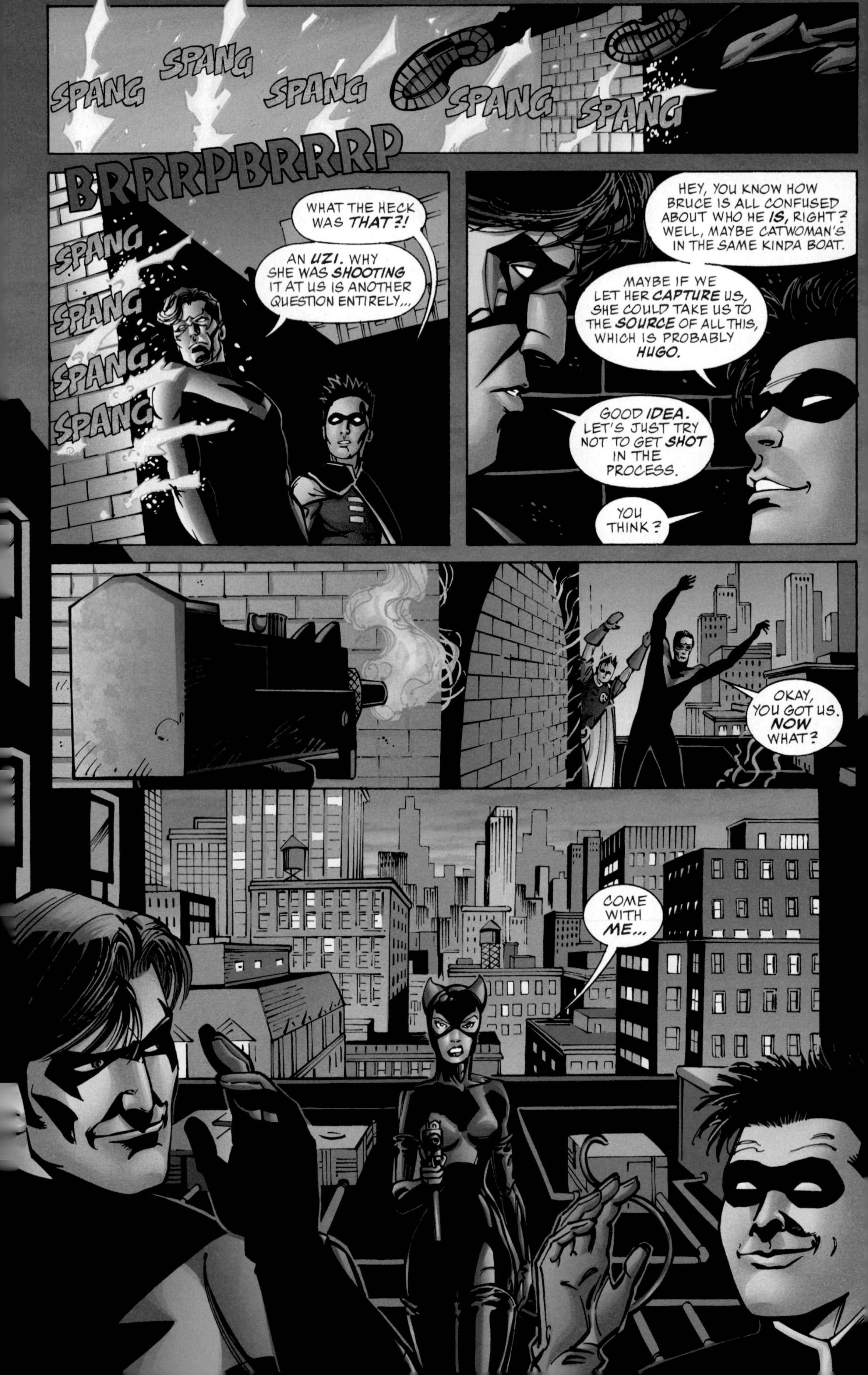
SPANG SPANG SPANG SPANG SPANG
BRRRPBRRRRP
SPANG SPANG SPANG SPANG
WHAT THE HECK WAS THAT?!
AN UZI. WHY SHE WAS SHOOTING IT AT US IS ANOTHER QUESTION ENTIRELY...
HEY, YOU KNOW HOW BRUCE IS ALL CONFUSED ABOUT WHO HE IS, RIGHT? WELL, MAYBE CATWOMAN'S IN THE SAME KINDA BOAT.
MAYBE IF WE LET HER CAPTURE US, SHE COULD TAKE US TO THE SOURCE OF ALL THIS, WHICH IS PROBABLY HUGO.
GOOD IDEA. LET'S JUST TRY NOT TO GET SHOT IN THE PROCESS.
YOU THINK?
OKAY, YOU GOT US. NOW WHAT?
COME WITH ME...

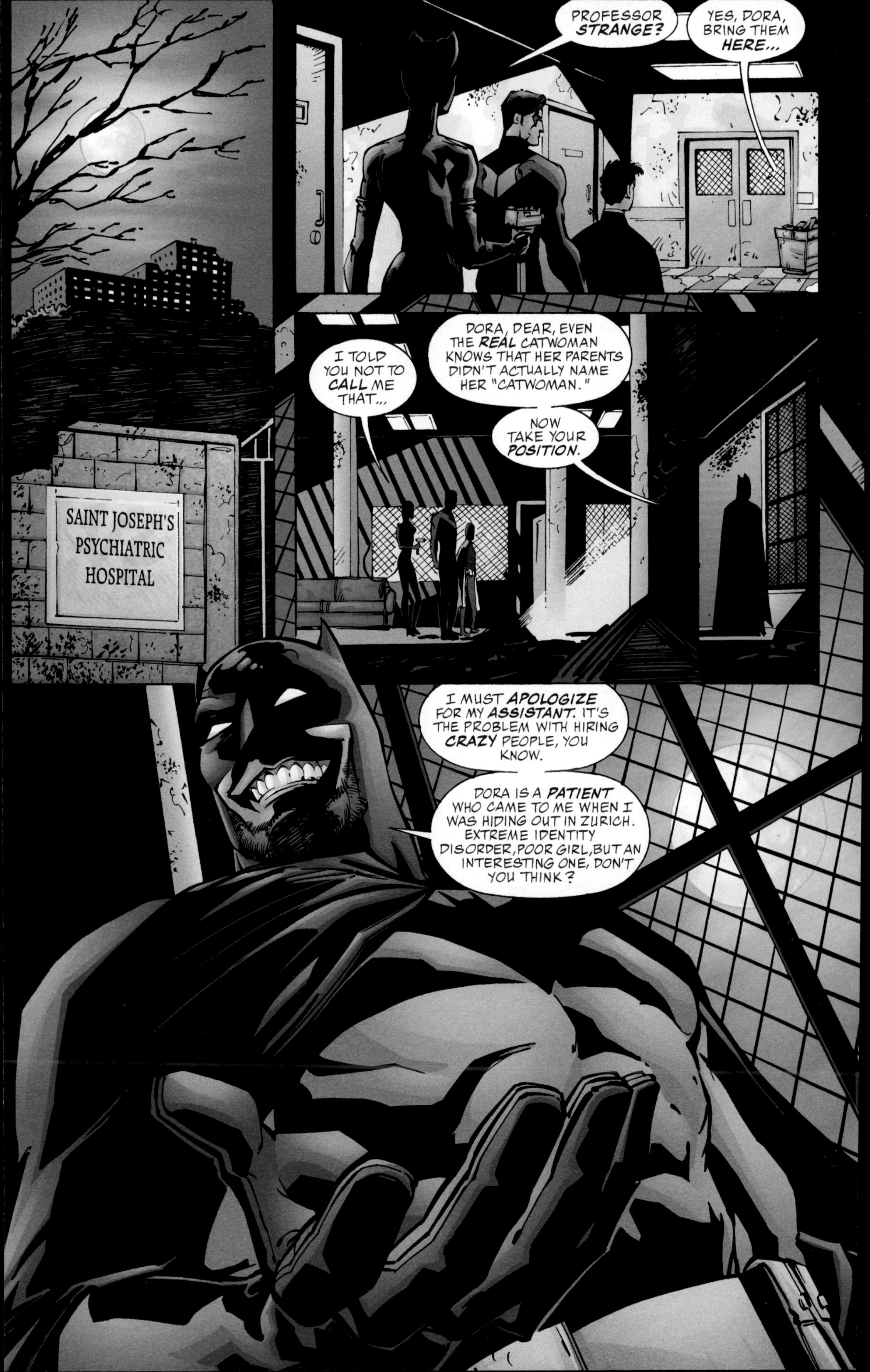
SAINT JOSEPH'S PSYCHIATRIC HOSPITAL
PROFESSOR STRANGE?
YES, DORA, BRING THEM HERE...
I TOLD YOU NOT TO CALL ME THAT...
DORA, DEAR, EVEN THE REAL CATWOMAN KNOWS THAT HER PARENTS DIDN'T ACTUALLY NAME HER "CATWOMAN."
NOW TAKE YOUR POSITION.
I MUST APOLOGIZE FOR MY ASSISTANT. IT'S THE PROBLEM WITH HIRING CRAZY PEOPLE, YOU KNOW.
DORA IS A PATIENT WHO CAME TO ME WHEN I WAS HIDING OUT IN ZURICH. EXTREME IDENTITY DISORDER, POOR GIRL, BUT AN INTERESTING ONE, DON'T YOU THINK?

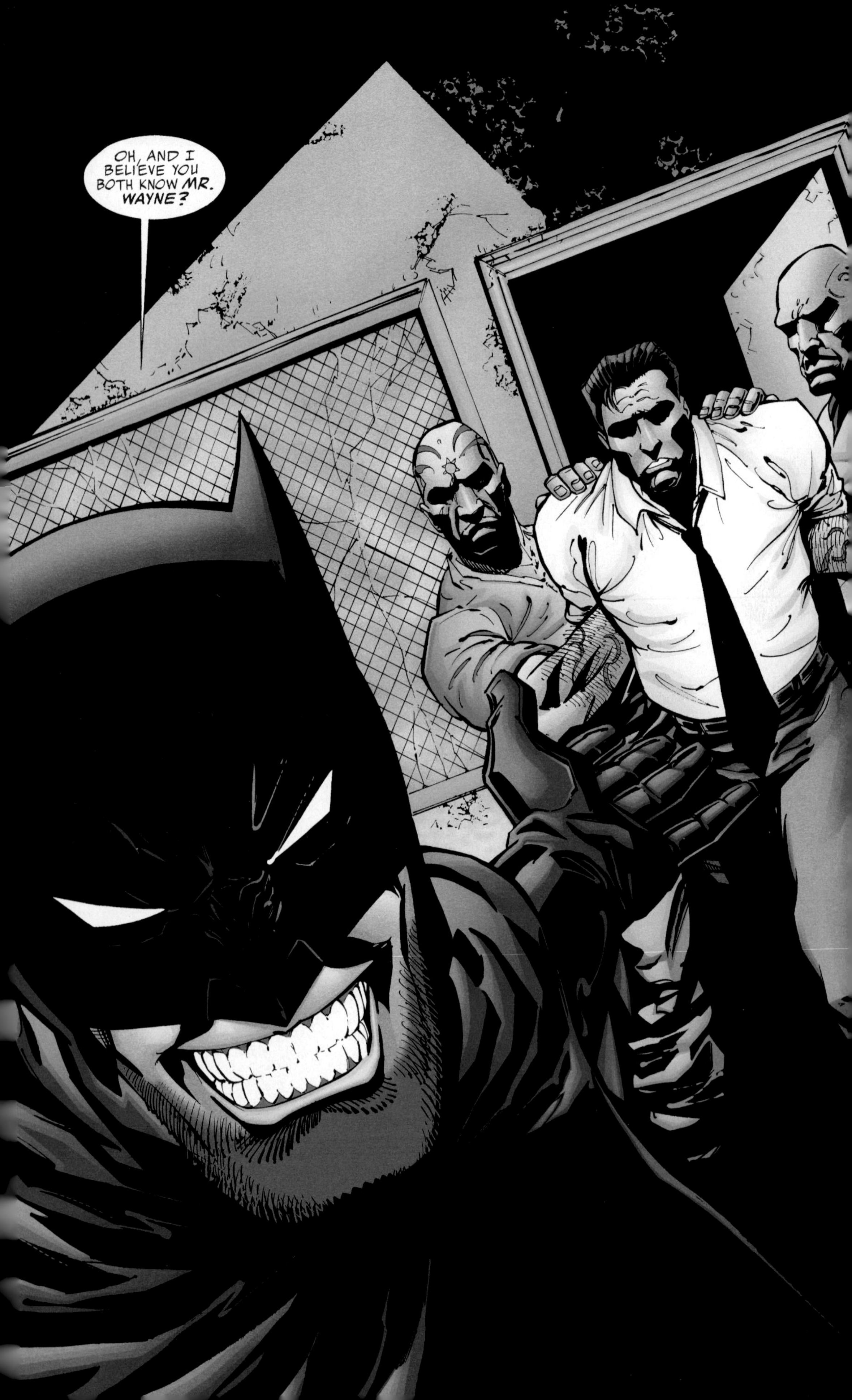
OH, AND I BELIEVE YOU BOTH KNOW MR. WAYNE?

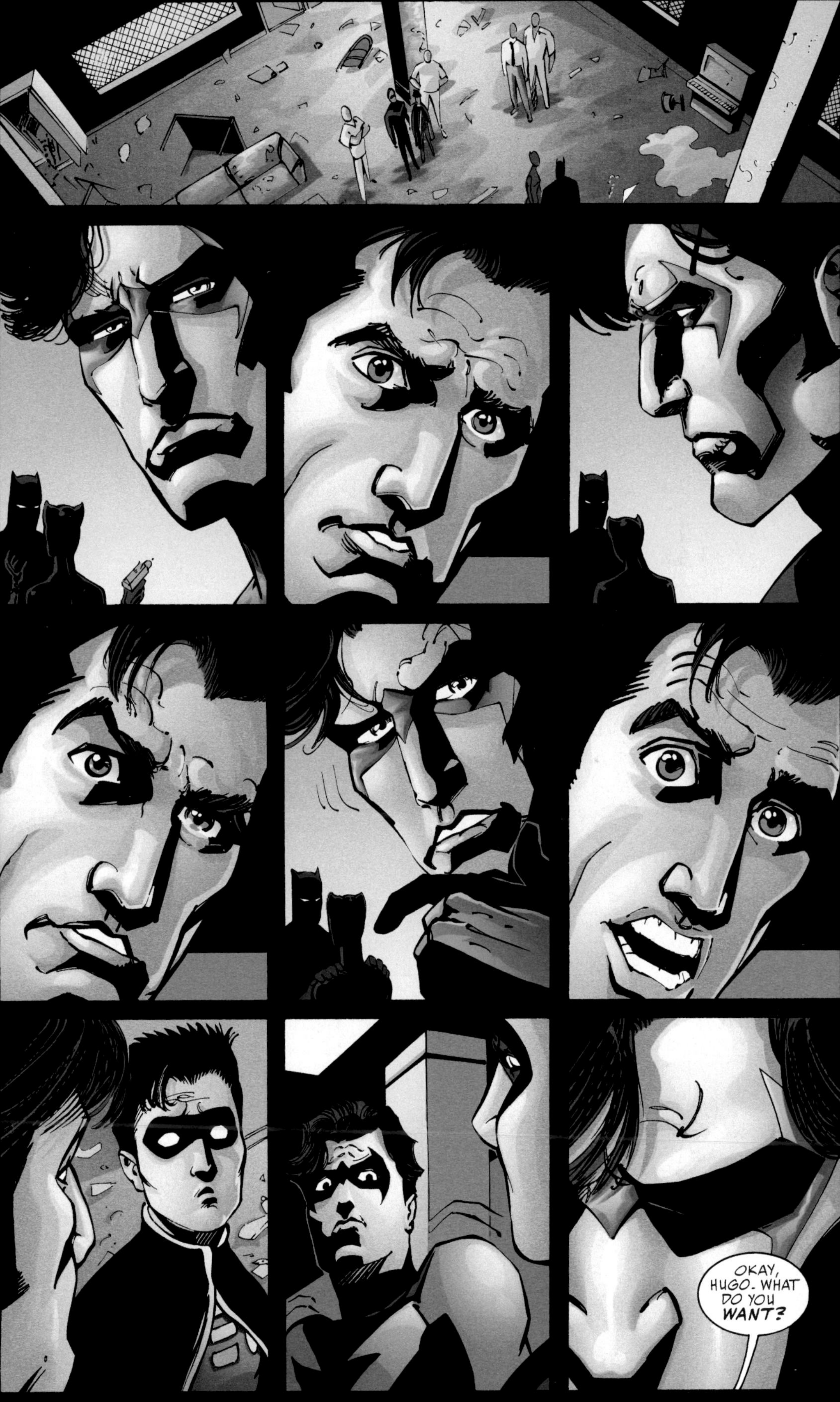
OKAY, HUGO. WHAT DO YOU WANT?

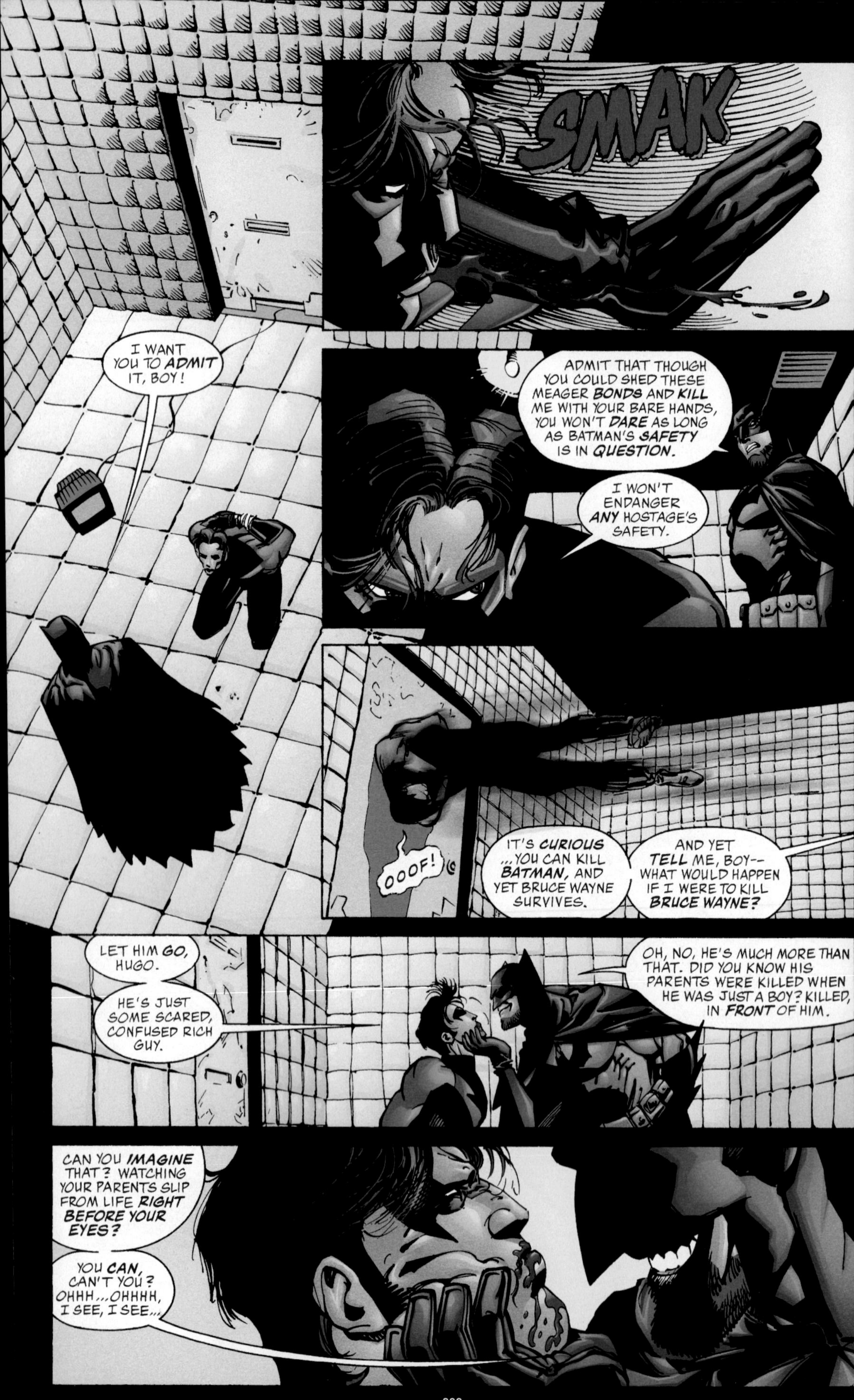
SMAK
I WANT YOU TO ADMIT IT, BOY!
ADMIT THAT THOUGH YOU COULD SHED THESE MEAGER BONDS AND KILL ME WITH YOUR BARE HANDS, YOU WON'T DARE AS LONG AS BATMAN'S SAFETY IS IN QUESTION.
I WON'T ENDANGER ANY HOSTAGE'S SAFETY.
OOOF!
IT'S CURIOUS ...YOU CAN KILL BATMAN, AND YET BRUCE WAYNE SURVIVES.
AND YET TELL ME, BOY-- WHAT WOULD HAPPEN IF I WERE TO KILL BRUCE WAYNE?
LET HIM GO, HUGO.
HE'S JUST SOME SCARED, CONFUSED RICH GUY.
OH, NO, HE'S MUCH MORE THAN THAT. DID YOU KNOW HIS PARENTS WERE KILLED WHEN HE WAS JUST A BOY? KILLED, IN FRONT OF HIM.
CAN YOU IMAGINE THAT? WATCHING YOUR PARENTS SLIP FROM LIFE RIGHT BEFORE YOUR EYES?
YOU CAN, CAN'T YOU? OHHH...OHHHH, I SEE, I SEE...

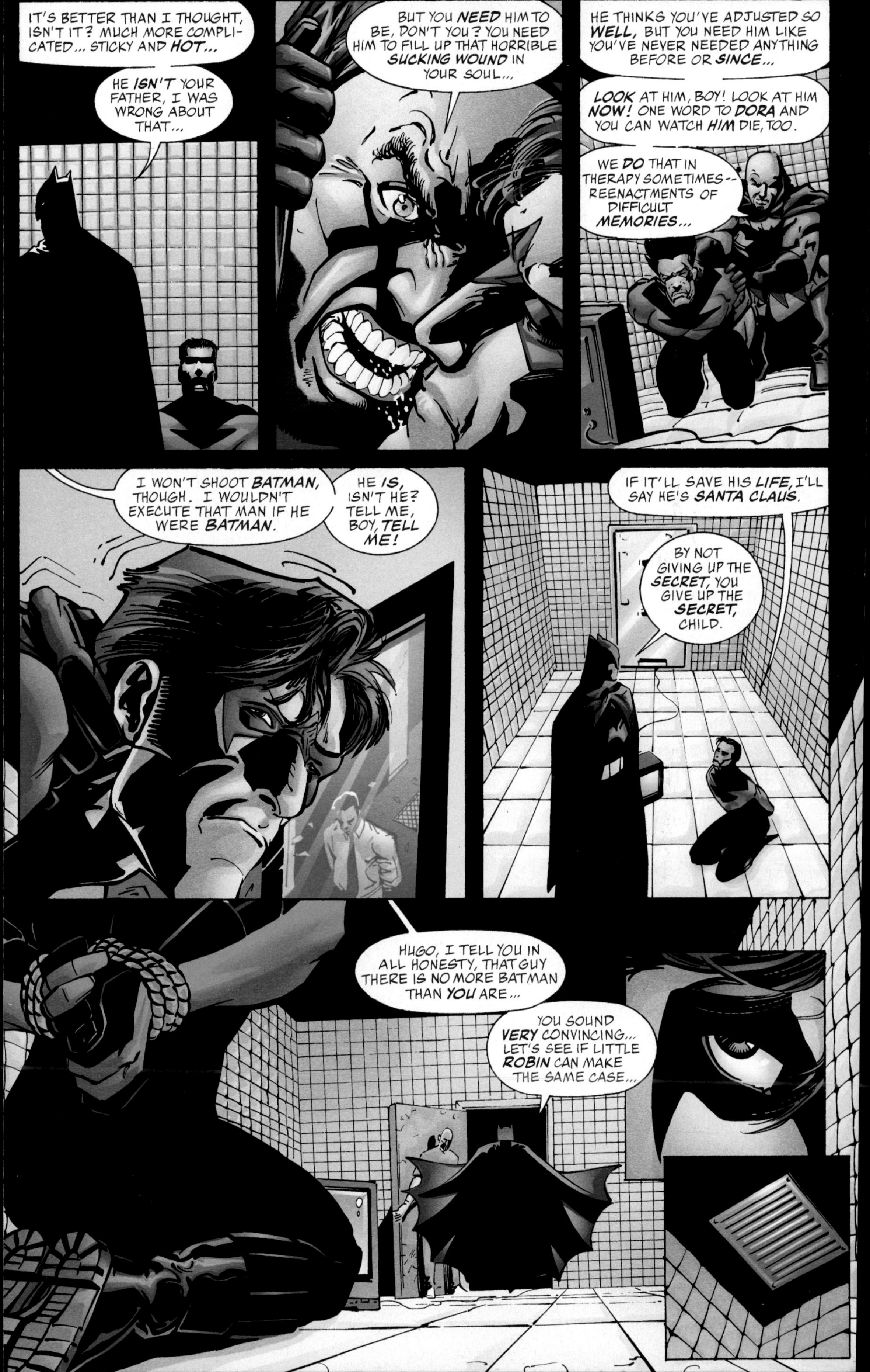
IT'S BETTER THAN I THOUGHT, ISN'T IT? MUCH MORE COMPLICATED... STICKY AND HOT...
HE ISN'T YOUR FATHER, I WAS WRONG ABOUT THAT...
BUT YOU NEED HIM TO BE, DON'T YOU? YOU NEED HIM TO FILL UP THAT HORRIBLE SUCKING WOUND IN YOUR SOUL...
HE THINKS YOU'VE ADJUSTED SO WELL, BUT YOU NEED HIM LIKE YOU'VE NEVER NEEDED ANYTHING BEFORE OR SINCE...
LOOK AT HIM, BOY! LOOK AT HIM NOW! ONE WORD TO DORA AND YOU CAN WATCH HIM DIE, TOO.
WE DO THAT IN THERAPY SOMETIMES--REENACTMENTS OF DIFFICULT MEMORIES...
I WON'T SHOOT BATMAN, THOUGH. I WOULDN'T EXECUTE THAT MAN IF HE WERE BATMAN.
HE IS, ISN'T HE? TELL ME, BOY, TELL ME!
IF IT'LL SAVE HIS LIFE, I'LL SAY HE'S SANTA CLAUS.
BY NOT GIVING UP THE SECRET, YOU GIVE UP THE SECRET, CHILD.
HUGO, I TELL YOU IN ALL HONESTY, THAT GUY THERE IS NO MORE BATMAN THAN YOU ARE...
YOU SOUND VERY CONVINCING... LET'S SEE IF LITTLE ROBIN CAN MAKE THE SAME CASE...

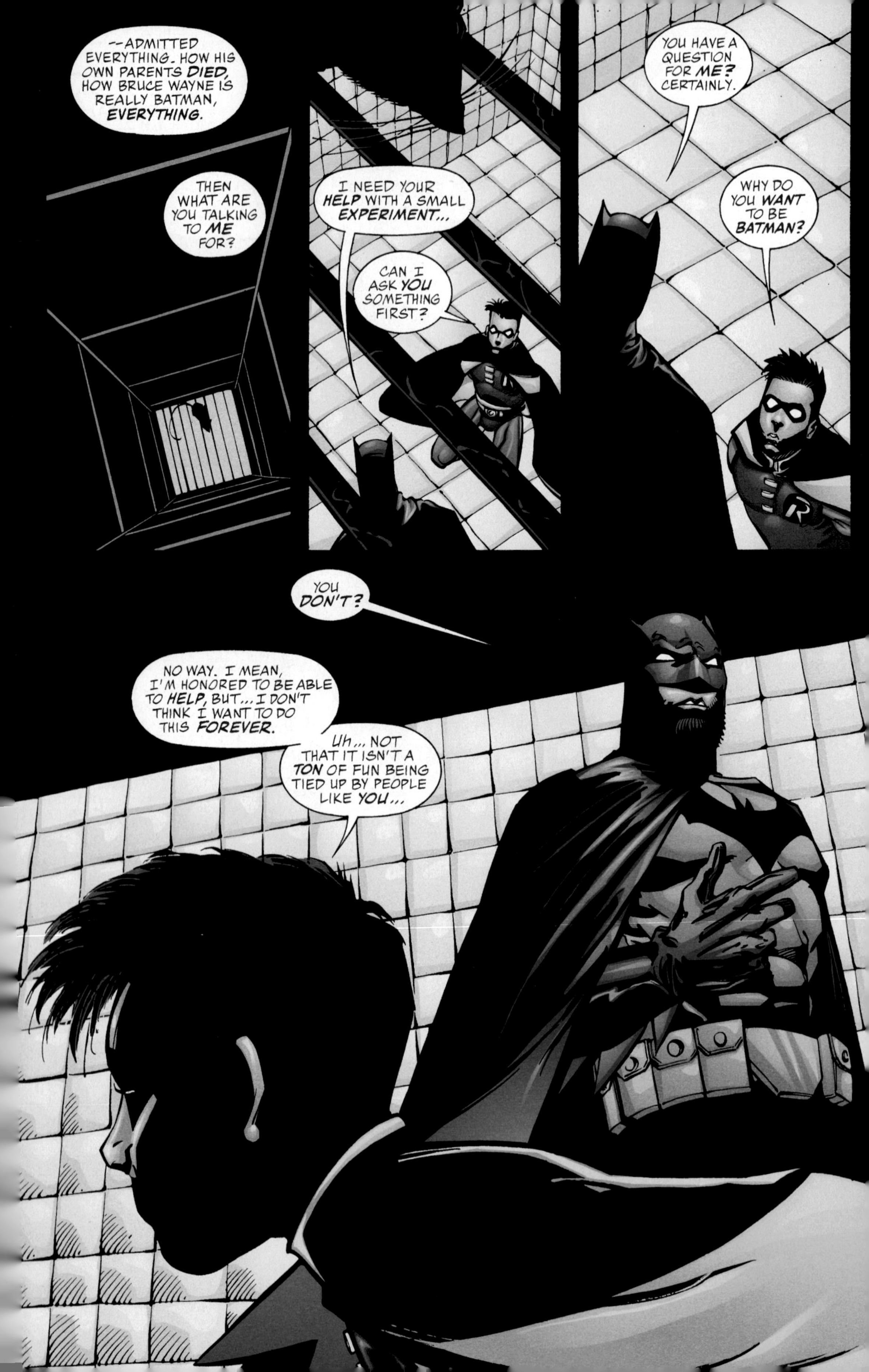
--ADMITTED EVERYTHING. HOW HIS OWN PARENTS DIED, HOW BRUCE WAYNE IS REALLY BATMAN, EVERYTHING.
THEN WHAT ARE YOU TALKING TO ME FOR?
I NEED YOUR HELP WITH A SMALL EXPERIMENT...
CAN I ASK YOU SOMETHING FIRST?
YOU HAVE A QUESTION FOR ME? CERTAINLY.
WHY DO YOU WANT TO BE BATMAN?
YOU DON'T?
NO WAY. I MEAN, I'M HONORED TO BE ABLE TO HELP, BUT... I DON'T THINK I WANT TO DO THIS FOREVER.
UH... NOT THAT IT ISN'T A TON OF FUN BEING TIED UP BY PEOPLE LIKE YOU...

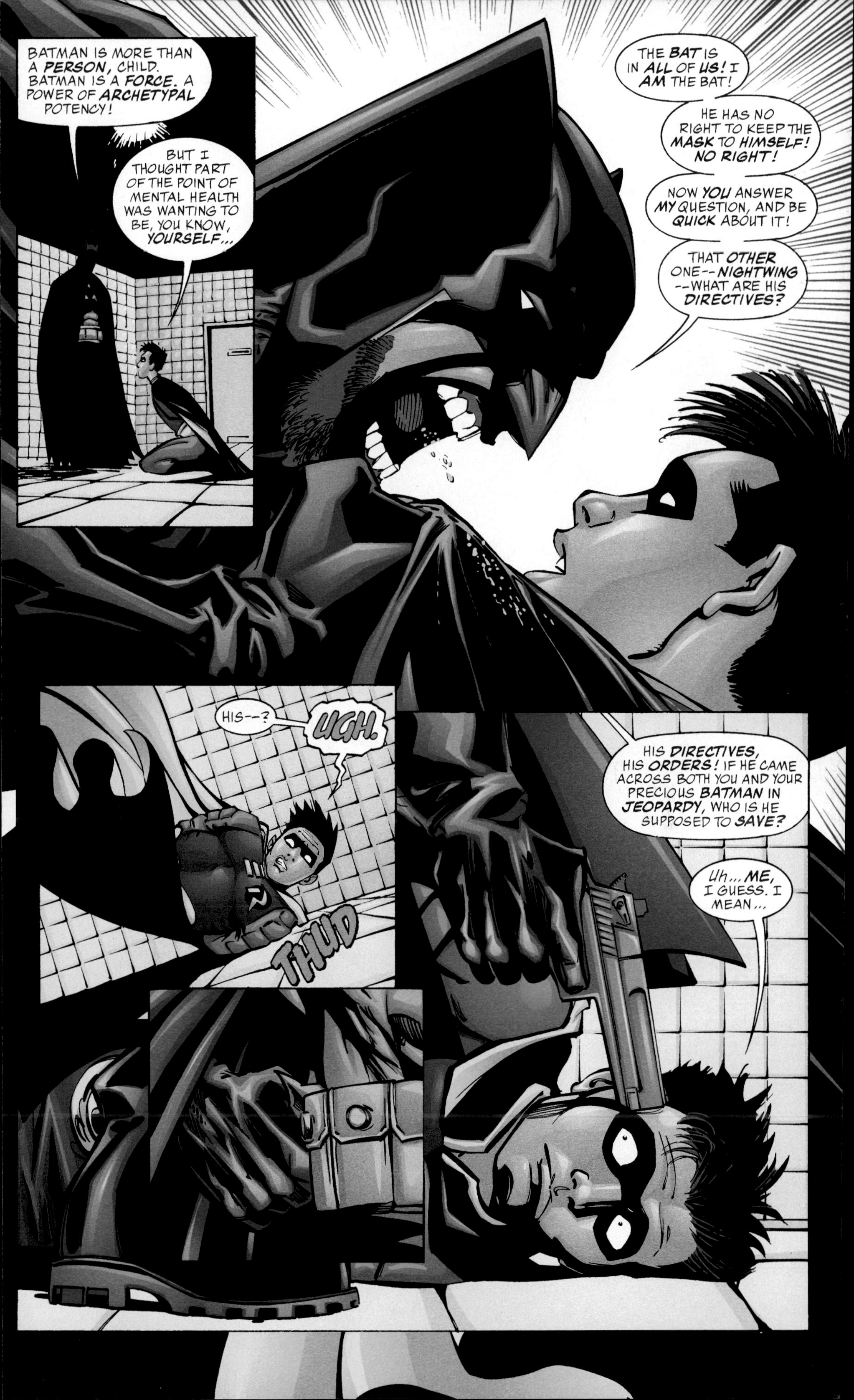
BATMAN IS MORE THAN A PERSON, CHILD. BATMAN IS A FORCE. A POWER OF ARCHETYPAL POTENCY!
BUT I THOUGHT PART OF THE POINT OF MENTAL HEALTH WAS WANTING TO BE, YOU KNOW, YOURSELF...
THE BAT IS IN ALL OF US! I AM THE BAT!
HE HAS NO RIGHT TO KEEP THE MASK TO HIMSELF! NO RIGHT!
NOW YOU ANSWER MY QUESTION, AND BE QUICK ABOUT IT!
THAT OTHER ONE--NIGHTWING--WHAT ARE HIS DIRECTIVES?
HIS--?
UGH.
THUD
HIS DIRECTIVES, HIS ORDERS! IF HE CAME ACROSS BOTH YOU AND YOUR PRECIOUS BATMAN IN JEOPARDY, WHO IS HE SUPPOSED TO SAVE?
Uh... ME, I GUESS. I MEAN...

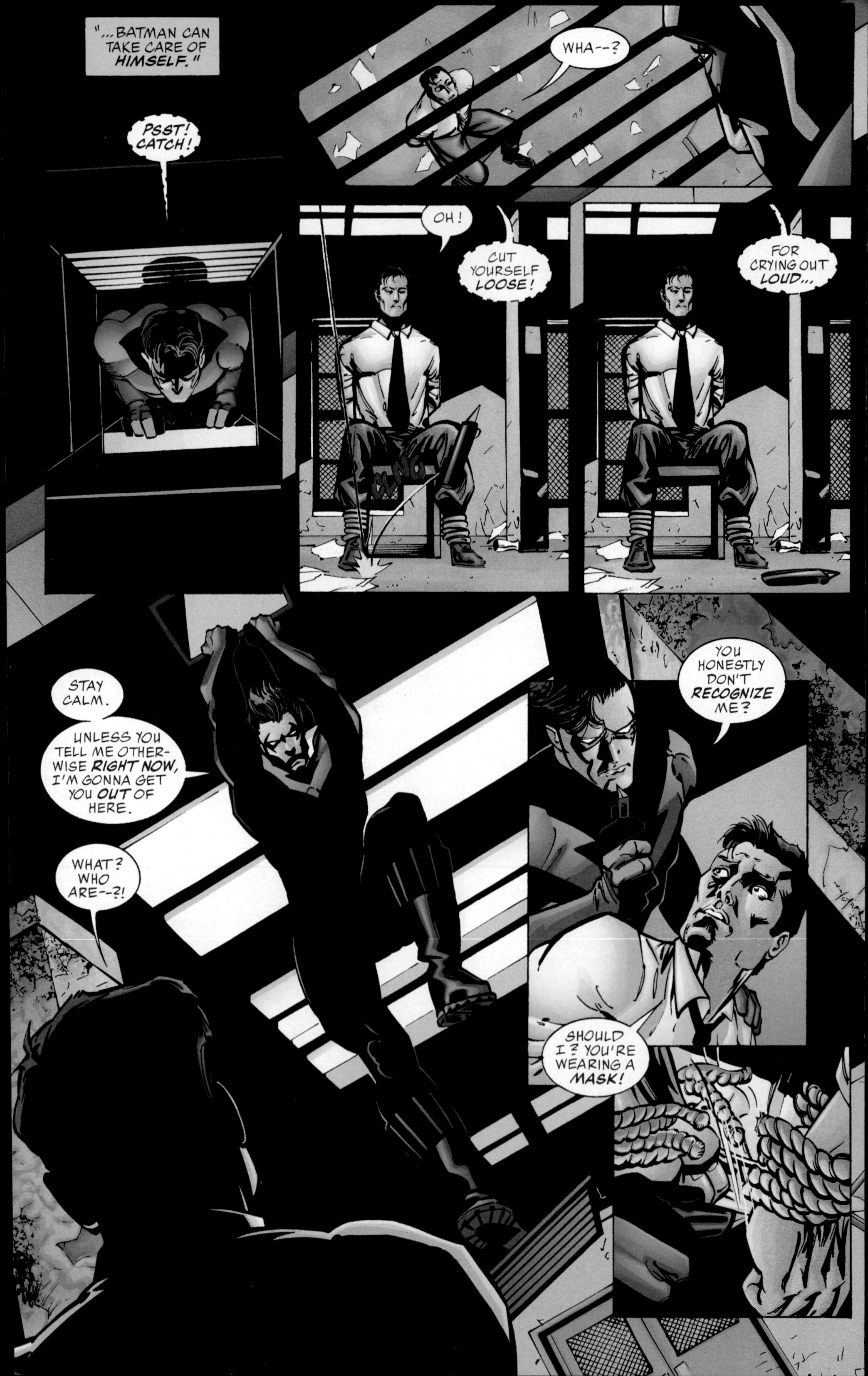
"...BATMAN CAN TAKE CARE OF HIMSELF."
WHA--?
PSST! CATCH!
OH!
CUT YOURSELF LOOSE!
FOR CRYING OUT LOUD...
STAY CALM.
UNLESS YOU TELL ME OTHER-WISE RIGHT NOW, I'M GONNA GET YOU OUT OF HERE.
WHAT? WHO ARE--?!
YOU HONESTLY DON'T RECOGNIZE ME?
SHOULD I? YOU'RE WEARING A MASK!

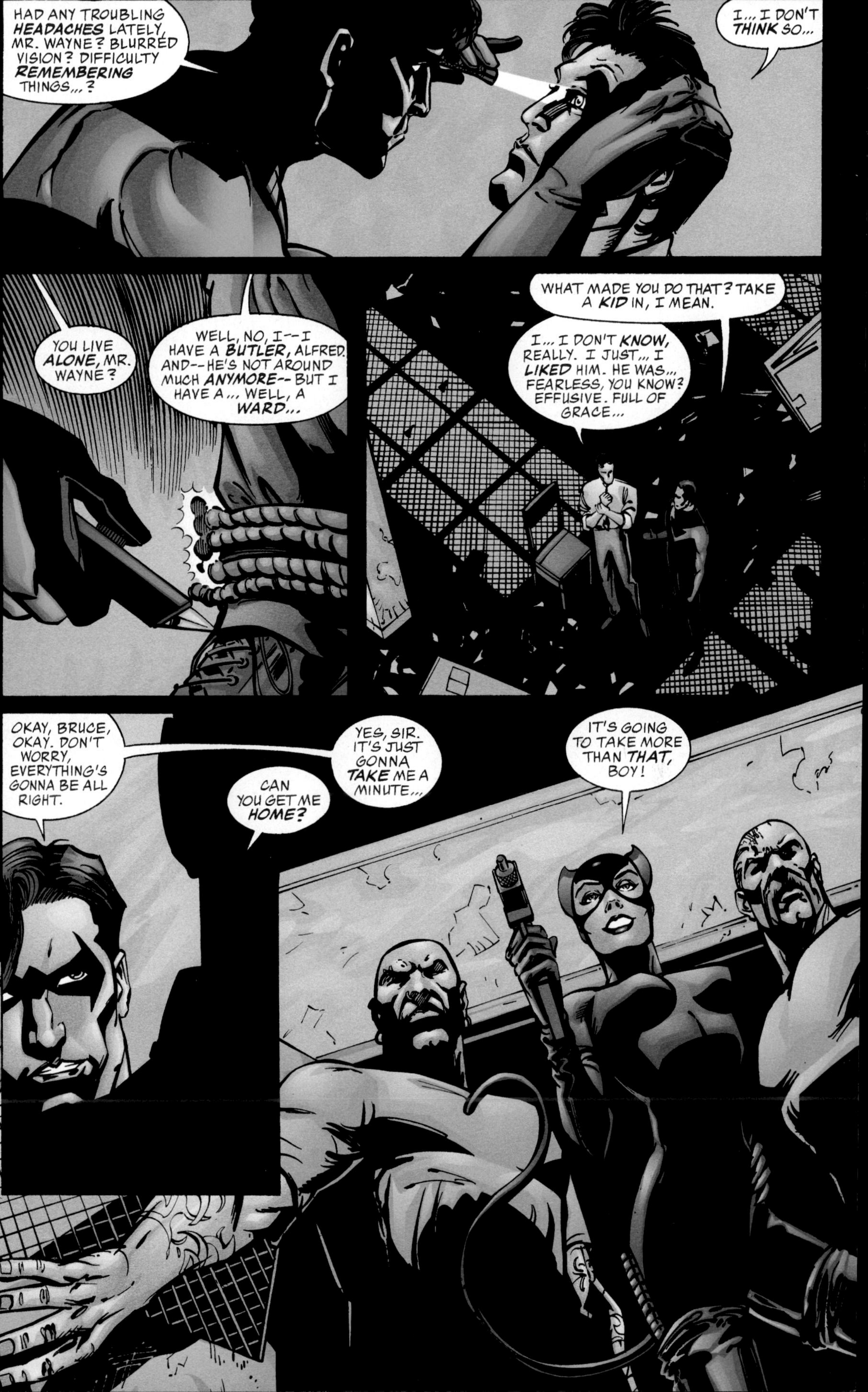
HAD ANY TROUBLING HEADACHES LATELY, MR. WAYNE? BLURRED VISION? DIFFICULTY REMEMBERING THINGS...?
I... I DON'T THINK SO...
YOU LIVE ALONE, MR. WAYNE?
WELL, NO, I--I HAVE A BUTLER, ALFRED. AND--HE'S NOT AROUND MUCH ANYMORE--BUT I HAVE A... WELL, A WARD...
WHAT MADE YOU DO THAT? TAKE A KID IN, I MEAN.
I... I DON'T KNOW, REALLY. I JUST... I LIKED HIM. HE WAS... FEARLESS, YOU KNOW? EFFUSIVE. FULL OF GRACE...
OKAY, BRUCE, OKAY. DON'T WORRY, EVERYTHING'S GONNA BE ALL RIGHT.
CAN YOU GET ME HOME?
YES, SIR. IT'S JUST GONNA TAKE ME A MINUTE...
IT'S GOING TO TAKE MORE THAN THAT, BOY!

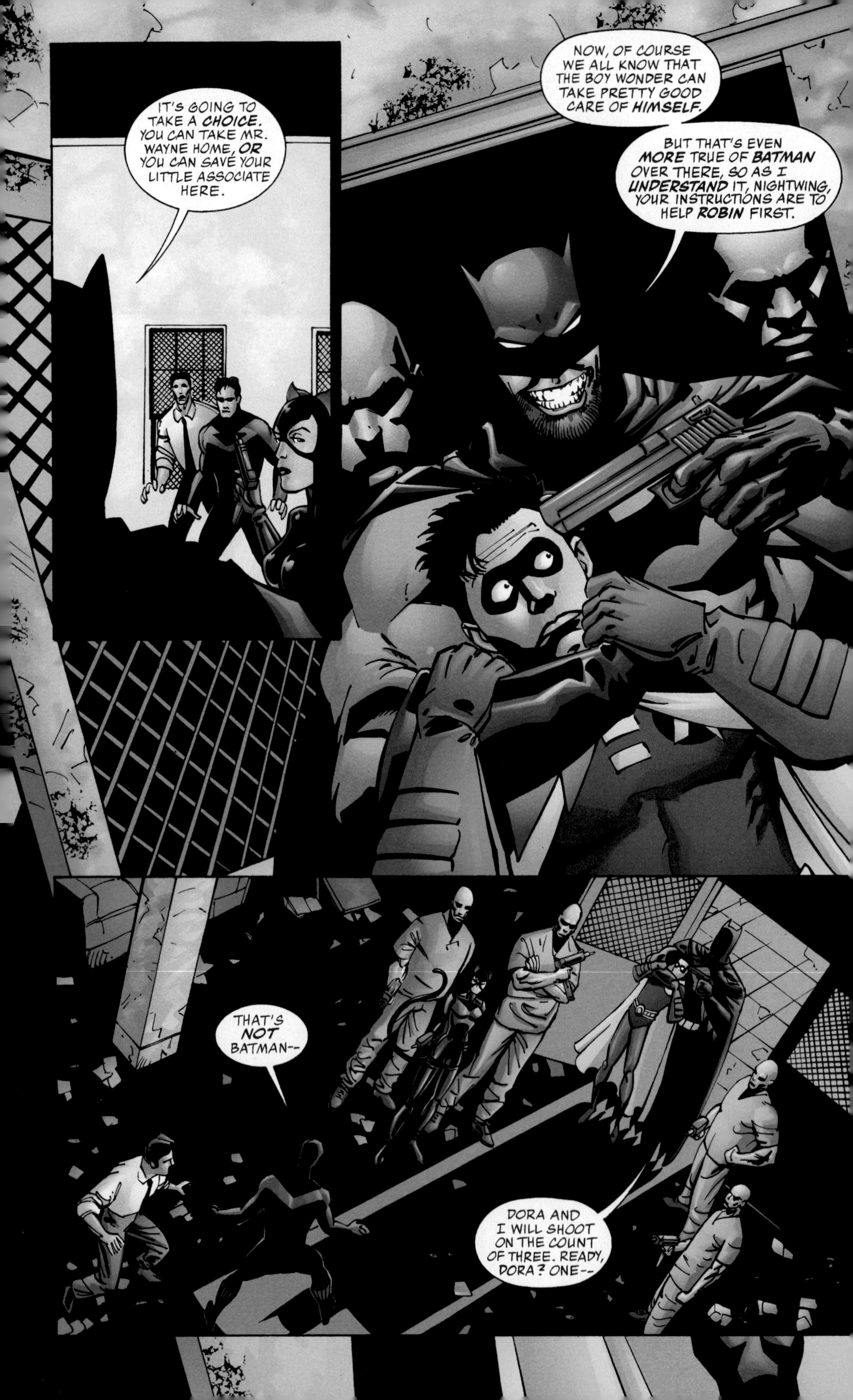
IT'S GOING TO TAKE A CHOICE. YOU CAN TAKE MR. WAYNE HOME, OR YOU CAN SAVE YOUR LITTLE ASSOCIATE HERE.
NOW, OF COURSE WE ALL KNOW THAT THE BOY WONDER CAN TAKE PRETTY GOOD CARE OF HIMSELF.
BUT THAT'S EVEN MORE TRUE OF BATMAN OVER THERE, SO AS I UNDERSTAND IT, NIGHTWING, YOUR INSTRUCTIONS ARE TO HELP ROBIN FIRST.
THAT'S NOT BATMAN--
DORA AND I WILL SHOOT ON THE COUNT OF THREE. READY, DORA? ONE--

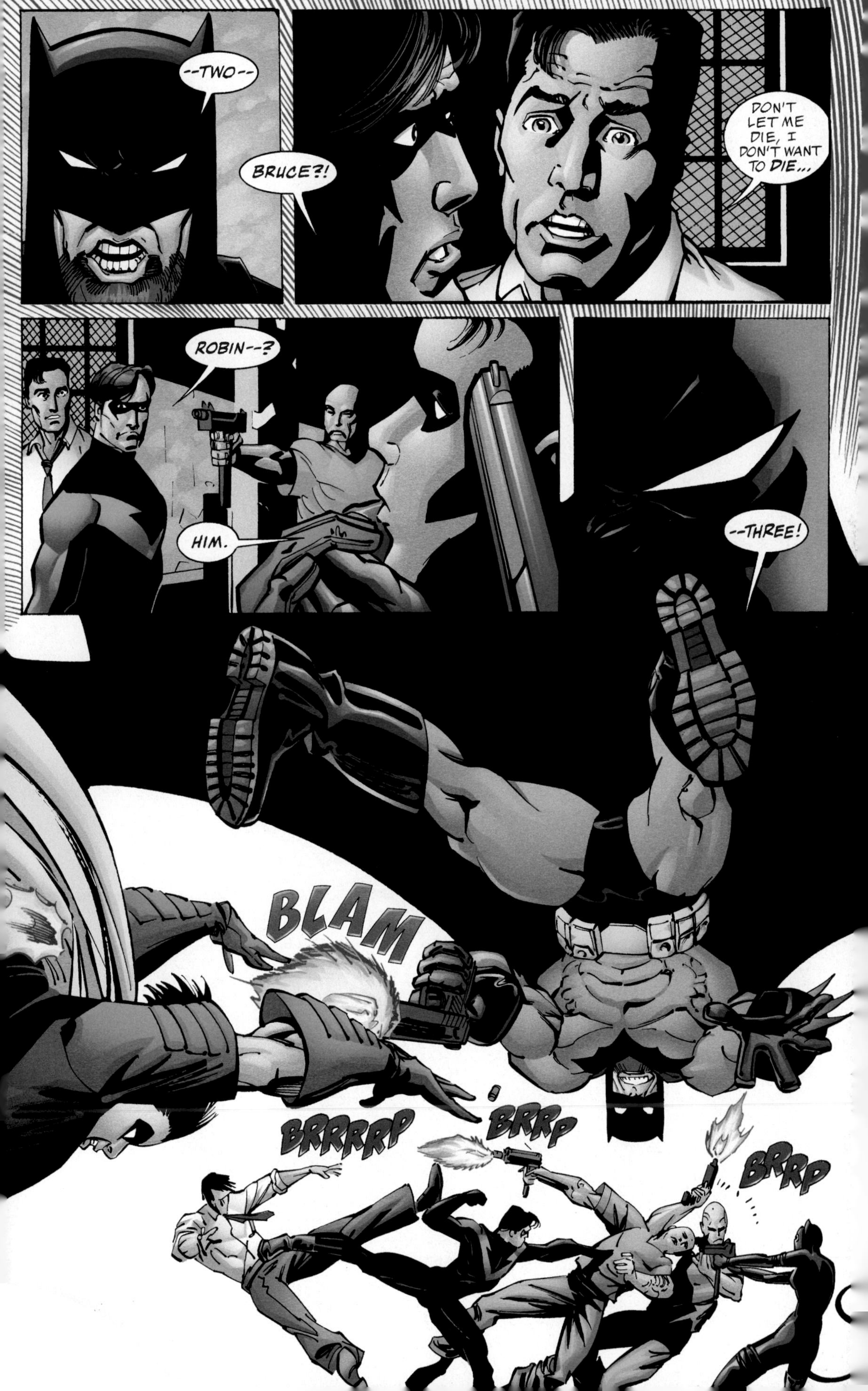
--TWO--
BRUCE?!
DON'T LET ME DIE, I DON'T WANT TO DIE...
ROBIN--?
HIM.
--THREE!
BLAM
BRRRRP
BRRP
BRRP

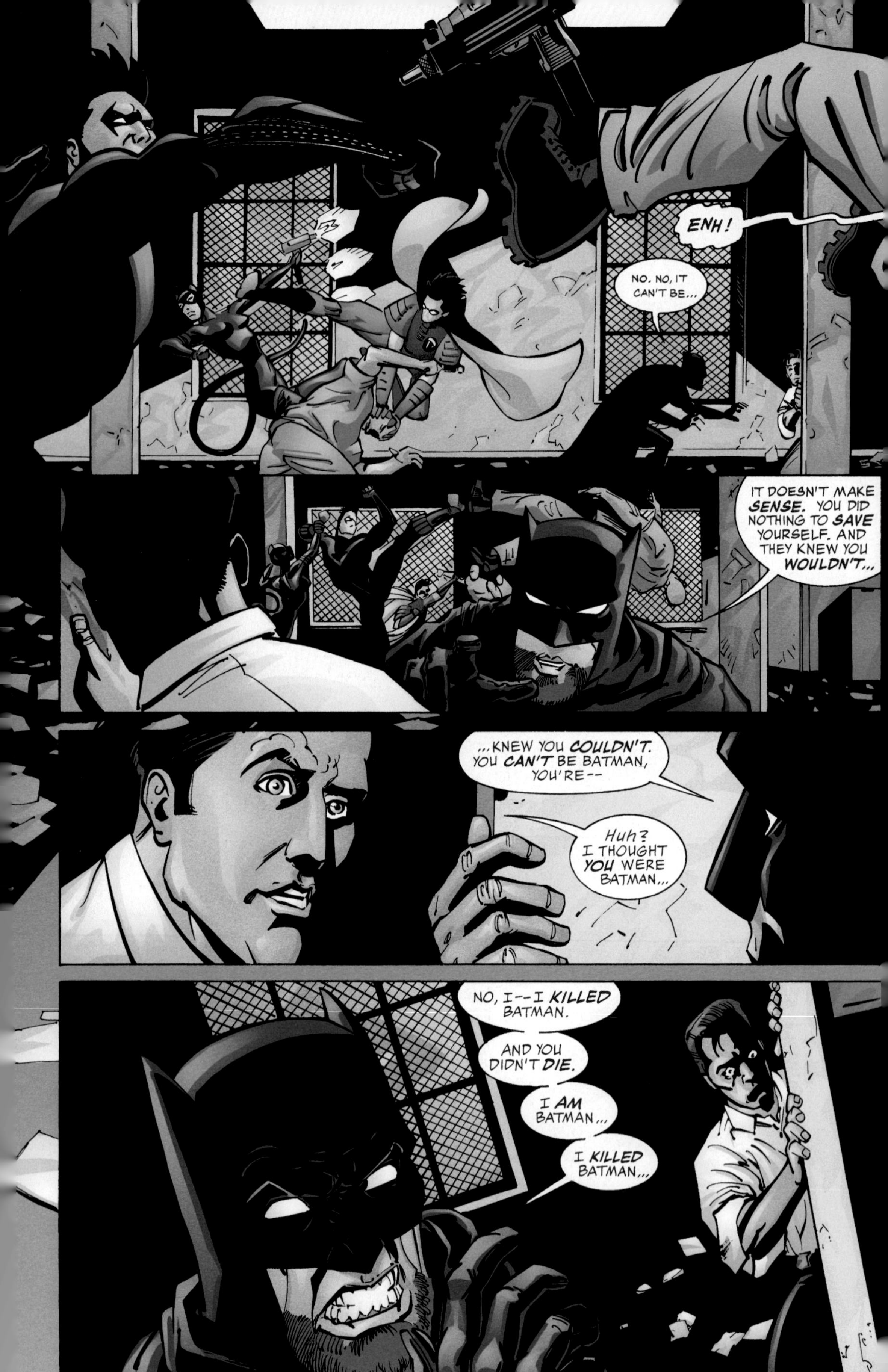
ENH!
NO. NO, IT CAN'T BE...
IT DOESN'T MAKE SENSE. YOU DID NOTHING TO SAVE YOURSELF. AND THEY KNEW YOU WOULDN'T...
...KNEW YOU COULDN'T. YOU CAN'T BE BATMAN, YOU'RE--
Huh? I THOUGHT YOU WERE BATMAN...
NO, I--I KILLED BATMAN.
AND YOU DIDN'T DIE.
I AM BATMAN...
I KILLED BATMAN...

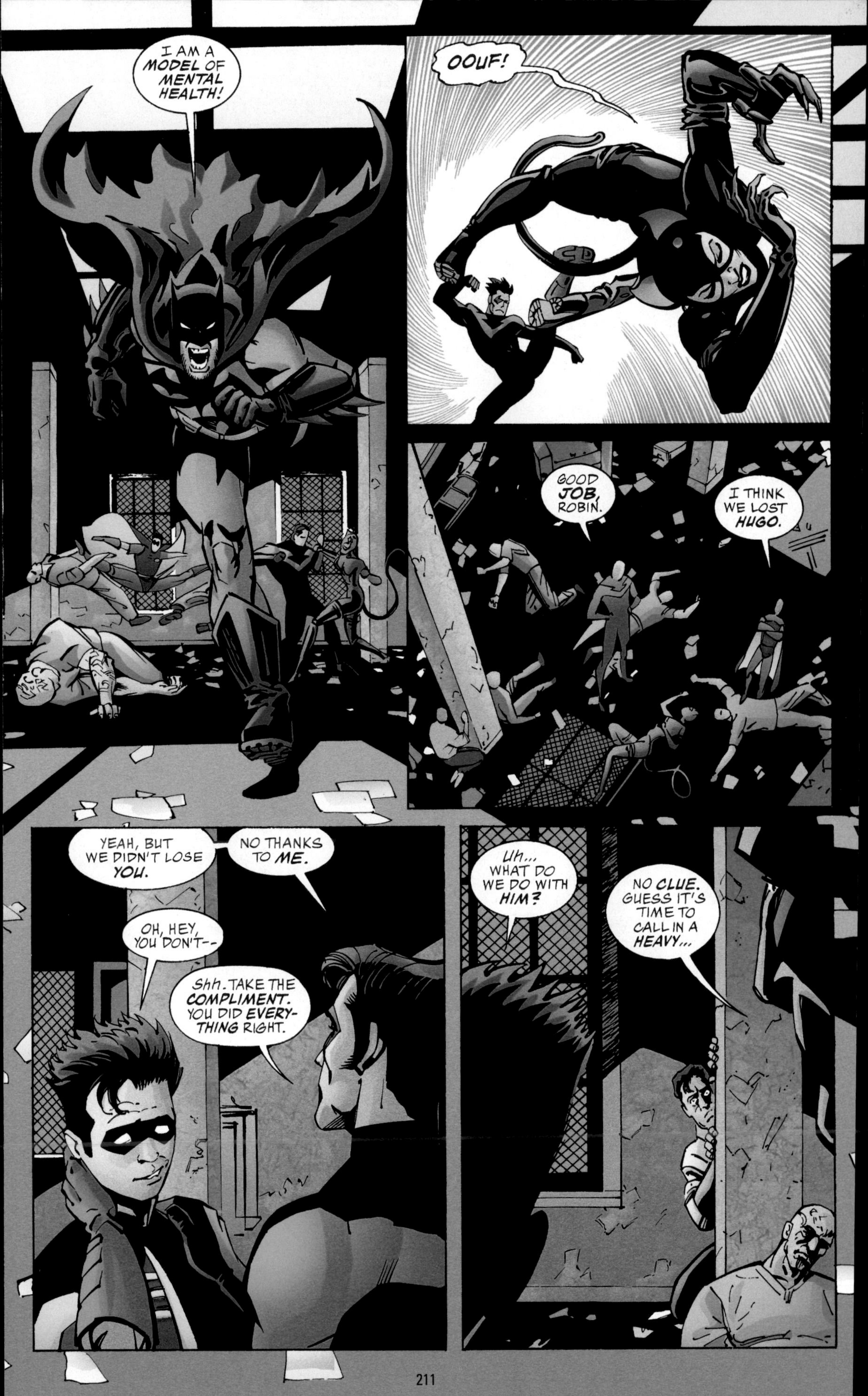
I AM A MODEL OF MENTAL HEALTH!
OOUF!
GOOD JOB, ROBIN.
I THINK WE LOST HUGO.
YEAH, BUT WE DIDN'T LOSE YOU.
NO THANKS TO ME.
OH, HEY, YOU DON'T--
Shh. TAKE THE COMPLIMENT. YOU DID EVERYTHING RIGHT.
Uh... WHAT DO WE DO WITH HIM?
NO CLUE. GUESS IT'S TIME TO CALL IN A HEAVY...

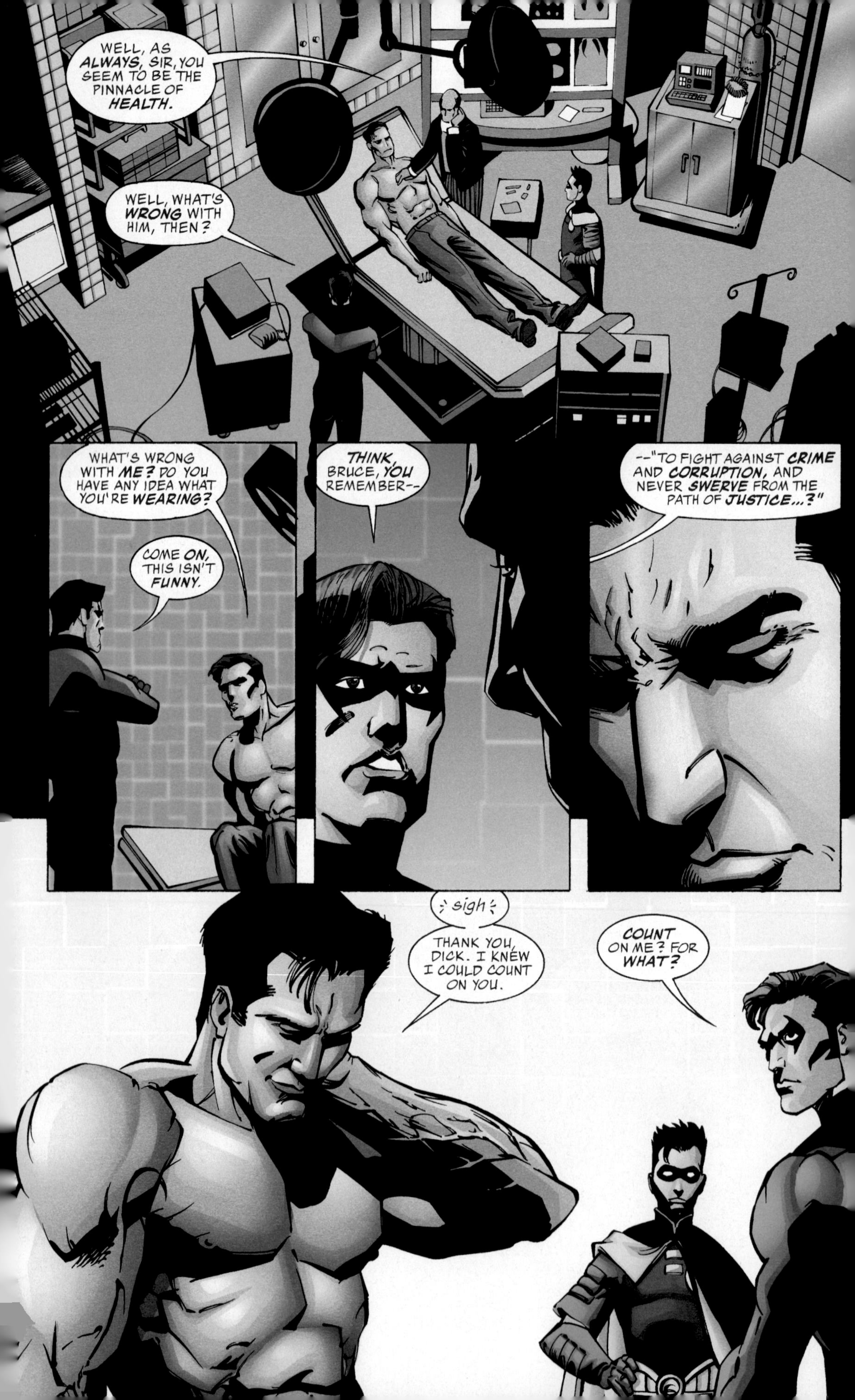
WELL, AS ALWAYS, SIR, YOU SEEM TO BE THE PINNACLE OF HEALTH.
WELL, WHAT'S WRONG WITH HIM, THEN?
WHAT'S WRONG WITH ME? DO YOU HAVE ANY IDEA WHAT YOU'RE WEARING?
COME ON, THIS ISN'T FUNNY.
THINK, BRUCE, YOU REMEMBER--
--"TO FIGHT AGAINST CRIME AND CORRUPTION, AND NEVER SWERVE FROM THE PATH OF JUSTICE...?"
sigh
THANK YOU, DICK. I KNEW I COULD COUNT ON YOU.
COUNT ON ME? FOR WHAT?

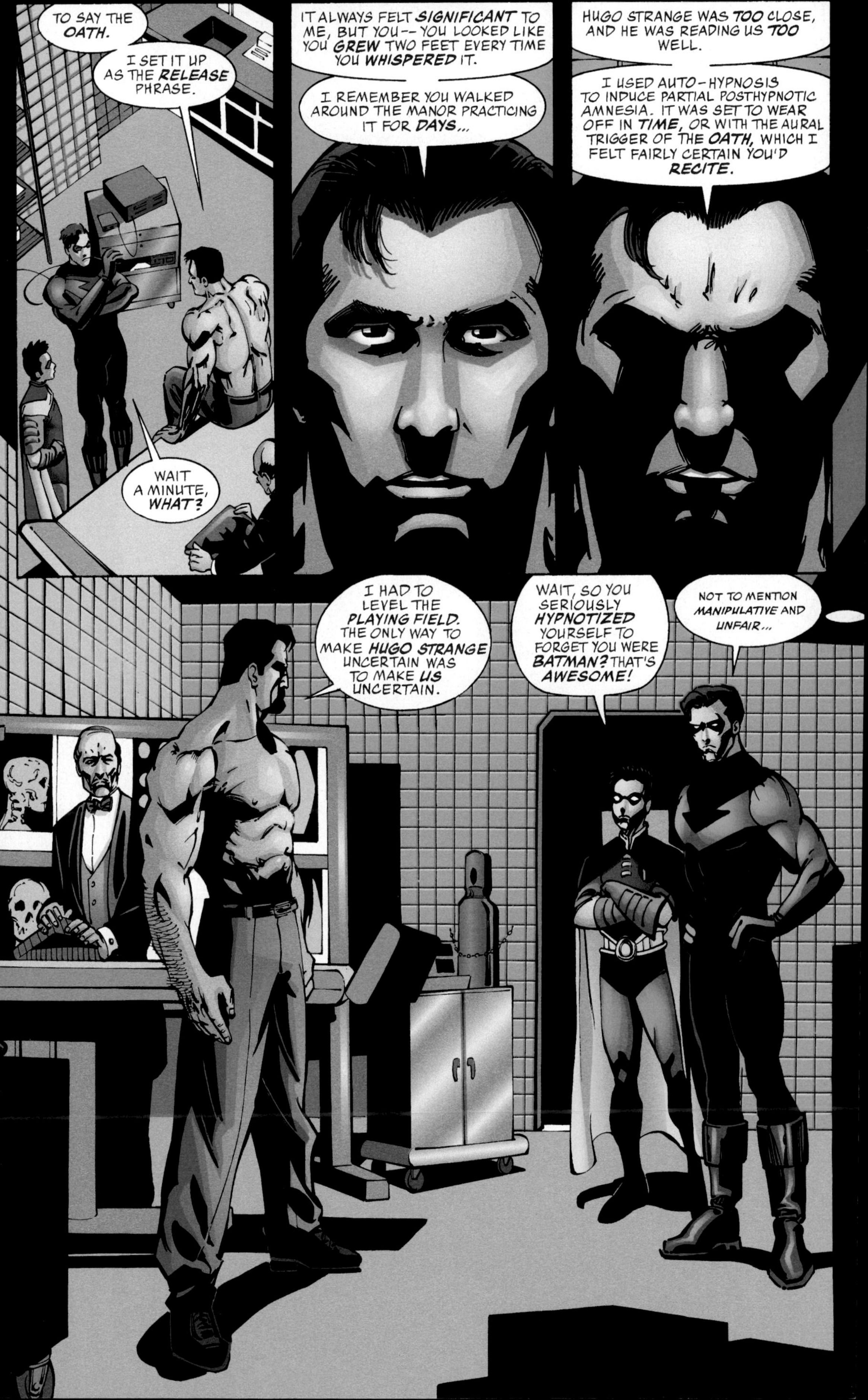
TO SAY THE OATH.
I SET IT UP AS THE RELEASE PHRASE.
WAIT A MINUTE, WHAT?
IT ALWAYS FELT SIGNIFICANT TO ME, BUT YOU-- YOU LOOKED LIKE YOU GREW TWO FEET EVERY TIME YOU WHISPERED IT.
I REMEMBER YOU WALKED AROUND THE MANOR PRACTICING IT FOR DAYS...
HUGO STRANGE WAS TOO CLOSE, AND HE WAS READING US TOO WELL.
I USED AUTO-HYPNOSIS TO INDUCE PARTIAL POSTHYPNOTIC AMNESIA. IT WAS SET TO WEAR OFF IN TIME, OR WITH THE AURAL TRIGGER OF THE OATH, WHICH I FELT FAIRLY CERTAIN YOU'D RECITE.
I HAD TO LEVEL THE PLAYING FIELD. THE ONLY WAY TO MAKE HUGO STRANGE UNCERTAIN WAS TO MAKE US UNCERTAIN.
WAIT, SO YOU SERIOUSLY HYPNOTIZED YOURSELF TO FORGET YOU WERE BATMAN? THAT'S AWESOME!
NOT TO MENTION MANIPULATIVE AND UNFAIR...

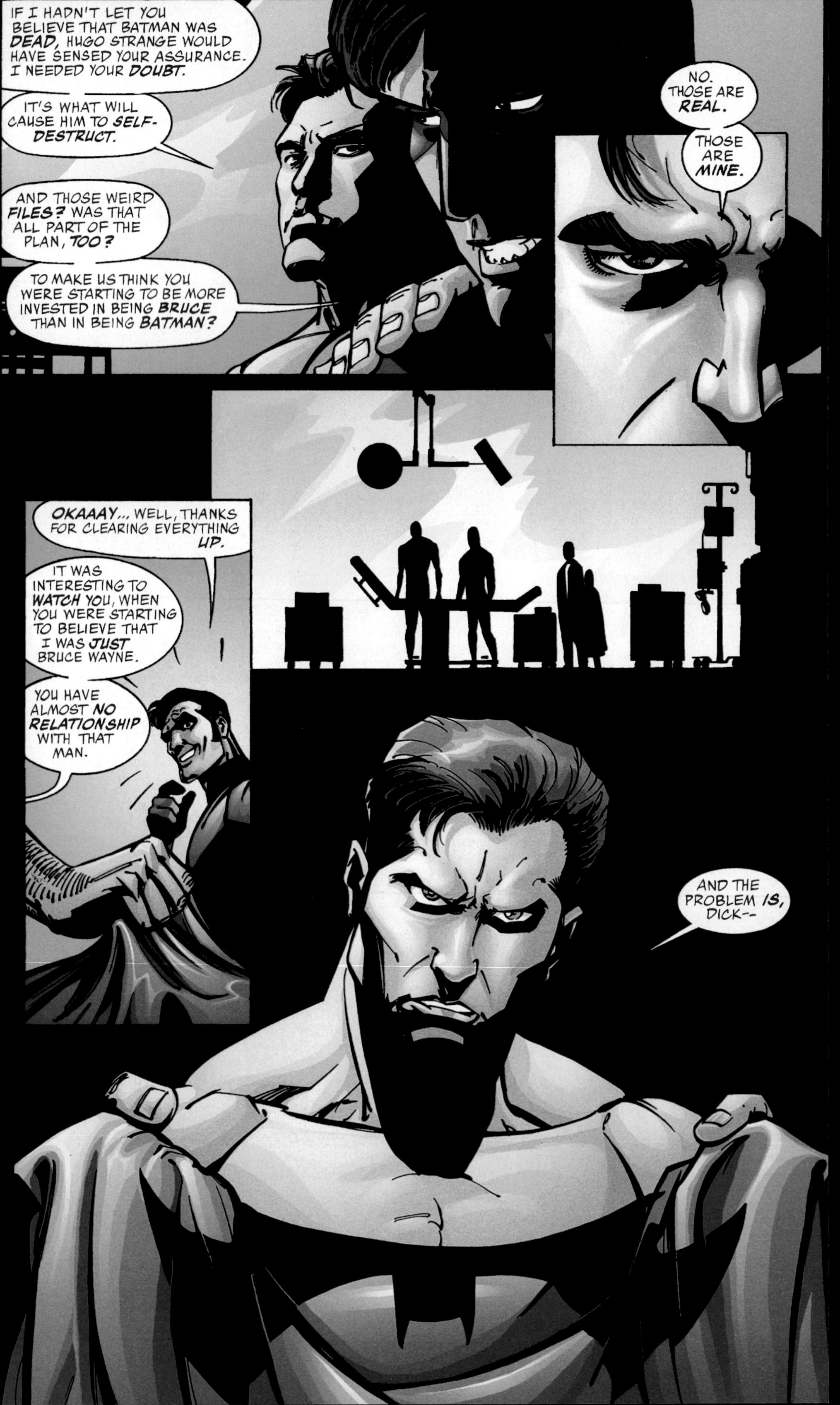
IF I HADN'T LET YOU BELIEVE THAT BATMAN WAS DEAD, HUGO STRANGE WOULD HAVE SENSED YOUR ASSURANCE. I NEEDED YOUR DOUBT.
IT'S WHAT WILL CAUSE HIM TO SELF-DESTRUCT.
AND THOSE WEIRD FILES? WAS THAT ALL PART OF THE PLAN, TOO?
TO MAKE US THINK YOU WERE STARTING TO BE MORE INVESTED IN BEING BRUCE THAN IN BEING BATMAN?
NO. THOSE ARE REAL.
THOSE ARE MINE.
OKAAAY... WELL, THANKS FOR CLEARING EVERYTHING UP.
IT WAS INTERESTING TO WATCH YOU, WHEN YOU WERE STARTING TO BELIEVE THAT I WAS JUST BRUCE WAYNE.
YOU HAVE ALMOST NO RELATIONSHIP WITH THAT MAN.
AND THE PROBLEM IS, DICK--

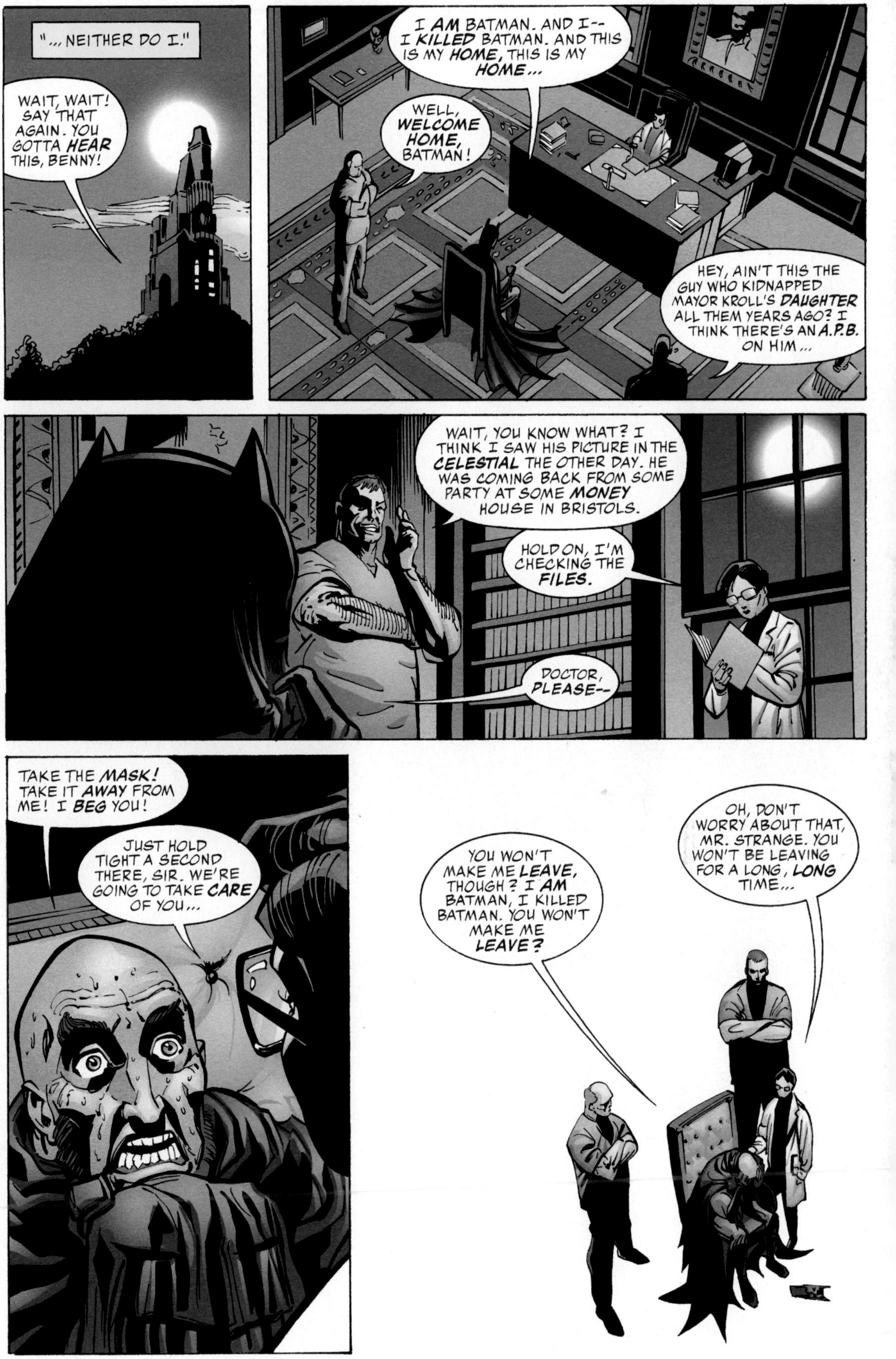
"... NEITHER DO I."
WAIT, WAIT! SAY THAT AGAIN. YOU GOTTA HEAR THIS, BENNY!
I AM BATMAN. AND I-- I KILLED BATMAN. AND THIS IS MY HOME, THIS IS MY HOME...
WELL, WELCOME HOME, BATMAN!
HEY, AIN'T THIS THE GUY WHO KIDNAPPED MAYOR KROLL'S DAUGHTER ALL THEM YEARS AGO? I THINK THERE'S AN A.P.B. ON HIM...
WAIT, YOU KNOW WHAT? I THINK I SAW HIS PICTURE IN THE CELESTIAL THE OTHER DAY. HE WAS COMING BACK FROM SOME PARTY AT SOME MONEY HOUSE IN BRISTOLS.
HOLD ON, I'M CHECKING THE FILES.
DOCTOR, PLEASE--
TAKE THE MASK! TAKE IT AWAY FROM ME! I BEG YOU!
JUST HOLD TIGHT A SECOND THERE, SIR. WE'RE GOING TO TAKE CARE OF YOU...
YOU WON'T MAKE ME LEAVE, THOUGH? I AM BATMAN, I KILLED BATMAN. YOU WON'T MAKE ME LEAVE?
OH, DON'T WORRY ABOUT THAT, MR. STRANGE. YOU WON'T BE LEAVING FOR A LONG, LONG TIME...

the end.

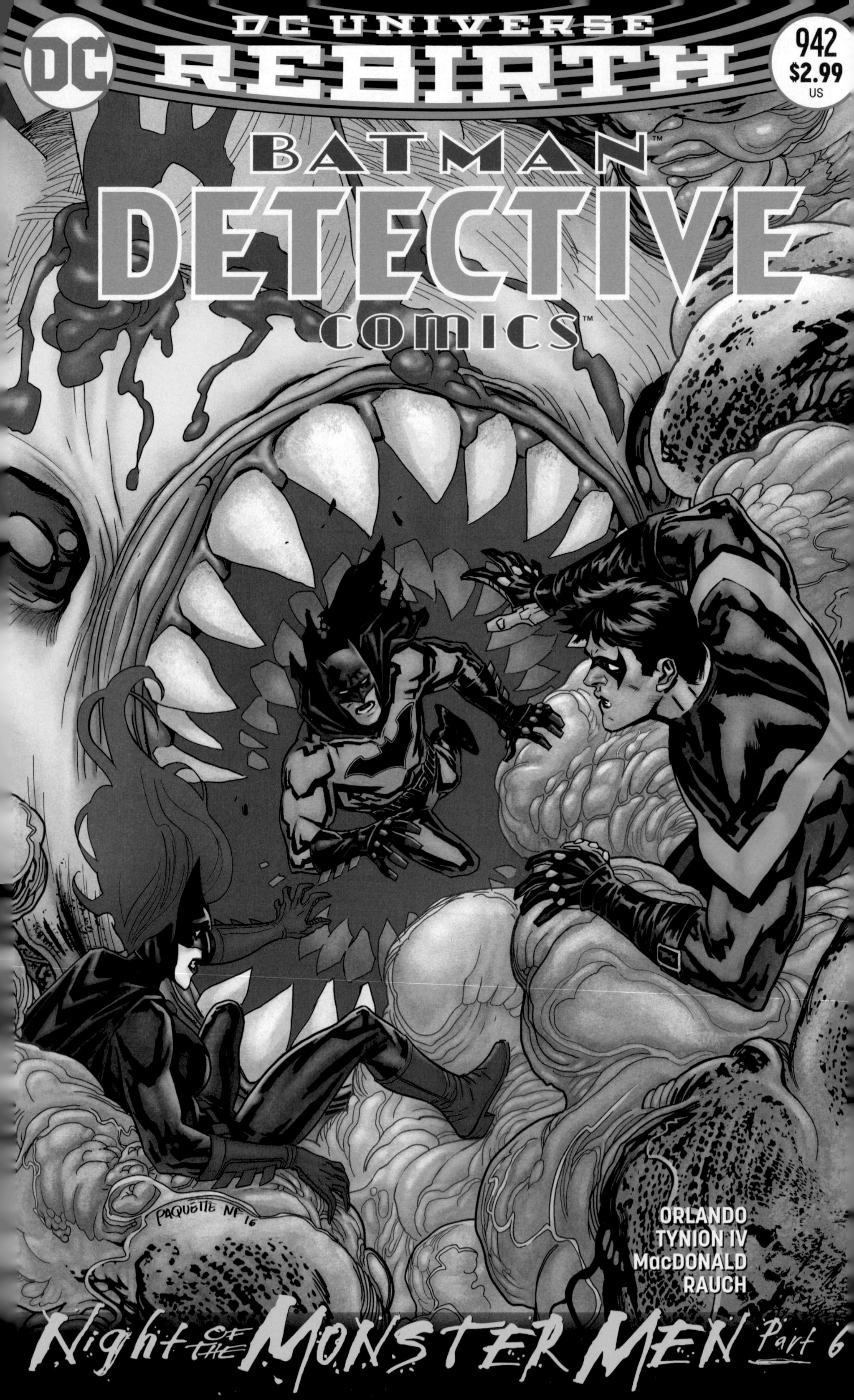
DC
DC UNIVERSE REBIRTH
942
$2.99
US
BATMAN™
DETECTIVE COMICS™
PAQUETTE NF '16
ORLANDO
TYNION IV
MacDONALD
RAUCH
Night of the MONSTER MEN Part 6

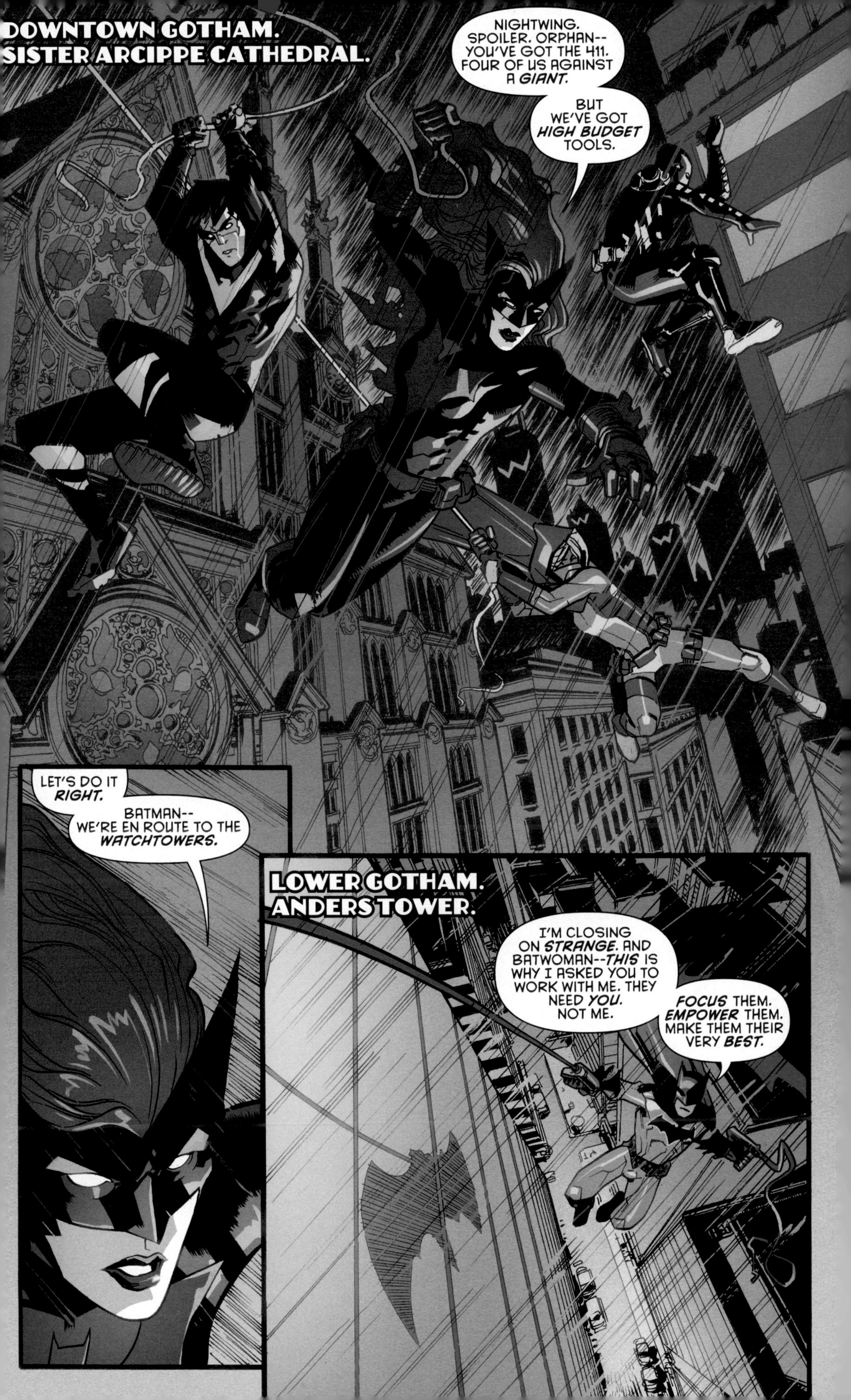
DOWNTOWN GOTHAM.
SISTER ARCIPPE CATHEDRAL.
NIGHTWING. SPOILER. ORPHAN-- YOU'VE GOT THE 411. FOUR OF US AGAINST A *GIANT*.
BUT WE'VE GOT *HIGH BUDGET* TOOLS.
LET'S DO IT *RIGHT*.
BATMAN-- WE'RE EN ROUTE TO THE *WATCHTOWERS*.
LOWER GOTHAM.
ANDERS TOWER.
I'M CLOSING ON *STRANGE*. AND BATWOMAN--*THIS* IS WHY I ASKED YOU TO WORK WITH ME. THEY NEED *YOU*. NOT ME.
*FOCUS* THEM. *EMPOWER* THEM. MAKE THEM THEIR VERY *BEST*.

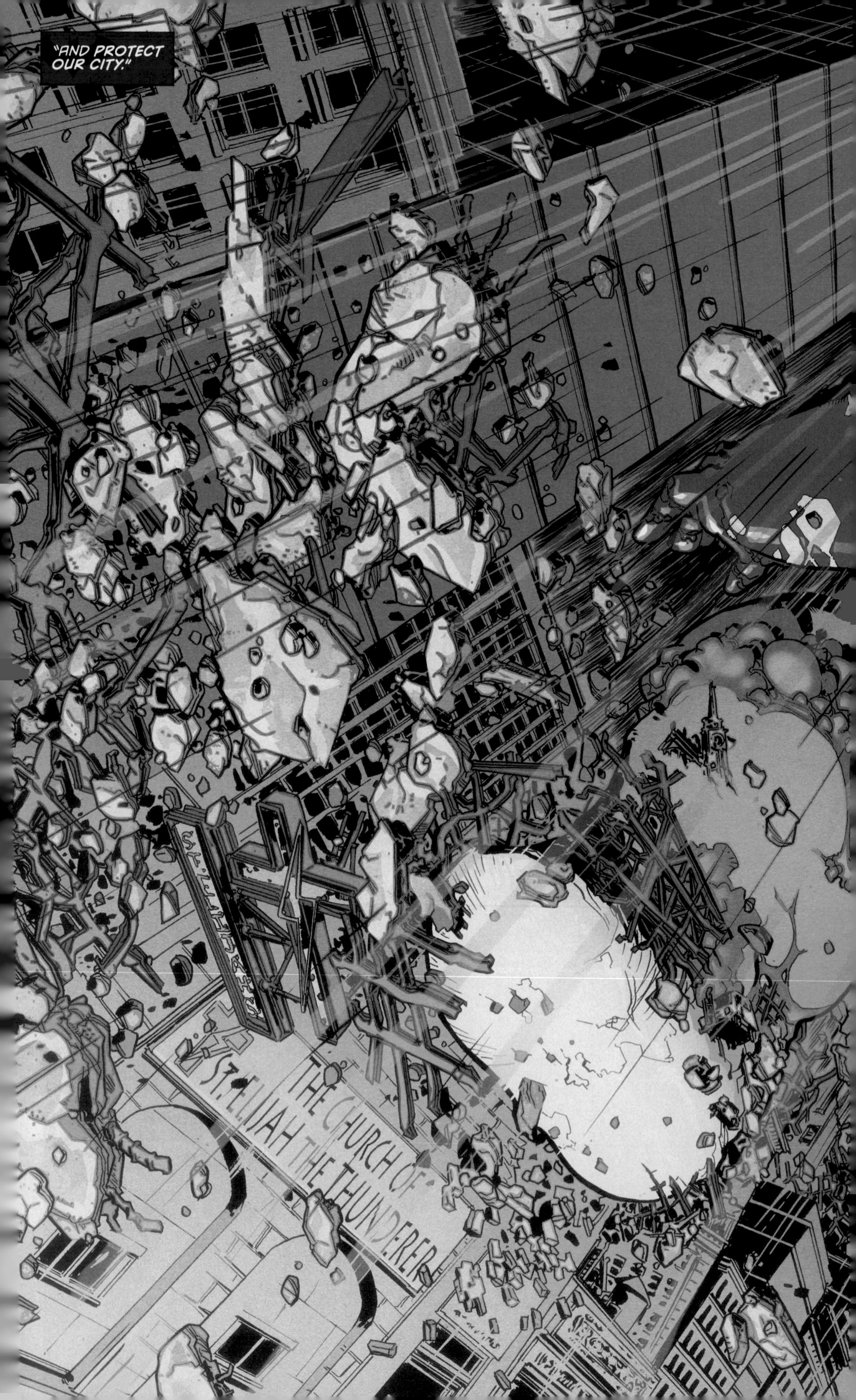
"AND PROTECT OUR CITY."
ST. ELIJAH'S
THE CHURCH OF ST. ELIJAH THE THUNDERER

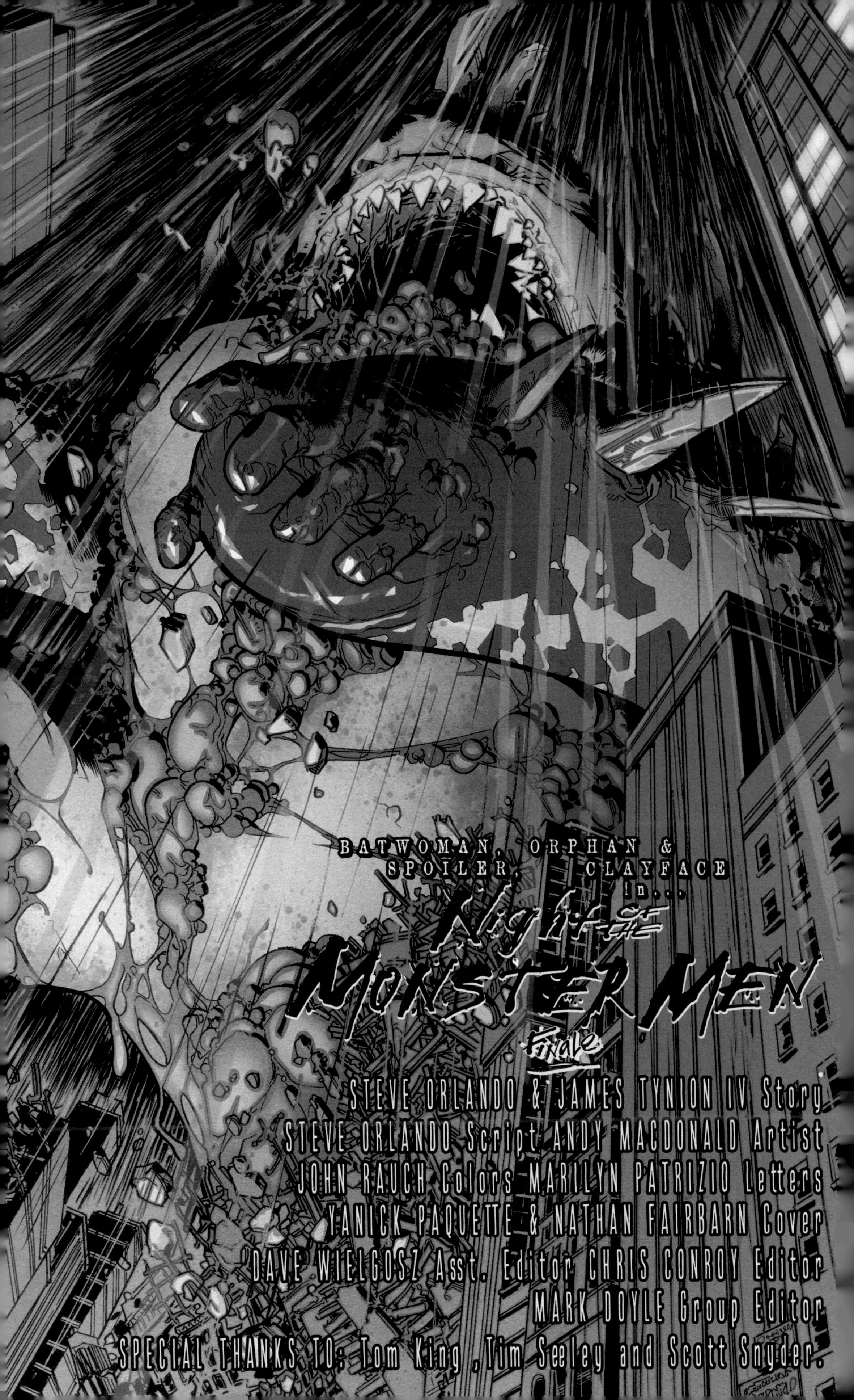
BATWOMAN, ORPHAN & SPOILER, CLAYFACE in...
Night of the MONSTER MEN
Finale
STEVE ORLANDO & JAMES TYNION IV Story
STEVE ORLANDO Script ANDY MACDONALD Artist
JOHN RAUCH Colors MARILYN PATRIZIO Letters
YANICK PAQUETTE & NATHAN FAIRBARN Cover
DAVE WIELGOSZ Asst. Editor CHRIS CONROY Editor
MARK DOYLE Group Editor
SPECIAL THANKS TO: Tom King ,Tim Seeley and Scott Snyder.

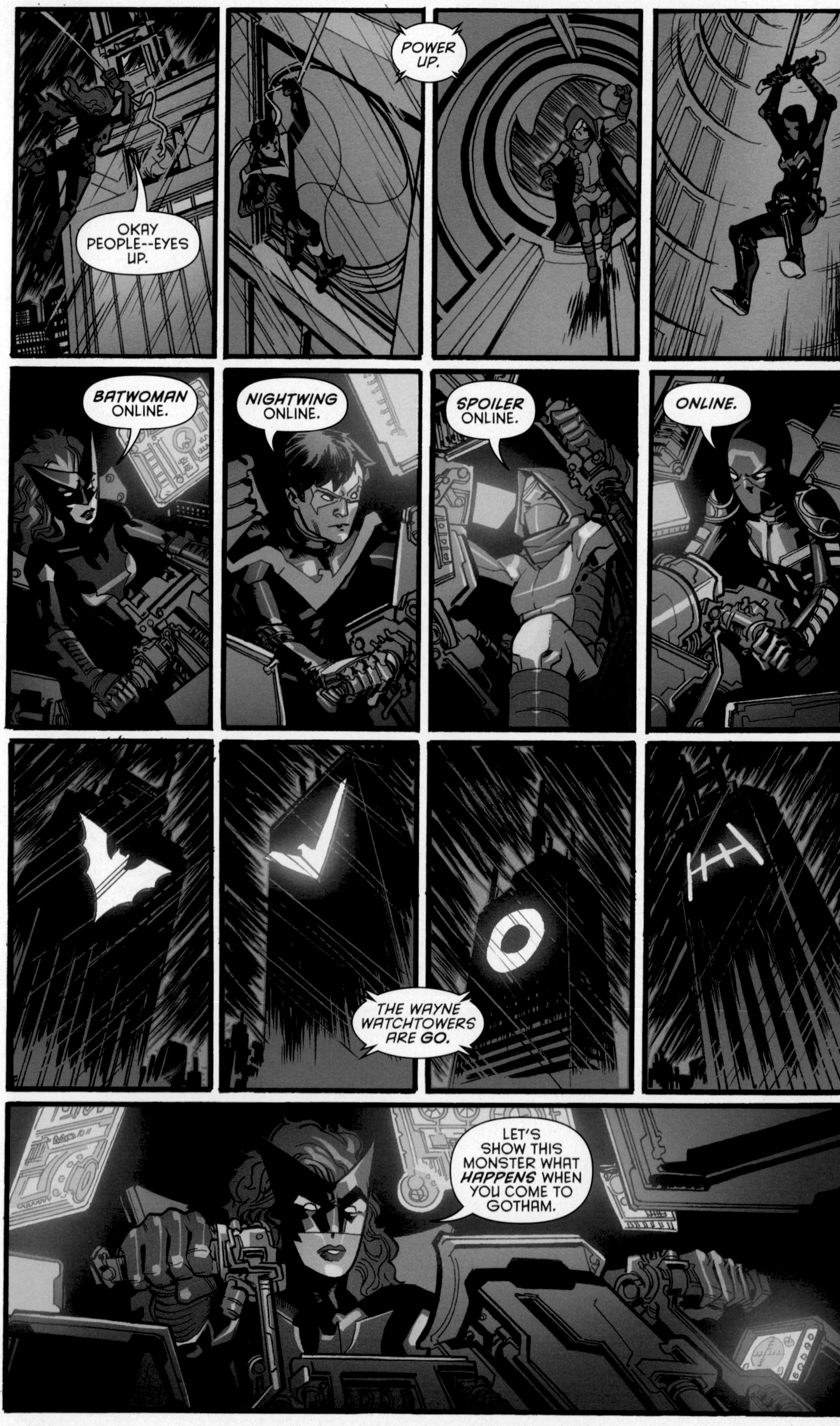
OKAY PEOPLE--EYES UP.
POWER UP.
BATWOMAN ONLINE.
NIGHTWING ONLINE.
SPOILER ONLINE.
ONLINE.
THE WAYNE WATCHTOWERS ARE GO.
LET'S SHOW THIS MONSTER WHAT HAPPENS WHEN YOU COME TO GOTHAM.

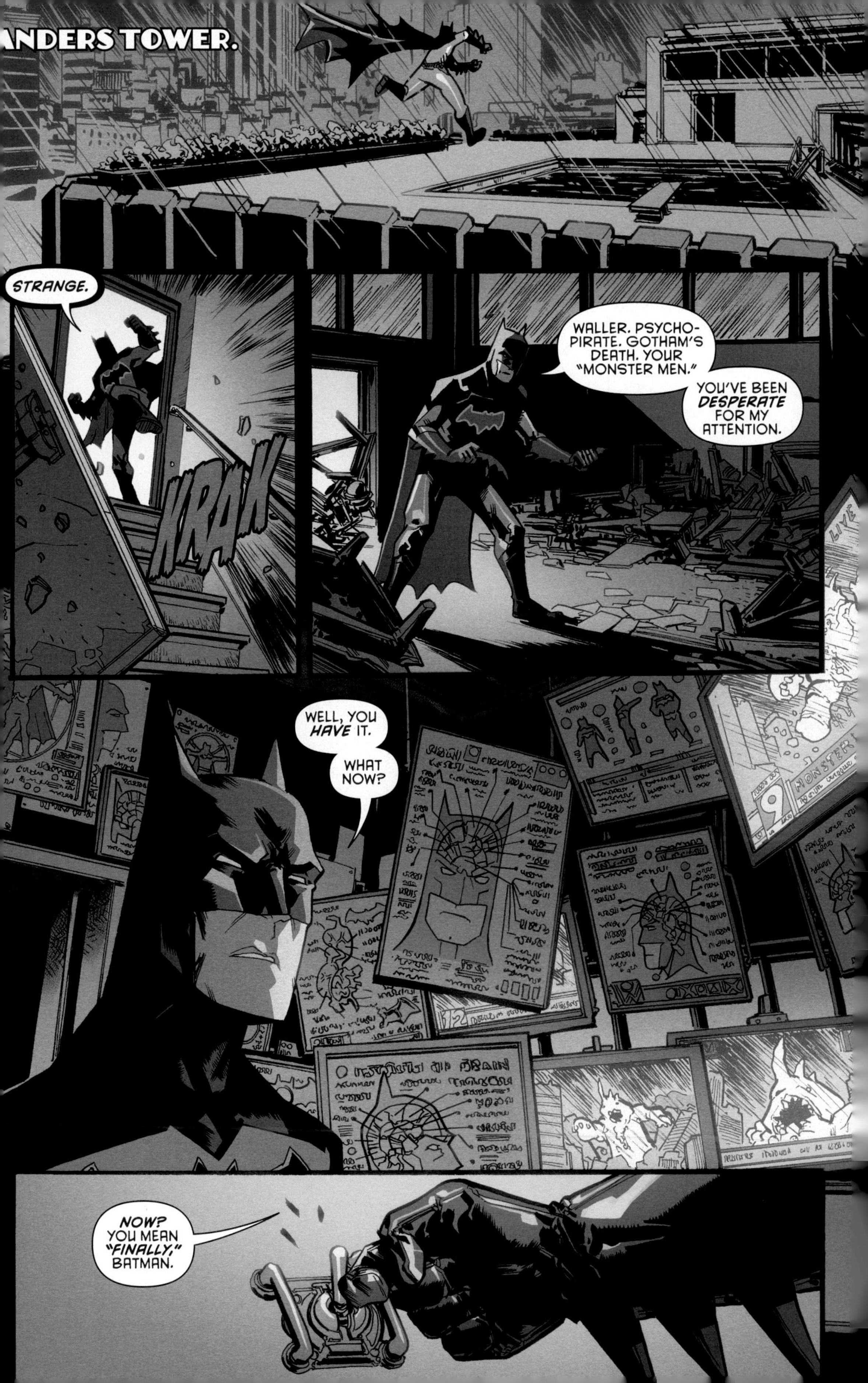
ANDERS TOWER.
STRANGE.
KRAK
WALLER. PSYCHO-PIRATE. GOTHAM'S DEATH. YOUR "MONSTER MEN."
YOU'VE BEEN DESPERATE FOR MY ATTENTION.
WELL, YOU HAVE IT.
WHAT NOW?
NOW? YOU MEAN "FINALLY," BATMAN.

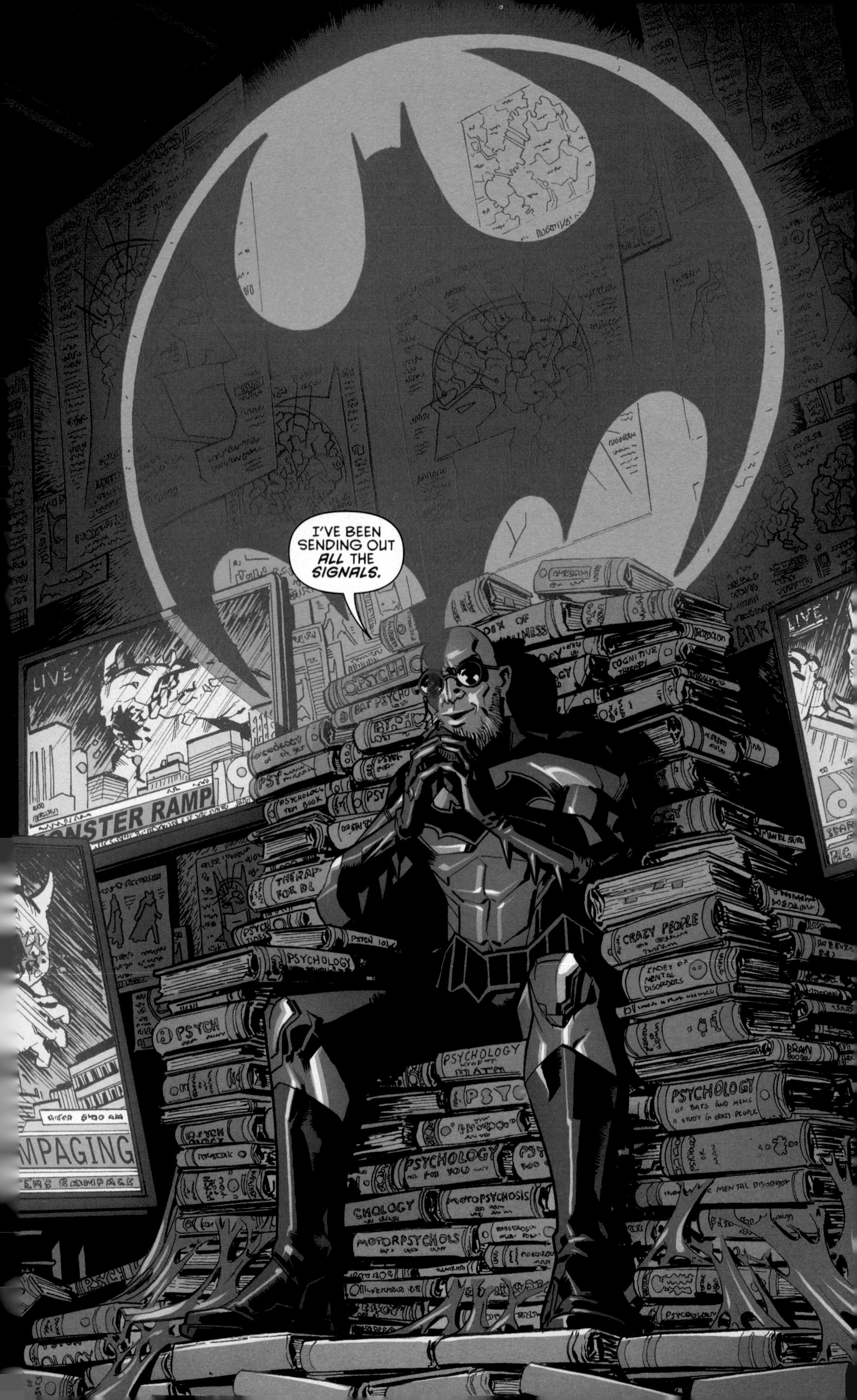
I'VE BEEN SENDING OUT *ALL* THE *SIGNALS.*
COGNITIVE THERAPY
CRAZY PEOPLE
INDEX OF MENTAL DISORDERS
PSYCHOLOGY OF BATS AND MENS A STUDY IN CRAZY PEOPLE
PSYCHOLOGY
PSYCH 101
PSYCHOLOGY TEXT BOOK
BAT PSYCHOLOGY
MOTOPSYCHOSIS
BRAIN BOOK
MENTAL DISORDERS
LIVE
PAGING

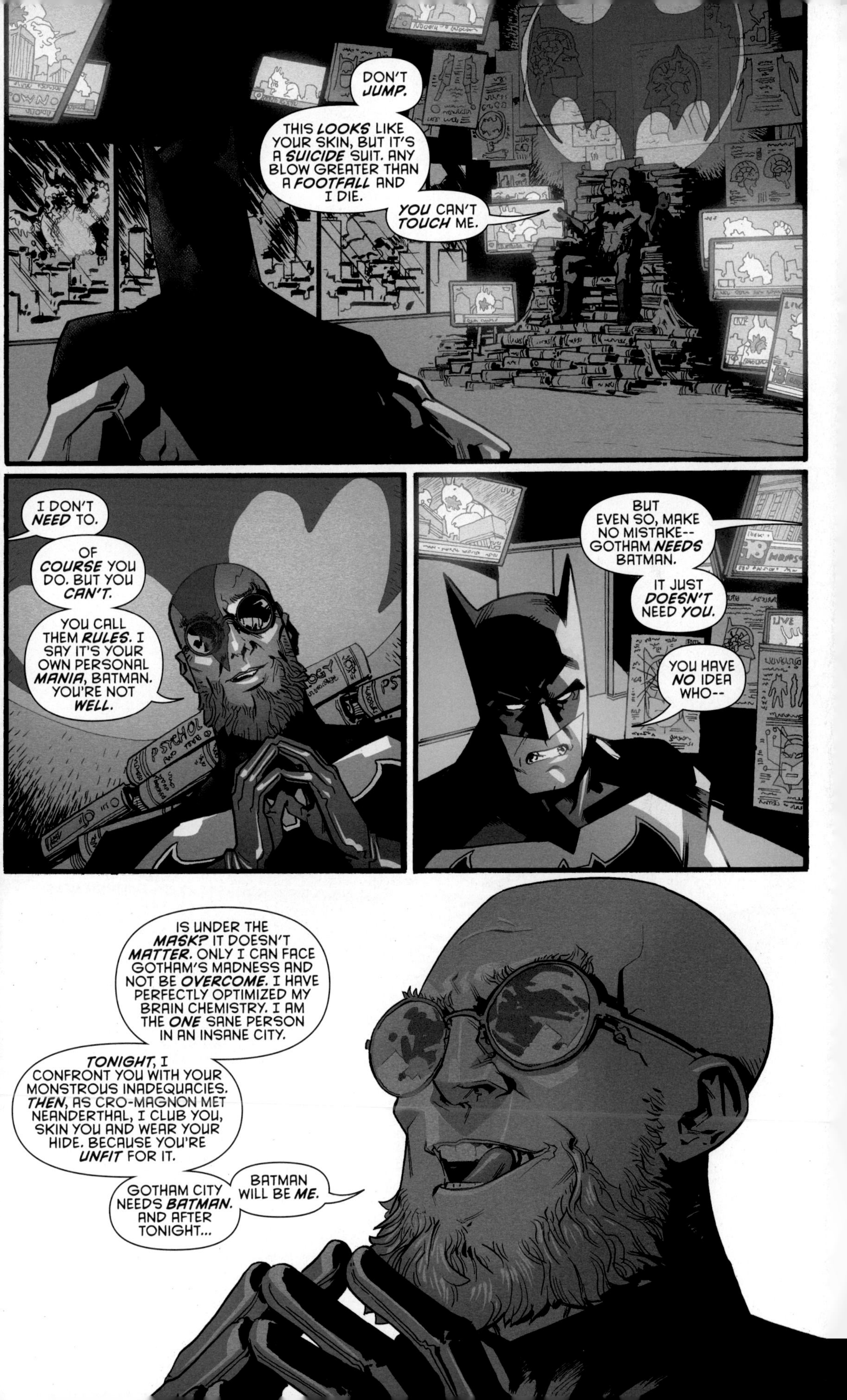
DON'T JUMP.
THIS LOOKS LIKE YOUR SKIN, BUT IT'S A SUICIDE SUIT. ANY BLOW GREATER THAN A FOOTFALL AND I DIE.
YOU CAN'T TOUCH ME.
I DON'T NEED TO.
OF COURSE YOU DO. BUT YOU CAN'T.
YOU CALL THEM RULES. I SAY IT'S YOUR OWN PERSONAL MANIA, BATMAN. YOU'RE NOT WELL.
BUT EVEN SO, MAKE NO MISTAKE-- GOTHAM NEEDS BATMAN.
IT JUST DOESN'T NEED YOU.
YOU HAVE NO IDEA WHO--
IS UNDER THE MASK? IT DOESN'T MATTER. ONLY I CAN FACE GOTHAM'S MADNESS AND NOT BE OVERCOME. I HAVE PERFECTLY OPTIMIZED MY BRAIN CHEMISTRY. I AM THE ONE SANE PERSON IN AN INSANE CITY.
TONIGHT, I CONFRONT YOU WITH YOUR MONSTROUS INADEQUACIES. THEN, AS CRO-MAGNON MET NEANDERTHAL, I CLUB YOU, SKIN YOU AND WEAR YOUR HIDE. BECAUSE YOU'RE UNFIT FOR IT.
GOTHAM CITY NEEDS BATMAN. AND AFTER TONIGHT...
BATMAN WILL BE ME.

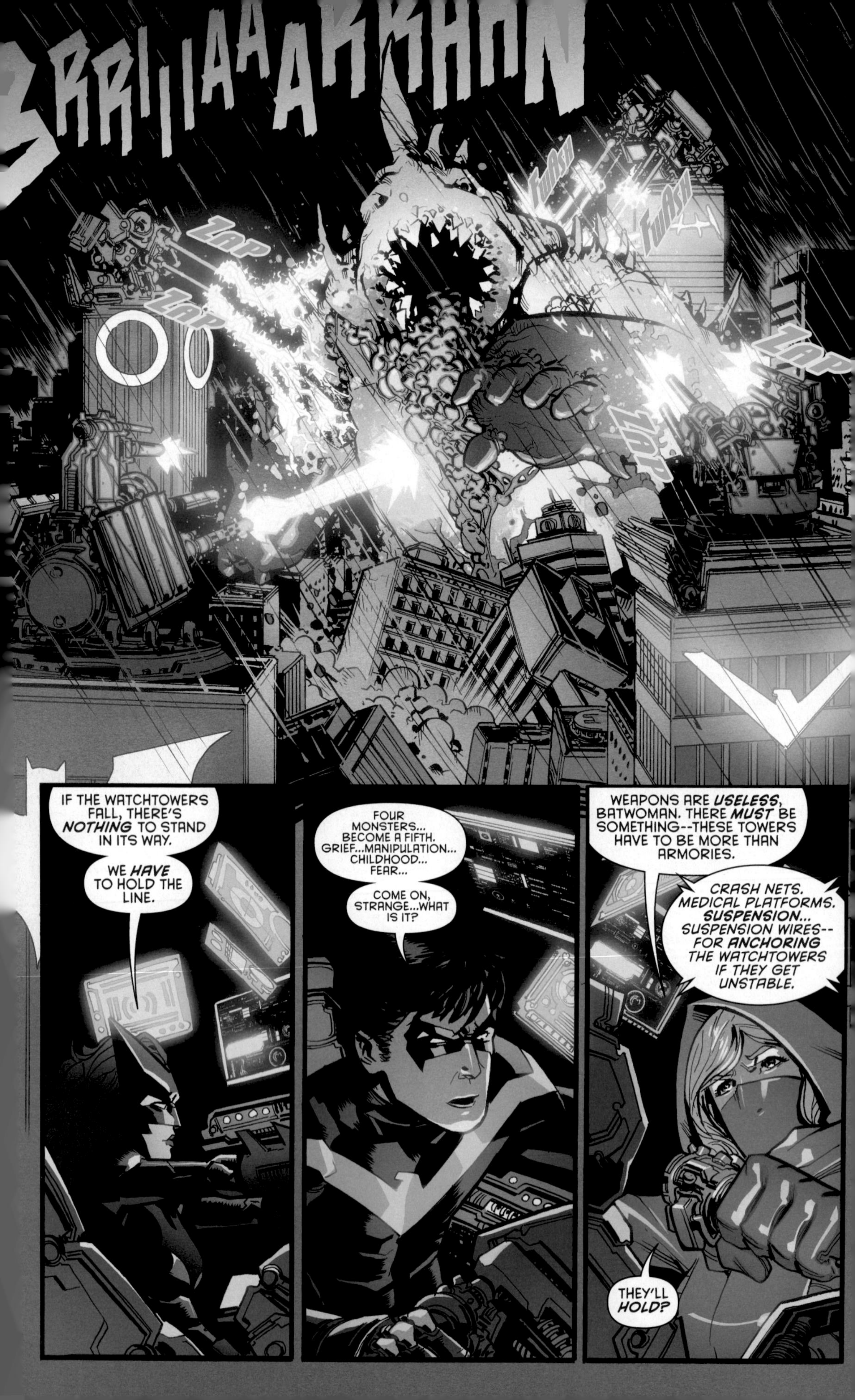

BRRIIIAAAKKHHN
ZAP
ZAP
FWASH
FWASH
ZAP
ZAP
IF THE WATCHTOWERS FALL, THERE'S NOTHING TO STAND IN ITS WAY.
WE HAVE TO HOLD THE LINE.
FOUR MONSTERS... BECOME A FIFTH. GRIEF...MANIPULATION... CHILDHOOD... FEAR...
COME ON, STRANGE...WHAT IS IT?
WEAPONS ARE USELESS, BATWOMAN. THERE MUST BE SOMETHING--THESE TOWERS HAVE TO BE MORE THAN ARMORIES.
CRASH NETS. MEDICAL PLATFORMS. SUSPENSION... SUSPENSION WIRES-- FOR ANCHORING THE WATCHTOWERS IF THEY GET UNSTABLE.
THEY'LL HOLD?

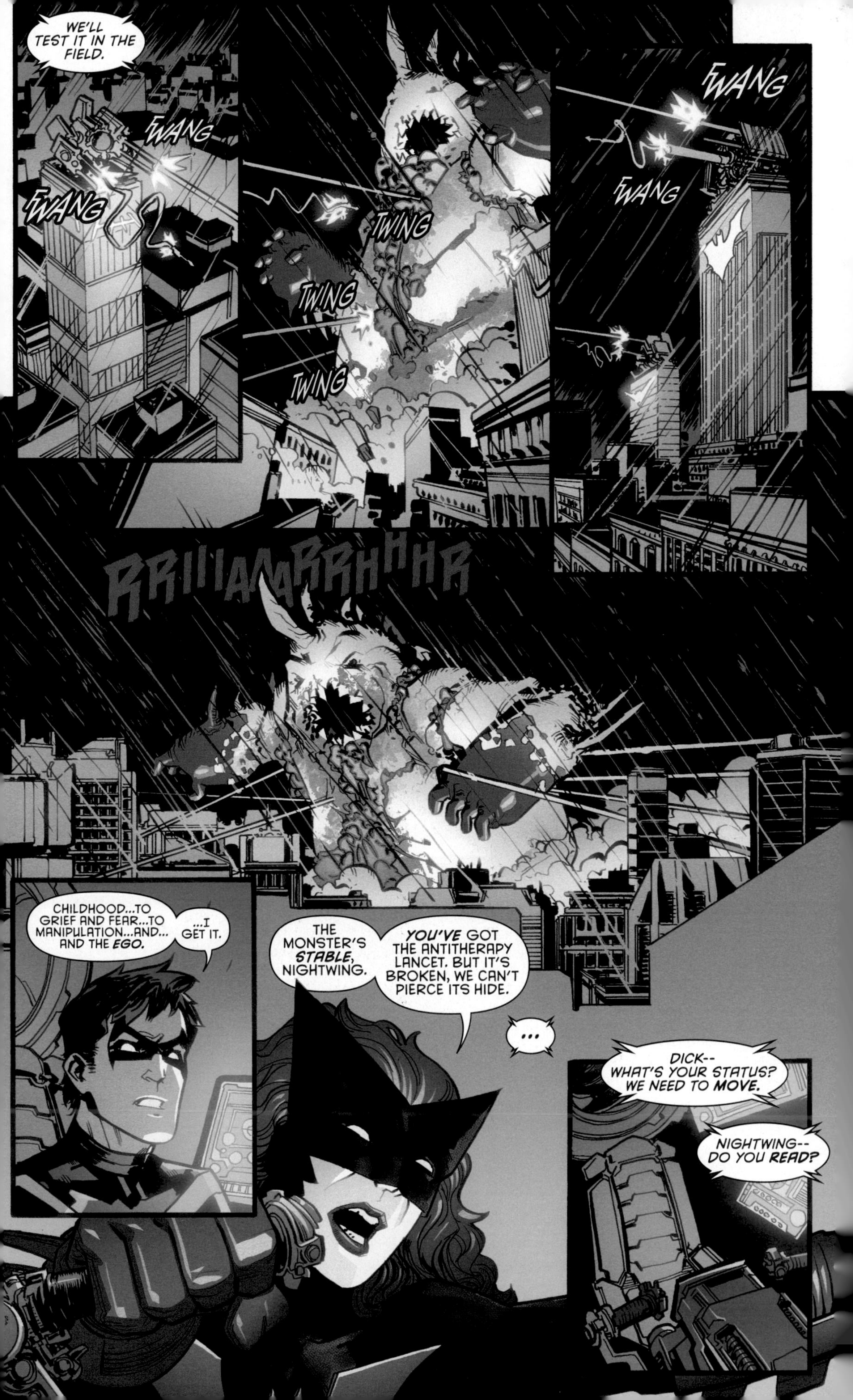
WE'LL TEST IT IN THE FIELD.
FWANG
FWANG
TWING
TWING
TWING
FWANG
FWANG
RRIIIAAGRRHHHR
CHILDHOOD...TO GRIEF AND FEAR...TO MANIPULATION...AND... AND THE EGO.
...I GET IT.
THE MONSTER'S STABLE, NIGHTWING.
YOU'VE GOT THE ANTITHERAPY LANCET. BUT IT'S BROKEN, WE CAN'T PIERCE ITS HIDE.
...
DICK-- WHAT'S YOUR STATUS? WE NEED TO MOVE.
NIGHTWING-- DO YOU READ?

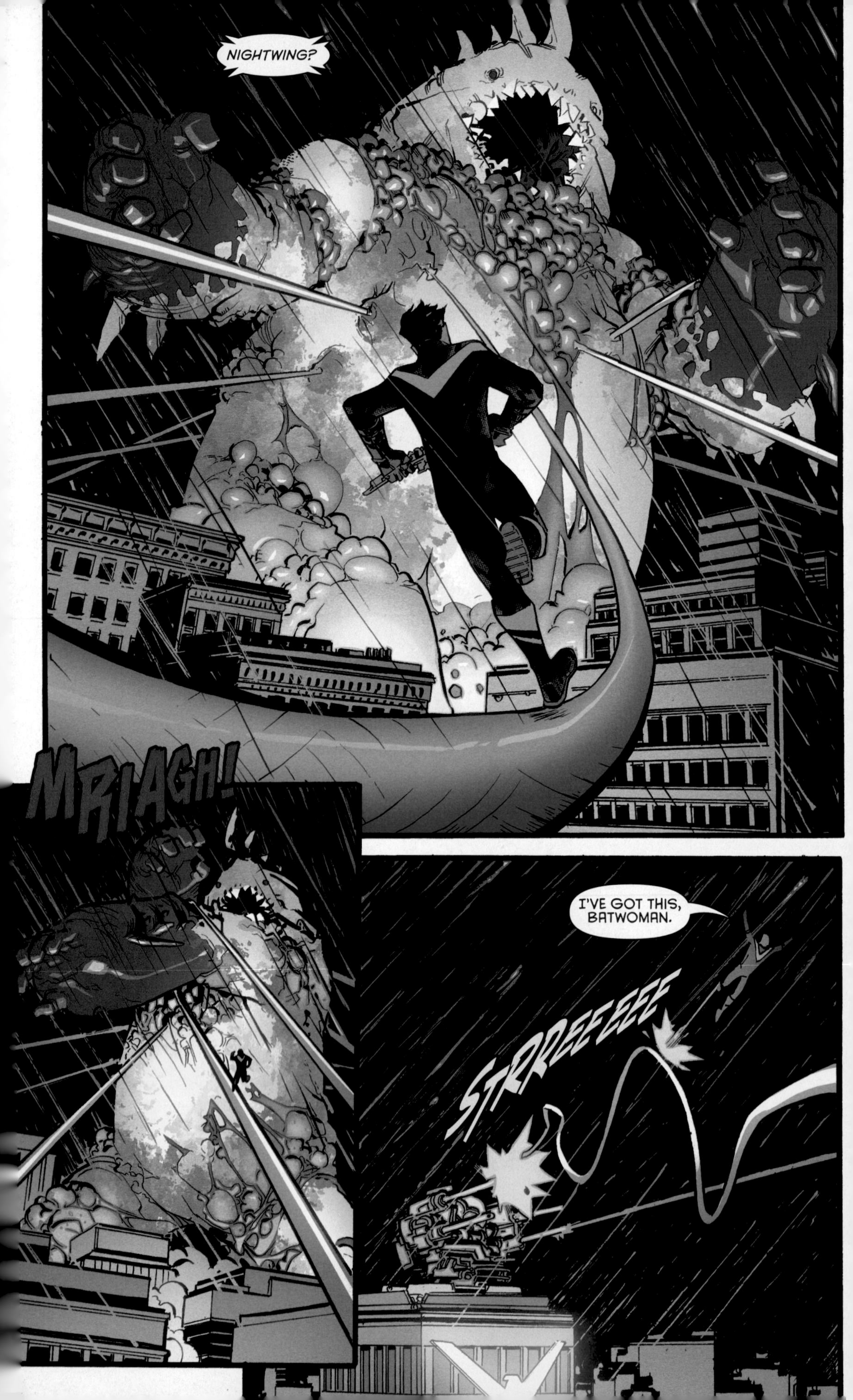
NIGHTWING?
MRIAGH!
I'VE GOT THIS, BATWOMAN.
STRREEEEEE

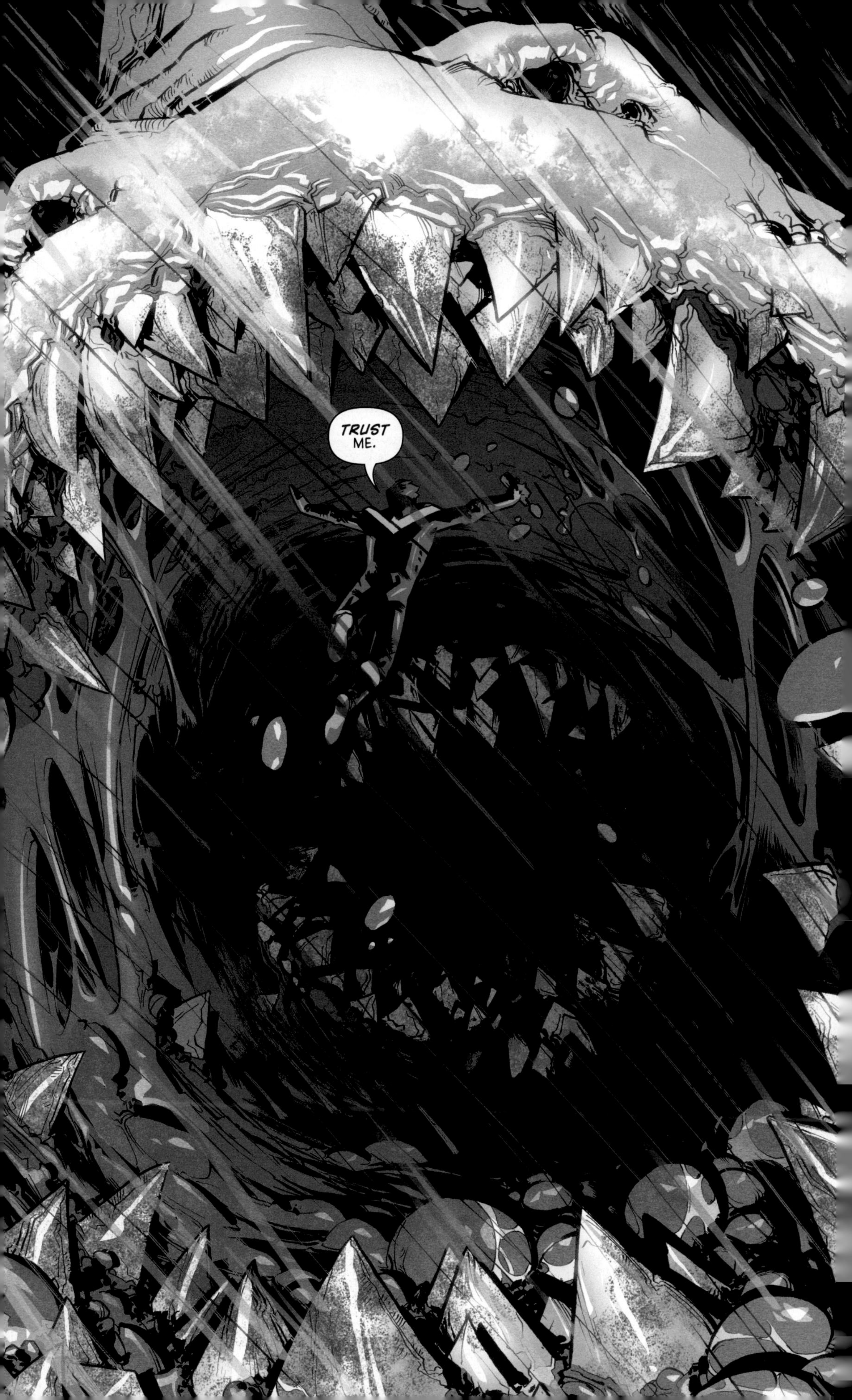
TRUST ME.

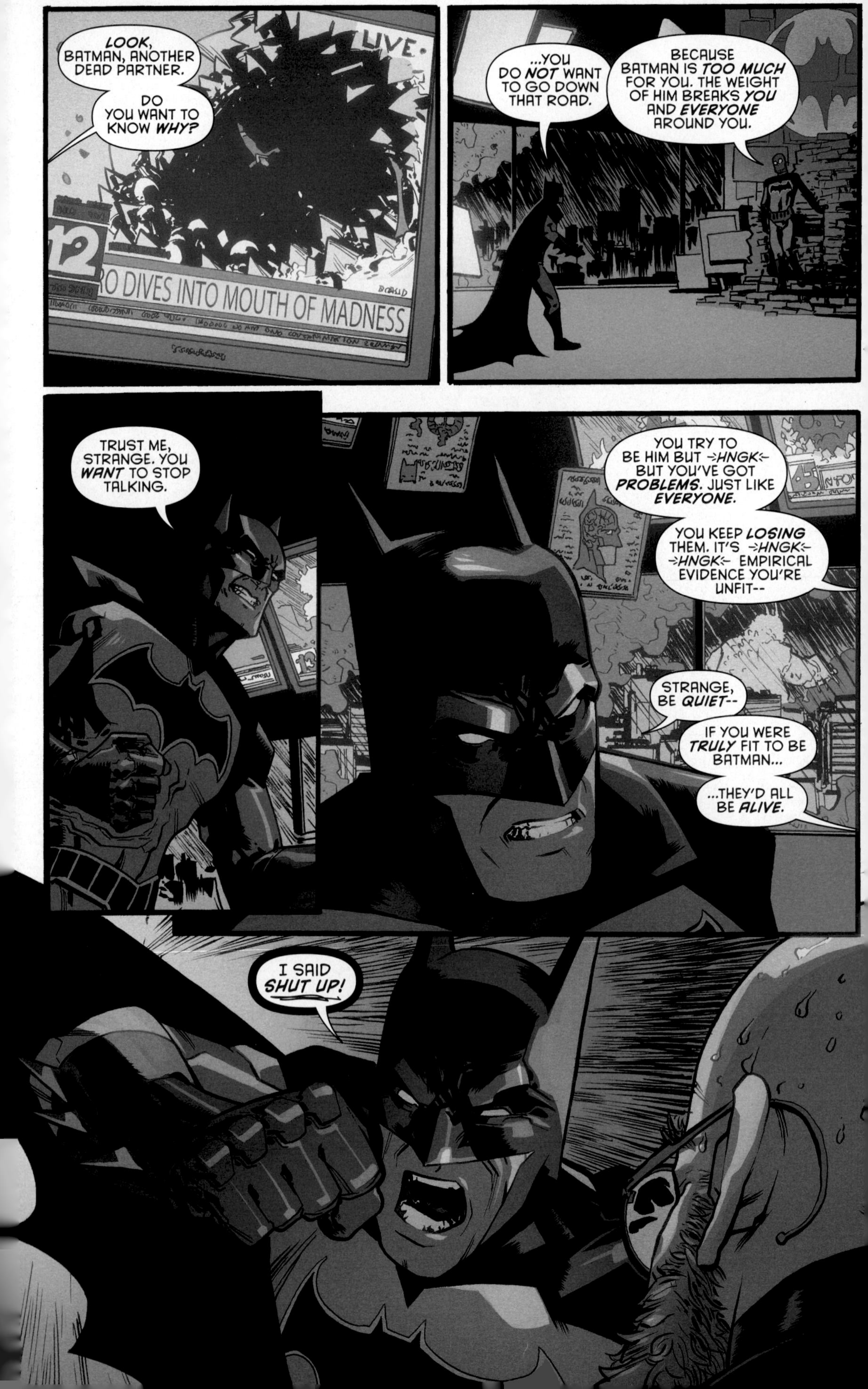

LOOK, BATMAN, ANOTHER DEAD PARTNER.
DO YOU WANT TO KNOW WHY?
LIVE.
RO DIVES INTO MOUTH OF MADNESS
...YOU DO NOT WANT TO GO DOWN THAT ROAD.
BECAUSE BATMAN IS TOO MUCH FOR YOU. THE WEIGHT OF HIM BREAKS YOU AND EVERYONE AROUND YOU.
TRUST ME, STRANGE. YOU WANT TO STOP TALKING.
YOU TRY TO BE HIM BUT ⇒HNGK⇐ BUT YOU'VE GOT PROBLEMS. JUST LIKE EVERYONE.
YOU KEEP LOSING THEM. IT'S ⇒HNGK⇐ ⇒HNGK⇐ EMPIRICAL EVIDENCE YOU'RE UNFIT--
STRANGE, BE QUIET--
IF YOU WERE TRULY FIT TO BE BATMAN...
...THEY'D ALL BE ALIVE.
I SAID SHUT UP!

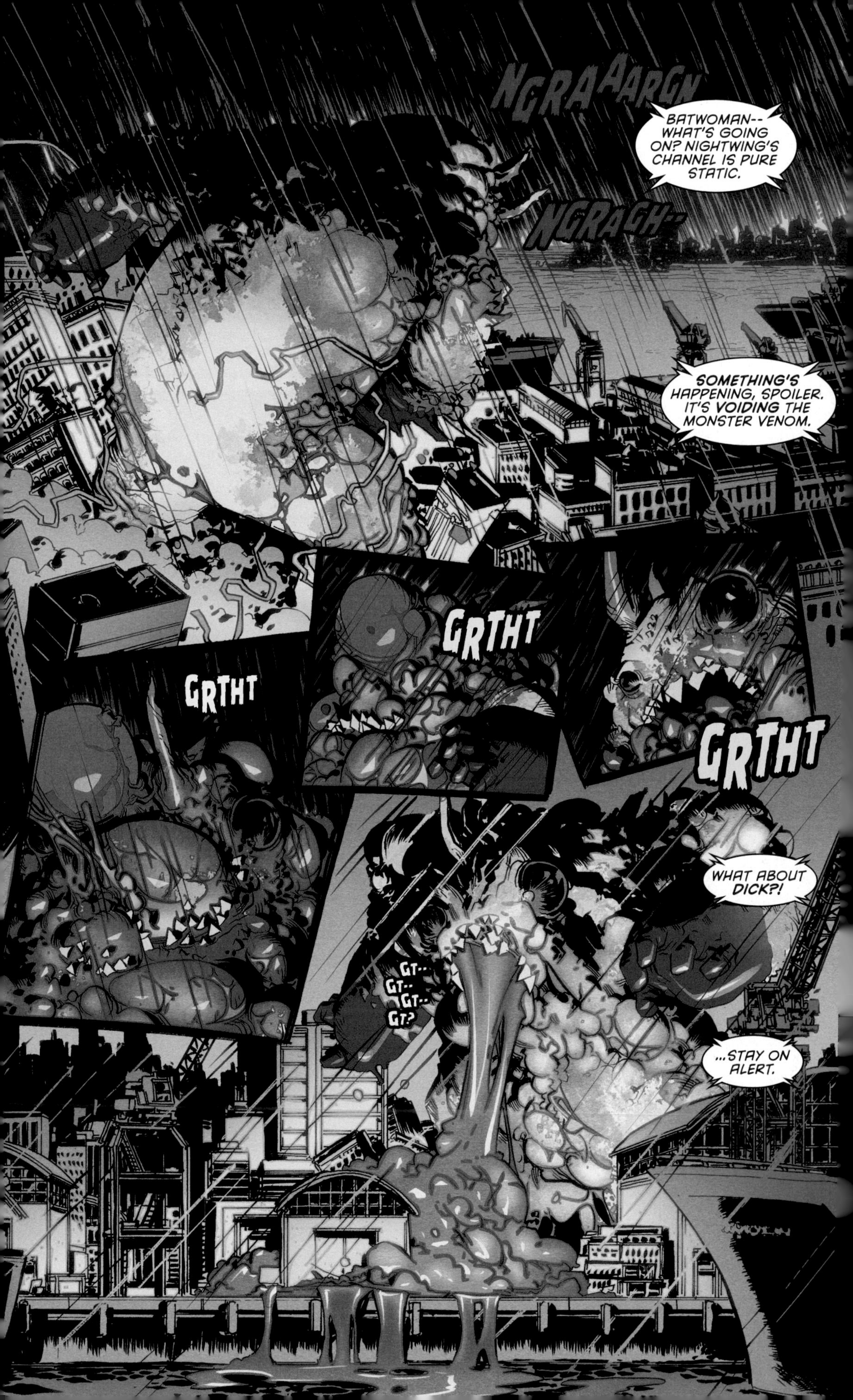
NGRAAARGH
BATWOMAN--WHAT'S GOING ON? NIGHTWING'S CHANNEL IS PURE STATIC.
NGRAGH--
SOMETHING'S HAPPENING, SPOILER. IT'S VOIDING THE MONSTER VENOM.
GRTHT
GRTHT
GRTHT
WHAT ABOUT DICK?!
GT--
GT--
GT--
GT?
...STAY ON ALERT.

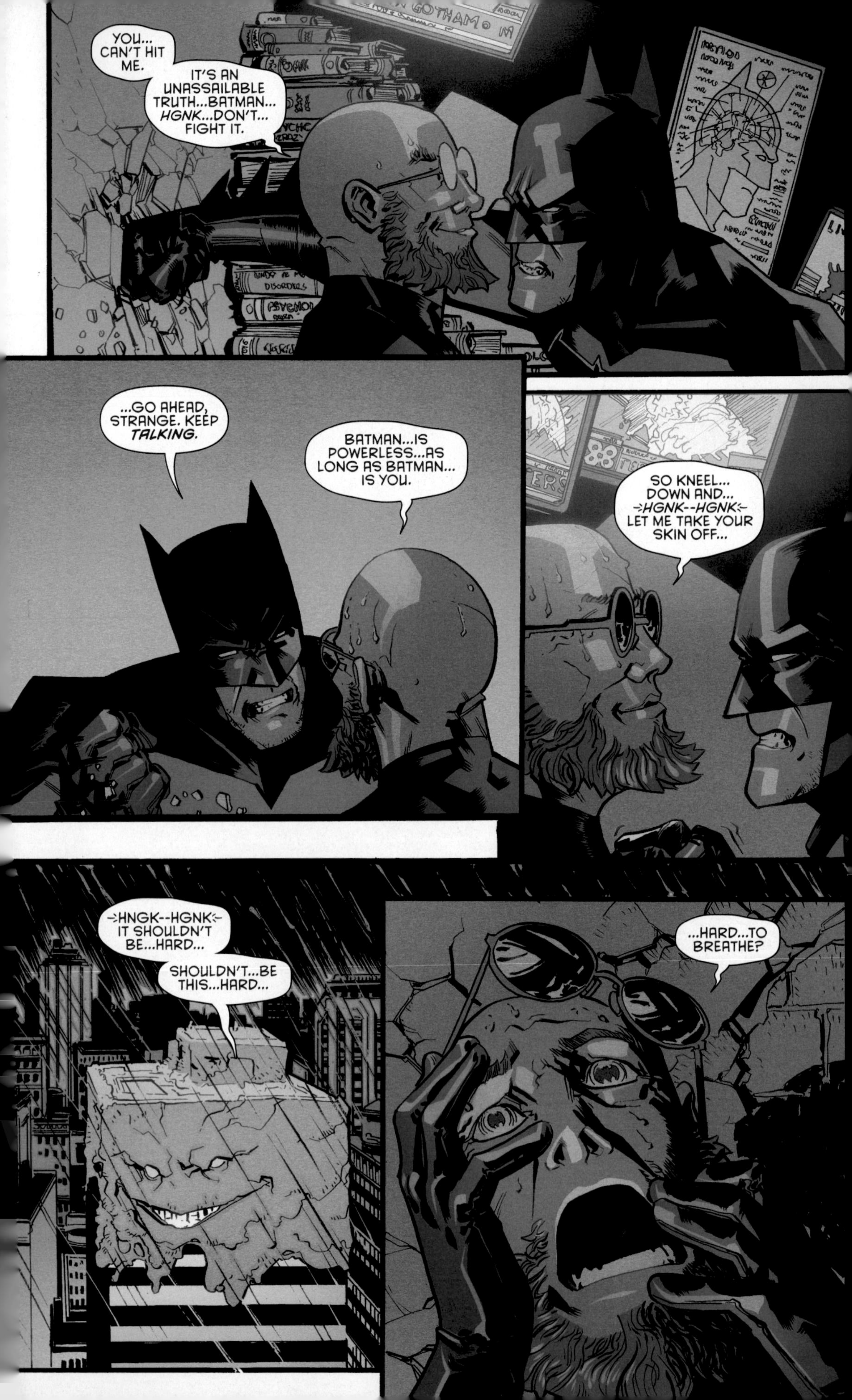
YOU... CAN'T HIT ME.
IT'S AN UNASSAILABLE TRUTH...BATMAN... HGNK...DON'T... FIGHT IT.
...GO AHEAD, STRANGE. KEEP TALKING.
BATMAN...IS POWERLESS...AS LONG AS BATMAN... IS YOU.
SO KNEEL... DOWN AND... HGNK--HGNK LET ME TAKE YOUR SKIN OFF...
HNGK--HGNK IT SHOULDN'T BE...HARD...
SHOULDN'T...BE THIS...HARD...
...HARD...TO BREATHE?

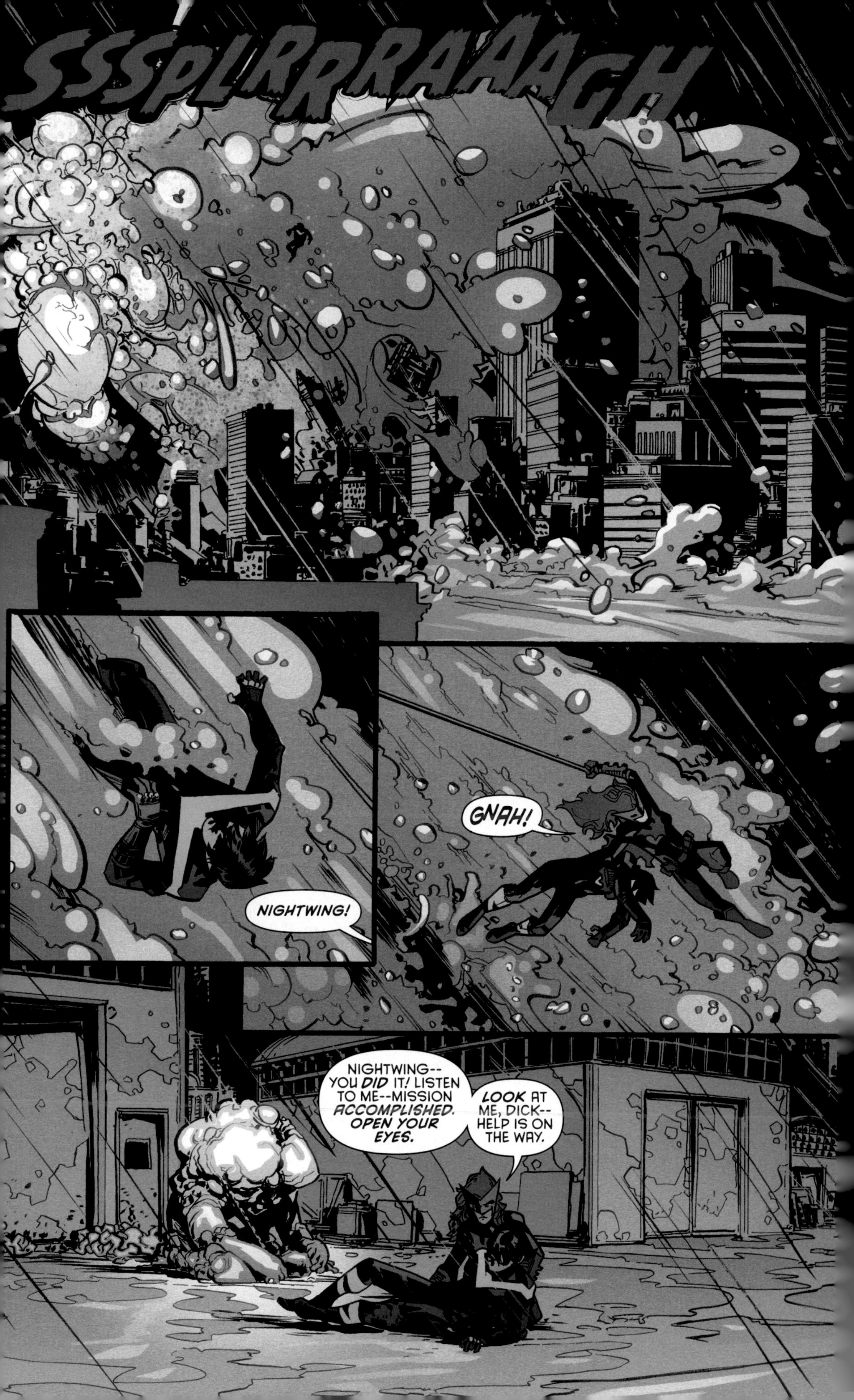
SSSPLRRRRAAAACH
NIGHTWING!
GNAH!
NIGHTWING-- YOU DID IT! LISTEN TO ME--MISSION ACCOMPLISHED. OPEN YOUR EYES.
LOOK AT ME, DICK-- HELP IS ON THE WAY.

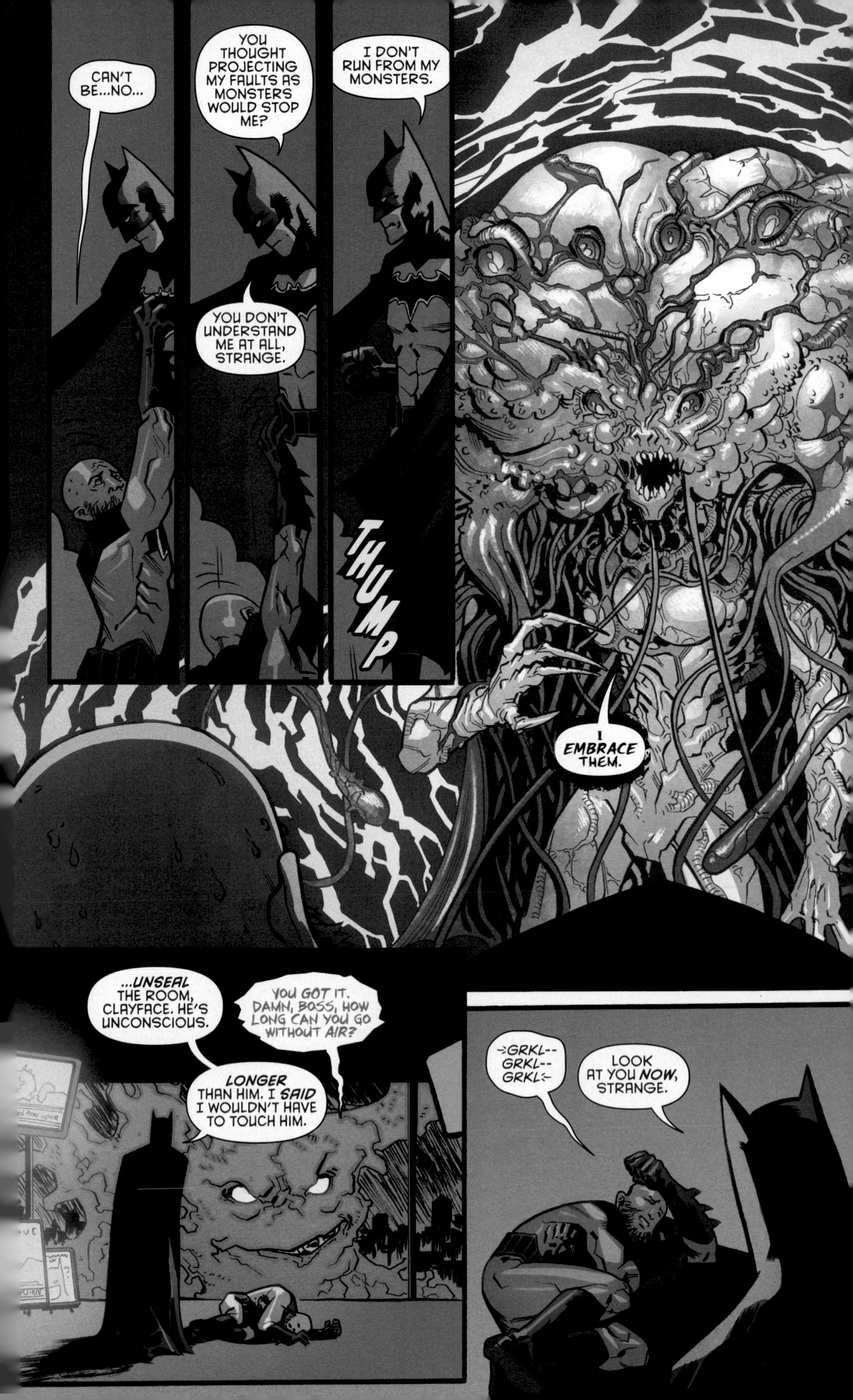
CAN'T BE...NO...
YOU THOUGHT PROJECTING MY FAULTS AS MONSTERS WOULD STOP ME?
YOU DON'T UNDERSTAND ME AT ALL, STRANGE.
I DON'T RUN FROM MY MONSTERS.
THUMP
I EMBRACE THEM.
...UNSEAL THE ROOM, CLAYFACE. HE'S UNCONSCIOUS.
YOU GOT IT. DAMN, BOSS, HOW LONG CAN YOU GO WITHOUT AIR?
LONGER THAN HIM. I SAID I WOULDN'T HAVE TO TOUCH HIM.
-GRKL-- GRKL-- GRKL-
LOOK AT YOU NOW, STRANGE.

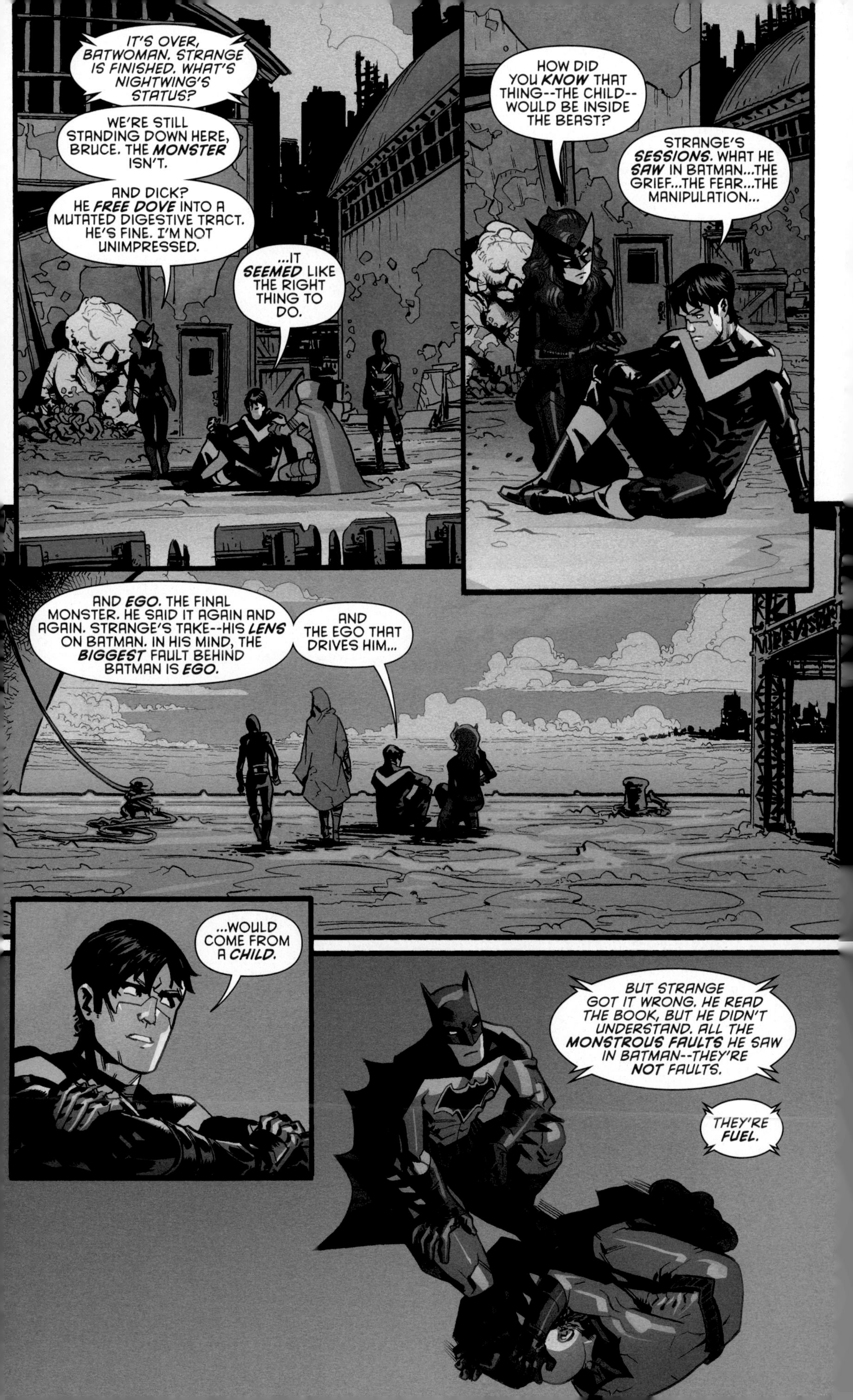

IT'S OVER, BATWOMAN. STRANGE IS FINISHED. WHAT'S NIGHTWING'S STATUS?
WE'RE STILL STANDING DOWN HERE, BRUCE. THE MONSTER ISN'T.
AND DICK? HE FREE DOVE INTO A MUTATED DIGESTIVE TRACT. HE'S FINE. I'M NOT UNIMPRESSED.
...IT SEEMED LIKE THE RIGHT THING TO DO.
HOW DID YOU KNOW THAT THING--THE CHILD--WOULD BE INSIDE THE BEAST?
STRANGE'S SESSIONS. WHAT HE SAW IN BATMAN...THE GRIEF...THE FEAR...THE MANIPULATION...
AND EGO. THE FINAL MONSTER. HE SAID IT AGAIN AND AGAIN. STRANGE'S TAKE--HIS LENS ON BATMAN. IN HIS MIND, THE BIGGEST FAULT BEHIND BATMAN IS EGO.
AND THE EGO THAT DRIVES HIM...
...WOULD COME FROM A CHILD.
BUT STRANGE GOT IT WRONG. HE READ THE BOOK, BUT HE DIDN'T UNDERSTAND. ALL THE MONSTROUS FAULTS HE SAW IN BATMAN--THEY'RE NOT FAULTS.
THEY'RE FUEL.

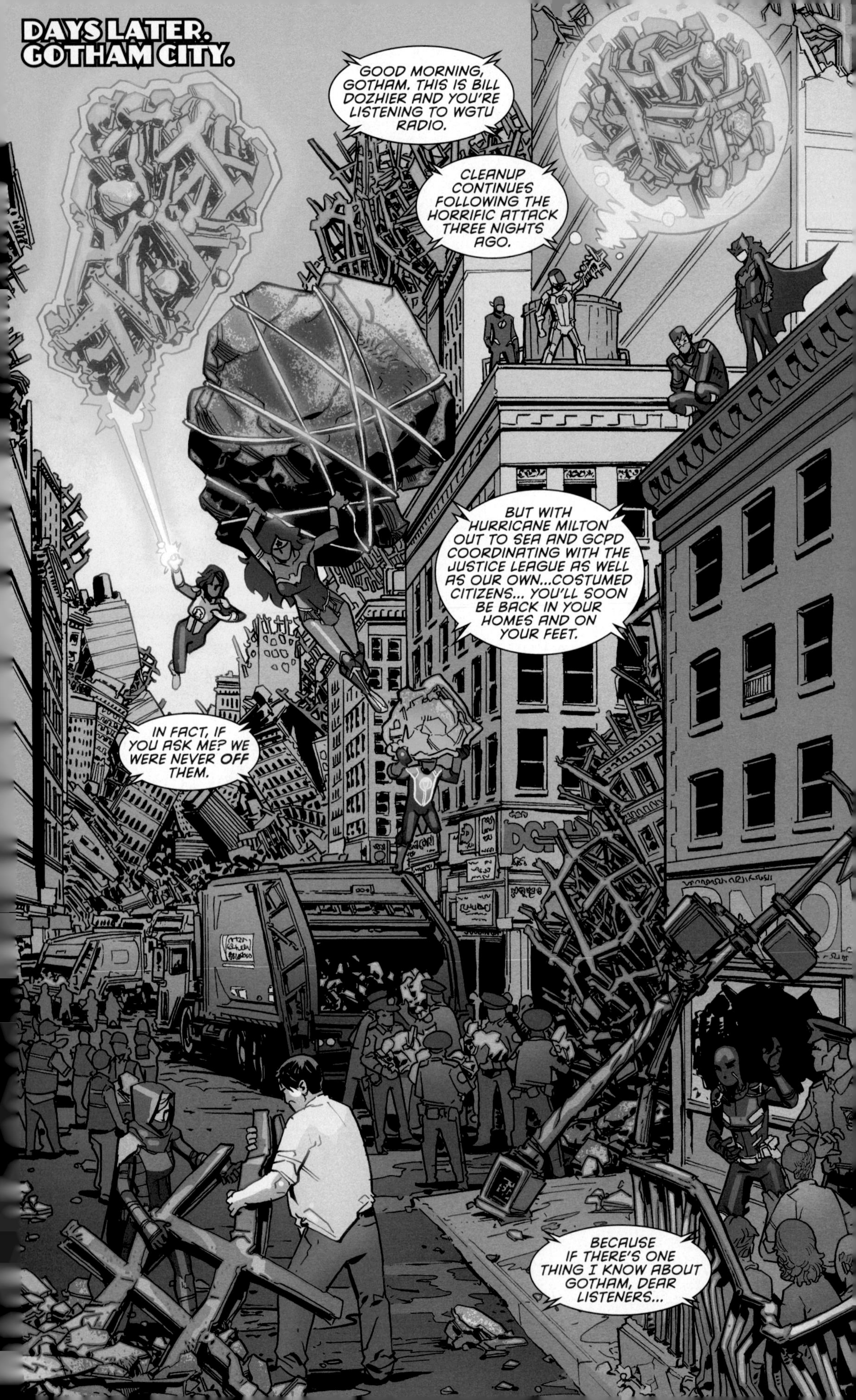
DAYS LATER. GOTHAM CITY.
GOOD MORNING, GOTHAM. THIS IS BILL DOZHIER AND YOU'RE LISTENING TO WGTU RADIO.
CLEANUP CONTINUES FOLLOWING THE HORRIFIC ATTACK THREE NIGHTS AGO.
BUT WITH HURRICANE MILTON OUT TO SEA AND GCPD COORDINATING WITH THE JUSTICE LEAGUE AS WELL AS OUR OWN...COSTUMED CITIZENS... YOU'LL SOON BE BACK IN YOUR HOMES AND ON YOUR FEET.
IN FACT, IF YOU ASK ME? WE WERE NEVER OFF THEM.
BECAUSE IF THERE'S ONE THING I KNOW ABOUT GOTHAM, DEAR LISTENERS...

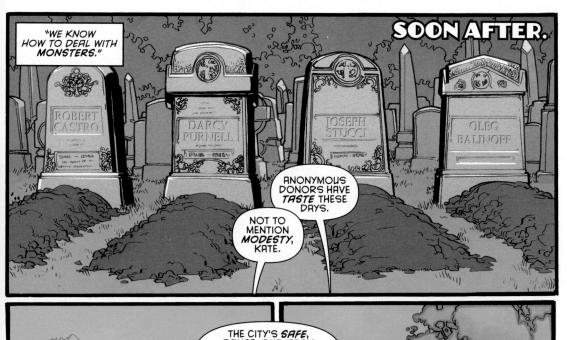

"WE KNOW HOW TO DEAL WITH MONSTERS."

ROBERT CASTRO

DARCY PURNELL

JOSEPH STUCCI

OLEG BALINOFF

ANONYMOUS DONORS HAVE *TASTE* THESE DAYS.

NOT TO MENTION *MODESTY,* KATE.

THE CITY'S *SAFE,* BRUCE. OUR *TEAM* PERFORMED WELL. AND WAS THAT A *SARCASTIC BARB* FROM *DEEP* IN YOUR UTILITY BELT?

YOU MUST HAVE MISHEARD. *STRANGE* IS IN CUSTODY. TIGHTLY.

ARKHAM?

NO. SOMEWHERE...BETTER *EQUIPPED* FOR HIS MIND.

AND HIS *MONSTER VENOM?*

DARCY PURNELL

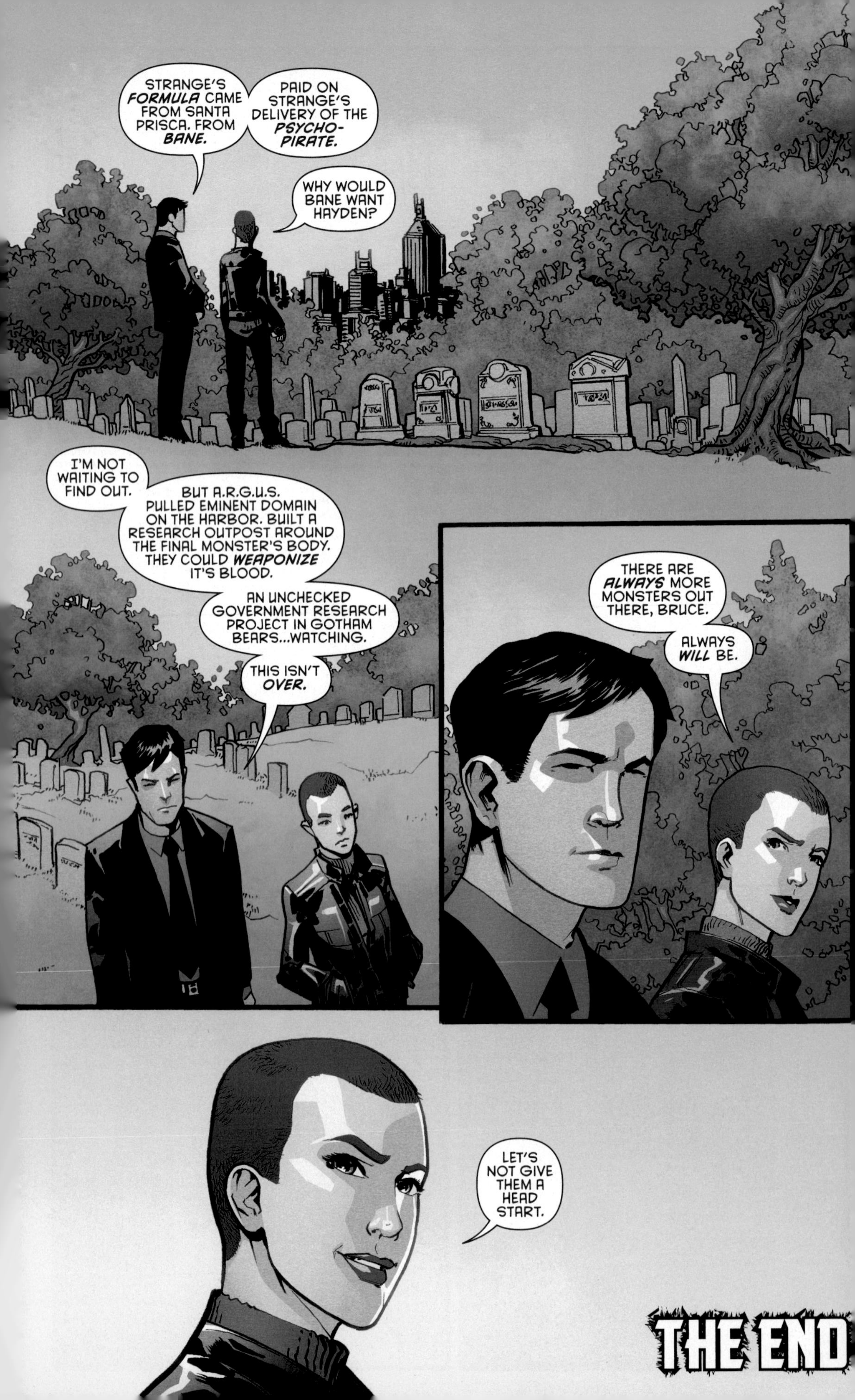
STRANGE'S FORMULA CAME FROM SANTA PRISCA. FROM BANE.
PAID ON STRANGE'S DELIVERY OF THE PSYCHO-PIRATE.
WHY WOULD BANE WANT HAYDEN?
I'M NOT WAITING TO FIND OUT.
BUT A.R.G.U.S. PULLED EMINENT DOMAIN ON THE HARBOR. BUILT A RESEARCH OUTPOST AROUND THE FINAL MONSTER'S BODY. THEY COULD WEAPONIZE IT'S BLOOD.
AN UNCHECKED GOVERNMENT RESEARCH PROJECT IN GOTHAM BEARS...WATCHING.
THIS ISN'T OVER.
THERE ARE ALWAYS MORE MONSTERS OUT THERE, BRUCE.
ALWAYS WILL BE.
LET'S NOT GIVE THEM A HEAD START.
THE END

## PERSONAL DATA

*Alter Ego:* None
*Occupation:* Criminal Scientist
*Marital Status:* Single
*Known Relatives:* None
*Group Affiliation:* None
*Base of Operations:* Gotham City
*First Appearance:* DETECTIVE COMICS #36
*Height:* 5′10½″ *Weight:* 170 lbs.
*Eyes:* Gray
*Hair:* Bald with gray beard

## HISTORY

One of the first and greatest of The Batman's foes (see *Batman I, II*), Professor Hugo Strange is one of the world's leading scientific geniuses and criminal strategists. Strange first clashed with The Batman when he used a gigantic electrical generator to blanket Gotham City with thick fog. Strange's men then looted the city. The Batman sent Strange and his men to prison, but Strange soon broke free and used chemicals to transform five mental patients into monstrous, super-strong giants. The giants were to terrorize the city while Strange's men looted it, but The Batman again defeated Strange.

Months later, Strange attempted to use his fear-inducing dust to take over first Gotham City, and eventually the world. The Batman and his new partner Robin (see *Nightwing*) thwarted Strange, who apparently fell to his death.

But Strange survived and spent years as a successful criminal in Europe. Seeking a challenge, Strange returned to Gotham to pit himself against The Batman. He launched an insidious blackmail scheme against powerful Gotham figures, and finally captured and unmasked The Batman. Obsessed with usurping his foe's identities, Strange masqueraded as The Batman's other self, Bruce Wayne, and plotted to plunder Wayne Enterprises. He also intended to auction off the secret of The Batman's true identity, but corrupt politician Rupert "Boss" Thorne captured Strange, and had his men brutally beat him to force him to reveal who The Batman is. Strange refused, saying the knowledge of the secret must be earned. Then Strange used yoga techniques to fool Thorne into thinking him dead. Robin eventually freed Wayne. Strange later used holograms of himself to make Thorne think his ghost was haunting him and thus to drive him insane.

Still seeking to usurp The Batman's two identities, Strange pitted a robot double of himself against The Batman. The robot, which Batman believed to be the real Strange, was destroyed.

Later, through various illegal means, Strange deprived Wayne of his home and fortune. Strange planned to frame The Batman as a criminal and then expose him as Wayne. The Batman and the new Robin (see *Robin II*) defeated Strange and turned him over to the police, along with proof of his recent crimes. Wayne thus regained his home and fortune. The Batman told the police that he had hypnotized Strange into believing he was Wayne to conceal his true secret identity, which Strange knew. When Strange was told this, he became utterly confused as to whether or not Batman was Wayne. Strange is now in prison.

## POWERS & WEAPONS

Professor Hugo Strange is a genius in many scientific fields and a master criminal strategist. He is a good hand-to-hand combatant.

# PROFESSOR HUGO STRANGE

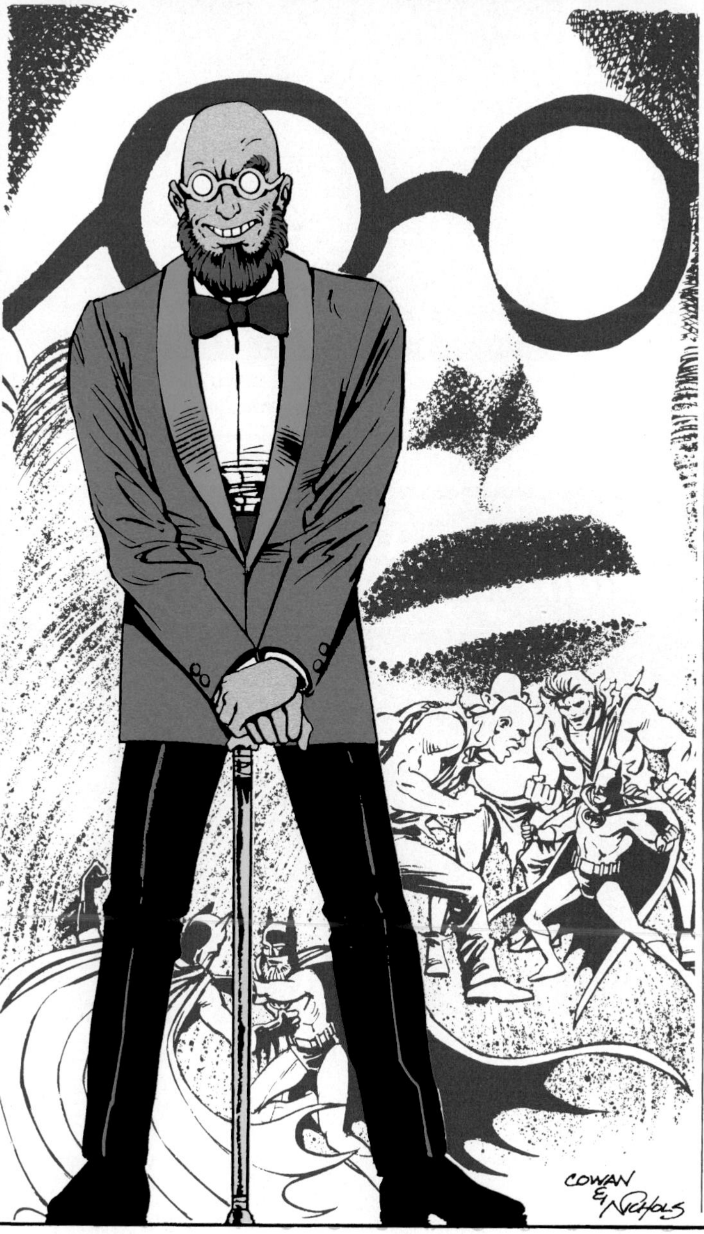

COWAN & NICHOLS


*Art by Denys Cowan & Art Nichols*

**DC UNIVERSE REBIRTH**

# BATMAN

## VOL. 1: I AM GOTHAM

### TOM KING
### with DAVID FINCH

VOL. 1 **I AM GOTHAM**
TOM KING * DAVID FINCH

**ALL-STAR BATMAN VOL. 1:**
**MY OWN WORST ENEMY**

**NIGHTWING VOL. 1:**
**BETTER THAN BATMAN**

**DETECTIVE COMICS VOL. 1:**
**RISE OF THE BATMEN**

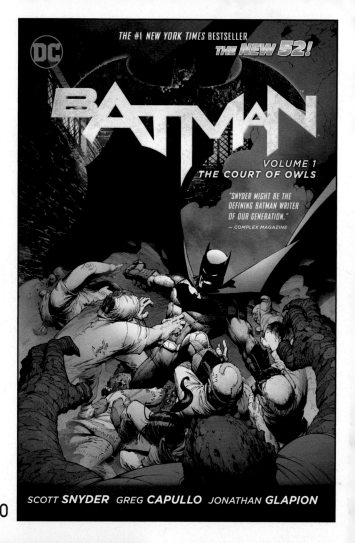
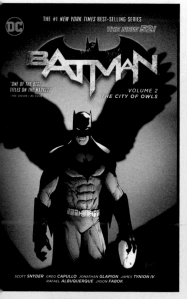
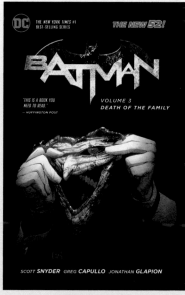

# BATMAN & ROBIN
## VOL. 1: BORN TO KILL
### PETER J. TOMASI
### with PATRICK GLEASON

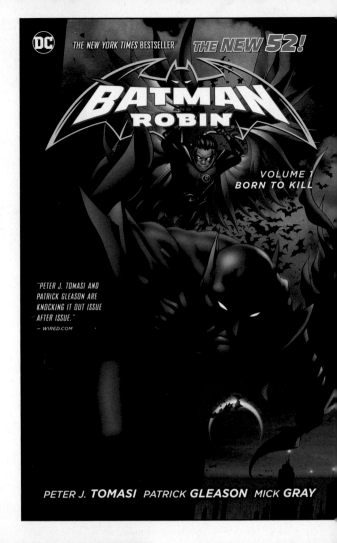

**BATMAN & ROBIN VOL. 2: PEARL**

**BATMAN & ROBIN VOL. 3: DEATH OF THE FAMILY**

## READ THE ENTIRE EPIC

BATMAN & ROBIN VOL. 4
REQUIEM FOR DAMIAN

BATMAN & ROBIN VOL. 5
THE BIG BURN

BATMAN & ROBIN VOL. 6
THE HUNT FOR ROBIN

BATMAN & ROBIN VOL. 7
ROBIN RISES